Federalism
in Canada

"The Hon. Attorney General promises us that Lower Canada will be the sun of Confederation. Since we cannot find a comparison on this poor earth emblematic of our future greatness, let us borrow one from the heavens at the risk of losing ourselves in the clouds with the advocates of Confederation; I propose the adoption of the rainbow as our emblem. By the endless variety of its tints the rainbow will give an excellent idea of the diversity of races, religions, sentiments and interests of the different parts of the Confederation. By its slender and elongated form, the rainbow would afford a perfect representation of the geographical configuration of the Confederation. By its lack of consistence – an image without substance – the rainbow would represent aptly the solidity of our Confederation. An emblem we must have, for every great empire has one; let us adopt the rainbow."

Henri Joly de Lotbinière
Confederation Debates, *Parliament of Canada 1865*

Federalism

---

in Canada:

Selected Readings

Edited by

Garth Stevenson

Canadian Cataloguing in Publication Data

Main entry under title:

Federalism in Canada

Includes bibliographical references.
ISBN 0-7710-8246-0

1. Federal government – Canada. 2. Federal-provincial relations – Canada.* I. Stevenson, Garth, 1943-

JL27.F43 1989   320.971   C89-093562-9

Printed and bound in Canada

McClelland & Stewart Inc.
The Canadian Publishers
481 University Avenue
Toronto, Ontario
M5G 2E9

Contents

Preface

This book has been compiled as a service to teachers and students of political science, and it reflects my own experience teaching courses on Canadian federalism at four different universities. Like most instructors in such courses I have used a core text supplemented by an assortment of articles and portions of other books dealing with specific aspects of the topic. Like other instructors I have wrestled for years with the problems of tracking down articles and chapters to be placed "on reserve" and then listening to students' complaints that they were nonetheless unobtainable. I have also experimented with the distribution of photocopies to the students, a practice that is expensive, morally objectionable, and now prohibited, however ineffectively, by Canadian law.

The only solution seemed to be to compile an anthology of articles that I thought students of Canadian federalism should read. No two persons, faced with this task, would produce exactly identical lists of articles to be included. In defence of the selections here included, I can only cite the general criteria that influenced my choices. First, I have defined the scope of "federalism" to include legal, socio-economic, political, and administrative aspects of the subject. Also, I have not succumbed to the fashionable prejudice that anything older than yesterday's news is "outdated." Several of the selections date from earlier decades, and one was published before I was born. Finally, I have tried to include only selections that have genuine intellectual merit, which does not necessarily mean either that they are all well known or that I agree with their conclusions. This criterion, however, does exclude press releases, political speeches, and official statements of the positions espoused by various governments or meetings of governments. Such material is ephemeral, and I can testify, as one who is professionally required to read a great deal of it, that it is usually tiresome, intellectually barren, and self-serving.

The four sections of the book include brief introductions. These are designed to explain the articles, to place them in historical context, and to highlight some of their main arguments. In these introductions I have also referred to relevant events or developments that have occurred since the articles were first published.

The appendices to the book include those sections of Canada's written constitution that are most directly relevant to the study of federalism and intergovernmental relations. These include, most obviously, the sections of the Constitution Act, 1867 that distribute legislative powers between the two levels of government and the sections of the Constitution Act, 1982 that outline the various procedures for constitutional amendment. It was decided not to reprint the Canadian Charter of Rights and Freedoms, since that document is essentially concerned with relations between the individual and the state, rather than with relations between the central government and the provinces. The Meech Lake Accord was also excluded since, as this book goes to press, it seems unlikely that it will be accepted by the legislatures of Manitoba and New Brunswick. In any event, both the Charter and the Accord appear as appendices to my *Unfulfilled Union*, which the present work is intended to supplement.

One final assertion is in order, which may or may not be applauded by purchasers and readers of this volume. I have not edited, shortened, or otherwise tampered with any of the articles, except to translate the one that was not available in English. It would have been possible to include more articles by shortening some of the longer ones, but I thought it more important to include the complete text of each, rather than to leave the reader wondering about what was omitted.

In conclusion I must thank my editor, Michael Harrison of McClelland & Stewart Inc., for his constant help and encouragement. The idea for this book had been germinating in my mind for several years, but it was his visit to my office at Brock University in the spring of 1988 that began the process of turning the idea into reality.

Garth Stevenson
St. Catharines, Ontario
April, 1989

PART ONE

The Constitutional

Division of Powers

and the Courts

The study of Canadian federalism should begin, although not end, with Canada's written constitution, particularly the Constitution Act of 1867. This document, known until 1982 as the British North America Act, sets out the terms under which Quebec, Ontario, New Brunswick, and Nova Scotia were united into a single federal state. Because those provinces were already familiar with parliamentary responsible government and because that form of government, in countries that follow the British tradition, relies more on unwritten convention than on formal enactment, the framers of the Act saw no reason to specify the complex and subtle relationships between prime minister, cabinet, and Parliament, relationships that are fundamental to the understanding of how Canada is governed. In fact, the office of Prime Minister is not even mentioned. On the other hand, the Act did specify in great detail the relationships between the government of Canada (now usually known as the "federal" government) and the governments of the provinces. It did this for two reasons. In the first place the existence of two distinct levels of government with constitutionally entrenched powers, that is, federalism, was a radical departure from British traditions and thus no conventions had developed, in Britain or in Canada, regarding the operation of such a system. Secondly, Confederation had been the result of various agreements and understandings among the political leaders of the day (now usually known as the Fathers of Confederation) and the terms of those agreements and understandings had to be specified in writing.

There may or may not be a logical connection between federalism and the power of the courts to declare that a statute is unconstitutional, but in practice most federations recognize such a power, whether or not it is explicitly specified in the constitution. Federalism provides a convenient and plausible argument for individuals and organizations that wish to challenge an act by either level of government: they can claim that it trespasses on the powers the constitution grants to the other level. Less frequently, governments themselves can challenge one another's acts using the same argument. In the course of resolving such disputes, the courts in most federations "interpret" the constitution and gradually cause the understanding of what the constitution means to evolve in response to new circumstances. As Archibald Cox, former solicitor-general of the United States, has written with reference to his own country: "The Court must preserve its legitimacy and the ideal of law by invoking a majestic sense of continuity, but it must also discover some composition with the dominant needs and aspirations of the present."[1]

To provide both change and continuity in this manner is a difficult task for any court. The courts that have interpreted Canada's constitution have not always succeeded in squaring the circle, and their rulings have often been controversial. This is partly the result of ambiguities in the written constitution itself and partly the result of fundamental conflicts of interest or ideology, which may cause Canadians to take sides in constitutional controversies. An additional reason is that the judges and courts themselves have lacked legitimacy. The Judicial Committee of the Privy Council, which served as Canada's highest tribunal until 1949, was located in England and, strictly speaking, was an advisory body to the British government rather than a court. It was thus increasingly viewed by Canadians as a relic of colonialism. The Supreme Court of Canada, which replaced the Judicial Committee as the last court of appeal, has been regarded by some Canadians as an instrument of the central government rather than an impartial umpire of federal-provincial disputes.

The articles in the first section of this book provide an introduction to the major problems in interpreting the division of legislative powers between Parliament and the provincial legislatures. Two of them, by Alan Cairns and Peter Hogg, are explicitly concerned with the problem of legitimacy and they defend the Judicial Committee and the Supreme Court, respectively, against the critics of those institutions. The other three articles discuss the techniques of interpreting sections 91 and 92 of the Constitution Act of 1867, and their authors reach somewhat different conclusions. Students will find it useful to read sections 91 and 92 before reading the articles, and perhaps to keep a copy of the Constitution Act within reach while they are reading the articles.

The article by Bora Laskin, first published in 1947, is a classic statement of the view that the Judicial Committee misinterpreted the constitutional distribution of powers. Laskin was subsequently, from 1973 to 1984, a distinguished Chief Justice of Canada, and his opinions on the bench generally promoted the broad and generous understanding of federal powers that he espoused in this article. He also wrote a widely used textbook on Canadian constitutional law. However, the importance of this article is not dependent on the eminence later attained by its author; it stands on its own merits.

Laskin wrote at a time when the Judicial Committee was still Canada's final court of appeal, but when the end of its jurisdiction over Canada was already in sight. The Judicial Committee itself had ruled following an appeal by several provinces against an earlier Supreme Court decision that Canada's Parliament had the right to abolish all appeals to the Judicial Committee, even those that concerned provincial legislation. The efforts to eliminate the right of appeal were the culmination of a growing disillusionment with the Judicial Committee's interpretations. One expression of this, referred to by Laskin, was a report written in 1939 by the legal counsel to the Senate, W.F. O'Connor, who argued that the Judicial Committee had deliberately distorted the meaning of section 91 by treating its introductory paragraph as a supplement to the enumerated sub-sections, rather than treating the latter as illustrations of the general power conferred by the former.[2] Laskin largely agreed, but he argued that this "judicial rearrangement of the terms of section 91" was not the main issue. More significant, according to Laskin, was the reluctance of the Judicial Committee, beginning in the 1890s, to accept federal legislation that had even the slightest and most indirect effect on provincial fields of jurisdiction. Only in wartime, and in the immediate aftermath of war, was the Judicial Committee inclined to take a more generous view of federal powers. Furthermore, the Supreme Court of Canada, and particularly Sir Lyman Duff, who sat on that court from 1906 until 1944, usually interpreted the constitution in much the same way as did the Judicial Committee. In fact, Laskin suggests that Duff was at least as influential as Viscount Haldane, his contemporary on the Judicial Committee, in narrowing the scope of the "peace, order, and good government" power.

The fundamental mistake of both Duff and Haldane, according to Laskin, was their attempt to classify legislation in terms of the subjects on which it had an impact, rather than in terms of the purposes it was intended to serve. This led to a rigid and mechanical approach, and a failure to consider the social and economic realities with which legislators were trying to deal. Canada's ability to respond creatively to economic and social problems had suffered as a result. While appeals to the Judicial Committee would soon end, Laskin recognized that its accumulated opinions would probably continue to be influential, since courts normally view the prior decisions of a higher tribunal as binding their own freedom of action. At the conclusion of his article he suggested how the federal government might act to encourage more innovative interpretation of Canada's constitution.

F.R.Scott was one of the leading critics of the Judicial Committee in the 1930s, but the article reproduced here was written after appeals to the Judicial Committee had been abolished. Scott lived most of his life in Quebec and taught constitutional law at McGill University. He was also one of the founders of the CCF, the predecessor of the NDP, and a major Canadian poet. Like most Quebec Anglophones, he favoured a centralized version of federalism, a preference reinforced in his case by his belief in economic planning and the welfare state and by his opposition to the right-wing Duplessis government in Quebec and its frequent attacks on civil liberties. Like Laskin, Scott argued that the Judicial Committee had distorted the meaning of the constitution with the result that the central government could not deal effectively with social and economic problems. Although narrowing the scope of federal power theoretically strengthened the provinces, Laskin and Scott both considered that this was not true in practice, since the provinces could not effectively exercise the powers that judicial interpretation had assigned to them. Scott makes the point more explicitly than Laskin that the beneficiaries of this situation are private corporations, which can do as they please in the absence of effective regulation by either level of government.

Although Parliament by this time had eliminated the possibility of appeals to the Judicial Committee, Scott was not very hopeful that the Supreme Court of Canada would abandon the Judicial Committee's narrow interpretation of federal powers. He referred to the Manitoba Court of Appeal's narrow definition of federal powers over aviation in the *Johannesson* case, unaware that its decision would soon be reversed by the Supreme Court in an opinion that affirmed a broad definition of peace, order, and good government.[3] On the other hand Scott predicted, erroneously, that if the cold war lasted for a long time the courts might make extensive use of the power over "militia, military and naval service, and defence" to uphold federal legislation on the basis of Haldane's emergency doctrine. Since he deplored the increasing level of tension in international relations, Scott did not take much pleasure in this prediction.

Writing at a time when Premier Duplessis and other Quebec nationalists routinely denounced the federal government for what they perceived as its centralizing tendencies, Scott suggested that Quebec would not benefit from decentralization and had not done so in the past. Quebec had managed to protect its culture and way of life even in periods when it lacked an autonomous provincial government, and decentralization would benefit mainly Anglophone corporations over which Quebec exercised little or no influence. To some extent Scott's analysis anticipates Pierre Trudeau's later advice that the Québécois should pursue "French power" in Ottawa rather than provincial autonomy in Quebec. However, Scott, writing before the Quiet Revolution, apparently did not foresee that Québécois would use the provincial level of government to gain more control over their economy at the expense of Montreal's Anglophone bourgeoisie.

The article by Alan Cairns, one of Canada's leading political scientists, is an attack on the views expressed by both Laskin and Scott, among others, regarding the Judicial Committee's interpretation of the Canadian constitution. By 1971 Canadians had grown accustomed to a Supreme Court that hardly ever declared federal legislation *ultra vires*, and the conventional wisdom was that the judiciary had little or no influence on the evolution of Canadian federalism. Furthermore, Canadians were apparently less persuaded of the desirability of a strong central government than they had been two decades earlier. Futility and incompetence had often seemed to characterize the central government during the Diefenbaker-Pearson era, while on the other hand Quebec nationalism seemed more liberal and progressive after 1960 than it had been in the days of Duplessis. Even some of the other provinces appeared to be administered more competently than they had been in the past. Amid confusion about the elusive "Canadian identity," there was a growing preoccupation with regional diversities and a tendency to argue that they required a more decentralized regime.

Although Cairns himself would later part company with many of these attitudes, they were part of the climate in which "The Judicial Committee and Its Critics" was written. Cairns did not dispute the fact that the Judicial Committee's decisions had tended to decentralize Canadian federalism, but he argued that this was what most Canadians had wanted, that the decisions were suitable to the diverse nature of the country, and that in any event they had only reinforced a decentralizing trend that had other and more significant causes. Cairns admitted that the Judicial Committee had not always been well informed about Canada, that frequent changes in its composition had sometimes produced inconsistency in its judgements, and that it had not clearly elucidated the reasons for its judgements, but he considered that it had done its job quite well in spite of these handicaps.

The critics of the Judicial Committee, according to Cairns, were divided into two camps, which he called "fundamentalists" and "constitutionalists," although they shared a centralist perspective. The fundamentalists, such as W.F. O'Connor, emphasized the discrepancy between the centralizing intent and language of the constitution and the decentralizing effect of the Judicial Committee's decisions. The constitutionalists, on the other hand, emphasized what they perceived as Canada's need for a centralized constitution and blamed the Judicial Committee for not adapting the constitution to new realities. Cairns suggested that the fundamentalists were closer to the truth, since the Judicial Committee had not in fact interpreted the constitution literally, but that the Judicial Committee itself had confused the issue by pretending to follow a rule of strict statutory construction. The judges were in fact adapting the constitution to new realities, but the realities were the diverse interests and policy preferences of the provinces and regions, which demanded a more decentralized federalism.

W.R. Lederman, like Cairns, dissented from the centralist approach to constitutional interpretation typified by Laskin and Scott. Yet, although he praised the Cairns article as "the definitive study" of the Judicial Committee's work and paid the usual tribute to the importance of "cultural, social, and economic realities," his approach was quite different and his criticism, in a sense, more fundamental. Unlike any of the other authors, Lederman argued that the words of the constitution, to say nothing of practical considerations, provided support for a relatively narrow interpretation of federal powers. More specifically, Lederman suggested that the Judicial Committee had been logical and correct in drawing a sharp distinction between the opening paragraph of section 91 and the enumerated sub-sections, and in giving more weight to the latter than to the former. He thus directly challenged what Cairns called the "fundamentalists," who had argued for years that the sub-sections were merely illustrative examples of what was contained in the general power conferred by the first paragraph, and thus logically superfluous. On the contrary, according to

Lederman, the sub-sections were needed to specify the portions of "property and civil rights" that were subtracted from that potentially broad category of provincial legislative power, since, historically, "property and civil rights" had been understood to include practically the whole range of economic transactions that might be regulated by the state. While the critics of the Judicial Committee considered that the general "peace, order, and good government" power was virtually unlimited, or limited only by the specifically enumerated provincial powers in section 92, Lederman suggested that the provincial powers included at least two that were potentially almost as capable of expansion as the introductory paragraph of section 91 itself. The two in question were 92:13 "Property and Civil Rights" and 92:16 "generally all Matters of a merely local and private nature in the Province." Thus, while he admitted that the introductory paragraph of section 91 should not be considered a "mere appendage" of the enumerated powers, he stressed that it did not stand alone as a uniquely broad source of legislative power, the position argued by the centralists.

This analysis serves as the prelude to the consideration of a practical question with great contemporary relevance: how should the Supreme Court distribute the power to legislate over new subjects, not mentioned in the constitution, that arise because of social and technological developments? The conventional answer of the centralists, such as Laskin and Scott, is that since section 91 includes everything not found in section 92, all such subjects should be assigned to federal jurisdiction. The Supreme Court has not followed this advice, according to Lederman, because to do so would gradually reduce the provincial governments to a state of irrelevance. Instead, it has pursued a more even-handed approach so as to preserve a balance between federal and provincial powers. Subjects that were new, but not really of national importance, have been left to provincial jurisdiction in accordance with section 92:16. Broadly defined subjects, such as labour relations or pollution, have been divided into their component parts so that responsibility for them could be shared by both levels of government. On the other hand, Lederman agrees with the exclusive assignment of air transport and broadcasting to federal jurisdiction because these subjects are clearly identified with specific technologies and can be easily defined.

Lederman's article was published in 1975 as the Supreme Court celebrated its centennial, an event that was little noticed by the Canadian public. Almost immediately afterwards, however, the Court would begin to play a much more prominent and controversial role in Canadian life. Governments, at the federal level and in certain provinces, were pursuing more controversial policies that in some cases depended on broad definitions of their constitutional powers. The Supreme Court responded by pursuing its role as a judicial umpire more vigorously, and in the process became involved in such controversial issues as language policy, constitutional change, and the control of natural resources. Although the federal government suffered its share of judicial defeats, provincial governments were more inclined to complain, loudly and publicly, when the Court's decisions stood in the way of their objectives. Provincially minded persons in Quebec and the western provinces even suggested that the Court might be biased toward the federal government, presumably because the judges were appointed by that government.

Peter Hogg's article, published in 1979, replies to these critics of the Supreme Court and convincingly demolishes their arguments: provincial governments have won as many victories before the Supreme Court as they have suffered defeats; the Supreme Court has not departed very significantly from the doctrines laid down by the Judicial Committee before 1949; and there is no evidence that federal governments have deliberately appointed "centralists" to the bench or that they could do so if they tried. Provincial statutes have been struck down more frequently than federal ones, but this is because there are more of them, because provincial politics are more polarized and provincial governments more activist than is true at the federal level, and because some provincial statutes must be struck down because they have an impact outside the province's boundaries. Hogg might have added that federal legislation is more likely to be struck down in Canada than in other federations. The Swiss Federal Tribunal has no power to declare federal statutes *ultra vires*. The Supreme Court of the United States and the High Court of Australia do have such powers, but both have virtually abandoned the notion that there are fields of legislative jurisdiction reserved to the states.

The Constitution Act of 1982, incorporating a Charter of Rights and Freedoms, has greatly broadened the scope of judicial review since Hogg's article was published. Lingering suspicions that the Supreme Court might have, or acquire, a "centralist" bias contributed to the lack of enthusiasm with which most provincial governments greeted the Charter and to the inclusion of section 33, the "notwithstanding" clause, which allows judicial decisions to be overridden in certain circumstances. Nonetheless, the Supreme Court's early decisions on the Charter struck down more federal than provincial legislation. More recently Parliament and most provincial legislatures have ratified the Meech Lake Constitutional Accord, which would give the provincial governments an important and perhaps decisive role in appointments to the Supreme Court. Whether this will give the Supreme Court greater legitimacy remains to be seen.

Notes

1. Archibald Cox, *The Court and the Constitution* (Boston, 1987), p.70.
2. Canada, Senate, Session of 1939, *Report to the Honourable the Speaker by the*

Parliamentary Counsel relating to the Enactment of the British North America Act, 1867, any lack of consonance between its terms and judicial construction of them and cognate matters (Ottawa, 1961).

3. *Johannesson* v. *West St. Paul* (1952) 1 SCR 292.

1 BORA LASKIN

"Peace, Order and

Good Government"

Re-examined

I

It is not good husbandry to plow tilled land and it may be equally a display
of folly to venture on a re-examination of the judicially determined content
of the introductory clause of section 91 of the British North America Act.
That clause has been the favourite "whipping-boy" of most of the articles
and comments on Canadian constitutional law[1] and justification for
another inquiry into it might, understandably, be required to rest on some
substantial ground. But if the amount of literature on Canadian constitutional law is a reflection of the interest which the subject holds for the legal
profession, no one who dares to write on it need offer any apology, regardless of the weight of his contribution. Even if extenuation is necessary,
there is at least this to be said: (1) the opinion of the Privy Council in
Attorney-General of Ontario v. *Attorney-General of Canada (Reference re
Privy Council Appeals),*[2] making it possible for the Parliament of Canada
to vest final and exclusive appellate jurisdiction in respect of all Canadian
causes in the Supreme Court of Canada, is an invitation to review our
constitutional position; and (2) the opinions of the Privy Council in the
Canada Temperance Federation case[3] and in the *Japanese Canadians
Deportation* case[4] contain propositions bearing on the introductory words
of section 91 which, on one view, neutralize much of what had been said by
the Judicial Committee on the matter in the past twenty-five years and, on

Originally published in *The Canadian Bar Review*, 25 (1947). Reprinted with
permission of the Canadian Bar Foundation/La Fondation du Barreau Canadien.

another view, merely add to the confusing course of judicial pronouncements on the "peace, order, and good government" clause.

There are several high points in the judicial history of this clause which may well serve as focal points for any thorough consideration of its content. I nominate as members of this select company (1) *The Dominion Insurance Act* reference,[5] (2) the *Snider* case,[6] (3) the *Natural Products Marketing Act* reference,[7] and (4) the *Canada Temperance Federation* case. The *Local Prohibition* case[8] must, of course, be included in this group, but in some respects its stature is of a retrospective magnitude just as that of the *Russell* case[9] (also a "must" for the group) is, from a certain point of view, of retrospective insignificance.

The dominant judicial personalities in the history of the introductory clause of section 91 appear to be Viscount Haldane on the Judicial Committee and, on the Supreme Court of Canada, its former Chief Justice, Sir Lyman Duff. While the practice of the Privy Council to give but a single, ostensibly unanimous, opinion has hidden from view any possible dissenter, the freedom of the members of the Supreme Court to express their individual opinions produced an opponent to the Haldane-Duff viewpoint in the person of Sir Lyman's predecessor, the late Chief Justice Anglin.[10] Viscount Haldane's views on the distribution of legislative power under the British North America Act were not uninfluenced by his long apprenticeship, when at the Bar, as counsel for the provinces in at least ten cases, although this may be discounted by several appearances as counsel for the Dominion.[11] Sir Lyman's views on the "peace, order and good government" clause were not solely the result of the compulsion of Privy Council decisions. The "locus classicus" accolade bestowed by the Privy Council[12] on his judgement in the *Natural Products Marketing Act* reference[13] may, in part, have been merely a self-serving tribute to a skilful and faithful exposition of its own course of decision but Sir Lyman showed, as clearly as the *Board of Commerce* case,[14] that he had embarked on that course as much by his own choice as by the dictates of *stare decisis*.

Even on the most generous view of the Privy Council's labours in constitutional interpretation on behalf of the Canadian people, one must find them false to their own oft-declared purpose of discussing each question as it arose and refusing to lay down principles which might later be applied to unforeseen circumstances.[15] Unnecessary, if not also innocuous, dicta in various cases became precious formulae for the decisions in later cases. One can readily admit that any judge may yield to a well-nigh irresistible urge to go beyond what is strictly necessary for his decision, and he ought not to be blamed if his successors treat his dicta as binding upon them. The power of members of an ultimate court to bind their successors (something which the "sovereign" legislature does not admit in relation to its successors) is perhaps peculiar to the judicial function of the House of Lords. The Judicial Committee has, in words at least, declared that it is not absolutely bound by its own decisions,[16] but it has hastened to qualify this by the statement that "on constitutional questions it must be seldom indeed that the Board would depart from a previous decision which it may be assumed will have been acted upon both by governments and subjects."[17] It is unfortunate that this type of hindsight could not have been matched by an equal degree of foresight as to the possible consequences, for succeeding generations of Canadians, of introducing generalities into cases where they had no place.

It would be too much of a threshing of old straw to review at length those Privy Council opinions which resulted in (1) separating the introductory words of section 91 from the declaratory enumerations in that section, and (2) reducing the introductory clause to a position supplementary to the declaratory enumerations. It is sufficient for the purposes of this article merely to state these results, while pointing out that in terms (1) the introductory clause constitutes the Dominion's sole grant of legislative power, and (2) the enumerations are merely illustrations of what is included in the power to make laws for the peace, order, and good government of Canada.[18] The righteous indignation of many writers who have commented on this inverted interpretation of the introductory clause is understandable, but I believe that there has been an exaggerated belabouring of this judicial rearrangement of the terms of section 91; and its over-emphasis (as in the case of the O'Connor Report) has distracted attention from a more fruitful point of attack, namely, the lame and artificial application of the "aspect" doctrine to the introductory clause of section 91.[19] Any discussion of the scope of federal legislative power cannot, of course, be divorced from a consideration of the opening words of section 91 as being an original or a supplementary grant of authority. But a sufficient appreciation of "aspect" could have surmounted even the "supplementary" view which the Privy Council espoused. My understanding of the group of Canadian "new deal" cases indicates this to be so.[20]

The *Russell* case was the first occasion upon which the Judicial Committee was invited to sustain Dominion legislation under the introductory words of section 91. It rose to the invitation in an opinion in which it initially characterized the impugned legislation, the Canada Temperance Act. The emphasis in this characterization was laid not so much on the subject matter of the Canada Temperance Act as on the purpose to which it was directed. As later cases put it, the Privy Council ascertained the pith and substance of the legislation so as to discover its "aspect" because that was the cardinal inquiry in assessing its validity under sections 91 and 92 of the British North America Act.[21] The approach from the standpoint of "aspect" rather than "subject matter" has depended on giving due weight to the phrase "in relation to matters," which recurs in sections 91 and 92 and which precedes the reference and listing in those sections of "classes of subjects." In those cases (and there are a number)[22] where the Privy Council has talked of "subject matter" rather than of "aspect," it has been guilty, if I may paraphrase a sentence of Mr. Justice Duff (as he then was), of a failure to distinguish between legislation "in relation to" and legislation "affecting."[23] No such failure is evident in the *Russell* case, because throughout its opinion in that case the Judicial Committee measured its characterization of the legislation against a number of classes of subjects enumerated in section 92 as well as against the grant of legislative power to the Dominion in section 91.

The consideration which moved the Privy Council to uphold the Canada Temperance Act as a valid exercise of power to legislate for the peace, order, and good government of Canada may best be underlined in the Board's own words. Thus, "the primary matter dealt with" was "one relating to public order and safety"; the "declared object of Parliament in passing the Act is that there should be uniform legislation in all the provinces respecting the traffic in intoxicating liquors with a view to promote temperance in the Dominion"; "Parliament deals with the subject as one of general concern to the Dominion upon which uniformity of legislation is desirable, and the Parliament alone can so deal with it"; "there is no ground or pretence for saying that the evil or vice struck at . . . is local or exists only in one province"; "the present legislation is clearly meant to apply a remedy to an evil which is assumed to exist throughout the Dominion."[24] The feature of these statements is their suggested connection with data which would support the existence of a temperance problem on a national scale. Such an approach infuses some realism into the "aspect" doctrine, permitting it to reflect the social facts of Canadian life.

The Privy Council in the *Russell* case spoke of the Canada Temperance Act as "legislation meant to apply a remedy to an evil which is assumed to exist throughout the Dominion." Assumed by whom? The answer must be that the Parliament of Canada made the assumption and that the Judicial Committee was prepared to respect it. One could wish for a recital of the specific facts on which the assumption was made or given credence. But it is at least important that the judgement of the Parliament of Canada was persuasive for the Judicial Committee. While this is perhaps nothing more than the application of a doctrine of "presumption of constitutionality" its import is a far-reaching one if we remember that the *Russell* case was decided in a period when the use of extrinsic aids in interpretation was extremely narrow.[25] About forty years later, in the *Board of Commerce* case, the Judicial Committee in invalidating certain federal anti-profiteering legislation recited that "it can therefore be only under necessity in highly exceptional circumstances, such as cannot be assumed to exist in the present case, that the liberty of the inhabitants of the Provinces may be restricted by the Parliament of Canada and that the Dominion can intervene in the interests of Canada as a whole in questions such as the present one."[26] The Board is now unwilling to make any assumption in favour of the validity of Dominion legislation for the peace, order, and good government of Canada; and, what is more, we are left without any discussion by the Judicial Committee of the factual considerations which underlay the enactment of the rejected federal legislation. It may be as unwise for a court to make assumptions in favour of legislative power as against it, when it can easily call for factual material by which it can reach a conclusion on reasonable grounds. But given a decided judicial attitude against resort to extrinsic aids in interpretation, an assumption in favour of constitutionality offers a court a way of reconciling its enormous power of judicial review with the great responsibilities that rest upon Canada's democratically elected legislatures to satisfy the social wants of a free people. As I shall attempt to show, Viscount Haldane, during the period when he was spokesman for the Privy Council, gave his decisions in terms of cold abstract logic, purporting to find its points of reference within the four corners of the BNA Act, and uninformed and unnourished by any facts of Canadian living which might have afforded a rational basis for his constitutional determinations. The fact that extrinsic aids have been resorted to more freely in the last two decades has seemingly had no effect upon the rigid abstractions with which Canadian constitutional interpretation was surrounded at the close of Viscount Haldane's period of Judicial Committee service.

Honest men may well disagree on whether available data do or do not justify legislation of a particular character and on whether the reasonable inference from such data supports a federal "aspect" in such legislation. But a sense of unreality is the result of constitutional interpretation which has an anchorage only in the mind and unsupported predilections of the judge, whose task it is (as in the case of the British North America Act) to determine from time to time the reach of the governmental functions of the Dominion and the Provinces respectively.

The course of a decision respecting the meaning and content of the introductory clause of section 91 suggests that it can conveniently be discussed under three heads: (1) its relation to the so-called "trenching" and "ancillary" doctrines; (2) its position as an "emergency" power; and (3) its position as a "residuary" power.

II

The so-called "trenching" doctrine, the origin of which is usually ascribed to *Tennant* v. *Union Bank of Canada*,[27] is, at bottom, merely a bit of embroidery on the "aspect" doctrine. Unfortunately it has become, in the hands of some judicial potters, a kind of clay used to stop up alleged over-extensions of federal power to legislate for the peace, order, and good government of Canada. There is a disarming charm about the trenching doctrine when, in Privy Council terms, it champions the paramountcy of federal legislation enacted under the enumerated classes of subjects listed in section 91. But, on closer examination, it becomes merely an apology to the provincial legislatures for any validation of Dominion legislation. Its use to explain a privileged encroachment on provincial legislative authority is purely gratuitous because once a court is satisfied that impugned legislation carries a federal "aspect," no invasion of provincial legislative authority exists.

A similar conclusion must be the result of any close examination of the operation of the so-called ancillary doctrine or the doctrine of "necessarily incidental," the origin of which is usually ascribed to *Attorney-General of Ontario* v. *Attorney General of Canada*[28] (*Voluntary Assignments* case). To say that the Dominion in legislating in relation to a matter coming within an enumerated class of subject in section 91 can also enact provisions which are necessarily incidental to effective legislation under the enumerated class is a tortuous method of explaining the "aspect" doctrine. It has the effect, however, not only of bisecting Dominion legislation but of enlarging the area of exercise of provincial legislative power. The latter result (in the absence of conflicting Dominion legislation) is perhaps not particularly objectionable but the former makes a travesty of the "aspect" doctrine. Legislation, as the Judicial Committee has itself said from time to time, must be considered as a whole and its aspect ascertained in the light of all its provisions.[29] To make what can only be an artificial distinction between those provisions of a federal enactment which are strictly in a federal aspect and those necessarily incidental to the effective operation of the legislation, is to trifle with legislative objectives and with the draftsman's efforts to realize them. Even so close and critical a student of constitutional law as Dean MacDonald accepts the reality of a distinction between the aspect and ancillary doctrines, though it may be that he does so more in terms of resignation than of conviction. He puts the difference in this way:

> The distinction between the "aspect" and "ancillary" doctrines is that under the former the provision in question is validly within the scope of an enumerated Dominion power, the only peculiarity being that, from some other aspect or for some other purpose, similar legislation might also be enacted by a province; while, under the latter doctrine, the provision in question is invalid *per se* as being legislation within an exclusive provincial head but in its particular context it derives validity because of its necessity to effective legislation under an admitted Dominion head.[30]

To me this is a distinction without a difference, a super-refined and unnecessary embellishment of the aspect doctrine which can only divert attention from the need for close and careful consideration of the problem of aspect.

There was nothing in the *Russell* case to indicate any notion of "trenching" or the idea of "necessarily incidental"; nor did these ideas appear in the *Hodge* case[31] which, in upholding the validity of the Ontario Liquor Licence Act, proceeded simply on the "aspect" approach. Not until the *Local Prohibition* case is there a suggestion that the "trenching" and "ancillary" doctrines (which had been enunciated in the meantime) might operate to confine the exercise of federal power to legislate for the peace, order, and good government of Canada. The matter is mentioned in a queer isolated sentence in the *Manitoba Licence Holders' Association* case.[32] In *Montreal* v. *Montreal Street Railway*[33] the Judicial Committee woodenly repeats (and with an error which is also perpetuated by Chief Justice Duff in the *Natural Products Marketing Act* reference) statements in the *Local Prohibition* case.[34] In the *Dominion Insurance Act* reference in 1916, Viscount Haldane in a sweeping statement, unsupported by citation of authority but clearly resting on his understanding of the *Local Prohibition* case (in which he was one of counsel for the province), puts the matter in terms of finality:

> It must be taken to be now settled that the general authority to make laws for the peace, order, and good government of Canada, which the initial part of s. 91 of the British North America Act confers, does not, unless the subject-matter of legislation falls within some one of the enumerated heads which follow, enable the Dominion Parliament to trench on the subject-matters entrusted to the provincial Legislatures by the enumeration in s. 92. There is only one case, outside the heads enumerated in s. 91, in which the Dominion Parliament can legislate effectively as regards a province, and that is where the subject-matter lies outside all of the subject-matters enumeratively entrusted to the province under s. 92.[35]

It is my submission that the above statement is unwarranted not only in its finality but in its pose as a clear reflection of antecedent interpretation.

The *Local Prohibition* case involved a reference to the Supreme Court of Canada in which that court held unanimously that a provincial legislature has no legislative jurisdiction to prohibit the manufacture of intoxicating liquor within the province, and held by a majority that a provincial legislature has no legislative jurisdiction to prohibit the sale within the province of intoxicating liquor.[36] In reversing the Supreme Court, the Judicial Committee stated that a province could, *in the absence of conflicting legislation by the Parliament of Canada,* prohibit the manufacture of intoxicating liquor in the province if the manufacture were so carried on as to make its prohibition a merely local matter; and that the province could prohibit the sale of intoxicating liquor in so far as there was no conflict "with the paramount law of Canada." Lord Watson stated:

If the prohibitions of the Canada Temperance Act had been made imperative throughout the Dominion, their Lordships might have been constrained by previous authority to hold that the jurisdiction of the Legislature of Ontario . . . had been superseded.[37]

This then would indicate that with respect to the actual issues before it, the Judicial Committee recognized the paramountcy of federal legislation over provincial legislation in a situation where in the absence of Dominion legislation the province might competently legislate; in other words, even accepting the artificial "trenching" doctrine, the Dominion could "trench" in the exercise of legislative authority for the peace, order, and good government of Canada.

A long dictum in the *Local Prohibition* case seems, however, at variance with this position, and it is important to set this dictum out in full, as follows:

The general authority given to the Canadian Parliament by the introductory enactments of s. 91 is "to make laws for the peace, order, and good government of Canada, in relation to all matters not coming within the classes of subjects by this Act assigned exclusively to the legislatures of the provinces"; and it is declared, but not so as to restrict the generality of these words, that the exclusive authority of the Canadian Parliament extends to all matters coming within the classes of subjects which are enumerated in the clause. There may, therefore, be matters not included in the enumeration, upon which the Parliament of Canada has power to legislate, because they concern the peace, order, and good government of the Dominion. But to those matters which are not specified among the enumerated subjects of legislation, the exception from s. 92, which is enacted by the concluding words of s. 91, has no application; and, in legislating with regard to such matters, the Dominion Parliament has no authority to encroach upon any class of subjects which is exclusively assigned to provincial legislatures by s. 92. These enactments appear to their Lordships to indicate that the exercise of legislative power by the Parliament of Canada, in regard to all matters not enumerated in s. 91, ought to be strictly confined to such matters as are unquestionably of Canadian interest and importance, and ought not to trench upon provincial legislation with respect to any of the classes of subjects enumerated in s. 92.[38]

It may be observed, with respect to this long passage, that it is the source of Viscount Haldane's positive assertion in the *Dominion Insurance Act* reference, already quoted. Insofar as it applies the concluding clause of section 91 to all the enumerations of section 92 and not only to the 16th enumeration, it has been the subject of competent criticism elsewhere;[39]

and it can hardly be gainsaid that if the concluding clause of section 91 is necessary (as the Privy Council holds) to justify the exclusiveness of the Dominion enumerations as against the whole of section 92, this means that the classes of subjects in section 92 are the dominant ones save to the extent necessary to give scope to those enumerated in section 91. The legerdemain displayed by the Privy Council in dealing with the concluding clause of section 91 gives the surprising result that only the matters within the enumerations of section 91 are deemed to be outside of section 92, whereas any careful reading of sections 91 and 92 indicates that only the matters in section 92 are excluded from Dominion power under section 91 and that the content of the classes of subjects in section 92 is, moreover, cut down by the enumerations in section 91.

The passage previously quoted, in so far as it enjoins the Dominion, when exercising power to legislate for the peace, order, and good government of Canada, from trenching "upon provincial legislation with respect to any of the classes of subjects enumerated in Section 92," conflicts with what was actually decided in the case. Reconciliation of the contradiction is possible only if we ignore the language of the dictum and re-interpret it in terms of the "aspect" doctrine. On such a view, the pieces of an otherwise insoluble puzzle fall into place because there must be a ready acceptance of the proposition that power to legislate for the peace, order, and good government of Canada relates to matters which are "unquestionably of Canadian interest and importance."

I referred earlier to a "queer isolated sentence" in the *Manitoba Licence Holders* case. That case is the counterpart for Manitoba of the *Hodge* case and the *Local Prohibition* case, and it repeats what was said in the latter case that "it is not incompetent for a provincial legislature to pass a [liquor] measure ... provided the subject is dealt with as a matter 'of a merely local nature' in the province and the [provincial] Act itself *is not repugnant to any Act of the Parliament of Canada*."[40] Lord Macnaghten speaking for the Privy Council assigned the provincial enactment to section 92(16) rather than section 92(13), purporting to apply what he conceived to be the Board's opinion in the *Local Prohibition* case. He goes on, however, to say this: "Indeed, if the case is to be regarded as dealing with matters within the class of subject enumerated in No. 13 [of section 92] it might be questionable whether the Dominion Legislature could have authority to interfere with the exclusive jurisdiction of the province in the matter."[41] This sentence, a sort of biologic sport in the context of the whole opinion, appears to be an attempt to reconcile practically the actual results in the *Local Prohibition* and the *Manitoba Licence Holders* cases with the long dictum from the *Local Prohibition* case quoted earlier. Besides wearing a strange look in preferring a dictum to the actual ratio, the sentence drives a wedge between section 92(16) and the other enumerations of section 92. This seems the more remarkable when one considers how, in relation to the concluding clause of section 91, the Judicial Committee in the *Local Prohibition* case went out of its way to oppose *all* the enumerations of section 92 to those in section 91. It said, in that connection, that "all the matters enumerated in the sixteen heads of section 92 [were] from a provincial point of view of a local or private nature."[42] The suggestion of the *Manitoba Licence Holders* case goes beyond merely segregating section 92(16) from the other enumerations in section 92 and making it alone subservient to the federal power to legislate for the peace, order, and good government of Canada. Its necessary consequence is further to reduce the effectiveness of the peace, order, and good government clause, because by giving that clause a hollow paramountcy over section 92(16) (a sort of provincial residuary clause)[43] it can the more easily be dismissed in relation to other more effective enumerations of section 92, such as No. 13. It is significant in this connection that only in respect of liquor legislation has this dubious preference been accorded to the federal power, so that it represents a whittling down of the "aspect" doctrine as applied in *Russell* v. *The Queen* and *Hodge* v. *The Queen*. Viscount Haldane lends support to this conclusion because in the *Dominion Insurance Act* reference he refers to the aspect doctrine as "a principle which is now well established but [which] none the less ought to be applied only with great caution."[44] His statement in that case, already quoted, on the subordination of the peace, order, and good government clause to the enumerations in section 92 shows the extent to which he ignores the aspect doctrine. He speaks there of "subject matter of legislation" and of "subject-matters entrusted to the provincial legislatures"; and further on in his opinion in the case he refers to the *Russell* case as one where "the Court considered that the particular subject-matter in question lay outside the provincial powers." It is clear, of course, that the particular subject matter was within provincial powers in a local aspect and outside such powers only where the purpose of the legislation was such as to give it a federal "aspect."

A great deal has been made, both by Sir Lyman Duff[45] and by Viscount Haldane,[46] of the unreported *McCarthy Act* decision of the Judicial Committee. There the Board, without giving reasons, invalidated the Dominion Liquor License Act, 1883, affirming, in so doing, the opinion of the Supreme Court of Canada.[47] It is important to note that this decision followed decisions of the Judicial Committee upholding the Canada Temperance Act and the Ontario Liquor License Act. An examination of the Dominion Liquor License Act reveals it to have been a purely local licensing statute, contemplating decentralized administration through district Boards of License Commissioners. The whole tenor of the Act indicated that it was dealing with the liquor traffic as a purely local problem in local licence districts. It is hardly a matter of surprise that the Supreme Court of Canada should have invalidated the enactment; but even so, the majority of the court saved those parts of the enactment relating to the carrying into effect of the provisions of the Canada Temperance Act. It is difficult hence to understand why Viscount Haldane in the *Snider* case should have felt it was hard to reconcile the *Russell* case with the *McCarthy Act* decision; or why he so artfully says, "as to this last decision it is not without significance that the strong Board which delivered it abstained from giving any reasons for their conclusions."[48] For, if the *McCarthy Act* case affirms anything, it affirms the application of the aspect doctrine already referred to in the *Hodge* case.

There is, of course, a constant temptation to apportion legislative power under the BNA Act according to subject matter of legislation, to read sections 91 and 92 as if they distribute fields of law-making instead of legislative power directed to various purposes, whether those purposes be related to the peace, order, and good government of Canada or to matters within enumerated classes of subjects. To yield to this temptation involves ignoring the qualitative and quantitative character of a particular legislative problem. Moreover, having regard to the course of decision which reduced the peace, order, and good government clause to a supplementary position and having regard to the use made of the "trenching" and "ancillary" doctrines with respect to that clause, constitutional interpretation becomes a mechanical process in which the substantial inquiry in connection with the validity of federal legislation for the peace, order, and good government of Canada is whether the subject matter of the legislation is part of "property and civil rights in the province" within section 92(13).

III

There can surely be nothing more remarkable in judicial annals than the Privy Council's treatment of the peace, order, and good government clause from the *Russell* case in 1882 to the *Japanese Canadians Deportation* case in 1946. Beginning with the *Board of Commerce* case in 1921 and carrying through the *Fort Frances* case[49] and culminating in the *Snider* case in 1925, Viscount Haldane laboriously built a doctrine of "emergency" around the clause, only to have Viscount Simon puncture the doctrine in no uncertain fashion in the *Canada Temperance Federation* case in 1946. But at the close of 1946 the Judicial Committee, speaking through Lord Wright in the *Japanese Canadians Deportation* case, reverted to the language of emergency with a strange detachment and a seemingly innocent unconcern which expressed itself in an omission to mention the *Canada Temperance Federation* case decided earlier in the same year.

The germ of the "emergency" character of the introductory clause is attributed to two sentences in Lord Watson's opinion in the *Local Prohibition* case, reading as follows:

> Their Lordships do not doubt that some matters, in their origin local and provincial, might attain such dimensions as to affect the body

politic of the Dominion, and to justify the Canadian Parliament in passing laws for their regulation or abolition in the interest of the Dominion. But great caution must be observed in distinguishing between that which is local and provincial, and therefore within the jurisdiction of the provincial legislatures, and that which has ceased to be merely local or provincial, and has become matter of national concern, in such sense as to bring it within the jurisdiction of the Parliament of Canada.[50]

It is well to note that these sentences are more consistent with an appreciation of the aspect doctrine than of any doctrine of power in extraordinary circumstances. *Ex facie,* they make allowance for a social and economic development of Canada which might transform local problems into national ones, so that they might require federal rather than provincial solutions. When Chief Justice Duff comes to deal with these two sentences in his judgement in the *Natural Products Marketing Act* reference, not only does he drain them of any vitality but he makes them ridiculous.

The learned Chief Justice begins by warning that the two sentences must be read in their context, and this admits of no contradiction. He refers to them as being "in . . . carefully guarded language"; and he continues as follows:

> It has been assumed, apparently, that they lay down a rule of construction the effect of which is that all matters comprised in any one of the enumerated sub-divisions of section 92 may attain "such dimensions as to . . . cease to be merely local or provincial" and become in some other aspect of them matters relating to the "peace, order and good government of Canada" and subject to the legislative jurisdiction of the Parliament of Canada.
>
> The difficulty of applying such a rule to matters following within the first subdivision, for example, of section 92, which relates to the amendment of the provincial constitutions "notwithstanding anything in this Act," must be very great. On the face of the language of the statute, the authority seems to be intended to be absolute. In other words, it seems to be very clearly stated that the matters comprised within the subject matter of the constitution of the province "except as regards the office of Lieutenant-Governor" are matters local and provincial, and that they are not matters which can be comprised in any of the classes of subjects of section 91.
>
> Then the decision in . . . *Montreal Park and Island Railway* v. *City of Montreal* seems to be final upon the point that local works and undertakings, subject to the exceptions contained in subdivision no. 10 of section 92 and matters comprised within that description, are matters local and provincial within the meaning of section 92 and excepted

from the general authority given by the introductory enactment of section 91.

The same might be said of the solemnization of marriage in the province. Marriage and divorce are given without qualification to the Dominion under subdivision 26 of section 91, but the effect of section 92(12), it has been held, is to exclude from the Dominion jurisdiction in relation to marriage and divorce the subject of solemnization of marriage in the province. It is very difficult to conceive the possibility of solemnization of marriage, in the face of this plain declaration by the legislature, assuming aspects which would bring it within the general authority of the Dominion in relation to peace, order and good government, in such fashion, for example, as to enable the Dominion to prohibit or to deprive of legal effect a religious ceremony of marriage. The like might be said of no. 2, Taxation within the Province; the Borrowing of Monies on the Sole Credit of the Province; Municipal Institutions in the Province; and the Administration of Justice, including the constitution of the Courts and Procedure in Civil Matters in the Courts.[51]

This, with respect, merely sets up a man of straw in order that he may easily be knocked down. The term "matters" has no meaning apart from legislative issues which may call for the exercise of legislative powers. Those issues depend not on artificial presuppositions but on the existence of facts and circumstances which give rise to some social pressure for legislation. There is no difficulty hence in understanding that the "some matters" in Lord Watson's two sentences could well relate to issues finding concrete support for federal treatment and that they do not necessarily comprehend the abstractions in which Chief Justice Duff seeks to envelop them.

The learned Chief Justice's conclusions as to the meaning of the two sentences are as follows:

> As we have said, Lord Watson's language is carefully guarded. He does not say that every matter which attains such dimensions as to affect the body politic of the Dominion falls thereby within the introductory matter of section 91. But he said that "some matters" may attain such dimensions as to affect the body politic of the Dominion and, as we think the sentence ought to be read having regard to the context, in such manner and degree as may "justify the Canadian Parliament in passing laws for their regulation or abolition . . . ." So, in the second sentence, he is not dealing with all matters of "national concern" in the broadest sense of those words, but only those which are matter of national concern "in such sense" as to bring them within the jurisdiction of the Parliament of Canada.[52]

This statement involves a *circulus inextricabilis*. On the Chief Justice's analysis, only "some matters" which attain such dimensions as to affect the body politic of the Dominion fall within federal power. To the question, What are those matters?, the answer given by the Chief Justice seems to be that they are matters of national concern in such sense as to bring them within federal jurisdiction. Surely this is merely turning the phrase "some matters" in upon itself and amounts to a definition in the terms of the phrase to be defined. It is well to mention at this point that the Judicial Committee in the *Labour Conventions* case said of the judgement of Chief Justice Duff that "[it] will, it is to be hoped, form the *locus classicus* of the law on this point and preclude further disputes"; and again, that "they consider that the law is finally settled by the current of cases cited by the Chief Justice on the principles declared by him."[53] There is certainly a strange and hollow sound to these words when one considers that Viscount Simon in the *Canadian Temperance Federation* case categorically rejected any notion of "emergency" in an opinion which did not bother to mention either Chief Justice Duff's *locus classicus* or the approbation given it by the Privy Council.

It is in the *Board of Commerce* case that the notion of emergency appears in recognizable form. The federal legislation impugned in that case was clearly of a far-reaching character, but nowhere in their opinions in the case do the Supreme Court or Privy Council challenge the necessity for stringent legislation. Admittedly, this is no argument upon which to support a federal exercise of power – or any provincial exercise of power for that matter. But if the necessity for restrictive legislation rests on the existence of a condition which is not local or provincial but general, and the legislation enacted to cope with it is predicated on the generality of the evil to be struck at, a federal "aspect" may well be found in such legislation. There may, of course, be a difference of opinion as to what inferences may legitimately be drawn from facts in evidence and as to whether any questioned legislation is fairly based on reasonable inferences from proved facts. That, however, is part of the necessary travail of constitutional adjudication unless the adjudication proceeds without a firm basis in the facts and circumstances surrounding the question to be determined.

The Supreme Court in the *Board of Commerce* case was divided on the question of the validity of the federal legislation there considered. Mr. Justice Anglin, for half the court, was of the opinion that it was a valid exercise of legislative authority in relation to the regulation of trade and commerce and, moreover, that it was supportable as legislation for the peace, order, and good government of Canada. In this latter connection he said:

> Effective control and regulation of prices so as to meet and overcome
> in any one province what is generally recognized to be an evil – "profi-

teering" – an evil so prevalent and so insidious that in the opinion of many persons it threatens to-day the moral and social well-being of the Dominion – may thus necessitate investigation, inquiry and control in other provinces. It may be necessary to deal with the prices and profits of the growers or other producers of raw material, the manufacturers, the middlemen and the retailers. No one provincial legislature could legislate so as to cope effectively with such a matter and concurrent legislation of all the provinces interested is fraught with so many difficulties in its enactment and in its administration and enforcement that to deal with the situation at all adequately by that means is, in my opinion, quite impracticable.

Viewed in this light it would seem that the impugned statutory provisions may be supported, without bringing them under any of the enumerative heads of s. 91, as laws made for the peace, order and good government of Canada in relation to matters not coming within any of the classes of subjects assigned exclusively to the legislatures of the provinces, since, in so far as they deal with property and civil rights, they do so in an aspect which is not "from a provincial point of view local or private" and therefore not exclusively under provincial control.[54]

On the other hand, Duff J. held the legislation to be invalid, and it is instructive to note his reasoning. Thus he says:

> There is no case of which I am aware in which a Dominion statute not referable to one of the classes of legislation included in the enumerated heads of sec. 91 and being of such a character that from a provincial point of view, it should be considered legislation dealing with "property and civil rights," has been held competent to the Dominion under the introductory clause.[55]

It is a matter of surprise that such a generalization should be based on but a single decision, namely, the *Dominion Insurance Act* reference – especially when it can be countered by the *Russell* case. If we exclude the "company" cases,[56] these were the only cases up to the time of the *Board of Commerce* case in which the Judicial Committee was called on to sustain federal legislation under the introductory clause of section 91. And the "company" cases can by no stretch of the imagination qualify for inclusion under that clause if as a condition thereof "it is essential that the matter dealt with shall be one of unquestioned Canadian interest and importance as distinguished from matters merely local in one of the provinces."[57]

There is no suggestion of "emergency" in the passage quoted from Duff J.'s judgement but rather a playing up of the provincial power under section 92(13). The *Russell* case is dismissed with the statement that "it must be remembered that *Russell*'s case was in great part an unargued case."[58] This is, of course, a barb (repeated again by Sir Lyman in his judgement in the *National Products Marketing Act* reference[59]) directed to the admission, made by Mr. Benjamin as counsel for the appellant in the *Russell* case, that if the Canada Temperance Act had been made imperative throughout Canada without local option it would have been valid. There is certainly nothing in the *Russell* case to indicate that this admission was fatal; and since the Act was in fact a local option statute it might have been good tactics to make an admission which was relevant to something not before the court. Presumably, Mr. Justice Duff is pointing out that counsel failed to make an argument which might have produced a different result in the *Russell* case. This does not lead anywhere because it should be equally possible to overturn other decisions in the same way. And treated as a plea against the too rigid application of *stare decisis* to constitutional decisions, the argument of Mr. Justice Duff apparently defeats the purpose he has in making it.

Mr. Justice Duff comes to actual grips with the problem in the *Board of Commerce* case in a passage which delineates in terms more reasonable than abstract the objections to easy enlargement of the content of the introductory words of section 91. It is as follows:

> The scarcity of necessaries of life, the high cost of them, the evils of excessive profit taking, are matters affecting nearly every individual in the community and affecting the inhabitants of every locality and every province collectively as well as the Dominion as a whole. The legislative remedy attempted by section 18 is one of many remedies which might be suggested. One could conceive, for example, a proposal that there should be a general restriction of credits, and that the business of money lending should be regulated by a commission appointed by the Dominion Government with powers conferred by Parliament. Measures to increase production might conceivably be proposed and to that end nationalization of certain industries and even compulsory allotment of labour. In truth if this legislation can be sustained under the residuary clause, it is not easy to put a limit to the extent to which Parliament through the instrumentality of commissions (having a large discretion in assigning the limits of their own jurisdiction, see sec. 16), may from time to time in the vicissitudes of national trade, times of high prices, times of stagnation and low prices and so on, supersede the authority of the provincial legislatures. I am not convinced that it is a proper application of the reasoning to be found in the judgments on the subject of the drink legislation, to draw from it conclusions which would justify Parliament in any conceivable circumstance forcing upon a province a system of nationalization of industry.[60]

The argument which Duff J. makes, for all its plausibility, is directed to a question which was not before the court. The legislation in the *Board of Commerce* case established a board empowered to prohibit the formation and operation of combines and the making of unfair profits, to prevent the accumulation of (defined) necessaries of life beyond reasonable amounts, and to require the sale of any surplus at fair prices. The issue of national- ization raised by the learned justice almost appears as an attempt to parade the horrors which might ensue from an enlargement of the content of the "peace, order, and good government" clause. We may note that he omits to tell us whether nationalization would be more acceptable in provincial garb. But whether the issue be nationalization or anti-profiteering and anti-combine legislation, the "aspect" approach cannot admit of denial of legislative power "in any conceivable circumstance." The British North America Act does not enshrine, in its distribution of legislative power, any particular economic theory, although it does express some economic pol- icy, as for example, in section 121, which provides for free entry into each province of products of any sister province.[61] It is understandable judicial technique to worry about the next case, but the judge in a constitutional case cannot justifiably fix the sights so far ahead as to detach himself completely from his immediate surroundings. And no more should he loll about in the past if that would also place him in an unreal environment.

When the *Board of Commerce* case reached the Privy Council the notion of the "extraordinary" or "abnormal" character of federal power under the opening words of section 91 makes its appearance in the argument of provincial counsel; and in the opinion of Viscount Haldane this idea is given countenance by his reference to the facts that the impugned legisla- tion was (1) passed after the conclusion of the war of 1914-1918,[62] and (2) was not fashioned as a temporary control measure. Undoubtedly these facts may be relevant in determining whether the aspect of the legislation falls within the introductory words of section 91; but to fasten them to the exclusion of the actual circumstances and conditions which induced the legislation seems to be arbitrary. Yet that is what Viscount Haldane does, as the following passage reveals:

> The first question to be answered is whether the Dominion Parlia- ment could validly enact such a law. Their Lordships observe that the law is not one enacted to meet special conditions in wartime. It was passed in 1919, after peace had been declared, and it is not confined to any temporary purpose, but is to continue without limit in time, and to apply throughout Canada. No doubt the initial words of s. 91 of the British North America Act confer on the Parliament of Canada power to deal with subjects which concern the Dominion generally, provided that they are not withheld from the powers of that Parliament to legislate, by any of the express heads in s. 92, untrammelled by the

enumeration of special heads in s. 91. It may well be that the subjects of undue combination and hoarding are matters in which the Dominion has a great practical interest. In special circumstances, such as those of a great war, such an interest might conceivably become of such paramount and overriding importance as to amount to what lies outside the heads in s. 92, and is not covered by them. The decision in *Russell* v. *The Queen* appears to recognize this as constitutionally possible, even in time of peace; but it is quite another matter to say that under normal circumstances general Canadian policy can justify interference, on such a scale as the statutes in controversy involve, with the property and civil rights of the inhabitants of the Provinces. It is to the Legislatures of the Provinces that the regulation and restriction of their civil rights have in general been exclusively confided, and as to these the Provincial Legislatures possess quasi-sovereign authority.[63]

Having rebuffed the Dominion in any "normal" resort to the power to legislate for the peace, order, and good government of Canada, Viscount Haldane proceeds to place the power on an "abnormal" level, as follows:

It has already been observed that circumstances are conceivable, such as those of war or famine, when the peace, order and good Government of the Dominion might be imperilled under conditions so exceptional that they require legislation of a character in reality beyond anything provided for by the enumerated heads in either s. 92 or s. 91 itself. Such a case, if it were to arise, would have to be considered closely before the conclusion could properly be reached that it was one which could not be treated as falling under any of the heads enumerated. Still, it is a conceivable case, and although great caution is required in referring to it, even in general terms, it ought not, in the view their Lordships take of the British North America Act, read as a whole, to be excluded from what is possible. For throughout the provisions of that Act there is apparent the recognition that subjects which would normally belong exclusively to a specifically assigned class of subject may, under different circumstances and in another aspect, assume a further significance. Such an aspect may conceivably become of paramount importance, and of dimensions that give rise to other aspects. This is a principle which, although recognized in earlier decisions, such as that of *Russell* v. *The Queen,* both here and in the Courts of Canada, has always been applied with reluctance, and its recognition as relevant can be justified only after scrutiny sufficient to render it clear that the circumstances are abnormal. In the case before them, however important it may seem to the Parliament of Canada that some such policy as that adopted in the two Acts in question should be made general throughout Canada, their Lordships do not find any evidence that the standard of necessity referred to has been reached, or that the attainment of the end sought is practicable, in view of the distribution of legislative powers enacted by the Constitution Act, without the co-operation of the Provincial Legislatures.[64]

It is of some significance that Viscount Haldane makes no reference to Lord Watson's opinion in the *Local Prohibition* case; and it may hence be justifiably said that the "emergency" colouring given to the introductory clause of section 91 was a product of Viscount Haldane's craftsmanship. War, after all, was a serious matter and Viscount Haldane, as a former British War Minister, could be counted on to appreciate the wide sweep of authority that must be confided in a central authority during a time of war. Presumably, the problems of peacetime living were capable of decentralized treatment regardless of their proportions. But, that he should have sought to support his doctrine on the basis of the *Russell* case, which involved a local option statute, merely emphasizes its sham quality. It may be noted that the suggestion for co-operation between the Dominion and provincial legislatures to attain ends denied to federal legislation alone was not original with Viscount Haldane but was made earlier by Mr. Justice Duff.[65] As is well known, the co-operation theory, which was miraculously put to a concrete test in respect to the marketing of natural products, was dispatched in its first encounter with the Privy Council.[66]

The *Board of Commerce* case, in retrospect, was a companion case to *Fort Frances Pulp and Power Co.* v. *Manitoba Free Press,* and both were merely a dress rehearsal for *Toronto Electric Commissioners* v. *Snider.* The *Fort Frances* case involved a federal statute which, although enacted after the cessation of hostilities in the war of 1914-1918, provided for the continuation, until the proclamation of peace, of newsprint controls which had been inaugurated under the War Measures Act. Here was an enactment which met the *Board of Commerce* case test of a temporary statute strictly related to a condition of war and Viscount Haldane had no trouble in pulling himself up by his own bootstraps and finding the statute to be valid.

In so doing, however, he overextended himself even in relation to the *Board of Commerce* case. In the first place, he speaks of implied powers arising in time of war. This naturally makes one wonder why, if in time of war, the Dominion can rely on implied powers, it should have been necessary to fit the "peace, order, and good government" clause into an emergency jacket. As a constitutional "Houdini," Lord Watson succeeded merely in reducing the clause to a supplementary position; Viscount Haldane's magic is strong enough to make it disappear altogether and to make it reappear as a spirit. In the second place, it is clear that practical considerations are unimportant for Viscount Haldane in respect of his co-operation theory. The tensions in a federal state which make legislative co-operation practically impossible in normal times are ignored by him. A time of war is, practically speaking, the only sure guarantee of effective co-operation; but the exercise of legislative power in wartime, says Viscount Haldane, "is not one that can be reliably provided for by depending on collective action of the Legislatures of the individual Provinces agreeing for the purpose."[67]

In the *Snider* case, Viscount Haldane reaches his apotheosis. It is there that he tries to bury the *Russell* case which he had used as a springboard for his "emergency" doctrine in the *Board of Commerce* case. The passage in his opinion in which he explains the decision in the *Russell* case as predicated on intemperance being at the time "a menace to the national life of Canada," requiring intervention by the federal Parliament "to protect the nation from disaster," is well known and has been well heaped with the ridicule it deserves.[68] It is a typical "Haldane" touch to find in the *Snider* case the statement that "it is plain from the decision in the *Board of Commerce* case that the evil of profiteering could not have been so invoked, for provincial powers, if exercised, were adequate to it."[69] Here is the arbiter *sans peur et sans reproche* ready to solve any problem by a prepared formula, invariable in its compounds, regardless of the matter to be solved; not for him any stress or doubts such as have agitated the minds and hearts of great constitutional judges in other federal countries. He has fashioned the Procrustean bed; let the constitution, the British North America Act, lie on it.

The *Snider* case affords a typical example of a legislative problem which had undergone a change in character with the passing of years but which was met by the Judicial Committee with the inflexible concepts that are often the product of a neat mind, unwilling in the interests of some sort of formal logic to disarrange thought patterns that had been nicely fitted together. The Industrial Disputes Investigation Act, 1907, as amended, introduced a scheme for conciliation of labour disputes which involved the mandatory postponement of strikes or lockouts pending the termination of conciliation efforts. A number of serious work stoppages preceding and following the enactment of the statute had indicated and buttressed the need for legislative establishment of federal machinery of conciliation. All the factors that weighed so heavily with the Judicial Committee in the *Russell* case were evident in the *Snider* case: there was the need for public order in industrial relations, there was generality, there was uniformity, there was the attempt "to remedy an evil which [was] assumed to exist throughout the Dominion." The genuineness of the legislation in these respects was reflected in the reach of its provisions, which covered employers "employing ten or more persons and owning or operating any mining property, agency of transportation or communication, or public service utility, including ... railways, ... steamships, telegraph and telephone lines, gas, electric light, water and power works."[70] The Appellate Division of the Supreme Court of Ontario, with only one of its five members dissenting, found the Act to be valid as an exercise of federal legislative power in relation to the regulation of trade and commerce and in relation to the criminal law.[71] Certainly that seemed to be a substantial enough ground of decision, at least in relation to most, if not all, of the industries covered by the Act. Viscount Haldane had, however, disabled himself by previous opinions from finding any support for the legislation in the "trade and commerce" clause.[72] And in dealing with it as an exercise of the "criminal law" power, part of his reasoning makes for despair, as where he says:

> It is not necessary to investigate or determine whether a strike is *per se* a crime according to the law of England in 1792. A great deal has been said on the subject and contrary opinions expressed. Let it be assumed that it was. It certainly was so only on the ground of conspiracy. But there is no conspiracy involved in a lock-out; and the statute under discussion deals with lock-outs *pari ratione* as with strikes. It would be impossible, even if it were desirable, to separate the provisions as to strikes from those as to lock-outs, so as to make the one fall under the criminal law while the other remained outside it; and, therefore, in their Lordships' opinion this argument also fails.[73]

It could not, of course, have been very surprising to find Viscount Haldane rejecting the contention that the Industrial Disputes Investigation Act was an exercise of power to legislate for the peace, order, and good government of Canada. One is inclined to agree in this result but only because adequate power to regulate industrial relations (at least in respect of industries having an impact beyond the province of their location) ought to be found in the "trade and commerce" power. Recent judgements by the British Columbia Court of Appeal in *Reference re Hours of Work Act to C.P.R. Hotel Employees*[74] and by Bigelow J. of the Saskatchewan Supreme Court in *C.P.R. and C.P. Express Co.* v. *Attorney-General of Saskatchewan*[75] may well mark the development of a tendency to this view.

What makes the *Snider* case significant is the revealed impotence of the "peace, order, and good government" power in the face of the wide sweep given to section 92(13). Viscount Haldane does not treat the phrase "property and civil rights in the province" in the context of the British North America Act as a class of subject for the exertion of provincial legislative power, but rather as relating to attributes of the citizenry of the Dominion which are beyond the reach of Dominion legislation wherever any portion of them can be the subject of provincial legislation. It is this unusual conception of section 92(13) which has produced the paralysis in the Dominion power to legislate for the peace, order, and good government of Canada, a paralysis so forcibly exposed to Canadian view in the group of "new deal" cases decided by the Judicial Committee early in 1937. How else can one explain the following barren comment by Viscount Haldane in the *Snider* case: "It does not appear that there is anything in the Dominion Act which could not have been enacted by the Legislature of Ontario, excepting one provision. The field for the operation of the Act was made the whole of Canada."[76]

The Haldane conception of section 92(13) in association with his "emergency" doctrine stands responsible for the striking down of the Dominion legislation involved in the *Employment and Social Insurance Act* reference.[77] The Act provided for compulsory unemployment insurance, to be administered by a commission and supported by contributions from employer, employee, and government; and it was enacted in the midst of an unemployment crisis and with a view to forestalling for the future the degree of distress which then existed. It is interesting that Duff C.J., whose analysis of the introductory clause of section 91 in the *Natural Products Marketing Act* reference made it impossible for the Supreme Court to uphold the Employment and Social Insurance Act under that clause, was prepared to find the Act valid as an exercise of legislative power in relation to the public debt and property (section 91(1)) and the raising of money by any mode or system of taxation (section 91(3)).[78] There would certainly seem to be a greater heterodoxy involved in attempting to uphold it under these powers than if it were supported as an exercise of authority to legislate for the peace, order, and good government of Canada.

The Judicial Committee, when the case came before it, affirmed the invalidity of the Act in a short opinion, almost shocking in its casualness unless one remembers that the "emergency" fixation settled the fate of the Act so far as the introductory clause of section 91 was concerned and that the "insurance" cases likewise were a premonition of its doom as an encroachment on provincial power under section 92(13). On both heads, the Privy Council gives us the now monotonous formulae of earlier cases: "It is sufficient to say that the present Act does not purport to deal with any special emergency"; "It is an Act whose operation is intended to be permanent"; "this Act is an insurance Act affecting the civil rights of employers and employees in each Province."[79] Not even a pretence at analysis, no effort expended to give explicit consideration to the effects of years of national unemployment in the 1930s, to the need for legislating preventively as well as curatively; the "law" on the subject was beyond recall or redefinition. The whole sorry story of the Judicial Committee's decisions in the Canadian "new deal" cases was discussed in a special number of this Review in 1937.[80] In the perspective of the past decade, its performance in those cases is surely a monument to judicial rigidity and to a complacence which admits of no respectable explanation unless it be that the blinders fashioned by Viscount Haldane's opinions permitted no deviation from the course on which he set Canadian constitutional interpretation. This is far from convincing, but it serves to explain why the social, factual considerations in the "new deal" legislation were largely irrelevant. To admit their relevancy would make it impossible to maintain a mythical consistency predicated on a fixed notion of the meaning of "property and civil rights in the province."

Viscount Simon's opinion in the *Canada Temperance Federation* case may be likened to the removal of shutters from a house which has been kept dark for many years. From one point of view, namely in its affirmation of the *Russell* case and of the validity of essentially the same statute as was there involved, it is nothing more than an echo of the *Russell* case, perhaps doomed to the same isolation; and, unfortunately, the "emergency" language of the *Japanese Canadians Deportation* case threatens this consequence. Again, it is difficult to say what deduction may properly be drawn from Viscount Simon's failure to mention the "new deal" cases. Does this leave the authority of Duff C.J.'s *locus classicus* unimpaired or is this seemingly intentional ignoring of that judgement a prelude to re-invigoration of the "peace, order, and good government" clause? If language means anything, the second alternative must be favoured; because Viscount Simon goes much further than is strictly necessary in deflating the *Snider* case not only in its appraisal of the *Russell* case but also in its actual approach to the "peace, order, and good government" clause. Thus Viscount Simon expresses himself as follows:

> The first observation which their Lordships would make on this explanation of *Russell*'s case is that the British North America Act nowhere gives power to the Dominion Parliament to legislate in matters which are properly to be regarded as exclusively within the competence of the Provincial Legislatures, merely because of the existence of an emergency. Secondly, they can find nothing in the judgment of the Board in 1882 which suggests that it proceeded on the ground of emergency; there was certainly no evidence before that Board that one existed. The Act of 1878 was a permanent, not a temporary, Act and no objection was raised to it on that account. In their Lordships' opinion, the true test must be found in the real subject matter of the legislation: if it is such that it goes beyond local or provincial concern or interest and must from its inherent nature be the concern of the Dominion as a whole (as for example in the *Aeronautics* case [1932] A.C. 54 and the *Radio* case [1932] A.C.304) then it will fall within the competence of the Dominion Parliament as a matter affecting the peace, order and good government of Canada, thought it may in another aspect touch upon matters specially reserved to the Provincial Legislatures. War and pestilence, no doubt, are instances; so too may be the drink or drug traffic, or the carrying of arms. In *Russell* v. *The Queen* Sir Montague Smith gave as an instance of valid Dominion legislation a law which

prohibited or restricted the sale or exposure of cattle having a contagious disease. Nor is the validity of the legislation, when due to its inherent nature, affected because there may still be room for enactments by a provincial legislature dealing with an aspect of the same subject in so far as it specially affects that province.

It is to be noticed that the Board in *Snider*'s case nowhere said that *Russell* v. *Reg.* was wrongly decided. What it did was to put forward an explanation of what it considered was the ground of the decision, but in their Lordship's opinion the explanation is too narrowly expressed. True it is that an emergency may be the occasion which calls for the legislation, but it is the nature of the legislation itself, and not the existence of emergency, that must determine whether it is valid or not.[81]

And further:

Moreover, if the subject matter of the legislation is such that it comes within the province of the Dominion Parliament that legislature must, as it seems to their Lordships, have power to re-enact provisions with the object of preventing a recurrence of a state of affairs which was deemed to necessitate the earlier statute. To legislate for prevention appears to be on the same basis as legislation for cure. A pestilence has been given as an example of a subject so affecting, or which might so affect, the whole Dominion that it would justify legislation by the Parliament of Canada as a matter concerning the order and good government of the Dominion. It would seem to follow that if the Parliament could legislate when there was an actual epidemic it could do so to prevent one occurring and also to prevent it happening again.[82]

These words contain expressions of opinion such as have not been heard from the Judicial Committee since 1882. And brave as they are, must they not be diluted in the light of a further statement by Viscount Simon that "their Lordships have no intention, in deciding the present appeal, of embarking on a fresh disquisition as to relations between sections 91 and 92 of the British North America Act, which have been expounded in so many reported cases"?[83] One can also be disturbed in this respect by Viscount Simon's reference in the first of his quoted passages to the requirement that the subject matter of legislation go beyond local or provincial concern or interests and from its *inherent nature* be the concern of the Dominion as a whole. Does this contemplate some fixed category of Dominion objects of legislation, or are we, at long last, to be able to judge the validity of legislation in the context of our society and its contemporary problems?

A bold judiciary can find in Viscount Simon's opinion all the material necessary for "a fresh disquisition as to the relations between sections 91 and 92" and, that being so, it was unnecessary for that learned judge to embark on it himself.

No doubt some persons will be disquieted by Viscount Simon's view that an emergency may be the occasion for legislation but that it is the nature of the legislation and not the existence of the emergency which will determine its validity. This raises the question whether the emergency may be not only the occasion but also the justification for the legislation. If it is the justification for the legislation, what happens when the emergency ceases? Should the court be able to invalidate legislation the *raison d'être* of which rests on the existence of a state of war, for example? In the *Fort Frances* case Viscount Haldane suggested that such legislation may become *ultra vires* but that "very clear evidence that the crisis had wholly passed away would be required."[84] The *Japanese Canadians Deportation* case reiterates the "emergency" language of the *Fort Frances* case but adds something new in the following statement:

> Again if it be clear that an emergency has not arisen or no longer exists, there can be no justification for the exercise or continued exercise of the exceptional powers.... But very clear evidence that an emergency has not arisen or that the emergency no longer exists is required to justify the judiciary even though the question is one of *ultra vires*, in overruling the decision of the Parliament of the Dominion that exceptional measures were required or were still required.[85]

This passage expresses the view, seemingly contrary to what is indicated in the *Board of Commerce* case, that some kind of presumption exists in favour of the validity of Dominion legislation where the legislation is predicated on an emergency. It goes beyond the *Fort Frances* case, which went only the length of saying that, accepting the existence of an emergency and of legislation valid for that reason, the court will defer to some extent to the opinion of the federal authorities that the emergency is still operative and hence that the legislation is still valid.

It should be noted that Lord Wright in the *Japanese Canadians Deportation* case does not mention the *Canada Temperance Federation* case and one can properly speculate on how the opinions in the two cases fit together. It is clear that the *Fort Frances* case viewed the introductory clause of section 91 as conferring only an emergency power; and the *Japanese Canadians Deportation* case suggests the same thing. Viscount Simon, however, indicates a scope for the clause beyond conditions of emergency. In so far, however, as an emergency is both the occasion and justification for federal legislation, a question of *ultra vires*, in the sense of the *Japanese Canadians Deportation* case, may well arise once the emergency is gone or if, in fact, no emergency existed. Nevertheless, legislation may be validly enacted under the "peace, order, and good government" clause which needs no justification of emergency; and there is no room here for any subsequent declaration of invalidity. The opportunity certainly offered itself in the *Canada Temperance Federation* case but *stare decisis* bulked large in the Judicial Committee's affirmation of the validity of the Canada Temperance Act.

IV

The Judicial Committee has admitted some scope for invocation of the introductory clause of section 91 as a "residuary" power. In the terms of its own formulae of interpretation, the Board has recognized valid exertions of legislative power under the opening words of section 91 in relation to (1) the incorporation of companies with Dominion objects,[86] and (2) radio communication.[87] These are illustrations of a "residuary power of legislation beyond those powers that are specifically distributed by the two sections [91 and 92]."[88] The *Aeronautics* case reflected a little confusion in the minds of the Judicial Committee as to the "emergency" and "residuary" features of the introductory clause. In that case it stated that "aerial navigation is a class of subject which has attained such dimensions as to affect the body politic of the Dominion."[89] Certainly there was no emergency in the *Snider* case sense although it could reasonably be said, using Privy Council language, that aerial navigation did not come within a provincial class of subject or within a Dominion enumeration so that it must be within the Dominion's residuary power. In the *Labour Conventions* case, however, the Judicial Committee retrospectively assigned the legislation in the *Aeronautics* case to section 132 of the British North America Act.[90] On an "aspect" view it would seem, clearly enough, that the legislation fell within the scope of the "peace, order, and good government" clause, if not also within the "trade and commerce" power.

In its application of the introductory clause of section 91 to cover federal incorporation of companies, the Judicial Committee has sounded a few notes that seem dissonant when one recalls its tune in relation to that clause generally. Thus we are told that the clause confers an exclusive power; and further, that "the effect of the concluding words of s. 91 is to make the exercise of this capacity of the Dominion Parliament prevail in case of conflict over the exercise by the Provincial legislatures of their capacities under the enumerated heads of s. 92."[91] There is no sign here that the Dominion Parliament cannot "trench" when acting under the introductory clause of section 91. And we are also introduced to the notion, novel in the light of the Judicial Committee's prior interpretations, that the concluding words of section 91 secure the paramountcy of legislation under the introductory clause over legislation under the enumerations in section 92. This means, of course, that the Dominion's power under the introductory clause is covered by the phrase "classes of subjects enumerated in this section" in the concluding clause of section 91. It is a significant reading of section 91 but one which Viscount Haldane did not resort to in the *Board of Commerce* case or in the *Fort Frances* case or in the *Snider* case. It is a reading which is in line with the aspect doctrine and it is hardly required if the introductory clause of section 91 is deemed to confer effective federal legislative power only in the residuary sense suggested by the Privy Council in the "company" cases. It does become important, however, if the introductory clause is given a content compatible with the approach indicated in the *Russell* case.

V

The vicissitudes of the "peace, order, and good government" clause, the Dominion's general legislative power, indicate that the Judicial Committee sought to give it a fixed content in terms of subject matter of legislation. Thus, it might be read (at least before 1946) as empowering the Parliament of Canada to make laws for the emergencies of war, famine, or pestilence, for the incorporation of companies with Dominion objects, and for the regulation of radio communication. This nightmarish association of subjects is distinguished by the same sort of affinity that has characterized the Judicial Committee's numerous pronouncements on the Dominion's general power. It is quite a price to pay for realizing Lord Watson's wish, as expressed in the *Local Prohibition* case, to secure the autonomy of the provinces.[92]

But has provincial autonomy been secured? In terms of positive ability to meet economic and social problems of interprovincial scope, the answer is no. A destructive negative autonomy exists, however, which has as a corollary that the citizens of a province are citizens of the Dominion for certain limited purposes only. This does not, of course, herald the break-up of our federal system. The individual provinces have a considerable stake in federation, beyond the mere maintenance of autonomy, and the plenary federal taxing power in its rather rough way gives the people of all the provinces some sense of a Canadian community. Our international commitments have, of course, the same effect.

Some sixty years ago the Judicial Committee said in *Riel* v. *The Queen* that the words "peace, order, and good government" were words "apt to authorize the utmost discretion of enactment for the attainment of the objects pointed to."[93] The remark was not made in relation to sections 91 and 92 of the British North America Act and in the context of the Act it is undoubtedly too wide. But in its reference to legislative objects it indicates the type of problem which a court must face in interpreting sections 91 and 92. It is beside the point that the words of the introductory clause are too large and loose for comfortable adjudication. The Judicial Committee has not been reticent about its ability to give content to the large and loose provincial legislative power in relation to property and civil rights in the province, although it may be noted that it has done so largely in terms of thwarting exercises of federal legislative power, whether for the peace, order, and good government of Canada or in relation to the regulation of trade and commerce.

It has been said that the Judicial Committee's course of interpretation has been perhaps the inevitable result of its perhaps inevitable choice to treat the British North America Act as a statute rather than as a constitution.[94] My examination of the cases dealing with the Dominion's general power does not indicate any inevitability in the making of particular decisions; if anything, it indicates conscious and deliberate choice of a policy which required, for its advancement, manipulations which can only with difficulty be represented as ordinary judicial techniques. But since these decisions are with us, willy-nilly, can we expect for the future that an ultimate court, whether it be the Judicial Committee or the Supreme Court, will depart from them? Able commentators feel that this is asking too much of the judiciary and that we must, if we seek a change in our constitutional interpretation, seek a change in our constitution.[95] One is justified, however, in being as optimistic for the prospect of a change in interpretation as for the prospect of a change in the constitution. At least, one can point to a beginning in the erosion of the old decisions by the opinion in the *Canada Temperance Federation* case; and one can point as well to the "constitution" approach to the British North America Act expressed by Viscount Jowitt in the *Privy Council Appeals* reference.

It is clearly preferable that the constitution be kept fluid through judicial interpretation than through repeated amendment, and the "aspect" doctrine is a ready tool for the purpose. It would be rash indeed to state that the inertia of *stare decisis* can easily be overcome with respect to the accumulated body of Privy Council doctrine. But, viewing this as a consummation devoutly to be wished, its practical realization would seem to involve at least the following steps: (1) enactment of federal legislation to vest in the Supreme Court of Canada ultimate judicial power; (2) full exercise by members of the court of the privilege of writing separate opinions; and (3) care by the federal government to bring before the court, in its initial exercise of ultimate power, legislation drafted with the utmost possible skill and not having any subject matter connection or similarity to prior legislation invalidated by the Privy Council. This is worth a fair trial with a Canadian court operating in a Canadian climate of opinion; and amendment as a postulated alternative may not be without effect in the matter.

Undoubtedly, many will say that this would amount to a clear attempt to subvert the court. On the contrary, it would represent an attempt in a federal context to appeal to those sentiments in existing constitutional doctrine which express principles of growth. The present-day common-law lawyer is prone to forget that his forbears made the same appeal in trying to keep the common law flexible, and that he himself does this today notwithstanding the encrustation of *stare decisis*. Our constitutional case law offers enough choices for fresh beginnings to enable a court to mark out a new trail without doing violence to judicial techniques. It may be true that "Judges are not the most competent people to determine high matters of state."[96] But their tradition of impartiality and a security of tenure which mirrors their independence are offsetting compensations. We are saddled in any event with judicial review so long as our federal system subsists. We ought not to forgo the opportunity of trying to place it on the higher level of constitutional interpretation as opposed to keeping it on the lower level of statutory interpretation. Limiting judicial techniques are operative at both levels, as even the judgements of the Supreme Court of the United States reveal. We can always seek final refuge in amendment.

Notes

1. See: Kennedy, "The Interpretation of the British North America Act," *Cambridge Law Journal*, 8 (1943), 146; MacDonald, "Judicial Interpretation of the Canadian Constitution," *University of Toronto Law Journal*, 1 (1936), 260; Tuck, "Canada and the Judicial Committee of the Privy Council," *University of Toronto Law Journal*, 4 (1941), 33; Richard, "Peace, Order and Good Government," *Canadian Bar Review*, 18 (1940), 243; Jennings, "Constitutional Interpretation – The Experience of Canada," *Harvard Law Review*, 51 (1937), 1; O'Connor, *Report to the Senate on the B.N.A. Act* (1939), Annex 1, 52-78 (hereafter O'Connor Report).
2. [1947] 1 DLR 801.
3. *Attorney-General of Ontario* v. *Canada Temperance Federation*, [1946] 2 DLR 1.
4. *Co-Operative Committee on Japanese Canadians* v. *Attorney-General of Canada*, [1947] 1 DLR 577.
5. *Attorney-General of Canada* v. *Attorney-General of Alberta*, [1916] 1 AC 588.
6. *Toronto Electric Commissioners* v. *Snider*, [1925] AC 396
7. *Reference re Natural Products Marketing Act*, [1936] SCR 398, affirmed [1937] AC 377 (*sub nom. Attorney-General of British Columbia* v. *Attorney-General of Canada*).
8. *Attorney-General of Ontario* v. *Attorney-General of Canada*, [1896] AC 348.
9. *Russell* v. *The Queen* (1882), 7 App. Cas. 829.
10. See *In re Board of Commerce Act, etc.* (1920), 60 SCR 456; *The King* v. *Eastern Terminal Elevator Co.*, [1925] SCR 434.
11. As counsel for the provinces: *St. Catherines Milling & Lumber Co.* v. *The Queen* (1888), 14 App. Cas. 46; *Attorney-General of Ontario* v. *Attorney-General of Canada*, [1894] AC 189; *Brophy* v. *Attorney-General of Manitoba*, [1895] AC 202; *Attorney-General of Ontario* v. *Attorney-General of Canada*, [1896] AC 348; *Attorney-General of Canada* v. *Attorney-General of Ontario*, [1897] AC 199; *Brewers & Maltsters' Association of Ontario* v. *Attorney-*

General of Ontario, [1897] AC 231; *C.P.R.* v. *Notre Dame de Bonsecours*, [1899] AC 367; *Union Colliery* v. *Bryden*, [1899] AC 580; *Madden and Attorney-General of British Columbia* v. *Fort Sheppard Ry.*, [1899] AC 626; *Attorney-General of Manitoba* v. *Manitoba Licence Holders' Association*, [1902] AC 73. As counsel for the Dominion: *Attorney-General of Canada* v. *Attorney-General of Ontario*, [1898] AC 248; *Attorney-General of Canada* v. *Attorney-General of Ontario*, [1898] AC 700.

I do not discount the influence of Lord Watson, especially that stemming from his opinion in the *Local Prohibition* case; but so far as the introductory clause of section 91 is concerned, it was Viscount Haldane that gave it its particular character. It should be noted, however, that Viscount Haldane magnanimously has credited Lord Watson for the form of the British North America Act under judicial interpretation. In an article on the Privy Council in *Cambridge Law Journal*, 1 (1922), 150, Viscount Haldane says:

"Particularly [Lord Watson] rendered an enormous service to the Empire and to the Dominion of Canada by developing the Dominion Constitution. At one time, after the British North America Act of 1867 was passed, the conception took hold of the Canadian Courts that what was intended was to make the Dominion the centre of government in Canada, so that its statutes and its position should be superior to the statutes and position of the Provincial Legislatures. That went so far that there arose a great fight; and as the result of a long series of discussions Lord Watson put clothing upon the bones of the Constitution, and so covered them over with living flesh that the Constitution of Canada took a new form. The Provinces were recognized as of equal authority co-ordinate with the Dominion, and a long series of decisions were given by him which solved many problems and produced a new contentment in Canada with the Constitution they had got in 1867. It is difficult to say what the extent of the debt was that Canada owes to Lord Watson, and there is no part of the Empire where his memory is held in more reverence in legal circles."

12. In *Attorney-General of Canada* v. *Attorney-General of Ontario*, [1937] AC 326.
13. [1936] SCR 398.
14. (1920), 60 SCR 456.
15. E.g.,*Citizens Insurance Co.* v. *Parsons* (1881), 7 App. Cas. 96. In the *Manitoba Licence Holders' Association* case, [1902] AC 73, the Board referred in this connection to "the advice often quoted but not perhaps always followed."
16. E.g., *Tooth* v. *Power*, [1891] AC 284.
17. *Canada Temperance Federation* case, *supra*, note 3, at p. 6.
18. The subject is canvassed in the O'Connor Report and in Kennedy, "Interpretation of the British North America Act."
19. The "aspect" doctrine is laid down in *Hodge* v. *The Queen* (1883), 9 App. Cas. 117, in these words: "Subjects which in one aspect and for one purpose fall within Section 92 may in another aspect and for another purpose fall within Section 91."

20. These cases involved decisions on a group of ten federal enactments among which were the Natural Products Marketing Act, 1934, the Employment and Social Insurance Act, 1935, and three statutes implementing international labour conventions. The cases are discussed in MacDonald, "The Canadian Constitution Seventy Years After," *Canadian Bar Review*, 15 (1937), 401.
21. E.g., *Attorney-General for Ontario* v. *Reciprocal Insurers*, [1924] AC 328.
22. E.g., *Board of Commerce* case, [1922] 1 AC 191; *Dominion Insurance Act* reference, [1916] 1 AC 588.
23. *Gold Seal Ltd.* v. *Attorney-General of Alberta* (1921), 62 SCR 424, at p. 460.
24. 7 App Cas. 829, at pp. 841-42.
25. See MacDonald, "Constitutional Interpretation and Extrinsic Evidence," *Canadian Bar Review*, 17 (1939), 77.
26. [1922] 1 AC 191, at pp. 197-98.
27. [1894] AC 31.
28. [1894] AC 189. And see *Attorney-General of Canada* v. *Attorney-General of British Columbia*, [1930] AC 111 (*Fish Canneries* case), where the Judicial Committee summed up in four propositions its approach to the distribution of legislative power under sections 91 and 92. The second proposition, although hewing to the "no trenching" line in relation to the Dominion's general power, is more consistent with the "aspect" doctrine than with any notion of emergency.
29. E.g., *Great West Saddlery Co.* v. *The King*, [1921] 2 AC 91.
30. MacDonald, "Judicial Interpretation," 274, n. 52.
31. (1883), 9 App. Cas. 177.
32. [1902] AC 73.
33. [1912] AC 333.
34. Lord Atkinson in the *Montreal Street Ry*. case, in stating certain propositions in the words of the *Local Prohibition* case, says: ". . . The exception contained in s. 91 near its end was not meant to derogate from the legislative authority given to provincial Legislatures by the *16th subsection* of s. 92," etc. Lord Watson in the *Local Prohibition* case said the "16" subsections of s. 92, not the 16th.
35. [1916] 1 AC 588, at p. 595.
36. (1894), 24 SCR 170.
37. [1896] AC 348, at p. 369.
38. *Ibid.,* 360.
39. *Supra*, note 18. The concluding clause of s. 91 reads as follows: "And any matter coming within any of the classes of subjects enumerated in this section shall not be deemed to come within the class of matters of a local or private nature comprised in the enumeration of the classes of subjects by this Act assigned exclusively to the Legislatures of the Provinces." Jennings "Constitutional Interpretation," accepts the view finally taken by the Judicial Committee in the *Local Prohibition* case that the concluding clause of s. 91 refers to all 16 heads of s. 92 and not merely to s. 92(16).

40. [1902] AC 73, at p. 78.

41. *Ibid.*

42. [1896] AC 348, at p. 359.

43. See "Note," *Canadian Bar Review*, 24 (1946), 223.

44. [1916] 1 AC 588, at p. 596.

45. In the *Board of Commerce* case (1920), 60 SCR 456, at pp. 509, 511; and in the *Natural Products Marketing Act* reference, [1936] SCR 398, at pp. 409, 411.

46. In the *Snider* case, [1925] AC 396. See also another reference in the *Dominion Insurance Act* reference, [1916] 1 AC 588, at p. 596, which states the result accurately.

47. See schedule to 1885 (Can.), c. 74.

48. [1925] AC 396, at p. 411.

49. *Fort Frances Pulp & Power Co.* v. *Manitoba Free Press*, [1923] AC 695.

50. [1896] AC 348, at p. 361. In the *Labour Conventions* case, [1937] AC 326, at p. 353, the Judicial Committee said of Lord Watson's two sentences: "They laid down no principle of constitutional law, and were cautious words intended to safeguard possible eventualities which no one at the time had any interest or desire to define." This seems a little incongruous when the Judicial Committee proceeds in its next sentence to approve Chief Justice Duff's analysis of the introductory clause of section 91 in the *Natural Products Marketing Act* reference, an analysis which certainly treated the two sentences as expressing a principle of constitutional law. That it is difficult to understand its application is another matter.

51. [1936] SCR 398, at p. 418.

52. *Ibid., 419.*

53. [1937] AC 326, at p. 353.

54. (1920), 60 SCR 456, at p. 467.

55. *Ibid., 508.*

56. There was also, of course, the *McCarthy Act* decision in 1885 where no reasons were given. As to the "company" cases, see *John Deere Plow Co. Ltd.* v. *Wharton*, [1915] AC 330.

57. (1920), 60 SCR 456, at p. 506, *per* Duff J.

58. *Ibid.*, 507.

59. [1936] SCR 398, at p. 420.

60. (1920), 60 SCR 456, at p. 512.

61. Section 121 reads as follows: "All articles of the growth, produce or manufacture of any one of the provinces shall, from and after the union, be admitted free into each of the other provinces."

62. It was enacted, however, before the Treaty of Versailles became effective.

63. [1922] 1 AC 191, at p. 197.

64. *Ibid.*, 200.

65. (1920), 60 SCR 456, at p. 506.

66. *Attorney-General of Canada* v. *Attorney-General of British Columbia*, [1937] AC 377. Nevertheless, the Judicial Committee in this case still advised the

Dominion and provinces to try co-operation (p. 389). See Royal Commission on Dominion-Provincial Relations (1940), Appendix 7, Difficulties of Divided Jurisdiction, by J.A. Corry, ch. 2.

67. [1923] AC 695, at p. 704.
68. *Cf.* Anglin C.J. in *The King* v. *Eastern Terminal Elevator Co.*, [1925] SCR 434, at p. 438; Kennedy, "Interpretation of the British North America Act."
69. [1925] AC 396, at pp. 412-13.
70. 1907 (Can.), c. 20 s. 2(c).
71. (1924), 55 OLR 454, Hodgins J.A. dissenting.
72. By his opinions in the *Dominion Insurance Act* reference and in the *Board of Commerce* case.
73. [1925] AC 396, at p. 409.
74. [1947] 2 DLR 723.
75. [1947] 4 DLR 329.
76. [1925] AC 396, at pp. 403-04. This notion was expressed by Duff J. much earlier in *In re sections 4 and 70 of the Canadian Insurance Act, 1910* (1913), 48 SCR 260.
77. *Attorney-General of Canada* v. *Attorney-General of Ontario*, [1937] AC 355.
78. [1936] SCR 427. Duff and Davis JJ. dissented from the holding that the Act was invalid.
79. [1927] AC 355, at p. 367.
80. *Canadian Bar Review*, 15 (1937), 393-507.
81. [1946] 2 DLR 1, at p. 5.
82. *Ibid.*, 7.
83. *Ibid.*, 6.
84. [1923] AC 65, at p. 706.
85. [1947] 1 DLR 577, at p. 585.
86. *Great West Saddlery Co.* v. *The King*, [1921] 2 AC 91.
87. *In re Regulation and Control of Radio Communication in Canada*, [1932] AC 304.
88. *In re Initiative and Referendum Act*, [1919] AC 935, at p. 943.
89. [1932] AC 54, at p. 77.
90. [1937] AC 326, at p. 351.
91. [1921] 2 AC 91, at p. 115. Cf. Scott, "The Consequences of the Privy Council Decisions," *Canadian Bar Review*, 15 (1937), 488-89, where he says: "The concluding paragraph of sec. 91 was obviously intended to apply to every subject specified in 91, including the general power of the residuary clause...."
92. [1896] AC 348, at p.361.
93. (1885), 10 App. Cas. 675, at p. 678. This was said in relation to the British North America Act, 1871 (Imp.), c. 28, giving the Dominion power in s. 4 "to make provision for the administration, peace, order and good government of any territory not for the time being included in any province."
94. Jennings "Constitutional Interpretation." See also Kennedy, "The British

North America Act: Past and Future," *Canadian Bar Review*, 15 (1937), 393.

95. Kennedy, "British North America Act: Past and Future"; MacDonald, "The Canadian Constitution Seventy Years After," *Canadian Bar Review*, 15 (1937), 401.

96. Jennings, "Constitutional Interpretation," 39.

2. F.R. SCOTT

Centralization and

Decentralization in

Canadian Federalism

The Canadian constitution cannot be understood if it is approached with some preconceived theory of what federalism is or should be. The British North America Act of 1867 was not made to fit a theoretical pattern, but grew out of a peculiar set of historical traditions, experiences, and necessities. There is little evidence that its creators, outside perhaps of Macdonald himself, had made any serious study of federalism in general or even of American federalism,[1] though this model was frequently referred to during the pre-Confederation conferences and debates. The essential material for the new nation-state was in the people themselves and in their already considerable experiments with different constitutional devices.

The constitution which emerged in 1867 is remarkable as much for its continuity with the past as for its introduction of federal forms. The central position of the Crown, the relations of cabinet to legislature, the legal supremacy of the Parliament of the United Kingdom, the central power of disallowance of local laws, the single court of final appeal for all provinces, the belief in a strong central government, were not sacrificed on any altar of federalism. The purpose of Confederation was not to create more autonomy for the British North American provinces (subject to what is said later regarding Quebec and Ontario) but to unite them in a federal state: that is to say, to take away from local governments many of their existing powers and to place over them a new national government

Originally published in *The Canadian Bar Review*, 29 (1951). Reprinted with permission of the Canadian Bar Foundation/La Fondation du Barreau Canadien and by permission of William Toye, Literary Executor of the Estate of F.R. Scott.

endowed with a wide general jurisdiction extending territorially over the whole country. The post-Confederation provinces therefore started with their previous autonomy much reduced, but with the residue guaranteed against federal invasion and, subject to the power of disallowance, placed on an independent basis.

The legal analysis does not apply in the same fashion to the old Province of Canada. True, its legislature, like those of the other provinces, used to make every kind of law, civil and criminal, subject only to a very infrequent Imperial control. No province today has such wide powers. Yet Confederation brought about a change in central Canada that was unlike what occurred elsewhere. The Province of Canada was composed of the union in 1841 of the still earlier provinces of Upper Canada and Lower Canada. It was separated in 1867 into its two historic parts, renamed Quebec and Ontario. Confederation thus re-created the legal entity called Quebec, and by so doing provided for French Canada a degree of autonomy which it had never previously known, not even under the French regime when colonial freedom was minimal. It similarly provided for Ontario a freedom from the restraints imposed in the constitution of 1841, but this relief was not comparable to that felt in Quebec, since the English element had always possessed a majority of votes in the Union Parliament. Hence, to Quebec, Confederation represented a partial escape from centralized control, whereas to all other provinces Confederation represented an acceptance of a measure of centralized control. It is small wonder that Quebec has always insisted the most strongly that the constitution was designed to secure autonomy to the provinces. This was peculiarly her experience. It was not the same for the other parts of Canada.

It is nevertheless an historical fact that the French law and language, and the Roman Catholic religion, won the battle of *la survivance* under a regime of centralization and not under one of provincial autonomy. The interval from 1763 to 1867, from the Cession to Confederation, is longer than the period from 1867 to 1951; yet during that first century under British rule, when the French population grew from some 70,000 to 1,000,000, when the Catholic religion was guaranteed and the French language made an official language, the constitutions under which the French were successively governed placed complete jurisdiction over property and civil rights, education and religion in governments controlled by British Protestants. That was true of the conciliar governments that prevailed from 1763 to 1792, of the Lower Canadian constitution that lasted from 1792 to 1838, of the Special Council which governed from 1838 to 1841, and of the Act of Union of 1841, which deliberately secured an English-speaking majority in the legislature. The Quebec Civil Code became law by enactment of a legislature in which the French were a minority, and the same legislature was the first to introduce separate schools in Ontario. If Quebec's "way of life" had depended upon a constitution which gave her full control of the precious subjects that form the basis of a culture, there would be none of it today. Such a constitution did not exist until 1867.

To suggest that "centralization" is a matter of life and death for Quebec's culture is therefore a view that lacks historical perspective. On the other hand, merely because centralization would not necessarily be a danger to fundamental values in Quebec is no proof that in a given instance it is desirable. It might become a danger, say, to the way of life in some other province, or to the democratic way of life common to all provinces. The problem of centralization is not just a problem of Quebec versus the rest of Canada. It would exist as a problem were Canada all French or all British.

What Does "Centralization" Mean?

Centralization is a currently popular term used to describe the prevailing trend toward an increase in the powers of central governments as opposed to regional and local governments. Its antonym is decentralization, the reverse process, more in evidence today than is generally supposed, through the delegation of state power to subordinate agencies. The problem of centralization raises the age-old question of deciding how authority should be distributed as between various levels of government. This is a vital question for all states, whether unitary or federal. Unitary states possess a single central legislature, usually with unlimited jurisdiction, but they decentralize through the use of municipal, county, and regional administrations, and by delegating functions to various governmental agencies which stand in a greater or lesser degree of independence from the parent body. Even the private corporation is a state creature granted authority and personality to perform certain economic and social functions, and exercising powers differing only in some respects from those possessed by other decentralized "little governments." Within the private enterprise sector of the Canadian economy, centralized authority is very apparent.[2]

In federal states the problem of centralization is structurally more complicated but in essence the same. There is the primary division of legislative powers between the central and local governments – in Canada, between Ottawa and the provinces – each of which is independent of the others and of co-ordinate authority within its own sphere; the word "centralization" in this context means granting more jurisdiction to the central and less to the local legislatures. Yet each type of government is then free to delegate its powers to other bodies if it so desires, though apparently intergovernmental delegation is forbidden in Canada. Thus in Quebec in recent years there is evident a tendency to centralize the powers formerly exercised by municipalities and school boards in the hands of provincial departments or commissions, and similar trends are seen elsewhere.

The distribution of legislative power as between Parliament and provincial legislatures is one thing; that between Parliament and legislatures, on the one hand, and subordinate instrumentalities, on the other, is quite a separate thing. Sometimes, too, administration is decentralized where jurisdiction is centralized. The outstanding example of this in Canada is the criminal law, the enactment of which is federal and the enforcement, for the most part, provincial. The discussion in this paper is primarily directed to centralization in its federal sense, that is to say, to a discussion of the distribution of legislative powers between Ottawa and the provinces.

In Canada the contemporary discussion of this problem meets special difficulties. Some of these are semantic, arising from the connotations of the word itself; others are real, lying deep in the nature of Canadian life. Semantic difficulties exist because the term "centralization" has an ugly sound. It conjures up the vision of a horde of bureaucrats (another loaded word) ruling by decree. It implies totalitarianism. To certain sections of the population it carries a particular menace; for most Quebecers it suggests the loss of their provincial autonomy to Ottawa, centre of British influence and Protestant majorities, while for the business community, fearful of an expanding welfare state with its increased taxation and controls, the word seems a signpost on the road to serfdom. Thus an objective analysis of the reasons for and against any proposed change in the distribution of legislative powers is not easy to achieve, particularly when, as so often happens in this centralizing age, the proposal involves an increase in federal power.

To these semantic difficulties must be added the real difficulties in distributing legislative powers, when the word "centralization" is stripped of its emotional overtones. Canada's physical characteristics alone would make federalism difficult to apply, even were her population homogeneous. What division of powers is appropriate for a country where 90 per cent of the people live in a narrow ribbon of settlement, broken in the middle, stretching 4,000 miles across the continent, and now including the detached island province of Newfoundland, particularly when the principal regions vary so widely in their economic activities? The wheat economy of the West, even though broadened by new industrial growth, would make an uneasy companion for the manufacturing central provinces under any form of government.

Add to this the cultural differences within Canada and the picture becomes the more complicated. In Quebec and Ontario, and to an increasing extent in other provinces, the British-Protestant and French-Catholic groups create a bicultural community whose special claims the constitution must recognize. Already the expansion of the French-speaking element in New Brunswick is pressing hard upon the limitations of section 133 of the BNA Act, which, while making French an official language in the federal Parliament and federal courts, leaves Quebec as the only officially bilingual province;[3] and Catholic demands for separate school rights are being heard in provinces not now obliged to maintain them by the educational guarantees of section 93.[4] Governmental "efficiency" cannot be the only criterion where a large section of the population is more concerned with protecting its special French and Catholic way of life than with easing the headaches of federal administrators. Nor are the cultural problems solely related to the historic situation of Quebec within the confederation. Canada possesses minorities within minorities – Protestants in Quebec, Catholics and French elsewhere, Eskimos and Indians – who claim consideration. In the western provinces a special need exists, that of assimilating into some general Canadian pattern the new Canadians of most divergent races and creeds, many of whom hive off into colonies which set up claims to minority rights not imagined in the BNA Act.

Competing with these regional and cultural factors today are the insistent requirements of economic regulation and national defence in a time of inflationary pressures and world unrest. These push heavily toward centralization, but they are relative newcomers to the federal scene, and perhaps in our innocence, we tend to regard them as emergency problems to which the Constitution need not permanently adapt itself. The older factors touch deeper roots of national consciousness, and some of these make for centralization, others for decentralization. Statesmanship of a high order is demanded of Canadians if they would bring these conflicting forces into harmonious federal balance. But of one thing we can be sure if Canada is to remain a federal state, neither breaking up into separate pieces nor marching to unification under a single government: a rigid attitude either for or against centralization is quite indefensible. The problems faced by governments have to be assessed, and the distribution of authority determined, not only in relation to cultural guarantees, but also and in some instances primarily in relation to social need. To refuse centralization where the evil to be met is beyond provincial control is to court anarchy or to suffer the unchecked domination of private interests; to rush into centralization when the matter is not of serious national concern is to risk creating an overmighty state and depriving the people of their local democratic control.

Unitary Principles in the BNA Act

All the debates and discussions about the Canadian constitution at the time of its adoption emphasized the high degree of central authority which it was to provide. Friend and foe alike agreed on this characteristic.[5] The text of the BNA Act impresses one by its apparent preference for unitary principles as opposed to provincial sovereignty. At every important point provincial freedom is hedged with federal controls, many of which no strict theory of federalism can ever justify. These are evident in the legislative, executive, and judicial spheres.

Provincial legislative autonomy, for example, is subject to several restraints. No provincial bill can become law without the assent of a federal appointee, the Lieutenant-Governor. He may legally withhold that assent, or he may reserve the bill for Ottawa's acceptance or rejection. Even after it has become law it may be disallowed by the federal executive within one year, a power which in fact has been frequently exercised.[6] In cases of conflict between an *intra vires* federal law and an *intra vires* provincial law, in matters of concurrent jurisdiction, the federal law always prevails.[7] What is of greater significance, the residue of unallocated subjects is centralized by the opening words of section 91, thus contrasting sharply with the principle underlying the American constitution. Even the laws relative to "Property and Civil Rights" were intended to be progressively centralized for the common law provinces by section 94. Provincial executive autonomy is restrained by the fact that the head of the executive is the same Lieutenant-Governor who is appointed, paid, instructed, and removed by Ottawa. The constitution does not require him to be a native or resident of the province. Provincial judicial autonomy is restrained by the fact that the judges of provincial superior courts are federally appointed and paid; the province may appoint judicial officers to minor courts only.[8] In addition, the Supreme Court of Canada, whose members are also federally appointed, is the final court of appeal for all questions of provincial as well as federal law, thus making it a truly national court and not merely, as is the Supreme Court of the United States, a federal court.[9] Even in the delicate matter of denominational schools the federal Parliament is given an ultimate power by section 93 to make remedial laws, in defined circumstances, which will override provincial legislation. Moreover the provincial representatives in the Canadian Senate are neither elected by provinces nor chosen by provincial governments, but are nominated for life by the federal executive.[10] Provincial financial autonomy is restrained by the fact that the power of the provinces to tax is limited to the imposition of direct taxes,[11] and provincial governments are subsidized by federal grants.[12]

If one turns from what may be called the political structure of the constitution to its distribution of economic powers, a similar centralization is noticeable. What were the chief economic activities of the population of the various provinces at the time of Confederation? An answer which listed trade and commerce, agriculture, fishing, navigation and shipping, railways and canals would not be far wrong, and would not leave many classes of workers uncovered. Every one of these subjects is allotted by the constitution to the national Parliament. Trade and commerce, seacoast and inland fisheries, and navigation and shipping are exclusive federal powers;[13] agriculture is a concurrent power, with federal laws paramount;[14] railways and canals are exclusively federal if interprovincial,[15] and, if not, can be made exclusively federal at any time by a simple declaration by

Parliament that they are for the general advantage. Any other local "works" can be similarly removed from provincial autonomy by this form of declaration.[16] True, provinces were left with the ownership of their natural resources in such things as lands, mines, forests, and waterpowers,[17] but once these became developed their products would enter the stream of trade and commerce, generally using interprovincial services, and would thus come within federal jurisdiction. Naturally the subjects concomitant to trade and commerce, such as banks, legal tender, interest, weights and measures, were exclusively federal.[18] To cap it all, provincial tariffs were prohibited, and customs and excise laws were given to Ottawa.[19] Thus the BNA Act appears to have provided beyond question for a central authority over the economic life of Canada, and to have safeguarded us against any reappearance of the provincial economic autonomy which had so stifled progress and development among the pre-Confederation colonies. In the words of a leading authority on Canadian government, "The federation was thus intended to depart radically from the pure federal form in which the component local units are of equal or co-ordinate rank with the central government."[20]

It will be noted that every federal power mentioned in the two preceding paragraphs is derived, not from judicial interpretation, and not from mere surmises or inferences, but from some positive text of the constitution itself. It would be tedious to quote all the leading Fathers of Confederation who spoke in support of the idea of Parliament's predominant position, and impossible to quote any against. The compact of Confederation, in so far as it existed, was an agreement to prefer national power to provincial autonomy on all matters of general or national concern, leaving the provinces control over their local affairs only, but with guarantees as to language and separate schools. This basic contrast between "general" and "local" matters, which Clement has rightly called "The Cardinal Principle of Allotment,"[21] is explicitly stated in the second of the Quebec Resolutions of 1864 and of the London Resolutions of 1866. The relevant portion of the London Resolutions reads as follows:

> In the Confederation of the British North American provinces the system of government best adapted under existing circumstances to protect the diversified interests of the several provinces and secure efficiency, harmony and permanency in the working of the Union is a General Government charged with matters of common interest to the whole country and Local Governments for each of the Canadas, and for the provinces of Nova Scotia and New Brunswick, charged with the control of local matters in their respective sections. . . .

Words could not be clearer to show that the line of demarcation between what was to be centralized and what was to be decentralized ran along the division between matters of general or national concern and matters of local concern ("of a merely local or private Nature in the Province," to borrow words from section 92, head 16). Enumerated heads of jurisdiction under section 91 were examples of general matters, all other general matters being thought of as contained in the federal residue; enumerated heads of 92 were examples of local matters, education received special treatment in section 93, and immigration and agriculture in section 95. It was a sensible arrangement, seemingly forever free from the kind of exaggerated local sovereignty which had disrupted the United States by civil war, and which served as so clear an object lesson to the men of both races who drafted the agreements at Quebec and London.

The Constitutional Revolution

Everyone familiar with Canadian constitutional history knows that the original constitution is far from representing the realities of Canadian law and politics today. The whole emphasis has now changed. Since 1867 the jurisdiction of the central government has relatively decreased, and that of the provinces increased, to such an extent that in the opinion of many authorities the intentions of the Fathers of Confederation have been frustrated. Despite the wording of the constitution, and despite her growth in international prestige and importance, Canada is now, eighty-five years after Confederation, troubled with such a trend toward "States Rights" (to use Macdonald's name for it) that the federal government must rely more and more on a new legal doctrine of "national emergency" in order to legislate on matters of unquestioned national importance, and the national Parliament is increasingly obliged to defer to agreements made in a kind of General Assembly of Sovereign Provinces called a Dominion-Provincial Conference, where each government possesses a veto over decisions. This outcome is indeed a commentary on the impossibility of directing the course of history by even the most carefully drawn constitutional provisions.

To attempt an explanation of how this change occurred would be a long story. Influences making for the end result, however, would not be difficult to identify. A major one would be found in the cumulative work of the courts, particularly of the Judicial Committee of the Privy Council, now vanishing as a final court of appeal for Canada but still a powerful factor in Canadian politics as long as the doctrine of *stare decisis* remains.[22] In the United States, a looser federalism was unified by the judgements of a Marshall, while in Canada a stronger union was decentralized by a Watson and a Haldane. Other influences would be found in the political, economic, and social forces that form the climate in which the constitution must work. The worldwide depression that began in 1873 forced the federal government to reduce its program of national development, and compelled Canadians to turn to "the older and more obvious realities of provincial and local community life."[23] An increasingly influential factor to be noted is the growing political and economic strength of French Canada, whose people have won for themselves, by their tenacity, productivity, and ability, a far wider recognition of their distinctive cultural rights than was accepted in 1867. Though now past their first struggles for mere *survivance*, and with about one quarter of their people living in other provinces, most French-speaking Canadians are generally persuaded that every limitation on Ottawa's constitutional powers means more strength in their "citadel" of Quebec and hence more autonomy for the French-speaking element. In other regions, notably the Maritime provinces, a tradition of autonomy is also strong. Of perhaps equal importance today are the prevailing notions of "free enterprise" held by wide and powerful sections of the community whose political philosophy inclines to a provincial autonomy from which they have little interference to fear, and whose influence on public opinion through agencies of mass communication and through direct party support it is difficult to exaggerate. *Le Devoir* and the *Montreal Gazette*, apt spokesmen for Quebec nationalists and powerful business interests respectively, share many constitutional opinions.

Counter influences making for centralization are found chiefly in claims for protection for special groups such as organized labour and farmers, in the growing demands for social insurance, and in the ever insistent pressures of defence planning and international collaboration. The growing industrialization tends towards centralization, despite what autonomists may say, though at the same time it increases the duties of local governments as well. Time, as Professor Angus once said, is running against the provinces,[24] but in Canada time seems often to move at the speed of a glacier. It is the law of the constitution which will be emphasized here, and the law of the constitution, in so far as the distribution of legislative powers is concerned, is now in certain respects out of line with the facts of modern Canadian life.

Judicial Preference for Decentralization

The decentralizing influence of judicial interpretation resulted from a piecemeal whittling away of certain important clauses allocating legislative powers to the Parliament of Canada. The story is not, of course, totally one-sided; a few notable decisions favoured Dominion jurisdiction. Some of these affected executive and judicial functions rather than legislative powers. For instance, the federal power of disallowance of provincial laws and the Lieutenant-Governor's power to reserve bills were upheld in the *Reference re the Power of Disallowance and Reservation*.[25] The right of the Parliament of Canada to abolish appeals from all Canadian courts to the Judicial Committee of the Privy Council in England, and to establish the Supreme Court of Canada as the final court of appeal, was upheld in *A.-G.*

for Ontario v. *A.-G. for Canada*.[26] The very unfederal power of Parliament to declare local "works" to be for the general advantage of Canada, and thus to transfer them from provincial into federal jurisdiction, has survived many tests.[27] The federal appointment of judges has not been questioned in the courts, though the definition of what constitutes a "Superior, District or County Court," whose members under the constitution must be appointed by Ottawa, has been reasonably framed so as to exclude various types of provincial administrative tribunal, thus leaving the provinces a freer hand in the development of their governmental services.[28] Under the "emergency" doctrine, the full authority of Parliament to legislate for the "peace, order, and good government of Canada," which was originally thought to be an ample residuary power covering new peacetime matters of "general interest" as well as emergency situations, has prevailed, so that Canadians know they can at least engage in wars without constitutional difficulties.[29]

These are examples of some significant Dominion successes in the law courts on matters of broad constitutional principle. Their effect was rather to stem the drift toward decentralization than to open new fields to Dominion jurisdiction. The two most important decisions since 1867 enlarging federal legislative power were the references which held that the subjects of radio broadcasting and aeronautics belonged to the Dominion sphere.[30] These judgements are scarcely surprising; the notion of local governments attempting separate control of flying and broadcasting within a single country is difficult to image. Yet even so the chief ground on which aeronautics was attributed to Ottawa was that an "Empire treaty" existed (the Aeronautics Convention of 1919) binding on Canada, and hence section 132 of the constitution could be applied. Aerial navigation was not held to fall within the enumerated head of "Navigation and Shipping." Just what might be Ottawa's position if there were no treaty it is hard to say, since the question has not been decided; already doubts have been raised in *Johannesson* v. *West St. Paul* as to the federal right to choose the location of aerodromes for peacetime commercial aviation.[31]

Over against these decisions we must set the series of leading cases on particular words and phrases in sections 91, 92, and 132 of the BNA Act, and particularly on the opening words of section 91, which reshaped Canada's federal system. Very few of the federal heads of jurisdiction, other than perhaps banks and banking, the criminal law, interest, and telegraphs, have received anything but the narrowest interpretation, while the provincial powers, notably property and civil rights, have received a broad and liberal one. The federal residuary power, surely one of the most important powers to distribute in a federal state, has been reduced to an "emergency" doctrine, virtually useless in normal circumstances, the provincial jurisdiction over "Property and Civil Rights" being the effective residue.

The turning point of this line of cases came with the *Ontario Liquor License* case of 1896,[32] which Lord Haldane himself described as "the watershed."[33] Here it was said by Lord Watson that

> the exercise of legislative power by the Parliament of Canada, in regard to all matters not enumerated in s. 91, ought to be strictly confined to such matters as are unquestionably of Canadian interest and impor- tance, and ought not to trench upon provincial legislation with respect to any of the classes of subjects enumerated in s. 92. To attach any other construction to the general power which, in supplement of its enumer- ated powers, is conferred upon the Parliament of Canada by s. 91, would, in their Lordships' opinion, not only be contrary to the intend- ment of the Act, but would practically destroy the autonomy of the provinces.[34]

The phrase "ought not to trench upon provincial legislation," meaning ought not to "affect" or "interfere with" the provincial laws, departs radically from the opening words of section 91 where the only limit upon the residuary power is that laws based on it must not be "coming within the classes of subjects by this Act assigned exclusively to the Legislatures of the Provinces." A law on banking may affect, trench upon, and interfere with "Property and Civil Rights," but it does not "come within" that subject; so too it was intended to be with laws on the new subjects of equivalent national importance such as trade unions and unemployment insurance. The weakness in the present position, from the governmental point of view, lies in the dependence upon an "emergency" situation for the validity of a federal law on almost all unenumerated subjects, and, while the courts in the most recent case seemed to suggest that they would not look behind a declaration of Parliament that an emergency existed, "unless the contrary were very clear," thus making of the emergency power almost a second declaratory power similar to that existing for local works,[35] the jurisdiction thus possessed is no substitute for a plain, untrammelled residuary power over matters of genuine interprovincial concern, such as was in the original constitution. War emergencies are only one form of "general interest," but they are the only form the courts seem willing to accept, though "pesti- lence" has been quaintly hinted at as equally justifying central authority under the residuary clause.[36] Nothing in the great economic crisis of the 1930s, not even mass unemployment and disrupted agricultural markets, was an emergency. A recent attempt has been made by Lord Simon, in the *Canada Temperance Federation* case,[37] to bring Canadian law on this point back to its source in the constitution, but his admirable logic and common sense seem about to suffer the same polite dismissal that was previously accorded a similar statement of the law made in *Russell* v. *The Queen* back in 1883.[38]

The whole story of this major constitutional amendment is too familiar to need repetition,[39] but it may be pointed up by comparing these words of Macdonald, spoken during the Confederation debates:

> We have strengthened the General Government. We have given the General legislature all the great subjects of legislation. We have conferred on them, not only specifically and in detail, all the powers which are incident to sovereignty, but we have expressly declared that all subjects of general interest not distinctly and exclusively conferred upon the local governments and local legislatures, shall be conferred upon the General Government and Legislature.[40]

and those of Lord Carnarvon in the House of Lords discussion on the BNA Act:

> It will be seen, under the 91st clause, that the classification is not intended 'to restrict the generality' of the powers previously given to the central parliament, and that those powers extend to all laws made 'for the peace, order and good government' of the Confederation, terms which, according to all precedents, will, I understand, carry with them an ample measure of legislative authority.[41]

with those which a distinguished Canadian barrister could publish in 1940:

> Clearly there is in the Act no such thing as a general power to make laws for peace order and good government. The very words of the clause itself (without even a comma to separate them) exclude from such general power everything that falls within sec. 92. It has been therefore the duty of the courts first to determine the limits of the powers conferred upon the Provincial Legislature, and only when these powers have been exhausted is the general power of the Dominion open for consideration.[42]

Obviously something drastic has occurred between 1867 and 1940. The Sirois Report muddied the historical waters by contending, with a fine appearance of impartiality, that there are grave doubts about the fundamental ideas of the Fathers, and that little light can be gained from a resort to history.[43] It cited five authorities on the side here maintained and two on the other. It might have cited a great many more than the five, but few more than the two.[44] The point immediately at issue is not whether there should be more or less centralization today, and not whether the BNA Act is a compact, but solely whether the Fathers of Confederation thought they had created a federal state with a general power to make laws outside the enumerated heads, and with a leaning toward centralization rather than toward provincial autonomy. On this there can be no serious debate. The courts have virtually eliminated the general power and have created a leaning toward provincial autonomy.

Next to suffer reduction after the residuary clause was another equally significant federal power, namely the regulation of trade and commerce. An intention clearly enunciated at Confederation, and on which much was said, was that the new Dominion of Canada was to be freed from the petty provincial economic policies and barriers to trade which bedevilled the first half of nineteenth-century Canadian history. Hence the constitution did not reserve to the provinces intraprovincial trade, as the United States constitution reserved intrastate commerce. However, this provincial reservation, omitted in the law, was supplied by a line of decisions beginning with the *Parsons* case.[45] On the merits that case appears sound, since it merely held that the ordinary contracts relating to a trade were matters of property and civil rights – a proposition difficult to quarrel with. It was the *dicta* in that case, now firmly established as law, which did the damage, particularly the rule excluding particular trades (later extended to cover groups of trades[46]) from federal regulations unless expressly mentioned in section 91 outside the trade and commerce clause. This rule was clinched in the insurance cases.[47] It may make sense according to the narrowest rules of interpretation for ordinary statutes, but it makes little sense in a national constitution. The historian sees the problem differently: "The enumeration of these definite powers did not exhaust the trade and commerce clause anymore than the trade and commerce clause exhausted the economic powers implied in the general authority to make laws for the peace, order and good government of Canada."[48] The judicial view, besides refusing to see the enumerated heads as mere examples of the general power, assumes that the drafters of the constitution wished for no federal authority over any individual trade other than the only one specially mentioned, namely banking, regardless of the size it might assume or the degree of dependence of the whole economy upon it. This does not harmonize with the concept of "general interest" as a source of federal power. Hence even so major a trade as that in wheat has had to have its legal base in federal law bolstered by the clumsy device of declaring all grain elevators in the Prairies to be works for the general advantage of Canada.[49] Add to this the later judicial holding that the word "regulation" excluded prohibition,[50] so that the prohibition of production and trading (for example, in margarine[51]) is a provincial matter, and the hollowness of federal authority over this all-important and highly emphasized subject is evident. Even the federal control of prices is of dubious validity in peacetime,[52] though it is not easy to see how ten local governments can control prices in a country with internal free trade. True, federal trade policies through credit control, international trade agreements, tariffs, and the criminal law are of great importance, but the direct reliance upon the words "Regulation of Trade and Commerce" is of little use.

Dominion regulation of agriculture and fisheries has received similar treatment. The federal law protecting the dairy industry by prohibiting the production of margarine,[53] and the federal Wheat Act itself,[54] were not considered laws relating to agriculture, nor was the Natural Products Marketing Act of 1934.[55] The all-embracing property and civil rights clause prevailed in these fields also. The Dominion's "exclusive" power to regulate fisheries has long since ceased to be exclusive. Moreover, "fisheries" does not include putting fish in cans or in refrigerating cars.[56] Once a potato or a codfish comes to be packed, processed, shipped, and sold it is trade and commerce, not agriculture or fisheries, and if confined to intraprovincial trade falls under provincial control. Under a constitution the text of which gives exclusive jurisdiction over the regulation of trade and commerce, and over seacoast and inland fisheries, to the central government, as well as concurrent jurisdiction over agriculture, a provincial Natural Products Marketing Act covering the following extensive operations was held to be a matter of "property and civil rights":

> The control and regulation in any or all respects of the transportation, packing, storage and marketing of natural products within the Province, including the prohibition of such transportation, packing, storage and marketing in whole or in part,

a natural product being defined as any product of

> agriculture, or of the forest, sea, lake or river, and any article of food or drink wholly or partly manufactured or derived from any such product.[57]

A federal Marketing Act of similar scope has been held to be invalid as trenching on the provincial field.[58] The enlargement of provincial control of trade and commerce was crowned by Lord Haldane, overruling the Supreme Court, when he held that companies created by a province had the capacity to do business anywhere across provincial boundaries, if granted permission from the outside authority.[59] Hence nationwide trade and commerce can be carried on by a provincial creature.

Treaty legislation is a matter of growing import to all states, both federal and unitary, in a shrinking world. Goods manufactured in and exported from a Canadian province, if produced under working standards and conditions below those of the country of import, carry with them a dangerous power to destroy the higher standards. Provincial legislation or its absence may thus affect vitally the lives of people in foreign countries. Any treaty binding Canada or even one province of Canada, if between the Empire and a foreign country, can be implemented exclusively by Ottawa under section 132 of the constitution. But by defining an Empire treaty as one made by the King on the advice of an Imperial executive, excluding those made on the advice also of the Canadian executive, the courts removed the Canadian-made treaty from section 132; and, after stating in the *Radio* case[60] that it would therefore fall in the Dominion residue under peace, order, and good government, changed their minds in the *ILO Conventions* reference and held such legislation to be within the competence of whichever legislature had jurisdiction over the subject matter of the treaty under sections 91 and 92.[61] Thus the only single treaty-enforcing power was in effect removed from the constitution, since Empire treaties have vanished with the Empire. Today the fact that a subject of legislation becomes of such international importance as to reach treaty formulation does not necessarily endow Ottawa with legislative jurisdiction over it. The question of jurisdiction is tested by the courts as if there were no treaty at all. The fact that is all important becomes non-existent. Canadian provinces, which under the BNA Act are specifically deprived of jurisdiction even over a ferry connecting them with a foreign country,[62] have full jurisdiction over the implementation of conventions treating of wages, hours of labour, and other matters otherwise within section 92, even though made between Canada and many foreign countries.

Admittedly the treaty-making power is a difficult one to distribute in a federal state. Recognition of this fact is seen in the special provisions in the charter of the International Labour Organization on the implementation of its conventions by countries whose powers are subject to limitations. There is an inescapable dilemma: either the central government has jurisdiction over all treaties, in which case the local governments are no longer sure of their autonomous powers, since at any moment a treaty may be made which will remove its subject matter from their competence, or else the central government, which alone may make and ratify the treaty, must defer to local governments for the implementation of some or all of them, in which case the freedom of the state to assist in building international co-operation is sharply curtailed. A choice must be made between the two values, one of local sovereignty, the other of world peace.

The subject is too wide for full treatment here, but some comment is relevant to the problem of centralization in Canada. The question is, Which attribution of jurisdiction is the more consistent with Canada's type of federalism? If the argument is sound, as used by the Privy Council in the *ILO Conventions* case, that to give Ottawa the same jurisdiction over Canadian treaties as it unquestionably has over "Empire" treaties would "undermine the constitutional safeguards of provincial constitutional autonomy," one is tempted to ask why this argument did not prevent the Fathers of Confederation from placing in Ottawa's hands those numerous powers (disallowance, Empire treaties, declaratory power for local works, etc.) which more seriously threaten that autonomy. Provincial autonomy is expressly limited to matters "in the province," while the essence of a treaty is that its subject matter is of international significance. The *Radio* decision put the problem in a truer light when it pointed out that a Canadian convention, though not a treaty within section 132, "came to the same thing," because, as their Lordships said:

> This idea of Canada as a Dominion being bound by a convention equivalent to a treaty with foreign powers was quite unthought of in 1867. It is the outcome of the gradual development of the position of Canada vis-à-vis to the mother country, Great Britain, which is found in these later days expressed in the Statute of Westminster. It is not, therefore, to be expected that such a matter should be dealt with in explicit words in either s. 91 or s. 92. The only class of treaty which would bind Canada was thought of as a treaty by Great Britain, and that was provided for by s. 132. Being, therefore, not mentioned explicitly in either s. 91 or s. 92, such legislation falls within the general words at the opening of s. 91 which assign to the government of the Dominion the power to make laws, 'for the peace, order and good government of Canada in relation to all matters not coming within the classes of subjects by this Act assigned exclusively to the legislatures of the Provinces.'
>
> In fine, though agreeing that the Convention was not such a treaty as defined in s. 132, their Lordships think that it comes to the same thing.

and further:

> The result is in their Lordships' opinion clear. It is Canada as a whole which is amenable to the other powers for the proper carrying out of the convention; and to prevent individuals in Canada infringing the stipulations of the convention it is necessary that the Dominion should pass legislation which should apply to all the dwellers in Canada.[63]

It is difficult not to believe that this view harmonizes better with the whole intent and spirit of the BNA Act than the opposite view adopted only five years later by a Judicial Committee whose personnel was totally different from that which decided the *Radio* case. And if the fanciful notion exists that Ottawa might use the treaty power as a device to extend its jurisdiction unwarrantably at provincial expense, the firm rule that colourable legislation – the attempt to dress up *ultra vires* statutes in some pretended constitutional form – is prohibited is available to the courts to prevent the invasion. No doubt other principles of control would be found if the necessity were to arise – for example, that the special and exceptional provision for federal remedial legislation in educational matters under section 93 precludes any other form of federal legislation such as might occur in implementing a treaty touching on education.

In the result, whereas up to 1937 the federal Parliament was able to legislate on all treaties and conventions binding on Canada, and had in fact so legislated so as to override provincial authority in four instances,[64] after 1937 the treaty-enforcing power in Canada was decentralized and Ottawa was deprived of a power held effectively for seventy years. A major constitutional limitation in international affairs was imposed on the Canadian nation in the very decade in which she finally achieved full national status. No other federal state in the world is so restricted, and in an age desperately seeking new bases for international co-operation such national weaknesses become something more than domestic problems. The Sirois Report recommended that Parliament be given power to implement ILO conventions, but this seems but a partial solution. Many other international organizations besides the ILO are engaged in important international work which Canada should be free to assist. The only way out now, short of further judicial interpretations and distinctions, would seem to be by amendment to the BNA Act granting Ottawa a treaty power hedged with defined safeguards against its possible use to overthrow the existing minority rights which everyone in Canada is agreed should be protected.

When a court declares that Ottawa is incapable of legislating on a certain subject it nearly always follows that the provinces have the jurisdiction. What is not centralized is decentralized. This is not always true, since some matters are withheld altogether from Canadian legislative competence and can only be dealt with through constitutional amendment adopted in the United Kingdom Parliament. For example, there is a prohibition in section 125 against taxing Crown lands, which applies to both Parliament and the provinces, and in 121 against establishing interprovincial tariffs. Then too a particular statute, as distinct from a "class of subjects," may be held *ultra vires* because it contains two or more matters which are unseverable, some of which are legitimate to Parliament and others not. But in general the denial of a specific power to the central government is the same as attributing it to the local governments.

Hence, in the process of judicial interpretation narrowing federal powers, large accretions of jurisdiction have come into provincial hands. The regulation of intraprovincial trade and commerce, including trade in the products of fisheries and agriculture, is no mean power for provinces the size of several in Canada, especially when it includes control of production. The jurisdiction over industrial disputes, even when between nationwide industries and nationwide trade unions, is a truly vast extension of the concept of "Property and Civil Rights in the Province," yet the Privy Council overruled Canadian courts which had held the federal Industrial Disputes Investigation Act to be a matter of regulation of trade and commerce, for the protection of national peace, order, and good government, and criminal law.[65] A national scheme of unemployment insurance of a type usual today was also held beyond federal jurisdiction,[66] and now it is generally assumed that any contributory health or pension scheme is a provincial matter except where constitutional amendment has changed the original law. A whole range of international conventions relating to wages, hours of labour, weekly day of rest, and employment of women and children, even after Canada has ratified them, must be made law in ten provincial legislatures before they take effect, which is another way of saying that no Canadian legislature ever sees them. Provincial control of marketing is so wide that a carefully drawn federal statute on the same subject, attempting to steer clear of the provincial field, was upset in the courts, even though every provincial legislature in Canada had passed supporting legislation so that for once legislative consent was unanimous that the federal law was needed. Just as in the United States, until the spirit of the New Deal had transformed public opinion and with it judicial opinion, the courts were adverse to new forms of social legislation, so in Canada they appear to have built the same constitutional barriers to social change, with this difference that whereas between 1937 and 1947 the United States Supreme Court, recognizing the inevitable, overruled its previous decisions thirty-two times,[67] the courts of last resort in Canada have shown no equivalent flexibility. Whenever the Privy Council has attempted a more liberal approach, as in the *Radio* and *Temperance Act* cases, a later Board has restored the judicial *status quo.*[68]

Besides these decisions affecting the distribution of powers as between sections 91 and 92, the provinces also benefited by the two leading cases which (a) established their possession not of delegated but of sovereign powers within their spheres, including the power of delegation to subordinate agencies,[69] and (b) defined the position of Lieutenant-Governor as the direct representative of the Crown, possessed of the attendant royal prerogatives.[70] While these decisions did not greatly enlarge the provincial sphere of jurisdiction, they added much prestige to the claims of provincial autonomists. Well might J.B. Haldane, as he then was, write as far back as 1899 of the work of Lord Watson, whose provincial leanings he so flattered by later imitation:

[Watson] made the business of laying down the new law that was necessary his own. He completely altered the tendency of the decisions of the Supreme Court, and established in the first place the sovereignty (subject to the power to interfere of the Imperial Parliament alone) of the legislatures of Ontario, Quebec and the other Provinces. He then worked out as a principle the direct relation, in point of exercise of the prerogative, of the Lieutenant-Governors to the Crown. In a series of masterly judgments he expounded and established the real constitution

of Canada. The liquor laws, the Indian reserve lands, the title to rega-
lia, including the precious metals, were brought before a Judicial Committee, in which he took the leading part, for consideration as to which
of the rival claims to legislate ought to prevail. Nowhere is his memory
likely to be more gratefully preserved than in those distant Canadian
provinces whose rights of self-government he placed on a basis that was
both intelligible and firm.[71]

Years later he repeated the same idea, remarking how under Lord Watson
"The constitution of Canada took a new form."[72] This avowal of the
political role of the Privy Council at least does not lack frankness.

Centralization by Amendment

The trend to decentralization in the law of the Canadian constitution has
had less damaging results on national policy than otherwise would inevitably have occurred, because the advent of war in 1939 brought the "emergency" doctrine into play. Instantly provincial autonomy gave way, to the
extent considered necessary by Ottawa to overcome the emergency. No
single federal wartime control of any importance met constitutional difficulties. When the war ended, a theory of transitional emergency operated,
and such continuing measures as survived the policy of "orderly de-
control," like rent control, were upheld in the courts as late as 1950 on the
ground that the emergency had not ceased.[73] Now a "cold war" exists
which might easily (who knows?) be a new emergency of indefinite dura-
tion. Certainly the notion of what constitutes "defence" has greatly
enlarged, and with it federal authority. It is possible that much of the law of
the constitution discussed here will never again see the light of day because
of world events, and that the centralization issue will be settled outside the
law courts and outside Canada. But this notion, like the fear of world
destruction in an atomic war, is scarcely one on which life can be planned.

Despite war emergency powers, the Canadian people have found it desirable to overcome some of the effects of judicial interpretation by constitutional amendment. In 1940 the subject of unemployment insurance was
made an exclusive federal power, becoming section 91, clause 2A, thus
doing away with the effects of the 1937 *Reference* decision. Then in 1951 the
Parliament of Canada was given power to legislate for old age pensions, by
the addition of section 94A to the BNA Act. These are the only two changes
in the distribution of legislative power between Ottawa and the provinces
by direct amendment to the BNA Act since 1867. Both have made for a
further degree of centralization.

The latest amendment, however, has introduced an entirely new principle to Canadian constitutional law. Hitherto all legislative power in Canada has been definable as either exclusive, that is to say exerciseable by
either Parliament or the legislatures alone, or concurrent, as in the case of

agriculture and immigration under section 95, exerciseable by either authority but with the federal law always prevailing. Judicial interpretation had evolved a notion of overlapping powers, but here again federal law was paramount. The wording of the recent pensions amendment is quite different. It states that any federal law "shall not affect the operation of any law, present or future, of a provincial legislature in relation to old age pensions." In other words, the attribution of the pensions power to Ottawa is subject to the condition that it must not affect the provinces' right to establish any provincial pension plan they desire at any time. If there is a conflict, present or future, between the two systems, national and local (which is an improbable but not impossible eventuality), the national must give way. Thus for the first time in Canadian constitutional history a matter within federal competence has been rendered subordinate to provincial law. Whereas the Quebec and London Resolutions each provided that,

> In regard to all subjects over which jurisdiction belongs to both the General and Local Legislatures, the laws of the General Parliament shall control and supersede those made by the Local Legislature, and the latter shall be void so far as they are repugnant to or inconsistent with the former...,[74]

the trend to decentralization in Canada has changed the compact of Confederation and introduced the opposite principle. Canada now has the American doctrine of nullification, that is, the right of a state to set aside national laws, written into this part of her constitution. She seems almost ready for the Hayne-Webster debate that took place in the United States Senate in 1830.[75]

The Present Situation

To say that judicial interpretation has whittled down federal powers, to such an extent as to alter the original balance of the constitution, is not the same as saying that it has, as a political fact, enlarged provincial powers to an equivalent extent. Provinces have much more status and legal authority now than they started with – that is obvious. But this is not the same thing as saying that provincial governments can exercise their jurisdiction. Many considerations may prevent or render ineffective the exercise of a constitutional power. Not a single Canadian province has directly implemented an ILO convention. Since they do not take part in the international processes by which the conventions are drawn up and adopted, and since no one province can be sure the others will follow its lead if it sets an example, they are not likely to. Provinces now have the power to protect their dairy industries by prohibiting the production and sale of margarine, and Quebec, for example, has done so. But Quebec's dairy farmers are not in fact protected by Quebec law, since margarine production elsewhere in Canada directly affects the Quebec butter price. Only the fact that Ottawa puts a floor price under butter helps the Quebec farmers. Similarly, the control of labour relations outside the limited Dominion field, even in many nation-wide industries organized by a single trade union, comes within provincial jurisdiction. Yet provincial law may be quite powerless to control the situation that develops when a whole industry is struck by that one union, as the history of the Canada-wide Packinghouse Workers strike in 1947 clearly showed. The helplessness of the national government in that situation, and the pathetic attempts of several provincial premiers to settle the dispute by provincial action, were sufficient commentary on false notions of provincial autonomy. This autonomy is equally hollow in face of the present challenge of inflation. If to these examples are added the numerous types of social insurance where the financing of legislative schemes is far beyond the resources of some if not all the provinces, the natural limits of a policy of decentralization are readily seen. Provincial autonomy becomes national inactivity. When governments are incapable of acting, private interests have a freer hand, and since within the private enterprise sphere a high degree of centralized control has developed, this in turn means that decentralization in provincial hands protects centralization in private hands. Thus centralization is not avoided by provincial autonomy, but is encouraged in another form – one over which the French-Canadian element has far less influence than it has in Ottawa. A discussion of the social consequences of this situation is not relevant to the subject of this paper, but should the Canadian people desire a larger measure of economic control and social security than they now possess, they will find their path bristling with legal obstacles. The constitutional problem is not always a valid excuse for Ottawa's inaction, but it constantly appears as an almost insuperable barrier to the adoption of certain kinds of national policy.

A solution frequently put forward by provincial leaders, particularly those from the wealthier provinces, is that the provinces should be granted wider powers of taxation by direct constitutional amendment, by increased federal grants, or by the withdrawal of Ottawa from existing provincial fields like the income tax so as to allow of provincial increases. A proposal to give provinces limited powers of indirect taxation was close to adoption both in 1936 and at the time of the recent pensions amendment. With more income, it is argued, provinces could finance more of their own services, and the dangers of centralization could be avoided. Up to a point this argument has force. There is no doubt that the financial arrangement at Confederation, which confined provinces to "Direct Taxation within the Province," supplemented by limited federal subsidies, is quite unsuited to the new responsibilities provincial governments must assume as a result of judicial interpretation and growing industrialization. Public finance and constitutional law cannot be based on two opposing theories of federalism, without a serious decrease in governmental efficiency and an increase in social tensions.

The Sirois Report gave one answer to this problem. Its proposals, however, were not adopted. Wartime taxation agreements with all provinces took their place, and post-war agreements of similar type with all provinces but Ontario and Quebec enabled Canada to carry on. The refusal of the two central provinces to accept the post-war agreements was the reason given by Ottawa for its inability to proceed with the social security provisions offered in 1945.[76] The social cost of reliance on unanimous provincial consent was thus made very evident. While the case for more permanent provincial income is strong, certain objections to it are equally plain. The disparity in wealth between economic regions in Canada means that too great a reliance on a provincial tax base produces marked inequality of social services in different provinces. The accident of birth means the difference between good health, education, and opportunity for Canadian children in more developed provinces and severe handicaps in the poorer ones. Production and industrial location are adversely affected by varying tax burdens, and low-standard areas threaten the stability of achievements in the more advanced provinces. These differences create political tensions and perpetuate conflicts between regions. Under-developed provinces within Canada cause the same kind of unrest as under-developed countries create in the international world.

Other ways around the problem, short of outright amendment, are being tried. *Ad hoc* arrangements worked out at Dominion-Provincial conferences seem the order of the day. They provide no certainty of solution, and at best only a temporary stability. No province can be compelled to agree; no law prevents provinces repudiating any agreement when made. In any event, the matters on which agreement can be reached are mostly confined to financial relations. It is impossible in such a conference to agree on an intergovernmental delegation of responsibility, since that kind of delegation is prohibited.[77] Hence, unless there is agreement to amend the constitution, no such problem as is presented by Dominion lack of jurisdiction over price control, or marketing of agricultural produce, or industrial relations in nationwide industries, can be faced. If the result is merely to augment Ottawa's payments to provinces, leaving them free to spend the money as they will, then a dangerous gulf between the tax gathering and expending authorities is created, with provincial governments becoming dependent on federal largesse.

In so far as the conferences attempt to develop into constituent assemblies for the amendment of the constitution, as they did with respect to the pensions amendment of 1951 and during the discussions seeking to find a new procedure for amendment in 1950, they suffer from two serious defects – first, the requirement of unanimity, so that, for example, the province of Prince Edward Island, with 0.7 per cent of the population, can frustrate the will of the rest of the country, and, secondly, the unrepresentative character of the conferences, which speak for the political party in power at the moment in the Dominion and in each province and not for the opposition parties as well. It is generally recognized in Canada that the present constitutional state of affairs is unsatisfactory, and particularly that a method for amending the constitution of the country inside Canada must be found. So strong is the fear of centralization, however, particularly in Quebec, that the constitutional conference summoned in 1950 adjourned at the end of the year *sine die*.[78]

The most important political factor in the problem of centralization, as in so many other Canadian matters, lies in the power relations existing between Quebec and Ottawa, which in turn reflect the basic racial factors in Canadian life. This at the moment is a more difficult relationship to bring into satisfactory balance than is the other great factor, the power relationship between business and government. The consolidation of Quebec as a bastion of the French-Canadian race is a firm policy of every Quebec government, made more explicit in recent years under the Union Nationale party of Premier Duplessis. Centralization appears to threaten this bastion, therefore it must be opposed in principle. This does not mean that Quebec will oppose every suggestion of an increase of federal powers, but that it will look at each proposal on its merits and decide for itself whether it is desirable or not. Quebec wishes to retain the right of veto, which as a matter of recent constitutional convention she appears to have achieved. Hence the difficulty of attaining any general method of amending the Constitution by which the Parliament of Canada and a majority of provinces could impose a change not acceptable to Quebec. So far the willingness of all other provinces to surround the minority rights in the constitution with special safeguards against amendment by majority vote has not brought the parties to agreement.

In so far as the original constitution is concerned, it is significant that the BNA Act protects Quebec's rights in respect of language, denominational schools, and the civil law, but not in respect of those other forms of centralized authority referred to. Quebec's lieutenant-governor, senators, and judges are selected by the same centralized power of appointment as is provided for the other provinces, There were no special political privileges accorded Quebec in the Constitution, only cultural ones. Politically, all Canadians are on an equal footing, except the Indians. Quebec laws are subject to the same disallowance as other provincial laws. What then is threatened in Quebec's special position by the advance of federal jurisdiction in matters of national concern? Not language rights, since federal laws and courts must use the two languages. Indeed, an extension of federal control means an extension of the two official languages throughout Canada. It is unlikely that there would be French radio stations on the Prairies today if radio broadcasting had been held to be provincial. As regards educational matters, it is difficult to take seriously the fear that the school rights defined in section 93 are threatened by an extension of federal power, since all groups in Canada are agreed that these rights must be entrenched against amendment without unanimous vote of all provinces. The question whether Ottawa should make grants to provinces for educational purposes is thus quite separate from the question whether there should be a shift in legislative powers; Ottawa could make and has recently made such grants without any constitutional amendment, since no province is obliged to accept them and no legislative jurisdiction is changed. It is the third of Quebec's guarantees, her jurisdiction over "Property and Civil Rights in the Province," and hence over her civil law, which seems to be most affected by centralization. A federal control of rents, for example, does affect the civil law contract of lease and hire, and no one could pretend the contrary.

Yet the history of the survival of the civil law suggests that it has much the same kind of change to fear from provincial autonomy as it has from centralization. In either case, the civil law, like all systems of private law, is going through constant adaptation to new social needs. We can observe that since 1867 the legislature of Quebec in the exercise of its autonomy has adopted a truly formidable list of statutes which have superimposed upon the civil law a body of new rules affecting or restraining its application. Many of these rules are barely distinguishable from the statutes of common law provinces on the same subjects. Laws dealing with corporations, workmen's compensation, minimum wages, hours of labour, industrial standards, pensions, public health, traffic regulation, collective bargaining, rent control, and so forth, have a common content throughout Canada because they confront a common social and economic situation. The more Quebec becomes industrialized, the more this will be true. As Professor Keirstead has said:

> Quebec cannot maintain its cultural values intact by attempting to maintain a separate economy and distinct political entity, for the provincial area is inadequate for proper economic controls and the Quebec economy would continue to reflect the exploitation and instability of the national economy. Even if Quebec were an independent state the process of exploitation of the French worker, the gradual denudation of the countryside, the gradual undermining of the small-town, small-scale French-Canadian entrepreneur would continue with the consequent corruption of French-Canadian culture. The only salvation for Quebec as a cultural entity, we hope to show, must be in common effort with all Canadians to resolve economic conflict and establish economic stability on a national scale.[79]

What is happening, and what nothing can prevent, is the emergence of new aspects of property and civil rights, which have to be dealt with on new principles not found in either the civil or the common law. Most of these new aspects the courts have classified as belonging to the old category of property and civil rights, and hence have placed under provincial jurisdiction. It is only in these fringe subjects, that is to say subjects of recent development, that there is any need or desire for centralization, and only for some of them which clearly are of national scope and importance. No federal government is ever going to attempt to enact a general body of private law which could become a code for all Canada, replacing the Civil Code of Quebec. In these fringe subjects, there is little that is purely cultural. The problem created by a provincial truck when competing with a federal railway can scarcely be classed as a cultural one, yet the national railway system and freight rate structure is today being undermined by the absence of a national control over highway trucking.

Too much centralization invites tyranny, too little creates anarchy. Both tyranny and anarchy are a threat to the cultural survival of both the British and French traditions in Canada. The argument here submitted is that although there is an increasing pressure for some further centralization of authority in Canada, notably in relation to economic regulation, insurance against calculable risks of modern society such as old age and ill health, and international obligations, this development is not in conflict with the basic principles of Canadian federalism but on the contrary is their proper expression in this day and age. It is submitted also that the cultural values of Quebec in particular, and of other regions also, are in less danger of being crushed out by this limited degree of centralization than they would be if it did not take place. It may be that the constitutional issue is already settled in favour of much greater centralization than is here contemplated, because we are in the midst of a period of such prolonged international unrest as to make the "emergency" in effect permanent.[80] It may be that the one word "defence" in section 91 will grow to be a new residuary clause in the constitution. We can but hope that this will not prove true. Already it has made the federal government the biggest employer, the biggest landlord, and the biggest contractor in the country. Defence needs, however, do not give Canadians social security, and do not settle the vexed question of the proper procedure for constitutional amendment. There is still need for agreement on the basic issues here raised. A plea for adherence to the original concepts of Canadian federalism wisely embodied in the constitution of 1867 may not be out of order. Under that constitution we can all be Canadians without ceasing to enjoy our political and cultural freedoms.

Notes

1. See Trotter, *Canadian Federation* (1924), 104.

2. An authoritative analysis of this centralization will be found in Lloyd G. Reynolds, *The Control of Competition in Canada* (1940). See also *Report of Royal Commission on Price Spreads*, 1935, and *Canada and International Cartels*, published by the Department of Labour, Ottawa, 1945.

3. The Manitoba Act of 1870, section 23, gave the French language an official status in the province, but this was repealed by the legislature of Manitoba. See RSM, 1940, c. 152. The French constitute approximately 40 per cent of the population of New Brunswick.

4. The right to separate schools supported by state funds is guaranteed in some only of the Canadian provinces.

5. Some of these comments are collected in my article, "Political Nationalism and Confederation," *Canadian Journal of Economics and Political Science* [*CJEPS*], 8 (1942), 399ff.

6. BNA Act, ss. 58, 90; Forsey, "Disallowance of Provincial Acts, Reservation of Provincial Bills, and Refusal of Assent by Lieutenant-Governors since 1867," *CJEPS*, 4 (1938), 47.

7. BNA Act, s. 95.

8. *Ibid.*, s. 96.

9. *Ibid.*, s. 101.

10. *Ibid.*, ss. 24, 29.

11. *Ibid.*, s. 92, head 2.

12. *Ibid.*, s. 118, as amended.

13. *Ibid.*, s. 91, heads 2, 10, 12.

14. *Ibid.*, s. 95.

15. *Ibid.*, s. 92, head 10(a).

16. *Ibid.*, s. 92, head 10(c).

17. *Ibid.*, s. 109.

18. *Ibid.*, s. 91, heads 15, 20, 19, 17.

19. *Ibid.*, ss. 121, 122.

20. Dawson, *The Government of Canada* (1947), 36.

21. Clement, *The Law of the Canadian Constitution* (3rd ed.), ch. 32.

22. Cf. Laskin, "The Supreme Court of Canada," *Canadian Bar Review*, 29 (1951), 1038.

23. Sirois Report, Vol. I, 47.

24. Angus, "The Canadian Constitution and the United Nations Charter," *CJEPS*, 12 (1946), 135.

25. [1938] SCR 71.

26. [1947] AC 127.

27. See discussion in *Dominion Law Annotations*, Revised, Vol. III (1951), 206.

28. For a recent discussion of this problem, see Shumiatcher, "Section 96 of the British North America Act Re-examined," *Canadian Bar Review*, 27 (1949), 131.

29. Laskin, "'Peace, Order and Good Government' Re-examined," *Canadian Bar Review*, 25 (1947), 1054.

34. *Ibid.*, 360-61.
35. *Reference as to the Validity of the Wartime Leasehold Regulations*, [1950] SCR 124.
36. *Toronto Electric Commissioners* v. *Snider*, [1925] AC 396, at p. 412.
37. [1946] AC 193.
38. See remarks of Lord Morton in *Canadian Federation of Agriculture* v. *A.-G. for Quebec*, [1951] AC 179, at p. 197.
39. For a thorough recent discussion, see Laskin, "'Peace, Order and Good Government.'"
40. At p. 33.
41. Hansard, Parliamentary Debates, 3rd Series, Vol. 185, col. 566.
42. McWilliams, Letter in *Canadian Bar Review*, 18 (1940), 516.
43. Vol. I, 32ff.
44. The following authorities have emphasized the degree to which the courts have departed from the original intention of the constitution: H.A. Smith, "The Residue of Power in Canada," *Canadian Bar Review*, 4 (1926), 432; Brooke Claxton, "The Amendment of the B.N.A. Act," Supplement to *McGill News* (June, 1929), 16; W.P.M. Kennedy, "Law and Custom in the Canadian Constitution," *Round Table*, 20 (1929) 143ff.; Kennedy, *The Constitution of Canada* (2nd ed.), 488ff.; Kennedy, "The Interpretation of the B.N.A. Act," *Cambridge Law Journal*, 8 (1943), 146; F.R. Scott, "The Privy Council and Minority Rights," *Queen's Quarterly*, 37 (1930), 677; Scott, "The Development of Canadian Federalism," *Proceedings of the Canadian Political Science Association*, III (1931), 231; J.S. Ewart, "Comments," *ibid.*, 248, 252; A. Brady, *Canada* (1932), 45ff.; Brady, in Innis and Plumptre, eds., *The Canadian Economy and Its Problems* (1934), 475; Brady, in *Democracy in the Dominions*, 44ff.; H.Carl Goldenberg, "Social and Economic Problems in Canadian Federalism," *Canadian Bar Review*, 12 (1934), 422; N.A.M. MacKenzie, "The Federal Problem and the B.N.A. Act," in *Canadian Problems*, 247; O.D. Skelton, evidence before Special Committee on the B.N.A. Act (1935), 23; V.C. MacDonald, "Judicial Interpretation of the Canadian Constitution," *University of Toronto Law Journal*, 1 (1935-36), 281; E.A. Forsey, in *CJEPS*, 2 (1936), 595-96; C.H.Cahan, address to Canadian Club of Toronto, Sept. 15, 1937; Cahan, in *House of Commons Debates*, April 5, 1937, 2574ff., and April 8, 1938, 2157; J.T. Thorson, *ibid.*, April 5, 1937, 2582; R.B. Bennett, *ibid.*, 2587ff.; A.-K. Hugessen, address to Junior Board of Trade, Montreal, reported in *Montreal Gazette*, Oct. 20, 1937; J.B. Coyne, *Canadian Neutrality* (1938), 30ff.; F.H.Underhill, "Edward Blake, The Supreme Court Act, and the Appeal to the Privy Council 1875-6," *Canadian Historical Review*, 19 (1938), 261; C.J. Burchell, in *The Canadian Constitution* (1938), 124-25; D.G. Creighton, "British North America at Confederation," Appendix 2 of Sirois Report, 49ff. (on the intentions of the Fathers); F.C. Cronkite, "Comment on the O'Connor Report," *CJEPS*, 5 (1939), 507; W.F. O'Connor, *Report on the B.N.A. Act* (1939), *passim*; O'Connor, "Property and Civil Rights in the

Province," *Canadian Bar Review*, 18 (1940), 331; E.R. Clark, "The Privy Council and the Constitution," *Dalhousie Review*, 19 (1939), 65; René Richard, "Peace, Order and Good Government," *Canadian Bar Review*, 18 (1940), 259; R.B. Hanson, *House of Commons Debates*, Nov. 12, 1940, 40; Raphael Tuck, "Canada and the Judicial Committee," *University of Toronto Law Journal*, 4 (1941-42), 34, 64; A.R.M. Lower, *From Colony to Nation* (1946), 334; Laskin, "'Peace, Order and Good Government.'" Similar views will be found in the briefs to the Sirois Commission presented by the province of Manitoba, the Native Sons of Canada, and the League for Social Reconstruction. This list is exhausting but not exhaustive. On the other side of the debate, besides the two authorities cited in the Sirois Report, Vol. I, 35, n. 37, will be found McWilliams, *supra*, note 42; and McWilliams, "The Privy Council and the Constitution," *Canadian Bar Review*, 17 (1939), 579. As long ago as 1884 Mr. Justice Loranger was arguing that the residue of powers in Canada was in provincial hands: *Letters upon the Interpretation of the Federal Constitution Known as the British North America Act, 1867* (Quebec, 1884), 46.

45. *Citizens Insurance* v. *Parsons* (1881), 7 App. Cas. 96.
46. *The Natural Products Marketing* case, [1937] AC 377.
47. Particularly the *Reference* case in [1916] 1 AC 588.
48. Creighton, *British North America at Confederation*, 55.
49. To overcome the effect of *The King* v. *Eastern Terminal Elevator Co.* [1925] SCR 434. See 3 Geo. VI, 1939, c. 36, s. 68.
50. In the *Ontario Liquor License* case, [1896] AC 342, at p. 363.
51. [1951] AC 179.
52. Since the *Board of Commerce* case, [1922] 1 AC 191.
53. *Supra*, note 51.
54. *Supra*, note 49.
55. *Supra*, note 46.
56. *A.-G. for Canada* v. *A.-G. for B.C.*, [1930] AC 111.
57. The British Columbia statute of 1936, held *intra vires* in *Shannon* v. *Lower Mainland Dairy Products Board*, [1938] AC 708.
58. *Supra*, note 46.
59. *Bonanza Creek Gold Mining Co.* v. *The King*, [1916] 1 AC 566.
60. [1932] AC 304.
61. [1937] AC 326.
62. BNA Act, s. 91, head 13.
63. [1932] AC 304, at pp. 312-13.
64. The four examples are: (i) The Japanese Treaty Act of 1913 overrode a British Columbia statute applying to employment of Japanese, *Brooks-Bidlake and Whittall Ltd.* v. *A.-G-. for B.C.*, [1923] AC 450; (ii) The Migratory Birds Convention Act of 1917 overrode a contrary provision in the Game Protection Act of Manitoba, *Rex* v. *Stuart*, [1924] 3 WWR 648; (iii) the Radio Convention of 1927 upheld the Dominion jurisdiction over broadcasting, though a second

ground was found in s. 92, head 10(a) of the BNA Act, *Radio Reference*, [1932] AC 304; (iv) the Aeronautics Convention of 1919 gave validity to Dominion regulations based upon it, *Aeronautics Reference*, [1932] AC 54.

65. *Toronto Electric Commissioners* v. *Snider*, [1925] AC 396.
66. *Employment Insurance Reference*, [1937] AC 355.
67. See Pritchett, *The Roosevelt Court* (1948), 57.
68. As in the *I.L.O. Conventions and Margarine References, supra,* notes 61 and 51.
69. *Hodge* v. *Regina* (1883), 9 App. Cas. 117.
70. *Liquidators of the Maritime Bank* v. *Receiver General of New Brunswick* [1892] AC 437.
71. *Juridical Review*, 2 (1899), 279-80.
72. From the *Cambridge Law Journal* (1922), cited in *Canadian Bar Review*, 8 (1930), 439.
73. *Supra*, note 35.
74. QR 45; LR 44.
75. On nullification and its history, see, for example, Swisher, *American Constitutional Development* (1943), 234ff.
76. The story of these arrangements will be found in Buck, *Financing Canadian Government* (1949), chs. 9-10. See also Eggleston, *The Road to Nationhood* (1946).
77. *A.-G. for Canada* v. *A.-G. for Nova Scotia*, [1951] SCR 31, now in appeal.
78. See the two volumes published by The King's Printer, Ottawa, 1950, entitled, respectively, *Constitutional Conference of Federal and Provincial Governments*, Ottawa Jan. 10-12, 1950 and *do.* Quebec, Sept. 25-28, 1950.
79. In Brady and Scott, *Canada after the War* (1943), 17-18.
80. See for example the remarkable degree of centralization provided in the Emergency Powers Act and the Defence Production Act adopted by the Parliament of Canada in 1951.

3. ALAN C. CAIRNS

The Judicial

Committee and

Its Critics

The interpretation of the British North America Act by the Judicial Committee of the Privy Council is one of the most contentious aspects of the constitutional evolution of Canada. As an imperial body the Privy Council was unavoidably embroiled in the struggles between imperialism and nationalism that accompanied the transformation of Empire into Commonwealth. As the final judicial authority for constitutional interpretation, its decisions became material for debate in the recurrent Canadian controversy over the future of federalism. The failure of Canadians to agree on a specific formula for constitutional amendment led many critics to place a special responsibility for adjusting the BNA Act on the Privy Council, and then to castigate it for not presiding wisely over the adaptation of Canadian federalism to conditions unforeseen in 1867.

Given the context in which it operated it is not surprising that much of the literature of judicial review, expecially since the Depression of the thirties, transformed the Privy Council into a scapegoat for a variety of ills that afflicted the Canadian polity. In language ranging from measured criticism to vehement denunciation, from mild disagreement to bitter sarcasm, a host of critics indicated their fundamental disagreement with the Privy Council's handling of its task. Lords Watson and Haldane have been caricatured as bungling intruders who, through malevolence, stupidity, or inefficiency, channelled Canadian development away from the centralized federal system wisely intended by the Fathers.[1]

Reprinted by permission of the journal and the author from *Canadian Journal of Political Science* (1971).

This article will survey the controversy over the performance of the Privy Council. Several purposes will be served. One purpose, *the provision of a more favourable* evaluation of the Privy Council's conduct, will emerge in the following discussion. This, however, is a byproduct of the main purpose of this article: an assessment of the quality of Canadian jurisprudence through an examination of the most significant, continuing constitutional controversy in Canadian history. The performance of the Privy Council raised critical questions concerning the locus, style, and role of a final appeal court. An analysis of the way in which these and related questions were discussed provides important insights into Canadian jurisprudence.[2]

Varieties of Criticism

Criticisms of the Privy Council can be roughly separated into two opposed prescriptions for the judicial role.[3] One camp, called the constitutionalists in this essay, contained those critics who advocated a flexible, pragmatic approach so that judges could help to keep the BNA Act up to date. Another camp, called the fundamentalists, contained those who criticized the courts for not providing a technically correct, logical interpretation of a clearly worded document.

According to the fundamentalists the basic shortcoming of the Privy Council was its elementary misunderstanding of the Act. The devotees of this criticism, who combined a stress on the literal meaning of the Act with a widespread resort to historical materials surrounding Confederation, had four main stages in their argument.[4] Naturally, not all critics employed the full battery of arguments possible.

1. The initial requirement was the provision of documented proof that the Fathers of Confederation intended to create a highly centralized federal system. This was done by ransacking the statements of the Fathers, particularly John A. Macdonald, and of British officials, for proof of centralist intent. Given the known desire of some Fathers for a "legislative union," or the closest approximation possible in 1867, a plethora of proof was readily assembled.

2. The next logical step was to prove that the centralization intended was clearly embodied in the Act.[5] This was done by combing the Act for every indication of the exalted role assigned to Ottawa and the paltry municipal role assigned to the provinces. This task required little skill. Even the least adept could assert, with convincing examples, that the division of powers heavily favoured Ottawa. If additional proof seemed necessary the dominance of the central government could also be illustrated by referring to the provisions of the Act dealing with the disallowance and reservation of provincial legislation, and with the special position of the lieutenant governor as a federal officer.

Once concordance was proved between what the Fathers intended and what they achieved in the Act, the critics could then delve into a vast grab bag of pre-Confederation sources for their arguments. This greatly increased the amount of material at their disposal and strengthened their claim that a prime reason for Privy Council failure was its unwillingness to use similar materials.

3. The third feature of this fundamentalist approach was a definition of the judicial role that required of judges no more and no less than the technically correct interpretation of the Act to bring out the meaning deliberately and clearly embodied in it by the Fathers. Where necessary the judges were to employ the methods of historical research in performing this task. This point was explicitly made by H.A. Smith in his criticism of the English rule against extrinsic evidence in the interpretation of statutes. This, he asserted, was to forbid the courts "to adopt historical methods in solving a historical problem." The consequences were grave:

> . . . an arbitrary and unreasonable rule of interpretation has produced the very serious result of giving Canada a constitution substantially different from that which her founders intended that she should have. A study of the available historical evidence gives us a clear and definite idea of what the fathers of Canadian confederation sought to achieve. By excluding this historical evidence and considering the British North America Act without any regard to its historical setting the courts have recently imposed upon us a constitution which is different, not only in detail but also in principle, from that designed at Charlottetown and Quebec.[6]

In brief, the judge, like Ranke's ideal historian, was to find out "the way it really was," and then apply his historical findings to the cases that came before him.

4. Proof that the Fathers had intended and had created a centralized federal system in the terms of the BNA Act, coupled with the transformation of the judge into an historian, provided conclusive evidence of the failure of the Judicial Committee. This was done by contrasting the centralization intended and statutorily enacted with the actual evolution of the Canadian polity toward a more classical decentralized federalism, an evolution to which the courts contributed. Since the judges were explicitly directed to apply the Act literally it was obvious that they had bungled their task. As W.P.M. Kennedy phrased it, their "interpretations cannot be supported on any reasonable grounds. They are simply due to inexplicable misreadings of the *terms* of the Act."[7] The same point was made in more polemical fashion by J.T. Thorson in a parliamentary debate on the Privy Council's treatment of the Bennett New Deal legislation:

> ...they have mutilated the constitution. They have changed it from a centralized federalism, with the residue of legislative power in the dominion parliament, to a decentralized federalism with the residue of legislative power in the provinces – contrary to the Quebec resolutions, contrary to the ideas that were in the minds of the fathers of confederation, contrary to the spirit of confederation itself, and contrary to the earlier decisions of the courts. We have Lord Haldane largely to blame for the damage that has been done to our constitution.[8]

In summary, the fundamentalists simply asserted that the Privy Council had done a bad job in failing to follow the clearly laid out understandings of the Fathers embodied in the BNA Act. O'Connor, the author of the most influential criticism of the Privy Council, viewed their decisions as indefensible interpretations of a lucidly worded constitutional document. He felt that the Act was a marvellous instrument of government, the literal interpretation of which would have been perfectly consonant with the needs of a changing society.[9] The same literal criticism was brandished by a critic of the decision in *Toronto Electric Commissioners* v *Snider* who "arose in his place in the House of Commons and protested against 'a condition which allows the Judicial Committee . . . to shoot holes in our constitution.' "[10] For such critics the failure was technical, a simple case of misinterpretation. All critics who appealed to the intentions of the Fathers or to the clearly expressed meaning of the Act when criticizing the "deviations" of the Judicial Committee fell into this category. Since this gambit was almost universal, this fundamentalist criticism was widespread.[11]

In documenting the emasculation of federal authority, critics concentrated on the opening "peace, order, and good government" clause of section 91 and on section 91(2), dealing with "the regulation of trade and commerce." The former, "the foundation of Macdonald's whole federal system,"[12] was the "favourite whipping-boy of most of the articles and comments on Canadian constitutional law . . . ."[13] According to critics, the peace, order, and good government clause was clearly designed to be the primary grant of federal authority with the enumerated clauses being illustrative, or "for greater certainty but not so as to restrict the generality" as section 91 declared. The destruction of the utility of the residuary clause, and its subsequent partial revival as a source of emergency power, evoked a series of violent critiques from a host of embittered commentators.[14]

The Privy Council's handling of the trade and commerce power evoked only slightly less indignation. W.P.M.Kennedy, the most influential constitutional analyst of the period from the early twenties to the middle forties, spoke for the bulk of the critics when he protested that it "is reduced to the almost absurd position of being a power which the Canadian Parliament can only call in aid of a power granted elsewhere . . . ." It had been "relegated to a position utterly impossible to defend on the clearest terms of the Act, and one which makes any reliance on it barren and useless."[15]

The decline of peace, order, and good government and the virtual nullification of trade and commerce on the federal side were counterbalanced by the remarkable significance that came to be attached to "property and civil rights" in section 92.[16] It was this provincial head that H. Carl Goldenberg described as "wide enough to cover nearly all legislation outside of criminal law," including the whole field of social legislation.[17]

In brief, the critics argued, the Privy Council seriously misinterpreted the division of powers in sections 91 and 92, to the extent that the provinces were left with responsibilities they were neither intended nor competent to handle. Several key decisions raised the status of the provinces,[18] while other decisions enhanced the significance of provincial jurisdiction in section 92, especially property and civil rights. Conversely, the federal government, originally endowed with potent problem-solving and nation-building capacities, had its powers cribbed and confined to such a degree that the Fathers would not recognize their creation. As a consequence, an explicitly centralized federal system was transformed into its reverse, a decentralized system approximating a league of states.[19]

The previous approach defined the judicial role in terms of the literal, almost technical, task of correctly interpreting a historic document in terms of the intention of its framers. From this perspective the trouble with the Privy Council was that it had got its history wrong, or had misinterpreted the clear phraseology of the BNA Act.

The second stream of criticism rested on contrary assumptions. These critics, the constitutionalists, took their stand with John Marshall's assertion that judges must not forget that they were expounding a constitution.

Critics of this school were hostile to the Privy Council for treating the BNA Act as a statute to be analysed by "the ordinary rules of statutory construction." They asserted that the Judicial Committee should have been an agent for constitutional flexibility, concerned with the policy consequences of their decisions. They flatly rejected the Judicial Committee's own interpretation of its task, to treat "the provisions of the Act in question by the same methods of construction and exposition which they apply to other statutes."[20]

Contrary to the narrow statutory approach officially adopted by the Privy Council, the critics favoured a more generous, flexible, liberal approach that clearly recognized the constitutional significance of judicial review, with its corollary of a policy role for judges. In positive terms these critics spoke variously and vaguely of the need to keep the BNA Act up to date, particularly in its federal aspects. In a variety of ways they believed that a Canadian version of the United States Supreme Court was required. They spoke especially favourably of Lord Sankey, the closest approximation to a hero they could find on the Privy Council, and they delighted in the analogy of the "living tree" he had applied to the BNA Act.[21]

The general tenor of the desired approach is readily apparent from the felicitous phrases used. MacDonald spoke of the need for interpreting the Act "progressively so as to keep it as apt an instrument of government in new conditions as it was in the conditions current at its enactment."[22] Elsewhere he wrote of the necessity for "constant effort to bring and keep the Constitution up-to-date as the source of power adequate to present needs,"[23] and the desirability of "the flexible interpretation that changing circumstances require."[24] Laskin wrote favourably of "those sentiments in existing constitutional doctrine which express principles of growth." He contrasted "the higher level of constitutional interpretation" with the "lower level of statutory interpretation."[25] F.R. Scott, one of the most prolific critics of the Privy Council, praised the "clear recognition" by courts in the United States "that a constitution is primarily intended, not to rivet on posterity the narrow concepts of an earlier age, but to provide a living tree capable of growth and adaptation to new national needs."[26] To A.R.M. Lower, the Act should have been interpreted "as the vehicle for a nation's growth. If the Act is the vehicle of a nation, then the broadest construction must be put on it in order that under it all parts of the nation may have adequate life."[27]

Essentially, these critics were strong on general exhortation and weak on specifics. What they disliked was very clear. Positively, they were concerned with consequences. They recognized the policy role of the judiciary and the dangers of being tied down to the constitutional assumptions of a previous era. The difficulties of formal amendment encouraged them to look to the courts for the injection of flexibility into an ancient document. They also frequently noted the necessity of incorporating a broader range of facts into the judicial decision-making process. From this perspective their orientation was salutary, for the brunt of their message was to make judges more self-conscious than hitherto.

Inevitably the advocates of a living tree, liberal, flexible approach to constitutional interpretation were hostile to *stare decisis*. MacDonald spoke of the "shackles of previous decisions,"[28] Laskin of "the inertia of *stare decisis*," and the "encrustation of *stare decisis*,"[29] and W.P.M. Kennedy of "that uncanny stranglehold with which *stare decisis* seems doomed to rob the law of creative vitality."[30] They were far more concerned with the suitability of the developing constitution to new circumstances than with a narrow fidelity to previous constitutional case law.

Underlying the specific criticisms of the Privy Council was the overriding assumption that a powerful central government endowed with broad-ranging legislative authority and generous financial resources was an essential requirement of modern conditions. "The complications of modern industry and of modern business," asserted W.P.M. Kennedy in 1932, "will sooner or later demand national treatment and national action in the national legislature."[31] In the mid-thirties Vincent MacDonald favourably noted "prevailing political theories which indicate the propriety or necessity of a greater degree of national control over, and governmental intervention in, matters of social welfare and business activity."[32] The general centralist basis of the critics is most clearly found in the writings of the socialist law professor, F.R. Scott, the "unofficial constitutional advisor" of the CCF.[33] On numerous occasions Scott criticized the Privy Council for departing from the centralist federalism established in 1867 and for leaving Canada with a constitution that gravely hampered attempts to solve important public problems. In 1931 he stated:

> Canadian federalism has developed continuously away from the original design. Constitutionally we have grown disunited, in spite of the fact that in other respects, as a result of the increased facility of communication, the rise of our international status, and the general spread of what may be called our national consciousness, we have grown more united. The Dominion Parliament does not play today the full part which the Fathers of Confederation planned for her. . . . Just at the time when the exigencies of the economic situation call for drastic action, for increased international co-operation and for a planned internal social order, we find ourselves with cumbrous legislative machinery and outworn constitutional doctrines.[34]

The same point was made by Laskin in an article shortly after the Second World War. After noting the provincial bias of the Privy Council, he continued: "But has provincial autonomy been secured? In terms of positive ability to meet economic and social problems of interprovincial scope, the answer is no. A destructive negative autonomy exists, however, which has as a corollary that the citizens of a province are citizens of the Dominion for certain limited purposes only."[35]

In the thirties, when the impotence of the provinces was highlighted by the Great Depression, this kind of opinion was greatly strengthened.[36] The interdependence of a modern economy, the growth of national corporations, national unions, and a national public opinion inevitably focused attention on the need for a strong national government. The recently formed CCF with its centralist orientation was inevitably hostile to the decentralizing tenor of Privy Council decisions. The intellectual spokesmen of the left in the League for Social Reconstruction viewed the provinces as reactionary supports of the business community.[37] The Conservatives, who had seen their New Deal program harshly treated by the Privy Council, reacted by raising the issue of abolishing appeals.

In the international arena a different set of factors required strong central governments capable of decisive action by means of treaties that could be negotiated, ratified, and implemented without the inhibitions of a federalist division of powers. In these circumstances Lord Atkins's decision in the Labour Conventions case was viewed as an unmitigated disaster. "While it is true," his judgement stated, ". . . that it was not contemplated in 1867 that the Dominion would possess treaty-making powers, it is impossible to strain the section [132] so as to cover the uncontemplated event."[38]

This particular decision elicited a veritable flood of intemperate, polemical abuse of the Judicial Committee, both at the time and subsequently. The critics found it insulting to Canadian dignity and incompatible with Canadian autonomy that the evolution of Canadian independence from Great Britain should leave the federal government so seriously hampered in its relations with foreign states. F.R. Scott dramatized the choice as between local sovereignty and world peace.[39] W.P.M. Kennedy asserted in 1943 that the treaty situation was fraught with grave consequences for Canadian performance of post-war peace treaties.[40] Vincent MacDonald satirically noted:

> The Dominion's power of treaty implementation is absolute as to types of treaty now obsolete. It is, however, almost non-existent as to many types of treaty called for by modern conditions; for these latter tend in point of subject matter to fall, entirely or largely, within Provincial heads of jurisdiction, as greatly expanded by judicial interpretation. This is a fact of the utmost importance in a day requiring co-operative action of many nations to control international forces of an economic, social or political character.[41]

Thus the critics, particularly the constitutionalists, were convinced that both domestic and foreign policy requirements necessitated the dominance of the central government in the federal system. Their opposition to the Privy Council on grounds of policy was backed by a growing Canadian nationalism. Even some of the early supporters of the Privy Council had recognized that in the fullness of time the elimination of appeals was inevitable. Nationalist arguments had been used by Edward Blake when the Supreme Court was established in 1875.[42] They were later to form a staple part of John S. Ewart's long campaign for Canadian independence in the first three decades of this century. To Ewart the appeal was "one of the few remaining badges of colonialism, of subordination, of lack of self-government."[43] A later generation of critics reiterated Ewart's thesis. In 1947 F.R. Scott stated that the continuation of appeals "perpetuates in Canada that refusal to shoulder responsibility, that willingness to let some one else make our important decisions, which is a mark of immaturity and colonialism."[44] The nationalist argument was incorporated in the official justifications of the Liberal government when appeals were finally abolished in 1949.[45]

The fact that the elimination of appeals occurred simultaneously with the admission of Newfoundland to Canada and a renewed attempt to find a domestic amending procedure was not accidental. On the one hand the meaning and value of the Commonwealth was not what it had been prior to the Second World War. A weakened Britain and an attenuated Commonwealth combined with a stronger and more self-confident Canada to diminish the significance of ties with the mother country, a phrase that had begun to sound quaint and archaic.[46]

The nationalist attack on the Privy Council was fed by the special pride with which many Canadian writers asserted the superiority of Canadian over American federalism. The centralized variant of federalism established north of the "unguarded frontier," in reaction to the destructive effects of a decentralized federalism the American Civil War allegedly displayed, was for many critics part of the political distinctiveness of Canada they prized. In these circumstances, for a British court to reverse the intentions of the farsighted Fathers was doubly galling. This helps to explain the bitterness with which Canadian writers frequently contrasted the divergent evolutions of the American and Canadian federal systems away from their respective points of origin.

Explanations of the Judicial Committee

Critics of the Privy Council attempted to explain, as well as condemn, the results they deplored. In additional to explanations in terms of incompetence, critics offered specific interpretations of the Privy Council's conduct. One explanation was legal, the assertion that it was natural for judges to attempt to reduce the discretion involved in interpreting vague phrases such as peace, order, and good government. Frank Scott held that the decline of the federal residual power was due to the displeasure of a court of law at the task of having to distinguish between local and general matters. "Rather than commit themselves they have on the whole preferred to support legislation under some specific power, and thus the general residuary power has died of non-use."[47] A legal explanation of the Privy Council's conduct has been given recent support by Professor Browne's attempted justification of the claim that the BNA Act was in fact properly interpreted in the light of its evident meaning.[48]

Occasionally critics suggested that Privy Council decisions were influenced by political considerations inappropriate to a court. While the nature of these considerations was seldom made clear, the most frequent accusation was that imperial interests were best served by a weak central government.[49] This explanation was consistent with the political bias most frequently attributed to the court, the protection and enhancement of the position of the provinces in Canadian federalism.[50] Proof of this was found in cases favouring the provinces, or restricting federal legislation, and in the provincialist statements these cases frequently contained. Critics also pointed to the several occasions on which the Privy Council referred to the BNA Act as a compact or a treaty.[51] Further proof could be found in the speeches by Lord Haldane explicitly noting a protective attitude to the provinces, especially by his predecessor, Lord Watson.[52] Haldane's candid admissions are of special significance because of the propensity of Canadian critics to single out these two judges for particularly hostile treatment.[53] Haldane stated of Watson:

> ... as the result of a long series of decisions, Lord Watson put clothing upon the bones of the Constitution, and so covered them over with living flesh that the Constitution of Canada took a new form. The provinces were recognized as of equal authority co-ordinate with the Dominion, and a long series of decisions were given by him which solved many problems and produced a new contentment in Canada with the Constitution they had got in 1867. It is difficult to say what the extent of the debt was that Canada owes to Lord Watson....[54]

Haldane was also explicit that a judge on the Privy Council had "to be a statesman as well as a jurist to fill in the gaps which Parliament has deliberately left in the skeleton constitutions and laws that it has provided for the British colonies."[55] In view of these overt indications of a policy role favouring the provinces there can be no doubt that Watson and Haldane consciously fostered the provinces in Canadian federalism, and by so doing helped to transform the highly centralist structure originally created in 1867.

An alternative policy explanation deserves more extensive commentary. This was to identify the court with more or less subtlety as defenders of free enterprise against government encroachments. Spokesmen for the Canadian left, such as Woodsworth and Coldwell, were convinced that "reactionary interests have sought to shelter and to hide" behind the BNA Act.[56] F.R. Scott asserted that the "large economic interests" opposed to regulation sided with the provinces, which would be less capable of their effective regulation than would the federal government.[57] The courts, as both Scott and Professor Mallory noted, responded favourably to the protection from control that business sought.[58]

Mallory's description is apt: "The force that starts our interpretative machinery in motion is the reaction of a free economy against regulation. ... In short the plea of *ultra vires* has been the defence impartially applied to both legislatures by a system of free enterprise concerned with preventing the government from regulating it in the public interest."[59] Business was opposed by labour, which has fought consistently for "greater Dominion jurisdiction, based on the facts of every day life as they must be met today by the Canadian working class population, looking to broader Dominion powers in questions touching the welfare of the wage earners."[60] The tactics of business and labour were pragmatic reflections of self-interest. A necessary consequence of a federal system is that each organized interest will seek to transform the most sympathetic level of government into the main decision-maker in matters which concern it. The evaluation to be put on these tactics, and the responses of the courts to them, however, is another matter. Regardless of the groups that align themselves with different levels of government at different times, it is far from clear that support for provincial authority is necessarily reactionary and support for federal authority necessarily progressive.

There is considerable evidence that influential groups in Canada, including prominent lawyers, opposed the growing regulatory role of the modern state. Sir James Aikins, founder and first president of the Canadian Bar Association, frequently spoke in satirical and hostile terms of modern legislation and the politicians who inspired it. Unlike former times, when harsh and antiquated law was softened by judicial fictions, "changes are dangerously empirical by reason of the easiness with which legislation can be secured, and the lack of comprehension in the legislator of the general principles of the law."[61] He deprecated the fact that experiments in social control had been transferred from courts to legislatures, which produce "an impromptu statute and try ... [it] ... out on a resigned public, amending or repealing according to the pained outcry." Legislatures, he felt, had an ephemeral membership, unlike courts or "organized law bodies." Their members were not experts in the law, "only amateurs, and their acts, too often crude and inartistic, run the gauntlet of interpretation and construction by courts and lawyers before they are put right, usually at the expense of some unfortunate litigant."[62] Aikins's antipathy to collectivism was shared by many. The report of the Committee on Noteworthy Changes in Statute Law in 1939 to the Canadian Bar Association expressed strong hostility to the growing role of government in the closing years of the Depression. It reported ominously on the extent of socialism in Canada and stated the belief that "private property is the pillar on which our whole civilization rests."[63] Critics of collectivism were disturbed by the "new despotism" of government by order-in-council and the developing authority of proliferating tribunals, which handled business felt to be the prerogative of the courts.[64]

In brief, collectivism, in Canada as elsewhere, had to be fought out in a variety of arenas, before mass electorates,[65] in parliaments, and in courts.[66] In each arena there were supporters and opponents of the emerging transformation in the role of public authority. The real question is not whether courts were embroiled in the controversy, or whether some judges sided with "reactionary" forces. It would be astonishing if such were not the case.

The important questions are more difficult and/or more precise. Were the courts more or less receptive than other elite groups to collectivism? Where did they stand in the general trend to the welfare, regulatory state.[67] What were the links between judges and courts and the various influential groups that appeared before them? How did the Privy Council compare with other final appeal courts, or with lower Canadian courts, in its response to collectivism? Research on these questions would be extremely informative in pinning down the role of courts in the transition from the nightwatchman state to the era of big government.

Supporters of the Judicial Committee

Depression criticism, followed in the next decade by the elimination of appeals, had the effect that the period in which the Privy Council was under strongest attack has probably had the greatest effect on contemporary attitudes to it. Some of the most influential academic literature dealing with judicial review comes from that period and its passions.[68] As a consequence the Privy Council has typically received a very bad press in numerous influential writings by historians, political scientists, and lawyers in the past forty years.

In these circumstances, it is salutary to remember that if its critics reviled it, and turned Watson and Haldane into almost stock figures of fun, the Privy Council nevertheless did have a very broad body of support. Many highly qualified and well-informed analysts gave it almost unstinting praise. Indeed, if its critics reviled it too bitterly, its supporters praised it too generously. Often they wrote in fulsome terms, replete with awe and reverence for this most distinguished court.[69]

It was described as "this splendid body of experts,"[70] as "one of the most unique tribunals in the world,"[71] as a body of judges that "possesses a weight and efficiency as a supreme Judicial tribunal unequalled in the history of judicial institutions . . . a tribunal supremely equipped for the task – equipped for it in unexampled degree."[72] In 1914 Sir Charles Fitzpatrick, the Chief Justice of Canada, claimed that "amongst lawyers and Judges competent to speak on the subject, there is but one voice, that where constitutional questions are concerned, an appeal to the Judicial Committee must be retained."[73] In 1921 the Hon A.C. Galt, Justice of the Court of King's Bench, Manitoba, replied to the objection that the Privy Council derogated from the dignity of Canadians with the assertion that it was always sensible to employ experts. "Now it so happens that the Privy Council possesses all the advantages, as experts, to deal with legal ailments which the Mayo Brothers possess in dealing with physical ones."[74] Howard Ferguson, Premier of Ontario, ended a eulogy of the Privy Council in 1930 with special praise for Haldane, who protected "the Constitution of this country . . . giving it sane and sound interpretation . . . . In this Country of ours we will ever revere the memory of that great man."[75] Another writer observed that it was neither necessary nor "in good taste" for counsel to cite authorities before the Privy Council, "as owing to the great learning and vast experience of the members of the Board, they are usually familiar with such as have a bearing on the matters in question."[76] Supporters referred in an almost bemused way to the diversity of jurisdiction, extent of territory, and range of cases it handled. "Imagination without actual experience," stated Justice Duff, "is hardly adequate to realize the infinite variety of it all. . . ."[77]

The defenders and supporters of the Judicial Committee typically inter-mingled judicial and imperial arguments. The alleged contribution of the board of uniformity of law between Britain and her colonies and dominions straddled both arguments,[78] while the general assertion that the court was a link of empire was explicitly imperial.[79] It was also from this vantage point – that of a British citizen across the seas – that appeals were viewed and defended as a birthright, and much sentiment was employed over the right to carry one's appeals to the foot of the throne.[80]

A reading of the eulogies of the Privy Council prior to 1930 makes it clear that its most important source of Canadian support was imperial, and only secondarily judicial. The bulk of its supporters regarded it as an instrument of Empire. Rather than viewing its dominant position in the judicial structure as a symbol of Canadian inferiority, they derived pride and dignity from the Empire of which it was a part. They were British subjects first, and Canadians second, although from their perspective there was no conflict between these two definitions. The sentiments that inspired them are well presented in a statement of Justice Riddell in 1910 in which he spoke of

> . . . the ideal of fundamental union in all British communities – made manifest in concrete form in one great Court of Appeal for all the lands beyond the seas . . . to me there is no more inspiring spectacle than that body of gentlemen in the dingy old room on Downing street, Westminster, sitting to decide cases from every quarter of the globe, administering justice to all under the red-cross flag and symbolizing the mighty unity of an Imperial people. . . . One name we bear, one flag covers us, to one throne we are loyal; and that Court is a token of our unity.[81]

The immediately preceding set of arguments was essentially imperial. One important set of arguments, however, was jurisprudential. This was the frequently reiterated thesis that the great virtue of the Privy Council was its impartiality, a product of its distance from the scene of the controversies it adjudicated, and, unlike the Supreme Court, its absence of any direct link with either level of the governments whose interests clashed in the courtroom. In the quaint phraseology of the time, the committee was without those local prepossessions, so the argument went, which inevitably influence the decisions of local courts and thus prejudice the impartiality necessary in the judicial role.[82]

In his presidential address to the Canadian Bar Association in 1927 Sir James Aikins spoke critically of the role of the American Supreme Court in augmenting national power, a court "appointed and paid by that central government, resident in the same place and within the influence and atmosphere of Congress and the Executive, consequently removed from any contact with the capitals or governments of the several states." He went on to mention that largely similar conditions prevailed in Canada, and similar results might be expected should the Supreme Court become the final appeal court. He concluded with the rhetorical question: "will it not be in the best interests of all to have constitutional interpretation made by an Empire Court which is not appointed or paid by or in the immediate environment of one of the parties interested."[83]

To the critics of the Privy Council, impartiality, or absence of local prepossessions, simply meant ignorance. Nevertheless, the argument is of some importance if only because of its durability. It is prominent in the contemporary debate over the Supreme Court. In recent years English Canadians have defended the Supreme Court on grounds of its impartiality, while French Candians have criticized it on grounds of its insensitivity to their distinctive culture and special position in Canadian federalism. Further, this particular image of a good court is a reflection of one of the enduring visions of the judicial role – the blind eye of justice. It is also very close to the ideals behind the principle of judicial independence, and it is integrally related to the positivist conception of the judicial role, to the concept of the impartial third party as chairman, and to the concept of neutrality. This image, in brief, includes one of the ubiquitous central values that inevitably and properly intrudes into discussions of the role of public officials in general and judges in particular.

Sociological Justification of the Judicial Committee

The defence of the Privy Council on grounds of its impartiality and neutrality is, however, difficult to sustain in view of the general provincial bias that ran through their decisions from the 1880s. This was the most consistent basis of criticism the Judicial Committee encountered. A defence, therefore, must find some support for the general provincialist trend of its decisions.

It is impossible to believe that a few elderly men in London deciding two or three constitutional cases a year precipitated, sustained, and caused the development of Canada in a federalist direction the country would otherwise not have taken. It is evident that on occasion the provinces found an ally in the Privy Council, and that on balance they were aided in their struggles with the federal government. To attribute more than this to the

Privy Council strains credulity. Courts are not self-starting institutions. They are called into play by groups and individuals seeking objectives that can be furthered by judicial support. A comprehensive explanation of judicial decisions, therefore, must include the actors who employed the courts for their own purposes.[84]

The most elementary justification of the Privy Council rests on the broad sociological ground that the provincial bias pervading so many of its decisions was in fundamental harmony with the regional pluralism of Canada. The successful assertion of this argument requires a rebuttal of the claim of many writers that the Privy Council caused the evolution of Canadian federalism away from the centralization of 1867.[85]

From the vantage point of a century of constitutional evolution the centralist emphasis of the Confederation settlement appears increasingly unrealistic. In 1867 it seemed desirable and necessary to many of the leading Fathers. "The colonial life had been petty and bitter and frictional, and, outside, the civil war seemed to point to the need of binding up, as closely as it was at all possible, the political aspirations of the colonies."[86] Further, it can be argued that what appeared as overcentralization in the light of regional pluralism was necessary to establish the new polity and to allow the central government to undertake those nation-building tasks that constituted the prime reasons for union.

It is, however, far too easily overlooked, because of the idolatry with which the Fathers and their creation are often treated, that in the long run centralization was inappropriate for the regional diversities of a land of vast extent and a large, geographically concentrated, minority culture. The political leaders of Quebec, employing varying stategies, have consistently fought for provincial autonomy. The existence of Quebec alone has been sufficient to prevent Canada from following the centralist route of some other federal systems. In retrospect, it is evident that only a peculiar conjuncture of circumstances, many of them to prove ephemeral, allowed the degree of central government dominance temporarily attained in 1867.[87]

In the old provinces of Canada and the Maritimes provincial loyalties preceded the creation of the new political system. Nova Scotia and New Brunswick were reluctant entrants into Confederation, while Lower Canada sought to obtain as much decentralization as possible. A striking series of successes for the new Dominion might have generated the national loyalty necessary to support the central government in struggles with the provinces. Instead, the economic hopes on which so much had been placed in the movement to Confederation proved illusory and contributed to the undermining of federal prestige. Intermittent depression for most of the first thirty years of the new polity seriously eroded the flimsy supports for centralization on which Macdonald and some of his colleagues depended. The military dangers, an important original justification for a strong central government, rapidly passed away. The thrusting ambitions of provincial politicians, bent on increasing the power and resources of their jurisdictions, wrested numerous concessions from the federal government by a variety of methods, of which resort to the courts was only one. Their conduct was sustained by the almost inevitable rivalry between politicians of the two levels of government, especially when belonging to opposed political parties.[88]

The provinces, which had initially been endowed with functions of lesser significance, found that their control of natural resources gave them important sources of wealth and power, and extensive managerial responsibilities. By the decade of the twenties, highways, hydroelectric power, a host of welfare functions, and mushrooming educational responsibilities gave them tasks and burdens far beyond those anticipated in 1867. By this time the centralizing effect of the building of the railways and the settlement of the West was ended by the virtual completion of these great national purposes.

As the newer provinces west of the Great Lakes entered the union, or were created by federal legislation, they quickly developed their own identities and distinct public purposes: their populations grew; their economies expanded; their separate histories lengthened; their governmental functions proliferated; and their administrative and political competence developed. They quickly acquired feelings of individuality and a sense of power that contributed to the attenuation of federal dominance in the political system.

Only in special, unique, and temporary circumstances – typically of an emergency nature – has the federal system been oriented in a centralist direction.[89] The focus of so many Canadian academic nationalists on the central government reflected their primary concern with winning autonomy from the United Kingdom. An additional and less visible process was also taking place. Canadian political evolution has been characterized not only by nation-building but by province-building.[90] Further, it is too readily overlooked that with the passing of time Canada became more federal. In 1867 there were only four provinces in a geographically much more compact area than the nine provinces which had emerged by 1905, and the ten by 1949. If a province is regarded as an institutionalized particularism the historical development of Canada has been characterized by expansion, which has made the country more heterogeneous than hitherto.

In response to this increasingly federal society the various centralizing features of the BNA Act fell into disuse, not because their meaning was distorted by the courts, but because they were incompatible with developments in the country as a whole. In numerous areas, decentralizing developments occurred entirely on Canadian initiative, with no intervention by the Judicial Committee. The powers of reservation and disallowance were not eroded by the stupidity or malevolence of British judges but by concrete Canadian political facts. The failure to employ section 94 of the BNA Act to render uniform laws relating to property and civil rights in the common law provinces was not due to the prejudice of Lords Watson and Haldane but to the utopian nature of the assumptions that inspired it and the consequent failure of Canadians to exploit its centralizing possibilities.

The preceding analysis of Canadian federalism makes it evident that the provincial bias of the Privy Council was generally harmonious with Canadian developments. A more detailed investigation provides added support for this thesis.

At the time when Privy Council decisions commenced to undermine the centralism of Macdonald there was a strong growth of regional feeling. During the long premiership of Oliver Mowat, 1872-96, Ontario was involved in almost constant struggle with Ottawa. The status of the Lieutenant-Governor, the boundary dispute with Manitoba and the central government, and bitter controversies over the federal use of the power of disallowance constituted recurrent points of friction between Ottawa and Ontario. Friction was intensified by the fact that, with the exception of the brief Liberal interlude from 1873 to 1878, the governing parties at the two levels were of opposed partisan complexion, and by the fact that Mowat and Macdonald were personally hostile to each other.[91] The interprovincial conference of 1887, at which Mowat played a prominent part, indicated the general reassertion of provincialism. The "strength and diversity of provincial interests shown by the conference," in the words of the *Rowell-Sirois Report*, "indicated that, under the conditions of the late nineteenth century, the working constitution of the Dominion must provide for a large sphere of provincial freedom."[92] Nationalism had become a strong political force in Quebec in reaction to the hanging of Riel and the failure of the newly opened West to develop along bicultural and bilingual lines. Nova Scotia was agitated by a secession movement. The Maritime provinces generally were hostile to the tariff aspects of the National Policy. Manitoba was struggling against federal railway policies. British Columbia was only slowly being drawn into the national party system after the belated completion of the CPR in 1885. It was entering a long period of struggle with the Dominion over Oriental immigration. In addition, the late eighties and early nineties constituted one of the lowest points of national self-confidence in Canadian history.[93] It was a period in which the very survival of Canada was questioned. By the late 1890s, when economic conditions had markedly improved, a new Liberal government, with provincial sympathies, was in office. The year of the much criticized Local Prohibition decision was the same year in which Laurier assumed power and commenced to wield federal authority with much looser reins than had his Conservative predecessors. "The only means of maintaining Confederation," he had declared in 1889, "is to recognize that, within its sphere assigned to it by the constitution, each province is as independent of control by the federal Parliament as the latter is from control by the provincial legislatures."[94]

The Privy Council clearly responded to these trends in a series of landmark decisions in the eighties and nineties.[95] Unfortunately, it is not possible to provide detailed information on whether or not their decisions were supported or opposed by a majority or minority of the Canadian people. What can be asserted is that provincial political elites vigorously used the courts to attain their objectives of a more decentralized federal system. Further, they apparently received widespread popular support for their judicial struggles with Ottawa.[96] Premier Mowat of Ontario, who used to go personally to London for the appeals,[97] was received as a hero on his return from his engagements with the federal government.[98] It can thus be safely asserted that the Privy Council was not acting in isolation of deeply rooted, popularly supported trends in Canada. For critics of the Judicial Committee to appeal to the centralist wishes of the Fathers is an act of perversity that denies these provincialist trends their proper weight and influence.

It would be tedious and unnecessary to provide detailed documentation of the relative appropriateness of the decisions of the Judicial Committee to subsequent centrifugal and centripetal trends in Canadian society. It can be generally said that their decisions were harmonious with those trends. Their great contribution, the injection of a decentralizing impulse into a constitutional structure too centralist for the diversity it had to contain and the placating of Quebec that was a consequence, was a positive influence in the evolution of Canadian federalism.[99] Had the Privy Council not leaned in that direction, argued P.E. Trudeau, "Quebec separatism might not be a threat today; it might be an accomplished fact."[100] The courts not only responded to provincialism. The discovery and amplification of an emergency power in section 91 may have done an injustice to the intentions of Macdonald for the residuary power, but it did allow Canada to conduct herself virtually as a unitary state in the two world wars in which centralized government authority was both required and supported.

The general congruence of Privy Council decisions with the cyclical trends in Canadian federalism not only provides a qualified sociological defence of the committee but also makes it clear that the accusation of literalism so frequently levelled at its decisions is absurd. Watson and Haldane in particular overtly and deliberately enchanced provincial powers in partial defiance of the BNA Act itself.[101] The Privy Council's solicitous regard for the provinces constituted a defensible response to trends in Canadian society.

Prior to the great outburst of criticism against the Privy Council in the Depression of the thirties, strong approval for its decisions and their consequences was voiced by a variety of commentators. In 1909 J.M. Clark pointed out "what is too well known to require argument, namely, that the earlier decisions of our Supreme Court would have rendered our Constitution quite unworkable," a fate prevented by the existence of appeals to the Privy Council.[102] A few years later another writer praised the Privy Council for the political astuteness it combined with its legal abilities: "Better for the Canadian Constitution that the highest tribunal is composed of judges who are also politicians, rather than of lawyers who are merely judges. The British North America Act is nearly forty-nine years old and works more easily every year; the American Constitution, admittedly a more artistic but less elastic document, is daily falling behind."[103]

In 1921 another supporter strongly criticized the opponents of the Privy Council "whose interpretations have evolved for us all that is great, splendid and enduring in the Constitution under which the Dominion has flourished."[104] An unsigned, eulogistic editorial in the *Canadian Law Times* (1920) sums up the approbation with which many viewed the work of the Judicial Committee:

> I have read many of the decisions of the Privy Council relating especially to the Constitutional questions of Canada which have come before it; and I say that if it never did anything else for the purification of our legal conceptions, it has by its interpretations of the BNA Act rendered services to this country which should assure to it an abiding and grateful memory. With steady, persistent, and continuous adherence to the true lines of demarcation it has kept the Province and Dominion apart; and it has built up the Provincial fabric into a semi-sovereignty independent alike of the Dominion and of the United Kingdom. Its declarations on the Provincial Legislative powers alone are worthy of our gratitude and endless admiration. They are reverberant of that splendid independency which the several entities of Canada enjoy. These powers which the Dominion at one time thought subject to its control and doubtless would have striven to make them so, the Privy Council has declared are not delegated at all or subordinate to any authority except the Crown, but on the contrary that they are powers granted and surrendered by the Imperial Parliament directly in favor of the Legislature of each Province of Canada, and not even through the medium of the confederate Dominion.
>
> How splendid an inheritance! This is not the letter of the BNA Act but its spirit interpreted or declared for us by the Sovereign through his Privy Council in the light of aspirant freedom and of future nationhood.
>
> Well may the upholder of our Constitution who stands aghast at the invectives of the would-be demolisher of the Privy Council say: *Si quaeris monumentum circumspice.*[105]

Any plausible defence of the Privy Council must come to grips with the *cause célèbre* that more than any other indicated to its critics its incompetence and insensitivity as a final appeal court. In 1937, in a series of decisions, the Privy Council largely invalidated the New Deal legislation of the Bennett government. By so doing it indicated, to the fury of its critics, that even the emergency of a worldwide depression provided insufficient justification for central government authority to grapple with a devastating economic collapse. In these broad terms the case of the critics seems irrefutable. The New Deal decisions, more than any other, are responsible for the general hostility to the Privy Council in the literature of recent decades. The critics, however, have ignored a number of factors that place the action of the Privy Council in a much more favourable light.

The constitutionality of most of the New Deal legislation was in doubt from the moment of its inception.[106] Further, the final decisions by the courts were entirely predictable to a number of critics. Ivor Jennings's British law class "correctly forecast five of the decisions; and we were wrong on the sixth only because we took a different view of 'pith and substance.' "[107] W.P.M. Kennedy anticipated every New Deal decision but one before they went to the Supreme Court or the Privy Council.[108] The decisions therefore were not wayward, random, or haphazard. The judges did what men trained in the law expected them to do.

Any impression of an aloof court slapping down a determined Canadian leadership backed by widespread support is wrong.[109] R.B. Bennett, the initiator of the legislation, was decisively beaten in the federal election of 1935. The victor, Mackenzie King, had questioned the constitutionality of the legislation from the outset, never displayed any enthusiasm for its retention on the statute books, forwarded it willingly, almost eagerly, to the courts for their opinion, and uttered no anguished cries of rage when the decisions were announced.

In brief, the decisions were legally predictable and politically acceptable. In addition, there were extremely powerful centrifugal forces operating in the Depression. Hepburn in Ontario, Duplessis in Quebec, and Aberhart in Alberta symbolized the developing regionalism unleashed by massive economic breakdown. French-Canadian separatists loudly resisted the claim that the Depression could only be fought by centralization.[110] In these circumstances it is at least arguable that the political situation of the time was scarcely the most apposite for the enhancement of federal authority. The centralist bias of the critics ignored this fact. They unquestioningly assumed that the scale and nature of the problems facing the Canadian people could only be handled by the central government, and that no other considerations mattered. The critics were supported by the contribution of the Statute of Westminster in 1931 to Canadian autonomy. They were also encouraged by the dramatic development of "an astonishing number of voluntary, non-political, national associations" dealing with social, cultural, and intellectual affairs.[111] Given these factors the critics' position is understandable and defensible. Equally so, however, is the conduct of the

Privy Council. The real controversy is not over the performance of the Judicial Committee but over the proper criteria for the evaluation of judicial decisions.

The Weakness of the Judicial Committee

The Judicial Committee laboured under two fundamental weaknesses, the legal doctrine that ostensibly guided its deliberations, and its isolation from the setting to which those deliberations referred.

The basic overt doctrine of the court was to eschew considerations of policy and to analyse the BNA Act by the standard canons for the technical construction of ordinary statutes. The objection to this approach is manifold. Numerous legal writers have pointed out that the rules of statutory construction are little more than a grab bag of contradictions. It is also questionable whether a constitution should be treated as an ordinary statute, for clearly it is not. In the British political system, with which judges on the Privy Council were most acquainted, it is at least plausible to argue that the doctrine of parliamentary supremacy, and the consequent flexibility of the legislative process, provides some justification for the courts limiting the policy role and assigning to Parliament the task of keeping the legislation of the state appropriate to constantly changing circumstances. The BNA Act, however, as a written constitutional document, was not subject to easy formal change by the amending process. Consequently, the premise that the transformation of the Act could be left to lawmaking bodies in Canada, as in the United Kingdom, was invalid. A candid policy role for a final appeal court seems to be imperatively required in such conditions.

Even in the absence of this consideration it is self-evident that no technical analysis of an increasingly ancient constitutional document can find answers to questions undreamt of by the Fathers. The Privy Council's basic legal doctrine was not only undesirable, therefore, it was also impossible. In reality, as already indicated, the Privy Council obliquely pursued a policy of protecting the provinces. The clear divergence between the Act as written and the Act as interpreted makes it impossible to believe that in practice the Privy Council viewed its role in the narrow, technical perspective of ordinary statutory construction. The problem of the court was that it was caught in an inappropriate legal tradition for its task of constitutional adjudication. It partially escaped from this dilemma by occasionally giving overt recognition to the need for a more flexible, pragmatic approach, and by covertly masking its actual policy choices behind the obfuscating language and precedents of statutory interpretations.

The covert pursuit of policy meant that the reasoning process in their decisions was often inadequate to sustain the decision reached. This also helps to explain the hypocritical and forced distinguishing of previous cases criticized by several authors.[112] Further, the impossibility of overt policy discussion in decisions implied the impossibility of open policy arguments in proceedings before the court. Inevitably, the court experienced severe handicaps in its role as policy-maker.

Caught in an unworkable tradition the Judicial Committee was unable to answer the basic question of constitutional jurisprudence, that is, how it should apply the discretion it unavoidably possessed. The application of a constitution to novel conditions provides a court with the opportunity for creative statesmanship. To this challenge the Judicial Committee evolved no profound theories of its own role. Its most basic answer was silence, supplemented by isolated statements of principle dealing with the federal system and occasional liberal statements concerning its role in contributing to the growth and evolution of the constitution. The confusion in Privy Council philosophy was cogently described by MacDonald:

> Uncertainty and inconsistence in ... matters which lie at the very threshold of the problem of interpretation have played a large part in making the ascertainment of the meaning of the Canadian constitution the precarious task that it is today; for the chief element of predictability of legal decision inheres in a known and uniform technique of approach. It is a prime criticism of the Privy Council that it has had no uniform technique of approach to the act; for it has sought now the intention of the framers of the act, now the meaning of its terms; sometimes excluding, sometimes being influenced by, extraneous matters, and sometimes interpreting the terms of the act as speaking eternally in the tongue of 1867, and sometimes in the language of contemporary thought and need.[113]

The second main weakness of the Privy Council was its isolation from the scene to which its judgements applied. Its supporters argued otherwise by equating its distance from Canada with impartiality. Judges on the spot, it was implied, would be governed or influenced by the passions and emotions surrounding the controversy before them. British judges, by contrast, aloof and distant, would not be subject to the bias flowing from intimate acquaintance.

The logic of this frequently espoused position was curious. The same logic, as J.S. Ewart satirically observed, implied the desirability of sending British cases to the Supreme Court at Ottawa, but no such proposals were forthcoming. "Local information and local methods," he continued, "are very frequently essential to the understanding of a dispute. They are not disqualifications for judicial action."[114]

The critics were surely right in their assertions that absence of local prepossessions simply meant relative ignorance, insensitivity, and misunderstanding of the Canadian scene, deficiencies that would be absent in

Canadian judges. "The British North America Act," Edward Blake had asserted in 1880, "is a skeleton. The true form and proportions, the true spirit of our Constitution, can be made manifest only to the men of the soil. I deny that it can be well expounded by men whose lives have been passed, not merely in another, but in an opposite sphere of practice.... "[115] The same argument was reiterated by succeeding generations of critics until the final elimination of appeals.[116]

The weakness flowing from isolation was exacerbated by the shifting composition of the committee, which deprived its members of those benefits of experience derived from constant application to the same task. "The personnel of that Court," stated a critic in 1894, "is as shifting as the Goodwin Sands. At one sitting it may be composed of the ablest judges in the land, and at the next sitting its chief characteristic may be senility and general weakness."[117] This instability of membership contributed to discontinuities in interpretation as membership changed. It also allowed those who sat for long periods of time, as did Watson and Haldane, to acquire disproportionate influence on Privy Council decisions.

The professed legal philosophy of the Judicial Committee helped explain away the disadvantages allegedly flowing from isolation, by stressing the mechanical, technical, legal character of the judicial task. This minimized the advantages of local understanding for judges. Conversely, the position of the critics was strengthened when they stressed the policy component in judicial interpretation. While a plausible case might be made that technical, legal matters could be handled as well, or even better, by a distant court, the same argument could scarcely be made of policy matters, where local understanding was obviously of first-rate importance. It necessarily followed that the Supreme Court of Canada, composed of men thoroughly conversant with Canadian social and political conditions, had a greater capacity to be a more sophisticated and sensitive court of appeal.

The understanding of Canadian politics held by British judges was well summarized by a sympathetic observer, Jennings:

> The Atlantic separates them from the political disputes of Canada. Their information about the controversies of the Dominion is obtained from the summary cables of the London press, which is far more interested in problems nearer home. If Mr. Dooley came to London he could not say that the Judicial Committee followed the Canadian election returns. Unless their functions make them particularly interested in Canadian news, they are probably as uncertain of the politics of the governments in power as is the average Englishman. The controversies which appear to them to be merely legal disputes as to the meaning of sections 91 and 92 of the Act often have a background of

party strife and nice political compromises. The judges may know enough to realize that politics are involved, but not enough to appreciate exactly why and how.[118]

These considerations add a special cogency to Vincent MacDonald's plea for abolition of appeals on the ground that "even in matters of dry law decision is affected by the national character and personal background of the judiciary." One could not ignore, he continued, "the temperament, the experience, the social background and training of the final court," especially when interpretation dealt with policy matters.[119] Tuck's argument was equally to the point:

> Resort to the Privy Council is unnecessary where the two tribunals agree; and where they disagree, since constitutional interpretation turns largely on matters of policy, its development would be best directed by a Canadian court with first-hand experience of Canadian conditions and needs. The Privy Council, with its constantly shifting personnel, working always at a distance from the scene of operations, is hardly the appropriate body for this kind of work.... It is unlikely, therefore, that the board will ever be thoroughly familiar with the spirit of the Canadian constitution, or the environment necessary to its successful working.[120]

Given the difficulties that inevitably flowed from its London location, and given the sterilities of the legal tradition it espoused, the decisions of the Privy Council were remarkably appropriate for the Canadian environment. The Privy Council, in its wisdom, was partially able to overcome some of the dangers caused by its own ignorance. That it did so imperfectly was only to be expected. Watson and Haldane have been criticized by McWhinney on the ground that if they were consciously influenced "by a bias in favour of provincial powers, their approach seems nevertheless to have been a vague, impressionistic one, without the benefit of a detailed analysis and weighing of the policy alternatives involved in each case."[121] Essentially the same criticism is made by MacGuigan, who criticizes the abstract natural law approach adopted by the Privy Council in coming to its policy decisions. They were policy-makers without the necessary tools of understanding.[122] These criticisms, while valid, reflect failings that were inevitable for a body of men who adjudicated disputes emanating from the legal systems of a large part of the world, and who could not be expected to become specialists in the shifting socio-economic contexts in which each legal system was embedded.[123] This particular weakness could not be overcome by a body of British judges. If local knowledge was a necessary attribute of a good court, the Privy Council could only be a second-best interim arrangement.

The context in which the Privy Council existed deprived it of the continual feedback of relevant information on which wise and sensitive judging depends. Superficially this could be described as a deficiency of local knowledge. This deficiency, however, is sufficiently complex and important to require elaboration.

An effective court does not exist in a vacuum. It is part of a complicated institutional framework for the amelioration of the human condition through the device of law in individual nation-states. Law is unavoidably national. It cannot be otherwise as long as the basic political unit is the nation-state. Laws are not designed for men in general, but for Canadians, Americans, Germans, etc.

Within these national frameworks a variety of procedures has been developed to make law sensitive to the needs of particular communities. This is readily recognized and admitted for legislatures and executives. For courts, however, the attributes of objectivity and impartiality, combined with the status of judicial independence, tend to distract attention from the task similarity between judges and legislators. Both, however, are concerned with the applicability of particular laws to particular communities. There is consequently an important overlap in their mutual requirements. Both must be provided with the institutional arrangements that facilitate an adequate flow of the relevant information for their specific tasks.

A strong and effective court requires a variety of supporters. It must be part of a larger system that includes first-class law schools, quality legal journals, and an able and sensitive legal fraternity – both teaching and practising. These are the minimum necessary conditions for a sophisticated jurisprudence, without which a distinguished judicial performance is impossible. Unless judges can be made aware of the complexities of their role as judicial policy-makers and sensitively cognizant of the societal effects of their decisions, a first-rate judicial performance will only occur intermittently and fortuitously. In brief, unless judges exist in a context that informs their understanding in the above manner, they are deprived of the guidance necessary for effective decision-making. Most of the conditions required as supports for a first-class court were only imperfectly realized in Canada prior to the abolition of appeals to the Privy Council. A shifting body of British judges, domiciled in London, whose jurisdiction covered a large part of the habitable globe, existed in limbo. This isolation of the court not only reduced its sensitivity to Canadian conditions but rendered it relatively free from professional and academic criticism.[124] A related part of the problem was noted by Ewart in his observation that the Privy Council either had the assistance of English barristers devoid of an intimate understanding of Canadian circumstances, or "Canadian barristers, who speak from one standpoint and are listened to from another."[125]

The position of the Judicial Committee at the apex of a structure of judicial review of global extent virtually necessitated the conceptualizing approach found offensive to so many of its critics. The court was not, and could not be, adequately integrated into a network of communication and criticism capable of transmitting the nuances and subtleties a first-class appeal court required.

The single opinion of the court, while it possibly helped to sustain its authority and weaken the position of its critics,[126] had serious negative effects. Jennings pointed out that "the absence of a minority opinion sometimes makes the opinion of the Board look more logical and more obvious than it really is. The case is stated so as to come to the conclusion already reached by the majority in private consultation. It is often only by starting again and deliberately striving to reach the opposite conclusion that we realize that . . . there were two ways of looking at it."[127] The absence of dissents hindered the development of a dialogue over the quality of its judgements. Dissents provide a lever for the critic by the indication of a lack of judicial unanimity, and by their provision of specific alternatives to the decisions reached. Unanimity of its published opinion thus made its own contribution to the isolation of the court. In addition, as a final appeal court, it had "no dread of a higher judicial criticism."[128] Finally, much of the debate that swirled around its existence and performance was so inextricably intertwined with the larger controversy between nationalism and imperialism that the question of the judicial quality of its task was not faced head on. These extraneous considerations partly account for the extremes in the evaluations made of the court, ranging between "undiscriminating praise and . . . over-criticism."[129]

The Confusion of the Critics

For the better part of a century the performance of the Judicial Committee has been a continuing subject of academic and political controversy in Canada. Even the elementary question of whether its work was basically good or fundamentally bad has elicited contrary opinions. The distribution of favourable and critical attitudes has shifted over time. From the turn of the century until the onset of the Depression of the thirties, informed opinion was generally favourable. Subsequently, English-Canadian appraisals became overwhelmingly critical. It is a reasonable speculation, sustained by Browne's recent volume,[130] by the contemporary strength of regional forces in Canadian society, and by the fact that Canadian judicial autonomy is now in its third decade, that more favourable evaluations of the Judicial Committee will begin to appear. For example, the Labour Conventions case (1937), which so aroused the ire of the critics who feared the emasculation of Canadian treaty-making, now seems to present a defensible proposition in contemporary Canadian federalism.

In the period up to and subsequent to the final abolition of appeals in 1949 there was a consistent tendency for opposed evaluations of the Judicial Committee to follow the French-English cleavage in Canada.[131] This divergence of opinion was manifest in French-Canadian support for the Judicial Committee,[132] with opposition on grounds of nationalism and its provincial bias largely found in English Canada. Many English-Canadian writers hoped that the Supreme Court, as a final appeal court, would adopt a liberal, flexible interpretation, eroding at least in part the debilitating influence of *stare decisis*. In practical terms, their pleas for a living tree approach presupposed a larger role for the central government than had developed under the interpretations of the Judicial Committee. In essence, one of the key attitudes of the predominantly English-Canadian abolitionists was to view a newly independent Supreme Court as an agent of centralization.[133] The very reasons and justifications that tumble forth in English-Canadian writings caused insecurity and apprehension in French Canada, which feared, simply, that if English-Canadian desires were translated into judicial facts the status and influence of the provinces fostered by British judges would be eroded.[134] The American-style Supreme Court sought by the constitutionalist critics of the Privy Council was justifiably viewed with apprehension by French-Canadian observers. They assumed, not unfairly, that if such a court heeded the bias of its proponents it would degenerate into an instrument for the enhancement of national authority. These contrary English and French hopes and fears are closely related to the present crisis of legitimacy of the Supreme Court.

An additional significant cleavage in Canadian opinion was between those fundamentalist critics who opposed the Judicial Committee for its failure to provide a technically correct interpretation of a clearly worded document and the constitutionalists who castigated it for its failure to take a broad, flexible approach to its task.

The fundamentalist approach, already discussed, imposed on the courts the task of faithfully interpreting a document in terms of the meanings deliberately embodied in it by the Fathers of Confederation. This approach was replete with insuperable difficulties:

1. If the task of the courts was to provide a literally correct interpretation of the agreement of 1867 it is possible to differ on the degree of their success or failure. The standard interpretation adhered to by MacDonald, O'Connor, and numerous others is that the performance of the Judicial Committee, from this perspective, was an abject failure. Recently, however, a new analysis by Professor G.P. Browne has lauded the Privy Council for the consistency of its interpretation and has categorically asserted that refined textual analysis of sections 91 and 92 indicates that they were given a proper judicial interpretation. According to Browne, British judges were not acting out a bias in favour of the provinces, but were simply applying the logic of the BNA Act to the legal controversies that came before them for adjudication.[135] Browne's revisionist thesis has been both praised and harshly criticized.[136] Its truth, if such a word can be applied to such a subject as constitutional interpretation, is not germane to our purposes.[137]

What is germane is the fact that a century after Confederation the question of the technically correct interpretation of the Act can still produce violently opposed positions among serious, competent scholars. One is tempted to ask if the pursuit of the real meaning of the Act is not a meaningless game, incapable of a decisive outcome.[138]

2. There is controversy over the relationship between the intentions of the Fathers and the BNA Act they created. The centralist argument is that the Fathers both intended and produced a centralized federal system. It has, however, been asserted by Professor Philippe Ferland that there is a discrepancy between the intentions and the result. This approach claims that the pre-Confederation statements of the Fathers favoured a legislative decentralization, but they drafted a text that devoured the provinces. The judges then, according to Ferland, concentrated on the text, ignored the external evidence, and thus damaged the interests of the provinces.[139] It is impossible to overlook the fact that here, as elsewhere, legal scholars have displayed an ingenious ability to locate evidence for the kind of intentions they sought.

3. LaBrie noted that even if it could be assumed that the Fathers of Confederation did have views on the newer areas of government, "there remains the question whether, in the light of our own greater experience in the problems of federal government, these intentions ought to rule us at the present day."[140] By implication the fundamentalists attempted to tie succeeding generations of Canadians down to the constitutional assumptions of a small body of men in the 1860s. For a completely static society, in which the original settlement was perfectly suited to existing social values and needs, such an approach has some plausibility. But as society changes, it seems evident that the faint glimmers of insights of the Fathers should be overruled by the more comprehensive understandings of their successors. Literalism, consequently, is an inadequate guide for judges. This was tacitly admitted by those fundamentalist critics who applied their literalism to the division of powers, but often proudly noted the flexibility of other portions of the Act. They were, for example, happy to accept the evolving conventions that transformed the roles of the Governor General and the Lieutenant-Governor. They tended to be literalist only when it suited their purposes.

Further, literalism, either as a description of what judges can or should do, is so clearly preposterous that its frequent employment as a tactic of criticism is, to say the least, surprising. M.R. Cohen's comment dealing with judicial review in the United States is no less applicable to Canada: "The pretence that every decision of the Supreme Court follows logically from the Constitution must ... be characterized as a superstition. No rational argument can prove that when the people adopted the Constitution they actually intended all the fine distinctions which the courts have introduced into its interpretation. Nor can we well deny the fact that judges have actually differed in their interpretations...."[141]

4. Most obvious, and noted by various writers, was the fact that the new and developing areas of government activity, where uncertainty was greatest, could not be fitted into the intentions of a previous generation ignorant of the problems involved.[142] The courts themselves have had to recognize the novelty of the issues they frequently encounter. When the Privy Council faced the question of whether a Canadian legislature could regulate appeals, the judgement stated that "it is . . . irrelevant that the question is one that might have seemed unreal at the date of the British North America Act."[143]

5. It can be argued that the relevant intentions of the Fathers include not only their specific intentions for the Canadian political system as they visualized it in 1867, but also their attitudes to the possibility that future generations might wish to transform the nature of their creation. Lord Haldane, for example, argued that the Fathers intended the courts to work out the constitution.[144]

6. The question of the intentions of the Fathers is part of the larger controversy over the desirability of going beyond the wording of the Act to a variety of pre-Confederation material that conceivably could throw light on its meaning.[145] Many critics recommended the use of the historical material surrounding Confederation as an aid to interpretation. Others asserted that not only was it the custom of the courts to exclude such materials, but that they were correct in doing so.[146] They agreed with Lord Sankey in the Edwards case that in interpreting the BNA Act "the question is not what may be supposed to have been intended, but what has been said."[147] Evan Gray, a critic of O'Connor, asserted that all pre-Confederation material "is illusory and inconclusive. It is not merely because a rigid rule of legal procedure binds our courts that we reject such material, but because as a matter of common sense we know that any other method of enquiry is unreliable, being speculative rather than logical and adding to uncertainty instead of resolving it."[148] The use of such materials was also undesirable, according to Vincent MacDonald, because the tying down of interpretation to the intentions of the Fathers "allows the horizon of that year [1867] to restrict the measures of the future." It was wiser, he argued, to interpret the words of the statute, which allowed flexibility and the incorporation of new meanings.[149]

The use of pre-Confederation material to document the intentions of the Fathers as an aid to interpretation would not have improved the Privy Council's performance. In addition to the much greater ambiguity of pre-Confederation speeches and resolutions compared to the BNA Act itself, their use is subject to all the criticisms of those who resist the binding of future generations by the restricted foresight of their predecessors. A living constitution incorporates only so much of the past as appears viable in the light of new conditions. A further weakness of the use of pre-Confederation material is that its contribution to understanding the BNA

Act was greatest at the general level of the nature of the Act as a whole, and weakest in the more specific areas covered by constitutional cases. It is significant that critics of the Privy Council tended to focus on pre-Confederation statements about the nature of the political system as a whole. Judges inevitably interpreted particular powers rather than the entire BNA Act, "because there was no machinery for the interpretation of the constitution as such."[150]

In summary, the intellectual rigour of the fundamentalist critics of the Privy Council leaves much to be desired. Their case is destroyed by its essential shallowness.

The constitutionalist critics of the Privy Council based themselves on a much more promising normative and analytic stand. They welcomed and recognized a policy role for the courts in judicial review. They appreciated both the impossibility and undesirability of complete fidelity to a statute conceived in former times by men who lacked the gift of foresight. To this extent, they were judicial realists. They could easily document, when so inclined, the inevitable policy content of judicial decisions and by so doing could puncture the slot machine theory of law. This was their achievement. Their recognition of a policy-making role helped to initiate normative discussions on what a final appeal court should do with the discretion inherent in its task.[151] However, their own prescriptive statements were frequently shallow and seldom placed in a carefully articulated philosophy of the judicial role. An important contributing reason for the inadequacy of their normative contribution was they they were not clearly distinguished in policy objectives from the fundamentalists. Unlike the United States, where the advocates of strict constitutional construction were usually state rightists,[152] Canadian centralists could and did find in the 1867 agreement constitutional support for their position. Thus the distinctions between the constitutionalists and the fundamentalists were blurred by the fact that both were centralists.[153] Constitutionalists, accordingly, could always fall back on literalist justifications for their centralist policy position. They were not therefore under an obligation to prescribe a carefully defined policy justification, either for their centralization or for the role of the court in helping to attain it. They thus lapsed into uncritical support for centralization on the general ground that it was required by the needs of the time.[154] This, however, as B.N. Cardozo pointed out, is not even the beginning of judicial philosophy:

> I have no quarrel, therefore, with the doctrine that judges ought to be in sympathy with the spirit of their times. Alas! assent to such a generality does not carry us far upon the road to truth. In every court there are likely to be as many estimates of the "Zeitgeist" as there are judges on its bench. . . . The spirit of the age, as it is revealed to each of us, is too often only the spirit of the group in which the accidents of birth or

education or occupation or fellowship have given us a place. No effort or revolution of the mind will overthrow utterly and at all times the empire of these subsconscious loyalties.[155]

The critics did not develop a consistent and meaningful definition of the judicial role in constitutional review. The much maligned Judicial Committee was criticized on two mutually exclusive grounds.[156] The fundamentalists, fluctuating back and forth between the Act itself and pre-Confederation material, charged it with departing from the clear meaning of the Act and the obvious intent of its framers. The constitutionalists, concerned with policy, charged it with a failure to interpret the Act in the flexible manner appropriate to a constitutional document. Their policy approach tended to be based on whether or not a given decision, or series of decisions, agreed with their values, which usually meant whether or not it facilitated government action regarded as desirable, or inhibited government action regarded as undesirable. The fundamentalists castigated the Privy Council for reaching decisions that every historian knew to be untrue, the very kind of decision the logic of the constitutionalists invited the bench to make. The fundamentalists demanded a technically correct performance of a mechanical act, the interpretation of a clearly worded document. The constitutionalists appealed less to the Act than to the contemporary conditions to which it was to be applied. While they did not write off the BNA Act as irrelevant, the constitutionalists tended to be hostile when the Act, or its judicial interpretation, stood in the way of their objectives. Their prime purpose was to allow the federal government to grapple with problems they deemed to be beyond provincial competence, or which they expected provincial governments to handle in some undesirable way. The simultaneous or sequential employment of these divergent fundamentalist and constitutionalist rationales was effective as a debating device. It was productive of great confusion over the basic question of the proper role for the court.

The critics of the Judicial Committee were moved more by the passions of nationalism and desires for centralization than by federalism. By the mid-thirties the two main perspectives on the judicial role agreed that the Act, as interpreted, was increasingly irrelevant to the environment to which it applied. Both groups of critics "took it as axiomatic that the application of the appropriate techniques of interpretation of the BNA Act, whether in the form of a larger dose of knowledgeable judicial statesmanship or greater fidelity to the true meaning of the constitutional text, could only be achieved by transferring the highest judicial power from English to Canadian judges."[157] Both groups of critics were centralists, although they found different constitutional justifications for their position. Neither group wrote favourably of the provinces, or expected much of them. They pinned their hopes on Ottawa. They shared Underhill's evaluation of the provinces: "The only province," he wrote in 1931, "which has not been subject to the regular alternation between short periods of comparatively good government and long periods of decay is Quebec. In Quebec they enjoy bad government all the time."[158] The critics assumed that industrial, technological, urban, or some other set of conditions required centralization. They stressed the difficulties of divided jurisdiction as barriers to the effective regulation of an interdependent economy. They placed great emphasis on the national structure of an economy no longer capable of meaningful delimitation by provincial boundaries. They assumed economic forces to be uncompromisingly centralist and never regionalist in impact. They shared Laski's thesis that federalism was obsolete, paid little attention to the varying kinds of pluralism rooted in non-economic factors, and were hostile to the institutional arrangements that preserved and protected federalism. They were prone to stress the national-local distinction as crucial to the proper understanding of the BNA Act, and thus they tended to employ a national dimension or general-interest justification for federal legislation. This was an approach to which French Canadians took strong exception because of its obvious threat to provincial autonomy.[159]

The really dramatic cleavage between the supporters and opponents, especially the constitutionalists, of the Privy Council was, as hinted above, in their opposition over the kinds of non-legal facts that should be of significance in constitutional adjudication. The supporters stressed either the governmental pluralism of the federal system or the underlying, regionally grouped diversities on which it was deemed to be based. Judicial decisions that protected and fostered this pluralism were praised. Judicial interpretation hostile to pluralism was opposed. The constitutionalists, by contrast, downplayed the significance of pluralism, which they frequently saw as a cover for vested interests seeking to avoid regulation. To them the paramount extra-legal factors were the ties of economic and technical interdependence and the corporate power behind them. These, by implication, had either undermined the sociological supports for pluralism or, by generating problems of national importance or scope that imperatively required central government authority for their resolution, had reduced pluralism to secondary significance.

There is no easy way by which these contrary definitions of relevant extra-legal facts can be categorized as more or less true. Both provided plausible justifications for the kind of federal system their advocates sought and the kind of judicial review required to achieve or sustain it.

Several speculations are in order. With the passage of time since 1867, ties of interdependence have been generated and have helped to knit the Canadian economy together. It seems clear, however, that an economic interpretation of Canadian history which presupposes that this economic interdependence has undermined pluralist values is largely wrong. Canadians have remained pluralist in spite of economic change.

Economic interdependence is an omnibus concept that conceals as much as it reveals. To the extent that it does exist it is not always seen as beneficial by all the parties caught in it. The National Policy incorporated the Prairies into the Canadian economy in a manner that has generated disaffection ever since Manitoba began to fight the railway monopoly of the CPR shortly after being constituted as a province. French-Canadian politicians have not been notably pleased with a system of interdependence in which capital and management were English and the workers were French.

The concept of interdependence is thus too general to be helpful in describing the nature of the Canadian economy or the kinds of political authority necessary to manage it. The concept also contributes to a disregard for the distinctive nature of the regional economies that have grown since Confederation. The importance of provincial control of natural resources and the foreign markets to which these resources are sent sustain distinct regional or provincial interests frequently hostile to a national approach. The nature of the Canadian economy has never been such as to offer unequivocal support for central government authority.

It is also probable that the alleged disastrous effects of Privy Council support for the provinces have been exaggerated. In recent years, at least, the provinces, particularly the larger and wealthier ones, have not been the impotent units of government that critics of the Privy Council assumed. They are neither synonyms for reaction nor backwaters of ineptitude. In the long view judicial support for the provinces has contributed to the formation of competent governments. It is also clear that the paralysing effect of judicial decisions on the federal government has been overstressed. For a decade and a half after the Second World War Canada was run in a highly centralist fashion despite nearly a century of judicial interpretation that was claimed to have reduced Ottawa to a powerless nonentity. Judicial review scarcely seems to have been as important a determinant of constitutional evolution as has often been imagined. Professor Corry has indeed speculated that judicial interpretation adverse to Ottawa precipitated the "spectacular refinement of the techniques of economic and fiscal powers after the war" on which post-war centralization was based. "Perhaps the Privy Council interpretations have, in the sequel, pushed effective centralization further and faster than it would otherwise have gone."[160]

Professor McWhinney is critical of the quality of the controversy over the Privy Council because it too frequently proceeded "in the form of a dispute over alternative rules of statutory construction, rather than in terms of the actual consequences to Canadian national life flowing from the individual decisions."[161] This is neither entirely true nor entirely fair. At bottom, the critics, of whatever school, were motivated by a concern for the consequences of constitutional interpretation. Especially in the Depression of the thirties, the perceived consequences of the New Deal decisions aroused their ire.

Hostility to the Judicial Committee was fed by the inability of Canadians to develop an amending procedure to facilitate transfers of power from the provinces to the central government. In this situation the courts were viewed as the last resort. When they failed to respond to the challenge in the thirties, their critics retaliated with passionate hostility as the federal system appeared impotent when confronted with economic breakdown and social dislocation. In general, criticisms resulted from an antipathy to the negative effects of Privy Council decisions on the capacity of Canadians to pursue certain objectives. The Privy Council left Canadians, in the phrase of one critic, with a "hardly workable polity."[162] In area after area, argued the critics, the situation was intolerable in terms of administrative efficiency, the scope of the problem, or the power of the interests requiring regulation.[163]

The constitutionalists, in particular, were much concerned with the consequences of judicial decisions. They inevitably sought legal justification for the decisions they favoured, but they can scarcely be faulted for that. They were simply playing the game in the accustomed manner. As indicated above, they exaggerated both the harmful consequences of the divisions and the role of the Judicial Committee in the evolution of Canadian federalism. They cannot, however, be criticized for lack of concern with policy. Their chief weakness lies elsewhere, in their failure to produce a consistent, comprehensive definition of what can legitimately be expected from a particular institution, a definition necessarily related to the specific task of that institution in the complex of institutions that make up the political system as a whole. In a discussion of the Privy Council's handling of the New Deal, A.B. Keith asserted that from a "juristic point of view" he was able to accord "cordial appreciation" to the decisions. It was, he continued, a "completely different question" whether the constitution was an apt instrument for the solution of new problems; but this, he concluded, was "a work for the statesmen and people of the Dominion, and not for any court."[164] The particular distinction made by Keith may or may not be valid. What is relevant is that he made a distinction. It is not necessary to fall into the textbook simplification between those who make the laws, those who administer them, and those who interpret them to suggest that different institutions are entrusted with different tasks. The failure to make any kind of differentiation denies the validity of the institutional division of political labour painfully evolved over centuries of Western history. To blame the milkman for not delivering bread or the doctor for the mistakes of the laundryman is a recipe for chaos. The basic, prior, and determining question is simply what can properly be expected of judicial review. In a constitutional system the function of judicial review must be more than simply allowing desirable policies to be implemented by whatever level of government so wishes. A worthwhile court of final appeal is bound on occasion to prevent one level of government from doing what a group of temporary incumbents or its supporters would like to do. Criticism of a court based on the fact that it has prevented a desirable objective from being attained is not good enough. Like the American legal realists, with whom the constitutionalists had some affinity, Canadian critics were effective at the task of demolition and weak at telling the judge what he should do.[165]

In sum, Canadian jurisprudence was deeply divided on the question of the relevant criteria for the guidance of judges in the difficult process of constitutional interpretation. Neither critics nor supporters of the Judicial Committee were able to develop consistent and defensible criteria for judicial review. Admittedly, Canadians were not alone in their confusion. Professor Corry asserted in 1939 that "one would have to search far to find a more confused portion of the English law" than "the rules to be followed in interpreting statutes and constitutions." He continued:

> The text writers and judges all insist that the basic rule is to find the "expressed intention" of the makers of the constitution and that, in the case of constitutions, this intention is to be liberally rather than narrowly construed. The trouble is that constitutions often do not have "expressed intentions" about many of the situations to which they must be applied. The Fathers of Confederation could not express any intention about aviation and radio. At best then, in such circumstances, the court can only argue by analogy, making inferences as to what the framers would have said if they had thought about the problem. Even then, there are numerous situations where no compelling inferences can be found by logical processes. Nor does it help to propose that the constitution should be liberally construed, for one must still ask for what purpose and to what end. Liberal construction of Dominion power is, at the same time, strict construction of provincial power and *vice versa*.[166]

In brief, if the performance of the Privy Council was, as its critics suggested, replete with inconsistencies and insensitivity, the confused outpourings of the critics displayed an incoherence completely inadequate to guide judges in decision-making. To contrast the performance of the Judicial Committee with the performance of its opponents is to ignore the dissimilarity of function between artist and critic. It is clear, however, that the Judicial Committee was much more sensitive to the federal nature of Canadian society than were the critics. From this perspective at least the policy output of British judges was far more harmonious with the underlying pluralism of Canada than were the confused prescriptive statements of her opponents.[167] For those critics, particularly on the left, who wished to transform society, this qualified defence of the Judicial Committee will lack conviction. However, such critics have an obligation not only to justify their objectives but also the role they advocated for a non-elected court in helping to attain them.

Whether the decline in the problem-solving capacity of governments in the federal system was real or serious enough to support the criticism the Privy Council encountered involves a range of value judgements and empirical observations of a very complex nature. The purpose of this paper has been only to provide documentation for the minimum statement that a strong case can be made for the Judicial Committee, and to act as a reminder that the basic question was jurisprudential, a realm of discussion in which neither the Privy Council, its critics, nor its supporters proved particularly illuminating.

The Abolition of Appeals and an Inadequate Jurisprudence

It is valid, if somewhat perverse, to argue that the weakness and confusion of Canadian jurisprudence constituted one of the main justifications for ending appeals to the Privy Council. The attainment of judicial autonomy was a prerequisite for a first-class Canadian jurisprudence.[168] Throughout most of the period of judicial subordination the weaknesses in Canadian legal education produced a lack of self-confidence and a reluctance to abolish appeals.[169] As long as the final court of appeal was an alien body the jurisprudence that did exist was entangled with the emotional contest of nationalism and imperialism, a mixture that deflected legal criticism into side issues. In these circumstances the victory of nationalism was a necessary preliminary to the development of an indigenous jurisprudence that has gathered momentum in the past two decades.

It is also likely that the quality of judicial performance by Canadian courts was hampered by subordination to the Privy Council. The existence of the Privy Council undermined the credibility of the Supreme Court and inhibited the development of its status and prestige. The Supreme Court could be overruled by a superior, external court. In many cases it was bypassed as litigants appealed directly from a provincial court to the Privy Council. Finally, the doctrine of *stare decisis* bound the Supreme Court to the decisions of its superior, the Privy Council. The subject status of the Supreme Court and other Canadian courts was further exacerbated by the absence of dissents, which reduced the potential for flexibility of lower courts in subsequent cases. In spite of the quality of its performance the dominant position of the Privy Council in the Canadian judicial hierarchy was an anomaly, incompatible with the evolving independence of Canada in other spheres, and fraught with too many damaging consequences for its elimination to be regretted.

The inadequate jurisprudence, the legacy of nearly a century of judicial subordination, which accompanied the attainment of judicial autonomy in 1949, has harmfully affected the Supreme Court in the last two decades. The Supreme Court, the law schools, the legal profession, and the political elites have been unable to devise an acceptable role for the court in Canadian federalism. Shortly after the court attained autonomy the institutional fabric of the Canadian polity, the court included, began to experience serious questioning and challenges to its existence. The Diefenbaker Bill of Rights was succeeded by the Quiet Revolution with its confrontation between rival conceptions of federalism and coexistence. Additional uncertainty has been generated by the proposed Trudeau Charter, which, if implemented, will drastically change the significance of the judiciary in our constitutional system. In the unlikely event that a significantly different BNA Act emerges from the present constitutional discussions, the court will face the task of imparting meaning to a new constitutional document delineating a division of powers different from the existing division. To these factors, as indications of the shifting world of judicial review, can be added the possibility that the court may be reconstituted with a new appointment procedure, with a specific entrenched status, and perhaps even as a special court confined to constitutional questions.

It would be folly to suggest that the above problems would not exist if Canadian jurisprudence had been more highly developed. Their source largely lies beyond the confines of the legal system. On the other hand, the confused state of Canadian jurisprudence documented in this article adds an additional element of difficulty to their solution.

Notes

In writing this article I have received assistance from numerous friends and colleagues, including Leo Barry, Ed Black, Alexander Brady, Ronald Cheffins, Peter Finkle, Martin Levin, Susan McCorquodale, Donald Smiley, Paul Tennant, and Walter Young.

1. "Within the last twenty years in particular," wrote G.F.G. Stanley in 1956, "it has been the common sport of constitutional lawyers in Canada to criticize, cavil and poke fun at the *dicta* of the judges of the Privy Council and their decisions in Canadian cases. Canadian historians and political scientists have followed the legal party line with condemnations of 'the judicial revolution' said to have been accomplished by Lord Watson and Lord Haldane, and the alleged willful nullification of the true intentions of the Fathers of Confederation." "Act or Pact? Another Look at Confederation," in Ramsay Cook, ed., *Confederation* (Toronto, 1967), 112.

2. I have not confined my sources to the writings of the legally trained. Historians and political scientists are also considered. Their approach, although less influenced by technical considerations, did not differ significantly in orientation from that of the lawyers.

   Canadian criticism of the Privy Council was part of the more general dissatisfaction present in many of the jurisdictions for which it was a final appeal court. See Hector Hughes, *National Sovereignty and Judicial Auton-omy in the British Commonwealth of Nations* (London, 1931), for an analy-sis.

3. Peter H. Russell, *The Supreme Court of Canada as a Bilingual and Bicultural Institution* (Ottawa, 1969), 34-35, identifies the same two streams of criticism singled out in this article. André Lapointe, "La jurisprudence constitution-nelle et le temps," *Thémis*, 7 (1956), 26-27, adds a third main criticism, the failure to use adequate legal arguments, but this is clearly subsidiary and is not in fact discussed in his article.

4. V.C. MacDonald, "Judicial Interpretation of the Canadian Constitution," *University of Toronto Law Journal* (hereafter *UTLJ*), 1 (1935-36), provides a general centralist interpretation of the intentions of the Fathers and the BNA Act they created, which he contrasts with the judicial interpretation of the act. See also H.A. Smith, "The Residue of Power in Canada," *Canadian Bar Review* (hereafter *CBR*), 4 (1926), 438-439.

5. MacDonald, "Judicial Interpretation," 267, after noting that a centralized federation was intended, observed "how closely the language of the act reproduces that intent . . ." W.F. O'Connor stated: "there are not any mate-rial differences between the scheme of distribution of legislative powers between Dominion and provinces as apparently intended at the time of Confederation and the like legislative powers as expressed by the text of Part VI of the British North America Act, 1867." *Report Pursuant to Resolution of the Senate to the Honourable the Speaker by the Parliamentary Counsel Relating to the Enactment of the British North America Act, 1867, and lack of consonance between its terms and judicial construction of them and cognate matters* (hereafter the *O'Connor Report*) (Ottawa, 1930), 11.

In his most recent publication, Donald Creighton states that the Fathers regarded federalism as a "suspect and sinister form of government . . . British American union, they admitted, would have to be federal in character; but at the same time it must also be the most strongly centralized union that was possible under federal forms. . . . This basic principle guided all the planning whose end result was the British North America Act of 1867." *Canada's First Century: 1867-1967* (Toronto, 1970), 10 (see also 44-46).

The extent of Macdonald's centralist bias is evident in his prediction in a letter to M.C. Cameron, dated December 19, 1864: "If the Confederation goes on you, if spared the ordinary age of man, will see both local govern-ments and all governments absorbed in the General Power." Cited in A. Brady, "Our Constitutional Tradition," mimeo, paper presented to the Pro-gressive Conservative Party Policy Conference, Niagara Falls, Autumn, 1969, 16n.

For additional support for the thesis that a centralized federal system was both intended and embodied in the BNA Act, see R.I. Cheffins, *The Constitu-tional Process in Canada* (Toronto, 1969), 37; D.G. Creighton, *British North America at Confederation* (Ottawa, 1939); R.M. Dawson, *The Government of Canada*, rev. by Norman Ward (4th ed., Toronto, 1963), chapters 2 and 5; W.P.M. Kennedy, *The Constitution of Canada, 1534-1937: An Introduction to Its Development, Law and Custom* (2nd ed., London, 1938), chapter 19; Kennedy, *Some Aspects of the Theories and Workings of Constitutional Law* (New York, 1932), 86-87; A.R.M. Lower, *Colony to Nation* (Toronto, 1946), 329-31; E. McInnis, *Canada: A Political and Social History* (rev. ed., New York, 1960), chapter 13; *Report of the Royal Commission on Dominion-Provincial Relations* (hereafter the *Rowell-Sirois Report*) (Ottawa, 1954), 1, 32-35; F.R. Scott, "The Development of Canadian Federalism," *Papers and Proceedings of the Canadian Political Science Association* (herafter *PPCPSA*), 3 (1931); Scott, "The Special Nature of Canadian Federalism," *Canadian Journal of Economics and Political Science* (hereafter *CJEPS*), 13 (1947); Scott, "Centralization and Decentralization in Canadian Federalism," *CBR*, 29 (1951); Scott, *Canada Today* (London, 1938), 75-78; R. Tuck, "Canada and the Judicial Committee of the Privy Council," *UTLJ*, 4 (1941-42), 41-43.

6. H.A. Smith, "The Residue of Power in Canada," 433. For additional assertions that the failure of the Judicial Committee to use pre-Confederation evidence was partially responsible for this misinterpretation of the BNA Act, see Tuck, "Canada and the Judicial Committee," 40-41. V.C. MacDonald, "Constitutional Interpretation and Extrinsic Evidence," *CBR*, 17 (1939), is a helpful discussion of the actual practice of the Privy Council.

7. W.P.M. Kennedy, "The Terms of the British North America Act," in R. Flenley, ed., *Essays in Canadian History* (Toronto, 1939), 129.

8. *Can. H. of C. Debates*, April 5, 1937, 584-85.

9. *O'Connor Report*, 11-14, and Annex 1.

10. R.W.S., "Criminal Appeals," *CBR*, 4 (1926), 410.

11. J.R. Mallory, *Social Credit and the Federal Power in Canada* (Toronto, 1954), 29, notes that generally historians, political scientists, and lawyers have argued that the courts misinterpreted the BNA Act. See, for example, Lower, *Colony to Nation*, 376-77; D.G. Creighton, *Dominion of the North* (Boston, 1944), 380-81; C.H. Cahan, *Can. H. of C. Debates*, April 5, 1937, 2575; W.P.M. Kennedy, "The Interpretation of the British North America Act," *Cambridge Law Journal*, 8 (1943), 156-57, 160; V.C. MacDonald, "The Constitution in a Changing World," *CBR*, 26 (1948), 29-30, 41; MacDonald, "The Privy Council and the Canadian Constitution," *CBR*, 29 (1951), 1035; Smith, "The Residue of Power in Canada," 434.

12. Creighton, *Canada's First Century*, 49.

13. B. Laskin, "'Peace, Order and Good Government' Re-examined," *CBR*, 25 (1947), 1054.

14. The vehemence that ran through many of these criticisms is evident in Laskin's assertion: "My examination of the cases dealing with the Dominion's general power does not indicate any inevitability in the making of particular decisions; if anything, it indicates conscious and deliberate choice

of a policy which required, for its advancement, manipulations which can only with difficulty be represented as oridinary judicial techniques." *Ibid.*, 1086. Kennedy, "Interpretation of the British North America Act," 153-56, and Tuck, "Canada and the Judicial Committee," 56-64, describe the development of the misinterpretation of this clause. See also Creighton, *Dominion of the North*, 380, 466-67; Dawson, *Government of Canada*, 94-102; MacDonald, "The Constitution in a Changing World," 33-34, 41; *O'Connor Report*, Annex 1, 52-78; E.R. Richard, "Peace, Order and Good Government," *CBR*, 18 (1940); D.A. Schmeiser, *Civil Liberties in Canada* (London, 1964), 8-9.

15. Kennedy, "Interpretation of the British North America Act," 156 and 156, n42. The situation was so anomalous that Anglin C.J. asserted that he found it difficult to accede to the proposition that "it should be denied all efficacy as an independent enumerative head of Dominion legislative jurisdiction." *King* v. *Eastern Terminal Elevator Co.*, [1925] SCR 434, at 441. Lionel H. Schipper, "The Influence of Duff C.J.C. on the Trade and Commerce Power," *University of Toronto Faculty of Law Review*, 14 (1956), discusses the influence of the provincial bias of Duff on the evolution of this clause. For critiques of the Privy Council interpretation, see B. Claxton, "Social Reform and the Constitution," *CJEPS*, 1 (1935), 419-22; A.B. Keith, "The Privy Council and the Canadian Constitution," *Journal of Comparative Legislation*, 7 (1925), 67-68; MacDonald, "The Constitution in a Changing World," 36-42; M. MacGuigan, "The Privy Council and the Supreme Court: A Jurisprudential Analysis," *Alberta Law Review*, 4 (1966), 421; F.R. Scott, "Constitutional Adaptations to Changing Functions of Government," *CJEPS*, 11 (1945), 332-33; A. Smith, *The Commerce Power in Canada and the United States* (Toronto, 1963); Tuck, "Canada and the Judicial Committee," 64-69.

16. Smith, "The Residue of Power in Canada," 433; H.A. Smith, "Interpretation in English and Continental Law," *Journal of Comparative Legislation*, 9 (1927), 162-63; Creighton, *Dominion of the North*, 381; Dawson, *Government of Canada*, 96–98; Thorson, *Can. H. of C. Debates*, April 5, 1937, 2584.

The critics asserted that the original and intended meaning of property and civil rights was much more restrictive than it came to be under judicial fostering. See W.F. O'Connor, "Property and Civil Rights in the Province," *CBR*, 18 (1940).

17. H. Carl Goldenberg, "Social and Economic Problems in Canadian Federalism," *CBR*, 12 (1934), 423.

18. *Hodge* v. *The Queen* (1883), 9 App. Cas. 117; *Liquidators of the Maritime Bank of Canada* v *Receiver-General of New Brunswick*, [1892] AC 437; *A.G. Ont.* v *Mercer* (1883), 8 App. Cas. 767. See Cheffins, *Constitutional Process in Canada*, 38-39, 107-08. Ramsay Cook, *Provincial Autonomy, Minority Rights and the Compact Theory, 1867-1921* (Ottawa, 1969), 21-22, discusses

the successful attempt of Premier Mowat of Ontario "to make the lieutenant-governor as much the representative of the Queen in the province as the governor general was the representative of the Queen in federal affairs." See also G.F.G. Stanley, *A Short History of the Canadian Constitution* (Toronto, 1969), 99-102, and J.C. Morrison, "Oliver Mowat and the Development of Provincial Rights in Ontario: A Study in Dominion-Provincial Relations, 1867–1896," in Ontario Department of Public Records and Archives, *Three History Theses* (Toronto, 1961), chapter 2.

19. This is the gist of comments by Mallory, *Social Credit and the Federal Power*, 29; Creighton, *Dominion of the North*, 381; J.M.S. Careless, *Canada: A Story of Challenge* (Toronto, 1963), 364-65; MacDonald, "The Constitution in a Changing World," 44.

20. *Bank of Toronto* v *Lambe* (1887), 12 App. Cas. 575, at 579. Critics of the Privy Council for its adoption of a narrow legal approach were legion. See, for example, Creighton, *Canada's First Century*, 49; Lower, *Colony to Nation*, 334; MacDonald, "The Privy Council and the Canadian Constitution," 1029-31; MacDonald, "Judicial Interpretation of the Canadian Constitution," 267-70; Kennedy, *Some Aspects of the Theories and Working of Constitutional Law*, 70-72; Kennedy, "Interpretation of the British North America Act," 151-52; MacDonald, "The Constitution in a Changing World," 23; Thorson, *Can. H. of C. Debates*, April 5, 1937, 2582; F.R. Scott, "Section 94 of the British North America Act," *CBR*, 20 (1942), 530; E. McWhinney, *Judicial Review* (4th ed., Toronto, 1969), 16-17, 29-30; Tuck, "Canada and the Judicial Committee," 36-41.

Even supporters of the Privy Council agree that this was its approach. In the midst of the furore over the New Deal decisions, Ivor Jennings wrote: "It is not reasonable to expect that the members of the Judicial Committee of the Privy Council would interpret the Act in any way different from that adopted in the interpretation of other statutes. The Act is an ordinary statute, passed by Parliament at the request of certain rather troublesome and very remote colonists on the other side of the world. The judges did not think of themselves as determining the constitutional development of a great nation. Here was a statute in essence not different from many other pieces of legislation; and the judges naturally interpreted it in the usual way, by seeing what the statute said. They were concerned not with the desires of the Fathers, but with the progeny they had in fact produced." "Constitutional Interpretation: The Experience of Canada," *Harvard Law Review,* 51 (1937), 3 (see also 35).

21. Lord Sankey's bias was "clearly against pettifogging lawyers' arguments that interfered with the effective control of social life and the freedom of Dominion action, and this led him to infuse a new spirit into the process of interpretation." Jennings, "Constitutional Interpretation," 36. He also suggested (p. 36) that had he been on the court at the time, the New Deal decisions might have been sustained. He discusses Sankey's "liberal" approach on 28-30. A "liberal" interpretation "implies a certain impatience with purely formal and

technical arguments" (p. 31). "Liberal" decisions most frequently favourably cited by critics of the Privy Council were *Edwards* v *A.G. Can.,* [1930] AC 124; *In re Regulation and Control of Aeronautics in Canada*, [1932] AC 54; *In re Regulation and Control of Radio Communication in Canada*, [1932] AC 304; *British Coal Corporation* v *The King*, [1935] AC 500; *A.G. Ont.* v. *A.G. Can. and A.G. Que.*, [1947] AC 127.

22. MacDonald, "The Privy Council and the Canadian Constitution," 1034.
23. MacDonald, "The Constitution in a Changing World," 24.
24. *Ibid.*, 41.
25. Laskin, " 'Peace, Order and Good Government' Re-examined," 1087.
26. A. Brady and F.R. Scott, eds., *Canada after the War* (Toronto, 1943), 77.
27. Lower, *Colony to Nation*, 334.
28. MacDonald, "The Constitution in a Changing World," 45.
29. Laskin, " 'Peace, Order and Good Government' Re-Examined," 1086-87.
30. Kennedy, "The British North America Act: Past and Future," *CBR*, 15 (1937), 399.
31. Kennedy, *Some Aspects of the Theories and Workings of Constitutional Law*, 92-93.
32. MacDonald, "Judicial Interpretation of the Canadian Constitution," 282. See also MacDonald, "The Constitution in a Changing World," 26, 44.
33. Michiel S.D. Horn, "The League for Social Reconstruction: Socialism and Nationalism in Canada, 1939-1945" (Ph.D. thesis, University of Toronto, 1969), 158.
34. Scott, "Development of Canadian Federalism," 247; see also Scott, *Canada Today*, 32-33, 80-82.
35. Laskin, " 'Peace, Order and Good Government' Re-examined," 1085.
36. In 1936 Vincent MacDonald wrote of the "inability of the Canadian constitution to meet the social, economic, and political needs of today and of the necessity for its revision . . . great problems affecting the social and economic life of the country demand legislative capacity and solution. The second great fact at the moment is that effective solution of these contemporary problems is, in part, handicapped, and, in part, rendered impossible by (a) the terms of the act of 1867, and (b) previous decisions thereon, which, together, withhold jurisdiction where it is necessary that jurisdiction should be, divide jurisdiction where unity of jurisdiction is essential, and in other cases, paralyse action because of doubt as to jurisdiction where certainty of jurisdiction is vital." "Judicial Interpretation of the Canadian Constitution," 282. According to A.R.M. Lower, "Objection to Privy Council appeals did not become considerable until about 1930, but it rapidly increased during the Depression when certain decisions visibly hampered the country's ability to cope with the situation." "Theories of Canadian Federalism – Yesterday and Today," in Lower *et al., Evolving Canadian Federalism* (Durham, N.C., 1958), 30. J.A. Corry, *Law and Policy* (Toronto, 1959), 26, notes how "the Great Depresssion of the thirties came perilously close to a breakdown in public order." See also

Jean Beetz, "Les attitudes changeantes du Québec à l'endroit de la constitution de 1867," in P.A. Crépeau and C.B. Macpherson, eds., *The Future of
Canadian Federalism/L'avenir du fédéralisme canadien* (Toronto, 1965), 134-
35.

37. Horn, "League for Social Reconstruction," 468.
38. *A.G. Can* v *A.G. Ont.*, [1937] AC 326, at 350.
39. Scott, "Centralization and Decentralization in Canadian Federalism," 1113.
40. Kennedy, "Interpretation of the British North America Act," 159.
41. MacDonald, "The Constitution in a Changing World," 42.
42. See Russell, *Supreme Court,* 11-17, for the controversy attending the establishment of the court and the failure to eliminate appeals at that time.
43. J.S. Ewart, *The Kingdom of Canada* (Toronto, 1908), 227; see also 22, and
Ewart, *The Kingdom Papers* (Ottawa, 1912), I, 88. For a study of Ewart, see
Douglas L. Cole, "John S. Ewart and Canadian Nationalism," Canadian
Historical Association, *Historical Papers, 1969.* "Canadian history as Ewart
viewed it had but one chief theme – Canada's fight for freedom from imperial
control" (p. 65).

    Nationalist criticisms of the Privy Council waxed and waned up until the
thirties. There was a brief flurry immediately prior to the First World War. See
W.E. Raney, "Justice, Precedent and Ultimate Conjecture," *Canadian Law
Times* (hereafter *CLT*), 29 (1909), 459; W.S. Deacon, "Canadians and the
Privy Council," *CLT*, 31 (1911), 9, and "Canadians and the Privy Council,"
CLT, 31 (1911), 126-27; J.S. Ewart, "The Judicial Committee," *CLT*, 33
(1913), 676-77; also "Address by W.E. Raney," *Proceedings of the Canadian
Bar Association* (hereafter *PCBA*), 5 (1920), 221-24. McWhinney points out
that the very low repute of Privy Council judges in the Depression represented not only dissatisfaction with "economically conservative judicial decisions ... [but] ... also, in part, an outpouring of local nationalism in that
the court ... was an alien (in the sense of English) tribunal ..." *Comparative Federalism* (Toronto, 1962), 21-22.
44. Scott, "Abolition of Appeals to the Privy Council: A Symposium," *CBR*, 25
(1947), 571; see also Scott, "The Consequences of the Privy Council Decisions," *CBR*, 15 (1937), 4939-94.
45. Hon. Stuart S. Garson (minister of justice), *Can. H. of C. Debates*, Sept. 20,
1949, 69, 74-75.
46. Michel Brunet, "Canadians and Canadiens," in R. Cook, ed., *French-
Canadian Nationalism: An Anthology* (Toronto, 1969), 289, discusses the
war and post-war nationalist drive to centralism, of which the abolition of
appeals was a part.
47. Scott, "The Development of Canadian Federalism," 245. See also J.A.
Corry, review of G.P. Browne, *The Judicial Committee and the British North
America Act* (Toronto, 1967), in *Canadian Journal of Political Science,* 1
(1968), 217-18; *Rowell-Sirois Report,* I, 57-59, and Browne, *The Judicial
Committee*, 40, 84, 158-59.

48. *Ibid.*, Browne.

49. As John Dafoe believed. See R. Cook, *The Politics of John Dafoe and the Free Press* (Toronto, 1963), 217. Modified versions of this view were also presented by A.R.M. Lower, "Theories of Canadian Federalism," 38; Jacques Brossard, *La Cour Suprême et la constitution* (Montreal, 1968), 172; and Guiseppe Turi, "Le déséquilibre constitutionnel fiscal au Canada," *Thémis*, 10 (1959-60), 38. Hughes, *National Sovereignty and Judicial Autonomy*, 98, 104-05, discusses the possibility of Judicial Committee bias "where the issue is one between a Dominion and the British Government or between a Dominion person or firm and a British person or firm. . . . This is based on its composition which is predominantly English and partly political. . . . "

    Unspecified allegations of political expediency are contained in Thorson, *Can. H. of C. Debates*, April 5, 1937, 2582, and MacDonald, "Judicial Interpretation of the Canadian Constitution," 285.

50. For discussions of the provincial bias of the Judicial Committee, see F.E. LaBrie, "Canadian Constitutional Interpretation and Legislative Review," *UTLJ*, 8 (1949-50), 318-23; McWhinney, *Judicial Review*, 51 n7, 67, 69; MacDonald, "The Privy Council and the Canadian Constitution," 1030-32, 1035; MacDonald, "The Constitution in a Changing World," 23; Mac-Guigan, "The Privy Council and the Supreme Court," 426-27. R.F. McWilliams, "The Privy Council and the Constitution," *CBR*, 17 (1939), 582, attempts to prove that the Privy Council was not a defender of the provinces or responsible "for whittling down the powers of the Dominion." See also Browne, *The Judicial Committee*, 77.

51. Privy Council treaty references are summarized in R. Arès, *Dossier sur le pacte fédératif de 1867* (Montreal, 1967), 66-68, and criticized in Mac-Donald, "Privy Council and the Canadian Constitution," 1030-31.

52. Cheffins, *Constitutional Process in Canada*, 130, provides a summary of the speculation on the reasons for the provincial bias of Watson and Haldane. Some interesting reflections on Haldane are contained in the "Address by the Right Honourable Sir David Maxwell Fyfe," *PCBA*, 37 (1954), 149-51. Jonathon Robinson, "Lord Haldane and the British North America Act," *UTLJ*, 20 (1970), and Scott, *Canada Today*, 77, refer to the relevant writings of Haldane. Robinson attempts to explain Haldane's provincial bias as an outgrowth of his Hegelian philosophy. See also the obituary of Watson given by Haldane, *CLT*, 23 (1903), 223-25.

53. See, for example, Creighton, *Dominion of the North*, 446; Thorson, *Can. H. of C. Debates*, April 5, 1937, 2585; Laskin, " 'Peace, Order and Good Government' Re-examined," 1077; MacGuigan, "The Privy Council and the Supreme Court," 425; Scott, *Canada Today*, 77-78.

    Jennings asserted that "Lord Watson held to the fixed idea that Canada was a true federation and that it was the function of the Board to maintain something called 'provincial autonomy' which was not in the Act." Jennings is an exception, however, in claiming that Haldane favoured the provinces reluctantly because of the "weight of the previous decisions." "Constitutional Interpretation," 35-36, 21.

54. Lord Haldane, "The Work for the Empire of the Judicial Committee of the Privy Council," *Cambridge Law Journal*, 1 (1923), 150.
55. Cited in Ewart, *Kingdom of Canada*, 20.
56. *Can. H. of C.Debates*, Feb. 1, 1937, 426, 444.
57. *Special Committee on British North America Act: Proceedings and Evidence and Report* (Ottawa, 1935), 82. R.M. Dawson, ed., *Constitutional Issues in Canada, 1900-1931* (London, 1933), 343-44, reprints a 1912 editorial from the *Ottawa Journal* strongly critical of several decisions in which the Privy Council supported "vested right against the public weal," while the decisions of the Canadian courts had been "in favour of the public." These cases are briefly noted by C.G. Pierson, *Canada and the Privy Council* (London, 1960), 47. For Depression fears that business would seek to shelter behind the provinces, see R.A. MacKay, "The Nature of Canadian Federalism," in W.W. McLaren *et al.*, eds., *Proceedings, Conference on Canadian-American Affairs* (Montreal, 1936), 202. F.H. Underhill wrote that the use of provincial rights to obstruct social reform was "largely camouflage put up by our industrial and financial magnates. None of these worthy gentlemen wants a national government with sufficient constitutional power to be able to interfere effectively with their own pursuit of profits." "Revolt in Canadian Politics," *Nation*, 139 (December 12, 1934), 673, cited in Horn, "League for Social Reconstruction," 439.
58. Scott, "Centralization and Decentralization in Canadian Federalism," 1116; Scott, "The Consequences of the Privy Council Decisions," 492; J.R.Mallory, "The Courts and the Sovereignty of the Canadian Parliament," *CJS*, 10 (1944), 166-73. Since the Revolution Settlement, asserted Mallory, British judges "have been activated by an acute suspicion of the motives of both the executive and the legislature and have conceived it their duty to confine the application of statute law to cases where its meaning could not be mistaken" (167). "Upon occasion the very novelty of government expedients has seriously strained the impartiality of the type of judicial mind which is shocked by the unorthodox" (173). See also Mallory, "The Five Faces of Federalism," Crépeau and Macpherson, *The Future of Canadian Federalism*, 6-7, and *Social Credit and the Federal Power*, 53-56 and chapter 3.

When Australia sought to restrict appeals to the Privy Council, the British Colonial Secretary, Chamberlain, stated: "The question of the right of appeal must also be looked at from the point of view of the very large class of persons interested in Australian securities or Australian undertakings, who are domiciled in the United Kingdom. Nothing could be more prejudicial to Australia than to diminish the security felt by capitalists who desire to invest their money there. One element in the security which at present exists is that there is the possibility of an ultimate appeal to the Queen in Council...." Cited in Ewart, *Kingdom of Canada*, 232. In 1909 J.M. Clark stated that the right of appeal "is also regarded as an important security and safeguard by British foreign investors." "The Judicial Committee of the Privy Council," *CLT*, 29 (1909), 352-53.

The high cost of appeals, which played into the hands of the wealthy and thus buttressed the position of the economically strong, was a frequent criticism of the Privy Council. See Editorial, "Procedure before the Judicial Committee," *CLT*, 25 (1905), 29-30; W.S. Deacon, "Gordon v Horne: Canadians and the Privy Council," *CLT*, 30 (1910), 877; Deacon, "Canadians and the Privy Council," *CLT*, 31 (1911), 128, and "Canadians and the Privy Council," *CLT*, 31, (1911), 10; C.E. Kaulbach, *Can. H. of C. Debates*, February 26, 1880, 241; "Labor's Views on Dominion-Provincial Relations," *Canadian Congress Journal*, 17 (February, 1938), 15; Pierson, *Canada and the Privy Council*, 41-42, 70.

Sir Allen Aylesworth, a former Liberal minister of justice (1906-11), admitted in 1914 that the wealthy had an advantage in appeals due to their high cost, but that was "after all, but one of the advantages which the possession of wealth carries with it in every walk of life." "Address of Sir Allen Aylesworth, 7th Annual Meeting of the Ontario Bar Association," *CLT*, 34 (1914), 144.

59. Mallory, "The Courts and the Sovereignty of the Canadian Parliament," 169.
60. "Labor's Views on Dominion-Provincial Relations," 10.
61. Presidential address, *PCBA*, 6 (1921), 110.
62. Presidential address, *ibid.*, 12 (1927), 112-13.
63. *Ibid.*, 24 (1939), 204-05. In their report the previous year the committee referred to the disallowance of Alberta legislation as a "reversion to sound thought. Disallowance in some cases is just as important as enactment." The report continued to warn, however, that "quite apart from certain notorious Acts, much of this year's product reveals an inspiration which is wholly alien to our usual habits of thought.... The Committee believes that it is the general view of the profession that unless we can govern ourselves according to settled and generally recognized principles of right and wrong, we are headed either for anarchy or despotism ... it can find no place in any civilized system of law for several Acts passed at the last Session of the Legislature of Alberta ... these are only high water marks which stand above the general level and are more conspicuous on that account." The committee went on to castigate open-ended legislation in British Columbia and Saskatchewan that gave significant, vaguely defined authority to the Lieutenant-Governor-in-Council to make regulations for the carrying out of legislation. *Ibid.*, 23 (1938), 191-93.
64. W.S. Johnson, "The Reign of Law Under an Expanding Bureaucracy," *CBR*, 22 (1944). Cheffins, *Constitutional Process in Canada*, chapter 3, contains a brief discussion of the factors behind this evolution in the procedures of government operation.

Cecil A. Wright stated in 1938: "we have to a great extent underestimated the importance of administrative tribunals and the place of modern legislation as regulating forces in modern society. Legislation has always been viewed with disfavour by the common law lawyer because of the traditional view of the common law broadening down from 'precedent to precedent,' and undoubtedly the general attitude of the profession today is not different from that of Lord Halsbury who is reputed to have said that 'the best Act you can have is a repealing Act.' One consequence of this is that our whole technique and approach to legislation is weak, and as a result antagonism between the legal profession and legislative and administrative bodies becomes more marked.

"We have, indeed, paid so much attention to past judicial policy, that courts and lawyers are frequently in danger of limiting present legislative policy by restrictive interpretations. The notion that a statute shall be deemed to have departed as little as possible from common law principles runs throughout many judicial decisions, yet, as a member of the House of Lords recently said, 'it is an unsafe guide in days of modern legislation, often or perhaps generally based on objects and policies alien to the common law.'"
"Law and Law Schools," *PCBA*, 23 (1938), 115.

65. See G.L. Caplan, "The Failure of Canadian Socialism: The Ontario Experience," *Canadian Historical Review*, 44 (1963), for the extreme anti-socialist campaign waged by business in the closing years of the Second World War.

66. For American experience, see Benjamin R. Twiss, *Lawyers and the Constitution: How Laissez-Faire Came to the Supreme Court* (New York, 1962).

67. W.H. Hamilton, "The Path of Due Process of Law, " *Ethics*, 48 (1938), 296, asserted that American courts were more resistant to laissez faire than other parts of the body politic. "It seems strange that so many jurists stood steadfast against the seductions of laissez-faire; history, political science, and economics can boast no such record ... does the whole story, in irony, paradox, and compromise, derive from the innate conservatism of the law – a rock of ages which even the untamed strength of laissez-faire could move but could not blast."

68. Stanley, "Act or Pact?" 112-13.

69. Given the strong criticism it subsequently received it is worthwhile to document the extent of its support in earlier years. See, for example, John T. Small, "Supreme Court and Privy Council Appeals," *CLT*, 29 (1909), 51-52; Clark, "The Judicial Committee of the Privy Council"; "Address of Sir Allen Aylesworth," 139; "By the Way," *CLT*, 36 (1916), 354-55, 662-63; W.E. Wilkinson, "Our London Letter," *CLT*, 41 (1921), 61, reporting Lord Cave; B[ram] T[hompson], "Editor's Note," *CLT*, 41 (1921), 62-63; "Editorial," *CLT*, 41 (1921), 83-86; Bram Thompson, "Editorial," *CLT*, 41 (1921), 161-65; Edward Anderson, "Address to Manitoba Bar Association," *CLT*, 41 (1921), 252-53; "Appeal to the Privy Council," *CLT*, 41 (1921), 525-26; Pierson, *Canada and the Privy Council*, 39.

70. A.C. Galt, "Appeals to the Privy Council," *CLT*, 41 (1921), 172.
71. W. Nesbitt, "The Judicial Committee of the Privy Council," *CLT*, 29 (1909), 252.
72. Sir L.P. Duff, "The Privy Council," *CBR*, 3 (1925), 278-79.
73. Sir Charles Fitzpatrick, "The Constitution of Canada," *CLT*, 34 (1914), 1031.
74. Galt, "Appeals to the Privy Council," 168-69.
75. *PCBA*, 15 (1930), 37. Another writer stated that Viscount Haldane was "recognized as the greatest living authority on the interpretation of the British North America Act." W.E. Raney, "Another Question of Dominion Jurisdiction Emerges," *CBR*, 3 (1925), 617.
76. Nesbitt, "The Judicial Committee," 244.
77. Duff, "The Privy Council," 278. See also Nesbitt, "The Judicial Committee," 243, 245-46; W.R. Riddell, "The Judicial Committee of the Privy Council," *CLT*, 30 (1910), 305-06; W.H. Newlands, "Appeal to the Privy Council," *CBR*, 1 (1923), 814-15.
78. Nesbitt, "The Judicial Committee," 250-51; Riddell, "The Judicial Committee," 304. Ewart, *Kingdom of Canada*, 228, argued that if the Privy Council did try to produce uniformity of laws in the Empire appeals should be abolished, for each community required its own laws, In fact, however, he asserted that the Privy Council endeavoured to keep the various systems of laws distinct.
79. Nesbitt, "The Judicial Committee," 250-51; Clark, "The Judicial Committee," 349, 352-53; "By the Way," *CLT*, 37 (1917), 624-25; "Address of Sir Allen Aylesworth," 140; Bram Thompson, "Editorial," *CLT*, 41 (1921), 162-63; Howard Ferguson, *PCBA*, 15 (1930), 37. The desire of the Macdonald Conservatives to retain appeals to the Privy Council when the Supreme Court Act of 1875 was under discussion was based "primarily on their concern for preserving Canada's links with the Empire." Russell, *Supreme Court*, 16.
80. Clark, "The Judicial Committee," 352; Galt, "Appeals to the Privy Council," 172.
81. Riddell, "The Judicial Committee," 304.
82. This argument was used by British officials in 1876 when the Liberal government attempted to cut off appeals to the Privy Council. See L.A. Cannon, "Some Data Relating to the Appeal to the Privy Council," *CBR*, 3 (1925), 460-62. In discussions on the Australian constitution in 1900 Chamberlain stated that "questions . . . which may sometimes involve a good deal of local feeling are the last that should be withdrawn from a tribunal of appeal with regard to which there could not be even a suspicion of prepossession." Cited in Ewart, *Kingdom of Canada*, 232. The British constitutional expert, A.B. Keith, asserted that the "true value of the appeal . . . lies in the power of the Judicial Committee to deal in perfect freedom from local or racial prejudice with issues deeply affecting the relations of the two nationalities in Canada,

or of the provinces and the Federation, or of the provinces *inter se.* " Cited in
W.E. Raney, "Appeal to the Privy Council," *CBR*, 5 (1927), 608.

For the widespread Canadian support for this line of reasoning, see "Editorial Review," *CLT*, 27 (1907), 403-04; Small, "Supreme Court and Privy
Council Appeals," 51; Nesbitt, "The Judicial Committee," 249; Riddell,
"The Judicial Committee," 304; Fitzpatrick, "The Constitution of Canada,"
1031; "Appeal to the Privy Council," *CLT*, 41 (1921), 525, reporting Premier
Taschereau of Quebec; James Aikins, "President's Address to Conference of
Commissioners on Uniformity of Legislation," *PCBA*, 6 (1921), 286; Brossard, *La Cour Suprême, 171.*
83. "Presidential Address," *CBR*, 5 (1927), 562-63.
84. Evan Gray made this point with vigour. "It is time the chief 'indoor sport' of
constitutional lawyers in 'lambasting' the Privy Council and cavilling at
decisions of that body was discontinued. The 'sport' never had any merit or
excuse and it violates 'good form' – an essential element of all 'sport'. All this
talk about distortion of the framework of Confederation and defeat of our
national purposes by judicial authority is silly and puerile. If there is distortion, we Canadians all must take the responsibility for the distortion. If there
is defeat of national purposes, let us do something worthy of our autonomy
rather than continue to accept and complain of the defeat. Our constitution
is what our forefathers made it and as we have applied it – not what British
judges gave us. If we do not like the constitution as it is, we have always had
leave to change it; let us change it – now – in an open, forthright and well-
considered manner." " 'The O'Connor Report' on the British North
America Act, 1867," *CBR*, 17 (1939), 333-34.
85. The issue was posed but not answered by R. Cheffins: "It could be argued
that the type of strong federal government envisaged by the political founders
of the Canadian nation was impractical and not realizable in a country as
large geographically and as culturally diverse as Canada. It could also be
argued that the Judicial Committee was recognizing the realities of the social
and political life of the nation in upholding the validity of provincial statutes.
On the other hand it could be maintained that if the Privy Council had not
ruled the way it did, then the provincial governments would never have
assumed the importance which they did, and thus their position would not
have to be continually sustained by judicial decisions." "The Supreme Court
of Canada: The Quiet Court in an Unquiet Country," *Osgoode Hall Law
Journal*, 4 (1966), 267.

Both Morton and Careless lay great stress on the contributions of the
Judicial Committee to the strong position of the provinces in the 1920s. W.L.
Morton, *The Kingdom of Canada* (Toronto, 1969), 444; Careless, *Canada*,
364. D.G. Creighton also emphasizes the causal role of the Judicial Commit-
tee in breaking down Macdonald's centralized federalism. "The Decline and
Fall of the Empire of the St. Lawrence," Canadian Historical Association,

Historical Papers, 1969, 24. See also Scott, "The Development of Canadian Federalism," 238-47; Goldenberg, "Social and Economic Problems in Canadian Federalism. "

86. Kennedy, *Some Aspects of the Theories and Workings of Constitutional Law*, 100.

87. See N. McL. Rogers, "The Genesis of Provincial Rights," *Canadian Historical Review*, 14 (1933), for an incisive analysis of the weakness of the centralist basis of Confederation from the moment of its inception.

88. "The failure of the Dominion's economic policies, which formed such important elements in the new national interest, discouraged the growth of a strong, national sentiment; and local loyalties and interests began to reassert themselves." *Rowell-Sirois Report*, I, 54. See also E.R. Black and A.C. Cairns, "A Different Perspective on Canadian Federalism," *Canadian Public Administration*, 9 (1966), 29, and Cook, *Provincial Autonomy, Minority Rights and the Compact Theory*, chapter 3, especially 19.

89. Black and Cairns, "A Different Perspective," 29.

90. *Ibid.*, 38-43.

91. Morrison, "Oliver Mowat," *passim.*

92. *Rowell-Sirois Report*, I, 55.

93. F.H. Underhill, *The Image of Confederation* (Toronto, 1964), 27.

94. Cited in A.Brady, "Quebec and Canadian Federalism," *CJS*, 25 (1959), 260-61.

95. See the *Rowell-Sirois Report*, I, 55-59, for a discussion. André Lapointe, "La jurisprudence constitutionnelle et le temps," is a suggestive impressionistic study to the effect that Privy Council decisions, 1880-84, constituted appropriate responses to the forces of regionalism developing at that time.

96. Gray, " 'The O'Connor Report,' " 334-35.

97. "The Late Lord Watson," *CLT*, 23 (1903), 224.

98. For Mowat's position on the role of the provinces, his success with the Privy Council, and his favourable reception by the people of Ontario, see Lower, *Colony to Nation*, 376-79. Creighton, *Canada's First Century*, 47, provides a critical assessment of Mowat's philosophy and conduct. G.W. Ross, *Getting into Parliament and After* (Toronto, 1913), 187-88, states that "Sir Oliver Mowat's success in the courts of Canada, and particularly before the Privy Council raised him greatly in the estimation of the whole people of Ontario. Were it not for these conflicts with the Dominion Government I doubt if Sir Oliver would have survived the general election of 1883." Morrison, "Oliver Mowat," provides the most detailed analysis of Mowat's strategy.

99. There is considerable academic support for the proposition that the federal system established in 1867 was too centralist for the underlying regional pluralism of Canadian society, and the related proposition that it was an act of creative judicial statesmanship for the Privy Council to adapt the constitution to pluralist realities. O.D. Skelton stated that the "provincial trend of court decisions paralleled or rather followed, with some time lag, the changes

in Canada itself." *Special Committee on the British North America Act: 1935*, 27. "In all justice to the Judicial Committee," asserted Professor Brady, "they probably did no more than what the majority of Canadians in the earlier period desired. They gave judicial expression to the upsurge of provincialism, evident from the early eighties to the decade after the First World War...." *Democracy in the Dominions* (2nd ed., Toronto, 1952), 45-46. See also Brady, "Our Constitutional Tradition," 16. Michael Oliver states of the centralist intentions of the Fathers: "It must be concluded that they either seriously overestimated the range of shared assumptions between the two cultures, or badly underestimated the degree of unity on fundamentals which was necessary to run the centralized state they had tried to create." "Quebec and Canadian Democracy," *CJS*, 23 (1957), 504. Cheffins states that the "ineffectiveness" of the centralist features of the BNA Act "serves as a classic example of the futility of written positive law in the face of a social environment which refuses to accept the original statutory intention." *Constitutional Process in Canada*, 37-38 (see also p. 132). G.P. Glazebrook states: "the Judicial Committee was a make-weight in scales that were otherwise uncertainly balanced. The committee did not create the provincial school of thought; and it is worthy of note that it was long after it had ceased to have jurisdiction that provincialism took on its most extreme form. Nevertheless the strong slant in the legal decisions ... may be regarded as influential in the years in which the constitutional debate began." *A History of Canadian Political Thought* (Toronto, 1966), 186-87. J.R. Mallory praised the political acumen of the Local Prohibition Case in 1896, but added that "No other judge since Lord Watson's time has attempted the judicial realignment needed by the times and comparable to that achieved by the Supreme Court of the United States after 1937." "The Courts and the Sovereignty of the Canadian Parliament," 177.

Even the leading Canadian constitutional expert, W.P.M. Kennedy, later to be so critical of the Privy Council, had strongly praised it in earlier writings. In 1930 he wrote: "I often wonder ... with the inevitable divergencies in our national life due to race, religion, geography and such like, whether after all the way of the Privy Council up to 1929 has not been the better way. We might, apart from the Privy Council, have followed paths of greater juristic cohesion. We might have created a stronger legal nation; but it is problematical, had we done so, whether our legal cohesion would not have been compelled, if federation was to have survived, to give ground ultimately to those more compelling forces ... and whether we should not have been forced ultimately, in the interest of continuing the union, to retrace our legal steps." Book review of E. Cameron, *The Canadian Constitution as Interpreted by the Judicial Committee, 1916-1929*, in *CBR*, 8 (1930), 708. Kennedy made the same point on several other occasions: see *Essays in Constitutional Law* (London, 1934), 59-60, 101-02; *Some Aspects of the Theories and Workings of Constitutional Law*, 93, 101-02.

See also J.A. Maxwell, "Aspects of Canadian Federalism," *Dalhousie Review*, 16 (1936-37), 277n; E. McWhinney, "Federalism, Constitutionalism, and Legal Change: Legal Implications of the 'Revolution' in Quebec," in Crépeau and Macpherson, *The Future of Canadian Federalism*, 159-60; McWhinney, *Judicial Review*, 25-26, 70-71; E. Forsey, "Concepts of Federalism: Some Canadian Aspects," in J.P. Meekison, ed., *Canadian Federalism: Myth or Reality* (Toronto, 1968), 349; Stanley, *A Short History of the Canadian Constitution*, 142.

100. P.E. Trudeau, *Federalism and the French Canadians* (Toronto, 1968), 198.

101. Cheffins, *Constitutional Process in Canada*, 130-31, and W.R. Lederman, "Thoughts on Reform of the Supreme Court of Canada," *Alberta Law Review*, 8 (1970), 3, both point out the inappropriateness of a literal criticism of Privy Council decisions.

102. Clark, "The Judicial Committee," 348.

103. E.W., "Random Remarks Regarding the Judicial Committee," *CLT*, 36 (1916), 370-71.

104. Bram Thompson, "Editorial," *CLT*, 41 (1921), 165.

105. "Editorial," *CLT*, 40 (1920), 261.

106. MacDonald, "Judicial Interpretation of the Canadian Constitution," 282-83.

107. Jennings, "Constitutional Interpretation," 38.

108. Kennedy, *The Constitution of Canada*, 550. See also F.C. Cronkite, "The Social Legislation References," *CBR*, 15 (1937), 478.

109. Left-wing critics of the time disagree with this interpretation. See *The Canadian Forum* (March, 1937), 4, and Dorothy Steeves in CBC, *The Canadian Constitution* (Toronto, 1938), 97-98.

110. R. Cook, *Canada and the French Canadian Question* (Toronto, 1966), 53.

111. Creighton, *Canada's First Century*, 213-14.

112. MacDonald, "The Privy Council and the Canadian Constitution," 1036.

113. MacDonald, "Judicial Interpretation of the Canadian Constitution," 281. MacDonald, "The Privy Council and the Canadian Constitution," 1034-35, reiterates his earlier statement, and adds that we do not even have certainty (p. 1036). Laskin, " 'Peace, Order and Good Government' Re-examined," 1056, accused the Privy Council of laying down too many unnecessary dicta and generalities. McWhinney, *Judicial Review*, 54, suggests that the need for compromise in the committee may have produced obscurities in their decisions. Some earlier technical criticisms may be found in "Editorial Review," *CLT*, 6 (1886), 375, and A.H. Marsh, "The Privy Council as a Colonial Court of Appeal," *CLT*, 14 (1894), 92. See, by contrast, E.W., "Random Remarks Regarding the Judicial Committee," 371-72, who praises the committee for its statesmanlike willingness to be inconsistent and to override legal quibbles. The caveat of H.A. Innis is also worthy of consideration: "But though interpretations of decisions of the Privy Council have been subjected to intensive study and complaints have been made about their inconsistency,

inconsistencies have implied flexibility and have offset the dangers of rigidity characteristic of written constitutions." "Great Britain, The United States and Canada," in M.Q. Innis, ed., *Essays in Canadian Economic History* (Toronto, 1956), 404.

114. Ewart, *Kingdom of Canada*, 226-28. Ewart repeated his opposition to this defence of the Privy Council on numerous occasions: *ibid.*, 20; *Kingdom Papers*, I, 88; "The Judicial Committee," *CLT*, 34 (1914), 221, 230-231; "The Judicial Committee," *CLT*, 33 (1913), 676-78; "Some Further Comments on Dominion-Provincial Relations," *PPCPSA*, 3 (1931), 253-58.

115. *Can. H. of C. Debates*, February 26, 1880, 253-55, and see Blake, cited in MacDonald, "The Privy Council and the Canadian Constitution," 1026. For Blake's later partial change of mind, see Russell, *Supreme Court*, 251, n173.

116. Raney, "Justice, Precedent and Ultimate Conjecture," 460; Thorson, *Can. H. of C. Debates*, April 5, 1937, 581-82; Scott, *Canada Today*, 77; Tuck, "Canada and the Judicial Committee," 71-73; Mallory, "The Five Faces of Federalism," 6.

117. A.H. Marsh, "The Privy Council as a Colonial Court of Appeal," *CLT*, 14 (1894), 94. See also Deacon, "Canadians and the Privy Council," 126-27. This criticism was popular among the opponents of the New Deal decisions. Cahan, *Can. H. of C. Debates*, April 5, 1937, 2574, and Scott, "The Consequences of the Privy Council Decisions," 493-94.

Jennings, "Constitutional Interpretation," is the best attempt to discuss the influence of Privy Council personnel on its judgements.

118. Jennings, "Constitutional Interpretation," 1-2.

119. MacDonald, "The Canadian Constitution Seventy Years After," *CBR*, 15 (1937), 426-27.

120. Tuck, "Canada and the Judicial Committee," 73 (see also pp. 55-56, 71-72). Versions of this point were made by various commentators. LaBrie, "Canadian Constitutional Interpretation and Legislative Review," 346; W.R. Lederman, "The Balanced Interpretation of the Federal Distribution of Legislative Powers in Canada," in Crépeau and Macpherson, *The Future of Canadian Federalism*, 111; Lederman, "Thoughts on the Reform of the Supreme Court of Canada," 3-4.

121. McWhinney, *Judicial Review*, 72.

122. MacGuigan, "The Privy Council and the Supreme Court," 425-26.

123. D.G. Creighton, speaking of the diversity of jurisdiction of the Privy Council, stated: "An expert knowledge of one of these legal systems might be regarded as a respectable accomplishment for an ordinary man. But the titans of the Judicial Committee, from long practice and profound study, have grown accustomed to the multifarious and exacting requirements of their office; and they apparently leap, with the agility of quick-change performers, from one legal metamorphosis to another. . . . To an outsider it might seem that there was at least the faint possibility of some bewilderment and confusion in these endlessly varied deliberations. The outsider might even be so far

misled as to conceive of a noble judge who continued obstinately to peruse the Koran when he ought to have been consulting the *British North America Act*." "Federal Relations in Canada since 1914," in Chester Martin, ed., *Canada in Peace and War* (Toronto, 1941), 32-33.

124. Ewart, "The Judicial Committee," 676. He also asserted that the Judicial Committee "suffers from a conviction of its own superiority – a conviction due (*a*) to the ruling character of the race to which its members belong, and (*b*) to the fact that, by sending our cases to it, we appear to acknowledge our incapacity."

125. *Ibid.*, 676.

126. "What gives its imposing respectability, its ponderous finality to a decision of the Privy Council is its unity. There may be considerable diversity of opinion, doubts, hesitations and dissents behind the curtain. But when the curtain goes up one judge delivers the opinion of the Court and it is law. It does not sprinkle like a garden hose; it hits like the hammer of Thor." A.T. Hunter, "A Proposal for Statutory Relief from the Privy Council Controversy," *CBR*, 4 (1926), 102. See McWhinney, *Judicial Review*, 52-53, for a discussion of the practice and suggested explanations for its survival.

127. He continued: "Though the reports summarize the arguments of counsel, the emphasis given to the written opinion minimizes the case that the majority did not accept. Finally, the opinion of the whole Board is given by one member. The substance is, no doubt, agreed to by the rest of the majority; but it is never certain that all the expressions would have been accepted by the majority if they had fully considered them. The type of opinion differs according to the judge who renders it. He comes to the conclusion desired by the majority and states the reasons acceptable to the majority; but anyone who has drafted a document knows that there are many ways of saying the same thing and that a draft often says more than is intended." Jennings, "Constitutional Interpretation," 2-3.

128. Ewart, "The Judicial Committee," 676.

129. E.W., "Random Remarks Regarding the Judicial Committee," 370.

130. Browne, *The Judicial Committee and the British North America Act*.

131. The reference is to a tendency, not to ethnic unanimity. Frank Scott was correct in pointing out in 1947 that Quebec had "no single view" on the question of the retention of the Judicial Committee, and in noting that a minister of justice from Quebec, Télésphore Fournier, who introduced the bill to establish the Supreme Court in 1875, stated that he "wished to see the practice put an end to altogether," and that Ernest Lapointe held similar views. "Abolition of Appeals to the Privy Council: A Symposium," 571. Scott had earlier argued that minority rights had received better protection from the Supreme Court than from the Privy Council. "The Privy Council and Minority Rights," *Queen's Quarterly*, 37 (1930). It is also worthy of note that the elimination of appeals occurred under a French-Canadian Prime Minister. Pierson, *Canada and the Privy Council,* 69-70, provides some

evidence of French-Canadian opposition to appeals. The 1927 Labrador decision of the Privy Council turned some French Canadians against the system of appeals. See Brossard, *La Cour Suprême*, 189, and Dale C. Thomson, *Louis St. Laurent: Canadian* (Toronto, 1967), 91, 208. Further, it is clear that there have been many English-Canadian supporters of the Privy Council right up to its final abolition. These observations do not, however, invalidate the statement about a tendency for opposed evaluations of the Judicial Committee to follow the French-English cleavage.

132. For French-Canadian support of the Privy Council's interpretation of the BNA Act and/or support for its continuation as a final appeal court, see L.P. Pigeon, "The Meaning of Provincial Autonomy," *CBR*, 29 (1951); Pigeon, "French Canada's attitude to the Canadian Constitution," in E. McWhinney, ed., *Canadian Jurisprudence* (Toronto, 1958); Jean Beetz, "Les attitudes changeantes du Québec à l'endroit de la constitution de 1867," 117-18; *CLT*, 40 (1920), 315, reporting a speech by Mr. Horace J. Gagne of the Montreal Bar; "Appeal to the Privy Council," *CLT*, 41 (1921), 525, reporting a speech of Premier Taschereau of Quebec. Russell notes that in the nineteenth century French-Canadian support for the Judicial Committee and opposition to the Supreme Court were primarily based on the belief that the composition, training, and background of the former was much to be preferred to that of the latter for interpretations of Quebec civil law. *Supreme Court*, chapter 1, *passim*. See also Brossard, *La Cour Suprême*, 125.

133. On this attitude of the abolitionists, see Jonas L. Juskaitis, "On Understanding the Supreme Court of Canada," *School of Law Review*, University of Toronto, 9 (1951), 7-8; and Leonard H. Leigh, "The Supreme Court and the Constitution," *Ottawa Law Review*, 2 (1967-68), 323. Jacques Brossard, "The Supreme Court and the Constitution," in Ontario Advisory Committee on Confederation, *Quebec in the Canada of Tomorrow* (Toronto, n.d.), translated from *Le Devoir*, special supplement, June 30, 1967, stated: "It was, moreover, in opposing the centralizing aims of the federal government that the Judicial Committee signed its own death warrant; it was accused, not without reason, of having violated the centralizing spirit of the BNA Act of 1867."

134. Beetz, "Les attitudes changeantes," 119-21. The divergent evaluations of the Judicial Committee and of a proposed independent Supreme Court are discussed by Peter Russell, "The Supreme Court's Interpretation of the Constitution since 1949," in Paul Fox, ed., *Politics: Canada* (2nd ed., Toronto, 1966), 117-18. See also Russell, *Supreme Court*, 31-32, 36-37. In addition to the ethnic-based opposition from French Canada there was also considerable provincial opposition to the unilateral nature of the federal action in abolishing appeals. P. Gérin-Lajoie, *Constitutional Amendment in Canada* (Toronto, 1950), xvii-xviii. By 1949 French Canadians had become critical of the Privy Council's treatment of French civil law, but this "was counterbalanced by approval of its interpretation of the BNA Act." Russell, *Supreme Court*, 31.

135. Browne, *The Judicial Committee and the British North America Act.*
136. J.A. Corry, while doubtful of the final validity of Browne's thesis, gives the book a very favourable review in *Canadian Journal of Political Science*, 1 (1968), 217-19. Critical reviews are provided by B. Laskin, *Canadian Public Administration*, 10 (1967), 514-18, and E.R. Alexander, *UTLJ*, 17 (1967), 371-77.
137. See the eminently sensible criticism by Corry, *ibid.*, 218-19. Jennings's observation is also relevant. "The idea that judges spend days on end in reading all the decisions on any particular topic is one which is sometimes assumed by academic writers; it can, however, be designated as clearly false by anyone who has watched a court give judgement immediately at the end of an argument." "Constitutional Interpretation," 27.
138. W.R. Lederman, after noting the antithetical literal interpretations of the BNA Act by Browne and O'Connor, states that in his view "Browne and O'Connor simply cancel one another out. The truth is that the BNA Act was simply ambiguous or incomplete in many respects as originally drafted and the answers just were not in the Act as to how these ambiguities were to be resolved and the gaps filled." "Thoughts on the Reform of the Supreme Court of Canada," 2.

    Note also the chronic "historical" controversy over the validity of the compact theory and between centralist and provincialist interpretations of the BNA Act and/or the intentions of the Fathers. Glazebrook's comment is apt: "one has only to sample the speeches and writings of politicians, academics, and jurists to appreciate the wealth of interpretation of the intent and terms of the original union. It needs a conscious effort to realize that they are describing the same episode in Canadian history. Confederation, in fact, was what you thought it was – or often what it should have been. Which seems to suggest that particular interpretations and points of view were rationalized by tailored versions of the Constitution." *A History of Canadian Political Thought*, 264 (see also pp. 153, 258).

139. Philippe Ferland, "La Confédération à refaire," *Thémis*, 5 (1954), 105. Stanley, "Act or Pact?" 114, asserts that the pre-parliamentary history of the BNA Act appears to confirm the interpretation of the Judicial Committee rather than that of the critics.

    The 1887 Interprovincial Conference, which advocated a much more decentralized federal system than prevailed under Macdonald's prime ministership, claimed that two decades of experience with the BNA Act have "disclosed grave omissions in the provisions of the Act, and has shown (when the language of the Act came to be judicially interpreted) that in many respects what was the common understanding and intention had not been expressed, and that important provisions in the Act are obscure as to their true intent and meaning." *Dominion, Provincial and Interprovincial Conferences from 1887 to 1926* (Ottawa, 1951), 20.

140. LaBrie, "Canadian Constitutional Interpretation," 310. K.N. Llewellyn's statement is also apt: "there is no quarrel to be had with judges *merely* because they disregard or twist Documentary language, or 'interpret' it to the despair of original intent, in the service of what those judges conceive to be the inherent nature of our institutions. To my mind, such action is their duty. To my mind, the judge who builds his decision to conform with his conception of what our institutions must be if we are to continue, roots in the deepest wisdom." "The Constitution as an Institution," *Columbia Law Review*, 23 (1934). 33.

141. M.R. Cohen, *Reason and Law* (New York, 1961), 84.

142. G.H. Ross, "Interpreting the BNA Act," *CBR*, 7 (1929), 704. LaBrie, "Canadian Constitutional Interpretation," 310, 318; *Rowell-Sirois Report*, I, 36.

143. *A.G. Ont.* v *A.G. Can.*, [1947], AC 127, at 154.

144. Robinson, "Lord Haldane and the British North America Act," 58. See also A.M. Bickel, "The Original Understanding and the Segregation Decision," *Harvard Law Review*, 69 (1955).

145. Various American writers have noted that the appeal to history in American constitutional interpretation has led to an abuse of history and does not in fact act as a control on the court. See, in particular, A.H. Kelly, "Clio and the Court: An Illicit Love Affair," in P.B. Kurland, ed., *The Supreme Court Review* (Chicago, 1965); J. Tenbroek, "Admissibility and Use by the United States Supreme Court of Extrinsic Aids in Constitutional Construction," *California Law Review*, 26 (1937-38), 448, 451; C.S. Hyneman, *The Supreme Court on Trial* (New York, 1964), 207-08. Felix Frankfurter, "Reflections on Reading Statutes," in A.F. Westin, ed., *The Supreme Court: Views from Inside* (New York, 1961), 75, 84-85, 88-92, argues the advantages in appealing to historical materials, although he also notes the difficult problems this entails. The difficulty in using historical material is also noted by W.O. Douglas, "Judges as Legislators," in Westin, *ibid.*, 68-69. A.A. North, *The Supreme Court, Judicial Process and Judicial Politics* (New York, 1966), 18-29, provides a neutral discussion. E. Bodenheimer, *Jurisprudence* (Cambridge, Mass., 1962), 348-53, is a good discussion of whether courts should take the original meaning at the time of statutory creation, or the contemporaneous ones understood at the time of decision.

146. See MacDonald, "Constitutional Interpretation and Extrinsic Evidence," for a discussion.

147. *Edwards* v *A.G. Can.*, [1930], AC 124, at 137.

148. He added: "it seems to us fallacious, as well as reckless, for the author to suggest that seventy years after Confederation he can assist us by such contemporary records to say that those who framed the Confederation Act intended to do other than what they embodied in the words of the statute.

"Indeed the matter goes deeper than that; what they are seeking to discover who speak of the pre-confederation intention of the framers of confederation or of the constituent provinces has no real existence. The search is pursuit of a 'will-o-wisp'; when once you leave the natural light afforded by the text of the BNA Act, you are in a realm of unreality....

"Neither should we continue the pretension of the author that by a miracle of understanding and foresight, the Canadian Fathers of Confederation provided in 1867 a constitution suitable to any future." Gray, " 'The O'Connor Report' on the British North America Act 1867," 316-18, 334.

See also Stanley, "Act or Pact?" 112, for the morass of contradictions involved in attempting to determine the "intentions" of the Fathers. "The one sure guide as to what the Fathers really agreed to agree upon, was the language of their resolutions, or better still, the language of the British North America Act itself. And in construing this Act in the way they have, the judges probably arrived at a more accurate interpretation than have the multitude of critics who have so emphatically disagreed with them."

149. MacDonald, "Judicial Interpretation of the Canadian Constitution," 280-81. His approach agreed with K.N. Llewellyn's assertion that with an ancient statute "the sound quest does not run primarily in terms of historical intent. It runs in terms of what the words can be made to bear, in making sense in the new light of what was originally unforeseen." *The Common Law Tradition* (Boston, 1960), 374. See also W. Friedman, *Law and Social Change in Contemporary Britain* (London, 1951), 252, 254-55.

150. Mallory, "The Courts and the Sovereignty of the Canadian Parliament," 173.

151. W.E. Rumble attributes the same achievement to the American legal realists. *American Legal Realism* (Ithaca, 1968), 232-33.

152. H.V. Jaffa, "The Case for a Stronger National Government," in R.A. Goldwin, ed., *A Nation of States* (Chicago, 1968), 121.

153. Browne suggests that the "constituent statute argument equates 'liberal' with 'federal' (and so 'literal' with 'provincial')." *The Judicial Committee and the British North America Act*, 31. This is not entirely true. As indicated in this essay there was also a critique of the Privy Council that was both "literal" and "federal."

154. The weak reasoning is similar to that noted by Smiley in "national interest" justifications for conditional grants. D.V. Smiley, *Conditional Grants and Canadian Federalism* (Toronto, 1963), 48-52.

155. B.N. Cardozo, *The Nature of the Judicial Process* (New Haven, 1960), 174-75.

156. Lapointe also notes the incompatibility of the two, and argues that the Privy Council conducted itself in accordance with the constitutional rather than the fundamentalist approach. "La jurisprudence constitutionnelle et le temps," 27-28.

"The manner of framing the question," writes Llewellyn, "is psychologically of huge importance. 'Is this within the powers granted by the Document?' throws the baseline of inquiry back a century and a half, constricts the vision to the static word, turns discussion into the channels of logomachy.

It invites, and too often produces, artificial limitation of attention to the non-essential, the accidental: to wit, what language happens to stand in the Document, or in some hoary – or beardless – text of its 'interpretation'. . . .

"Contrast the effect of framing the question thus: 'Is this within the leeway of change which our ongoing governmental scheme affords? And even if not, does the nature of the case require the leeway to be widened to include it?' The baseline then becomes so much of the past only *as is still alive,* and the immediate future comes to bear as well. The tone and tendency of the very question is dynamic. The 'nature of the case' invites attention to explicit policy. While that continuity with the past which, if not a duty, is wisdom quite as well as a necessity, is carefully preserved – only that the past concerned is that embodied not in an ancient Text, but in a living Government." "The Constitution as an Institution," 32-33.

157. Russell, *Supreme Court*, 35.
158. F.H. Underhill, "O Canada," *The Canadian Forum*, 11 (June, 1931), 332, cited in Horn, "League for Social Reconstruction," 433.
159. Ferland, "La Confédération à refaire," 106-07; Beetz, "Les attitudes changeantes du Québec à l'endroit de la constitution de 1867," 120.
160. Corry, "Commentaries," in Crépeau and Macpherson, *The Future of Canadian Federalism*, 38.
161. McWhinney, *Judicial Review*, 69.
162. Tuck, "Canada and the Judicial Committee," 75.
163. J.R. Mallory recently contrasted the capacity of the Supreme Court of the United Sates to "'follow the election returns'" with the Privy Council, which "was so deficient in both sense and sensibility that the allocation of power in the constitution, by the end of the 1930's, had achieved a remarkable incongruity between the resources, capacities, and responsibilities of the federal and provincial governments." "The Five Faces of Federalism," 7. See also MacDonald, "The Privy Council and the Canadian Constitution," 1032-33, 1035, 1027; MacDonald, "The Constitution in a Changing World," 43-44; MacDonald, "Judicial Interpretation of the Canadian Constitution," 278; Tuck, "Canada and the Judicial Committee," 34; B. Laskin, "Reflections on the Canadian Constitution after the First Century," in Meekison, *Canadian Federalism*, 139.
164. A.B. Keith, "Privy Council Decisions: A Comment from Great Britain," *CBR*, 15 (1937), 435.
165. Rumble, *American Legal Realism*, 220-21, 227, 232.
166. J.A. Corry, "Decisions of the Judicial Committee, 1930-9," *CJEPS*, 5 (1939), 511-12. See also Rumble, *American Legal Realism*, 231, on the difficulty of defining relevant criteria for judicial decisions. Herbert Wechsler, "Toward Neutral Principles of Constitutional Law," *Harvard Law Review*, 73 (1959), is an important attempt to define a judicial process that is "genuinely principled, resting with respect to every step . . . in reaching judgement on analysis and reasons quite transcending the immediate result . . . on

grounds of adequate neutrality and generality." He is hostile to criteria concerned with immediate results that turn the court into a "naked power organ" rather than a court of law. He describes the resultant *ad hoc* evaluation as the "deepest problem of our [American] constitutionalism" (pp. 15, 12).

167. A related question is whether or not Canadian federalism would have had a less turbulent history if the task of judicial interpretation had been undertaken by the Supreme Court. McWhinney, *Judicial Review*, 73-74, provides evidence on both sides of the question, although personally doubtful that the Supreme Court would have acted differently. Glazebrook, *A History of Canadian Political Thought*, 258, finds no proof that the Supreme Court would have done otherwise than the Judicial Committee. MacGuigan argues that, from the evidence, it is impossible to decide whether or not the Supreme Court approved of the decisions of the Judicial Committee. "The Privy Council and the Supreme Court: A Jurisprudential Analysis," 421. R.F. McWilliams, "The Privy Council and the Constitution," 579, also doubts that the Supreme Court would have differed in its interpretation from the Privy Council. Russell, *Supreme Court*, 255-56, n5, notes the difficulty in arguing that the Supreme Court was more pro-dominion than the Privy Council. On the other hand, supporters of the Supreme Court, who note that it and the Judicial Committee usually agreed, have been cautioned not to ignore the fact that the Supreme Court had to take the previous decisions of the committee as the major premise in its thinking. MacDonald, "The Canadian Constitution Seventy Years After," 426. Scott argues that an independent Supreme Court would have produced decisions much more favourable to the federal government. *Canada Today*, 77; "Development of Canadian Federalism," 246.

168. A point strongly made by W.E. Raney sixty years ago. "Justice, Precedent and Ultimate Conjecture," 461.

169. Innis, "Great Britain, The United States and Canada," 404. Sir Allen Aylesworth told the Ontario Bar Association that "It is . . . no disparagement to Canadian lawyers or to Canadian judges to say that the men, or some of the men at any rate, who constitute the Judicial Bench in England, and some of the men who sit at the Council Board as members of the Judicial Committee are better read lawyers, are stronger lawyers than any men we have, either at the Bar or upon the Bench, in Canada, and in these circumstances it is a matter of actual daily practical advantage to the people of this country that they should have still the right to take to that Court their complicated cases as between citizen and citizen for final adjudication." Address of Sir Allen Aylesworth, 143.

Bram Thompson stated: "The reader of the Law Reports is constantly confronted with cases which the Privy Council decisions prove to have been decided in our local Courts upon the grossest misconception of even elementary principles. Indeed, some of our Courts seem to delight in rendering judgements which are, to say the least of them, utterly perverse." "Editorial," *CLT*, 41 (1921), 164. Russell notes that the early weakness of the Supreme Court inhibited moves to abolish appeals. *Supreme Court*, 24.

4. W.R. LEDERMAN

Unity and Diversity

in Canadian Federalism:

Ideals and Methods

of Moderation

Canada is a federal country of great extent and variety in which we respect both unity and diversity. This is difficult to do, but we *have* been doing it with a large measure of success for well over 100 years. The total process of governing Canada revolves about a division and distribution of primary legislative capacities or powers by two lists of subjects, one list for the federal Parliament (primarily section 91 of the British North America Act)[1] and the other for each of the provincial legislatures (primarily section 92 of the British North America Act). Instead of subjects, one might speak of categories or classes. For the most part, sections 91 and 92 taken together comprise a complete system for the distribution of primary legislative powers and responsibilities in Canada over virtually the whole range of actual and potential law-making. The courts have held the distribution is complete, with some very few exceptions that prove the rule. The exceptions are concerned with certain specific rights to use of the French or English languages, certain specific rights to denominational schools, and free trade across provincial borders. Without disparaging the importance of these exceptions, it is fair to point out that nearly all of our constitutional jurisprudence in the courts for 100 years has concentrated on issues of the distribution of powers.

My concern in this article is to offer some thoughts on the nature and quality of the judicial interpretation of sections 91 and 92 of the British

Originally published in *The Canadian Bar Review*, 53 (1975). Reprinted with permission of the author and of the Canadian Bar Foundation/La Fondation du Barreau Canadien.

North America Act over the years. Until the end of 1949, of course, the dominant court was the Judicial Committee of the Privy Council in London. Only since 1949 has the Supreme Court of Canada emerged from the shadow of the Judicial Committee and become supreme in law as well as in name. So, while we are celebrating this year the hundredth anniversary of the creation of the Supreme Court of Canada, we are only celebrating the twenty-fifth anniversary of the supremacy of the Supreme Court of Canada as the final tribunal of appeal for Canadians.

The definitive study of the Privy Council period in constitutional interpretation was published in 1971 by Professor Alan C. Cairns. This is an essay of about forty-five pages in the *Canadian Journal of Political Science*, entitled "The Judicial Committee and Its Critics." I agree with Professor Cairns's conclusions, so I give them rather fully in his own words:[2]

> In brief, if the performance of the Privy Council was, as its critics suggested, replete with inconsistencies and insensitivity, the confused outpourings of the critics displayed an incoherence completely inadequate to guide judges in decision-making. To contrast the performance of the Judicial Committee with the performance of its opponents is to ignore the dissimilarity of function between artist and critic. It is clear, however, that the Judicial Committee was much more sensitive to the federal nature of Canadian society than were the critics. From this perspective at least the policy output of British judges was far more harmonious with the underlying pluralism of Canada than were the confused prescriptive statements of her opponents. For those critics, particularly on the left, who wished to transform society, this qualified defence of the Judicial Committee will lack conviction. However, such critics have an obligation not only to justify their objectives but also the role they advocated for a non-elected court in helping to attain them.
>
> Whether the decline in the problem-solving capacity of governments in the federal system was real or serious enough to support the criticism the Privy Council encountered involves a range of value judgements and empirical observations of a very complex nature. The purpose of this paper has been only to provide documentation for the minimum statement that a strong case can be made for the Judicial Committee, and to act as a reminder that the basic question was jurisprudential, a realm of discussion in which neither the Privy Council, its critics, nor its supporters proved particularly illuminating.

Note that Professor Cairns deplores the general confusion that has reigned concerning a positive philosophical jurisprudence of constitutional judicial review in Canada. Secondly, note that in any event he thinks the record of their Lordships of the Privy Council is a lot better in this regard than that of their critics. Note finally that he says the basic question was and is jurisprudential.

Accordingly, writing as a critic who has been both chastened and challenged by what Professor Cairns has said, I now offer some thoughts on the essential operating jurisprudence of Canadian federalism. I assume in so doing that judicial review at all levels, and especially at the highest level, is essential to the process of interpreting a federal distribution of primary legislative powers. I have made the case for this proposition several times in earlier published essays,[3] and I will return to it near the end of this article. What I now do is to select two points to develop about the essential operating jurisprudence of our federal distribution of legislative powers, and in the course of discussing them, I will offer some opinions on the quality of what judges have said they were doing, and on what other critics have said the judges should have been doing.

In the first place, I address the nature of the Canadian system for the distribution of legislative powers. This then leads in the second place to a consideration of the significance of what I prefer to call the federal general power, but which often is called the federal peace, order, and good government power.

Starting then with the nature of the Canadian federal system, we find that our way of distributing legislative powers has been to set up two rather detailed lists of federal and provincial legislative capacities. In an earlier essay, I described the two lists and the methods of interpreting them in these terms:[4]

> The federal distribution of legislative powers and responsibilities in Canada is one of the facts of life when we concern ourselves with the many important social, political, economic or cultural problems of our country. Over the whole range of actual and potential law-making, our constitution distributes powers and responsibilities by two lists of categories or classes – one list for the federal parliament (primarily section 91 of the *B.N.A. Act*), the other for each of the provincial legislatures (primarily section 92 of the *B.N.A. Act*). For instance, the federal list includes regulation of trade and commerce, criminal law, and a general power to make laws in all matters not assigned to the provinces. Examples from the provincial list are property and civil rights in the province. local works and undertakings, and all matters of a merely local or private nature in the province.
>
> These federal and provincial categories of power are expressed, and indeed have to be expressed, in quite general terms. This permits considerable flexibility in constitutional interpretation, but also it brings much over-lapping and potential conflict between the various definitions of powers and responsibilities. To put the same point in another way, our community life – social, economic, political, and cultural – is

very complex and will not fit neatly into any scheme of categories or classes without considerable overlap and ambiguity occurring. There are inevitable difficulties arising from this that we must live with so long as we have a federal constitution.

Accordingly, the courts must continually assess the competing federal and provincial lists of powers against one another in the judicial task of interpreting the constitution. In the course of judicial decisions on the *B.N.A. Act*, the judges have basically done one of two things. First, they have attempted to define mutually exclusive spheres for federal and provincial powers, with partial success. But, where mutual exclusion did not seem feasible or proper, the courts have implied the existence of concurrent federal and provincial powers in the overlapping area, with the result that either or both authorities have been permitted to legislate provided their statutes did not in some way conflict one with the other in the common area.

The words quoted imply the point I now wish to develop more explicitly. We have here two lists of powers that are in total competition one with the other in all their parts, total competition, that is, to embrace challenged provincial or federal statutes and to stamp them with legitimacy as exercises of provincial or federal legislative power respectively. The federal general power competes with the provincial general power, the federal criminal law power competes with the provincial property power and so on. Proper use of words – good grammar and syntax – is essential as a starting point for the expression of a scheme of division of powers. But it is only the starting point, and it is a mistake to think that the task of interpretation is grammatical and syntactical only, treating the constitutional document in isolation from the economic, social, and cultural facts of life of the society to which the constitutional document relates, both historically and currently. Yet this has frequently been done in Canada. The famous O'Connor *Report* of 1939[5] castigates the Judicial Committee because it perversely contradicted the so-called "plain words" of section 91 of the British North America Act. Many years later, Professor G.P. Browne, in his book on the Privy Council period,[6] discovered full justification for the Judicial Committee's results in the grammar and syntax of the same so-called "plain words" of sections 91 and 92. So, O'Connor and Browne simply cancel one another out, and in so doing demonstrate the truth of the following remarks by Professor Hans Kelsen, who said (speaking of the constitution of the United Nations):[7]

Since the law is formulated in words and words have frequently more than one meaning, interpretation of the law, that is determination of its meaning, becomes necessary. Traditional jurisprudence distinguishes various methods of interpretation: the historical, in contrast to the grammatical, an interpretation according to the "spirit", in opposition to a literal interpretation keeping to the words. None of these methods can claim preference unless the law itself prescribes the one or the other. The different methods of interpretation may establish different meanings of one and the same provision. Sometimes, even one and the same method, especially the so-called grammatical interpretation, leads to contradictory results. It is incumbent upon the law-maker to avoid as far as possible ambiguities in the text of the law; but the nature of language makes the fulfillment of this task possible only to a certain degree.

So I say one needs to insist that the power-conferring words and phrases of sections 91 and 92 must be related to the cultural, social, and economic realities of the society for which they were and are intended, both historically and currently, if they are to make sense as basic guide lines for government at both the provincial and federal levels.

To illustrate what I mean, I wish to take up a neglected historical point. I refer to the historically established meaning of the phrase "Property and Civil Rights" in central British North America from 1774 to 1867. The phrase comes from the Quebec Act of 1774 of the Imperial Parliament,[8] which provided that French law and custom were to obtain respecting property and civil rights in the royal colony of Quebec. This covered all the law except English criminal law, and except the English public law that came to Quebec as necessary context for English colonial government institutions. In her recent book on the subject, Dr. Hilda Neatby, a distinguished Canadian historian, has demonstrated from the official documents of the time that the phrase "Property and Civil Rights" in the Quebec Act had and was intended to have this very broad significance.[9] Moreover, these words retained this very broad significance in Upper and Lower Canada between 1791 and 1841, and in the United Province of Canada, 1841-1867. The Fathers of Confederation knew all about this – they lived with it every day – and naturally they took the broad scope of the phrase for granted. Accordingly, they realized that, in setting up a central Parliament in their new federal system, a considerable list of particular central powers would have to be specified in some detail as subtractions from the historically established meaning of "property and civil rights." Otherwise the use of that phrase in the provincial list would leave very little for the new central Parliament. Because of this, I reiterate, the Fathers of Confederation knew that a general grant of power to the central Parliament in all matters not assigned to the provinces would in and by itself *not* be enough to give the central Parliament all the powers they wished it to have, for example over banking, or marriage and divorce, or bills of exchange. I am not just speculating at large when I say this. One can see it in the text of both the Quebec and London Resolutions:[10]

Quebec Resolutions
  43 (15) Property and civil rights, excepting those portions thereof assigned to the General Parliament.
     (18) And generally all matters of a private or local nature, not assigned to the General Parliament.

London Resolutions
  41 (15) Property and civil rights (including the solemnization of marriage) excepting the portions thereof assigned to the General Parliament.
     (18) And generally all matters of a Private or Local Nature not assigned to the General Parliament.

The same point also emerges from a comparison of the penultimate draft of the British North America Act with the final draft that was enacted.[11] I infer from the comparison that the "notwithstanding" clause in the opening words of section 91 and the "deeming" clause in the closing words were designed to ensure that the twenty-nine specific categories in the original federal list were to be taken as withdrawn from the historic scope of the provincial property and civil rights clause, and withdrawn also from the new provincial category of things generally of a local and private nature in the province.

In other words, the implication is plain that this double-listing was done because the Fathers of Confederation, the Colonial Secretary, and the parliamentary draftsmen were all satisfied that it was necessary; that the rather long and particular federal list, supported by the "notwithstanding" clause and the "deeming" clause, was essential if items like banking, marriage and divorce, copyright, connecting railways, and so on were to be within the power of the new federal Parliament, where they wanted them to be.

Accordingly, it follows that the twenty-nine specific categories of federal parliamentary power originally listed in section 91 are not merely illustrations of what would have been embraced anyway by the federal general power to make laws in all matters not assigned to the provinces. For the reasons of historical fact that I have given about the phrase "property and civil rights," the federal list was not just superfluous grammatical prudence, it was compelled by historical necessity and has independent standing. Many if not most of the twenty-nine enumerated heads in section 91 confer powers on the federal Parliament that would not have been attracted to that Parliament by the federal general power alone in single-handed competition with the historic provincial property and civil rights clause.

The result of this reasoning about the nature of section 91 may be recapitulated as follows. The twenty-nine more particular powers, the so-called enumerated powers, add greatly to the competence that would have been invested in the federal Parliament by the federal general power alone, though no doubt there is a modest amount of overlapping. On the other hand, the federal general power is no mere appendage to the twenty-nine enumerated powers, an appendage labelled "for emergencies only." It covers considerable ground that the enumerated powers do not cover. What then do we see when we look at the complete picture afforded by sections 91 and 92? I say we see a total system of power-distribution wherein thirty heads of federal power, including a national general and residuary power, compete with sixteen heads of provincial power, one of which is a local general and residuary power. The grammar and syntax of sections 91 and 92 are as consistent with this result as with any other, and the history of central British North America from 1774 to 1867 confirms this alternative as the correct picture of the system. This is why I describe Canadian power-distribution as the total competition of thirty federal heads of power with sixteen provincial heads of power. Because of amendments since 1867 we should now speak of thirty-two and sixteen. So potentially the logical extent of this competition is all the permutations and combinations of thirty-two versus sixteen. The picture is indeed a complex one, but anything less is surely oversimplification.

When the time came to compose a federal constitution for Canada, we can count ourselves fortunate that the history of property and civil rights in the royal colony of Quebec and the successor colonies compelled the use of two rather long lists of federal and provincial powers. The many power-conferring phrases used were all equal in status as parts of a single system and thus had each to be read in a context that included all the others. As a result, there had to be restraint, moderation, and mutual modification in the scope that was to be given any one of them.[12] The federal trade and commerce clause could not be allowed to destroy all commercial significance for the provincial property and civil rights clause, or *vice versa*. The provincial property power could not be extended indefinitely at the expense of the federal criminal law power, or *vice versa*, and so on.

As Canada expanded westward geographically and accepted heavy immigration, the country became more and not less diverse. The kind of federal document that history gave us facilitated the development of a carefully balanced federalism that accommodated old and new diversities as well as ensuring essential unities. Unique flexibility for Canada comes from having *many* power-conferring phrases in competition with one another, and the equilibrium points established between them portray the critical detail of Canadian federalism. The power-conferring phrases themselves are given by the British North America Act, but the equilibrium points are not to be found there. They have necessarily been worked out painstakingly by judicial interpretation and precedent over many years. Furthermore, particular equilibrium points are not fixed for all time. As conditions in the country genuinely change and truly new statutory schemes are enacted, judicial interpretation can adjust and refine the equilibrium of the division of legislative powers to meet the new needs. So the high importance of sophisticated judicial interpretation as an ongoing process is obvious.

Let me now turn in the second place to one particular aspect of the interpretation – the proper scope to be given to the general power of the federal Parliament – the power to make laws for Canada in all matters not assigned to the legislatures of the provinces. There is also a provincial general power to make laws in all matters of a merely local or private nature in the province, and, theoretically, it raises the same interpretative problems as does the federal general power. But the cases have concentrated on the federal general power, so this analysis does likewise.

The basic interpretative problem here may be explained as follows. Leaving the two general powers out of the count, there are thirty-one specific grants of powers to the federal Parliament and fifteen specific ones to the provincial legislatures. Let us assume that a new statute has been passed by the federal Parliament and that its validity has been challenged. The federal government now claims that the statute is valid because its primary concern is a *new* subject entitled to be treated as within the residuary reach of the federal general power, and thus in effect to be added to the existing list of thirty-one specific federal subjects. Accordingly our question becomes this: when is such a claim allowed for a subject not specifically listed in either section 91 or 92, and when is it disallowed? In other words, when is it proper to enfranchise a new category to be added to the thirty-one existing specific federal categories by virtue of the residuary significance of the federal general power?

Well, look at some examples of what the courts have done about unlisted subjects. Aviation, atomic energy, and the incorporation of Dominion companies have each been enfranchised as additions to the list of federal subjects by virtue of the residuary reach of the federal general power.[13] But labour relations and pollution are also complete unlisted subjects. They too are real enough as subjects of concern in our society and they have not been enfranchised as new federal subjects by virtue of the federal general power.[14] Rather, each of these subjects has been itself subdivided into several parts that could be reclassified piecemeal according to some of the already established specific categories of thirty-one federal and fifteen provincial subjects. The parts are thus distributed accordingly, some to the federal Parliament and others to the provincial legislatures. Take the example of labour relations. If you have a business or industry that is under federal jurisdiction, like banks or interprovincial railways, power to regulate their labour relations is federal. If you have a business or industry under provincial jurisdiction, like a retail store or a coal mine, power to regulate their labour relations is provincial. The same sort of point can be made about the various powers to regulate the abatement of pollution of our air, land, or water. Why is the regulation of aviation made a new federal category, a unit in its own right, while labour relations is broken up and parcelled out piecemeal by the operation of several of the specific categories – the thirty-one federal ones and the fifteen provincial ones? What tests does the subject "aviation" meet that the subject "labour relations" fails to meet to warrant such radical differences in treatment? This is no frivolous question; it is a fundamental one about the positive operating jurisprudence of our federal system.

To answer this question, we must first take account of the many possibilities of multiple classification or cross-classification that exist by virtue of the philosophy of the classification process itself as it relates to the distribution of legislative powers. A prohibition against emitting noxious chemicals from an industrial plant into a river, for example, may be logically classified as property law, criminal law, fisheries law, pollution law, environmental law, recreational law, public health law, and so on. Logically the prohibition may be properly characterized as any or all of these things. But which classification is to dominate for the purpose of our federal distribution of powers? Clearly, as a first step, the significant classification of a challenged law for this purpose should be sought among the specific categories listed in the British North America Act. There are forty-six of them – thirty-one in the federal list and fifteen in the provincial list. If this first search among the forty-six categories does not result in a dominant classification of the challenged law satisfactory in terms of the social needs and facts of the country, then as a second step you consider invoking the federal general power. I suggest that you can take the second step and successfully invoke the federal general power if two conditions are met. First, the new subject must, as a matter of evidence, arise out of the needs of our society as something that necessarily requires country-wide regulation at the national level. Secondly, and leaving aside true emergencies, the new subject should also have an identity and unity that is quite limited and particular in its extent.

Note that whether we are assessing the impact of the forty-six specific subjects listed in the British North America Act, or considering the possibility of adding a new subject to the federal list, we are not simply engaging in philosophical speculation at large about the many dozens or indeed hundreds of logically possible classifications for the challenged law.

Yet this latter range of logically possible classifications cannot be entirely ruled out of the process. Counsel seeking to invoke the federal general power in order to support a challenged federal statute on a new basis will search the whole range of dozens or hundreds of philosophically relevant classifications in order to find the one unlisted class that may serve their purpose – the one which they can then propose as a new subject for the federal list by virtue of allegedly sufficient evidence of social fact and social need for this type of regulation at the national level. If we now shift from counsel to the judges, we have an alternative statement of the basic problem. By what tests do the judges determine the success or the failure of such propositions from counsel about a new subject?

Perhaps I can clarify this with the example of aviation. Both the Judicial Committee and the Supreme Court of Canada have held that aviation was a subject that deserved to be added as a new specific category to the federal list by virtue of the federal general power. Why did they do this? Because technologically and industrially aviation has a factual unity as a transportation system and implications for transportation as a force in the life and development of Canada that make provincial boundaries frustrating or irrelevant, in relation to the legal regulation necessary. Read the judgement of Lord Sankey in the *Aeronautics* case of 1932[15] and that of Mr. Justice Locke in the *Johannesson* case of 1952,[16] and you will see this reasoning well expressed, especially in the words of Mr. Justice Locke. This illustrates the way in which new subjects win entitlement to be added to the federal list.

It is interesting to note that this is the way Viscount Haldane thought of the national emergency power. Speaking of it in the *Board of Commerce* case, in 1922, he located the subject of national emergency under the federal general power because it involved "conditions so exceptional that they require legislation of a character in reality beyond anything provided for by the enumerated heads in either s.91 or s.92. . . ."[17] That is exactly the right reasoning, in accordance with my analysis. Nevertheless, as we know, Viscount Haldane went too far when he also said, in effect, that national emergency of some sort was the *only* subject that could qualify for status as a new subject under the federal general power. That is not in accordance with the analysis I am offering here. My analysis leads to the conclusion that the possibilities of enfranchising new specific subjects as within the federal general power are always open. They are never closed. But getting a new specific subject added to the federal list in this way has never been easy, and this is as it should be. It should in principle be very difficult to add a subject in this way, either to the federal list by virtue of the federal general power or to the provincial list by virtue of the provincial general power, which speaks of unlisted matters local in character.

Why should it be very difficult in principle to invoke the federal general power? Because it is essential in our federal country that the balance between federal and provincial subjects of primary legislative powers should remain stable – reasonably constant – subject only to a process of gradual changes when these are rendered truly necessary by the demands of new conditions in our society from time to time. This applies not only to the federal general power, but of course also to the whole scheme of division of powers. Nevertheless, the cases concerned with the scope of the federal general power are the cases that raise most clearly issues of the overall nature of our federal system, hence my concentration on those cases in this article. The balancing and adjusting necessary is typically a task for sophisticated judicial interpretation – it is basically jurisprudential in the sense that it is an appeal to law as reason.

For the most part, I think the judges of the Judicial Committee and the Supreme Court of Canada, in their cases on the federal general power, have understood this necessity well, and have decided issues and given reasons accordingly. For me, the primary words of wisdom on the subject are those of Lord Watson, whom I consider the greatest of the Privy Council judges concerned with the Canadian constitution. In the *Local Prohibition* case of 1896, he said:[18]

> There may, therefore, be matters not included in the enumeration, upon which the Parliament of Canada has power to legislate, because they concern the peace, order, and good government of the Dominion. But to those matters which are not specified among the enumerated subjects of legislation, the exception from s. 92, which is enacted by the concluding words of s. 91, has no application; and, in legislating with regard to such matters, the Dominion Parliament has no authority to encroach upon any class of subjects which is exclusively assigned to provincial legislatures by s. 92. These enactments appear to their Lordships to indicate that the exercise of legislative power by the Parliament of Canada, in regard to all matters not enumerated in s. 91, ought to be strictly confined to such matters as are unquestionably of Canadian interest and importance, and ought not to trench upon provincial legislation with respect to any of the classes of subjects enumerated in s. 92. To attach any other construction to the general power which, in supplement of its enumerated powers, is conferred upon the Parliament of Canada by s. 91, would, in their Lordships' opinion, not only be contrary to the intendment of the Act, but would practically destroy the autonomy of the provinces. If it were once conceded that the Parliament of Canada has authority to make laws applicable to the whole Dominion, in relation to matters which in each province are substantially of local or private interest, upon the assumption that these matters also concern the peace, order, and good government of the Dominion, there is hardly a subject enumerated in s. 92 upon which it might not legislate, to the exclusion of the provincial legislatures. . . .
>
> Their Lordships do not doubt that some matters, in their origin local and provincial, might attain such dimensions as to affect the body politic of the Dominion, and to justify the Canadian Parliament in passing laws for their regulation or abolition in the interest of the Dominion. But great caution must be observed in distinguishing between that which is local and provincial, and therefore within the jurisdiction of the provincial legislatures, and that which has ceased to be merely local or provincial, and has become matter of national

concern, in such sense as to bring it within the jurisdiction of the Parliament of Canada.

Then, after Viscount Haldane's aberration about emergency, we come back on track with the judgement of Viscount Simon in the *Canada Temperance Act* case of 1946.[19] He cited the *Local Prohibition* case with approval, and proceeded to re-state the test of the scope of the federal general power in words that are in substance the same as those of Lord Watson:[20]

> In their Lordships' opinion, the true test must be found in the real subject matter of the legislation: if it is such that it goes beyond local or provincial concern or interests and must from its inherent nature be the concern of the Dominion as a whole (as, for example, in the *Aeronautics* case and the *Radio*[21] case), then it will fall within the competence of the Dominion Parliament as a matter affecting the peace, order and good government of Canada, though it may in another aspect touch on matters specially reserved to the provincial legislatures. War and pestilence, no doubt, are instances; so, too, may be the drink or drug traffic, or the carrying of arms. In *Russell* v *The Queen*,[22] Sir Montague Smith gave as an instance of valid Dominion legislation, a law which prohibited or restricted the sale or exposure of cattle having a contagious disease. Nor is the validity of the legislation, when due to its inherent nature, affected because there may still be room for enactments by a provincial legislature dealing with an aspect of the same subject in so far as it specially affects that province.

In the period since 1949, the Supreme Court of Canada has consistently followed and upheld what I would call the Watson-Simon conception of the scope of the federal general power; the Supreme Court justices have exhibited the caution and restraint that the Watson-Simon view embodies.

But this does not entirely answer the dilemma I put earlier; why was aviation treated as a new federal subject while labour relations was denied the benefit of the federal general power, divided into several parts, and distributed piecemeal in accordance with the more particular relevance of the parts to some of the original specific federal and provincial powers? In his recent distinguished essay on "Sir Lyman Duff and the Constitution," Professor Gerald Le Dain has expressed the dilemma in these terms:[23]

> Many matters within provincial jurisdiction can be transformed by being treated as part of a larger subject or concept for which no place can be found within that jurisdiction. This perspective has a close affinity to the notion that there must be a single, plenary power to deal

effectively and completely with any problem. The future of the general power, in the absence of emergency, will depend very much on the approach that the courts adopt to this issue of characterization.

What I am trying to explain and illustrate in this analysis is what Professor Le Dain has perceptively pinpointed as "this issue of characterization." In other words, am I able to answer my own question about the different treatment of aviation and labour relations as unlisted legislative subjects? I said earlier that, in normal circumstances, leaving aside true emergencies, to qualify under the federal general power a new subject should genuinely need regulation at the national level, and should also have a natural unity that is quite limited and specific in its extent – a natural unity that can be given quite particular definition philosophically. Aviation meets this test. It was a new form of transportation with a natural industrial and technological unity necessarily nationwide in scope so far as need for legislative action was concerned. Also, as a subject, aviation is quite limited and specific in extent, relatively speaking. It is just one of many forms of transportation, and as a legislative subject it does not imply large-scale trespass upon major areas of existing provincial powers. Aviation is an important subject, of course, but in its legislative implications it does not take over great portions of the laws of property and civil rights or municipal institutions.

But contrast with this labour relations as a unitary legislative subject. This is no limited subject or theme, this is a sweeping subject or theme virtually all-pervasive in its legislative implications. Every employer in every business or industry there is has labour relations, from the corner store to General Motors. If "labour relations" were to be enfranchised as a new subject of federal power by virtue of the federal general power, then provincial power and autonomy would be on the way out over the whole range of local business, industry, and commerce as established to date under the existing heads of provincial power. The same point can be made about environmental pollution or economic growth or language requirements as unitary legislative subjects.

Notice too that this reasoning cuts both ways, it is a double-edged sword. If it were claimed that something called "culture" is, in all its aspects and as a unit, a subject that falls entirely within provincial jurisdiction because of the provincial general power over all matters of a local or private nature in the province, this would be equally contrary to the spirit and philosophy of our Canadian system for the division of legislative powers. Let me illustrate this point by a quotation from an editorial in the newspaper *La Presse*, for Friday, November 9th, 1973. The editorial writer, M. Guy Cormier, is asking for some definition of the phrase "cultural sovereignty." He says:[24]

The word "culture" is a catch-all besides being a trap. One of the major weaknesses of the famous Laurendeau-Dunton Commission was that its work started under the terms of a mandate which gave no definition of the word "culture". So, why repeat the same foolish mistakes?

Nowadays, everything is cultural. A book is certain a cultural product, as is a film, a record, or a song. But is not a song factory, or a word factory, like the C.B.C. also a cultural reality? In a way oil is also "cultural", since oil is automobiles, home comforts, a whole manner of existence and a life style.

Nowadays, therefore, everything is cultural. A notion which used to be reserved for delicate, manual or mental exercise, for literature, music, painting, or needlework, is today extended to tools and computers. In this perspective, the "Boeing 747" is a modern cultural phenomenon.

In general, what we see here is the need to keep the power-conferring phrases of our federal-provincial division of powers at meaningful levels of specifics and particulars. And from this it follows that federal and provincial statutes should be drafted with sufficient detail and particularity that they take due account of those characteristics of our division of primary legislative powers. These are two sides of the same coin. No one has expressed this better than Mr. Justice Rand of the Supreme Court of Canada. In the *Saumur case* in 1953 he said:[25]

Conceding, as in *Re Alberta Legislation*,[26] that aspects of the activities of religion and free speech may be affected by provincial legislation, such legislation, as in all other fields, must be sufficiently definite and precise to indicate its subject-matter. In our political organization, as in federal structures generally, that is the condition of legislation by any authority within it: the courts must be able from its language and its relevant circumstances, to attribute an enactment to a matter *in relation to which* the legislature acting has been empowered to make laws. That principle inheres in the nature of federalism; otherwise, authority, in broad and general terms, could be conferred which would end the division of powers. Where the language is sufficiently specific and can fairly be interpreted as applying only to matter within the enacting jurisdiction, that attribution will be made; and where the requisite elements are present, there is the rule of severability. But to authorize action which may be related indifferently to a variety of incompatible matters by means of the device of discretionary licence cannot be brought within either of these mechanisms; and the court is powerless, under general language that overlaps exclusive jurisdictions, to delineate and preserve valid power in a segregated form. If the purpose is street regulation, taxation, registration or other local object, the language must, with sufficient precision, define the matter and mode of administration; and by no expedient which ignores that requirement can constitutional limitations be circumvented.

It is true as stated earlier that all legislative powers are distributed in Canada but that does not mean that there is a single power, either federal or provincial to embrace any problem or subject that can be philosophically identified as such, out of the thousands of logically possible identifications. All problems or subjects can be fitted into the total of forty-eight categories in sections 91 and 92 of the British North America Act one way or another, and Mr. Justice Rand's point is that this must be done if federal or provincial statutes are to have validity – that they must be drafted with a particularity that has this requirement in mind. So I claim that the words of Mr. Justice Rand which I have quoted support the main thrust of my reasoning on the Canadian division of legislative powers.

A vital point about my main thesis here should now be made. As a student of Canadian federalism, I have complained by way of example of the sweeping character of "labour relations" as a single category and have said that it should in effect be treated as outside the distribution-of-powers system and broken down into several more particular parts. These parts are then each allotted, some one way and some the other, according to their particular relevance to some of the thirty-one specific federal categories and the fifteen specific provincial ones. But in breaking down one of these all-pervasive classes or subjects, we may find one or more of the resulting parts left over, so to speak. We may find that we have one or more of the several parts that do not have relevance to one of the thirty-one specific federal categories or the fifteen specific provincial categories. Now, with respect to these leftover parts, we are down to interpretative competition between the two residuary clauses. In these circumstances, the federal general power then embraces the leftover part or parts of inherent national significance or importance. The provincial residuary power in section 92(16) would likewise embrace any leftover part or parts of a merely local or private nature in the provinces.

Another example of one of these sweeping or all-pervasive categories is language – language requirements or options. Virtually all communication, thought, and social organization depend on the use of language. In the case of *Jones* v *Attorney General of Canada et al.* last year,[27] the full Supreme Court gave judgement on the constitutional validity of the federal Official Languages Act.[28] Chief Justice Laskin gave the unanimous judgement of the court upholding the validity of the statute as within the powers of the federal Parliament. I believe that the extent to which he used the federal general power to uphold the validity of the statute is in harmony with the general analysis I am offering here. He said:[29]

Apart from the effect of s. 133 and s. 91(1), to be considered later in these reasons, I am in no doubt that it was open to the Parliament of Canada to enact the *Official Languages Act* (limited as it is to the purposes of the Parliament and Government of Canada and to the institutions of that Parliament and Government) as being a law "for the peace, order and good Government of Canada in relation to [a matter] not coming within the Classes of Subject ... assigned exclusively to the Legislatures of the Provinces". The quoted words are in the opening paragraph of s. 91 of the *British North America Act, 1867*; and, in relying on them as constitutional support for the *Official Languages Act,* I do so on the basis of the purely residuary character of the legislative power thereby conferred. No authority need be cited for the exclusive power of the Parliament of Canada to legislate in relation to the operation and administration of the institutions and agencies of the Parliament and Government of Canada. Those institutions and agencies are clearly beyond provincial reach.

Chief Justice Laskin then goes on to point out that the federal general power likewise supports the validity of the provisions of the federal Official Languages Act concerning the use of the English or French languages in courts properly established by federal statute, and in all criminal courts and proceedings in Canada. He adds that these are *also* matters respectively within the power of the federal Parliament under section 101 of the British North America Act, concerning the establishment of courts for the better administration of the federal laws of Canada, and the federal criminal law and procedure power in section 91(2) of the British North America Act. Criminal law and procedure generally are not of course in the list of provincial powers, and so here is one very important respect in which the federal general power is indeed illustrated and re-affirmed by one of the later enumerated powers in section 91. As I said earlier in this analysis of our power-distribution system, there is some overlapping of this kind in section 91 of the British North America Act. This does not impair my main thesis that the overlapping is far from complete in the whole area of property and civil rights, in the broad historical extent of that phrase in British North America from 1774 to 1867. In any event, as I read Chief Justice Laskin, he is not saying and did not intend to say that all mandatory language requirements and options form a single subject for the purposes of the power-distribution system, a subject that would be embraced by the federal general power. I believe he is saying in effect that the subject requires considerable subdivision into several parts, which is in accordance with my analysis in this article.

Pollution affords a further example of a sweeping category or theme that needs this piecemeal treatment for purposes of our power-distribution system. Recently the Supreme Court of Canada faced an example of this issue also, in the case of *Interprovincial Co-operatives Limited* v. *The Queen in Right of the Province of Manitoba.*[30] They gave judgement on March 26th of this year. The majority opinion was given by Mr. Justice Pigeon. The problem concerned interprovincial rivers flowing into Lake Winnipeg, and mercury pollution of the rivers originating at points on the rivers in Saskatchewan and Ontario that allegedly ruined the fisheries in Lake Winnipeg. Mr. Justice Pigeon held that certain Manitoba legislation on the subject was beyond provincial powers, and was exclusively within federal power by virtue of the federal general power in its residuary character. But he carefully confined what he said to the pollution of *interprovincial* rivers bringing residents of different provinces into legal conflict with one another as to their respective legal rights and duties. This was not property and civil rights *in the province of Manitoba.* This is just one of the many parts or aspects into which the general subject of pollution may be sub-divided. Note that Mr. Justice Pigeon did not say or suggest in any way that pollution was a single subject for purposes of power-distribution, embraced in all its aspects by the federal general power.

Returning now for a moment to the proposition that Professor Le Dain correctly isolated as having some currency in our constitutional jurisprudence – "the notion that there must be a single plenary power to deal effectively and completely with any problem" – I claim that this is a dangerous fallacy. To me, it is a dangerous oversimplification that could lead to constitutional chaos or to the end of federalism. I infer that Professor Le Dain does not like the proposition any more than I do, though he does not commit himself explicitly on the point. In any event, this danger deserves some further explanation.

The philosophy of classification systems is such that any doctrinaire group that wants to push its special cause to the limit can find a subject-label for that cause that is new, so far as the established lists in the British North America Act are concerned. Then the group proceeds to urge that the great importance of this new subject means that the federal Parliament can and should give them the legislation that they want under the federal general power. Special interest groups of all kinds can be expected to urge legislative salvation for themselves in this way, and, up to a point, this may be legitimate advocacy, but it is only advocacy and should be critically evaluated as such.

As Professor Cairns has remarked:[31] "A necessary consequence of a federal system is that each organized interest will seek to transform the most sympathetic level of government into the main decision-maker in matters which concern it." One should also add that the same dangerous misuse could be made of the provincial general power in section 92(16) of the British North America Act. Our society is full of a great variety of groups that in many respects have conflicting interests. These considerations emphasize why we must have the caution and restraint that I have tried to spell out as the full meaning of the Watson-Simon view of the federal general power. These same considerations emphasize why it is that the superior courts, as impartial and independent interpretative tribunals, must be the umpires of the federal system of division of legislative powers. To use a figure of speech from the gambling world, if you want federalism at all, this is the only game in town, like it or not.

Having said all that, I must now add that I do not deny the reality and importance of social problems grouped under headings such as pollution, economic growth, culture, quality of life, and the like. Of course these are important generalized concepts with social reality in our country. My point is rather that categories as all-pervasive as these ones are cannot be allowed to dominate our distribution-of-powers system from within, so to speak. They must be treated as outside the system, which means they should each be subdivided into appropriate parts so that necessary legislative action can be taken by some combination of both federal and provincial statutes. Co-ordination of these legislative efforts should come through co-operative federalism – that is, by complementary federal and provincial statutes co-ordinated by virtue of custom, practice, or inter-governmental agreements of some sort. This is a large subject in itself which I cannot develop further here.[32] Suffice it to say that *before* you can successfully practise co-operative federalism, you must have in place a fundamental distribution of legislative powers and resources between the central government and the provinces. The essence of co-operative federalism is federal-provincial agreement, whether tacit or explicit, about complementary uses of federal and provincial powers and resources. Hence, unless the constitutional definitions of such powers and resources remain reasonably stable as the basis of the autonomy of the parties, subject only to the process of gradual adjustment I have already described, the respective bargaining positions of the two levels of government will be too uncertain for federal-provincial agreements to be reached.

Recently, the conception of the necessary operating jurisprudence of Canadian federalism that I have given at some length in this article has come under almost total attack by Professor Paul C. Weiler, a distinguished Canadian legal scholar with long experience in the field of labour relations and collective bargaining.[33] Much as I respect Professor Weiler, I must say that, on this subject, I thoroughly disagree with nearly all of what he has said.

Professor Weiler has said that the words and phrases by which our federal constitution distributes legislative powers were relevant to society and full of meaning when the constitution was first drawn up in 1867, but that, as society changed over the years in our country, these words and phrases became increasingly unreal and irrelevant to prevailing social conditions. Hence, he tells us that, 100 years later, the Supreme Court justices can really get no guidance from the original text of the British North America Act, no guidance from the concepts denoted by the original words and phrases. Thus he alleges that, in making interpretative decisions today, the Supreme Court is really making up a new constitution piecemeal as it goes along, and not doing it very well at that. Now I would agree that a final judicial interpretative tribunal has important degrees of discretion here, as in other parts of the law, but Professor Weiler goes much too far in what he has said.

I think Professor Weiler has got his history backwards. I consider the true history of the development of the British North America Act by judicial interpretation to be almost the complete reverse of what Professor Weiler says it is. As I said early in this article, the greatest uncertainty about the meaning of the power-conferring words and phrases of the constitution, in relation to one another, occurred at the beginning. As time went on and precedents accumulated, many years of judicial interpretation greatly reduced this uncertainty and made the distribution-of-powers system much more meaningful. In other words, after 100 years of judicial interpretation, the British North America Act has become much more meaningful than it was in 1867, and of course it was by no means devoid of meaning in 1867. We are talking of matters of degree and of the main trends, positive or negative, in the development of the meaning and utility of the constitution. Moreover, judicial interpretation over the years has shaped the original power-conferring words and phrases, in relation to one another, so that they have been capable of affording guidelines for new problems of legislative power-distribution arising from social change. This parallels the function and operation of judicial precedent in other branches of the law, so there should be nothing surprising about it.

Now in saying this, I am definitely not saying that the British North America Act is complete and all-sufficient in the sense that it contains in its text detailed principles and concepts that automatically embody easy solutions for every problem in the division of legislative powers that may arise. If this were so, reading the Act would be all that was involved in constitutional interpretation. I know that this extremely simplistic view of interpretation and meaning is not valid. But Professor Weiler has gone to the opposite extreme. He says that the federal constitution has become virtually meaningless, so that the Supreme Court is really making up new constitutional rules as it goes along under the guise of interpreting the text of the British North America Act. This extreme is just as invalid as the other. It does not properly describe our true operating federal jurisprudence either. As usual, the truth lies at some middle position between these opposed extremes. I think Professor Weiler has gravely over-simplified the nature of constitutions and constitutional history.

Logically enough as a result of his views, however, Professor Weiler considers that we would be better off if the courts in general, and the

Supreme Court of Canada in particular, were out of the business of judicial review of the federal constitution altogether. He would look instead to the model afforded by collective bargaining in labour relations for the operational jurisprudence of our federal system – he would put the main issues of the federal constitution into rather constant negotiation at federal-provincial conferences of our elected political leaders of government. For my part, I think these latter gentlemen already have quite enough to do operating *within* the guidelines afforded by judicial review of the constitution.

In the latest version of his views, published last year, Professor Weiler does concede a marginal role for the courts.[34] If some unfortunate citizen is caught by actual conflict of federal and provincial statutes applicable to him, Professor Weiler would allow him to go to court. But, to me, this latest qualification simply makes Mr. Weiler's main position less credible than ever. Conflict or inconsistency is a complex and flexible idea. There are thousand of pages in the federal statute books, and tens of thousands of pages in the provincial statute books, to say nothing of subordinate legislation. A good counsel could nearly always find enough conflict or inconsistency of some kind to get into court, and you would be back to full-fledged judicial review.

In any event, I do not find the model afforded by labour relations jurisprudence in Canada to be satisfactory as a type of system for control of the operating fundamentals of our federal constitution. I repudiate the labour relations model as a substitute for sophisticated judicial review at the highest levels in these fundamental matters. It is to the latter that we must look for a satisfactory operating jurisprudence of Canadian federalism, and, while this is centred on the courts, it does not involve the courts alone. To quote Professor Cairns again:[35]

> A strong and effective court requires a variety of supporters. It must be part of a larger system that includes first-class law schools, quality legal journals, and an able and sensitive legal fraternity – both teaching and practising. These are the minimum necessary conditions for a sophisticated jurisprudence without which a distinguished judicial performance is impossible. Unless judges can be made aware of the complexities of their role as judicial policy-makers and sensitively cognizant of the societal effects of their decisions, a first-rate judicial performance will only occur intermittently and fortuitously.

I say "Amen" to that, but again I feel both chastened and challenged. I have not yet said anything about my own views on this thing called policy-making, and to leave that out these days is to risk being characterized as a mere technician.

I do maintain that respectable beliefs in the realm of values lie behind the views I have expressed here. In the first place, a good federal division of legislative powers honours the values of pluralism – of the diversities in our society – as well as the need for a certain amount of unity. This assumes sophisticated and socially sensitive interpretation of the power-conferring words and phrases by impartial courts, especially the Supreme Court of Canada. The jurisprudential problem then is to achieve a balance between carefully defined unities and carefully defined diversities, the definitions collectively being comprehensive or potentially so. I have argued that it is a necessary part of our system to hold the definitions of federal and provincial categories of powers to a meaningful level of specific identity and particularity. The value of this is that, when we analyse our legislative needs, the issues requiring value decisions are rendered specific and brought into focus one by one in particular terms, so that ordinary mortals of limited wisdom and moral insight can cope with them. We are all ordinary mortals, so it is no use setting up a system that only God could operate. Moreover, I prefer federal systems to unitary ones because I believe in countervailing power among human institutions. I like to see our federal government having to compromise with provincial governments, and *vice versa*. I feel more secure as a citizen when the system requires this.

In the second place, it is necessary that impartial superior courts should act as umpires of the essential guidelines for the respective federal and provincial responsibilities given by the federal constitution. Of course the value assumptions of the judges will enter into their decisions. We would complain if this were not so. They must weigh such matters as the relative values of nationwide uniformity *versus* regional diversity, the relative merit of local *versus* central administration, and the justice of minority claims, when provincial or federal statutes are challenged for validity under the established division of powers. Inevitably, widely prevailing beliefs in the country about these issues will be influential and presumably the judges should strive to implement such beliefs. Inevitably there will be some tendency for them to identify their own convictions as those which generally prevail or which at least are the right ones. On some matters there will not be an ascertainable general belief anyway. In the making of these very difficult decisions of relative values, policy decisions if one prefers that word, all that can rightly be demanded of judges is straight thinking, industry, good faith, and a capacity to discount their own prejudices with due humility. No doubt it is also fair to ask that they be men or women of high professional attainment, and that they be somewhat representative in their thinking of the better standards of their times and their fellow citizens.

Notes

1. 1867, 30 & 31 Vict., c. 3, as am. (U.K.).

2. Alan C. Cairns, "The Judicial Committee and Its Critics," *Canadian Journal of Political Science*, 4 (1971), 343-44.

3. W.R.Lederman, "The Independence of the Judiciary," *Canadian Bar Review*, 34 (1956), 769, 1139; Lederman, "The Balanced Interpretation of the Federal Distribution of Legislative Powers in Canada," in Macpherson and Crépeau, eds., *The Future of Canadian Federalism* (1965), 91.

4. W.R.Lederman, "The Concurrent Operation of Federal and Provincial Laws in Canada," *McGill Law Journal*, 9 (1962-63), 185.

5. Report by W.F. O'Connor, The Parliamentary Counsel to The Honourable the Speaker of the Senate relating to "The enactment of the *B.N.A. Act,* 1867, any lack of consonance between its terms and judicial construction of them and cognate matters" (1939).

6. G.P. Browne, *The Judicial Committee and the British North America Act* (1967).

7. Hans Kelsen, *The Law of the United Nations* (1951), xiii-xv.

8. 14 Geo. III, c. 83 (U.K.).

9. Hilda Neatby, *Quebec, 1769-1791* (1966), *passim.*

10. Joseph Pope, *Confederation* (1895), 47, 106.

11. *Ibid.,* 233-36.

12. *Citizens' Insurance Company* v. *Parsons* (1881-82), 7 AC 94, at pp. 106-10.

13. *In re Regulation and Control of Aeronautics in Canada*, [1932] AC 54; *Johannesson* v. *West St. Paul*, [1952] 1 SCR 292; *Pronto Uranium Mines Ltd.* v. *O.L.R.B.* (1956), 5 DLR (2d) 342 (Ont. HC).

14. *Toronto Electric Commissioners* v. *Snider*, [1925] AC 396. *Reference re Industrial Relations and Disputes Investigation Act*, [1955] SCR 529.

15. *Supra*, note 13.

16. *Ibid.*

17. *In re The Board of Commerce Act, 1919, and the Combines and Fair Prices Act, 1919,* [1922] 1 AC 191, at p.200.

18. *Attorney General for Ontario* v. *Attorney General for the Dominion and the Distillers and Brewers Association of Ontario*, [1896] AC 348, at pp. 360-61.

19. *Attorney General for Ontario and Others* v. *Canada Temperance Federation and Others*, [1946] AC 193.

20. *Ibid.,* 205.

21. *In re Regulation and Control of Radio Communications in Canada*, [1932] AC 304.

22. (1882), 7 App. Cas. 829.

23. Gerald Le Dain, "Sir Lyman Duff and the Constitution," *Osgoode Hall Law Journal*, 12 (1974), 293.

24. Translation by the translation service, Ministry of Treasury, Economics and Intergovernmental Affairs, Government of Ontario (multigraphed).

25. *Saumur* v. *City of Quebec and the A.G. for Quebec*, [1953] 2 SCR 299, at p. 333.

26. *In the Reference re the Accurate News and Information Act of Alberta*, [1938] SCR 100.

27. (1974), 45 DLR (3d) 583 (SCC).

28. RSC 1970, c. 0-2.

29. *Supra*, note 27, 588-89.

30. (1975), 53 DLR (3d) 321.

31. Cairns, "The Judicial Committee and Its Critics," 315.

32. W.R.Lederman, "Cooperative Federalism: Constitutional Revision and Parliamentary Government in Canada," *Queen's Quarterly*, 78 (1971), 7; Lederman, "Some Forms and Limitations of Co-operative Federalism," *Canadian Bar Review*, 45 (1967), 409.

33. Paul C. Weiler, "Law and Social Change," in Ziegel, ed., *Osgoode Hall Lecture Series* (1973), ch.3, with critical comment by W.R. Lederman.

34. Paul C. Weiler, *In the Last Resort* (1974), ch. 6.

35. Cairns, "The Judicial Committee and Its Critics," 331.

5. P.W. HOGG

Is the Supreme Court
of Canada Biased
in Constitutional Cases?

I. The Issue

In recent public discussions of the Supreme Court of Canada the allegation has occasionally surfaced that the court has been biased in favour of
the federal interest in constitutional cases.[1] The allegation has been especially stimulated by the decisions in the two broadcasting cases,[2] which
denied provincial power over cable television, and by the *CIGOL*[3] and
Potash[4] cases, which limited provincial power to tax and regulate the production of natural resources located in the province. It is true that over the
last few years there has been an increase in both the number and the
importance of the constitutional cases before the Supreme Court of Canada, and the federal interest has fared much better than the provincial
interest.[5]

When a province loses a case which engages vital provincial policies it is
only to be expected that the province's politicians will be upset with the
result, and that their criticism will depart from the conventions of polite
legal discourse. But in my view the allegation of bias has to be taken
seriously by lawyers and political scientists. It casts doubt upon the efficacy
of judicial review as a means of resolving federal-provincial controversies.
It underlies the proposals to entrench the court in the constitution and to
provide a role for the provinces in selecting the judges. The purpose of this
article is to examine the allegation of bias on its merits.[6]

Originally published in *The Canadian Bar Review*, 57 (1979). Reprinted with
permission of the author and of the Canadian Bar Foundation/La Fondation du
Barreau Canadien.

We must start with the trite proposition that the law rarely supplies a clear answer to the questions which come before the Supreme Court of Canada. A litigant is not likely to spend good money taking an appeal to the Supreme Court of Canada unless he is convinced that there is a fair chance that the Supreme Court will reverse the decision which was arrived at by the provincial (or federal) court of appeal. The Supreme Court is not likely to give leave to appeal if a simple point of law is involved. The fact is that the Supreme Court often does reverse the court of appeal, and is often divided itself. All of the constitutional controversies which come before the court are cases where the language of the constitution does not speak clearly with respect to the question at hand, and the precedents either do not quite cover the question at hand or are conflicting. Obviously, differences of opinion as to the "correct" result in such cases do not imply bias on the part of anyone.

There is a long-standing controversy among legal scholars as to how judges do decide these difficult cases where a judge has to choose between competing interpretations of the existing legal materials. The extreme "positivist" point of view that a judge simply applies the pre-existing rules to the case at hand is entirely unhelpful, because it is the ambiguous or vague condition of the pre-existing rules which has caused the litigation, and the judge's decision will itself define for the first time the rule which is applicable to the case at hand (and like cases). In this situation a new rule has been created (or developed or elaborated). In formulating that new rule the judge exercises a choice which cannot be wholly explained by the pre-existing rules. How is that choice made? The extreme "realist" point of view would be that judges are inevitably free to indulge their own personal policy preferences in choosing between competing interpretations of the pre-existing rules. But it seems clear that judges do not feel that they have this kind of freedom, and the shared assumption of appellate advocacy is that the judge is not free to develop the law along lines which would be congenial to his own preferences. The moderate position, which seems to me to be accurate, is that the judicial choice is primarily governed by the body of legal policies and principles which underlie the more specific rules and which emerge from the statutes, cases, and other conventional sources of law; the judge formulates the legal rule which seems to him to flow most plausibly from those conventional sources of law, even if the result does not accord with his own policy preferences.[7] But it is undeniable that the decision of a difficult case may, as Oliver Wendell Holmes said long ago, "depend on a judgment or intuition more subtle than any articulate major premise";[8] and precisely because that crucial judgement or intuition is inarticulate, it can be influenced – unconsciously no doubt – by the judge's predispositions.[9]

I conclude that it is at least possible for a judge to be biased in federal-provincial controversies. Of course, the Supreme Court of Canada consists of nine judges at any one point of time, and a total of fifty-seven judges have sat on the court. In investigating the charge of bias in federal-provincial controversies it is necessary to ask whether the numerous judges of the court are likely to share a predisposition to favour the federal or centralist side of the case.

II. Federal Appointment of Judges

The simplest form of the argument for bias is that the judges are appointed and paid by the federal government, and will feel beholden to the federal government. Sometimes this argument is reinforced by the argument that the institution itself – the Supreme Court of Canada – was created by a federal statute, and could be abolished the same way. These facts, it would be said, may serve to inculcate gratitude or fear (or a mixture of the two) in the minds of the Supreme Court judges, predisposing them to render decisions pleasing to the federal government. It is obviously not necessary to embark on a detailed rebuttal of this argument. The fact is that once a judge has been appointed – admittedly by the federal government – he has nothing to hope for or fear from the federal government. Constitutional guarantees and powerful political traditions of judicial independence render the judge invulnerable to any kind of governmental action.[10]

The objective fact of judicial independence would not preclude the existence of a sycophantic psychology on the part of the judges. The fact here, however, is that the judges are all long-standing members of the legal profession; in most cases they have been engaged in the private practice of law; they have all been nurtured in a professional tradition which is highly unsympathetic to governmental authority, especially when exercised from Ottawa; and they are unlikely to have developed attitudes which are unduly deferential to the federal government. The strong likelihood is that they value the assessment of their work by the legal profession infinitely more highly than they value the opinions of the members of the federal cabinet and civil service. The reputation of a judge in the legal profession is established partly through scholarly writing but mainly through informal discussion among lawyers, and it develops primarily as a result of professional assessment of craftsmanship and fairness. The judge who could always be counted on to vote for the federal government would be regarded with contempt by the profession.

A more subtle form of the bias argument holds that the federal government exercises its appointing power in favour of people with known centralist predispositions. It is only to be expected, so the argument runs, that a government intent on strengthening its power would make such appointments. In fact, however, it seems unlikely that the government does engage in this kind of court-packing. It is not easy to find eminent lawyers and judges who are in favour of increased centralization of power in Ottawa. If obvious candidates for appointment were being passed over in favour of committed centralists, or if inquiries were being made about the constitutional opinions of potential candidates, I think it is obvious that these facts would become known and would be the subject of a considerable protest.[11]

To be sure, there are well-qualified candidates who have publicly recorded their views on some aspects of federal-provincial relationships. It is well known that Chief Justice Laskin, as a law professor, was a vigorous critic of the Privy Council decisions which strengthened provincial power at the expense of the federal government.[12] It is less well known that Mr. Justice Pigeon and Mr. Justice Beetz before their appointments had published articles which vigorously defended the decisions of the Privy Council.[13] So far as I am aware, none of the other judges had before appointment recorded his opinions on constitutional law.[14] On the basis of the precedents of Laskin C.J., Pigeon and Beetz JJ., it is impossible to substantiate any charge of court-packing. In any case it is impossible to predict with confidence how a person will vote when he assumes judicial office. For example, Laskin C.J. has written the court's opinion, or a separate concurring opinion, in every case in which a federal statute has been held unconstitutional;[15] Pigeon and Beetz JJ. have often written or agreed to opinions holding a provincial statute to be unconstitutional.[16]

It must be remembered, too, that constitutional cases form only a very small part of the work of the Supreme Court of Canada. The great majority of cases are appeals in civil or criminal cases which involve no constitutional issues at all. One of the factors which is taken into account by the federal government in making appointments is the securing of an appropriate mix of legal experience and expertise among the judges. It would be impossible for the federal government to give due weight to this consideration, as well as conforming to the conventional regional balance of the judges,[17] at the same time as it was pursuing judges who could be relied upon to vote the "right" way in constitutional cases.

The truth is, I suspect, that the federal government does not see the winning of constitutional law cases as a major policy objective, does not see the role of the Supreme Court in constitutional cases as being of major importance in determining the balance of power between the centre and the provinces,[18] and does see that any evidence of packing the court would provoke a storm of protest. If these viewpoints correspond with reality, as I believe they do, then one must conclude that it is good politics to make good appointments.

III. Frequent Invalidation of Provincial Statutes

The only remaining argument for bias is based on the outcomes of constitutional cases[19] decided in the Supreme Court of Canada from the abolition of appeals to the Privy Council on December 23rd, 1949, to the present.[20] I have looked at all those cases, and I find that sixty-five provincial statutes were attacked in the Supreme Court of Canada and twenty-five of them were held to be unconstitutional in whole or in part,[21] or to be inoperative through paramountcy. In the same period thirty-seven federal statutes were attacked in the Supreme Court of Canada and four of them were held to be unconstitutional in whole or in part.

This kind of raw data must be treated with the utmost caution. Consider some of the complicating factors.

First of all, there are ten legislative bodies busy enacting provincial laws and only one legislative body enacting federal laws. Even allowing for the fact that many provincial statutes duplicate those of other provinces, the volume and variety of provincial laws are so much greater that there are bound to be, and there are, more challenges to the constitutionality of provincial laws. In the period of my study, January, 1950, to May, 1979, inclusive, as I have just indicated above, there were sixty-five decisions on the validity of provincial laws, and thirty-seven decisions on the validity of federal laws. Of course, this point goes to explain the number of challenges to provincial laws, not the ratio of success to failure.

Secondly, in such a large and diverse country as Canada, the provinces really are the "social laboratories" that they are supposed to be. Innovative and even radical political ideas tend to find political expression at the provincial level. Federal governments, by contrast, cannot get elected except on middle-of-the-road policies which appeal to a broad cross-section of the country. Since the Second World War cautious or weak federal governments have undertaken few initiatives which would invite a plausible constitutional challenge. The Trudeau government was quite exceptional in its willingness to intervene in the economy. The provinces, however, especially in the West and in Quebec, frequently elect governments with strong mandates to intervene in the economy. These interventions naturally provoke constitutional challenges.

Thirdly, technological developments have tended to diminish provincial powers of economic regulation and increase federal powers.[22] Even in 1867 shipping and rail could move products from their producers to distant markets; but those means of transportation have now been joined by the highways and the airlines. Similarly, the printing press has now been joined by the motion picture, the telephone, radio, and television. The improvements in transportation and communication, and other technological developments, have led to larger and larger business units which can take advantage of the techniques of mass production, mass distribution, and mass advertising. This has led to the gradual disappearance of locally produced consumer goods. The general tendency of technological change is to convert activities which were once local and private, and which could be governed by the private law of contract, tort, and property, into activities which extend across the entire nation, make use of public facilities, and require regulation in order to protect the public from predatory or monopolistic practices. These developments do not necessarily answer the question of which level of government should be the regulator. But in many instances the need for a single national policy is so clear that the federal claim is very plausible.

Fourthly, in a federal system – any federal system – provincial laws are vulnerable to constitutional challenge on the basis of their extraterritorial impact. Various doctrines are either expressed in the constitution or are inferred by the courts to limit the power of a provincial legislature, which is elected by and answerable to the people of only that province, to enact policies which will have an impact on the people of other provinces. This is the underlying policy behind many of the limits on the powers of the provinces, even though the limits may be expressed in terms of encroaching on interprovincial trade and commerce, imposing indirect taxation, as well as the more straightforward prohibition on extraterritorial laws. The federal Parliament, by contrast, is elected from all over the country. No doctrine has developed and none is needed to prevent it from overreaching in a territorial sense.[23]

Fifthly, in Canada, and apparently in all modern federations,[24] provincial laws are vulnerable to constitutional challenge on the basis of their inconsistency with federal law. This is a judge-made doctrine in Canada, to be sure, but one for which the Privy Council, and not the Supreme Court of Canada, bears the responsibility. In any event, I think there would be little quarrel with the general proposition that where national and provincial laws come into conflict it is the national law – the law with the broadest political support – which should prevail.[25] The doctrine of federal paramountcy provides a ground for challenging provincial laws which is not available in respect of federal laws.[26]

What all this means is that we must expect many more successful constitutional challenges to provincial laws than federal laws. This situation stems from the nature of the Canadian federal system, not from any bias on the part of the judges. Even during the Privy Council period this was true. I only have figures from 1919 to the end of appeals, but that was the period when the Privy Council established doctrines highly favourable to the provinces. In that period there were thirty-five challenges to provincial statutes of which nineteen were held invalid in whole or in part, and twenty-two challenges to federal statutes of which eight were held invalid in whole or in part.[27] The Privy Council was less restrained in judicial review than the Supreme Court of Canada. Therefore the rate of invalidation is higher for both classes of statutes. But a similar discrepancy in the numbers of challenges and in the proportions of successful challenges is obvious.

IV. Doctrines Established by the Court

1. Legacy of the Privy Council

Let us now move away from the raw data and ask whether the doctrines established by the judges indicate a pro-centralist bias.

The legacy left by the Privy Council was a very broad provincial power over property and civil rights in the province, and correspondingly narrow federal powers over the peace, order, and good government of Canada and over the regulation of trade and commerce. As new kinds of legislation emerged, even when the initiative had come from the federal Parliament, the Privy Council had often allotted the new law to provincial jurisdiction, usually, property and civil rights in the province. The regulation of insurance, and therefore of other industries and occupations, most labour relations, trades and professions, wages and prices, combinations, health and welfare, and the marketing of natural products were all topics which the Privy Council ruled were outside the competence of the federal Parliament, except in time of war. During the depression of the 1930s the federal Parliament did not have the power to undertake measures designed to alleviate the distress and prevent its recurrence. Federal laws providing for unemployment insurance, minimum wage and maximum hours laws, as well as marketing regulation, were all held to be unconstitutional.[28]

The decisions of the Privy Council were widely if not universally deplored by English-Canadian constitutional lawyers, although not by French-Canadian constitutional lawyers.[29] From a doctrinal point of view, however, there was surely force in the criticism that the decisions had virtually emptied the major federal powers of content. It was not a particularly plausible interpretation of the peace, order, and good government power that it applied only in wartime. It was not a particularly plausible interpretation of the trade and commerce power that it would not permit the regulation of any intraprovincial trade and commerce. Indeed, the Privy Council itself had left a number of decisions and dicta which reflected quite different opinions than those which became dominant during the Haldane period.

2. Peace, Order, and Good Government

When we look at the extensions of the peace, order, and good government power which have occurred since 1949, we have to remember how severely that power had been attenuated by the Privy Council and how inevitable it was that there would be a movement away from the Privy Council's more extreme views. In fact, the decisions of the Supreme Court of Canada have been quite cautious in departing from Privy Council precedents. The "national concern" branch of peace, order, and good government has been used to uphold federal power over aviation,[30] the national capital commission,[31] the minerals off the shore of British Columbia,[32] and the control of narcotics.[33] None of these outcomes would surprise a visitor from another federation. But in the *Anti-Inflation Reference* (1976),[34] a case which shows up in the raw data as a federal victory, the Supreme Court of Canada refused to extend the national concern test to wage and price controls. These could only be enacted as a temporary emergency measure in wartime or in a peacetime crisis. To be sure, the court found that the requisite crisis existed, and upheld the Anti-Inflation Act; but the court emphasized that permanent controls were outside federal competence. I suggest that a visitor from another federation would be surprised that permanent wage and price controls cannot be enacted by the federal Parliament. This means, of course, that they cannot be enacted at all, because provincial controls could not be effective while there is free movement across provincial boundaries of personnel, capital, goods, and services. The opinions in the *Anti-Inflation Reference*, and especially that of Beetz J., abundantly demonstrate the continuing life of the Privy Council extension of property and civil rights in the province.

3. Trade and Commerce

The history of the trade and commerce power is similar. Few people would quarrel with the Supreme Court of Canada's acceptance of federal marketing legislation for wheat[35] and oil,[36] products which flow across provincial boundaries.[37] But when the federal government sought to use the trade and commerce power to uphold a law which afforded a civil remedy for loss caused by an act or business practice which was "contrary to honest industrial or commercial practice in Canada" the Supreme Court of Canada in *MacDonald* v. *Vapor Canada* (1976)[38] unanimously condemned the law. Once again, the viability of the old cases on property and civil rights in the province was reaffirmed. In the *Anti-Inflation Reference* (1976),[39] counsel for the federal government did not even argue that the trade and commerce power could sustain the wage and price controls, and the tenor of the opinions makes clear that at least five of the nine judges would have emphatically rejected such an argument.

The Supreme Court of Canada has used an expanded view of the trade and commerce power to strike down several provincial marketing schemes, including Manitoba's egg marketing scheme[40] and Saskatchewan's scheme to control the production and price of potash.[41] The essential basis of these decisions is that the provincial law had too severe an impact on interprovincial trade and commerce. In my opinion, these decisions are hard to reconcile with earlier decisions and therefore do represent a shift in doctrine by the Supreme Court of Canada;[42] it is a shift which is unfavourable to provincial power. But, as I noted earlier, every federal system has to define limits on the power of its provincial (or state) governments to affect people in other parts of the country. The litigation which this same issue has spawned in the United States[43] and Australia[44] demonstrates that this is a real problem upon which people of equal intelligence and equal good faith are simply not going to agree. Moreover, while the provinces have lost some of the cases where the effects of provincial laws have rippled outside the province, they have won others, most notably *Carnation Co.* v. *Quebec*

Agricultural Marketing Board (1968),[45] in which a provincial marketing scheme was held applicable to a processor of milk who shipped the bulk of the processed product out of the province,[46] and *Canadian Indemnity Co.* v. *A.-G. B.C.* (1976),[47] in which the creation of a provincial monopoly of automobile insurance was upheld despite the interprovincial character of the business of writing automobile insurance. The latter case reaffirmed the Privy Council precedents upholding provincial jurisdiction over the insurance industry. In the United States, by contrast, initial holdings of state jurisdiction over insurance were reversed in 1944 on the basis that the nationwide character of the industry brought it within the commerce clause and thus within federal jurisdiction.[48]

One must conclude that while the federal trade and commerce power has expanded at the hands of the Supreme Court of Canada, it has not expanded very much. As a support to federal jurisdiction the expansion has been very cautious, confined to marketing schemes over wheat and oil and (with co-operative provincial supplementation) eggs. An observer from the United States would be astonished to learn that the trade and commerce power cannot be employed to regulate the insurance industry, or to impose nationwide wage and price controls, and that the constitutional validity of federal regulation of foreign ownership and anti-trust and securities regulation still comprises matters of argument among constitutional lawyers. As a barrier to provincial jurisdiction, the trade and commerce power has been applied more boldly – to the chagrin of some of the provinces. Even here, however, the results have not been uniformly unfavourable to provincial power to regulate activity which spills outside provincial borders; and the difficulty of drawing the line between that which is predominantly local, and that which is predominantly interprovincial, is one which simply cannot be denied.

4. Cable Television

The recent decisions affirming federal regulatory authority over cable television[49] and denying provincial authority over cable television[50] came as a blow to Quebec, where the issues were perceived in terms of the protection of French-Canadian language and culture. However, federal jurisdiction over broadcast (non-cable) radio and television had been established by the Privy Council in the *Radio Reference* (1930),[51] and the argument over cable television boiled down to the question of whether it was feasible to regard the cable system as a local undertaking separate from the undeniably federal broadcasting system. The Supreme Court's decision that the cable system should not be regarded as separate was in accord with a virtually unanimous accumulation of prior decisions and published articles.[52] The point was still open, as is evidenced by the dissents of the three French-Canadian judges, but it should be noted that the Federal Court of

Appeal in the *Capital Cities* case and (more significantly, perhaps) the Quebec Court of Appeal in the *Dionne* case were each unanimously of the same opinion as the majority in the Supreme Court of Canada.

My opinion, for what it is worth, is that the competing federal and provincial claims to regulate cable television are each founded on real interests. A judicial decision which allocates jurisdiction to one level of the government or the other cannot be entirely satisfactory, whichever level of government emerges as the winner. It is most unlikely that the judicial resolution will turn out to be final. What is required is an agreement for the sharing of jurisdiction, either spelled out in a revised constitution, or embodied in sub-constitutional arrangements.

5. *Taxation*

In *Canadian Industrial Gas and Oil* v. *Government of Saskatchewan* (1977),[53] the Supreme Court of Canada struck down a provincial tax on oil produced in the province. The tax was designed to appropriate to the province the dramatic increase in the price of oil which had started in 1973. Because of the huge sums involved the decision was a serious blow to the province of Saskatchewan, and it attracted severe criticism from the government of that province. The legal issue before the court was whether the tax was direct or indirect, because the provinces are confined to direct taxes by section 92(2) of the BNA Act. Previous decisions established that a tax which tended to enter into the price of a commodity was an indirect tax and was incompetent to the provinces. The Saskatchewan Court of Appeal held that this tax was direct because the price of oil determined the tax rather than the other way around. This was also the view of Dickson J. (with de Grandpré J.) dissenting in the Supreme Court of Canada. But Martland J. for the seven-judge majority of the Supreme Court of Canada viewed the facts differently, emphasizing the power which the statute conferred on the provincial minister to fix the price at which oil was to be sold when the minister was of opinion that oil had been sold at less than fair value.

CIGOL must be accounted an important loss to the provinces in federal-provincial litigation. I find the majority opinion of Martland J. much less persuasive than the minority opinion of Dickson J. I do not see the answer to Dickson J.'s point that "purchasers would be paying the same price whether the tax existed or not."[54] The ministerial power to fix the price, which was relied upon by Martland J., seems to me to be satisfactorily explained by Dickson J. as a subsidiary provision to block evasion of the tax by "such practices as sale of oil between related companies at artificially low prices."[55] However, the legal issue turned on one's perception of exactly how the tax and associated regulations would impinge on the price of Saskatchewan oil. Differences of opinion on complex issues of this kind should not lay the judges open to a charge of bias.

The Supreme Court of Canada recently made another decision upon the provincial taxing power. In the *Ontario Egg Reference* (1977),[56] the court held that marketing levies were not indirect taxes; the levies were regulatory charges which could be imposed by the provinces as an incident of a valid provincial marketing scheme. This holding involved an unprecedented overruling of the decision of the Privy Council in the *Crystal Dairy* case,[57] which had decided that marketing levies were indirect taxes which were incompetent to the provinces. It was also necessary to overrule (on this point) a previous decision of the Supreme Court of Canada, the *Farm Products Marketing Act Reference* (1957).[58] The court applied the new doctrine by striking down a federal statute authorizing the imposition of marketing levies by provincial marketing boards, notwithstanding the fact that the federal statute had been enacted in 1957 in reliance on the fact that the *Crystal Dairy* doctrine had been reaffirmed by the Supreme Court of Canada in the *Farm Products Marketing Act Reference* in 1957. This unanimous holding is a remarkable example of judicial activism, and of course its effect was to augment provincial power.

6. Administration of Justice

Federal power over the administration of justice by federal courts, which is granted by section 101 of the BNA Act, has been severely limited by the decisions of the Supreme Court of Canada in *Quebec North Shore* (1976)[59] and *McNamara Construction* (1977),[60] which hold that the federal Parliament can confer jurisdiction on federal courts only over issues governed by federal statute law. This has gravely undermined or rendered uncertain much of the jurisdiction of the Federal Court of Canada, introduced terrible complexities to multi-party litigation, especially where the federal Crown (which can only be sued in the Federal Court) is involved, and spawned a flood of litigation which is now working its way up through the system.[61] I have criticized these decisions elsewhere.[62] For present purposes it suffices to note that the new doctrine is highly unfavourable to federal power.

Provincial power over the administration of justice in the province has been contentious in recent years. In *Di Iorio* v. *Montreal Jail Warden* (1976),[63] the Supreme Court of Canada decided by a majority that the province of Quebec had the jurisdiction to establish an inquiry into organized crime, despite the close relationship with the federal subject of criminal law. However, in the *Keable* case[64] the court decided unanimously that the province of Quebec did not have the jurisdiction to establish a broad-ranging inquiry into the policies, procedures, and methods of the Royal Canadian Mounted Police, although the inquiry could be continued in respect of particular criminal acts allegedly committed in Quebec by the force. In *The Queen* v. *Hauser* (1979),[65] the court decided by a majority that the federal Parliament had the jurisdiction to provide for the federal prosecution of offenses under the Narcotic Control Act. This decision, like *Keable*, was unfavourable to the provincial point of view, but, also like *Keable*, it was based on rather narrow grounds. The court in *Hauser* did not affirm federal power to provide for the prosecution of criminal law (as many observers expected); a majority of the court managed to avoid this vexed issue by holding that the Narcotic Control Act was not really a criminal law after all,[66] which enabled the Court to decide the case on the basis that the federal Parliament had the power to provide for the enforcement of its non-criminal laws.

Frequent attacks on provincial administrative agencies (or inferior courts), based on the allegation that the agencies (or courts) were exercising judicial powers analogous to those of a superior court in contravention of section 96 and the other judicature provisions of the BNA Act, have met with success in three cases,[67] but have usually failed. The court has emphasized that "it is not the detached jurisdiction or power alone that is to be considered but rather its setting in the institutional arrangements in which it appears and is exercisable under the provincial legislation."[68] This pragmatic contextual approach is of course favourable to the provincial power to set up administrative agencies.

7. Civil Liberties

In the 1950s the Supreme Court of Canada rendered decisions which tended to limit if not deny provincial power to legislate in relation to speech and religion. The *Saumur* case (1953)[69] held that Quebec City could not prevent the distribution of religious tracts in the streets. *Switzman* v. *Elbling* (1957)[70] held that a provincial law prohibiting the use of a house to propagate communism was invalid. These cases were unfavourable to provincial power, to be sure, but they had their roots in well-respected dicta by Duff C.J. and Cannon J. in the *Alberta Press* case (1938),[71] and they were widely applauded for their support of civil libertarian values. Recently, however, the court has upheld provincial restraints on civil liberties. In *Nova Scotia Board of Censors* v. *McNeil* (1978),[72] provincial censorship of movies was upheld as being merely the regulation of a business (the movie business) and of property (films) in the province; and this despite the absence of any explicit criteria laid down by the statute or regulation or by the censorship board itself to limit the kinds of movies which could be forbidden. In *A.-G. Can. and Dupond* v. *Montreal* (1978),[73] a Montreal by-law prohibiting all demonstrations in the streets and parks of the city for a specified period of time was upheld as a regulation of the use of the municipal public domain.

It is difficult to believe that *McNeil* and *Dupond* would have been decided the same way by the Supreme Court of the 1950s. For present purposes, the point is, of course, that the value of provincial autonomy over local matters has been held to encompass even speech and assembly despite the nationwide implications of speech and assembly for the democratic process. Whatever else one may say about the recent decisions, they are certainly favourable to provincial power.

8. *Paramountcy*

The BNA Act says nothing explicit about conflict between federal and provincial laws. The Privy Council early developed the rule of federal paramountcy: in the event of conflict the federal law was to prevail. Surprisingly, however, there were only a few occasions for the application of this rule by the Privy Council, and their lordships never developed any jurisprudence as to the degree of inconsistency which would amount to a conflict which would attract the rule. Here then was an opportunity for the court to give effect to any centralizing predispositions. Given the overriding force of federal law, a wide definition of inconsistency would result in the defeat of provincial laws in the same "field" as a federal law. In the United States and Australia there are many precedents for this covering-the-field test of conflict. On the other hand, a narrow definition of inconsistency would allow provincial laws to survive so long as they did not expressly contradict the federal law.[74]

The Supreme Court of Canada has not followed the covering-the-field precedents of the United States and Australia. It has not taken the course of judicial activism in favour of central power. On the contrary, it has insisted upon a direct contradiction between the federal and provincial law to trigger the paramountcy doctrine. There are many cases in which the court has refused to render a provincial law inoperative for paramountcy,[75] and only two where the conflict was deemed sufficient to render the provincial law inoperative.[76] The cases have been described elsewhere,[77] but it is perhaps worth briefly describing one case. In *Ross* v. *Registrar of Motor Vehicles* (1973),[78] the court was concerned with the effect of a federal Criminal Code provision dealing with penalties for drunk driving and conferring a discretion on the sentencing court to prohibit driving on an intermittent basis – "at such times and places as may be specified in the order." In the *Ross* case this power had been exercised by prohibiting the defendant "from driving for a period of six months, except Monday to Friday, 8:00 a.m. to 5:45 p.m., in the course of employment and going to and from work." The question was whether the Criminal Code discretion, as exemplified by the *Ross* order, conflicted with a provincial law which automatically suspended the driving licence of anyone convicted of drunk driving. The provincial law had the effect of nullifying the spirit if not the letter of the carefully tailored order made under the Criminal Code because the order obviously contemplated that the defendant be free to drive in the periods which were exempt from the prohibition. Yet the Supreme Court of Canada held that the provincial law was not rendered inoperative by paramountcy. Ross's licence was suspended.

While the *Ross* case is the most extreme example, many others could be cited to show the length to which the court has been willing to go in support of provincial laws.[79] In this area the Supreme Court of Canada has developed doctrine highly favourable to provincial power.

9. Conclusion

My conclusion is that the Supreme Court of Canada has generally adhered to the doctrine laid down by the Privy Council precedents; and that where the court has departed from those precedents, or has been without close precedents, the choices between competing lines of reasoning have favoured the provincial interest at least as often as they have favoured the federal interest. There is no basis for the claim that the court has been biased in favour of the federal interest in constitutional litigation.

Notes

This article originated as a paper which I delivered to classes at the University of Victoria and the University of British Columbia in January, 1979. I have also tried it out on my own students and a number of my colleagues. It has been heard or read by a large number of people, and I have benefited from many comments. I should however specifically acknowledge the particularly helpful comments of law student Douglas Marshall and law professors Stanley Schiff, William Angus, and Katherine Swinton.

1. Charges of bias in the press prompted a defence of the court by the Chief Justice: Laskin, "Judicial Integrity and the Supreme Court of Canada," *Law Society Gazette* (1978), 116.

2. *Capital Cities Communications* v. *Canadian Radio-Television Commission,* [1978] 2 SCR 141; *Public Service Board* v. *Dionne*, [1978] 2 SCR 191; but compare *A.-G. Que.* v. *Kellogg's Co. of Canada*, [1978] 2 SCR 211.

3. *Canadian Industrial Gas and Oil* v. *Govt. of Sask.*, [1978] 2 SCR 545, hereinafter referred to as *CIGOL*.

4. *Central Canada Potash Co.* v. *Govt. of Sask.*, [1979] 1 SCR 42.

5. See K. Lysyk, "Reshaping Canadian Federalism," *U.B.C. Law Review*, 13, (1979), 16-21, who does not, however, allege bias.

6. There is an important study in existence, commissioned by the government of Quebec: Gilbert L'Ecuyer, *La Cour suprême du Canada et le partage des compétences 1949-1978* (Gouvernement du Québec, Ministère des Affairs intergouvernementales, 1978), which rejects the allegation of bias. The present article, while agreeing with L'Ecuyer's conclusion, investigates the issue by different methods.

7. Out of the vast literature on judicial decision-making, I cite as particularly useful on this point, Paul C. Weiler, "Two Models of Judicial Decision-Making," *Canadian Bar Review*, 46 (1968), 406; Paul C. Weiler, "Legal Values and Judicial Decision-Making," *Canadian Bar Review*, 48 (1970), 1.

8. *Lochner* v. *New York* (1905), 198 U.S. 45, at p. 76, per Holmes J. dissenting; see also "The Path of the Law," *Harvard Law Review*, 10 (1897), 466.

9. In *Lochner* v. *New York*. It will be recalled that the Supreme Court of the United States struck down a state law prescribing maximum hours of labour in bakeries as "an unreasonable, unnecessary and arbitrary interference" with freedom of contract.

10. The federal Parliament retains power over judicial salaries, and the Prime Minister decides who will be promoted to Chief Justice when that office is vacant. But the tradition of judicial independence ensures that these powers will not be used to punish or reward judges who render decisions adverse to or favourable to the federal government.

11. For an account of the procedure which is followed in making judicial appointments, see E. Ratushny, "Judicial Appointments: The Lang Legacy," in A.M. Linden, ed., *The Canadian Judiciary* (1976), ch. 2.

12. B. Laskin, "'Peace, Order and Good Government' Re-examined," *Canadian Bar Review*, 25 (1947), 1054.

13. L.-P. Pigeon, "The Meaning of Provincial Autonomy," *Canadian Bar Review*, 29 (1951), 1126; J. Beetz, "Les attitudes changeantes du Québec à l'endroit de la Constitution de 1867," in P.-A.Crépeau and C.B. Macpherson, *The Future of Canadian Federalism* (1965), 113.

14. Judges appointed to the Supreme Court of Canada from the bench of another court would normally have decided the occasional constitutional case.

15. *MacDonald* v. *Vapor Canada*, [1977] 2 SCR 134; *McNamara Construction* v. *The Queen*, [1977] 2 SCR 655; *Quebec North Shore Paper Co.* v. *Canadian Pacific*, [1977] 2 SCR 1054; *Reference re Agricultural Products Marketing Act*, [1978] 2 SCR 1198.

16. E.g., *Amax Potash* v. *Govt. of Sask.*, [1977] 2 SCR 576; *Canadian Industrial Gas and Oil* v. *Govt. of Sask., supra*, note 3; *A.-G. Que.* v. *Farrah*, [1978] 2 SCR 638.

17. The Supreme Court Act, RSC, 1970, c. S-19, s. 6, stipulates that three of the nine judges must come from Quebec. Until December, 1978, the practice was to appoint three judges from Ontario, two from the four Western provinces, and one from the Atlantic provinces. In December, 1978, on the retirement of Spence J. who had been appointed from Ontario, McIntyre J. was appointed from British Columbia. The present composition of the court therefore includes (as well as the three judges from Quebec and the one from the Atlantic provinces) two judges from Ontario, two judges from the Prairie provinces, and one judge from British Columbia. It remains to be seen whether this is now to be the permanent regional distribution of appointments.

18. The federal-provincial financial arrangements, which are made by agreement between the eleven governments and which encompass the sharing of tax "room," equalization grants, and shared-cost programs, are incomparably more significant. When a judicial decision does have a serious impact on the federal-provincial sharing of power, an accommodation is usually reached by agreement among the various governments. On three occasions that agreement has led to a constitutional amendment to reverse the effect of a judicial decision: s. 91(2A) of the British North America Act (added by British North America Act, 1940, 3-4 Geo. VI, c. 36 (U.K.)) and s. 94A (added by British North America Act, 1951, 14-15 Geo. VI c. 32 (U.K.) and revised by British North America Act, 1964, 12-13 Eliz. II, c. 73 (U.K.)), hereinafter referred to as BNA Act, were designed to abrogate *A.-G. Can* v. *A.-G. Ont.* (Unemployment Insurance), [1937] AC 355. More commonly, the effect of the decision can be overcome or modified by revenue-sharing arrangements (e.g., modifying effect of *Reference re Offshore Mineral Rights*, [1967] SCR 792) or by federal inter-delegations of various kinds (e.g., those upheld in *Lord's Day Alliance* v. *A.-G. B.C.*, [1959] SCR 497; *P.E.I. Potato Marketing Board* v. *Willis*, [1952] 2 SCR 392; *Coughlin* v. *Ont. Highway Transport Board*, [1968] SCR 569; *Reference re Agricultural Products Marketing Act, supra,* note 15, each of which was a response to a judicial decision). I predict that current controversies over the control and taxation of natural resources and over cable television will also be settled reasonably agreeably to the contending governments. Indeed, one scholar has argued that judicial review could be abolished in view of the existence of consensual methods of resolving federal-provincial controversies: Paul C. Weiler, "The Supreme Court of Canada and Canadian Federalism," *Osgoode Hall Law Journal*, 11 (1973), 225; Paul C. Weiler, *In the Last Resort* (1974), ch. 6.

19. I included only cases which raised a constitutional issue of federalism. Constitutional cases on points not bearing on the distribution of powers were excluded, for example, cases on the Canadian Bill of Rights, RSC, 1970, Appendix III. I excluded cases in which the majority opinion was not based on a constitutional issue, even though the point may have been strenuously argued, or even formed the basis of a dissenting opinion (as in *Breckinridge Speedway* v. *The Queen*, [1970] SCR 1975). I also excluded cases in which a constitutional point was referred to in the majority opinion, but was in my view either an *obiter dictum* or a subsidiary ground of decision; these exclusions are more controversial, but it must be appreciated that the constitution is argued in many cases and often receives passing reference in the decisions, for example, in administrative law cases.

20. The cases comprise all the decisions of which I was aware, from the beginning of 1950 up to June 1, 1970. This included all the cases reported in the Supreme Court Reports up to Part 2 of [1979] 1 SCR together with four cases decided, but unreported in SCR at that time, namely, *Construction Montcalm* v. *Commission du salaire minimum*, December 21, 1978; *Tropwood A.G.* v. *Sivaco*

Wire and Nail Co., March 6, 1979; *Mississauga* v. *Peel*, March 6, 1979; *The Queen* v. *Hauser*, May 1, 1979. I excluded *Winner* v. *S.M.T. Eastern*, [1951] SCR 887, because, although it was decided after 1949, it still went on appeal up to the Privy Council.

21. In six cases a statute was not held invalid, but "read down" or interpreted narrowly so that it was held inapplicable to the facts on the ground that a literal application of the statute would have been unconstitutional. On reading down, see Hogg, *Constitutional Law of Canada* (1977), 90-92. I counted these cases as holdings of partial invalidity.

22. Paralleling technological developments has been the rise of egalitarian values reflected in social policies to provide income support and security from illness, disability, and old age. Many of these policies are within provincial legislative jurisdiction, but there is also a heavy federal presence reflected in federal programs of unemployment insurance, family allowances, Canada pension plan, old age security, guaranteed income supplement, and in shared-cost programs of income support, hospital insurance, and medical care. Unlike economic regulation, programs of income distribution and social security rely primarily upon extensive spending powers and are rarely vulnerable to constitutional challenge.

23. It may be objected that the federal Parliament is subject to a comparable limitation in the sense that it is precluded from legislating in relation to matters which are local. Perhaps the answer is that this fourth point is really only a corollary to the third point, which is that fewer and fewer matters are genuinely local.

24. K.C. Wheare, *Federal Government* (4th ed., 1963), 74.

25. The practice of other federal systems (see Wheare, *ibid*.) supports this proposition. This is not to deny that in a revised Canadian constitution there may well be some areas of concurrent legislative power where the general rule should be reversed so that provincial laws would be paramount.

26. In the period under study, 1950-1979, *supra*, note 20, only two provincial statutes were actually held inoperative by reason of federal paramountcy. The paramountcy cases are discussed later in this article.

27. Weiler, *In the Last Resort*, 309, note 3.

28. See Hogg, *Constitutional Law*, chs. 14, 15, 17.

29. Compare the articles cited, *supra*, notes 12 and 13; and see Alan C. Cairns, "The Judicial Committee and Its Critics," *CJPS*, 4 (1971), 301.

30. *Johannesson* v. *West St. Paul*, [1952] 1 SCR 292.

31. *Munro* v. *National Capital Commission*, [1966] SCR 663.

32. *Reference re Offshore Mineral Rights, supra*, note 18.

33. *The Queen* v. *Hauser, supra*, note 20. This is a surprising decision, because it appears to resuscitate *Russell* v. *The Queen* (1882), 7 App. Cas. 829, a decision widely regarded as wrong, and because narcotics law had hitherto been generally regarded as criminal. But the allocation of narcotics law to federal power is not at all surprising.

Federalism in Canada: Selected Readings

34. [1976] 2 SCR 373.
35. *Murphy* v. *Canadian Pacific Railway*, [1958] SCR 626.
36. *Caloil* v. *A.-G. Can.*, [1971] SCR 543.
37. See also *Reference re Agricultural Products Marketing Act, supra,* note 15, where an egg marketing scheme was upheld. The scheme was the fruit of a federal-provincial agreement and supported by both federal and provincial statutes; the federal statute was carefully expressed in most of its provisions to be limited to interprovincial and export trade.
38. *Supra*, note 15.
39. *Supra*, note 34.
40. *A.-G. Man.* v. *Man. Egg and Poultry Assn.*, [1971] SCR 689; see also *Burns Foods* v. *A.-G. Man.* [1975] 1 SCR 494.
41. *Central Canada Potash Co.* v. *Govt. of Sask., supra*, note 4; see also *Canadian Industrial Gas and Oil* v. *Govt. of Sask., supra*, note 3.
42. Hogg, *Constitutional Law*, 311.
43. Laurence H. Tribe, *American Constitutional Law* (1978), ch. 6.
44. P.H. Lane, *The Australian Federal System* (1972), 597-675.
45. [1968] SCR 238.
46. See also *Reference re Agricultural Products Marketing Act, supra*, note 15, where provincial controls on the production of eggs were upheld, although the controls applied regardless of the ultimate destination of the eggs.
47. [1977] 2 SCR 504.
48. *United States* v. *South-Eastern Underwriters Assn.* (1944), 322 U.S. 533.
49. *Capital Cities Communications* v. *Canadian Radio-Television Commission, supra*, note 2.
50. *Public Service Board* v. *Dionne, supra*, note 2; but compare *A.-G. Que.* v. *Kellogg's Co. of Canada, supra*, note 2.
51. [1932] AC 304.
52. The case-law and commentary before *Capital Cities* and *Dionne* are discussed in Hogg, *Constitutional Law*, 336-42.
53. *Supra*, note 3. See also *Amax Potash* v. *Govt. of Sask. supra*, note 16.
54. *Ibid.*, 593.
55. *Ibid.*, 592.
56. *Reference re Agricultural Products Marketing Act, supra*, note 15.
57. *Lower Mainland Dairy Products Sales Adjustment Committee* v. *Crystal Dairy*, [1933] AC 168.
58. [1957] SCR 198.
59. *Quebec North Shore Paper Co.* v. *Canadian Pacific, supra*, note 15.
60. *McNamara Construction* v. *The Queen, supra*, note 15.
61. At the time of writing only one case had reached the Supreme Court of Canada, namely, *Tropwood A.G.* v. *Sivaco Wire and Nail Co., supra*, note 20, upholding federal jurisdiction in admiralty.
63. [1978] 1 SCR 152.
64. *A.-G. Que. and Keable,* v. *A.-G. Can.*, [1979] 1 SCR 218.

65. *Supra*, note 20.

66. *Supra*, note 33.

67. *Toronto v. Olympia Edward Recreation Club*, [1955] SCR 454; *Seminary of Chicoutimi v. A.-G. Que.*, [1973] SCR 681; *A.-G. Que. v. Farrah, supra*, note 16.

68. *Tomko v. Labour Relations Bd. (N.S.)*, [1977]1 SCR 112, at p. 120; see also *Reference re Quebec Magistrate's Court*, [1965] SCR 772; *Dupont v. Inglis*, [1958] SCR 535; *Brooks v. Pavlick*, [1964] SCR 108; *Tremblay v. Commission des relations de travail du Québec*, [1967] SCR 697; *Jones v. Edmonton School Trustees*, [1977] 2 SCR 873; *Mississauga v. Peel, supra*, note 20. This pattern of judicial restraint in support of provincial power had been established by the Privy Council in *Labour Relations Bd. (Sask.) v. John East Iron Works*, [1949] AC 134.

69. *Saumur v. City of Quebec*, [1953] 2 SCR 299.

70. [1957] SCR 285.

71. *Reference re Alberta Statutes*, [1938] SCR 100.

72. [1978] 2 SCR 662.

73. [1978] 2 SCR 770.

74. For general discussion, see Hogg, *Constitutional Law*, ch. 6.

75. The leading cases are *Reference re s. 92(4) of the Vehicles Act 1957 (Sask.)*, [1958] SCR 608; *Smith v. The Queen*, [1960] SCR 776; *O'Grady v. Sparling*, [1960] SCR 804; *Stephens v. The Queen*, [1960] SCR 823; *Mann v. The Queen*, [1966] SCR 238; *Ross v. Registrar of Motor Vehicles*, [1975] 1 SCR 5; *Bell v. A.-G. P.E.I.*, [1975] 1 SCR 25; *Robinson v. Countrywide Factors*, [1978] 1 SCR 753; *Construction Montcalm v. Commission du salaire minimum, supra*, note 20.

76. *A.-G. B.C. v. Smith*, [1967] SCR 702; *A.-G. Ont. v. Policy-holders of Wentworth Insurance Co.*, [1969] SCR 779.

77. Hogg, *Constitutional Law*, ch. 6.

78. *Supra*, note 75.

79. *Ibid*. Also, see especially the decisions in *Reference re s. 92(4) of the Vehicles Act 1957 (Sask)*, *Smith v. The Queen* and *Mann v. The Queen, supra*, note 75.

PART TWO

The Social and

Economic

Background

of Canadian

Federalism

Although constitutional law has rightly been a preoccupation for all serious students of Canadian federalism, it is equally obvious that neither the written constitution nor the history of its interpretation by the judiciary can fully explain the way in which Canadian federalism has evolved. John A. Macdonald, the principal architect of Confederation, made no secret of his preference for a unitary rather than a federal state. Soon after Confederation, he confidently predicted that the provincial governments would become insignificant, since most powers had been given to the central government.[1] Not only has this failed to happen, but the provincial governments today enjoy more power than their counterparts in any other federation, with the possible exception of Yugoslavia.

Whether one approves of it or not, this triumph of the provincial governments over Macdonald's plans and predictions requires explanation. While the Judicial Committee of the Privy Council contributed to this outcome, Alan Cairns correctly observed that it "strains credulity" to suggest that their decisions were the only or even the principal contributing factor.[2] Some other explanation, or explanations, must be found.

A persistently popular approach to explaining the relatively decentralized nature of Canadian federalism is one that relates it to the diversity of Canadian society. Henri Joly de Lotbinière, an opponent of Confederation and later Premier of Quebec, sarcastically suggested in 1865 that Canada's symbol should be the rainbow, which had an endless variety of colours, an elongated shape, and no substance.[3] More than a century later, Joe Clark described Canada as a "community of communities." Countless other commentators have rung variations on the same theme. This kind of explanation is plausible, but, like Joly de Lotbinière's rainbow, it lacks substance when examined more closely. Canada is not a particularly diverse country by world standards, or even in comparison to its nearest neighbour, the United States. Furthermore there is no necessary link between diversity and decentralized government. The United Kingdom has more genuine regional diversity than Australia, but the United Kingdom is a unitary state and Australia is a rather decentralized federation. New Mexico, Louisiana, and Minnesota are far more culturally distinctive than Alberta or British Columbia, but "states' rights" are practically defunct as a political issue in the United States, while the demands of Canadian provinces for more autonomy have grown increasingly strident.

A more fruitful explanation would seem to be one that concentrates less on Canada's alleged cultural diversity and more on the structure of its economy. The great economic historian Harold A. Innis emphasized in his work three aspects of Canada's economic development: its reliance on natural resources, the difficulty of extracting those resources due to the vast distances and harshness of the environment, and the resulting reliance of Canada on external markets and sources of capital. Although he was not primarily concerned with politics, and although most of his research concentrated on the period before 1867, Innis made several observations relating the strength of the provincial governments, which was already evident in his lifetime, to these circumstances.[4] Innis's work has greatly influenced scholars of a later generation.

Andrew Jackson's paper, published here for the first time, is an excellent example of the "political economy" approach to political science that became popular in the 1970s. Jackson criticizes Innis for neglecting the importance of class conflict, an omission that is rectified in his own paper, but at the same time his intellectual debt to Innis is obvious. Jackson's purpose is to explain the declining power of the central government and the growing importance of the provinces between 1867 and 1929, an era during which most countries experienced a growth in the power of the central government. He considers various explanations for this phenomenon, including that of Innis, and finds all of them partially valid but insufficient. The missing factor in these explanations, he finds, is class.

Prior to Confederation, the provinces of British North America had generally similar economies, but Confederation and Sir John A. Macdonald's National Policy produced patterns of regional specialization. Some provinces, particularly Ontario, developed economies largely based on manufacturing. Others, such as British Columbia, specialized in extracting and processing natural resources. A third group, the Prairie provinces, specialized in producing agricultural commodities, particularly wheat, for export. Each type of economy developed a characteristic pattern of class relations and class conflict within its own boundaries, and each was related in different ways to Canada as a whole and to the dominant class fraction that controlled finance, commerce, and transportation. Both the industrial capitalists of Ontario and the farmers of the Prairies needed strong provincial governments to express their interests and to perform tasks that the central government in Ottawa was unable or unwilling to perform for them. Neither group was strong enough or numerous enough to unite on a national basis and control the central government. The urban working class was divided, and therefore weak, because in some provinces it joined with industrial capitalists to support high tariffs while in others its interests appeared to have more in common with those of the farmers. Those capitalists who were interested in transportation, banking, and commerce, as opposed to manufacturing, were influential in Ottawa, as they generally are in countries that depend heavily on the export of commodities. However, once the West had been opened to settlement by Confederation and the building of the Canadian Pacific Railway, the interests of this group no longer required a strong central government. They, and the federal government itself, placed few obstacles in the way of growing provincialism, at least prior to the depression that began in 1929.

Harvey Lithwick, an economist at Carleton University, also uses a political economy approach to examine whether federalism is good for regionalism. Lithwick is perhaps closer to the classical political economy tradition of Innis than is Jackson, since the concepts of class and class conflict do not play a significant part in his analysis. While Jackson's analysis is historical, Lithwick's is contemporary. Another difference is that while Jackson is only concerned with explaining the decentralizing tendencies in Canadian federalism, Lithwick seeks to identify and explain both the decentralizing forces and those that have a unifying effect.

Lithwick agrees with Jackson that there are different patterns of economic development in different regions of Canada and that the regional boundaries are largely defined by those differences. However, he disagrees with him by suggesting that the boundaries of the regions cannot be equated even approximately with those of the ten provinces. The provincial boundaries are essentially irrelevant to genuine economic regionalism, although they may have been relevant to it at the time when Confederation took place. Thus federalism, meaning the existence of provincial governments with powers guaranteed by the constitution, is not really good for regionalism because it does not represent regions as such. Most of the provinces incorporate two distinct regions: a metropolitan centre that trades in goods and services with other metropolitan centres in Canada, and a rural hinterland that specializes in extracting natural resources and shipping them mainly to foreign markets. The metropolitan centres are linked to one another on an East-West basis, reinforcing Canadian unity. The resource hinterlands, as Innis noted half a century ago, have few ties with one another but are closely linked with their markets and sources of capital in the United States. They thus produce tendencies toward provincial autonomy. The balance between these two sets of forces explains the survival of Canada as a decentralized, but still united, federal state.

This analysis seems to explain some Canadian political phenomena not referred to in the article itself. The Prairie populist movements of the interwar period, which challenged the National Policy, arose in the rural areas and had little impact on the cities. Social Credit in British Columbia, with its strident provincialism, arose and had its greatest strength in the resource-producing outback of the province, while Vancouver remained the stronghold of the provincial Liberals and New Democrats. In the Quebec referendum of 1980 Montreal surprised many observers by rejecting sovereignty-association and voting for federalism, even in neighbourhoods where there were few Anglophones. The resource-extracting constituencies in northern Quebec did vote for sovereignty-association in the referendum and gave strong support to the Parti Québécois in the elections of 1981 and 1985.

The last two articles, by Quebec political scientists Anne Legaré and Gérard Boismenu, are both explicitly Marxist in their approach. While a somewhat adulterated version of Marxism has gained a foothold in the social science faculties of Anglophone Canadian universities, its influence on Québécois social science has been much greater. This phenomenon may be attributed partly to the weakness of American intellectual influences in Quebec, partly to the perception that Quebec was an oppressed and colonized nation, and partly to the fact that the social sciences in Quebec developed very late and had little indigenous tradition.

While Marxism had its attractions for Quebec academics, the attractions of nationalism, which has far deeper roots in Quebec, were considerably stronger. The obsession with the "national question" and the belief (until the referendum of 1980) that Quebec was progressing inexorably toward independence led Quebec social scientists, whether Marxist or not, to concentrate almost exclusively on their own province. Quebec was analysed in isolation, as though it were already the sovereign state that most of its intelligentsia wished it to become.

The articles by Legaré and Boismenu were both written after the referendum and after the Canadian constitution had been amended and "patriated" on the initiative of Prime Minister Trudeau and over the objections of the Quebec government. These events suggested that Quebec could not in fact be considered in isolation from the rest of Canada, and the two articles explicitly repudiate the assumption that it could be. The subject matter of the articles also suggests an increased interest in, although not necessarily affection for, Canadian federalism.

Anne Legaré begins by distinguishing between the form of the state and the form of the regime. By the form of the state she means the relationship that exists between economics and politics: mature capitalism requires a more interventionist type of state, with a broader range of functions, than the primitive capitalism of John A. Macdonald's era. The modern Canadian state is of the same form as those of other advanced capitalist countries. Federalism is merely the form of the regime, which is of secondary importance. The changing form of the state (from laissez faire to interventionism) has had an impact on the regime (federalism) but the form of the regime also has an impact on the evolution of the state. The state's tendency toward interventionism is evident at both levels of government, and the fact that the regime requires certain functions to be performed at the provincial level has implications for the exercise of class power.

Like most contemporary Marxist scholars, Legaré emphasizes the notion of the relative autonomy of the state. This means that, while the state must reproduce the conditions conducive to the survival of the capitalist economy, its policies are not literally dictated by the capitalist class, let alone by individual capitalists. To pursue the long-term interests of capitalism, and to retain the loyalty and support of the population, the state must have some degree of independence. Legaré suggests that federalism contributes positively to this requirement by making the relationship between class power and the state more complex and less visible. On the other hand, federalism may be counterproductive, from a capitalist point of view, if it makes it more difficult for the state to perform essential tasks such as responding to an economic crisis.

Legaré's interpretation of the controversies over the constitution between 1980 and 1982 is based on these assumptions, and also on the notion that the power bloc (the alliance of economic and political power whose influence is ultimately decisive) is the synthesis of the power relations operating at the federal level and in each of the ten provinces. Constitutional changes are one means by which the nature of this synthesis can be readjusted from time to time. The need for a more interventionist form of state, according to Legaré, was the basic reason for the constitutional changes of 1982, although the outcome of the Quebec referendum facilitated the changes. The governments of the Anglophone provinces accepted the changes because those governments did not represent fundamentally different interests from those represented by the federal government.

Although the Quebec government opposed the constitutional changes, Legaré argues that "bourgeois" Quebec nationalism (in which category she includes the Parti Québécois) is compatible with Canadian federalism and may actually help to perpetuate it. Legaré doubts that the regionalism of Anglophone Canada, in the absence of Quebec, would be strong enough to prevent Canada from becoming a *de facto* unitary state.

Gérard Boismenu's essay covers some of the same ground, asserting even more emphatically than does Legaré that Quebec cannot be considered in isolation from the Canadian state and society of which it is a part. This perception does not make him a federalist; in fact, he insists that the Québécois suffer from "national oppression" and that this fact makes Quebec nationalism qualitatively different from the provincialism of the other provinces. At the same time, Boismenu appears to take the provincialism of Anglophone Canada more seriously than does Legaré. It is interesting that of the six propositions that form the heart of his analysis of Canadian federalism, only one refers specifically to Quebec.

Boismenu is critical of a type of analysis that allegedly underestimates the interdependence of the two levels of government and the strength of the federal level. According to Boismenu, the Canadian capitalist class does not lack strength and cohesion when its fundamental interests are at stake, and it is far more than the sum of provincial capitalist classes with distinct and conflicting interests. Furthermore, Boismenu asserts, it is misleading to assert an instrumental relationship between particular class fractions and particular governments or levels of government. The reality is one of complex and overlapping alliances and of governments that enjoy a large degree of relative autonomy.

These assertions by Boismenu have considerable merit. Still, Boismenu concedes that each "regional space" in Canada has a somewhat distinctive pattern of class relations and political alliances, and that a particular class or class fraction may have more influence over one government, or one level of government, than over others. Thus the objectives of governments may conflict in ways that reflect these differences. Even Quebec's relations with the federal government can be largely explained in this manner, although "national oppression" gives them an additional dimension not found in the other provinces. As Boismenu notes, the "national question" also makes it easier for the Quebec government than for other provincial governments to mobilize public opinion in support of its demands.

Although Boismenu's analysis is difficult and at times excessively verbose, it deserves careful study as a subtle and sophisticated effort to explain the dynamics of federalism and regionalism in terms of Marxist categories. He has used the same analytical framework in a book-length study of Quebec under Maurice Duplessis. For Anglophone students who use this anthology the Legaré and Boismenu essays may serve as an introduction to an unfamiliar world: the vigorous tradition of neo-Marxist social science in Canada's other official language.

Notes

1. Joseph Pope, ed., *Correspondence of Sir John Macdonald* (Toronto, 1921), 74-75.
2. Cairns, in this volume, p. 81.
3. Quoted in Frank H. Underhill, *In Search of Canadian Liberalism* (Toronto, 1961), ii.
4. Harold A. Innis, *Essays in Canadian Economic History* (Toronto, 1956), 209, 236, 251, 279, 317-18.

6. ANDREW JACKSON

Divided Dominion:

Class and the Structure of

Canadian Federalism from

the National Policy

to the Great Depression

Introduction: The Structure of Federalism and the Economic Role of the State

The state structure created at Confederation was a compromise between several objectives, but those forces pressing for a centralized variant of federalism were to be successful in making the minimum possible concessions to Quebec and Maritime "particularism." Material imperatives largely took precedence over cultural heterogeneity. Imperial commercial interests, the exigencies of welding the disparate colonial relics of a superseded mercantilism into a unified national market, and orchestration of the expansion of Canadian commercial empire to the West tended in a single direction and effectively dictated a Dominion monopoly of all important economic powers in an age when the purposes of the state were pre-eminently material.[1] The nation-building role assumed by the state in the Macdonald-Laurier period demanded the active exercise of those powers beneath the rubric of the National Policy and its associated instruments. The result was a federal system that, by the 1880s, was such as to "exclude the provinces from interfering with the direction, control and operation of the economy."[2] While it would be misleading to talk of a centralized state in the period before World War One, the Dominion was clearly pre-eminent in terms of substantive state action and constituted the principal focus of political conflict concerning those issues germane to economic development.[3]

It has been argued by the "political economy tradition"[4] that this outcome was determined by the specific contextual circumstances that granted a distinctly "statist" flavour to Canadian capitalism.[5] Mobilization of credit in conditions of capital shortage, varied forms of participation in infrastructural development, the alienation of natural resources to bring them within the orbit of market relations, transportation and tariff policies to promote East-West economic integration, and tentative attempts to promote industrialization were the central economic functions of the Dominion in the "heroic period" and underlay its relative dominance. If the role of the state was one almost akin to "strategic economic planning,"[6] the dynamic of development of these functions has been variously interpreted with reference to the exigencies of dependent capitalist development (Innis), "nationalist imperatives" (Creighton, Aitken), or the accumulation needs of a dominant financial commercial bourgeoisie (Naylor). Each of these interpretations implies a specification of the manner in which a changing field of economic forces, largely defined in relation to the issue of dependency, would ultimately serve to influence the structure of the state. Despite differences of emphasis and interpretation, the common defining categories of political economy rooted in staples theory have stressed the crucial weight of economic forces in shaping the institutional anatomy of government and have sought to relate concretely state functions to state structure. It is the central purpose of this paper to discuss these perspectives insofar as they bear upon the changing character of federalism, and on that basis to outline the manner in which the economic and class structure created within the pre-World War One path of national capitalist development served to help "fragment" or "disaggregate" the state by the interwar period. In broad terms it is argued that there is a need for a shift of emphasis within political economy toward a view of the state as the product of political class conflict.

Two qualifications concerning this approach should be made at the outset. First, it is not held that socio-cultural factors – and, most centrally, the internal national cleavage[7] – were without importance in shaping federal state institutions. Interpretations stressing the manifest heterogeneity of Canadian social relations as expressed in the salience of the "limited identities"[8] of nation, region, and ethnicity have sought the anatomy of the state within a plural society that promises an always contentious survival-oriented unity in diversity.[9] While this dominant perspective discounts the material and class bases of regionalism and expresses an implicitly celebratory functionalist view of federalism as an *integrative* mechanism,[10] it may be acknowledged that the forces shaping Canadian federalism were not those of economy and class *tout court*. Here it is argued only that the nature of dependent capitalist development and the consequent patterns of political class conflict concerning the economic role of the state were of central and critical importance. Further, the development of the institutional structure of the state in the period cannot be analytically isolated from its substantive role as an economic agent.[11]

Second, the evolution of federalism cannot be explained without an appreciation of the independent effects of inherited governmental institutions in shaping the expression of political conflict. As historical-institutionalists have cogently argued, the prior existence of a federal political system has served to grant plural points of access to the political process and a high degree of expression to regional interests through provincial governments.[12] Province-building signified the emergent phenomenon through which the regions came to play an active role in their own development by steadily extending their areas of constitutional competence into the economic field, broadly construed, and access to an expanding revenue base.[13] Federalism was to be manifestly shaped by the actions of plural mini-states that were important actors in their own right.[14] The dynamic impelling or pre-figuring such developments cannot, however, be best grasped with reference to the peculiarities of the Canadian constitutional structure but must be situated against the existence of a highly "disarticulated" economic and class structure, considered in regional terms.

What serves to mark off the Canadian experience in any comparative perspective is the marked attenuation of the powers of the Dominion in an era when the expansion of government has ineluctably led to concentration and centralization.[15] While Canadian state spending on current account alone rose from 4 per cent to 15 per cent of GNP during the period 1870-1933,[16] the Dominion share fell from over 50 per cent to a mere quarter by the latter year.[17] In the 1920s public expenditure on capital account constituted some 30 per cent of domestic capital formation,[18] of which the federal government accounted for only about one-third.[19] Most strikingly, federal current-account spending fell by 20 per cent from 1921 to 1926, while provincial expenditures increased by almost 50 per cent.[20] By 1921 total provincial departmental employment was 50 per cent greater than that of the Dominion.[21] This relative decentralization within a process of very pronounced governmental expansion (non-military state spending in the 1920s being broadly comparable to the 1950s level) in turn coincided with what might be termed state "disaggregation."

Clearly, by the Great Depression the party system could only with difficulty constitute the factor of cohesion within the state. The dominant national two-party division was reproduced only on the Maritime periphery and, in a far more problematic fashion given the character of Hepburn liberalism, in Ontario.[22] Emergent fragmentation as expressed through overt federal-provincial conflict had existed since the days of Mercier and Mowat and came to concern issues of economic policy in the struggle over Manitoba railway legislation in the 1880s and in the pronounced tension between pre-World War One Ontario conservatism and Laurier liberalism.

The fight for better terms by B.C. and the Maritimes and western dissatisfaction over the resources question, among others, were standard features
of Canadian political life from an early period. Such conflict did, however,
reach unprecedented heights in the depression with the emergence of
strong and assertive provincial governments under the varied populist
auspices of Pattullo, Aberhart, Hepburn, and Duplessis, whose intransigence led in large part to the search for a new federal formula with the
appointment of the Rowell-Sirois Commission.

By at least the 1920s the vision of a centralized variant of federalism had
clearly faded as the nation that had indeed been built seemed to find its
truest reflection in the ascendant and innovative provincial governments
and, emergently, within the substantively rather inert edifice of King liberalism. The future government party might mediate a host of antagonisms
with considerable political finesse to preserve unity, but it would barely
begin even to contemplate a new vision of the role of the state that would
push the Dominion to the fore. Bennett's belated and half-hearted attempt
to do so ended in a defeat that all but annihilated his party for a generation.
Considered together, these developments clearly mark off the Canadian
experience from that of even broadly comparable federal states such as
Australia, let alone the wider world of democratic capitalist states. As
noted above, the origins of fragmentation may be located in the historical
specificities of Canadian capitalist development and in the structure of
economic and class conflicts it engendered. These issues may be best
approached through a critical discussion of the theoretical perspectives of
Canadian political economy.

Dependent Capitalism and the State

By placing the dialectic of state and economy as encountered within the
unique defining circumstances of Canadian historical development at the
centre of its analysis, the political economy perspective has put forward the
most powerful existing explanation of the evolution of the state structure.
It will, however, be noted that an implicit centralism in part discounted the
importance of federalism within the classical tradition's view of the state, a
lacuna that has not been rectified within the recent translation of staples
theory into the new political economy. Further, a degree of economic
determinism and of class-based functionalism has relatively downplayed
the role of class *conflict* in shaping state institutions.

"Classical" political economy may be usefully divided into two interrelated modes of analysis associated with Innisian staples theory and the
schema of nation-building Laurentian historiography it served to inform.
Taken together, the two united in a coherent synthesis the dynamic or
independent logic of a national economy based on the development of
staples trades in response to external forces, the specifically economic role
of the state, and the federal state structure in the period before World War

One. Very schematically, the relatively centralized state[23] performing the functions briefly alluded to above was necessary to create an integrated transcontinental staples-based economy on the Laurentian axis in conditions given by the external field of forces on the North Atlantic triangle. In short, state economic orchestration of development was central to the evolution of the Canadian political economy, by contrast to the liberal model of capitalist development. The key question is to discuss the manner in which the pronounced economic role of the state has been explained to isolate the dynamic of change within the state structure.

For Innis, the fundamental relation between the economic structure and state action is one of functional determination by the exigencies of staples production in "new" countries as shaped by the market forces of the metropole and their export of capital and technique. Staple economies are subject to a dependent logic of development. They must maximize their opportunities by rapidly expanding staples production in response to external market demand and investment. This subordinate relationship is continuously reproduced as the rigidities encountered as the product on one period of expansion constrain further development along the staples path, which constitutes the cutting edge of economic growth.[24] In large detail the role of the state is that of a credit instrument, creating the necessary conditions for expansion (infrastructural development, assistance to domestic capital formation) and orchestrating shifts in the orientation of the economy in response to a changing field of external forces.[25] Policies and the structure of state institutions are in essence the given requirements of a particular path of expansion cemented about the character of the dominant staple.[26] The state may also *contingently* perform a *regulative* function to counter the inherent instability of an economy dependent on fluctuating external demand and investment and subject to the rapid drawing off of resources without lasting benefit to the domestic economy. Boundary conditions surrounding the development of new countries do permit some flexibility to promote diversification on the basis of the growth of the national market and the construction of forward linkages, i.e., the further processing of the staple prior to export.[27]

Innis is, however, fundamentally an economic determinist and the state is granted a highly limited degree of flexibility given the defining market context of dependency, the exigencies of financing external debt, infrastructural rigidities created in past periods of expansion, and the structure of state finance.[28] Thus his marked "dehumanization"[29] of history brilliantly specifies what may be termed the accumulation function of the state as encountered within the process of dependent capitalist development and convincingly delimits the objective structural constraints surrounding the role of the state. However, Innis remains largely silent concerning the role of specifically *political* action in working within or upon those constraints. Also, his structural model makes no attempt to account for or even notice the existence of class relations as an intervening factor between the needs of economic development and state action.

For Aitken and Creighton, by contrast, the patterns of state action are understood with reference to the staples dynamic, broadly understood, but the state as an economic agent acts according to a nationalist imperative.[30] Defensive expansionism (Confederation and the National Policy) was directed to the creation of the material pre-conditions for the continued political independence of British North America within the political and economic context of the North Atlantic triangle. An integrated transcontinental economy constructed on the Laurentian axis, also supportive of the political and economic relation to the British Empire, had to be constructed to counter the threat of American continental expansion and to unite the disparate economic interests of the scattered colonies. As Aitken argues with reference to the key economic role of the Dominion: " . . . the overall objective of the policy was to make possible the maintenance of Canadian political sovereignty . . . and to build a national state that could guide its own economic destiny . . . *within limits no more restrictive than those necessarily applicable to an economy dependent upon staple exports.*"[31]

The central question is posed as one of precisely how restrictive those limits were, and to what extent state action would seek to *counter* rather than to promote relations of dependent development. The acid test of the nationalist basis of the Canadian state[32] would lie in its response to the changing field of external forces as the dominant metropolitan influences on the staples-based national economy became the continental rather than the British Imperial nexus.[33]

The thrust of the Innis argument is that new opportunities would be responded to via appropriate readjustments. Hence the "colony to nation . . . to colony" depiction of Canadian history as one of transition between two forms of external dependency based on the logic of development of the hinterland's staples-based economic structure. Continental economic integration and the displacement of an East-West by a North-South axis of development would strengthen regionalism and the importance of the provinces as economic agents performing the requisite new functions to sustain a new form of expansion. The accumulation function would be displaced from the Dominion to the provinces, given their control of the new resources demanded by an ascendant American empire.[34]

The defensive expansionist thesis was developed with close reference to the heroic nation-building period before World War One and thus inadequately sustains the view of the role of the state as consistently nationalist in economic terms. The view that "[e]ach phase of expansion in Canada has been a tactical move designed to forestall, counteract or restrain the northward extension of American economic and political influence"[35] remains largely unsupported with reference to the interwar period, which saw the rise of the new staples industries. These decades saw the active promotion of precisely such American influence by the state, largely in the form of the provinces, and certainly did see the assertion of a coherent national economic policy to succeed the completed objectives of the Macdonald and Laurier governments.[36]

This *relative* abdication of the economic field by the Dominion has been noted and vilified by nationalists such as Creighton. Viewed as an effect of petty Liberal provincialism and inherent Quebec parochialism that served to undermine the essentially unitary vision of Confederation, such fragmentation is not coherently related to emergent tensions within the earlier integrated national political economy. It is precisely for that reason that nation-building perspectives do little to illuminate the structural trans-formation of the post-National Policy political economy.[37] Economic nationalism in retrospect was, in large part, a function of the dominance of the British Imperial nexus. Against the nationalist and centralist perspec-tive, even in the heroic period the economic policies of the provinces could be no more defensive or regulative in relation to the thrust of American expansion than the Dominion would willingly countenance. The economic nationalism of Macdonald conservatism is itself highly suspect given the tariff policy's explicit objective of promoting American branch-plant man-ufacturing investment.[38] In short, an excessive "politicism," which views the economic role of the state as pre-eminently directed to sustaining the material basis for national integration and independence, is unable to comprehend adequately the dynamic of state economic action within the context of dependent capitalist development.

The New Political Economy and the State

The "new political economy" most closely associated with the important work of Naylor[39] has taken these deficiencies of the classical tradition as its point of departure while building on the central insights of Innis. Akin to Innis, the dynamic of development of the political economy and of the state structure is broadly understood as a consequence of the logic of staples production, which is theorized as a specific form of capitalist development. The critical thrust of re-interpretation is directed to estab-lishing the logic of development of the economic and political structure in terms of class. The specific character of the dominant class becomes the missing variable in the framework of Innisian determinism and the key to the ambiguous nationalism of the Canadian state.

Within Naylor's terms, the economic functions of the state are not viewed as simple effects of structural dependency but as expressions of the accumulation needs of a dominant financial-commercial "comprador" bourgeoisie. Mediation of the relations of exchange between the domestic and external markets that define the cutting edge of dependent capitalist development serves to create a dominant fraction of capital that extracts

surplus within the sphere of circulation rather than through direct participation in production.[40] This attempt to "stand Creighton on his feet"[41]
stresses the unity of centralist and dominant class objectives in the
Confederation-National Policy period, given the defining stuctural framework of the British Imperial nexus and the dominance of the wheat staple,
which created the market and investment-based metropolitan "pull" to
weld the new state into an integrated transcontinental economy. East-West
economic integration was founded on the construction of a third commercial empire of the St. Lawrence through the joint action of the state,
indigenous Canadian capital in the sphere of circulation, and British commercial capital. The dominant class created in Canada within the context
of dependent capitalist development would, however, be only contingently
nationalist, that is, directed to sustaining East-West integration, and it
would be ultimately determinant of the direction of development. The
logic of Canadian history is the logic of the truncated horizons of its
dominant class.[42]

A mercantile-financial bourgeoisie, created within the nexus of
exchange relations between the centre and the periphery of the world
economy, adjusts to the new needs of the metropolitan power and organizes the shifts of investment and infrastructural development from one
export staple to another. It further undertakes to mediate the changing
relations between the domestic economy and a changing external order.
The function of mediation in the sphere of circulation underlies the reproduction of relations of dependent capitalist development because there is
no impetus to transform mercantile into industrial capital. Industrial capitalism, which would perform the progressive role of deepening and divers-
ifying the economic structure, is "strangled."[43] The developmental needs of
the two forms of capital are ultimately contradictory, easy credit, low
transportation costs, and cheap raw materials defining the prerequisites of
industrialism that were denied by financial-mercantile dominance *encountered in both the economic and political spheres.*

Lacking a dynamic for the industrialization that could have countered
dependency, the Canadian political economy made an easy transition from
the British to the continental orbit. American *direct* investment in the new
natural resources industries and branch-plant manufacturing created a
new *modus vivendi* between indigenous and foreign capital. Relatively
separated within the discrete economic spheres of production and circulation, there was little conflict of purposes between them. Most importantly,
this transition eroded the material basis of national integration given the
increasingly salient North-South axis of trade and investment, the consequent creation of discrete regional economies, and the rise of competition
among the provinces as each sought a greater share of the inflow of foreign
capital. These factors eroded the paramount economic role of the Dominion, which was a feature of the period of British metropolitan dominance.

The fall of the third commercial empire of the St. Lawrence thus saw the rise of direct linkages between the provinces, holding jurisdictional authority over the new staples, and American capital. Thus, "(t)he new staple industries and the rise of branch plant industrialism provided the provincial governments with the means to regain the financial powers they had been robbed of by Confederation."[44] Such concentrations of direct investment "tend to fragment national markets and balkanize the state structure."[45] Thus, for Naylor, "(t)rends in the federal-provincial division of effective power during this century reflect little more than the ratio of American direct to British portfolio investment."[46] From the Innis-Naylor perspective the rise of the provinces from at least the eary 1920s was first and foremost a reflection of the transition of the Canadian political economy between two forms of external dependency.[47] The relative diminution of the economic role of the Dominion expressed the lack of a need on the part of the dominant classes to perpetuate the relatively centralized state structure that had been necessary to promote expansion in the pre-World War One period. Thus the theory of dependent capitalist development and its associated view of the state, unlike alternative perspectives, coherently explains both the period of centralization and that of disaggregation from a theoretical specification of the nature of state *economic action within the context of peripheral capitalism.*

Dependent Capitalism and the State: A Critique

This perspective is of central importance in situating the changing structure of the state against the background of the changing field of economic forces defining the nature of Canadian development. However, an adequate theory of the state and of federalism must further bring the dynamic of political conflict to the fore. This has been relatively downplayed within the political economy tradition as a whole with the signal exception of the hinterland theorists.[48]

While for Creighton and others the structure of the state is grasped as a function of nation-building and for left nationalists as a function of dominant class needs, both share a nationalist-based centralism that at least implicitly accords an illegitimacy to "provincialism." The latter appears as either divisive in the face of external domination or as the product of continentalism.[49] In historical terms this centralism is reflected in defining the dynamic of institutional development with reference to imperatives defined at the centre, rather than in terms of the patterns of economic and political conflict between that centre and the *internal* peripheries. Yet, the tensions characteristic of the period of national economic "unity" and integration that *preceded* continentalism served equally to undermine the vision of a centralized state. As Mallory and Macpherson[50] have argued, Western agrarian revolt against a centre that fused the power of the Dominion with commercial and financial interests expressed subordinate class interests that found an important point of expression at the provincial level. Agrarian political action encountered the limits of the national two-party consensus and thus increasingly turned to the province as a more accessible means of redress against external domination. Effective hegemony at the provincial level was in turn expressed in the demand for widened provincial powers. While this perspective was in a sense the mirror image of Laurentian centralism – viewing the National Policy from the critical standpoint of the wheat economy's periphery – such an analysis may be extended to the rise in importance of the other provinces. Regionally based fractions of business, farmers, and labour could, in certain circumstances, find their interests bound to the extension of provincial powers given the close ties between the Dominion and the nationally dominant financial-commercial class that had created an East-West integrated economy in its own image.

To be sure, continentalism and regionalism are closely associated phenomena, but the latter was as much the product of a particular form of unity as it was of the former. The advent of continental integration served to reinforce rather than create a regionally disarticulated national economy. Further, the evolution of class relations was a product of the path development took before continentalism, and the impact of the latter must be understood within those terms. The assertion of provincial economic powers had its origins in the period before World War One, and in part had an anti-continentalist thrust, as in Ontario's nationalization of American hydroelectric interests. This action, among others, encountered federal opposition. A focus on the linkages between the provinces and American capital may thus discount the crucial role of regionally based business in defining integration on its own terms, at both the national and international levels. Province-building entailed mediation of the emergent North-South axis of development and the assertion of policies in opposition to the imperatives defined at the centre. Certainly as Innis, Drache, Naylor, and others have argued, dependent capitalism largely defined the accumulation function of the state in terms of its response to the changing external development. Further, this function would be increasingly displaced to the provinces with the emergent continentalism based on the new resource industries under their jurisdiction. So long as the cutting edge of capital formation underpinning the development of the economy as a whole remained situated in relation to the development of the international sector, expanded staples development in the context of American expansion would certainly serve to reinforce provincialism. However, the economic role of the state, as Innis noted, would not be *just* defined in relation to staples development since a regulative function could be contingently performed in order to promote diversification and industrialization. As Naylor demonstrates, such regulation would entail conflict between the industrial and financial-commercial fractions of capital. In very large detail he argues that no such conflict took place since indigenous industrial capital was so weak as to be practically non-existent as a political force. By contrast, it is argued here that such conflict did exist among other cleavages and was important in shaping the structure of federalism. An overemphasis on the accumulation function of the state as shaped by dependency and the political hegemony of financial-commercial capital tends to downplay the regulative functions within the economy. This important dimension of state economic action sought to counter the logic of development of market forces in the interests of specific constituencies and emerged as an outcome of political conflict over economic policy.

Canadian Capital and Canadian Industry

Though no extended discussion of the issues involved is possible here, staples theory and the dependency model generally have discounted the extent of indigenous Canadian industrialization in the period under consideration. As will be noted below, the interpenetration of the international and domestic sectors of the economy had important implications concerning the structure of class relations and patterns of conflict over state economic policy. The growth of domestic industry has, however, been little studied within a dominant framework of economic historiography founded on staples theory.

After the implementation of the National Policy tariffs and the extension of numerous state bounties and subsidies to manufacturing, the gross value of production in secondary manufacturing grew by over 50 per cent from 1880 to 1890[51] and by a further 150 per cent from 1890 to 1910.[52] Again doubling over the World War One period, which had a pronounced expansionary effect, such production reached $1 billion by 1919 and expanded further, by more than one-third, in the brief boom of the later 1920s. Over the period as a whole, secondary manufacturing increased by a substantial factor of 14, somewhat higher than that of primary manufacturing (largely export staples).[53] As early as 1920, secondary manufacturing accounted for more than one-quarter of national income.[54] The manufacturing labour force more than doubled, 1880-1920, and grew slowly in the later 1920s to reach 666,000 by 1929.[55] Concentration of industry was particularly marked in the pre-World War One period, the number of businesses declining by more than 75 per cent during the 1890-1915 period.[56] A number of recent studies by labour historians point to the associated creation of a specifically industrial working-class over the same period.[57]

This evidence, as well as the suggestive accounts contained in company histories and the contemporary business press, suggests the classical features of capitalist industrialization: uneven rhythms of expansion followed by contraction and concentration.[58] The second generation of late nineteenth-century industrialism was created by Canadian capital, dominant in such industries as iron and steel, textiles, agriculture implement production, and transportation equipment, including railway rolling stock. To be sure, the new industries of the post-World War One period (autos, rubber, chemicals, electrical goods) were often under the control of American branch plants, but by 1929 American capital controlled "only" about a quarter of all manufacturing.[59] The central point is simply that Canadian industrial capital grew substantially with the expansion of the western and northern hinterlands and the domestic market. While undoubtedly subordinate within the economic structure as a whole, which remained highly dependent on integration within the world economy,[60] the domestic manufacturing sector was hardly unimportant. Given the objective structural constraints on industrialization specified by dependency theorists, attention here is drawn to the need for supportive state action and to the possibility of political conflict between those pressing for industrial policies and the dominant financial-commercial class. Before we consider the implications this held for federalism, a schematic depiction of the Canadian economic and class structure as created by the path of development set in motion by the nation-building role of the Dominion should be outlined.

Economic Structure and Class Structure

Schematically, by the 1920s the economic structure created in Canada by the wheat economy and emergent industrialization contained two distinct economic sectors resting in part on different relations of production. Commodity production by individuals in the internationally oriented agrarian sphere co-existed with capitalist relations of production in the resource, industrial, and manufacturing sectors. The latter were themselves divided between sectors oriented to international and domestic markets. These sectoral divisions could underline differences within both the "dominant" and "subordinate" classes and serve to create different class coalitions at the political level.

A key element of the international sector rested on agrarian production by individual farmers (the wheat economy), a relatively homogeneous class compared to the more polarized agrarian class structures characteristic of export economies. Given that financial and commercial profit was at the direct expense of the farmer who needed to minimize costs, opposition between farmers and the banks, the railway companies, and the grain companies defined the most important axis of class conflict generated from within the early pattern of economic development. It was, of course, a conflict with a pronounced regional dimension, and the forms it took were to be of some importance in shaping the pattern of state institutions.[61]

Despite the development of the wheat economy by centralized capital owned and controlled in the domestic metropoles of Montreal and, to a lesser extent, Toronto, smaller commercial capital did exist in the West. The Winnipeg business community in particular had developmental objectives that could conflict with those of eastern capital.[62] Massive infrastructural development associated with creating and maintaining the wheat economy also demanded the creation of a western working class in construction and transportation (a high component of the Canadian labour force from the late nineteenth century to the 1920s). Frequently highly mobile and in the process of accumulating savings to purchase land, labour was by no means absent from the western hinterland.

The second major element in the international sector was production in the new staples industries. Resource industry capital in forestry, pulp and paper, and mining had varied origins. In a capital-intensive sector it frequently (though by no means predominantly) relied on American investment, which carried with it market access, or on the large pools of Canadian capital in the financial-commercial sphere, for example, the early entry of the CPR into mining and of Toronto finance into northern Ontario. In any case, the new staples sector was characterized by sharp antagonism between labour and capital. Again, this antagonism had a pronounced regional dimension with traditions of labour militancy on the resource frontier, particularly in British Columbia, being defined through a structure of class relations more crudely exploitative than was the case in manufacturing production.

The domestic sector of the economy contained secondary manufacturing industry geared to the production of both consumer and producer goods. Growth and concentration steadily eliminated the artisanal basis of earlier industrial production from at least the 1850s and created a skilled and unskilled working-class.[67] The relatively limited size of the secondary manufacturing sector and the capital-intensive character of industrialization in a context where mature techniques were available militated against the emergence of a numerically predominant manufacturing-sector working class. Indeed, from an early period industrialization expanded the white-collar section of the labour force and the service sector at a relatively more rapid rate, a phenomenon common to North American industrialization.[64] The existence of a surplus agrarian population in both Ontario and Quebec and high levels of immigration, as well as a pronounced boom-bust cycle of development, created a particularly fluid labour market that tended to militate against the organization of all but the skilled working class. Ethnic and religious divisions – and the internal national division – militated against the emergence of a politically cohesive industrial proletariat. Nevertheless, labour was of some political importance, as will be discussed below.

The relation of financial-commercial to industrial capital in the period from the late nineteenth century to the 1920s is problematic. Certainly there was some tension between the two before the merger wave of the pre-World War One slump,[65] and closer interpenetration as a result of industrial growth did not overcome the division in any absolute sense. The origins of Canadian industrialization frequently saw the rapid growth of small-scale production on the basis of accumulation and re-investment of capital, as in the growth of Massey-Harris – Marx's "revolutionary path" of capitalist development, which was rather more typical of the period before the merger wave than was the entry of mercantile capital into industrial production. At a later stage, expansion relied on access to large pools of financial capital, as in the Stelco merger. The political objectives of finance and industry could be in conflict, given the primary orientation of the former to the expansion of the international sector and its particularly close links to foreign capital. As Naylor has underlined, the contradiction between staples development and national industrial development would serve to create at least the possibility of political cleavages within business. This problem will be examined in greater detail below.

The regionally heterogeneous consequences of the path of development cemented through the National Policy were particularly marked. The Maritimes were largely isolated from the thrust of expansion as early industrialization was annihilated by competition and concentration from the early twentieth century on[66] and as the old staples industries shaped within the structure of British mercantilism began their long decline. As Naylor demonstrates, the savings of the region flowed out to the more dynamic sectors of the economy and left behind an increasingly marginalized economic structure based on farming, fisheries, and forestry. Apart from the Cape Breton industrial complex, employment opportunities were substantially lacking and resulted in widespread migration.

Secondary manufacturing was concentrated in southern Ontario and Quebec (about 80 per cent of production from the 1890s) in a near-constant proportion of 3:2, and was based primarily on a low-wage, labour-intensive specialization, particularly in the more competitive sector of consumer goods production (boots and shoes, textiles, clothing). These two provinces, like B.C., were also at the forefront of the development of the new staples industries from the early twentieth century, with development in Quebec occurring somewhat later. Though Quebec was rather more "backward" in terms of the character of the manufacturing sector and the mechanization and market orientation of agriculture, the picture of a traditional agrarian society resisting industrialization is pure myth. The pace of urbanization lagged only slightly behind that of Ontario while the agrarian sector was itself transformed between the late nineteenth century and the 1920s.[67] Though there were certainly differences between the class structures of the two provinces in terms of the composition of both business and the working class, these were clearly of secondary importance to cultural differences in shaping political patterns.

Outside the central core, the western hinterland's economy was dominated by the different forms of staples production. While the monolithic character of the wheat economy has been overstated, it was dominant on the Prairies, though ranching and coal mining were of importance in Alberta, and Winnipeg was a commercial and industrial sub-metropole with a local business class and a substantial working class. Even in the "company province" of British Columbia, whose industrial staples-based development created the most urbanized and class-divided regional economy of the 1920s, the existence and importance of indigenous capital cannot be discounted. This was particularly the case in the forestry industry and in spheres ancillary to staples production. Certainly the dependent position of the western hinterland was, within the context of a federal democratic state, subject to political redress. The economic dynamism of the region and its extraordinarily rapid development created the conditions for an assertion of provincial powers in response to a number of forces that might in certain instances challenge the external domination of central Canadian capital. This development largely failed to take place on the Maritime periphery, where the struggle for equal rights took the form of demands for increased federal subsidies and adjustments of freight rates but was rarely expressed in activist policies of economic development by the provincial governments.

One important point that deserves to be underlined is that the economic structure of Canada as a whole was dominated by agrarian production until well into the period under consideration, the transition from a predominantly rural to an urban society taking place only in the early 1920s. Again, agrarian class structures were defined on a distinctively regional basis. The uneven transition to mixed farming in Ontario and Quebec generated by industrialization and urbanization frequently depended on a high capitalization and created a less homogeneous farmer constituency than was the case in the West. Certainly the market orientation of western and eastern farmers was distinct, as was their relative susceptibility to the economic cycle and to the decisions of highly centralized forms of financial and commercial capital.

The industrial development that increasingly eroded a predominantly rural society was located in the largely discrete sectors of manufacturing and resource development, and in both cases was heavily dependent on the state action. The agrarian constituency could and did regard such state preference with considerable antipathy. The most salient issues of economic policy with which the state as a whole would have to deal concerned, then, not just the relation between the domestic and international sectors, that is, dependency versus national industrial development, but also the relation between the agrarian and industrial sectors. This issue under pinned the most significant political class conflict of the period and, though other antagonisms were of importance, they were in turn shaped by it. In summary, divisions within a regionally and sectorally disarticulated national economy were the product of the particular path of development begun by the National Policy and the establishment of the wheat economy.

These divisions could only be reinforced by the emergence of a North-South axis of dependency, but they were hardly the product of continental-ism *per se*. A number of antagonisms could be expected to emerge at the political level over the determination of state economic policies. The central argument to be developed here is that the manner in which these conflicts and interests intersected precluded the emergence of a centralizing axis of political cleavage and underlay the increasing importance of the provinces as economic actors.

The Working Class and the State

The emergent conflict between capital and labour in Canada has usually been viewed as a politically centralizing cleavage reflecting the strength of limited identities or cultural heterogeneity and the weakness of industrial-ization.[68] Yet in numerical terms wage labour probably constituted at least one-third of the national labour force by the early 1920s. While it is important to note the cultural obstacles intervening between objective class situation and class action,[69] attention has less often been drawn to the importance of the *internal* composition of the working class and the ongoing terms of political conflict into which it entered. Both served to weaken the emergence of labour as an independent political force with important implications for the development of the state structure.

The division between the international and domestic sectors and between resources and manufacturing industry served to "fractionalize" the working class as well as capital. This helped create regionally distinctive labour traditions, particularly noticeable in the period of the 'wheat boom' and immediately after W.W.1. The existence of a largely unskilled industrial proletariat in the resource industries of the West and in transportation was related to the development of the region by large-scale and concentrated forms of capital. This sharply polarized class structure gave rise to a combative labour movement and political milieu, variously expressed in the continued strength of the industrial unionism from the early years of the century, syndicalism, and even revolutionary socialism.[70] Strongest in B.C. and in the coalfields of Alberta, a distinctive western radical labour tradition would, by the end of World War One, encompass most of the organized working class from Winnipeg to Vancouver.

By contrast, the dominant thrust among organized craft and skilled workers in the eastern Trades and Labour Congress was, at most, toward labourism. In large part, this sectoral division was reinforced by the American Federation of Labour domination of the nascent labour movement, which benefited from the marked industrial expansion of the Laurier years. AFL hegemony destroyed earlier embryonic forms of industrial unionism and strongly militated against independent political action.[71] The thrust to the former was blunted equally by the internal structure of the manufacturing-sector working class. Business could countenance with relative equanimity the organization of skilled workers into the AFL unions, accommodate their interests, and count on the latter to exclude the unskilled. The more polarized class structure of the West and the more highly capital-intensive character of the industrial context worked against such an easy accommodation. The western labour movement was frequently divided by dual unionism as radicals denounced craft organizations, and even the latter displayed strong schismatic tendencies long before the One Big Union split. Industrial unionism, moreover, strongly favoured independent political action, and early electoral successes, most notably in B.C. but also in Winnipeg and in the coalfields of Alberta, strengthened the greater politicization of the western movement.

Perhaps most importantly, organized labour in manufacturing and the eastern working class more generally found their political interests closely bound up with those of industrial capital *given real barriers to industrialization*. Thus the marked Tory political domination of urban Ontario from the late nineteenth century, even more marked at the provincial level, was at least in part dependent on conscious mobilization of labour support. At the provincial level, rather meagre rewards – limited social insurance measures and regulation of the worst abuses of an untrammelled labour market – were not so forthcoming from the agrarian-based Liberals. Most importantly, policies oriented to industrial development, such as the nationalization of Ontario Hydro and measures to promote forward linkages from the northern resource base, were presented in terms of a general objective of promoting "the manufacturing condition."[72] Tory nationalism successfully spoke to the interests of labour in a context where protectionism, subsidies to capital, and state interventionism generally were subject to strong opposition from agrarian Grit radicalism. At the federal level, support for the tariff – of which the Conservatives were certainly the most consistent champions – could drive a wedge between labour and agrarian interests when the trade issue was politically dominant, as in the elections of the 1880s and of 1911.

The fundamental cleavage between labour and farmers existed even in Ontario where mixed farming increasingly directed to the domestic market was predominant. Electoral co-operation between agrarians and labour was indeed stronger the further west one moved – lasting for some fifteen years in Alberta under the United Farmers of Alberta by contrast to the short-lived UFO coalition in Ontario. For western labour the tariff was not a fundamental issue, and for organized workers it was certainly insufficient to constitute a basis for political identification with their employers. Another barrier to farm-labour unity at the national level was the structure of agrarian class relations. By contrast to Australia and other economies based on export-oriented agriculture, the dominance of an independent petit bourgeoisie on the land created a relatively homogeneous farmer constituency that saw little basis for an identification with labour. In

Australia, paid agricultural workers would find common cause with labour in the Labour Party. While attempts to realize such a unity certainly existed in Canada – most notably in the CCF – pronounced tensions always existed. Further, the very size and regionally concentrated character of the radical agrarian constituency in Canada implied either a domination of agrarian over labour interests where some unity was achieved, as Johnson has argued,[74] or a lack of interest in maintaining or seeking such co-operation. The tension between radical agrarians and labour spokesmen in the CCF indicated the continuing difficulties of such an association even after a large section of the agrarian movement had consciously broken with radical liberalism.[75]

Thus the internal structure of a working class shaped within the context of dependent capitalist development, and the ongoing terms of political conflict into which it entered, strengthened the impact of ethnic heterogeneity, the instability of the business cycle, and the continuously inflated labour market as forces militating against a strong national labour movement. The failure of labour to constitute itself as a strong, independent political force at the national level was strikingly demonstrated in the massive labour upsurge that greeted the end of the First World War. It was not so much the weakness of labour *per se* that became apparent, for general strikes in a large number of centres and a series of electoral successes in B.C., Alberta, Manitoba, and Ontario and even Nova Scotia testified to the marked estrangement of labour from the dominant parties and its ability to independently challenge the political system. Rather than the political docility of the working class or any corporatist thrust on the part of the Liberals or Conservatives – near hysteria concerning the Western movement in particular being the dominant response – the political inability to institutionalize this inchoate radicalism effectively was decisive. This owed much to the East-West division, both doctrinal and organizational, and to the contradictory relation to the agrarian movement, though other factors were not without importance.

Two important consequences followed from the post-war defeat. First, labour traditions of political action would be increasingly defined at the provincial level. Even when the CCF later sought to unite labour politically on a national basis, its limited areas of strength would possess rather different characteristics. The B.C. section in particular could regard the national party's labourism with a degree of radical scepticism that found expression in a rather greater focus on the possibility of achieving its goals at the provincial level. Centralists from the League for Social Reconstruction looked askance at proposals to "provincialize" financial institutions.[76] In a wider sense, the very weakness of labour at the national level served to focus attention on the means of redress available at a level where labour could sometimes wield a greater influence. Social welfare, industrial regulation, and legal definitions of the framework of collective bargaining were emergently important provincial responsibilities that permitted some incorporation of labour interests. Though strength at the provincial level should not be exaggerated, it certainly impelled the expansion of provincial spending in the field of social services and, in Ontario and B.C., labour was a constituency that could be won to support activist policies of provincial economic development. Labour political action at the provincial level in turn shaped rather different labour movements in each province.

Second, and most importantly, the national political weakness of labour implied that brokerage politics would continue to be dominant, that labour would fail to bring about a political unity on the part of its opponents. This permitted a continued high degree of expression of the myriad competing regional and sectional interests of business, which might otherwise have been forced to coalesce and find common cause in a party of the right. The conditions within which labour political action was shaped were thus of importance in shaping the structure of the state since a decentralized federalism was very much the product of divisions within the national business community and of their specific developmental needs.

Business and the State

The relation between the dominant fraction of business and the state cannot be seen as one of instrumental subordination, even in the period of near interpenetration of private and public agencies of development. Such policies as freight rate regulation and abolition of the CPR western monopoly in response to agrarian pressures in the early twentieth century[77] and the *de facto* recognition of unionism in the creation of the Department of Labour[78] demonstrated the relative autonomy of the state. Class politics in a democratic society established clear limits on the hegemony of business. State support for capital was certainly the *sine qua non* of development in "new" countries, as Innis argued, given enormous investment needs far in advance of future returns, but he further noted that the state would attempt to impose these risks and the costs of later rigidities on private capital. Insofar as it was possible, the state had good reason to avoid a mushrooming debt and the consequent strengthening of ridigities in periods of downturn.[79] However, to a large extent it was unable to do so, particularly in the nation-building period, and in periods of contraction the role of the state was further extended, as in the nationalization of the CNR. The state was thus forced to assume for capital much of the costs of rigidities as well as those of expansion through debt and revenues derived from tariffs and freight rates. These in turn exerted highly unequal burdens on different business groups and defined the wider framework of economic development (in terms of establishing metropolitan areas, securing the relative position of domestic industrial development, etc.). The important point is that the economic role of the state generated issues that could also divide business into distinct constituencies.

The relation between capital and the state had two dimensions. Business, at least by the late nineteenth century, was politically united in defence of high tariffs and the extension of state subsidies to capital formation in the face of agrarian and some small business opposition. The state, however, would also have to mediate cleavages *within* this consensus. The relation of the state to capital and its institutional development was thus shaped both by patterns of conflict between business and the subordinate classes *and* by divisions within the former. Further, the political needs of capital would be subject to change as the economic structure matured in the aftermath of the wheat boom.

Before 1911 one may readily discern, with Myers[80] and Naylor, singularly close associations between specific private interests and the dominant parties. The rival railways were particularly inclined to a close alignment with their respective champions, together with associated constellations of financial interests.[81] Nation-building and political corruption were inextricably linked, though an instrumentalist interpretation discounts the extent to which the expansion secured through such collaboration served wider interests. Beyond this business manipulation of partisian politics,[82] the relative closeness of the Liberals to agrarian interests before the late 1880s and their espousal of the Grit vision of the limited state engendered a near unanimity of nationally organized business behind "the old man and the old flag" when the trade issue became dominant.[83] Strong consensus concerning the key elements of the National Policy in the face of agrarian (and perhaps some small business and hinterland) opposition was amply demonstrated in 1911, particularly by the defection of the Toronto Eighteen from the Liberals. Opposition to statist development could thus unite business despite distinct partisan proclivities[84] and sectional objectives.

From at least the late nineteenth century to the 1920s, both Montreal finance and Toronto financial and industrial capital were more closely aligned with the federal Tories,[85] who stood for high protectionism, advocacy of industrial subsidies, and defence of the Imperial nexus. Both parties after 1911, however, were sufficiently attuned to the broad statist consensus to dispel any real illusions of neutrality so far as organized agrarian and emerging labour interests were concerned. This consensus constituted the boundaries beyond which class-based third-partyism would be defined after World War One. If the state was more than a class instrument – though it frequently acted as the agent of specific interests – it still set clear limits upon which interests could be accommodated, and to what degree.

The very strength of agrarian and other radical democratic opposition to the singularly close association between the federal state and the business interests combined with the increasing internal complexity of capital itself to create a new relative autonomy after the war. The remarkable expansion of industrial capital was such as to change in part the relation between business and the state.[86] Certainly the nationalization of the bankrupt transcontinental railways saw the inability of the powerful and previously decisive voices of the CPR and Montreal finance to press their own solution of amalgamation. Excessive compensation would be paid to maintain confidence, but farmers and industry would not tolerate a CPR and with it Montreal mercantile hegemony. The diminution of patronage and the creation of regulatory commissions to deal with freight rates and tariffs, which began before the war, were means of distancing the state from the close associations of public and private power that had been characteristic of a far less complex economic structure. Even the Conservatives under Meighen distanced themselves from the sectional demands of Montreal finance,[87] though they continued to pay a high electoral price for their explicit denial of agrarian, labour, and hinterland regional demands. By the 1920s resolute defence of the autonomy of the CNR, further attempts to depoliticize the tariff issue, and the rapid dismantling of the wartime controls, which had signified qualitatively new forms of state intervention and state-business interpenetration, marked the decrease of "clientilism." Most importantly, the earlier association between business and the federal state was not to be replaced by "quasi-corporatist" forms as the political needs of business became more limited. Prime Minister Mackenzie King in particular had a well-founded fear of too close an association with "the interests," the Beauharnois scandal constituting a rather exceptional episode. The wider imperatives of brokerage in a context of emergent class politics were simply too great to permit the continued existence of earlier forms of association.

The autonomy of the federal state from business can, however, be seriously overstated. The banks, other constellations of financial power, and the internationally oriented financial-commercial sector more generally remained the decisive voices and could set clear limits on demands for new state initiatives. King's adept handling of the tariff issue signified a strong awareness of the limits within which progressivism could be responded to,[88] as did both parties' handling of the Wheat Board issue. The later creation of the Bank of Canada indicated an extreme deference by both parties to the views of the bankers in the face of considerable pressures for the socialization of credit and planned inflation, not least within the dominant parties themselves.[89]

Again, responses to politically popular anti-trust campaigns at the outset of the depression were greeted only through symbolic action, given the accepted imperative of sustaining efficient and therefore concentrated forms of capital.[90] Progressive opinion called largely in vain for federal action in the social services field in the fiscally propitious 1920s, business hostility being far more crucial than the constitutional impasse.[91] Examples could be repeated *ad nauseam*. The central point is that personalist elite linkages, the pronounced ideological congruency of businessmen and dominant party politicians, the exigencies of campaign financing, and, most importantly, the independent power of capital outside the state all circumscribed the limits of state intervention in the interests of the lower classes. This further implied that the patterns of state action would be primarily determined by the needs of capital and by the expression of divisions within business. Though largely defined at the economic rather than the political level, such cleavages were of importance in shaping state institutions.

As the previously dominant financial and commercial companies were joined by increasingly monopolistic national market-based industry, divisions within capital were potentially sharpened. However, the merger wave signalled some interpenetration of the two sectors. A product of the speculative proclivities of finance stressed by Naylor and of the search for profitable long-term investment, consolidation under financial auspices also flowed from the specifically industrial imperatives of rationalizing over-expansion in relation to the size of the domestic market and gaining access to the capital required for integration and innovation. By no means all of the leading national industries were the product of financial interventions (e.g., Massey-Harris), and state support was certainly needed to bridge the gap between the requirements of industry and the rigidities of the domestic capital market (e.g., bonuses and subsidies to the primary iron and steel industry). Increased interpenetration nevertheless eliminated some of the older hostility between industry and finance.[92]

Financial-industrial penetration was, however, rather less marked in Ontario than was the case within the orbit of Montreal.[93] Ontario industry was far more decentralized in terms of control, contrasting to the exertion of Montreal financial hegemony over Quebec, the Maritimes, and eastern Ontario.[94] It is interesting to note that, despite the reorganization of the Canadian Manufacturers' Association in 1900, which was directed to the creation of a specifically industrial organization to counter the power of the banking and transportation interests in the areas of tariff and freight rate policy,[95] manufacturers had considerable difficulty in finding a common political voice at the national level. The contrast to the usually authoritative and united stance of the bankers is striking. Industrial political unity was largely founded on the tariff and subsidies issues in the face of opposition, but the detailed structure of tariffs and freight rates produced a plethora of sectional contradictions such as those between users of raw materials and their domestic producers. Other differences, as with freight rates, had a regional basis, as demonstrated by the schismatic position of Winnipeg and Vancouver industrialists within the CMA.[96] Thus in the 1920s the CMA "more or less ceased to act as a unified pressure group and came to concentrate upon the provision of services."[97] At the same time, individual manufacturers were hardly powerful voices at the federal level. They could not even obtain their own department and remained amalgamated within

Trade and Commerce. This pronounced organizational disunity of manufacturing – disguised by the consensus that did appear on occasion in the
face of fundamental challenges – implied that the interests of specific
constituencies might be better met at the more accessible provincial level of
the state.

Within this context one may discern, most centrally in Ontario, the
assertion of industrial interests within emergently important provincial
policies of economic development. The evolution of natural resources
policy in particular had a far more nationalist and industrial development-
oriented thrust than would be readily countenanced by the Dominion
(Laurier) government. The establishment of linkages from and between
the staples industries and the deepening of the domestic industrial market
encountered some financial opposition precisely because it entailed legislative and fiscal measures directed against the free flow of international
capital. This further suggests that the rise of the importance of the provinces as economic actors can by no means be attributed to continentalism.
The attempt to create forward linkages, as in the timber export ban of 1898
and its (unsuccessful) extension to nickel in 1900, was resisted by the banks
and the federal government on the basis of a feared loss of confidence by
American capital.[98]

The issue became even clearer with that pioneering example of regulative
state intervention, the creation of Ontario Hydro, which split bankers from
industrialists and aligned them with different levels of the state.[99] Public
development of Hydro and the timber policy ensured not only the rapid
expansion of the pulp and paper industry (i.e., integration between basic
staple industries), but also the deepening of a secondary manufacturing
structure that had been hindered by the high costs of coal. The Toronto
CMA and boards of Trade across the province vigorously pressed for public
ownership, opposing equally strong financial opposition and some ambivalence on the part of the Whitney Conservatives. As Nelles has argued,
"From the outset the crusade for public power was a businessmen's movement [which] meant cheap electricity for the manufacturer."[100] The economic policies of the provincial Conservatives saw a vigorous extension of
state controls over the pattern of development, a "struggle against continental integration on American terms" that "resolved itself into a struggle
between the Province of Ontario and the federal government."[101] Support
for domestic industry was also expressed in the virtual exemption of manufacturing from provincial (and often municipal) taxation and the extension
of numerous bounties and subsidies, particularly to the primary iron and
steel industry. The huge integrated industrial complex developed at Sault
Ste. Marie by Clergue required massive provincial involvement through
grants and resource cessions.

Though the cleavage between the domestic and international sectors of
capital may have receded in importance after the war, a Ferguson-

Taschereau alliance would defeat grandiose federal projects for private power developments geared to the American export market,[102] while the St. Lawrence power development issue tended to align the provinces against financial interests working through the federal government. Ontario industry certainly resisted any power exports.[103] In the same period Ferguson vigorously campaigned for a national fuel policy that would have removed freight rate impediments to the entry of Alberta and Nova Scotia coal to Ontario markets and thus help to integrate a national industrial economy.[104] Federal inactivity in this area was matched by lack of interest in funding industrial education until well after the province had intervened. Similarly, the creation of the Ontario Research Foundation in 1928 was directly geared to industrial needs and filled a gap where the federal government was unwilling to intervene.[105]

Close relations between the provinces and regional fractions of business had, by the end of the interwar period, reached the point where the CMA would justly complain of the tendency of provincial taxation to create a *de facto* internal tariff structure.[106] Intraprovincial users of raw materials were favoured by taxation while the provinces sought greater leverage by insisting on the right to incorporate companies that were national in scope, insurance constituting a major case in point, with the objective of retaining internally generated savings. Tentative attempts to create more integrated provincial economies certainly reflected the interests of smaller capital. Provincial action could work to strengthen the national position of regional business communities. Manitoba railway legislation in the 1880s sought to establish Winnipeg as a commercial and industrial sub-metropole by challenging the CPR monopoly, and concessions won privately and publicly were ultimately to be successful.[107] The construction of the two new transcontinentals before World War One was made possible by generous subsidies from the provinces and, in the case of B.C. and Manitoba, these were linked to controls and agreements over freight rates with the objective of countering regional disabilities. The provinces could also independently engage in railway building, as in the construction of the Temiskaming and Northern Ontario, though this was more directly reducible to the extension of the new staples frontier. Thus the distinct interests of regional and sectorally based fractions of capital, which were relatively weak at the federal level, could be expressed within provincial policies of economic development. The impact of such policies should not be overstated, but they probably served to strengthen domestic industry and, in the case of the West, to weaken Montreal's metropolitan hegemony.

To be sure, the rise in importance of the provinces as economic actors was due in greater part to the extension of their northern staples frontiers from the early years of the twentieth century. This was closely associated with the rising influence of American capital, particularly in the 1920s. Road and railway construction and other forms of infrastructural development saw the reproduction of the National Policy at the provincial level, and with it particularly close relations between provincial governments and specific business groupings. The ties of Cochrane, Ferguson, and Hepburn to the northern Ontario mining interests, of McBride to the B.C. lumber barons, and of Taschereau and Duplessis to *les trustards* of the pulp and paper industry were singularly close. A mutually beneficial accommodation was reached as (extremely low) resource revenues and provincial expenditures flowed into infrastructural development, the rise of unionism was strongly resisted, and campaign contributions and other largesse flowed back in response.

However, as Nelles argues, provincial natural resource policies could at least serve wider interests, and province-building certainly cannot be seen as subordination to American capital *tout court*. Even in mining, American companies controlled less than 40 per cent of production in 1936 and the Canadian share within these companies was almost one-third.[108] Similarly, American capital controlled just over one-third of pulp and newsprint production in the same year.[109] Many companies – as in the case of B.C. forestry industry – might be geared primarily to production for export but were under the control of provincially owned capital. Tentatively, it can be argued that provincial developmental strategies flowed from the structure of the provincial business class – the absence of a countervailing force to large American and Montreal financial capital being particularly marked in Quebec, which showed rather greater deference to the resource industry giants. In B.C., policies of forward linkage under McBride parallelled those in Ontario, showing some disposition to maximizing the gains accruing to the provincial economy. The greater influence of labour in both provinces may also have strengthened more regulative policies of development, given the need to expand employment. However, in large detail the rise of the new staples was certainly central to the rise of the stronger provinces and saw the close instrumental ties between private interests and the state that had been earlier characteristic of the Dominion. The fact that a new and increasingly North-South directed axis of development pushed the province to the fore was, (then), of importance in bringing about the relative decline in the economic role of the Dominion, though other factors were at play.

The 1920s represented the national stage in the "colony to colony" path of development discerned by Innis and, though provincial action in relation to the development of the new staples moved to the fore, state involvement in the economy was relatively minimized. In a new period of upturn a greater degree of maturity on the part of industry, achieved through concentration and production for a considerably widened market, permitted internal financing of expansion. The more dynamic sectors of industry – automobiles, rubber, chemicals, electrical goods – were frequently under the control of American branch plants and thus had no need to look to the state for the mobilization of capital. As Innis noted, "(T)he marked expansion of credit and of capital equipment in the twenties assumed the efficiency of private enterprise."[110] The rise of American investment in Canada implied a decreased role for the state in a period of expansion, a contrast to earlier periods, but this also signalled the increased integration and deepening of the domestic market. New forms of federal intervention in the post-war period were thus largely limited to managing the rigidities inherited from the past period of expansion, most notably the management of the railway system. The costs of future downturns were viewed as avoidable through a greater reliance on private capital.

Thus the expansion of state economic activity in the 1920s remained broadly similar to the earlier pattern – mobilization of capital (itself minimized) and infrastructural development in relation to a new staples frontier. To a large extent the quasi-corporatist forms of interventionism that underpinned the rising importance of the state as an economic actor in the larger world of capitalist nations remained absent, as did the centralization of power that would accompany such intervention. State-sponsored mergers, restructuring of and investment within industry, as well as the enforcement of cartel agreements to promote greater efficiency, stability, and international competitiveness, were emergently important features of state action in Europe and Britain in the 1920s that had been anticipated within wartime controls.[112] The lack of such developments in Canada may be attributed to the lack of industrial maturity in terms of ability to compete on the world market, but probably reflected equally the highly monopolistic structure of domestic industry, which was hardly characterized by unmanageable forms of competition. The rapid expansion of new industries created a particularly buoyant economy in contrast to the relatively greater stagnation elsewhere. Equally significant were the patterns of class conflict characteristic of the period. The weakness of the labour movement constituted an important barrier to the development of new forms of state action,[113] while the strength of the agrarian constituency impeded the extent to which the state could continue to sustain industrial needs given the political popularity of anti-monopoly sentiment.

Further, there is little evidence of business demands for new forms of federal state support. Wartime controls were rapidly dismantled at their behest and business had a firm faith in fiscal stringency, not least because of the massive debt accumulated within the earlier period of development and during the war. As Neatby remarked concerning the economic role of liberalism in the late 1920s, "Instead of urging the federal government to intervene as they had in the days of Macdonald and Laurier, [business] now argued that the federal government was spending too much and that federal taxes were an unfortunate burden upon their enterprises."[113]

A "sound" financial policy akin to that of Baldwin or Hoover was all that business generally would seem to have demanded of the federal state[114] and reflected the particularly strong influence of the financial sector. Business objectives could be secured privately through renewed concentration and intra-industry negotiation while statism implied for most an unwelcome intrusion into their private domain. On balance, the Canadian experience in the early twentieth century was that the state was called on to perform needed developmental functions and on occasions to strengthen the relative position of specific business groupings, but nationally organized business as a whole remained rather aloof from the political sphere except when core assumptions were challenged. A decentralized federalism represented an adequate enough means of securing sectional developmental objectives and of mediating differences, and was an important means of delaying unwelcome pressures for social legislation. To that extent, Canadian federalism reflected the existence of an essentially limited state.

The Depression began to shift business attitudes in a more interventionist direction but the existence of some pressures from the domestic sector dependent on the expansion of the national market encountered opposition from more internationally oriented sectors of capital.[115] Both Bennett before 1935 and subsequently King remained wedded to the traditional solutions of fiscal stringency and trade policy. In large detail, new forms of state interventionism were espoused well before the war by more progressive businessmen and the federal bureaucracy (e.g., the National Employment Commission) and quasi-corporatist forms of planning were implicit in elements of the Bennett New Deal and proposals made by the Stevens Commission, but the construction of a new consensus on the economic role of the federal state would await the later rise in strength of the labour movement and of the CCF. Specifically "modern" forms of state interventionism in Canada were very much the product of the post-war period. Interestingly, some of the earlier anticipations existed at the provincial level, as in Pattulo's "Little New Deal" for British Columbia and in the Hepburn-Duplessis negotiation and enforcement of an intra-industry agreement within the vastly over-extended pulp and paper industry.[116] Certainly in the 1920s, however, the economic role of the federal state remained predicated on the traditional axioms, and this explains in no small part the existence of a decentralized variant of federalism in the period.

Farmers, Small Business, and the State

The relative dominance of farmers and small business within the Canadian class structure until well into the interwar period constitutes an important dimension of Canadian exceptionalism. As Corry implied, this predominace blunted the thrust to social welfarism that has generally contributed to the growth of the state and to relative centralization. The laissez-faire values of small capital and of many farmers emphasized fiscal stringency and the values of self-reliance, and, indeed, they did not themselves rely on the state to any great extent.[117] The attachment of the small producer and trader to the values of laissez-faire liberalism is hardly surprising, and the populist gestures of many provincial governments and the rhetorical espousals of free enterprise made by politicians at all levels expressed a response to the association made between the state and "the interests," which was so characteristic of this constituency. Duplessis's campaign against *les trustards* in Quebec, Hepburn's invocation in Ontario of the value of the little man, and the campaigns of the agrarian radicals against the plutocrats were all expressive of the populist vision of the limited state. While concealing the nexus of relations between the provinces and large-scale capital, the sentiment in favor of fiscal stringency and non-interventionism could certainly see in the provinces a first line of defence. The strength of agrarian and small business interests at the provincial level thus constituted one point of opposition to what appeared as the reckless expense of nation-building in the interests of the privileged few.

Exceptional episodes such as H.H. Stevens's heroic crusade of 1935 aside, small business failed to appear as an independent national political force. Development always implied state support for concentrated forms of capital, and independent businessmen benefited from growth in the short term as much as they might ultimately suffer the consequences. Concentration inexorably swallowed up small capital even as growth gave rise to new forms, the virtual absence of national organizations testifying to the inability to define a common political stance across myriad divisions of interest.

The position of farmers in the West was exceptional in that the dominance of the wheat staple defined a common market position and a common antagonism to large-scale capital at the centre among a cohesive and regionally concentrated class of individual commodity producers. Western agrarian revolt against the structure of the wheat economy has been so extensively discussed elsewhere that it suffices to identify schematically some of the consequences for the federal state structure.

Liberal mediation of organized agrarian interests before World War One proved capable of countering some of the worst abuses of transportation and grain trade monopolies, but the limits of the balancing act between farmers and capital became clearly apparent in the Progressive episode. King had the signal advantage of Conservative intransigence, but the long process of reincorporation of farmers within Liberalism demonstrated the limits of brokerage politics in the face of class radicalization. As a result the organized agrarian movement increasingly turned to the provincial state as a means of redress. Publicly owned elevators, support for cooperatives, the establishment of credit agencies, demands for provincial control of land and resources, and infrastructural subsidies to counter monopolies were all means of confronting the dominance of central Canadian capital through the assertion of provincial powers. The national revolt embodied in progressivism did, of course, turn to the provincial sphere in

Alberta and Manitoba, while in Saskatchewan the Liberals could hardly fail to be responsive to the organized agrarian movement. As I have argued elsewhere, divergent patterns of western hinterland revolt defined distinctive provincial political traditions as farmers turned to the more accessible level of the state as a means of redress and severed their relations with the dominant national parties.[118] One outcome, Social Credit, constituted the most far-reaching assertion of provincial powers against the centre in Canadian history. Some of the wider implications of this axis of class conflict have been noted above. Agrarian revolt contributed in no small way to state disaggregation, while the political expression of agrarian dissatisfaction at the federal level both weakened labour and constrained a consensus among business that concealed important differences. These in turn militated against perpetuation of the leading economic role of the Dominion.

Conclusions

By the late 1920s the relatively centralized state structure created to assume the tasks of nation-building was demobilized to a degree that serves to distinguish sharply the Canadian experience from that of the wider world of democratic capitalist states. The roots of this exceptionalism may be in part located in the peculiarities of the economic and class structures that had been created within the process of national development. A regionally disarticulated national economy, the division between the domestic and international sectors, and the cleavage between the agrarian and industrial spheres engendered complex patterns of conflict concerning the economic role of the state. The political expression of these conflicts and the manner in which they intersected served largely to preclude the centralizing cleavages that might have pushed the central government to the fore. Class and intra-class conflict and the specific developmental and political needs of capital further served to strengthen the position of the provinces. Such a perspective on the Canadian state entails a somewhat changed emphasis on the theme of dependent capitalism that has been dominant within the political economy tradition. While invaluable in defining the external context within which Canadian capitalism was shaped and some of the consequent internal ramifications, this emphasis has tended to discount the development of political class conflict as one of the most important forces shaping the form and development of the state.

Notes

I want to thank Alan Cairns, Ken Carty, Frank Longstreth, Rianne Mahon, Phil Resnick, and Doug Williams for comments on earlier versions of this paper.

1. See *Report of the Royal Commission on Dominion-Provincial Relations*, Book 1 (Ottawa, 1939) [hereafter Rowell-Sirois Report]; W.A. Mackintosh, *The Economic Background of Dominion-Provincial Relations* (Ottawa, 1939); D. Creighton, *British North America at Confederation* (Ottawa, 1939); and V.C. Fowke, *The National Policy and the Wheat Economy* (Toronto, 1957).
2. J.R. Mallory, *Social Credit and the Federal Power in Canada* (Toronto, 1976), 25.
3. Most notably, the tariff issue in the elections of the 1880s and of 1911. The issue of railway financing was also politically important.
4. The best survey is D. Drache, "Rediscovering Canadian Political Economy," *Journal of Canadian Studies* (August, 1976).
5. See H.J. Aitken, "Defensive Expansionism: The State and Economic Growth in Canada," in W.T. Easterbrook and M.H. Watkins, eds., *Approaches to Canadian Economic History* (Toronto, 1967); and H.A. Innis, "Government Ownership and the Canadian Scene," in Innis, *Essays in Canadian Economic History* (Toronto, 1956).
6. H.J. Aitken, "Government and Business in Canada: An Interpretation," *Business History Review* (Spring, 1964).
7. Thus some importance must be granted to the absence of an "integral nationalism" capable of subsuming the specific nationalisms of French and English Canada. In this sense Canada has always constituted a "political nation." Cf. D.V. Smiley, *The Canadian Political Nationality* (Toronto, 1967). The attempt to impose an imperialist definition of the nation prior to and during World War One in contradistinction to Bourassa's, and less obviously Laurier's, pan-Canadian nationalism prefigured the emergent identification of French Canada with the Quebec state. However, the Duplessis period in part excepted, the economics/culture trade-off and elite accommodation at the federal level implied that Quebec would be relatively quiescent in terms of shaping federal state institutions. Conservative nationalism was not concerned with aggrandizement of provincial powers, though the internal national question was of importance in shaping federalism since it impeded the development of pan-Canadian class politics. Further, Québécois nationalism would work against too tight an integration with the British metropole.
8. J.M.S. Careless, "Limited Identities in Canada," *Canadian Historical Review* [hereafter *CHR*] (March, 1969). On the importance of cultural interpretations of Canadian history, see C. Berger. *The Writing of Canadian History* (Toronto, 1976).
9. On socio-cultural interpretations of federalism, see W.S. Livingston, *Federalism and Constitutional Change* (Oxford, 1956).
10. For a critique in these terms, see J. Porter, *The Vertical Mosaic* (Toronto, 1965), ch. 12.
11. Following Leo Panitch in "The Role and Nature of the Canadian State," in Panitch, ed. *The Canadian State* (Toronto, 1977), one may argue that the

accumulation function of the state as specified by J. O'Connor (*The Fiscal Crisis of the State* [New York, 1973]) was dominant in the Canadian context in the period under consideration.

12. See in particular Mallory, *Social Credit*, and more generally the work of D.V. Smiley and A.C. Cairns.

13. E. Black and A. Cairns, "A Different Perspective on Canadian Federalism," in J.P. Meekison, ed. *Canadian Federalism: Myth or Reality?* (Toronto, 1968).

14. A. Cairns, "The Governments and Societies of Canadian Federalism," *Canadian Journal of Political Science* [hereafter *CJPS*] (December, 1977).

15. See A. Peacock and J. Wiseman, *The Growth of Public Expenditures in the United Kingdom* (Princeton, N.J., 1961), on the concentration effect of the expanding role of the state; and R. Miliband, *The State in Capitalist Society* (London, 1969), ch. 1.

16. O.J. Firestone, *Canada's Economic Development, 1867-1953* (London, 1958), 127.

17. *Ibid*. These figures probably overstate the case compared to alternative series, but the general trend is clear.

18. K. Buckley, *Public Investment and Capital Formation* (Ottawa, 1945), 24, Table B. The figure is gross domestic capital formation including repair and maintenance.

19. *Ibid*., 26, Table F.

20. Rowell-Sirois Report, Tables 13-17.

21. R. Bird, *The Growth of Government Spending in Canada* (Toronto, 1970), 300.

22. Indeed, from an early period the national parties would seem to have been crucially dependent on their provincial counterparts. J. English, *The Conservatives and the Decline of the Party System, 1911-21* (Toronto, 1977), argues that the Conservative victory of 1911 was highly dependent on the provincial organizations established by Roblin, Whitney, and McBride. R. Whitaker, *The Government Party* (Toronto, 1977), argues in a similar vein with reference to the Liberal victory of 1935.

23. In terms of the division of legislative powers, the allocation of fiscal capabilities, and the power of disallowance vested in the Dominion. See Fowke, *The National Policy*; Mallory, *Social Credit*.

24. See Innis, *Essays*, particularly "Government Ownership and the Canadian Scene" and "The Canadian Economy in the Great Depression"; D. Drache, "Stapleisation: A Theory of Canadian Capitalist Development," in J. Saul and C. Heron, eds., *Imperialism and Nationalism in Canada* (Toronto, 1977), is an excellent summary.

25. For example, the analysis of the external economic forces leading to Confederation; British abrogation of mercantilism; the rise of American protectionism; the competitive expansion to the West.

26. For example, analysis of the relation between the National Policy and the development of the wheat staple. See Fowke, *The National Policy*.

27. Thus Innis saw the tariff as not just a fiscal measure but as "a crude instrument designed to obtain a share of new resources." *Essays*, 81.

28. This emerges particularly clearly in Innis's "Government Ownership" and in his general pessimism concerning the scope for free action in the face of overwhelming economic forces.

29. Berger, *The Writing of Canadian History*, 98.

30. Aitken, "Defensive Expansionism." For Creighton, see *Dominion of the North* (Toronto, 1944), and *Canada's First Century* (Toronto, 1970).

31. Aitken, "Defensive Expansionism," 209.

32. Considered at a minimum as an instrument that could unite the interests of French and English Canada in remaining politically independent of the United States.

33. See R.T. Naylor, "The Rise and Fall of the Third Commercial Empire of the St. Lawrence," in G. Teeple, ed., *Capitalism and the National Question in Canada* (Toronto, 1973).

34. See Innis, *Essays*, 154. Innis offers only scattered remarks on the subject and generally neglected the importance of the provinces as economic actors within his analyses of state action.

35. Aitken, "Defensive Expansionism," 221.

36. See D. Smiley, "Canada and the Quest for a National Policy," *CJPS* (March, 1975).

37. See Berger, *The Writing of Canadian History*, for his defence of the non-centralist perspectives of W.L. Morton and J.M.S. Careless.

38. M. Bliss, "Canadianizing American Business: The Roots of the Branch Plant," in I. Lumsden, ed., *Close the 49th Parellel* (Toronto, 1970).

39. Naylor, "Rise and Fall," and Naylor, *The History of Canadian Business, 1867–1914*, 2 vols. (Toronto, 1976). See also D. Drache, "The Canadian Bourgeoisie and its National Consciousness," in Lumsden, ed., *Close the 49th Parallel*; W. Clement, *The Canadian Corporate Elite* (Toronto, 1975); R. Laxer, ed., *(Canada) Ltd.* (Toronto, 1973); Teeple, ed., *Capitalism and the National Question*; and numerous articles in *Canadian Dimension* and *This Magazine*. The historical essays in Panitch, ed., *The Canadian State*, seem to discount the perspectives of the dependency theorists.

40. That is, through interest on loans to producers, the provision of services, transportation and carrying charges, mark-ups on commodities, speculative gains on resources held from production, etc.

41. Letter from Naylor to *Canadian Dimension* (Nov.-Dec., 1974), 63.

42. See also Drache, "The Canadian Bourgeoisie."

43. Hence the introductory quotation from Marx cited by Drache in "Stapleisation": "We sufffer not only from capitalist development but also from the incompleteness of that development."

44. Naylor, "Rise and Fall," 32.
45. *Ibid.*
46. *Ibid.*
47. Innis, *Esays*, 396-99.
48. On whom, see Drache, "Rediscovering Canadian Political Economy"; Berger, *The Writing of Canadian History*.
49. Hence the calls for a "new national policy" and the associated critique of balkanization.
50. C.B. Macpherson, *Democracy in Alberta: Social Credit and the Party System* (Toronto, 1953); Mallory, *Social Credit*.
51. M.C. Urquhart and K. Buckley, eds., *Historical Statistics of Canada* (Toronto, 1969), 490. Secondary manufacturing is defined as production primarily for the domestic market and excludes manufactured export staples.
52. *Ibid.*
53. *Ibid.*
54. *Ibid.*, 141. This overstates the domestic market-oriented sector.
55. *Ibid.*, 463.
56. *Ibid.*
57. See G. Kealey and P. Warrian, eds., *Essays in Canadian Working-Class History* (Toronto, 1976).
58. See K. Buckley, *Capital Formation in Canada, 1896–1930* (Toronto, 1955), Appendix, Table C. These tables also indicate a fairly high degree of market control by domestic industrial producers, particularly in the areas of farm implements, transportation equipment, and even industrial, electrical, and mining machinery (one-third to one-half of the domestic market after 1920).
59. See H. Marshall *et al.*, *Canadian-American Industry* (New Haven, 1936).
60. Thus about one-quarter in GNP in the 1920s was exported, predominantly in the form of raw materials and semi-processed staples.
61. The classic Marxist interpretation is Macpherson, *Democracy in Alberta*.
62. See J.M.S. Careless, "Frontierism, Metropolitanism and Canadian History," *CHR* (March, 1954), on the importance of dispersed metropolitanism in Canada. On Winnipeg, see J.A. Artibise, *Winnipeg: A Social History of Urban Growth* (Montreal, 1975).
63. H.C. Pentland, "The Development of a Capitalist Labour Market in Canada," *Canadian Journal of Economics and Political Science* (1959); M. Cross, ed., *The Workingman in the Nineteenth Century* (Toronto, 1974).
64. See G. Kolko, *Main Currents in Modern American History* (New York, 1976), ch. 5.
65. T.W. Acheson "Changing Social Origins of the Canadian Industrial Elite 1880–1910," *Business History Review* (Summer, 1973).
66. T.W. Acheson, "The Social Origins of Canadian Industrialism: A Study in the Structure of Entrepreneurship, 1880–1910" (Ph.D. thesis, University of Toronto, 1971), and his "The National Policy and the Industrialization of the Maritimes, 1880–1910," *Acadiensis* (Spring, 1972).

67. See *Economie Québécoise*, Cahiers de l'Université du Quebec, 1969; J. Hamelin and Y. Roby, *Histoire Economique du Québec, 1851–96* (Montreal, 1971).

68. See Porter, *The Vertical Mosaic*, and various essays by Gad Horowitz in *Candian Dimension*, 1967–70.

69. That is, ethnic, religious, and regional divisions.

70. See A.R. McCormack, *Reformers, Rebels and Revolutionaries: The Western Canadian Radical Movement, 1899–1919* (Toronto, 1977).

71. R. Babcock, *Gompers in Canada* (Toronto, 1974).

72. M. Bliss, *A Living Profit: Studies in the Social History of Canadian Business, 1883–1911* (Toronto, 1974), chs. 3, 5.

73. Macpherson, *Democracy in Alberta*.

74. Leo Johnson, "The Development of Class in Canada in the Twentieth Century," in Teeple, ed., *Capitalism and the National Question*.

75. See W. Young, *The Anatomy of a Party: The National C.C.F.* (Toronto, 1969), chs. 2, 3.

76. M. Horn, "The League for Social Reconstruction" (Ph.D. thesis, University of Toronto, 1969), 162-63.

77. Fowke, *The National Policy*, chs. 7–9.

78. Bliss, *A Living Profit*, ch. 4, demonstrates considerable business hostility to unionism in the period.

79. Innis, *Essays*, 90–91.

80. G. Myers, *A History of Canadian Wealth* (Toronto, 1975).

81. Thus the Conservative Party-Bank of Montreal-CPR nexus was succeeded by the Liberal Party-Grand Trunk-Toronto finance alignment under Laurier.

82. On the early material bases of this, see F.H. Underhill, "The Development of National Parties in Canada," in *In Search of Canadian Liberalism* (Toronto, 1960).

83. See Bliss, *A Living Profit*, ch. 5, though Naylor's *History of Canadian Business*, ch. 15, suggests some division.

84. Acheson, "Changing Social Origins."

85. And to their provincial counterpart in the case of the latter.

86. See English, *The Conservatives*, on the attempts of Borden Conservatism to create a "modern" programmatic party structure in the period and the perceived need for a relatively autonomous state.

87. See the discussion in R. Graham, *Arthur Meighen*, vol. 2 (Toronto, 1963).

88. H.B. Neatby, *Mackenzie King: The Prism of Unity, 1924–32* (Toronto, 1963), 14–20.

89. See L. Grayson, "The Formation of the Bank of Canada, 1913–38" (Ph.D. thesis, University of Toronto, 1974), chs. 3–4.

90. M. Bliss, "Another Anti-Trust Tradition: Canadian Anti-Combines Policy, 1889-1910," in R. Porter and G. Cuff, eds., *Enterprise and National Development* (Toronto, 1973).

91. As demonstrated by the relative ease with which such legislation was passed

both post-World War Two and when necessary before that, as in the case of old age pensions.

92. Particularly noticeable in early issues of the CMA journal, *Industrial Canada*.

93. Acheson, *The Social Origins of Canadian Industrialism*, chs. 3–4.

94. Perhaps also reflected in the less overwhelming metropolitan dominance of Toronto over southern Ontario compared to that of Montreal over Quebec industrial development.

95. S.D. Clark, "The Canadian Manufacturers' Association," *Canadian Journal of Economics and Political Science*, 4 (1938), 508.

96. S.D. Clark, *The Canadian Manufacturers' Association* (Toronto, 1939), ch. 5.

97. *Ibid.*, 69.

98. C. Armstrong, "The Politics of Federalism: Ontario's Relations with the Federal Government, 1896–1941" (Ph.D. thesis, University of Toronto, 1972), 112–22.

99. *Ibid.*, 172. See also C. Armstrong and H.V. Nelles, "Private Property in Peril: Ontario Businessmen and the Federal System, 1898–1911," in Porter and Cuff, eds., *Enterprise and National Development*.

100. H.V. Nelles, *The Politics of Development: Forests, Mines and Hydro Electrical Power in Ontario, 1890–1940* (Toronto, 1973), 249.

101. *Ibid.*, 310.

102. Armstrong, "The Politics of Federalism," 283–88.

103. *Ibid.*, 275.

104. P. Oliver, *Howard Ferguson: Ontario Tory* (Toronto, 1977), 199 and ch. 10 *passim*.

105. P. Oliver, *Public and Private Persons: The Ontario Political Culture, 1913–34* (Toronto, 1975), ch. 7.

106. Submission to the Rowell-Sirois Commission, Part 2, p. 4.

107. See Artibise, *Winnipeg*.

108. Marshall *et al.*, *Canadian-American Industry*, 87.

109. *Ibid.*, 36.

110. Innis, *Essays*, 126.

111. On the origins of European corporatism in the 1920s, see C. Maier, *Recasting Bourgeois Europe* (Princeton, N.J., 1975). On the U.S., see Kolko, *Main Currents in Modern American History*, and J. Weinstein, *The Corporate Ideal in the Liberal State* (Boston, 1968).

112. Leo Panitch, "Corporatism in Canada," *Studies in Political Economy*, No. 1 (Spring, 1979), 43-92.

113. Neatby, *Mackenzie King*, 217.

114. See Graham, *Arthur Meighen*, concerning Lord Atholstan and the *Montreal Star*'s virulent campaign against Meighen for his alleged departures from this objective.

115. A. Finkel, "Origins of the Welfare State in Canada," in Panitch, ed., *The Canadian State*, 352-55.

116. Nelles, *The Politics of Development*, 461.
117. J.A. Corry, *The Growth of Government Activities since Confederation* (Ottawa, 1939).
118. A. Jackson, "Patterns of Hinterland Revolt: Alberta and Saskatchewan in the Inter War Period," *CPSA Papers* (1977).

7. N.H. LITHWICK

Is Federalism
Good for
Regionalism?

Introduction

Regionalism constitutes the spatial dimension of pluralism. As such, it can serve as a useful way of identifying within society subgroups that are distinguishable in non-trivial ways as a result of their physical location. Of necessity, these subgroups would have interests that are at once relatively widely supported within the group and, in certain spheres, quite distinct from the interests of other subgroups.

The basic political dilemma of pluralism is to reconcile the common interests of the society as a whole with the particular interests of its subgroups. Obtaining political representation for widely scattered ethnic, linguistic, or class interests is a continuing challenge for democratic societies. The spatial basis for social partitioning inherent in regionalism offers a very attractive solution to this problem, for territoriality provides clearly demarcated zones of jurisdiction.

As a result, many societies have evolved multi-tiered political systems, with a centralized authority responsible for essentially national issues, and regional authorities catering to those interests essentially of a local nature. Most formal among these arrangements is federalism, in which the independent legitimacy of the regional authorities in terms of fiscal powers and responsibilities is spelled out in the constitution.

Central to the logic of the federalist solution, therefore, is the concept of regionalism. However, its intrinsic simplicity may create difficulties. If

Reprinted from *Journal of Canadian Studies*, 15, 2 (1980), with permission of the journal and the author.

spatial factors are not of primary significance in social differentiation, such as in a small country, or in one where other divisions (e.g., class) dominate, then federalism would be little more than a convenient administrative arrangement and would have little to do with regionalism. Such a case may arise where a phony regionalism is promoted to divert attention from more basic cleavages. It may also occur when initial conditions of regionalism warrant a federalist solution but those conditions subsequently undergo radical transformation. In such circumstances, continuing to assume that federalism is attuned to regionalism will not only be misguided but can aggravate social and political tensions.

This paper is an attempt to demonstrate how and why the latter situation occurred in Canada. It is argued that regionalism has evolved in ways that are no longer consistent with the structure and the orientation of the originally created federal system of government. Moreover, the federal system has itself developed in a way that makes it increasingly unresponsive to the new dimensions of regionalism.

Major institutional changes and constitutional proposals, practical as well as theoretical, can be seen as attempts to force regionalism into the straitjacket of federalism. To the extent that such efforts misconstrue genuine problems of regionalism, they can only serve to exacerbate a variety of difficult situations.

I. Characteristics of Canadian Regionalism and Federalism

If regionalism constitutes the spatial partitioning of society, then understanding regionalism requires that we identify the mechanisms leading to that spatial partitioning. In other words, what determines the distribution of populations in space and under what circumstances will those populations acquire spatially identifiable interests? The latter part of this question is important because if there are no important differences between spatially separate groups, it is difficult to understand what regionalism could mean.

Central to the determination of population distribution as well as private and group interests are economic phenomena. Economic conditions are among the most important determinants of voluntary migration, international no less than internal. Moreover, economic status, occupation, etc. are important determinants of values and interests. Hence, while regionalism may have as its focus concerns that range far beyond the economic, economic influences, especially of a non-transient sort, can be expected to play a major role in shaping those diverse interests. As a result, the nature of Canadian regionalism and its evolution will be very much dependent on the underlying structure and development of the Canadian economy.

Federalism is a sharing of political authority among various *levels* of government to achieve a more or less acceptable blend of economies from centralized provision of certain public services and responsiveness to local needs from decentralized provision of other public services. The constitutional assignment of functions and of revenue sources among levels means that shifts in the relative importance of either or both of these realms influence the overall distribution of power. Hence, the evolution of political and fiscal arrangements plays a central role in determining the nature of Canadian federalism.

II. The Historical Congruence Between Regionalism and Federalism

Regionalism in pre-Confederation Canada reflected very strongly the early structure of the Canadian economy. That structure derived from the sequential exploitation of natural resources for export, and hence the development of those territories or regions encompassing the respective staples, from cod to beavers to forestry to wheat and minerals. National economic development therefore consisted of several somewhat parallel lines of regional development.[1] Each region's economic structure was based primarily on its particular location and resource endowments so that, even though necessarily linked to national centres and foreign export and import markets for trade as well as labour and capital supplies, each region tended to be quite autonomous and unique. Certainly links with other regions were weak at best.

The spatial segregation of economic activities provided a strong basis for regionalism. The different areas clearly required political mechanisms closely identified with their respective interests. The existing and newly emerging provinces were ideally situated to pay just such a role. Hence provinces provided the formal spatial partitioning of the country in line with regional interests. The provinces provided the territorial definition for regionally differentiated societies and provincial governments became the official spokesmen within Confederation for those societies. It should be noted as well that provinces were the *only* sub-national entities with essentially inviolable spatial boundaries and independently legitimate political status. Due no doubt to the rather well-defined nature of provincial society at that time, no other regional interests were recognized or legitimized.

This convenient mapping of discrete economic activities and their social superstructure onto spatially separable territories provided a strong rationale for province-based regionalism. Each province was relatively homogeneous in terms of economic structure and quite distinguishable from the others. So long as economic development was centred on resource exploitation, the provincial boundaries matched the basic structural and associated spatial characteristics of the economy. Moreover, regional development was a building block in national development. The relationship was essentially additive, and the whole (national) economy was not much more than the sum of its (provincial-regional) parts. In such a situation regionalism and federalism were correctly perceived to be consistent, mutually supportive forces.

III. Parting of the Ways
(1) The Evolution of Regionalism

Because of the persistence of the belief in congruence between regionalism and federalism, changes in both regionalism and federalism make a re-examination of that relationship timely. Starting with regionalism, it should be obvious that the above "model" of the Canadian economy as an assembly of quasi-autonomous regions that map neatly into provincial boundaries is too simplistic. Important changes in the nature of the Canadian economy have occurred, fundamentally altering its historical economic structure, modifying and complicating thereby the nature of spatial relationships and hence the characteristics of regionalism.

Central to these changes was Macdonald's National Policy after Confederation, in which a deliberate attempt was made to alter the traditional staple-based nature of the economy. In pursuing a policy of encouraging non-resource sectors, especially manufacturing, through tariff protection and a national transportation policy, the foundations were laid for a radically transformed national economy in terms of both its structure and its spatial characteristics.

The technological requirements of modern industry are such that specialization in production, economies of scale, and mass, accessible markets impact in new ways on spatial organization. Industry tends to locate in or close to large centres, and draws on inputs from and markets in other large centres. In other words, these technical requirements lead both to nodalization of activity and integration among the nodes.

This transformation affected the provinces in two ways. First, it led to a reorientation of spatial relationships *within* provinces. Whereas towns and cities formerly existed to service the resource hinterland of the province, those which had the potential to benefit from the new drive for industrialization as a result of locational and related advantages developed economic roles increasingly autonomous from their former resource hinterland. The most fully developed cities came to dominate much of their hinterland. Subsequent economic development of the emerging metropolitan field was explained less and less by resource development, and increasingly by the sequential development of advanced sectors in and among the dominant economic centres.[2] Those portions of provinces outside the metropolitan field tended to develop in a more autonomous and often pathological manner, which created substantial economic and social differentiation within provinces.

This same process had no less significant an impact on transprovincial relationships. Spatial polarization requires extensive patterns of exchange with other centres, in terms not only of commodity flows, but labour, capital, and innovational flows as well. Since many of the key centres are found within other provinces, the result will be an erosion of the relevance of provincial boundaries as limits on the spatial extent of economic activities. The National Policy was designed to break down such spatial barriers and to foster instead spatial interdependencies. The promotion of transportation, manufacturing, and the emergence of the financial sector, of communications, and of services reinforced the process of intraprovincial differentiation and interprovincial integration.[3]

Demonstrating the empirical validity of these hypotheses is constrained to some extent by the retention of our strong emphasis on provincial units as the key economic entities of the nation. Not only are "regional" economic data restricted almost exclusively to the provincial level of aggregation[4] but data on interprovincial linkages are very sparse. Interestingly, one result is that much analysis of provincial economic performance is forced to ignore interregional factor and product flows, a procedure which is not only conceptually inadmissable but one which gives a strong element of support for the notion that one can continue to treat provinces as if their economies were in fact independent.[5] While problematic for research, this assumption about the separability of provincial economies has led to serious misunderstanding about the nature of the Canadian economy. For example, the overwhelming integrative role of major metropolitan centres is almost everywhere discounted.[6] Once this dimension of spatial interaction is admitted into the discussion, the separability assumption becomes tenuous indeed.[7]

We can proceed to examine the assumption of separable provincial economies by considering first some evidence on metropolitan dominance and urban-rural differentiation. Then we will consider the nature and scope of interprovincial integration.

The former hardly requires extensive documentation. Virtually all studies indicate the urbanization of modern activities[8] and the consequent polarization of society into rural and urban segments. Perhaps the most conclusive evidence on intraprovincial economic disparities is that on income distributions: as Table 1 shows, metropolitan incomes are not only much higher than non-metropolitan incomes in all provinces, but they are much more homogeneous and have become increasingly so. The real spatial distinctions in income would therefore appear to be rural-urban rather than interprovincial. Since income is highly correlated with most key social indicators, it seems reasonable to conclude that intraprovincial differentiation exists and is significant. Indeed, it would appear that most of the diversity in incomes *between* provinces is due to variations among their respective non-metropolitan sectors. When these latter are removed, the interprovincial (intermetropolitan) differences are significantly reduced.

Table 1
Average Family Income, 1977*
($ 000)

Province	Total	Metropolitan Areas	Non-Metropolitan Areas
Newfoundland	16.5	19.9	15.6
Prince Edward Is.**	16.0	—	16.0
Nova Scotia	16.5	18.4	15.1
New Brunswick	16.9	19.4	15.6
Quebec	19.1	19.9	17.3
Ontario	21.6	22.6	18.8
Manitoba	18.4	20.3	15.7
Saskatchewan	18.0	20.8	17.0
Alberta	21.3	22.6	19.4
British Columbia	21.0	22.0	19.5
Canada	20.1	21.5	17.7
Coefficient of Variation			
1977	.10	.07	.10
1973	.13	.09	.11

* Data include transfer payments likely to reduce rural/urban disparities.
** Prince Edward Island has been excluded from our calculations due to the
  absence of a metropolitan area in the province.
SOURCE: Statistics Canada, *Income Distribution by Size in Canada,* Cat. No.
  13-207, 1977. Table 3, pp. 42ff. (August, 1979): 1973, Table 3, pp. 26ff.
  (July, 1975).

These findings are consistent with our expectations about interprovincial integration, but are somewhat indirect. One can assess the degree of
integration more directly by examining linkages between product markets
(trade relationships) and factor markets (labour and capital flows). Data
on commodity flows are extremely scarce and unreliable in Canada. The
only widely (and improperly) quoted study (Table 2) presents data on
interregional (metaprovincial) and international shipments of manufactured goods in one year, 1974. While it tends to confirm that interregional
flows are important, in the absence of an historical benchmark little more
can be concluded. More important is the fact that it considers manufacturing alone, which contributes only 20 per cent to Gross Domestic Product.
Since economic integration relates to all sectors, and since there is reason to
believe that other sectors, such as finance, communications, trade, and
services, have very strong interregional linkages, drawing economy-wide
conclusions from manufacturing data is at best unreliable.

Table 2
Interregional and International Shipments of
Manufactured Goods, Canada, 1974 (per cent)

Origin	Atlantic	Quebec	Ontario	Prairie	British Columbia	Intra Reg'l	Inter Reg'l	Inter Nat'l	Other	Total
Atlantic Region	41	9	8	1	1	41	18	34	7	100
Quebec	4	50	19	4	2	50	30	14	7	100
(Montreal)	(4)	(52)	(20)	(5)	(5)	(52)	(32)	(9)	(7)	
Ontario	3	11	50	6	3	50	23	20	6	100
(Toronto)	(3)	(11)	(56)	(6)	(3)	(56)	(23)	(14)	(7)	
Prairie Region	1	6	6	62	9	62	22	8	7	
British Columbia	1	2	3	8	40	40	14	38	9	100
(Vancouver)	(1)	(2)	(4)	(11)	(56)	(56)	(18)	(14)	(13)	
Canada						50	24	20	7	100

SOURCE: Statistics Canada, *Destination of Shipments of Manufacturers, 1974*, Cat. No. 31-522, Occasional, June, 1978, Table I, p. 13, for provincial shipments and Table 3, p. 224, for CMA shipments.

Additional information from the manufacturing study substantiates the advantage of an urban focus. Data are provided on manufacturing ship-ments from major metropolitan areas that can be compared with ship-ments from their respective provinces. In all cases, international shipments from the metro areas are much less significant and shipments to other regions more significant. This admittedly limited evidence tends to support the view of provinces as essentially dualistic, with rural areas relatively more tied to foreign markets and metro areas more tied to other regions in Canada.

At this point, it is appropriate to modify our methodology. For if the major economic interdependencies between provinces are the result of linkages between metropolitan areas, and the degree of provincial interde-pendence is concealed when provincial units are used because of the non-interdependence of rural areas, then we can discover more about spatial economic integration in Canada by considering inter-metropolitan rela-tionships.[9]

If direct flow evidence on product market interdependence is lacking, it is possible to examine the consequences of interdependence. Close links would tend to produce relatively interdependent markets with similar out-comes as measured by secular price trends (discounting distance costs).

Data for metropolitan areas since 1971 tend to confirm similar trends in prices for a variety of different products (Table 3).

Table 3
Consumer Price Indexes, Selected Regional Cities
Jan. 1980 (1971 = 100)*

	Halifax	Montreal	Toronto	Edmonton	Vancouver
All items	195.9	197.9	198.7	200.6	198.0
Food	237.4	242.3	238.3	232.6	240.8
Housing	193.3	185.4	192.1	210.5	191.2
Clothing	161.8	164.7	171.0	180.4	169.3
Transportation	189.9	194.7	190.7	188.1	191.9
Health and personal care	176.0	192.0	200.0	173.6	184.4
Recreation and education	157.6	168.0	164.9	170.3	159.0
Tobacco and alcohol	164.9	180.0	173.0	154.0	173.8

* The indexes measure within city trends and cannot be used to compare levels between cities.

SOURCE: Statistics Canada, *Consumer Price Index*, January, 1980, Cat. No. 62-001.

Much more appropriate for examining economic integration is the interdependence of factor markets. The migration of labour in particular is central to the process of social and economic reorganization. So also is the pattern of diffusion of new ideas, new fashions, etc.

Data on capital flows are not easily available, but the nature of Canada's branch banking system alone would lead us to expect a very significant degree of interregional integration. The data on migration confirm a very high degree of interprovincial mobility, the dominant proportion of which is interurban.

More than a half million Canadians migrated between provinces between 1956 and 1961; of these over 65 per cent moved between urban centres. In the period 1966-71, the number of interprovincial migrants increased to 840,000, of which 71 per cent moved between urban centres.[10]

Since the dominant reasons for migration are job related, and the major labour markets are metropolitan areas, these findings provide direct and strong confirmation of the degree of interprovincial labour market integration, and further confirm the central role of metropolitan areas as the conduit for that integration.[11]

Research on the diffusion of new ideas, and especially innovations, indicates that they flow through the urban system via the hierarchical structure. Although evidence on this for Canada is meagre, the importance of interurban linkages in the process of economic development appears to be well established.[12]

Additional evidence of spatial integration consists of cyclical interdependence between units. In Table 4, we provide data on the correlations of cyclical unemployment performance between metropolitan areas. The high correlations among the largest areas further demonstrate their close functional interdependence.

Table 4
Interurban Correlation of Unemployment, 1966-75*

	Montreal	Vancouver	Calgary	Edmonton	Winnipeg	Hamilton	Ottawa-Hull	London	Windsor	St. Catharines	Halifax	St. Johns	Victoria	Chicoutimi	Quebec
Toronto	•	•	•	•	•	•	•	•	0	0	•	•	•		
Montreal		•	•	•	•	•						0			
Vancouver			•	•	•	0	0						0		
Calgary				•	•						0	0	0		
Edmonton					•	0									
Winnipeg														0	
Hamilton							•	•	0	0					
Ottawa-Hull								•		•	0				
London									•	•	•	0			
Windsor										•		0			
St. Catharines															
Halifax												•			
St. Johns													•		
Victoria															
Chicoutimi															
Quebec															

* After 1975, the unemployment data are non-comparable.
0 denotes a correlation coefficient that is significant at the 97.5 per cent level.
• denotes significance at 99 per cent level.
SOURCE: Statistics Canada, Labour Force Survey Division (mimeo).

While far from conclusive, these findings are consistent with the following hypotheses that derived from our examination of the spatial consequences of Canadian economic development:

    i) The Canadian economy has become integrated across provincial boundaries to some substantial extent.

    ii) Much of this integration is the result of the emergence of and interaction between metropolitan areas.

It may be useful to provide a schematic representation of the altered basis of regionalism. Panel (a) of Figure I depicts the original situation in which the boundaries between provinces were sharply defined and the linkages within provinces predominated: the situation of provincial societies and economies. Panel (b) depicts the current situation, in which interprovincial linkages due to metropolitan development and interdependence have been augmented, and the intraprovincial separation between rural and urban has probably deepened.

Figure 1
A Schematic Representation of Spatial Relationships

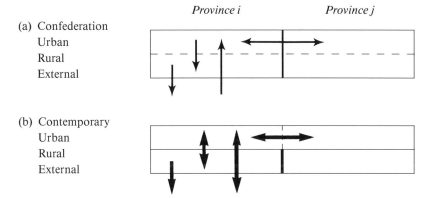

(2) Evolution of Federalism

If the economic determinants of regionalism have been subjected to fundamental transformations, no less significant has been the evolution of the federal system. Much of that evolution derives from the constitutional legitimation of provinces as the spokesmen for local concerns. Assigned responsibility for entities such as metropolitan areas that would in time come to dominate their respective provinces and, in several cases, outstrip in economic and social significance all but two or three of the larger provinces, provincial governments were able to become the chief beneficiaries of that expansion.[13]

The causes of this growth included both the expansion in demands for public services (education, health, etc.) in those areas of traditional provincial jurisdiction, and the transfer of funds from the federal government to help finance the provision of such services (Table 5). In addition, there has been growing dependence of local governments on provincial governments to help provide increased services at the local level, a factor which has helped to consolidate provincial power (Table 6).

Table 5
Expenditure by Level of Government Before and After
Intergovernmental Transfers, Selected Years, 1950-78
(national accounts basis)

Year	Gross Expenditures (before transfers)*				Direct Expenditures (after transfers)**			
	Fed.	Prov.	Local	Hospitals	Fed.	Prov.	Local	Hospitals
1950	58%	24%	18%	—	52%	26%	22%	—
1956	62	20	18	—	56	21	23	—
1965	52	30	18	—	43	23	27	7%
1970***	49	35	15	—	37	30	25	8
1978***	51	36	11	—	40	30	22	7

* Transfers paid to other levels of government are included as expenditures of the transferring government, but excluded from expenditures of recipient governments. Reflects per cent of *costs* to level of government of services provided or activities undertaken by all governments combined.

** Transfers paid to other levels of government are excluded from the expenditures of the transferring government, but included in the expenditures of the recipient government. Shows percentage of total direct expenditures *administered* by each level of government, or costs of services provided by each level of government.

*** Shares allow for CPP and QPP expenditures as follows:

Year	$(mil.)	%
1970	134	.4
1971	200	.6
1972	284	.7
1973	406	.9
1974	542	1.0
1975	777	1.1
1976	1099	1.4
1977	1427	1.7
1978	1781	1.9

SOURCES: Strick, "Trend Analysis of Government Revenues"; Statistics Canada, *National Income and Expenditure Accounts*.

Much of the argument in favour of the growth of the power of provincial governments has been based on their presumed greater sensitivity to the regionally differentiated needs of Canadians. That regionalism has been used to augment provincial powers is not surprising. Why the assumptions underlying this argument have remained unchallenged requires further examination.

Table 6
Components of Local Government Revenue, 1969-76
(financial management data)

	1969	1973	1976
Taxes	47%	40%	39%
Total own sources	56	52	49
Provincial transfers			
General purpose	4	6	6
Specific purpose	38	40	42
Federal transfers	1	1	1
Total transfers	44	47	51
Total revenue	100	100	100

SOURCES: See Strick, "Trend Analysis of Government Revenues"; Statistics
Canada, *Government Finance.*

IV. Redefined Regionalism

If the Canadian economy has evolved as described above, then the new
patterns of social-economic structure would tend to be at odds with the
simple provincial subdivision. The Canadian economy is such that spillovers beyond provincial boundaries are a virtual certainty, so that the
provinces are in one sense too limited in scope to deal efficiently with the
new regional realities.[14] In another sense, the emergence of metropolitan
areas as the key spatial units in functional economic and social terms
makes provinces too big to be *sensitive* to local requirements.[15] In other
words, the very same factors that led to creation of a federal system when
Canada was a simple society might now appear to call for a revised political
structure to promote efficiency and relevance in government.

In fact, such an adaption of our political structure is virtually precluded
by the previously noted growth of provincial power in the name of "regionalism." It is vital, therefore, to examine more precisely how this term has
come to be redefined.

A major contributing factor has been the ability of provincial governments to use their power so as to claim to speak for their citizens. Indeed,
the word "provinces" is used to describe both the territories and their
governments without distinction.

The reason for this association of governments with community relates
to the dynamics of governmental expansion. As provincial power grew,
identification of particular *interests* with the authority most capable of
serving their needs expanded. These interests included ordinary citizens,
who are clients of their provincial governments for an increasing range of
services, along with business interests, public-sector employees, and so

forth. This history of provincial government has been argued to constitute proof that provincial "societies" have been created even if they were originally only administrative units, and that therefore provinces have become even more meaningful units for capturing Canada's true regional social structure than ever before.[16]

While superficially attractive, this view is based on a very questionable assumption regarding the role of provincial public services in creating a well-defined social entity.[17] This approach disregards the fact that spatial choices regarding location are primarily dependent on where economic opportunities lie. Hence, employment prospects in particular explain labour mobility. While provincial policies may have some impact on employment opportunities, their impact can be expected to be minor compared to the overriding market forces at work.[18]

The major structural changes we noted above produced very significant internal mobility in Canada, which in turn has led to rapidly changing communities both in sending and in receiving areas (Table 7). The result is that the notion of provinces as homogeneous, closed communities with common sets of interests, which is implicit in the idea of provincial societies, is of diminishing accuracy particularly for the metropolitan areas that now dominate the economy. These metropolitan areas are the precise opposite of closed societies, featuring instead enormous diversity of populations, of lifestyles, and hence of economic interests. Moreover, the fact that so much of the population in any one city comes from other cities creates a network of intermetropolitan social ties that contributes greatly to their interdependence.[19]

Table 7
Role of Migration To and From Selected
Metropolitan Areas, 1966-71

	In Migrants As % of '71 Pop.	Out Migrants As % of '66 Pop.	Immigrants As % of '66 Pop.
Halifax	16.1	17.3	2.9
Montreal	6.3	6.5	4.5
Toronto	8.5	9.0	11.5
Edmonton	17.9	15.5	5.1
Vancouver	13.1	9.1	7.7

SOURCE: Frederick I. Hill, *Canadian Urban Trends*, Vol. 2, *Metropolitan Perspective* (Toronto: Copp Clark and Supply and Services Canada, 1976), Table 1.6, p. 7.

If there is any persistence of traditional values and sentiment about provincial attachments, it is more likely to be found in the more static, non-metropolitan segments of the province. The rural-urban dichotomy in virtually every province in Canada is more profound and more reflective of alternative "regional" values in their truest form than the readily accepted distinctions between provinces. Simply put, the communities of Halifax, Toronto, and Vancouver and possibly even Montreal are likely to be more similar in their overall interests than they will be relative to other residents in the non-metropolitan areas of their respective provinces.

Nevertheless, the notion of province as a regional entity not only persists, but thrives. A second and more important reason may lie in the emphasis that has been placed on the widely accepted goal of regional equality and, more recently, on regional development. The most significant attempt by Ottawa to deal with this perceived problem entailed equalization payments *to provincial governments*. In the name of equalizing service levels to Canadian citizens, these payments reinforced the power of provincial governments. This in turn imparted an increasingly restrictive interpretation to the concept of regional economies and hence their relationship to the national economy. Such an interpretation was abetted by what might be called the neo-Keynesian, public economy view, in which the emphasis is placed primarily on the public sector of the economy and its role as a provider of public services.

Such a focus provides the framework developed by economists to analyse federalism, namely fiscal federalism.[20] The problem of fiscal federalism is first and foremost the assignment of *public-sector* functions among existing levels of government. The concern is almost exclusively with efficient assignment among levels, and not whether the particular level being considered constitutes a reasonable choice.[21] Our prior question, of the correspondence between spatially defined interests (regionalism) and provincial governments, has not been raised. The critical consequence of acceptance in practice of this framework with its approach to provinces as spaceless public economies has been the deliberate enhancement of provincial fiscal power in the name of regionalism.

Fiscal federalism, and this public-sector orientation in general, is not designed to provide insights into the behaviour of the rest of the national economy. However useful the Keynesian (demand) emphasis on the public sector might have been, it was appropriate only to stabilization activity over relatively short periods of time in which changes in the rest of the economy were sharply circumscribed.[22] By ignoring longer-term (supply) considerations, the frame of reference fails to deal with the structure and development of the national economy as a whole. The spatial implications of the evolution of the economic system cannot be conceived in the absence of these latter considerations.

The low priority attached to issues in the non-governmental domain of the Canadian economy in the post-war period and the increasing fiscal and political power of the provinces have been used to legitimate an interventionist role by provinces in the management of economic affairs. Provinces are now able to claim responsibility for "their" regional economies, and there are few who would challenge the underlying premise.

If our view that social and economic transformation has transcended these historical boundaries is correct, then the persistence of this narrower conception is likely to pose problems both for the efficient and equitable management of the Canadian economy and for its long-term rate and pattern of development.

It seems clear that the only working concept of regionalism in Canada today is provincialism.[23] One can appreciate why provincial governments perpetuate this view of regionalism. It gives substance to their very considerable claims on national resources intended to deal with problems of regional economic disparities and underdevelopment. And, as post-war history has shown, these resources can constitute a vital means of expanding the fiscal and political power of provincial authorities.

Less obvious are the reasons why the federal government has accepted this notion of provinces as economic regions. It appears to be the case that federal authorities have simply not moved beyond their neo-Keynesian, managerial understanding of the Canadian economy. They tend to see all economic issues in terms of public economics, and hence the regional economic concern must be interpreted exclusively within the framework of fiscal federalism. Regional economic issues find resolution by means of the many highly innovative instrumentalities of federal-provincial co-operation[24] such as equalization payments. Significantly, these latter are designed to achieve public-sector equality but *not* individual equity.[25] In other words, the economic dimensions of regionalism are hardly conceivable by Ottawa outside the federal political system.

This might, of course, constitute not conceptual shortsightedness but a mature recognition of political facts of life, namely that Ottawa cannot realistically challenge the legitimacy of provinces on such a key issue. Certainly the federal effort to deal with urban Canada was initially constrained and then terminated in deference to provincial hostility to such efforts largely on constitutional grounds, despite the overwhelming importance of metropolitan areas to the Canadian economy.

If such constitutional propriety were costless, in that the provincial assumption of responsibility for regional economies created no fundamental problems for the Canadian economy, such benign neglect would indeed be astute. However, there is reason to believe the costs may be extremely high. Several analysts have already explored the efficiency costs of reduced labour and capital mobility, of barriers to commodity flows, and so forth.[26] In addition to these, however, are a variety of broader, systemic consequences that we turn to in the concluding section.

V. Some Consequences

One important consequence of distracting attention from regionalism as pluralism is that provinces, in failing to capture important dimensions of Canadian regionalism, may actually harm genuine regional interests. For example, to the extent that there are common regional interests among the Maritime provinces that could be more adequately served by collective action, the existence of provinces and their pursuit of more narrowly defined provincial goals in the name of regionalism will fracture and thereby frustrate those potentially more significant regional interests.

In a similar vein, the evidence strongly suggests that metropolitan interests are quite distinct from and in conflict with rural interests. Provinces which try to serve both types of regional interests may do great disservice to both. Certainly, large cities have long argued that provincial policies have retarded their efficient development, and, if so, this would entail potentially high costs for all Canadians.

Even for the traditional concerns of federalism, a faulty identification of Canadian regionalism can prove costly. Consider first the attempt to remove regional economic disparities. It is widely believed that federal initiatives in this area have failed. This view derives from evidence that gaps in income and unemployment *between* the provinces have persisted despite major efforts to eliminate them. The cause is often attributed to inadequate federal sensitivity to "regional" interests, which flaw, it is believed, can only be removed by decentralizing this task to the authorities genuinely reflecting regional interests, the provinces.

Our understanding of economic influences on modern Canadian regionalism raises questions about this diagnosis. If provinces are not closely integrated economic entities, then economic policies which assume them to be are unlikely to work, and may make matters worse. Regional development policies aimed at particular locations (urban or rural) within a province will transmit improvements primarily to economically linked regions. These will probably be only a limited subset of the province, and may well include regions in other provinces. While there is reason to expect regional equalization to result between these integrated units, there is no basis for assuming economic disparities between provinces as a whole will be eliminated. Indeed, they may well be exacerbated.

A more critical issue concerns the demand for greater decentralization of the federal system. The provinces have argued vigorously and on the whole effectively for the devolution of powers, largely on the grounds that they are best situated to deal with the centrifugal forces of regionalism.

Our discussion suggests that this claim may be at best only partially valid. Many interests for whom the provinces presume to speak because they reside in the territory may have a wider focus, either because of spillovers and related linkages, because of broader redistributional goals, or because they share economic and social concerns with other citizens of Canada. This is not to deny the existence of legitimate provincial interests, but these will tend to derive primarily from the public economy roles of the province, as provider of provincial public services and employer of public-sector workers. It remains to be demonstrated, logically or empirically, that other interests, and especially those dependent on the performance of the national economy, have a significant attachment to the province as a place. Their attachment may be wider (e.g., national or multinational corporations, national labour markets, etc.) or narrower (e.g., city, suburb, or town), but it is difficult to conceive of a persuasive argument as to why their attachment would be exclusively or even primarily to the province.

Perhaps the most questionable political use of the notion of regionalism has occurred in the cases of Quebec and Alberta. In its White Paper on Sovereignty-Association, the Parti Québécois government discusses "our community," "our people," "francophones," and "Quebeckers," as if they are, and indeed always were, interchangeable descriptions for a single group with common regional interests.[27] This view led to the successful pursuit of greater fiscal autonomy under Prime Minister Pearson, which in turn contributed quite naturally to the struggle for political autonomy (however labelled) as well. Alberta, meanwhile, although not as far advanced as Quebec, is pursuing and, encouraged by most other provinces, is gaining fiscal autonomy.

While it is not possible to trace a causal relationship between fiscal autonomy and political autonomy on the basis of a very small sample, the nature of bureaucratic and political power makes it foolish to ignore the likelihood of such a relationship. And when combined, these are likely to lead to a third stage in autonomy, namely general economic autarky. Such autarky provides maximum provincial control over "their" economies and leads to unenlightened intervention in the national economy. In part this process has begun with renewed attention being paid to resource industries. Provinces are inclined to promote activities such as oil exploration, hydro and mineral development, and the like because they permit quick profits and greater independence from federal economic direction (not to mention the great tax advantages to provincial Crown corporations).

What is not so clear is whether what is good individually for the *governments* of Alberta, Ontario, Quebec, or Newfoundland is necessarily in the long-run interests either of their own citizens (past, present, and/or future) or of all Canadians. For this process of "provincialization" of the economy will not only reduce the advantages from interregional economic integration, but may lead to far-reaching and undesirable structural changes. For example, the high capital requirements in the resource industries will increase our dependence on foreign investment. The implication for domestic interest rates and for exchange rates is such as likely to weaken other sectors of the economy (e.g., manufacturing) where technical progress has traditionally been high.

More important, the historical attempt to build Canada as an integrated society, in which citizens are free to move and share in the fruits of progress, is giving way to a divisive parochialism that is a throwback to earlier days. Rather than adjusting our political institutions to the new patterns of regionalism inherent in modern society, we appear to be in the process of freezing our society into forms that enhance the power of those institutions. Certainly regionalism as we have defined it cannot be well served by these developments. Hopefully some clarity about regionalism might help us to assess the costs entailed.

Notes

I should like to acknowledge the helpful suggestions of my colleagues, Stan Winer and Michael Ray.

1. An excellent attempt to use a structural explanation, including the staple model, as the basis for an integrated approach to regional and national economic development is Richard E. Caves and Richard H. Holton, *The Canadian Economy, Prospect and Retrospect* (Cambridge, Mass., 1961), 141.

2. For an analysis of the leading role of metropolitan growth in national economic development, see Brian J.L. Berry, *The Human Consequences of Urbanization* (New York, 1973), ch. 12.

3. Clearly the process of sectoral specialization and spatial integration has been incomplete. The continuing importance of resources and resource exports in certain provinces precludes *total* integration of those regions into the rest of the Canadian economy. Similarly, the absence of a highly developed capital goods industry, and hence the need to import machinery and equipment, leaves a structural gap and hence less than complete economic integration. But this only confirms less than total integration.

4. Indeed, the statistical agencies at both the provincial and federal levels are assigning top priority to producing "regional" accounts for the provinces, and national economic models (Candide) are being "regionalized" to incorporate the "behaviour" of these provincial economies.

5. See, for example, Ludwig Auer, *Regional Disparities of Productivity and Growth in Canada* (Ottawa, Supply and Services, 1979).

6. For a useful summary of the substantial evidence on the nature of the Canadian urban system, see J.W. Simmons, *The Canadian Urban System: An Overview*, Centre for Urban and Community Studies, University of Toronto, Research Paper No. 104, January, 1979.

7. In order to focus on the central point of the paper, we have not attempted to articulate the precise forms of spatial organization and integration, such as urban structure, hierarchy, networks, and the like.

8. The three largest metropolitan areas, Montreal, Toronto, and Vancouver, all ship between 40 and 50 per cent of the goods manufactured in their respective provinces. They also account for almost 40 per cent of all manufacturing shipments despite constituting less than 30 per cent of the population; Statistics Canada, *Manufacturing Industries of Canada: sub-Provincial Areas*, 1961, Cat. no. 31-209 (Ottawa, January, 1980), Fig. 1, xvii.

9. The importance of urban units is discussed by the Economic Council of Canada in *Living Together, A Study of Regional Disparities* (Ottawa, 1977). However, the concern of that study was the significance of cities or intraprovincial city systems for regional (provincial) disparities. Our concern is with interprovincial urban relationships.

10. *Census of Canada*, 1961, Vol. 4:1-9; *Census of Canada*, 1971, Vol. 1:2-7.

11. Attempts to re-estimate spatial interdependencies, such as migration, based on spatial units that are more defensible in terms of economic theory have yielded much improved results. See, for example, G. Alperovitch, J. Bergsman, and C. Ehemann, "An Econometric Model of Migration Between United States Metropolitan Areas," *Urban Studies* (June, 1977), 135-45.

12. B.J.L. Berry, "Hierarchical Diffusion: The Basis of Development Filtering and Spread in a System of Growth Centres," in Niles M. Hansen, ed., *Growth Centres in Regional Economic Development* (New York, 1972), 108-38.

13. For historical trends, see Richard M. Bird, *The Growth of Government Spending in Canada*, Canadian Tax Foundation, Canadian Tax Papers, No. 51, July, 1970. A more thorough assessment of the current situation and in particular the increasingly dominant provincial role vis-à-vis cities is provided in John C. Strick, "Trend Analysis of Government Revenues, Expenditures and Intergovernmental Transfer Payments," *Report of the Tri-Level Task Force on Public Finance*, Special Studies, Vol. II (mimeo), 1976, available from Canada Mortgage and Housing Corporation.

14. "Public decisionmaking is faulty insofar as important interactions either cannot be co-ordinated or must be disregarded." Jerome Rothenberg, "Local Decentralization and the Theory of Optimal Government," in Julius Margolis, ed., *The Analysis of Public Output* (New York, 1970), 33.

15. Paradoxically, provinces have used precisely this argument of capturing spillovers to create "regional" governments at the local level, while not confronting it at the interprovincial level.

16. This position is taken by The Task Force on Canadian Unity in its document *A Future Together, Observations and Recommendations* (Ottawa, 1979), ch. 3, and especially 30-31.

17. One of the more innovative attempts to explain how mobility can lead to more efficient provision of public services through creating communities with homogeneous tastes was that of Charles M. Tiebout, "A Pure Theory of Local Expenditures," *Journal of Political Economy* (October, 1956), 416-24. For the problems involved in applying this model to the real world, see Harvey E.

Brazer, "Some Fiscal Implications of Metropolitanism," in Guthrie S. Birkhead, ed., *Metropolitan Issues: Social, Governmental, Fiscal* (Syracuse, N.Y., 1962), 61-82.

18. Thomas J. Courchene, "Interprovincial Migration and Economic Adjustment," *Canadian Journal of Economics*, III, 4 (November, 1970), 550-76.

19. Almost one-quarter of immigrants to Montreal between 1966-71 were from Toronto, and slightly over one-quarter of those to Toronto were from Montreal. Frederick I. Hill, *Canadian Urban Trends*, Vol. 2, *Metropolitan Perspective* (Toronto, 1976), Table 1.7, 8-9. The difficulty of finding "native" Albertans in Alberta is symptomatic of the same rapid social turnover.

20. Early contributions to this literature include A.D. Scott, "A Note on Grants in Federal Countries," *Economica*, XVII, (November, 1950); J.M. Buchanan, "Federal Grants and Resource Allocation," *Journal of Political Economy*, LX (June, 1952); A.D. Scott, "Federal Grants and Resource Allocation," *Journal of Political Economy*, LX (December, 1952), and Buchanan's "A Reply," same issue. The most formal statement of the issue is Wallace E. Oates, *Fiscal Federalism* (New York, 1972). A closely related recent Canadian study is Albert Breton and Anthony Scott, *The Economic Constitution of Federal States* (Toronto, 1978).

21. For example, certain functions are allocated to "the provincial" level as if it included homogeneous units. The vast differences in size alone among Canadian provinces would undermine the applicability of many of the theoretical conclusions.

22. The Economic Council's concern with regional interdependencies emphasized spending *leakages* rather than functional *linkages*, the former being a short run, demand concept, the latter being a long run, supply-determining concept. *Living Together*, ch. 6.

23. For a well-reasoned statement of this case, see J.E. Hodgetts, "Regional Interests and Policy in a Federal Structure," *Canadian Journal of Economics and Political Science*, XXXII, 1 (February, 1966), 3-14. Reprinted in N.H. Lithwick, ed., *Regional Economic Policy: The Canadian Experience* (Toronto, 1978), ch. 5a. The term "provincialism" was used in a similar context by Paul W. Fox, "Regionalism and Confederation," in *Regionalism in the Canadian Community, 1867-1967* (Toronto, 1967). Also reprinted in Lithwick, *ibid.*, ch. 5b.

24. The machinery of federal-provincial co-operation is analysed in Richard Simeon, *Federal-Provincial Diplomacy, The Making of Recent Policy in Canada* (Toronto, 1972).

25. Vincent Bladen cautioned against the confusion of provincial political interests with the welfare of individuals some forty-five years ago. "The Economics of Federalism," *Canadian Journal of Economics and Political Science*, 1 (1935), 348-51. For an empirical demonstration of the failure of province-based regional economic policies to redistribute interpersonal income, see W.I.

Gillespie and Richard Kerr, "The Impact of Federal Regional Economic Expansion Policies on the Distribution of Income in Canada," Economic Council of Canada Discussion Paper 85, 1977.

26. Carl S. Shoup, "Interregional Economic Barriers: The Canadian Provinces," in *Issues and Alternatives, 1977, Intergovernmental Relations*, Ontario Economic Council, 81-100. See also A.E. Safarian, *Canadian Federalism and Economic Integration*, Constitutional Study for Privy Council (Ottawa, 1974).

27. See Chapter 1 of *Quebec-Canada: A New Deal* – the Quebec government's proposal for a new partnership between equals: sovereignty-association, as reprinted in *The Globe and Mail*, November 2, 1979, p. 9.

8. ANNE LEGARÉ

Canadian Federalism
and the State

Marxist analysis has often conceptualized federalism in the very terms of liberal discourse: as an object in itself, an autonomous and distorting legal form. In an attempt to escape this tendency, federalism will be considered here as a form of regime, a cosubstantial element of the general definition of the capitalist state, and particularly of the Canadian state.

The state designates a field of class relations which is broader than the regime which organizes its sites of power. While the state cannot exist without a regime, its aims go beyond that of the regime, because the state reproduces, through a series of concrete means, the conditions necessary to maintain social relations, and relations of production marked by class domination. The ways in which this domination is exercised, the material- ity of state power, are objects of analysis which cannot be reduced to the regime. It is not the Canadian state which has a federal form, but rather its regime. We must therefore clarify what is meant by the Canadian state through definition which takes account of the juridico-political forms of organization/distribution of institutional power and which extends to the spaces of class power.

The approach to federalism which I propose here is found at the heart of a conception of the state which has come to the fore in Marxism over the last ten years. This current, critical of the economism of the Third Interna- tional, has raised questions about the historical biases that have led both Western Communist parties and those in the "actually existing socialist"

Published in *Studies in Political Economy* (1982) as "Towards a Marxist Theory of Canadian Federalism." Reproduced with permission of the journal and the author.

countries along the path of failure of revisionism. We have thus come to see that Marx, in *Capital*, started from the principle of non-correspondence between the base and the superstructure and of the non-exteriority of instances to explain the relation of the political and of the state to the economic. Consider the place occupied by factory legislation in the chapter on "Machinery and Modern Industry"[1] and the law presiding over the genesis of the industrial capitalist in *Capital*. The Factory Acts Extension Act and the Workshop Act are both considered from the standpoint of the constitutive role of the state vis-à-vis the new capitalist division of labour.

The work of N. Poulantzas has helped to rescue this conception of the state as a constituent element of capitalist relations of production and other theorists have also emphasized the fact that the relative autonomy of instances does not imply that the effect of one on another comes totally from the outside. Suzanne de Brunhoff has formulated this principle of non-exteriority by means of concepts such as "state management of labour power."[2] Along with Poulantzas, Hirsch, and others, she explains how the state is present in the constitution of capitalist relations of production right from the formation of the mode of production. Poulantzas has also helped to distinguish the various forms of the capitalist state which involve changes in its relation to classes and to the economic, according to each of the states of capitalist development. This has proved particularly enlightening with regard to the Keynesian stage.[3]

However, Poulantzas and most present-day Marxist theorists do not seem to have perceived the link of interdependence and the reciprocal action between the form(s) of the *regime* and the *state*, precisely with regard to the constituent presence of the political in the relations of production. For example, Poulantzas writes: "Political regimes are seen here as variables within the limits set by the form of state of a typical stage. The relations and concrete functioning of the parties, in relation to a regime, are seen as variables within the limits set by the power bloc, corresponding to the form of state of this stage."[4]

This statement by Poulantzas appears static. I will develop my analysis from the idea that the form of regime, as an organization/distribution of the sites of exercise of state power, has a specific effect on the expansion of the forms of the state and is incorporated as a constituent part of the latter, particularly in its relation to classes. Moreover, to the extent that the form of regime is essentially given by the constitution, its transformations and adaptations to the state, following the stages of the mode of production in each social formation, act on the state through tendential relations of resistance/submission of the regime to the state. Each form of regime, each given historical case, will be a concrete variant of this interdependence. Thus a form of regime is not, as Poulantzas puts it, a mere "variable within the limits set by the form of state." The case of Canadian federalism and its difficulties in the state demonstrate that things are much more complicated.

The following propositions for the analysis of federalism and of the state in Canada originated partly in *local* preoccupations. Inasmuch as certain ideological state apparatuses of education and culture, demarcated as provincial by the Canadian federal regime, were bastions of rising nationalism, the project – a study of class relations formed in the state apparatuses given by federalism – was rooted in the Quebec conjuncture.

More broadly, Marxist writing in both Canada and Quebec seemed to disdain the study of federalism, treating the latter as simply a juridical representation of power. We knew of no concrete study of the Canadian state which treated the constituent action of federalism in the relation between classes, the state, and the relations of production. At best, federalism was taken into account through its function of separation/segmentation of power in various sites – the provinces. These analyses effectively accepted the liberal discourse which treats the Canadian state as the sum of provincial and federal powers. Each province accordingly is presented as an autonomous space and Quebec is separated from its constituent relation to the Canadian state. In thus abstracting Quebec from the Canadian ensemble by enclosing it within an opaque and self-sufficient regional limit, these studies convey an empirico-positivist and ethnocentric conception of the state.

In the following analysis, a particular effort has been made not to apprehend the Canadian state as the sum of its apparatuses, nor to reduce it to these. Thus, Quebec is a given region, a province defined according to the constitutional division of powers, a given site of power, a given space containing certain institutions materializing certain apparatuses. As is any other case, Quebec is thus the site of a particular, specific, and historically determined realization of the relations of force between the classes within the totality of the social formation designated by the Canadian state. In this analysis, the general, clearly, is present in the particular.

The following text, as it analyses Canadian federalism, will deal with provinces, political regions, and centres defined by the regime as distinct sites of power, with various spaces designating the totality of the relations materialized in the apparatuses of these provinces, or in these regions, or at the centre, but never in isolation; always it is in relation to the whole given by the Canadian state, whose generality and historicity run through each particular site. Each site of power, each region, is a microcosm of the whole. The Canadian state, in its concrete meaning, points to a complex overlapping and entanglement of levels, apparatuses, and sites of power rather than to a chain of so many successive links. The political reality covered by the term "Canadian state" represents the synthesis of a great many determinations of which federalism is one element. By "Canadian state" is designated thus the unique new entity produced by the articulation of all the sites of power.

I shall now propose a series of five theses centred on the position put forward above. These theses concern the relation between the state and federalism. They attempt to show that the dialectical analysis of power must start from a definition of the state as a relation and not the sum of the addition and separation of powers, as is the case with technico-juridical division of institutions given by the constitution. Moreover, the propositions attempt to assign a place to the various sites of class power (for example, the power bloc and the regional political spaces), starting from the specific conceptual unity of the Canadian state. First, the principle of the articulation between federalism and the state will be posed, then the relation of each to the various sites of class power, and finally the figure of the federal regime state. Last of all, the Quebec national question will be considered as the nodal point of the reproduction of the Canadian state.

First Thesis: The Articulation between Federalism and the State

In Marxism, there can be no autonomous theory of federalism or of the form of regime, but rather a theory of articulation between the form of regime and the state.

Posing the question this way runs counter to the custom established in Canada of speaking of the "federal state" or the "federal form of the state." But the form of the state, whether liberal or interventionist, designates something different from the form of regime – although the two are connected. We must therefore get to the bottom of what is the real object of each of these concepts.

The expression "federal state" is inappropriate, from a dialectical point of view, because the state cannot be reduced to the central level of power, to the sum or the separation of all the apparatuses, or to the federal regime. The state represents rather the *synthesis* of all the struggles marked by the *domination* of a set of class interests over those of other classes.

By the form of state is designated the type of relation which is instituted between the political and the economic, dictated by the stage of mode of production in the given social formation, within the context of a separation of instances which remains only relative. The form of the state, then, points to the interpenetration which is established between these instances according to the more or less clear limits of the autonomy governed by the historical forms of the capital-labour contradiction. The state will be more or less liberal, more or less interventionist in the totality of these relations with the economic and with the classes. In this way its form can be said to be dominated by a liberal, interventionist, or authoritarian tendency.

On the one hand, the form of *regime* points to the juridical organization/distribution of the powers and jurisdictions between the various public institutions formally coming under the state power. The form of regime can be, for example, federal or unitary, according to the degree of concentration of the legislative and executive powers granted to each level of government. As Michel Miaille writes:

> We mean by form of régime the concrete modalities in which a form of state appears.... We refer to the precise historical conditions which created the society under consideration, to the particularities of the relations between social classes; in short, to the specificity of the political in the social formation.[5]

The form of government is distinct from the form of regime in that it designates exclusively the rules of organization of the governmental apparatuses: the party system and representation, elections, parliamentarism, etc. Miaille defines it as "the way in which governments are designated and in which they exercise power."[6]

If the theoretical principle raised here is that of the necessity of analysing the articulation between the form(s) of state and the form(s) of regime, it is because, first of all, these two realities are quite distinct. *The form of state points to the nature of the relation which is established between classes and the state, to the more or less liberal or authoritarian manner in which the state, a contradictory complex of class relations, ensures the reproduction of the relations of production.* This latter function shows the necessity for homology between the state and the mode of production, and also the possibility for the realization of this relation through various historical paths. The form of the state in each of these stages, then, corresponds to the degree of directivity of the state in the means employed to reproduce the relations of production and the politico-ideological relations of domination.

In this sense, each form of state, each historical phase of a given state in the relations between classes and the instances of power, will establish a particular and different relation with the concrete forms of the political. Thus the organization/distribution of the powers of the state, federalism as a form of regime, and other forms of the political, will be neither indifferent nor completely autonomous vis-à-vis the form of the state.

For example, at the competitive stage of the capitalist mode of production, the liberalism of the state in its relation to the classes present will tolerate a flexible and decentralized distribution of the power sites. On the other hand, when capitalism is in its imperialist stage, while a certain autonomy remains, the room to manoeuvre enjoyed by the political and the state will be less and will lead to a more and more authoritarian interventionism. After this stage, the regime will tend to be subject to the imperatives of the state. On the other hand, the very coherence of the regime and, in this case, the characteristics of federalism will, to a certain extent, resist, or adapt to, the constraints of the form of the state.

In the present phase, it can be supposed that the constitutional crisis created by the centralizing policies of the federal government reveals the necessity for the Canadian state, in its present form, to adapt the various concrete forms of the political, federalism in particular, to the rules of its new relation to classes. Federal initiatives, then, reflect the tendency toward authoritarian intervention noted above.

The first thesis suggests that the state and the form of regime, corresponding to reciprocal finalities, should not be confused. The task of Marxist analysis is to develop the theory of the relations that each form of state can maintain with each form of regime. At the monopolist stage to which corresponds the interventionist form of the state, the exercise of autonomy by the provinces in the areas of their jurisdiction may hinder the directive process, which is not guaranteed by federalism *per se*. Each example of federalism must thus be studied in its relation to the historical forms of the state and these relations must be grasped at a theoretical level.

The state, taken in one of its various forms, then designates a reality which can be neither reduced to nor confused with the form of regime. These two entities, of different qualitative and conceptual levels, establish mutual relations which must be explained on a theoretical basis.

Second Thesis: A Historical Relation of Interdependence

The process which articulates the regime and the state makes federalism a constituent element of the Canadian state. In fact, the form of the regime is not in a position of exteriority vis-à-vis the state, just as law is neither the effect nor cause but a constituent element of the bourgeois state. While they cannot be reduced to each other, the regime and the state are interdependent.

The form of regime is a process of distribution of the institutional sites of class power – the apparatuses of political society, according to Gramsci – and unifying/separating the regions and the centre. Thus, the regime assigns places to the sites of material realization of the relations of power located within the state. This distribution/separation forms an integral part of the state. It is for this reason that federalism is considered a constituent element of the Canadian state.

Only in an exclusively juristic or institutionalist discourse could the state be confused with or reduced to the regime which distributes its powers. In a study of the articulation of the sites of power, the conceptual framework must recognize the distinction between the co-ordinates of a general type governing the particular case and the historical peculiarities which specify it. In this case, the Canadian state will first of all be determined by capitalist relations of production, etc. Its form of regime will be in large part marked by the general characteristics of federalism. However, once we have admitted the principle of the interaction of the reality designated by the state and that designated by federalism, the specific historical modalities of this interaction remain to be discovered.

The interaction of two phenomena implies that they are at once distinct and concomitant. Their alterity entails opposites, their alternation means that they are, in certain respects, dependent on each other. The two should not be confused, as they are in the institutionalist approach to the state. Nor should they be isolated from each other, as in the debate on the constitution. That is why, as a pair of opposites, these terms are not totally external or foreign to each other. Separate yet indissociable, these realities act on each other. The great principles which define the class state assign limits to the regime which, giving their own characteristics, tend to act on the state in return. Thus, federalism is distinct from the state, and has its own life, but also contributes to its make-up.

On the other hand, in traditional political science, largely dominated by the institutionalist approach, the phenomena of law, the juridical, are considered as autonomous facts. The juridical is a given and the products it isolates are studied for and in themselves. As Engels writes:

> Similarly with law. As soon as the new division of labour which creates professional lawyers becomes necessary, another new and independent sphere is opened up which, for all its general dependence on production and trade, has also a special capacity for reacting upon these spheres. In a modern state, law must not only correspond to the general economic conditions and be its expression, but must also be an *internally coherent* expression which does not, owing to inner contradictions, reduce itself to nought. And in order to achieve this, the faithful reflection of economic conditions suffers increasingly. All the more so the more rarely it happens that a code of law is the blunt, unmitigated, unadulterated expression of the domination of a class – this in itself would offend the conception of right.[7]

The form of regime, given by constitutional law, is approached in the same spirit, as if it did not directly reflect interests of the dominant classes, but operated rather through an inversion, as if the fact of law had been established *a priori*. Thus Engels adds: "And it seems to me obvious that this inversion, which, so long as it remains unrecognized, forms what we call *ideological outlook*, reacts in its turn upon the economic basis and may, within certain limits, modify it."[8]

This separation of law from the economic is also reflected in materialist writings, inasmuch as the juridical is neglected, under the pretext that law, like ideology, is only a representation of the real. In relation to the state, this conception leads to the view that the political regime has no class significance because it is only, as it were, a mystification of the struggles between them. But the process of distribution of the powers of the state provides the very materiality of political class domination. By making the juridical at fault in an ideological shift of the real stakes, thought itself here operates this shift by making itself the subject of juristic discourse and by neglecting the interdependence of each form of regime and the state. That is why the reciprocal action which separates and connects in a specific way the state and federalism in Canada needs to be understood.

The concrete illustration of this thesis is based on the following theoretical principles:

a) the state points to a complex of class relations;
b) these class relations, condensed by the state, are concretely and materially realized in state apparatuses/institutions;
c) the exercise of state power takes place through the material substratum that is the chain of apparatuses:
d) each particular social formation, each given society shows a particular configuration of the relations of forces materialized in the state apparatuses;
e) the form of regime, whether federal or unitary, is a particular way of organizing and qualitatively distributing the state apparatuses among various political sites/spaces;
f) what distinguishes different forms of regime is the degree of separation/integration of these apparatuses vis-à-vis the whole, the state;
g) federalism is thus a particular mode of organization/distribution of the powers of the state marked by the dominance of the *separation* of the sites of power over their unification;
h) this last observation does not mean that federalism only separates the sites of power; it also tends to unite them, but this characteristic is its second aspect, while the reverse is true for the unitary regime;
i) it is the state which realizes the unity of the sites of power, which the regime separates.

The fact that federalism is a constituent element of the state can be illustrated as follows. Canadian federalism stipulates, for example, that the federal level has jurisdiction over defence, currency, and banking. On the other hand, education, municipal institutions, etc. come under the provinces. In view of the specific historical relations that each of these spaces of reproduction maintains with the various classes and fractions allied in the state, it can be said that their allocation/distribution at the federal or provincial level establishes a particular link, which is different in each case, with the power of the state. It can be supposed that at the monopolist and interventionist stage the banking system, at the federal level, functions in close relation with the hegemonic fraction at this stage – monopoly capital. On the other hand, the education systems, while they are linked in accordance with the interests of class power at the level of the entire social formation, will adapt in different ways to the alliances in each province or region. Thus, the process of distribution of these sites of power – federalism – has a role to play in the composition of power in the state. The

Canadian federal regime, in fact, formed in 1867 from the existence of the regions (the former colonies), in turn structures these by governing the juridico-political conditions of their reproduction and, as such, provides structural conditions for the power of the state.

The Canadian state, on the one hand, finds itself operating the synthesis of the relations of forces present in the apparatuses of the regions and the centre which, on the other hand, are separated by federalism. It is in this way, in this close symbiosis with the process of the formation of the power of the state through the separation/unification of the sites of power that federalism is a constituent element of the Canadian state.

However, while we can isolate the facts of constitutional law, for example, from their relations to the state, it remains that it is because of this very separation that the regime can serve as a support for the relative autonomy of the political vis-à-vis the economic, a proposition which will be developed in the thesis that follows. It is thus thanks to its "internal coherence," to use Engels's expression, that federalism, in the case of Canada, can realize this autonomy, and do so in a characteristic way.

Third Thesis: Canadian Federalism and the Relative Autonomy of the Political

As a material organization-distribution of the institutional powers of the state, the political regime realizes the separation between the political and the economic, between the state and the classes present in a social formation. Federalism in Canada, through its various phases and forms, realizes the relative autonomy of the political by a process of dislocation/unification of the forms of the state between the centre and the regions, themselves subject to a constant movement of formation/dissolution.

In terms of federalism as a form of regime, a key question concerns its specific effect on the relation of state and class. It should be remembered that the relative autonomy of the political in the capitalist mode of production conforms to a definition of the state which poses it as not only the instrument of the interests of a class but especially as a synthesis of the totality of all the relations of struggle between the classes, under the domination of the bourgeoisie. The apparatuses of the state are the concrete sites where this autonomy operates, inasmuch as it is there that interests of opposed classes are in constant confrontation. This domination in the state is not univocal. It is produced through a series of mediations which fulfil the principle of this autonomy, indispensable for the reproduction of capitalist relations of production. It is only relative inasmuch as the class state must ensure, in the last instance, the hegemony of capital over the totality of classes in the social formation.

The function of the state, then, is to reproduce the conditions of production, and, to do this, it retains a certain distance vis-à-vis the classes which constitute it, while making sure that the power of the bourgeoisie is maintained. In a specific way, by the fetishistic character that it attributes to power, by the mode of separation it institutes between political power and social classes, federalism is the process par excellence by which the state can cause itself to be seen as separate from class power. As Pasukanis puts it:

> Beside direct and immediate class domination is constituted a *median*, *reflected* domination, in the form of official power as a particular power *detached* from society. . . .[9] Any juridical theory of the state[10] . . . must necessarily pose the state as a powerful entity *separate and autonomous* from the society.[11]

That is how the form of regime, as a juridico-political agent of the organizations of state power, is a constituent element of the state, and provides, in the case of Canada in particular, the conditions for the relative separation of the classes (and in particular the hegemonic fraction), a relative separation which is both ideological and real.

To understand the relation between the form of regime and classes, it should be remembered that the regime is not only the positive and unifying principle that the law claims to institute. It is as subordinate as any state phenomenon to the class relations which go beyond it. Thus, the political regime collides with the dynamics of social relations in its path. In the same way, federalism in Canada has to deal with the relation of forces created and destroyed through the concrete spaces that federalism separates and that the state unifies. The weight of the interests of regionally circumscribed classes has a specific effect on the regime. Federalism fulfils the principle of relative autonomy of the state vis-à-vis the classes by a movement of dislocation-unification among the concrete spaces of struggle that are the regions. As supports for this movement, the regions provide the principle of the articulation between federalism, classes, and the state. In Canada the regions, as specific objects of class struggle, impose on the state and the realization of its autonomy a tendency toward the differentiation of its forms between the centre and its regions. This movement of dislocation/unification of the forms of the state, which is consecrated by federalism, has the regions as a support.

Before proposing definitions of the notions of region, "regional question," and regionalism, it would be useful to attempt to illustrate the argument sketched above. The following points have been put forward: a) federalism attributes a fetishistic character to power; b) it represents a particular mode of separation between the classes and power; c) federalism separates the sites of power that the state unifies; d) through the dislocations in the relations between the political and the economic at the centre and in the regions, created by federalism, the state is characterized by a tendency toward autonomization vis-à-vis the classes present.

In capitalism, the relation of the state to class, as explained in the first thesis, takes successive forms which correspond to so many degrees in the autonomy existing between the political and the economic. This thesis maintains that because of federalism there is a strong tendency running through the degrees of this autonomy, whatever the form of the state may be. In other words, the variation in the degrees of this autonomy from one form of state to the other, and more particularly *the relative reduction of its autonomy in the interventionist or authoritarian state,* is effected in a much more contradictory manner in federalism. From this may follow a relative delay in the hegemonization of one form over all the sites of power or, in the case of a transformation of the state, a structural difficulty in the formation of the unity of the power bloc.

This thesis can be clarified by the following example. We know that in Canada just before the Second World War, social legislation was appreciably behind that in other dominant social formations. The federal government decided to make the implementation of the Marsh report proposals dependent on the result of federal-provincial conferences. It was to be the provinces which pushed ahead with the various forms of health insurance. As a result, the period 1945-60 was marked by strong counter tendencies. The phase of the hegemonization of monopoly capital consequently was accompanied by a delay in the form of the state vis-à-vis the economic.[12]

Our analysis maintains that federalism has been the delaying factor in the generalization of the interventionist form of the state in Canada. While this form of separation of powers is suitable for relatively liberal articulation of the political and the economic up to 1945, this form of regime offers serious resistance to a univocal and enlarged transformation of the apparatuses. If we infer the establishment of the Keynesian state form by reducing the state to federal or provincial policies, we can see that the process of generalization/unification of the interventionist form took a long time to be fully realized in Canada.

This thesis may also be illustrated by reference to the recent crisis in Canadian federalism. The emphasis on constitutional reforms has fetishized power at all levels: only a generalized and centralized authoritarianism will break the present mediation in the overall relation of the classes to the state, effected through each space as a possible site of dislocations. Finally, it can be stated that any form of regime, federal or unitary, is a support for the relative separation of the classes vis-à-vis the state inasmuch as each form of regime operates, to varying degrees, the separation of the apparatuses of power within the state and sanctions thus a relative autonomy of each of these vis-à-vis the synthesis of the whole. This separation between the apparatuses or sites of power, whether it is centralized or decentralized (unified or federal), is necessary for the reproduction of the capitalist relations of production, inasmuch as it fetishizes each site of power as separate from the others: thus is provided the institutionalization necessary for the formally separate domination of the bourgeoisie.

To clarify this point, let us cite Hirsch:

> The reproduction of the classes in the process of valorization of capital and the reproduction of political domination are not identical.... Therefore capitalism is characterized by the fact that the coercive violence of the bourgeoisie, concentrated in the means of physical repression, undergoes necessarily, by reason of the social mode of class exploitation and reproduction, an *institutionalization separate* from the individual bourgeois. *It takes a form which separates it formally* from the dominant class: this separation of the apparatuses of physical coercion vis-à-vis the proletariat and the bourgeoisie is the fundamental element in the form of domination of the bourgeois classes.[13]

This proposition maintains, then, that the degree of separation/segmentation of the state apparatuses produced by federalism fetishizes and institutionalizes in an enlarged way, in a vast number of sites of power and in particular through regional divisions, the necessary separation between the domination of the bourgeoisie and the state. This appears concretely in the political use which is made of the weight of the provinces in the process of the legitimization of the state in Canada.

We must then ask the question: what is a region? I shall propose a distinction between the notions of region, regional question, and regionalism. Unfortunately, a full treatment of these distinctions lies beyond the scope of this article. The first characteristic of the *region* is that it covers a series of political processes in a constant movement of formation/ dissolution. In the capitalist mode of production, the region is not, therefore, a static fact: the region is, by definition, relative to other regions and to the state, part of the uneven succession that makes up the space of the state. The presence of the state in the process of the formation/dissolution of the region is thus central, a presence which can be negative or positive. I believe that the region tends to be subjected to a movement of alienation/ identification vis-à-vis the state. I shall define it with regard to two interdependent aspects; a) in its relation to the classes, the region covers a totality of social relations having its own coherence (unity and diversity) centred on spatial, cultural, economic, and political stakes; b) in its relation to the state, the region is the process of formation/dissolution of a juridico-political space of reproduction. This process of formation/dissolution of the region tends to conflict with a movement of formation, a movement of assimilation or autonomization. Finally, what makes for the unity and the interdependence of these two dimensions of the concept of region (relation to the classes and relation to the state) is that in both cases, the region constitutes the support for contrary tendencies between the class processes on the one hand and the state movement on the other. The region is at once the support for movements of dissolution of juridico-political spaces of state reproduction, of movements of alienation/identification vis-à-vis the state, of movements of dislocation/unification of the forms of the state running through the various sites of power, of movements of assimilation of the region by the state or of movements of autonomization by classes, etc.

The *regional question* is precisely the expression of the movement of resistance to one or another process of formation or dissolution of a region. The regional question is the expression of objective interests centred on stakes linked to the position of regional limits and preceding or accompanying the formation-consolidation of a region or accompanying and succeeding the tendency to disappearance-dissolution of a region. That is why the regional question, raised by the formation-transformation or dissolution of a region, is a movement in the order of class relations which cannot be reduced to the state. There can exist a regional question before or after the process of formation/dissolution of a region.

In addition, I shall define *regionalism* as the totality of the habits, behaviours, beliefs, representations of one or several classes concerning a region. Regionalism is therefore an ideology whose aim is to unify the representation of separate social wholes; in this sense, there may be, for the same region, several regionalisms, according to the interests of the classes: a state regionalism whose goal is to mask the internal and external social divisions of the region and, precisely, to unify separate wholes; a regionalism of the local bourgeoisie whose aim is to obtain a regional consensus to consolidate its representation in its relations with the state and with the power bloc; a regionalism of the dominated classes whose goal is to give themselves a regional hegemony breaking with that of the local and/or national dominant classes. Regionalism, as an ideology of several classes, may be either an agent of the regional question or a condition of the reproduction of the state on the base of the region. The regional question and regionalism are class manifestations imprinted on the region as a power space of which federalism is the principle of mediation and of autonomy vis-à-vis the state. Thus, we can say that federalism, as a process of separation of regional spaces, reinforces, to a certain extent, the relative distance of the totality that is the state vis-à-vis the classes.

Fourth Thesis: The Composition of the Power Bloc and Federalism

The Canadian state is neither the sum of the numerous federal and provincial power sites, nor the sum of the regional and central apparatuses, but represents the synthesis of all these power sites. Consequently, the Canadian power bloc is neither the sum of all the regional powers, nor exclusively the sum of the federal alliances. The power bloc, through Canadian federalism, is structurally articulated to the process of unification-dislocation which runs through the form of the state, and in each conjuncture, its make-up follows the transformations which are current in this process.

I shall not come back to the question of the definition of the state, nor the principle of the articulation between federalism, the classes, and the state, which has the division into regions as a support. I shall merely recall that while the power bloc has as its subject the unity of the diverse interests which constitute it as an alliance, it also owes its make-up, from a structural point of view, to the conditions which define the state. In the Canadian case, federalism is articulated to the state through a series of more or less unified or dislocated power sites whose supports, the regions, are in a constant movement of consolidation/disappearance.

That is why the make-up of the power bloc is based, on the one hand, on the diversity of those tendencies which affect the regions and provide certain conditions for the make-up and rules of the alliance. On the other hand, this bloc is formed around its unitary pole, according to the reproduction of the conditions of production, which is entrusted to the state, under the supervision of the hegemonic fraction. Federalism in Canada thus provides, by its very materiality, the conditions for the movement of differentiation of the regional interests which are, in turn, unified by the relation of the power bloc to the state.

The classes allied in the power bloc come together in it insofar as their specific regional interests are only partly hampered by their participation in the alliance and insofar as they derive some benefit from it, beyond their differences, on the basis of reciprocal compromises. It is therefore a question of dependence/independence of each fraction vis-à-vis this political project of the whole of the bourgeoisie which governs the make-up of the power bloc. The capacity of one of the fractions to act on the political regime by putting its very existence at stake is evidence of its position. Federalism links the parties to this alliance in the state by laying the foundations of its relative autonomy, and being at the same time the principle of its division. *In a context of constitutional crisis, the parties redefine the conditions of participation in the power bloc.* In the Canadian case, it is through a reform of federalism that this renegotiation is achieved.

This many-sided articulation to the power bloc is carried out, however, inside very precise co-ordinates. As we know, the unity found within the power bloc contravenes and must contravene all conjunctural divergences and guarantee, at all times, the supremacy of the whole of the bourgeoisie over the other classes reproduced through the state. This unity is consolidated by the action of a fraction which, by its strength and its hegemonic capacity, rallies all the others, despite their differences, around this common project of domination. In adversity, the state will sanction, through its various sites of power, this cohesion of the social formation. By its very nature, hegemony tends to be exercised everywhere through all the central and regional power sites – otherwise we would see a generalized movement toward the demolition of the state.

Such a case of decomposition can only be a feature of a very exceptional conjuncture. From the structural point of view, that is, from the point of view of the profound tendency which is at work in a social formation characterized by capitalist relations of production, the unity of the various fractions of the bourgeoisie realized by a hegemonic fraction is, by definition, an enlarged process, one which unceasingly tends to be realized in all power sites.

At the other end of this pole of domination, the strengthening of the autonomy of one of several regional fractions vis-à-vis the power bloc is not irreconcilable with the reproduction of the whole. However, this autonomization vis-à-vis the power bloc is a process which is only achieved in very specific conditions. In particular, these conditions must show an advanced maturation of the autonomist political project of that fraction, as is the case for the Quebec bourgeoisie, transformed into a social force by the formation of its own political party, with political effects on other parties and on other class interests, etc. Thus, the formation in an autonomous class fraction, vis-à-vis the power bloc, does not mean a *de facto* break with the domination of the whole of the bourgeoisie over the dominated classes. It means rather a particular situation either of relative alienation or of more or less achieved independence. Moreover, it acts on its own internal conditions and gives rise to the transformation of other relations.

This autonomous fraction of the bourgeoisie, according to its alienation or its separation from the power bloc, as was the case of the non-monopolist Quebec bourgeoisie since Duplessis, expresses its disagreement with the manner of realizing the domination, the unity of the alliance, that is, with the historical conditions of this unity, at a given moment. To do this, it must be strong, organized, but it still may not have a full hegemonic capacity. It only goes against the prevailing pattern of hegemonic domination to a certain extent, and this shows the contradictory nature (strength/weakness) of its project. The support of other classes must help the fraction to succeed in its project of autonomous development. This introduces a new element in the particular relation of forces that is represented by the state. This has been clearly illustrated by the PQ power in Quebec.

Between the hegemonic fraction and the fraction or fractions which tend to be autonomous is found the totality of the other interests which, while they are not undifferentiated, form a consensus on the concrete modalities of the exercise of their domination as a totality. These fractions, like the autonomous fractions vis-à-vis the power bloc, derive their specificity from the particularities of a region, or from interests which run through several regions such as non-hegemonic banking interests. That is why the common reduction of the make-up of the power bloc to the representatives of the non-monopolist regional fractions is an oversimplification. We should not forget that in the Canadian case, the relations between classes and the state are marked by the form of regime with a tendency toward diversification/autonomization.

This thesis can be illustrated in the following way. Various important fractions in the Canadian bourgeoisie (fractions which have provincial economic-political bases and are, as well, linked to the Canadian state as a whole) agree on the fact that their dominant position depends on the organization of state power approximately as it is: that is, for example, on a segmentation/separation of the material sites of power as is given by Canadian federalism, apart from some minor adjustments. By its economic supremacy, one of these fractions imposes the rationality and the modalities of accumulation on the others, and is thus led to subject all ideological and political processes to its own determinations. this is the mission, in the present phase of capitalism in Canada, of the monopolist bourgeoisie. The other fractions may have to deal with distinct interests *to a certain extent* but the fact remains that they agree above all with the juridico-political conditions of their relation to the state. These fractions, then, form with the hegemonic fraction an alliance called the power bloc. This alliance was recently illustrated by the agreement of nine provincial premiers on the formula for the repatriation of the constitution. After numerous conflicts pointing to the historical particularity of class domination in each region/province, which takes the form of dislocations between the regional power sites vis-à-vis the interventionist form of the Canadian state as a whole, each of the fractions making up the alliance, with the exception of Quebec, rallied to the hegemonic interests personified by Pierre Elliott Trudeau *and thus promoted the project of a more centralized federalism, with its authoritarian tendency.*

The Canadian constitutional crisis has thus revealed that the Canadian power bloc was suffering severely from the structural gaps produced by federalism which affect the process of unification of the form of the state as well as hegemony: a directive intervention initiated by the strongest interests had become necessary. The recent crisis was the pretext for a new distribution of places within the alliance, a distribution more favourable to the centralist hegemony shown by the authoritarianism of the Prime Minister. None of the allied fractions really challenged the basic project: Canadian-style federalism.

In a 1977 study of class structure in Quebec, I had suggested that "the Quebec faction of the non-monopolist bourgeoisie, whether independentist or not, is not part of the Canadian power bloc."[14] This has been shown by recent events: it is not part of the power bloc because it refuses to accept federalism, while accepting nonetheless the hegemony of monopoly capital. This position, based on the primacy of the national question in Quebec, reiterates the formal alienation of the classes within Quebec from the Canadian state. Thus more than ever, divergent political projects are authorized within the Canadian state and dislocations are produced in its unification. This double contradictory movement runs through the very figure of the Canadian state – a point to be developed in the last thesis.

Thus Canadian federalism realizes, as the material condition of state power, the principle of the relative autonomy of the state vis-à-vis the classes, and thus becomes a primary political stake defining the contours of the power bloc. On the one hand, the hegemonic fraction in its function of ensuring the reproduction of the relations of production by the state initiates any unifying measure necessary for its supremacy. On the other hand, its allied fractions will use federalism as the raw material for their alliance. Finally, the fraction or fractions which are autonomous vis-à-vis the power bloc will tend to take a position of exteriority vis-à-vis the prevailing regime, that is, they will refuse to share the conditions of the alliance which define the power bloc and will give themselves other strategies for domination.

Fifth Thesis: The Quebec National Question, the Structural Principle of the Break-up of the Canadian State

The figure of the articulation between the form of regime, and the state, in Canada, is characterized by a structural tendency toward break-up. The federal form of regime is the factor of the reproduction of this tendency induced by the Quebec national question.

It has been shown above that federalism gives to the Canadian state a form which tends to work for a movement of differentiation between the regions, and then between the centre and the regions. The federal regime provides the materiality of this movement, and is at the same time the reason for the confrontations and alliances of the power bloc. The power bloc is the real site of domination, and it follows from this fact that the power of the state and the power bloc have distinct objects inasmuch as the capitalist state maintains a certain distance (whose modalities and degrees vary) from the dominant classes. At the same time, federalism, a principle of unification between the state and the power bloc, gives the Canadian state a tendency toward break-up.[15] This tendency is in fact constantly reproduced by the contradictory region/federalist regime, so that it is the very figure of the unity of the Canadian state, a form constantly reunified, constantly renegotiated at each of the great phases in the history of the Canadian social formation. The regional forces, more or less manifest, more or less coherent at a given time; the dislocations between the modalities of realization of the separation of the state and the classes; the greater or lesser unity and stability of the power bloc in a given conjuncture; the various degrees of the initiative of the hegemonic fraction to ensure the cohesion of the power bloc: all these elements punctuate the close interaction of federalism as a form of regime and the historical forms of the Canadian state, that is, the periodization of the forms of its relation to the social classes.

It is here that the Quebec national question comes in as a nodal point in the structure of the Canadian state. Certainly the national question may be seen above all as the emergence of the collective consciousness of the oppression of the nation, and as the exacerbation of the contradictions involved in this question. The national question is thus, of course, the effect of struggles and as such is located in the various conjunctures. However, through the link between the process of formation-assimilation of the dominated nation and the structural modalities of class domination in the Canadian state, through federalism, the national question is also situated in the structure of the social formation as a sort of disruptive structural *nodal point* of class relations. It is a matter of structure, then, as well as of conjuncture. In fact, the development and the strengthening of the national question in Quebec, a recurrent phenomenon of the political scene, a catalyst for social consciousness, a pole of identity, appears at first glance as an element of the conjuncture. While it brings profound changes, the Quebec national question is almost exclusively considered and ana-lysed as a conjunctural element. But the national question is not merely a phenomenon of opposition appearing at a given time. The presence of nations, and in particular the Quebec nation, is also an element of the structure of the Canadian social formation which has its own effect on the state and an action which is not external to the Canadian state, such as nationalist struggles or confrontations.

In the structure of the Canadian social formation, the Quebec national question is not an isolated element. In fact, the reproduction of this domi-nated nation intersects a process of formation-consolidation of a region of the Canadian state – Quebec – of which it is impossible, unfortunately, to enumerate here all the facets. However, the essential point is that the national question transforms, at the conjunctural level, the process of formation of this region as simply a regional question, through the emer-gence of new politico-ideological class relations identified with the region.[16] In the Canadian social structure, the nation has primacy over the region, and, as it were, overdetermines it and gives it shape. In certain conjunctures this leads to a position of relative differentiation of the inter-ests of the classes of this nation vis-à-vis the other classes and vis-à-vis the power bloc.

From a structural point of view, the contradictory movement which defines the dominated Quebec nation and transforms it into a regional question induces a particular relation between this region and the Cana-dian state. On the one hand, the Quebec region is assigned a distinct place in the relation of forces covered by the state and, on the other hand, it controls measures of redeployment of hegemony in the relation of the state to the masses. It becomes thus a principle of break-up/consolidation of the state.

The existence of the Quebec nation, transformed into a national and regional question, in Canada points to these structural dimensions. As the particularity of a region with specific cultural, economic, and political aims being transformed into a regional question, next with a position of alterity vis-à-vis the power bloc, finally as a principle of the redeployment of the state, realized through the double tendency of federalism toward unification and differentiation, the national question contributes, in a contradictory manner, to the consolidation of the form of regime, in its relation to the Canadian state.

As long as profound conditions for a break with the Canadian state are absent, the national question is not only a factor of opposition but also a positive element in the articulation of the relations between regions, federal regime, and state in Canada. This division introduced by the presence of Quebec in the Canadian state is, as it were, a mode of reproduction of the Canadian state in its intrinsically broken-up figure: this internal division is a contradictory dimension of its unity. It is once more the federal form of regime, as the materiality of the political struggles within the Canadian state, in this case at the same time the object and the condition of reproduction of the nation linked to the regions, which produces this tendency toward break-up.

In more concrete terms, we can say that the existence of the national question in Quebec is an aspect, a dimension even, of Canadian federalism. The more this national question is politically exacerbated, the more federalism undergoes pressure in its relation to the state. Thus, it is not surprising that the centralizing measures of Trudeau were initiated soon after the defeat of the Quebec referendum, as if the Canadian federal regime had just reached the height of its tolerance. The interventionism of Ottawa is a counter tendency in the fact of the cosubstantial presence of a break-up in the state, a presence manifested in the fact that the Quebec bourgeoisie has been able to give itself, precisely because of the regional powers granted by federalism, a project which is foreign to the power bloc.

The national question and federalism in the state are like the two faces of the same thing: the tendentially conflictual articulation of the regions to the state as a contradictory and unifying whole. The Quebec national question and federalism are interdependent terms, in their origin and in their present form. Inasmuch as federalism is a constituent element of the Canadian state, the national question is a special support of this structural tendency toward break-up as long as it does not realize its project of national independence. It is thus a constituent of the Canadian state.

As the mode of realization of the separation between the political and the economic, federalism, as a political stake, is as it were the reply, at the structural level, to the specific weight of the Quebec nation relying on the region. It is in this sense that the Quebec national question, as a space of class relations on the one hand, and federalism, as a state space on the other, are the two faces of this same broken unity of the state in Canada.

In this article we wanted first of all to raise points on which we could focus for the concrete analysis of class relations in the Canadian totality. We have also attempted to pose the terms of an alternative discourse to the present constitutional debate. Although limited in scope, the article has, we hope, raised some important questions.

Notes

Translated by Sinclair Robinson, Department of French, Carleton University.

1. Karl Marx, *Capital*, v. 1 (New York, 1967), 371-93.
2. Suzanne de Brunhoff, *The State, Capital and Economic Policy* (London, 1978), 9-36.
3. See in this regard Christine Buci-Glucksman and Göran Therborn in *Le défi social-démocrate* (Paris, 1981).
4. N. Poulantzas, *Political Power and Social Classes* (London, 1973), 154.
5. M. Miaille, *L'Etat du droit* (Grenoble, 1978), 28.
6. *Ibid.*, 26.
7. Engels to C. Schmidt, October 27, 1890. Marx and Engels, *Selected Works* (Moscow, 1968), 686-87.
8. *Ibid.*, 687.
9. E.G. Pasukanis, *La Théorie générale du droit et la marxisme* (Paris, 1970), 127. Emphasis added.
10. That is, the state is given through law and the way in which it can be seen is part of what it is.
11. Pasukanis, *La Théorie*, 133.
12. A long concrete analysis carried out by Nicole Morf (Département de science politique, UQAM) on the periodization of the forms of the state since 1930 demonstrates the slow growth of Keynesianism in Canada. The results of this research will be published in 1982.
13. J. Hirsch, *La crise de l'état* (Paris, 1976), 107-08. Emphasis added.
14. A. Legaré, *Les classes sociales au Québec* (Montreal, 1977), 188.
15. The foundations and concrete manifestations of this tendency of the Canadian state have been analysed with Gilles Bourque in *Le Québec, la question nationale* (Paris, 1979), 215-25.
16. In its historical genesis, the national question derived, as it were, its state aspect from federalism.

9. GÉRARD BOISMENU

The Federated State
and the Heterogeneity
of Space

When one undertakes to analyse the social, economic, and political reality of Quebec, one is confronted with a major dilemma. Either one maintains the implications, mistakes, and misunderstandings of an already existing literature, and consequently places oneself within that tradition, or else one decides to confront the problem directly and must make a theoretical detour in order to employ a new methodology. The following propositions are presented as a consequence of clearly opting for the second approach.

As Daniel Salée emphasizes, Quebec society appears, in most of the existing studies, to be detached from Canada as a whole. Attention is concentrated on the specificity of Quebec and on the Quebec "state," leaving unexamined the relations between Quebec society and Canadian society, neglecting to situate the Quebec state within the whole of the Canadian federated state. On the pretext that it is a federated state, everything proceeds as though the Canadian state were dismantled into distinct parts endowed with an independent logic and coherence.

The theoretical and practical consequences of such a concept for research are numerous. Notably, the concept has a certain influence on studies of Quebec that are founded on the concept of class struggle and inspired by historical materialism. This influence shows itself in turn, or all at once, in three ways.

1. Quebec is at best located in the Canadian social formation in an intuitive or descriptive way. Quebec's "regional specificity" can be sum-

Translated by Garth Stevenson. Published by permission of Les éditions du Boréal, originally published in Boismenu et al., *Espace Regional et Nation* (Montréal, 1983).

marily outlined without being rigorously based in theory.[1] Despite certain terminological propositions, the conceptualization is inadequate in the way it inserts Quebec into the whole of Canada, both at the economic and at the political-ideological level. However, this is still better than the analyses which, beginning with the fact of national oppression, end by viewing the structures of Canada/Quebec as parallel and separate.[2]

2. The Canadian state is perceived in terms of a model of the state that is the product of two different modes of analysis, analysis of the bourgeoisie in terms of its fractions, which are assumed to have no relations that can be perceived, and analysis of the two levels of government in terms of relations that also cannot be perceived. This means that each fraction or layer of the bourgeoisie is assigned to one level of government, with some other fraction assigned to the other level.[3] This approach lends to a mechanistic view of class relations in the Canadian state. I will return to this subject.

3. Class relations vis-à-vis the provincial level of the state are not studied in their totality. The provincial level is analysed as a state, perhaps qualified as a "truncated" state, tending to materialize a distinct power. Consequently, one seeks, at least implicitly, to locate the class direction that is the basis of the power materialized by the state. The provincial level of the state is then placed in relation more specifically with the classes more influenced, in their composition, by the territorial limits of the province (the non-monopolist bourgeoisie, the middle class, and the farmers), significantly underestimating the main component of the power bloc – a component that directs the power structure within the federated state – the big bourgeoisie.[4]

It seems quite essential, in an effort to escape from these effects and theoretical tendencies, to present some conceptual tools that enable us to establish the relations between the specific reality (society and state apparatus) of Quebec and the whole of the Canadian reality, and to uncover the social base that produces the specificity of the class relations being analysed. In this perspective, the spatial configuration in which these relations are connected is placed at the heart of the discussion. We must inevitably approach the problem of the social space as it appears in Canada and place Quebec in relation to that space. Thus I will deal, in the first place, with the connection between class relations in the space of the Canadian social formation and those in the regional space of Quebec. Secondly, I will attack the question of the mediatized reproduction of the connection between these relations in and through the Canadian federated state.

To treat this project in depth would surpass the framework of this chapter – I will limit myself especially to formulating propositions that will allow me to outline a methodology. More specifically, presenting the concept of a social formation space associated with Canada will allow me to introduce the concept of a regional space. These are starting points that can lead to a discussion concerning the Canadian federated state and the mode of expression of the contradictory class relationships that pervade it.

Social Formation Space and Regional Spaces in Canada

The concept of "space" that guides the discussion is mainly inspired by the work of Alain Lipietz. The social space is understood as the dynamic product of the spatial deployment of the connections between class relations, as they appear at the economic, political, and ideological levels. Considering that the connection between social structures defines the "morphology" of space, the specific modes of connection between the structures engender a differentiation of concrete spaces. Thus one can say, with Lipietz, that "the structuring of space is the spatial dimension of social relations and, since these are class struggles, the structuring of space is class struggle, not only in the sense that it is the product of class struggle, but in the sense that it is the object, and even an instrument of class struggle."[5] This comprehension of social space, which sees in it the differentiated materialization of a form of inscription of the class struggle, takes us far from a primary locating of territory in the reality of space.

The deepening of this understanding of space allows one to grasp the complexity of the configuration and of the modes of articulation of class relations in Canada in their spatial setting. To begin with, it must be recognized that Canada, as a socio-economic space and as a state, has been constituted and formed similarly to other societies dominated by capitalism, notwithstanding its distinctive characteristics. Conceptually, one must not lose sight of the fact that Canada is a capitalist social formation.

The Process of Establishing the Social Formation in Canada

In the British colonies of North America the beginning of class struggles in the mid-nineteenth century was marked by the development of capitalism and became part of the process of constituting a social formation space, a process whose political object revolved around the formation of the Canadian federation.[6] A many-faceted fundamental tendency gave impetus to the constitution of a unified space and of a state uniting the British colonies. This movement grew mainly out of the interests of the mother country, the rise of a commercial and financial bourgeoisie, the plans of the railway companies, the development of industrial capital, and the need to enlarge the field of capital accumulation and to create an internal market.

This movement, however, was not one-sided and straightforward; it encountered resistance and opposition that necessitated the political compromise of federalism. I will return later to this compromise. I would like to emphasize at this point that the process of constituting the Canadian space, as a social formation, was highly contradictory. On the one hand it was directed by the bourgeoisie and had the tendency to provide an overall unity of the development of economic, political, and ideological relations; it was a process of constituting an overall direction of class relations on the basis of which developed a typical organization of political power relations. But on the other hand, this process was influenced from the beginning by a striking regional specificity of class relations and it is known that subsequently the process could only develop by way of renewing and reinforcing this specificity. Historical perspective makes it possible to affirm that the structuring of the unity of the Canadian social formation was marked by the competitive existence of opposing tendencies, of varying intensity, expressing the regional specificity of class relations.

Historically, it thus appears that the establishment of the Canadian space and state was part of a general process of establishing the capitalist social formation and state but that this process was only completed by overcoming, always provisionally, the contradictory tendencies that indicate a diversified class base. Locating this contradictory character requires a theoretical reflection on the form of articulation of social relations that makes the social formation and differentiates this space.

The Space of the Social Formation

Contrary to what a simplistic view might suggest, the domination of capitalist production in society has not eliminated all the other forms of production; thus it must be recognized that other types of productive relations lead to the production of material goods. The concept of a social formation, created to express the complexity of social relations, allows us to understand the concrete social reality, which is structured by the way different coexisting productive relations are combined. Far from coexisting in an anarchic manner or in mutual isolation, the different productive relations are connected in such a way that one type of productive relations is dominant and its laws have a decisive influence on the others.

Following the historical process of class struggles, the capitalist mode of production becomes dominant in the social formation, attaining a certain coherence and a certain correspondence between its different levels of social relations (economic, political, and ideological). The arrival of capitalist domination assumes a spatial dimension of the first importance. In effect, the transformation of the social formation under the direction of rising capitalism is accompanied by the structuring of new social space[7] (whose matrix differs from those of the ancient or medieval societies) and by the destruction of economic, political, ideological, and linguistic barriers. These barriers are contrary to the existence of a broader market and field of accumulation and to the organization of political power in a state that controls the major processes of organization of the space. This new space has typically, although not always, taken the form of the nation-state.

In the course of consolidating its dominance, the capitalist mode of production determines the principal organization of the whole of social relations, both at the level of the economic base and at that of the super-structure, and it reproduces itself on a larger scale. In these circumstances, within the capitalist social formation space, appear the problems of the "persistence" of the dominated forms of production, the connection of these forms to capitalism, and the effect the reproduction of capital has on them.

The reproduction of capital, as enlarged social reproduction, carries in its wake the totality of social relations – capitalist and non-capitalist – and produces two kinds of significant effects on the development of non-capitalist relations. Firstly, it tends toward the dissolution – decay and destruction – of the non-capitalist forms of production. Secondly, it tends to conserve and maintain them, subsuming them within itself and restructuring them. In the capitalist social formation the non-capitalist forms of production, subordinated and restructured, reproduce their social and material conditions of existence under the auspices of capital in such a way that these conditions are henceforth an integral part, and even a condition, of the reproduction of capital.

The social formation, as a space based on the overall connection of the dominant capitalist mode of production with the non-capitalist forms of production, is the historical product of the class struggle at the moment of the consolidation of the power of the bourgeoisie. It has taken the typical form of the nation-state. On this last point, a clarification is required. In many situations, including Canada, the process of constituting the capitalist social and political space has given rise, within the same state and within a social formation space recognized as unitary, to the establishment, under the direction of the dominant class, of relations of national oppression between the agents of two nations. In fact, the national question is not a directly pertinent factor for the designation of the social formation space. If the social formation space is often thought of by reference to the nation-state, it cannot be reduced to that.

To sum up, the capitalist social formation represents a given space[8] for the investment of capital and for the manifestation of the class struggle under the domination of the bourgeoisie. In it are defined an overall connection of the development of all kinds of social relations, a general structure of class relations, and an organization of political power relations manifested by and in the state.

Regional Differentiation of the Social Formation

Although the social formation depends on a process of unification of space, in which is located an overall connection, a general structure of classes, and an organization of power, this space cannot be considered, in its development, as uniform and homogeneous. In fact, the connection of social relations only manifests itself uniformly within the whole of the social formation.

It is known that the enlarged reproduction is dominated by the reproduction of capital. This reproduction is fundamentally contradictory. First, the reproduction of capital, tending toward the decay of the non-capitalist forms of production, constantly modifies the contradictory relations between those forms and capital. The relations assume in the end, by their exacerbation, brutal and violent forms. Next, the reproduction of capital signifies as much the reproduction of the social and material conditions for the existence of capital as the reproduction of contradictions inherent in capitalism, such as uneven development or the antagonistic and non-antagonistic relations between classes. In other words, the enlarged social reproduction of capitalism necessarily brings about a regional differentiation in the ways in which social relations are connected across the social formation space.

The regional specification of the manifestation of social relations is based principally on five sets of circumstances:

1. The concrete modalities of the "persistence" of non-capitalist modes of production, especially in agriculture, and their connection with capitalist production. If agriculture, historically, has experienced an external connection, and then integration, it must be noted that on the one hand this progression has followed various evolutionary paths (the Anglo-Prussian, American, and French versions) and on the other hand the present phase of integration is far from absolute proletarianization; instead, there is a differentiation of the exploitative relations.[9]
2. The spatial deployment of monopoly capital in its relations with the other layers and fractions of the bourgeoisie, particularly with non-monopoly capital and "big family-regional capital."
3. The specialization and inequality of capitalist development. In the prolongation of what precedes it, the economic regions exist as arenas tending to group different types of branches and different types of work with productive networks (head offices, centres of skilled production, centres of "unskilled" labour).[10]
4. The spatial segregation of labour forces, which is a set of circumstances associated with the foregoing. With the segmentation and regionalization of the labour market is found a differentiation of pools of manpower, of salary zones, etc.[11]
5. The globalization of the economy and its effects of dislocating the economic space. We should emphasize, especially in Canada, that the penetration of foreign capital is combined with the preceding factors, which contribute to the specification of regional spaces, and even to balkanization.[12]

The utilization of these sets of circumstances in an objective economic analysis allows us to measure the "determination in the last instance at the economic level of spatial heterogeneity and its mutations."[13] But if this determination alone delineates the outline of the space, it is far from accounting for the multifaceted relations that compose its real appearance. Before exploring this question in depth we can state at this point that the connection between capitalist and non-capitalist modes of production and the manifestation of the contradictions inherent in the development of capital constitutes the social formation space, as well as, by the regional specifications of this connection, a certain number of regional spaces. The specified regional spaces, as spatial morphologies of the social formation, contribute to the contradictory unity of this formation.

The Contradictory Unity of the Canadian Social Formation

The Canadian social formation, a spatial configuration produced by a complex social structure, develops itself and enhances its unity while reproducing the regional spaces which, without becoming uniform, participate in this unity in a contradictory manner – so much so that, in a general way, Canada has a structural unity, both economic and political (the latter aspect will be considered carefully in another section), which comprises the overall site of the manifestation of class struggles under the domination of the bourgeoisie. At the same time, however, this structural unity only exists in and through the specificity of its materialization of regional spaces.

It must be understood that the unity of the social formation and of the regional specificity are two contradictory aspects that imply one another, under the domination of the former aspect. This raises the problem of the simultaneous perception of these two aspects in the same situation, in the sense that each phenomenon is part of the regional specificity and a concurrent element, in a contradictory way, to the unity of the formation. This also raises the problem of the more or less unstable domination of unity over regional specificity. The latter problem is crucial for Canada; on this subject I will not provide a definitive response but will be content to advance some hypotheses that have not yet been investigated in depth.

In Canada, no doubt more than elsewhere, the unity of the social formation cannot be related to any uniformity or any harmonization of social relations. The structural unity of the social formation is not a given. Quite the contrary, this unity is realized by and through a multiplicity of social, economic, political, and ideological contradictions. In addition, the economic and political unity of Canada is always in question, because it must contend with the increased differentiation of regional spaces and the deepening of inequalities, with the regional specificity of class struggles, with national oppression and the resistance it provokes, with ideological regionalisms and Quebec nationalism, with struggles inside the state and conflictual relations between the levels of government. Economic and political unity is thus particularly affected by an endemic tendency toward disintegration, which means that in Canada the question of the reproduction of the unity of the social formation is constantly, or rather regularly, on the agenda.

The Role of the Political System in the Formation of Space

At this stage of the discussion it is necessary to emphasize a major point in the formation of space, namely the role of the political system.

The social formation space, as a structural site determined by the development of the class struggle, is an overall space in which are defined the political power relations that are expressed, organized, and condensed in and by the state. This state, which embodies typical power relations, reinforces and renews the domination of the bourgeoisie, particularly by participating actively in the contradictory reproduction of capital and of class relations. In this regard the state, according to its traditional modalities throughout history but from the beginning, plays a significant role in the spatial inscription and materialization of class struggles and of their reproduction. In fact, by its unitary or federal organization, by its structure and by the apparatus with which it demarcates the boundaries of the space and divides up its internal diversity, the state overdetermines the constitution of social space.[14]

The overdetermination of the constitution of space has more than one dimension. The state fixes the boundaries, on the one hand, for the exercise of class power (law, citizenship, legitimate force, administrative decentralization, a system of political relations, a unifying ideology) as much by organized public violence as by its hegemony over the masses. It also fixes the boundaries for the concrete manifestation of the class struggle (at the economic, political, and administrative levels) and in effect designates the settings in which that struggle is most likely to be expressed. In addition, the state overdetermines the constitution of space by intervening spatially to organize and reproduce relations of exploitation; this "administration of territory" takes the concrete forms of urbanization, facilities for transport and communications, restrictions on the use of land, etc. Finally, the state, while indicating in its institutional-administrative network the specific ways in which social relations are connected, acts upon these ways to consolidate, transform, or dissolve them.

If the development of the state consists of making the boundaries of the social formation space correspond with its own boundaries, the action of the state is generally less clear in shaping political spaces that reproduce the contours of economic regionalism. Nonetheless, this phenomenon has its own varied effects on the network of political, social, and ideological relations. Although these effects can express themselves by the state taking regionalism into account, designating regional centres for special attention, and arranging its administrative apparatus accordingly, political (state) boundaries rarely coincide exactly with those of economic regions. However, at the margin of the state, or in relation with it, the formation of locally distinct systems of political or economic relations, of local strongholds for one or another party or faction, of ideological or cultural traditions and ways of resisting metropolitan domination, forms regional hegemonic systems within the "local society" and thus at least begins to outline political and ideological regions that rival the economic regions.[15] Even if these different types of diversities do not necessarily coincide exactly, they tend to reinforce one another in shaping the character of the regional space.

The federated state, by the characteristic features of its organization, accentuates the tendency for economic, political, and ideological relations to take place within coinciding regional boundaries. It can also give this regionalism a definite shape by designating formally both the sites for the polarization of multidimensional class relations and the corresponding territorial spaces. Conversely, the very functioning of the unitary state blurs and complicates the outlines of the natural region – without dissolving it – because regional "spaces" corresponding to different types of relations seem to be superimposed on one another with distinct and eventually distant centres of convergence. These different types of "spaces" do not really coincide.[16]

Overdetermination of the Canadian Federated State and Regional Spaces

The Canadian state fully assumes this overdetermining role in the formation of the "social formation" space; it must, however, be emphasized that this overdetermination is subject to the federated organization of this state. First of all, the Canadian space, formed in the beginning from British colonies that were independent of one another, produces, on the bases of the complex and differentiated connection between capitalist and noncapitalist modes of production, as well as the unequal redistribution of capital, a spatial unity that includes a large degree of regional specificity. That being the case, the action of the Canadian state, in overdetermining the formation of space, defines concretely both the unity of the social formation space and the differentiation of regional spaces.

The federated Canadian state, and especially its provincial level, has come sometimes to perpetuate the characteristics of the economic and social development of the regions, including the unequal distribution of capital investment, and sometimes to determine the specificity of social relations. It does this by defining the areas for the exercise of power, by designating the locations for the expression of conflict, by supporting varying policies for the administration of territory, and by acting differently in different places toward the varying development of class relations.

So much is this the case that the regional spaces produced by the different patterns of class relations and overdetermined by the organization and activity of the federal state can be designated as provincial spaces.

Although they are not the basis for designating regional spaces, statistical data on the provinces (such as data on per capita revenue, unemployment, and economic specialization) illustrate the formation of such provincial spaces.[17] Overall, the requirements of the capitalist economy in Canada imply a tendency to divide the country into provincial spaces. This division takes on a structural character as much from the relations that bring it about as from its existence as illustrated by the statistical data.

I must make two things clear. First, if I have mentioned that the Canadian space is differentiated at a first level into regional spaces roughly corresponding with the provinces, it is because these regional spaces have a degree of complexity which, at another level, allows a distinctive and in-depth analysis of an internal spatial heterogeneity. To be precise, given that the formation of spaces depends on the specific mode of connection of social relations, when I designate a regional space that I identify with a provincial space, I am not designating a space that appears homogeneous, harmonious, or uniform. Instead, it should be understood as a site for the emergence of intense contradictions and specific conflicts. Furthermore, many studies have described the internal economic differentiation of the Quebec regional space.[18] Second, it appears that to really understand this internal differentiation in Quebec (for example) one must face the problem that the outlines of the "sub-regional" spaces are blurred by the not completely identical boundaries of "specific spaces" defined by economic, political, or ideological relations. This is the same problem encountered from the very first in unitary states.

The Regional Space of Quebec

How can Quebec be described within Canada? The present discussion leads me to consider Quebec as a regional space within the Canadian formation.

Quebec is marked by a given mode of connection between class relations, overdetermined by the provincial level of the state. Quebec's mode of connection must be analysed concretely in its many aspects that correspond to class realities. These aspects go beyond, although they include, national oppression. To understand this connection between class relations requires that we return to the five categories of principal factors upon which spatial heterogeneity is based. These factors as well as the political and ideological relations and practices that accompany them and the discriminatory relations, such as national oppression,[19] which transcend the reality of classes, trace the outlines of class relations and practices in the Quebec regional space.

In addition, the regional space of Quebec participates in the formation of the Canadian economic, social, and political space and in its contradictory unity. Quebec's distinctiveness is in part a function of its insertion into the overall Canadian reality. As a result, the contradictory unity of the political power relations and the unity of the overall structure of classes cannot be correctly understood by limiting oneself only to the specific reality of Quebec. On the contrary, they must be understood in a pan-Canadian context. However, the specific reality of Quebec, at whatever level of relations, is not dissolved in the whole of Canada; it is recognized and situated within Canada. The economic, political, and ideological characteristics of Quebec can only be understood as peculiar manifestations of the class struggle within the regional space of Quebec, which is part of the Canadian formation.

Basing myself on these considerations, I am going to explore more specifically the contradictory unity of political power relations in Canada and its complex realization by and in the federated state.

The Exercise of State Power in Canada

The unitary state is often considered to be the typical capitalist state, as though the federal state were only a poor approximation of the materialization of the political power of the bourgeoisie. Certainly the analysis of the materialization of power in the federated state must be more complex than that of its counterpart in the unitary state.

To appreciate this complexity it is useful to note some conditions basic to the formation of a federated state. We can ask ourselves under what circumstances the capitalist state adopts this form of organization. Generally, the federated state reveals a political compromise inherent in the formation of a state that tries to transcend a set of exacerbated social contradictions – not by resolving them, but by absorbing them into its structures and by decentralizing the exercise of power. These contradictions,[20] which express themselves in acute clashes and conflicts, include the balkanization of economic spaces, the heterogeneity of the virtually dominant class, national oppression, religious rivalries, and the rigidity of the political and ideological superstructure prior to the formation of the new state.

The conditions that historically accompanied the formation of the Canadian federated state correspond to this scenario. There was a multifaceted fundamental movement conducive to the establishment of a unified space and of a unifying, if not unitary, state. The aspiration toward a unitary state was defeated by an assortment of resistances, oppositions, and obstacles that necessitated the federal compromise.

These resistances, oppositions, and obstacles consisted essentially of the contradictory class relations within the colonies. The state of these relations was the product of an economic, political, and ideological regionalism encouraged by colonial history and geography, of the diversity of economic development of the colonial provinces, of the specialization of the provincial bourgeoisies and their varying degrees of formation, of the opposition to the hegemony of the Anglo-Canadian bourgeoisie of the Province of Canada, of Quebec's resistance to national oppression, and of the opposition to the conservative and undemocratic political project of the bourgeoisie.[21] Generally speaking, the differentiation and specific character of the class struggles in the different colonies made a federated state essential.

The federal compromise, which allowed the creative of the Canadian state, confirmed the existence of the social (economic and political) spaces of the different provinces. It recognized the two historic and national components (Ontario and Quebec) of the Province of Canada by re-dividing them to give each a provincial level of government with constitutional powers. The federal compromise made possible the creation of the Canadian state, but it was far from resolving the contradictions that had provoked it. On the contrary, by transforming the conditions in which they were manifested, the federated state absorbed these contradictions into the organization of its internal relations, as modes of existence of power relations in Canada.

It is clear that the realization of the domination and direction of the bourgeoisie in Canada through two levels of government raises problems with respect to the way their concrete manifestations are understood. A certain model of the Canadian state tries to pass over these problems by reducing the dynamics of the Canadian state to some particular aspects and by adopting a mechanistic perspective on class relations within the state. This consists of a conception of the state that identifies for each level of government some layer or fraction of the bourgeoisie.

Several writers employ, at least implicitly, this model of the Canadian state although they do not all arrive at the same conclusions: the way they conceptualize the difference between levels is not the same. Consider three examples. In his analysis of "the political economy of the Canadian state," Garth Stevenson views the levels of government as specializing in defending the interests of one or another layer, class, fraction, or category of interests.[22] He defines three chronological periods characterized by different types of distinctions between levels. In the first period the central government represented the bourgeoisie and the provincial governments placed the interests of independent commodity producers in the forefront. In the second period the provincial level was linked with the natural resource industries while the central government represented the interests of the railways, manufacturing industries, and banks. In the present day, finally, Canada, which is now no more than a collection of regional economies, sees the provincial level dominated by a regionalized and specialized bourgeoisie that can only unify itself in an uncertain and precarious manner through the central government. On the other hand, Alfred Dubuc, in contrast to Stevenson for the contemporary period at least, recognizes the existence of a Canadian big bourgeoisie.[23] In this case the distinction is more along horizontal lines. Thus the big bourgeoisie basically expresses its interests through the central government, while the autonomist tendencies at the provincial level represent the interests of the middle classes, either "traditional" or "new."

In discussing the era of Duplessis, Denis Monière also draws the distinction horizontally. However, he recognizes its paradoxical nature in practice.[24] At first sight the provincial government of Quebec is identified with the interests of the petty bourgeoisie (by which I believe he means the non-monopolistic bourgeoisie) and the central government operates on behalf of the big bourgeoisie. The paradox of the Duplessis regime is that, contrary to what is suggested above, it represented the interests of a fraction of the big bourgeoisie. Now I suggest that this consisted only of the American fraction.

This model of the state, which is applied especially to Canada,[25] leads to a formalistic and mechanistic perception of political power relations in the federated state. I introduce the concept of paradox to emphasize that this model can only lead to the accumulation of paradoxes when it is applied to the analysis of political realities. Although it bears some relation to reality, it excessively simplifies and caricatures the reality of political power relations in Canada. Besides, this model does not permit us to establish a coherent and effective methodology to analyse the materialization of power relations through the ten provincial governments and at the same time through the central government.

It is thus appropriate to develop a methodology for the analysis of the exercise of power through and in the Canadian federated state. I am thus going to advance some propositions to clear the way for a general understanding of the question and for the beginning of a methodology. To do so, it is necessary to return to certain conclusions from the preceding discussion about space.

I have said that a contradictory structural unity develops in the Canadian social formation as a result of an intense regional specialization. From the uneven development of capitalism joined to other forms of production, an overall class structure is established on which are based the relations of political power. These relations, on the one hand, determine the configuration of the power bloc and, on the other hand, take shape through and in the Canadian federated state.

The overall unity of the social formation necessarily includes the great diversity of conditions and of the manifestation and expression of classes in the different regional spaces. Furthermore, the unity of political power relations, as well as the contradictory unity of social relations, develops through the many forms in which the class struggle is realized within the

Canadian space. As a result, the study of the specific characteristics of class struggles in a regional space allows us to understand the determined forms of existence both of capitalist development and of the domination of the power bloc in Canada through the federated state. In this order of ideas, questions arise regarding the unity of political power relations, which includes the numerous political forms of the class struggle and simultaneously includes the determined forms of domination that are registered on the federated state.

In short, the discussion of the contradictory unity of the Canadian social formation and of the overall structure of class relations leads us to ask ourselves about the exercise of political power by the federated state and about the determination of forms of domination at both the central and provincial levels of government.

Proposition I. The unity of the social formation, despite its spatial differentiation, is combined with the unity of the federated state and with the consolidation of a dominant class, as contradictory as one is with the other.

The formation of the Canadian state appeared historically as a necessary corollary of the establishment of the social formation space. The Canadian federated state was intrinsically linked with the organization, consolidation, and development of the Canadian space under the direction of, and at the initiative of, the bourgeoisie.

This obvious situating of the Canadian state in relation to the Canadian space must be understood as a precondition to understanding the organization of power and of the state. I stated earlier that there is only one social formation, even though it is differentiated into regional spaces. The regional spaces, which have their distinctive characteristics, compose and participate in the contradictory unity of the Canadian space. All the same, we must recognize that there is only one Canadian state, despite its federated form. The form of the state must not mislead us as to its unity. Federalism is a mode of existence of the capitalist state that embodies a given organization of power relations, and thus the federated form does not mean that several juxtaposed states embody distinct organizations of power relations. In Canada there is only one state, albeit federated in form, which embodies a general organization of political power relations.

The federated Canadian state embodies the power of the bourgeoisie in Canada. Before going further, we must specify that this class is not homogeneous. Without falling into a crude generalization that would only lead to a tautological argument, let us outline several aspects of the composition and morphology of the bourgeoisie in Canada.[26] It is composed as follows: (a) the Canadian monopolist bourgeoisie, divided into financial groups whose spheres of influence and bases of accumulation are very unequal and whose elements are distinguished by differences in their relations with foreign imperialist interests and in their positions within the global system of accumulation; (b) the comprador bourgeoisie, subordinated to foreign interests which it directly represents and including, at this stage in the internationalization of productive capital, both the agents and direct representatives of the owners of foreign corporations and the partial or nominal owners of the branch plants; (c) the "provincialized" non-monopolistic bourgeoisie, whose bases of accumulation rarely extend beyond a single province, divided into fractions and reproducing within itself the contradictions of the monopolist bourgeoisie. Finally, let us note that national oppression appears within the bourgeoisie although its effects vary among the levels and fractions; these effects have an impact on the positions occupied by agents within the bourgeoisie and on the political options they defend.

However, as divided as the bourgeoisie may seem when we focus on its composition and morphology, it exhibits its unity and cohesion, as a class, in its relations of domination over the working class and the masses. To this effect the state, which expresses and confirms the place of the bourgeoisie in the relations of power, represents a special factor of organization for the bourgeoisie where its unity and cohesion, resting on a given set of relations among its elements, are fashioned and developed. Thus the homogeneity and uniformity of the bourgeoisie and the disintegration and fragmentation of the bourgeoisie are both caricatures that distort the overall reality of that class.

Proposition II. The political power of the bourgeoisie in Canada is mediated by the whole of the federated state, that is to say, by both the central and the provincial levels of government.

Let us remember that the political power of the alliance of layers and fractions of the bourgeoisie in Canada found its form of existence in the federated state; it is precisely all the components of that state that function to maintain and reproduce that power. Thus it is quite incorrect to reduce the exercise of that power to one or the other level of government. This means that the political power of the alliance of layers and fractions of the bourgeoisie is diffused throughout the Canadian state. Although they appear dispersed, fragmented, and contradictory, the political practices at each level of government proceed from the same basic organization of class power relations. At the same time, these practices give consistency to the existence of this power.

It is necessary to stress this idea, that the fundamental organization of power relations, consolidated on the basis of an alliance between the layers and fractions of the bourgeoisie, supports the federated state and is the constantly renewed result of the practices of the political agents of this alliance, as diverse as they are and at whatever level of government they act.

If I return to it, it is because, in these terms, there would seem to be a direct link and even a coincidence or identity between the fundamental organization of class power relations and the concrete functioning of the totality of levels and branches of this federated state, which ensures the maintenance and reproduction of this power. But this is not so, perhaps because in capitalist society, especially, political power is exercised indirectly.[27] In a less general way, I will suggest that this relation between the diffusion of political power and the functioning of levels of government is indirect because it is conditional and only operates via the specific organization of political relations in each of the political arenas. The key to this relationship is thus given to us by the general combination of precise configurations of each of the political arenas. This leads us to inquire about the determination of these configurations.

Proposition III. The specific organization of political relations in the political arenas must be understood as relevant political effects of the differentiated development of the class struggle in the Canadian space and in each of the regional spaces.

The Canadian federated state, it has been said, overdetermines the constitution of the Canadian space (social formation) and the differentiation of the regional (provincial) spaces. From this discussion of the space differentiated following the joining of social structures can be deduced a distinction that designates the starting point for the analysis of the Canadian state and the political arenas.

The distinction, which will be reviewed and elaborated, is as follows: the political effects that can be observed in each of the political arenas at the provincial level are produced and reinforced by the specific pattern of class relations that constitutes each regional space. In addition, the political effects that appear in the political arena at the level of the central government are brought about by the overall pattern of class relations, which creates the social formation space in its entirety.

Beginning at this point, the reasoning must be clarified because when the distinction is made between the political effects of the specific and of the overall patterns of class relations, it must be remembered that these patterns are not unrelated or mutually isolated. In fact, we know instead that the social formation is the spatial inscription of a unifying – but not homogenizing – organization of the regional spaces. This organization reproduces itself through this contradictory unity so well that the regional spaces, despite their specific characteristics, are simultaneously integral parts of the social formation. This leads me to conclude that the relevant political effects imposed on the political arenas are brought into existence on the basis of spaces (regional and Canadian) that are closely related. It is thus artificial to separate them into water-tight compartments and then to view them as external to one another.

Within the framework of bourgeois domination and on the basis of the differentiation of the social formation, the classes, layers, and fractions organize themselves and intervene as social or political forces whose behaviour is molded by the boundaries of the federated state and its levels of government. In organizing themselves and intervening as social or political forces the classes, layers, and fractions express in terms of political interests the class effects of the numerous economic and social contradictions that appear in the Canadian space as a whole and in each of the regional spaces.[28] In other words, these class effects do not appear uniformly in the Canadian space; the types of contradictions that produce the most striking effects, the intensity of these contradictions, and the way they express themselves all vary from one regional space to another and from the regional spaces to the whole of the social formation. For its part, through its own organization the federated state comes to reveal, to channel, and to accentuate this reality.[29]

In effect, within the framework of the fundamental organization of political power relations the federated state provides different sites for the political expression of the class struggle. For each of these sites, the history of the contradictions that occurred in the past and the history of political and social forces that were present shape the way the political power of the bourgeoisie becomes a reality. In each political arena, whether at the central or provincial level, different prevailing circumstances determine the objects, the sense, the limits, and the general outcomes of political struggles. This is so because each political arena refers back to a more or less limited space, and thus to a specific class struggle, and to a given expression of the struggle, and thus to a particular political history.

In particular, it should be observed that, considering the distribution of constitutional powers, the central government is structurally and institutionally concerned with the totality of the class struggle in Canada, the reproduction of capital, the position of Canada in the world economy, etc. All of this, moreover, lessens the impact of certain contradictions which, at the regional level, appear with great intensity. The provincial level of government, in terms of preponderance, is made aware of this overall situation through the contradictions most acute within the given regional space.

Proposition IV. Taking account of the political effects of the development of the class struggle in a differentiated space and of the different sites for the manifestation of political power that comprise the federated state, the federal and provincial governments, with their different characteristics, embody types of political alliances between the dominant layers and fractions.

Governments, both at the central and provincial levels, embody types of political alliances in the sense that they express, in a fairly stable manner, distinct stratified organizations, historically and concretely determined, of the interests of dominant class layers and fractions. These types of political alliances, as specific modes of exercising power, are determined by several categories of factors, including:

- the relations within the bourgeoisie as they develop in the different spaces;
- the relations between the bourgeoisie and one or more supporting classes;
- the importance of different political forces and the concrete forms of development of the class struggle;
- the history of the parties, of their political orientation, and, more generally, of the political arenas.

Evidently these factors vary enormously from one regional space to another and throughout the history of each. Furthermore, they vary according to circumstances in a way that highlights the strictly political and ideological dimensions.

The specific characteristics of each type of alliance represented by governments must be analysed concretely. They cannot be mechanically equated with different levels of government. Thus it is incorrect to identify *a priori* a type of political alliance, or a class or fraction, with the central or with the provincial level of government. Also, it should be emphasized that the levels of government, as sites for the formation of different types of alliances between dominant layers and fractions, do not operate exclusively for any one layer or fraction. None of these layers or fractions is excluded, by definition, from either level of government. If there is an exclusion, it can only occur through a particular ideological or political process that is not dictated by the structure of the Canadian federated state. Thus, generally, the types of alliances represented by governments do not bring about clear divisions within the bourgeoisie.

While they have specific characteristics that are more or less pronounced, the types of political alliance represented by the governments of the ten provinces and by the central government all fall within the framework of the exercise of power by the bourgeoisie. These types of alliance together comprise the effective structure of the overall alliance of dominant layers and fractions for the whole of Canada. For this reason, the types of alliance are part of the struggles for influence, rank, hegemony, etc. between the elements of the bourgeoisie. All of the alliances, neither alien nor fundamentally opposed to one another, participate in and reproduce the contradictory unity of the Canadian federated state, each in its own fashion.

Proposition V. While intergovernmental relations in Canada occupy a prominent place on the agenda, it is useful to consider that the more or less acute differences between the types of political alliance, which represent quite faithfully the contradictions within the bourgeoisie, correspond to the essential basis, apart from the national question, of the contradictions within the Canadian state.

The contradictions within the state include several dimensions that contribute to the formation of certain types of political alliance in government.[30] Before considering some of them, it must be understood that the fundamental issue, which underlies federal-provincial discussions and, to an even greater extent, constitutional conflicts, is the respective capacity (or at best the fashioning of means) of intervention of the two levels of government.[31] What is effectively at stake is the definition of the sites in which the hierarchization of dominant interests takes place. This hierarchization appears, from one government to another, as so many distinct types of political alliance. Evidently this definition of the sites where power is exercised directly concerns the dominant layers and fractions because, bearing in mind the relative position of each as regards their political effectiveness in the federated organization of the exercise of power, it is a question of their capacity to assure themselves a significant influence over the sites where the political alliances that affect them most directly are formed. In addition to this question of the first importance, some dimensions combined with it must also be considered.

The precise type of political alliance represented by a government is determined by the concrete social and political conditions under which the class struggle is conducted. These conditions vary depending on whether we refer to the whole of the social formation or to one or another regional space. To understand these conditions, let us emphasize certain aspects, such as:

- the concrete specific conditions of the exercise of power over the masses;
- the degree of development and the political mode of expression of the labour movement, including the unions;
- the place of non-capitalist relations, particularly in agriculture, and the political behaviour of classes linked to them, such as the small farmers;
- the place of the middle class (new and traditional) in politics and the class position of its fractions.

These conditions lead, in the political process dominated by the bourgeoisie, to the elaboration of particular modes of exercising power and, more specifically, of given political strategies. As a result, the types of political alliance, determined by the condition of the class struggle in each of the spaces concerned, form part of the struggles of tendencies within the bourgeoisie.

Furthermore, the formation of a type of political alliance indicates the political effectiveness of the dominant layers and fractions in each of the political arenas. In this sense, the conflicts and debates between specific alliances often coincide with the differentiation of the political efficacy of the components of the dominant class in the federated state. Two questions should be borne in mind. First, these conflicts reveal, on the one hand, the divergent interests of the different fractions and/or of distinct sectors of the economy that predominate in one or another political alliance. Secondly, these conflicts express the unequal capacity for influence and action of the monopolist bourgeoisie and of the non-monopolist bourgeoisie at different levels of government. While recognizing that the levels of government don't function exclusively on behalf of the dominant layers and fractions, it must be emphasized that the big bourgeoisie, as compared to the middle bourgeoisie, is more able to achieve coherence and political effectiveness at the level of the central government. On the other hand, the middle bourgeoisie can attain its greatest political coherence at the provincial level. This intervention of the middle bourgeoisie at the provincial level, tending to be more systematic and consistent, can significantly and decisively affect the type of political alliance represented by one or other provincial government.

Also, together with the tendency of constitutional powers to become concentrated in the central government, the accentuation of regional inequalities, the movement of capital to the west, the unceasing disparities within the regional spaces, and the deterioration or necessary consolidation of the bourgeoisie in the regions all demand a regional policy conceived and implemented at the provincial level. The political effects of class relations within the regional spaces, in terms of popular struggles and especially of the redefinition of alliances at the provincial level, impel the political representatives of these alliances[32] to recognize the capacity for a massive intervention at the provincial level in order to regulate capitalist development and to mitigate class contradictions in the regional spaces. As a result, there is a desire to maintain at the provincial level a significant role in the exercise of power and a genuine capacity to intervene in the development of the class struggle.

The totality of elements that have been discussed with regard to the differentiation of regional spaces, the formation of specific class alliances, and more generally the economic, political, social, and ideological class struggles, based on the reality of the regions, comprise the multiple dimensions of the regional question in Canada. The regional question delineates the endemic centrifugal tendency that punctuates the evolution of the Canadian state and social formation.

Proposition VI. National oppression in Quebec, which transforms the regional question into a national question, accentuates the contradictions of the federated state to the point at which its disintegration is a real possibility, or at least to the point at which the compromise pertaining to the modalities of exercising power must be renewed.

Quebec, considered as a space and as a level of government, is different from the other regional spaces in Canada. Quebec is the space in which the Québécois nation exists and consolidates itself. It is also the site of national subordination, which takes a number of concrete forms, and at this point the effects of the totality of discriminatory political and ideological relations, which appear in every sphere of social activity, provide the basis of the national question and provoke resistance and counter-attacks. Moreover, it is the site, mediated by the constitution of the federated state, of the political organization of national oppression. This is so because politics overdetermines not only the structuring and reproduction of the nation, but also its place in the relations of national oppression.[33]

National oppression develops in the cracks of the structure of power relations. Also, overcoming this national oppression directly indicates the question of political power, but also of power relations more generally, such as in the economic domain. In addition, insofar as national oppression affects, in varying ways, all classes in Quebec, nationalist discourse, profoundly influenced by the interests of the bourgeoisie and of the middle class, is still capable of mobilizing the different classes and uniting them in pursuit of their demands. (This does not negate the fact that, at the same time, national oppression has the effect, for the exploited classes, of making their exploitation more obvious.) In fact, national oppression and nationalist ideology are the elements of the evolution and development of the class struggle, not only in relation to bourgeois domination over the masses, but also in relation to the internal conflicts within the bourgeoisie.

In short, the Quebec provincial government is the special place for the representation of "national interests," which are by no means confined to the domains of language and culture, since they include the economic and political fields in particular. The supervision and orientation of capitalist accumulation in Quebec presents itself as one of the issues uniting these two fields. The provincial political representatives of the bourgeoisie and of the middle class are oriented, historically with popular support, toward preserving and even enlarging the constitutional powers at the disposal of the Quebec provincial government. In addition, by what seems a cumulative process, the question of political self-determination appears as the necessary means of overcoming national oppression.

It must be understood that the Quebec question is deeply rooted in the national question, but that the numerous effects of national oppression in Quebec transform the regional question, which can be observed elsewhere in Canada, into a national question. This means that the national question does not eliminate the aspects, mentioned above, which provide the basis for regional concentrations but that it is combined with them to form a whole new dimension that transforms the totality and gives it a qualitatively different significance. The national question exacerbates the contradictions of the federated state by posing, in the destabilizing struggles and demands that perpetuate it, the alternative of the economic and political disintegration of Canada. As a result Quebec, by providing the basis for the crisis of the state, represents the weak link of the Canadian federation. However, there is nothing irreversible or cumulative about this process. In fact, insofar as the nationalist political movement and ideology do not lead to a genuine political self-determination and insofar as they conceal the reality of class relations, they participate in reproducing bourgeois domination and national oppression. At the same time they impose – as so many significant compromises – more or less complex and contradictory practices on the exercise of power and of hegemony.

These propositions are only intended as conceptual instruments for analysing the social, economic, and political reality of Quebec within Canada. They are the nucleus of a way of understanding social relations and the federated state in Canada and Quebec. They serve, for a particular subject, to state the problem, to indicate the way of understanding the given circumstances, and to mark the path of analysis. This analytical framework can only reveal its dynamic possibilities when it is applied to concrete situations.

As regards the analysis of the political position promoted by the government of Quebec, certain things should be noted. Like other governments in Canada, this one represents a type of political alliance that expresses a given stratified organization of the interests of dominant layers and fractions, even though it is affected by the national question, and which participates, contradictorily, in the political power of the bourgeoisie in Canada. The specific forms in which political power is exercised in Quebec are anchored in the particular pattern of class relations in this regional space and in the concrete organization of political forces and of political and ideological means of domination. In addition, and in contrast to other governments, the types of political alliance historically represented by the Quebec government have expressed, in one way or another and sometimes within narrow political limits, the resistance to national oppression, thus leading toward a readjustment of the real relations of subordination.

Notes

1. Gilles Bourque and Anne Legaré, *Le Québec, la question nationale* (Paris, 1979), 122-31, refer briefly to the "specificité régionale de l'articulation des

modes de production." However, the discussion that follows this valuable insight is rather sketchy. I hope that their ongoing work will pursue this line of inquiry, which requires further development.

2. It should be emphasized in passing that an incorrect understanding of the national question in Canada has given rise to analyses based on the idea of parallel structures (Canada/Quebec), which are mutually exclusive for all practical purposes. Specifically, it will be possible to speak of Canadian imperialism in Quebec, e.g., S. Moore and D. Wells, *Imperialism and the National Question in Canada* (1975), 87-89; C. Saint-Onge, "Imperialisme U.S. au Québec" (Thèse de doctorat, Paris VIII, 1975); D. Monière, *Le développement des idéologies au Québec* (Montréal, 1977).

3. Notably, G. Stevenson, "Federalism and the Political Economy of the Canadian State," in Leo Panitch, ed., *The Canadian State, Political Economy and Political Power* (Toronto, 1977), 71-100; A. Dubuc, "Les fondements historiques de la crise des sociétés canadienne et québécoise," *Politique aujourd'hui*, nos. 7-8 (1978), 29-53.

4. For example, Henry Milner as well as G. Bourque and N. Laurin-Frenette, who have produced analyses that are useful in more than one way, overestimate and exaggerate the role of the middle class in political relations, and particularly within the state. Bourque and Legaré, *Le Québec*, are sometimes inclined to give the non-monopolist bourgeoisie the role usually attributed to the middle class, while underestimating the position of the Canadian big bourgeoisie. Milner, *Politics in the New Quebec* (Toronto, 1978); Bourque and Laurin-Frenette, "Classes sociales et idéologies nationalistes au Québec (1960-1970)," *Socialisme québécois*, no. 20, 109-55.

5. A. Lipietz, *Le capital et son espace*, "Économie et socialisme" (Paris, 1977), 90.

6. A. Dubuc, "Une interpretation économique de la constitution," *Socialisme 66*, no. 7 (janvier, 1966), 4-13; S.B. Ryerson, *Le capitalisme et la confederation* (Montréal, 1972), 307-426; R.T. Naylor, "The rise and fall of the third commercial empire of the St. Lawrence," in Gary Teeple, ed., *Capitalism and the National Question in Canada* (Toronto, 1972), 1-41; G. Stevenson, *Unfulfilled Union* (Toronto, 1979), 27-49; J.C. Bonenfant, "Les origines économiques et les dispositions financiéres de l'Acte de l'Amérique du Nord Britannique de 1867," in Rodrigue Tremblay, *L'économie québécoise* (1976), 194-208; Bourque and Legaré, *Le Québec*, 73-109.

7. N. Poulantzas, *L'Etat, le pouvoir, le socialisme* (1978), 110-18; P. Allis, *L'invention du territoire*, "critique du droit" (1980).

8. Lipietz, *Le capital*, 28. "Space" in the present context means a connected set of social relations that are manifested in a particular territory. It should therefore not be confused with the use of the term "space" by G. Bourque in a recent text. For Bourque "space" becomes in effect a synonym for the field or base of accumulation of a specific layer or fraction of the bourgeoisie. See "Petite bourgeoisie envahissante et bourgeoisie tenebreuse," *Les Cahiers du socialisme*, no. 3 (printemps, 1979), 138-39.

9. Lipietz, *Le capital*, 30-53. For Quebec, see my book, *Le Duplessisme: politique économique et rapports de force* (Montréal, 1981), 235-60; and D. Perreault, "Intégration capitaliste en agriculture québécoise et structure de classes en milieu rural" (Thèse M.Sc., Université de Montréal, 1981).

10. F. Caillet, B. Denni, and P. Kukawka, "Espaces et politique; éléments de recherche sur la region Rhone-Alpes," in *Espace et politique, I. la region dans la dynamique de la formation française* (Grenoble), III-3-III-99; Lipietz, *Le capital*, 92-101; A. Lipietz, *La dimension régionale du développement du tertiaire* (Paris, 1978), 65-127.

11. Lipietz, *La dimension*; J. Lafont, D. Leborgne, and A. Lipietz, *Rédéploiment industriel et espace économique: une étude intersectorielle comparative* (Paris, 1980), 54-63; B. Jobert, "Ville et reproduction des differences sociales," in B. Jobert and C. Gilbert, *Système scientifique et développement urbain* (Grenoble, 1976), 36-138.

12. A. Sales, "Système mondial et mouvements nationaux dans les pays industrialisés: l'exemple Québec-Canada," *Sociologie et sociétés*, XI, 2 (octobre, 1979), 69-94. See especially my monograph: *Notes pour l'analyse de la politique économique dépendante dans l'État fédératif canadien* (Colloque Strategies industrielles pour le developpement, Université de Montréal, 1979); G. Stevenson, "Canadian Regionalism in Continental Perspective," *Revue d'études canadiennes*, XV, 2 (été, 1980), 16-28; P. Marchak, "The Two Dimensions of Canadian Regionalism," *ibid.*, 88-97.

13. A. Lipietz, *Sur la question régionale en France* (Paris), 65.

14. Lipietz, *Le capital*, 135-38.

15. See the very informative studies on France: P. Vieille and E. Gilbert, "Espace et politique en Languedoc, de la viticulture aux institutions régionales," and Caillet, Denni, and Kukawka, "Espace et politique," in *Espace et politique I. La region dans la dynamique de la formation française*, II-44-II-119 and III-89-III-178; Lipietz, *Le capital*, 143-48, 159-63; R. Dulong, "La crise du rapport État/Société locale vue au travers de la politique régionale," in N. Poulantzas, ed., *La crise de l'État* (1978), 124-52.

16. Vieille and Gilbert, "Espace et politique en Languedoc," II-118-II-137; F. d'Arcy and C. Gilbert, "L'espace du capital et le remodelage des institutions," in Poulantzas, ed., *La crise de l'État*, I-14-I-127.

17. R. Parenteau, "Les problèmes du développement régional dans un État fédératif, l'experience canadienne," *Revue d'économie politique*, LXXIII, 2 (mars-avril, 1963), 161-222; T.N. Brewis, "Regional Development," *Canadian Economic Policy* (Toronto, 1965), 316-27; B. Bonin, "Repartition régionale des investissements depuis la guerre," *L'Actualité économique*, XXXV, 4 (janvier-mars, 1960), 566-95; P. Harvey, "Conjoncture et structure: les perspectives spatiales du plein-emploi au Canada," *L'Actualité économique*, XXIX (janvier-mars, 1954); Conseil économique du Canada, *Vivre ensemble, Une étude des disparités régionales* (Ottawa, 1977).

18. P.-Y. Villeneuve, "Classes sociales, régions et accumulation du capital," *Cahiers de géographie de Québec*, XXII, 56 (septembre, 1978), 159-72; P.-Y. Villeneuve, "Disparités sociales et disparités régionales: l'exemple du Québec," *Cahiers de géographie de Québec*, XXI, 52 (avril, 1977), 19-32; J.-L. Klein, "Du materialisme historique aux inégalites régionales: le cas de la région de Québec," *Cahiers de géographie de Québec*, XXII, 56 (septembre, 1978), 173-87; S. Côté and B. Lévesque, "L'envers de la medaille: le sous-développement régional," Communication presentee à l'AC-FAS, 14 mai 1980; F. Harvey, "La question régionale au Québec," *Revue d'études canadiennes*, XV, 2 (été, 1980), 74-87; S. Côté, "Enjeux régionaux et luttes pour le pouvoir," *Les Cahiers du socialisme*, no. 4 (automne, 1979), 202-11.

19. G. Boismenu, "Les classes et l'oppression nationale au Québec," paper presented to the 14th Latin American Sociology Conference, Puerto Rico, October, 1981.

20. C.J. Friedrich, *Tendances du fédéralisme en théorie et en pratique* (Belgian Institute of Political Science, 1971), 15-92.

21. See note 6, as well as A. Faucher, *Histoire économique et unité canadienne* (Montréal, 1970), 11-29; M. Lamontagne, *Le fédéralisme canadien* (Québec, 1954), 7-16; F.R. Scott, *Essays on the Constitution* (Toronto, 1977), 251-60; R. Arès, *Dossier su le Pacte fédératif de 1867* (Montréal), 223-50.

22. Stevenson, "Federalism and the Political Economy of the Canadian State."

23. Dubuc, "Les fondements historiques."

24. Monière, *Le développement des idéologies au Québec*, 296: "Les contrats gouvernementaux et le patronage renflouaient la petite bourgeoisie en concurrence inégale avec les monopoles, dont le développement était favorisé par le gouvernement fédéral et, aussi, paradoxalement, par l'Union nationale qui soutenait les intérêts américains contre les intérêts canadiens-anglais."

25. This concept is not unique to Canadian and Quebec authors; it is found even in the analysis of a unitary state like France. The studies of Dulong, cited above, are evidence of this. Lipietz brings out this aspect when he insists that the local dominant classes are also part of the national power bloc and that Dulong "sous-estime la participation au Pouvoir central des fractions hégémoniques régionales." Lipietz, *Sur la question régionale*, 66-67. It will be understood that in the case of the unitary state, as in that of the federated state, this concept results from applying a mechanistic and instrumental methodology of the state.

26. Boismenu, *Le duplessisme*, 29-47, 81-84; J. Niosi, *La bourgeoisie canadienne* (Montréal, 1980); W. Clement, *Continental Corporate Power* (Toronto, 1977).

27. E. Balibar, *Cinq études du matérialisme historique* (Paris, 1974), 90-101.

28. The class effects of the accumulation of capital, of the enlarged reproduction of capital, of the integration of dominated forms, of the development of underdevelopment, of national oppression, etc.

29. The federated form enshrines and encourages the political expression of the regional variations in the emergence and organization of contradictions. In

Canada this tendency is reinforced because the major agents of integration (such as political parties) have shown themselves to be ineffective and institutions at the federal level have had difficulty in accommodating regional interests. T.A. Levy, "Le rôle des provinces," *Le Canada et le Québec sur la scène internationale* (1977), 109-145; Commission de l'unité canadienne, *Se retrouver* (Ottawa, 1979), 11-33; R. Boily, "Les États fédéralistes et pluralistes, le cas canadien: processus de fédéralisation en éclatement," *Czasopismo Prawno-Historyczne*, XXXII, 1 (1980); Stevenson, *Unfulfilled Union*, 183-95; D.V. Smiley, "The structural problem of Canadian federalism," *Administration publique du Canada*, XIV, 3 (1981), 326-43; L. Jalbert, "Régionalisme et crise de l'Etat," *Sociologie et sociétés*, XII, 2 (1980), 66-72.

30. I refrain from mentioning here the sources of conflict, which are only significant in association with the fundamental contradictions, even if they seem to be important from the standpoint of narrative history, political parties, institutional interests, intergovernmental status rivalry and competition, administrative mechanisms and overlapping between them, and communication. R. Simeon, *Federal-Provincial Diplomacy* (Toronto, 1972), 184-96; Stevenson, *Unfulfilled Union*, 184-85, 195-203; G. Veilleux, *Les relations intergouvernementales au Canada et au Québec* (1977), 399-425; D.V. Smiley, "Canadian Federalism and the Resolution of Federal-Provincial Conflict," in F. Vaughan, P. Kyba, and O.P. Dwivedi, eds., *Contemporary Issues in Canadian Politics* (Toronto, 1970), 48-66; E. Gallant, "The Machinery of Federal-Provincial Relations: I," in J.P. Meekison, ed., *Canadian Federalism: Myth or Reality* (Toronto), 287-98; R.M. Burns, "The Machinery of Federal-Provincial Relations: II," *ibid.*, 298-304; R. Schultz, "The Regulatory Process and Federal-Provincial Relations," in G. Bruce Doern, ed., *The Regulatory Process in Canada* (Toronto, 1978), 128-46; G. Julien and M. Proulx, *Le chevauchement des programmes fédéraux et québécois* (1978); V. Lemieux, "Québec contre Ottawa: Axiomes et jeux de la communication," *Études internationales* (1978) 323-36.

31. G. Boismenu, "Vers une redéfinition des lieux d'exercice du pouvoir d'État au Canada," *Cahiers d'histoire*, II, 1 (1981), 11-30.

32. The necessity of a regional policy developed and implemented at the provincial level does not appear equally evident. The marginalization of the Atlantic provinces in relation to the development of Canada leads the governments of those provinces to consider that their own capabilities cannot compare with those of the federal government. See Simeon, *Federal-Provincial Diplomacy*, 163-65. However, simultaneously with the government of Quebec, which revived the COEQ at the beginning of the 1960s, six other provincial governments (including New Brunswick and Nova Scotia) established between 1962 and 1965 a consultative body to develop a more consistent interventionist economic policy. H.E. English, "Economic Planning in Canada," in *Canadian Economic Policy* (Toronto, 1965), 358-75.

33. G. Bourque, *L'État capitaliste et la question nationale* (Montréal, 1977), especially 115-16. The Canadian federated state in its traditional organization and operation, as well as in the recent reform of some of its principles and institutions, illustrates well the present observation. See G. Boismenu and A.J. Belanger, "Les propositions constitutionnelles: sens et portée," in *Québec: un pays incertain* (Montréal, 1980), 225-56; "Vers une redéfinition des lieux d'exercice du pouvoir d'État au Canada," *ibid*., 15-28.

PART THREE

Federalism and

Party Politics

The influence of political parties on federalism, and of federalism on the parties, is a fascinating subject that has not yet been adequately studied in Canada. Canadian political scientists who specialize in the study of parties have tended to take federalism for granted, and the relations between federal and provincial party organizations in most cases have not been a major theme of their work. In fact, there are surprisingly few books of any kind on the Liberal and Progressive Conservative parties, which between them have monopolized power at the federal level. Political scientists who specialize in federalism, on the other hand, give most of their attention to the constitution and to various aspects of intergovernmental relations. Most proceed from the premise that parties are irrelevant to the sources of conflict between federal and provincial governments, that intergovernmental relations are mainly between non-partisan bureaucracies, and that premiers and prime ministers treat their counterparts impartially regardless of whether or not they share a party label. This discounting of the importance of parties is part of a general tendency in political science to argue that parties have little influence on what government actually does, that their only purposes are to select candidates for high office, conduct electoral campaigns, and mobilize the voters on election day. The fact that many political scientists belong to parties might suggest that they are not really convinced of this in practice, but this is the view expressed in their teaching and research.

Political scientists who study other federations, however, have given somewhat more attention to the relations between parties and federalism. K.C. Wheare suggested that "a good party system" was essential to the effective operation of federalism.[1] He meant by this that the party system should allow for the expression of regional interests and viewpoints but should also permit their aggregation into some sort of national consensus. W.H. Riker suggested a more precise and more testable proposition: "The federal relationship is centralized according to the degree to which the parties organized to operate the central government control the parties organized to operate the constituent governments."[2] Other writers have reversed this relationship, suggesting that if a state has federal, as opposed to unitary, institutions it is likely to have decentralized parties. This seems to be particularly true of the United States, but the separation of powers between the President and Congress may be a more important contributing factor than federalism itself.

Canada perhaps meets K.C. Wheare's definition of a "good" party system since all three major parties (the only ones represented in Parliament since 1980) nominate full slates of candidates and try to appeal to voters in all parts of the country. Even in Quebec, where nationalist parties have held office at the provincial level, voters are apparently content to support one of the major national parties at the federal level. Efforts to create an explicitly regionalist, or even separatist, party in the western provinces have met with little success. The only time when the party system threatened to divide the country along regional lines was in 1917, when Anglophone Canada voted overwhelmingly for a coalition government pledged to introduce conscription and Quebec voted even more over-whelmingly for the Liberal opposition.

On the other hand, the fact that all three national parties try to overcome regional differences does not mean that they succeed in attracting equal levels of support across the country. The Liberals have been traditionally weak in British Columbia and Alberta, and more recently in Saskatchewan as well. On the other hand, the Conservatives were extremely weak in Quebec for most of the twentieth century, although their fortunes impro-ved dramatically in 1984. NDP electoral support has been largely confined to four provinces: Ontario, Manitoba, Saskatchewan, and British Colum-bia. It is possible to form a government with negligible support from certain regions, and such a government may have difficulty in aggregating the interests of all parts of the country. Some observers have suggested that a new electoral system, allowing for some degree of proportional represen-tation, would overcome this problem.

Even more striking than the disparities in party support across the country are the discrepancies between the party systems at the federal and provincial levels, often within the same province. As Steven Muller observed almost three decades ago, "the national party system has two distinct layers."[3] While the two traditional parties have monopolized the roles of government and official opposition at the national level, this has not been true at the provincial level in any province west of New Brunswick. New Democrats have formed governments in three provinces and are currently (1989) the official opposition in two others. Other parties that have governed in one or more provinces include Social Credit, United Farmers, Progressives, Co-operative Commonwealth Federation, Union Nationale, and Parti Québécois. Two provinces have had coalition govern-ments and in two others, including New Brunswick at the time of writing, the governing party has held every seat in the legislature. Some provincial parties, such as the Union Nationale and the Parti Québécois, have abstained completely from federal elections. In some provinces one or more of the major federal parties has at times played an insignificant role, or none at all, in provincial elections. Canadians are sometimes accused of "inconsistency" in their federal and provincial voting behaviour, but at times "inconsistency" is unavoidable because the choices available to the voters at the two levels are not the same. Even if they are the same, federal and provincial parties bearing the same name may stand for quite different policies.

What Riker calls party centralization has varied considerably over time and from one party and province to another. Sir John A. Macdonald's Conservative Party was highly centralized, with the provincial sections subordinate to the federal. In the Liberal or Reform Party at that time, and in both major parties after 1900, the provincial wings had much more autonomy and more influence over the federal wing. The New Democratic Party has a highly integrated organization, although the greater electoral success of that party at the provincial level, particularly in the West, has a decentralizing impact. Provincial sections of the NDP have sometimes been at odds with the federal party, despite their ostensibly shared ideology. The Progressive Conservative Party also has a fairly integrated organization, with the degree of centralization depending largely on whether or not the party holds office at the federal level. The Progressive Conservatives do not contest provincial elections in Quebec, the province where the possibility of conflict between the provincial and federal wings of the same party would be greatest. The Liberals since 1960 have developed a national party organization that is almost completely independent of the provincial parties, but the corollary of this is that the provincial parties are also independent of the federal party, so that the shared label has very little meaning. When the Quebec Liberal Party formally declared its independence from the federal party in 1964, the federal party offered little opposition.

In most federations, most of the time, the same parties compete at both levels of government, using the same electoral organizations to do so. Why is Canada different? As Edwin Black suggests in his study of the British Columbia Progressive Conservatives, trying to operate at both levels creates problems for party organizations. This is perhaps particularly true in provinces such as British Columbia and Quebec, where federal-provincial conflict seems to be more the rule than the exception. In British Columbia in the 1940s, as Black explains, the problems were enhanced because the Tories and Liberals formed an anti-socialist coalition at the provincial level while they remained opponents at the federal level. Yet conflict between the two wings of the Progressive Conservative Party continued long after the coalition had collapsed. In part this was because the provincial wing accused the federal wing of being too friendly with Social Credit Premier W.A.C. Bennett, a former Progressive Conservative. Not until the Columbia River Treaty had produced an open and bitter conflict between Bennett and the federal Progressive Conservatives was harmony among the Tories restored. However, the Progressive Conservative Party remains insignificant at the provincial level, as it has been since 1952.

The success of Social Credit in British Columbia, where that party still controls the government, illustrates two important facts about Canadian politics: provincial politicians can win votes by verbally abusing the federal government, and provincial parties affiliated with the federal government will share the blame for any failure of "Ottawa" to give the province what it wants. Parties like Social Credit and the Parti Québécois, having no federal affiliation, need not worry about this problem. Progressive Conservatives and New Democrats, whose parties rarely win federal elections, have managed to maintain largely integrated organizations, except in Quebec. Provincial Liberals, whose party usually controls the federal government, have sometimes resorted to formally severing their ties with the federal wing of the party. On the other hand, federal Liberals (and federal Tories in British Columbia) have sometimes regarded their provincial affiliates as a lost cause and have given them little or no support.

Even in Ontario, where the electorate is generally well disposed toward the federal government, relations between federal and provincial party organizations are affected by these circumstances. The studies of Hamilton by Henry Jacek *et al.* and of Thunder Bay by K.L. Morrison were conducted when the Liberals controlled the federal government and the Progressive Conservatives controlled the government of Ontario. (There were only eight years between 1943 and 1988 when the same party governed at both levels.) The party organizations studied in Hamilton were all ostensibly involved in politics at both levels, as one would expect in a province with a strongly centralist orientation and with no distinctive provincial parties analogous to Social Credit and the Parti Québécois. Nonetheless, the Hamilton organizations displayed significant variations in practice, with some being primarily federal and others primarily provincial. About a third of the individual activists were highly active at only one level. Liberals were the most inclined to limit their activity to one arena, usually the federal, a finding that may demonstrate the lingering effect of the bitter conflict between Premier Mitchell Hepburn and Prime Minister Mackenzie King, almost three decades before the study was conducted. Since the article was first published the fortunes of provincial Liberals in Ontario have significantly improved, and in 1985 they formed a government for the first time since the Second World War. Nonetheless, the improvement has been less pronounced in Hamilton, where the NDP won three out of four provincial ridings in 1985 and again in 1987.

Morrison's article attempts to explain the fact that many voters, localities, and entire provinces appear to support different parties in federal and provincial elections. While easily explicable in Quebec and British Columbia, where significant parties exist that contest elections at one level only, the phenomenon is harder to explain in Ontario, where the same three parties operate at both levels. Nonetheless, the tradition of "split" voting has deep roots in Ontario, dating back to the nineteenth century when Tory Prime Minister Sir John A. Macdonald and Liberal Premier Oliver Mowat simultaneously shared the support of the Ontario electorate. The positions of the two parties were reversed between 1943 and 1985, when Ontario had a Progressive Conservative government while it usually supported the Liberals in federal elections.

Morrison considers one plausible hypothesis: that different fractions within the business community support either the governing federal party or the governing provincial party, depending on which level of government has the greatest impact on their type of business. No evidence was found to support this interpretation. Instead, the evidence suggested that the business community of Thunder Bay arrived at a consensus to support the Liberals federally and the Progressive Conservatives provincially, partly to keep the NDP from winning seats and partly to have representation in the party that was most likely to form the government at each level. In the 1980s the federal Liberals were widely perceived as hostile to business and this strategy seems to have been abandoned. The Progressive Conservative vote in Thunder Bay increased sharply in 1984 and the NDP captured both seats. At the provincial level, however, Thunder Bay has remained on the winning side, electing two Liberals in 1987.

In the final essay here, David Rayside examines the Liberal Party, or rather parties, in Quebec. His data were collected in 1973, almost a decade after the creation of formally separate party organizations at the two levels. That separation took place following a long period of conflict, similar to the situation in British Columbia described by Black, and in spite of the fact that the federal wing of the Liberal Party in Quebec enjoyed a certain degree of independence from the Ottawa-based organization of the national party. It was still possible after the split to belong to both organizations, but Rayside found, as Jacek *et al.* found in Hamilton, that many party activists specialized in either federal or provincial politics, although federal and provincial activists shared similar views on political issues. Greater differences of opinion were found between Liberal Members of Parliament and Liberal members of the National Assembly, particularly on issues related to language and the constitution. Despite their similarities of background, both groups of politicians tended to conform to the views of their own level of government. Such pressures to conform are reinforced by the parliamentary system, under which backbenchers are expected to observe party discipline so as to maintain the government in office. Under this system the federal government cannot easily accommodate regional differences of opinion, and the task of expressing those differences is largely left to the provincial governments.

Rayside concluded that relations between federal and provincial wings of the same party were likely to be particularly difficult when both were in office, but subsequent events suggest that they are difficult even when this is not the case. When Prime Minister Trudeau took steps to patriate and amend the constitution despite the opposition of most provincial governments the provincial Liberals were in opposition, but most of them joined the Parti Québécois government in condemning the federal initiative. After the provincial Liberals returned to office in 1985 they supported the Canada-United States free trade agreement, which was negotiated by a Progressive Conservative federal government. The federal Liberals, now in opposition, vehemently opposed the agreement, which became the major issue in the federal election of 1988. Premier Robert Bourassa made little effort to conceal his hopes that the Progressive Conservatives would win the election. With his tacit support, they won an overwhelming majority of Quebec's constituencies.

Notes

1. K.C. Wheare, *Federal Government* (4th edition, New York, 1964), 82.
2. W.H. Riker, *Federalism: Origin, Operation, Significance* (Boston, 1964), 129.
3. Steven Muller, "Federalism and the Party System in Canada," in Aaron Wildavsky, ed., *American Federalism in Perspective* (Boston, 1967), 144.

10. EDWIN R. BLACK

Federal Strains

Within a

Canadian Party

Unity is a rallying cry within the ranks of political parties everywhere; that it must be voiced so often and in so many different circumstances reveals some of the extent to which political parties are subject to internally divisive forces. To state, then, that Canada's major parties are peculiarly susceptible to quarrels over leadership is to direct attention to an unusual aspect of such disputes in this country – the dimension imparted to them by the federal system. Canadian parties do, of course, have difficulties analogous to those of parties in other countries, difficulties such as the disputes between Hugh Gaitskell and Aneurin Bevan or between Harold Macmillan and Peter Thorneycroft. But equally noteworthy in Canada are the frequent public squabbles between federal party chieftains and the provincial leaders, their theoretical subordinates. A simple pairing of names suggests some of them: Mackenzie King and Mitchell Hepburn of Ontario, George Drew and Deane Finlayson of British Columbia, Lester Pearson and Ross Thatcher of Saskatchewan. Whatever may be the causes of leadership feuds, in Canada they are always likely to be complicated by the federal system, which with its plurality of independent centres of political power, makes country-wide party discipline more difficult to maintain than it is in comparable unitary countries.

Two subjects have been raised, party leadership and the impact of federalism on the party system; as yet, neither has been investigated systematically. This paper is designed to explore the fringes of these subjects by

From *The Dalhousie Review*, 45, 3 (1965). Reprinted with permission of *The Dalhousie Review* and the author.

examining a particular case – the dispute between the federal and provincial factions of the British Columbia Progressive Conservative Association – and by looking briefly at several other quarrels between federal and provincial leaders. Factors isolated from these disputes lead to a concluding statement of ten general propositions about the relationship of federalism to the party system. Special emphasis will be given to the peculiar problems of organization that a party faces in trying to operate at both the federal and provincial levels of the federal system.[1]

Quarrels within a political party can usually be traced to differences over policies and objectives, to conflicts of personalities and ambitions, or to differences in the perception of problems and their most appropriate solutions. It should be recognized, however, that these same differences impart vitality as well as discord to the system. The problem is to keep the expression of these differences within bounds, a task which becomes even more difficult if the party has an "open" tradition honouring healthy debate and the expression of diverse and even radically different viewpoints.

The course of debate and struggle within a party is analogous to an electrical system in which the leaders and clusterings of party opinion are represented by electrodes of varying capabilities. The party's *raison d'être* – its ultimate objective – is represented by the common field through which the electrodes interact. The system's activity depends upon maintenance of voltage differentials (i.e., opinion differences) between the electrodes, all or some of which are responsive to changes in the external environment. The organization's relative efficiency depends upon its ability to harmonize and integrate the different forces coursing through it. If the internal transmission and transforming facilities break down, the system's output of power is reduced. In most states the boundaries of the system are co-terminous with a single service area – the unitary state. But in a federation such as Canada there is a self-contained party organization within each province. This means that there is co-existing within the country whole series of similar parties which are frequently required to work together as national units. Attempts to combine these often disparate systems for the pursuit or maintenance of public office at the federal capital reveal the strengths and weaknesses of the overall integrating process.

Before considering a particular case, we should, perhaps, look briefly at the editorial-page model which rationalizes the twofold concerns of a major Canadian party. According to the model, the Conservative Party, for example, should be a unified, country-wide association of political activists who work through provincial subdivisions to achieve their goals. While the party's objectives – of ideological formulation, popular persuasion, and attainment of office – may be prosecuted at two independent levels of government, the party subdivision chiefs, the provincial leaders, are usually seen to be hierarchically inferior to the federal leader. The Progressive Conservative Party in British Columbia does not always conform closely to the model.

The Conservative Party has deep roots in the often rocky soil of British Columbia. The party's nineteenth-century attributes were those of trade and tariffs, of opportunity and opportunism, of damn-yankeeism and visioneering, with nearly all these traits summed up in "what's good for business is good for B.C." These political attributes found ready acceptance in the primitive coastal society which featured mansions for imperial cast-offs, easy money for timber pirates and railway buccaneers, and cold beans or worse for down-on-their-luck eastern and American gold-hunters. The Conservatives successfully promoted the colony's union with Canada in 1871 and enjoyed to the full the favour of federal voters for three decades.

The party was never one to worry much about policy or ideology in the province.[2] Although members were summoned to policy-making conventions as early as the 1920s, the party has always stressed attractive leadership, good organization, and a balanced geographical appeal as the best route to the council chamber at Victoria. The party was given its provincial shape by Richard McBride, who became British Columbia's first partisan premier in 1902. Unit that time, the provincial cabinet had been a coalition dedicated to the non-partisan principle of extracting as much as possible from Ottawa and concerned to keep the local community as healthy as possible for business.

To win the election of 1902 as a Conservative, McBride put together an assortment of personal supporters, existing federal associations, and a number of *ad hoc* legislative electoral committees. Many Tories protested McBride's conversion of the federal associations to provincial purposes, but his efforts to co-ordinate party campaigning found favour with Robert Borden, who was trying to reconstruct the Canadian party after Laurier's victories of 1896 and 1900. The fruits of victory soon provided solace for the protesting federal Tories, and all the more so because McBride's chief lieutenant, W.J. Bowser, employed his considerable talents and the advantages of office-holding to build a strong provincial organization. When Borden became prime minister, his supporters from British Columbia were indebted to McBride's provincial association for organizing their campaign.

British Columbia voters remained fairly faithful to the party until 1916, when the Conservatives were deposed from the provincial government benches. After twelve years in opposition, the party returned to office in 1928; there it remained until 1933, when the depression and political stupidity destroyed the party provincially. In the federal field, the Conservatives held the largest number of British Columbia seats from 1908 through to 1935, when they were reduced to only five of the sixteen parliamentary seats.

In the early 1930s, the provincial Conservatives found themselves leaderless, their ranks decimated, their association disintegrating, and their campaign machinery non-existent; the only Tories holding public office had made their way by their own energies. Provincial Conservatives wandered in the wilderness for some years, but by the end of the decade they had found new leaders and some legislative representation. Before either Dr. R.J. Manion or R.L. Maitland could remedy the party's weaknesses in the federal and provincial fields, the Second World War had begun. At Ottawa, Manion was rebuffed in his proposals for a union government, but at Victoria the Liberals found it expedient after the 1941 election to take Maitland and his eleven Tory seat-mates into a coalition government. This created an embarrassing anomaly for the party. In the federal capital, the Conservative Party stood as the champion of the provinces and in strong opposition to the Liberals. In the provincial capital, however, the Conservative leaders were committed to supporting a coalition cabinet in which they were junior partners to the Liberals.

British Columbia's political environment changed significantly during the 1930s and 1940s. Both the social outlook and the political allegiance of the people were shaped anew by the forces of depression, heavy immigration, and later boom periods. Many of the electorate that came to the fore at the mid-century lacked strong identification with either the Liberal or the Conservative Party. Without family or community political tradition relevant to their new society, these people saw partisan politics in terms of either protest or simple opportunism; to the political environment of the pre-depression era had been added, as well, the yeasty elements of militant socialism and radical conservatism.

Both war and depression had long inhibited vigorous provincial government action. The dominant Liberals changed their leader, began wearying of their alliance with the Conservatives, and eventually expelled the Tory leader, Herbert Anscomb, from his provincial cabinet post. Neither Liberals nor Conservatives, in preparing for the 1952 election, showed much awareness of the new electorate. A resulting lack of sensitivity to the voting public was reflected in preparations for the 1952 election – preparations which consisted chiefly in devising a mixture of voting schemes which would keep the socialists at bay. The CCF was denied office, but the electoral jimmying resulted in the election of a Social Credit government led by a renegade Conservative MLA whose party had twice rejected his bid for the leadership. The Conservatives were reduced by that election to four of the forty-eight legislative seats; the Liberals fared only a little better. In the 1953 election, Premier Bennett and his Social Crediters greatly improved their standing; the Conservatives were cut to one lonely member, and even he eventually left the party. Despite numerous by-election attempts and two more general elections, by the end of 1960 the Conservatives still had no representation in the legislature.

The party was stronger in the federal field. Conservatives held three of the province's federal seats through the 1949 and 1953 elections, seven in 1957, and eighteen of the twenty-two in 1958. Little of this support could apparently be swung to provincial candidates despite some effort made by the three senior members of Parliament, Howard Green, Davie Fulton, and George Pearkes. The Social Credit premier had succeeded, first, in identifying his group as the party of progress – in contrast with the coalition parties – and, secondly, in polarizing provincial politics into "Social Credit or Socialism." Even worse for the Tories, Social Credit had captured not only their former electorate but a good number of their followers who had toiled previously for the Tories in the provincial vineyards. Indeed, some people even worked for Social Credit in provincial campaigns and for the Conservatives in federal campaigns. Why was the Conservative Party in such a perilous state? The most significant reason, it may be suspected, was an ailment that can be termed "federal-provincial schizophrenia."

"Federal-provincial schizophrenia" is what Aristotle would probably call a degenerate form of the "right state" of a political party. Our model suggests this "right" form obtains when the same political organism functions with equal efficiency in both the federal and provincial areas of its responsibility. The schizophrenic forms of organization are probably more common in the Canadian provinces than is the efficiently operating, dual function type. To its great cost, the Conservative Party in British Columbia manifested its schizophrenic tendencies in a violent public quarrel; the resulting public attention made the situation especially difficult to repair.

The quarrel turned, essentially, on two issues: how federal activity in the province should be organized and who should direct it.[3] Following the provincial association's collapse in the early 1930s, federal work in the province was handled by a committee appointed by members of Parliament and other candidates. On coming to the federal leadership in 1942, John Bracken undertook to revitalize Conservative organization throughout Canada. Where a province had an effective Conservative Party association, full responsibility was vested in the provincial leader. Where the party was notably weak, as in Quebec, a special organizer was named. British Columbia presented an unusual problem. An active provincial association existed, but its leaders were in coalition with the Liberals. An effective CCF opposition was keeping the government on the defensive, and leading British Columbia Conservatives were frequently required to support or promote Liberal-inspired policies. To compound the problem, from Bracken's point of view, the provincial Tories tended to see the local picture in the same terms as did the Liberals and did not agree that there was any necessity for a thorough-going reorganization.

Deciding that a strong personal hand was needed, Bracken named Howard Green as his personal representative and gave him particular responsibility for all federal organization work in British Columbia. In practice, Bracken made the policy and tactical decisions and Green communicated them to the faithful in British Columbia. The then provincial leader (R.L. Maitland) accepted this arrangement, although his chief lieutenant, Herbert Anscomb, was angry at having to defer to Green or to anybody else in organizational concerns. Anscomb won the provincial leadership in 1946 but did little to improve the state of the party.

The coalition arrangement generated much internal party friction after the war. Anscomb and his close associates enjoyed many of the prerequisites of office and insisted on continuing with the coalition; they hoped thereby to gain both time and resources for rebuilding the party. But many other Conservatives thought that the coalition should have been terminated at the war's end. This group included the many who were out of favour with the gruff and sometimes arrogant provincial leader. More importantly, however, the dissidents also comprised returning veterans, older party workers who saw the organization degenerating, young party members eager for a change, and many party adherents who were concerned that the alliance with the Liberals was impairing the party's chances in the federal field. Liberal and Conservative party labels were not used during the 1945 and 1949 provincial elections, and the Conservative associations were ordered to work for the election of Coalition candidates no matter what their previous political stripe might have been. A sizable number of those discontented with Anscomb refused to participate, especially in the 1949 campaign; most prominent of all the abstainers were the members of Parliament and their close associates and supporters.

The provincial leader was openly challenged at the 1950 annual meeting. The federal wing of the party, the Young Conservatives, and others discontented with Anscomb supported W.A.C. Bennett in what proved to be that MLA's second futile bid for the leadership. After beating off Bennett's threat fairly easily, Anscomb went on to elect nearly all his own people to the association executive, and again sought to control all campaign funds and the selection of federal candidates. Drew, taking the advice of his MPs, refused to accede either to Anscomb's insistence on full organizational control or to his demand that the organizer be dismissed. The organizer, Frank Barker, was accused by the Anscomb faction of having directed Bennett's unsuccessful drive for leadership. Soon after the convention, Barker was summarily locked out of the provincial Conservative office and his files were thrust into the hall. With the approval of the federal group, Barker opened another office despite the provincial leader's strong objections.

The 1952 provincial election was a disaster for the Conservatives, and Anscomb resigned; a protégé, Deane Finlayson, came out of the ensuing leadership contest with a comfortable lead over the candidate of the federal wing (A.L. Bewley). Finlayson also sought to control federal organization work but was told that he would first have to demonstrate some competence both in the field and at the polls. He continued to insist on his "rights" as provincial leader. Finally, in 1954, to report the occasion from Finlayson's viewpoint,

> After years of frustration, after failing in every means including the changing of leadership in the province and the changing of presidents; after promises of cooperation that were never kept, after dismemberment of the party and what appeared to be a deliberate effort to emasculate the party so it could no longer be a factor in provincial politics, the Executive decided upon drastic action. It moved a motion of non confidence in the National Leader on July 17th (1954).[4]

The provincial leader urged the necessity of approving his executive's motion. He charged that Drew had had secret dealings with various party opponents, that Drew was arrogant and dictatorial, and that Drew and his organizers had made a "saw-off" deal with Social Credit to the effect that Drew's group would keep out of Social Credit's way in British Columbia in return for Social Credit agreement not to oppose federal Conservative candidates. The federal party leaders in the province were "agents of malice and misery," Finlayson said, and he went on to predict that within two years Drew would be supplanted as national leader by John Diefenbaker. Angry debate filled the air for several hours, charges were hurled freely, and individuals were slandered on all sides. Eventually, a ballot was taken. The federal leader stood condemned by an announced vote of 40 to 24. The party's three MPs jumped to their feet and stalked from the room followed by twenty-one supporters, several of them in tears and all of them enraged.

During the weeks that followed, Conservatives ranged themselves defiantly into two antagonistic camps. The party's bitter internal strife was fully reported and exposed for all the voters to see. On the one side were Provincial Leader Finlayson, most of the executive of the provincial association, and some constituency-association officers. On the other side were the members of Parliament, the Young Conservatives, and the other riding-association executives. Newspapers reported the dispute as a simple personality clash between Drew and Finlayson. The provincial leader's charge that the federal leader was denying him his rights as provincial leader and acting like a dictator seemed to accord with Drew's public image and was generally accepted outside the party. Many of those supporting the federal leader justified doing so on the grounds that the provincial executive had acted unconstitutionally and had thereby gravely injured the party. Chiefly, however, it would seem that they supported Drew because they refused to relinquish to an untried provincial leader and his friends the full control of the party's federal organization, an organization built largely through the efforts of such men as Leon Ladner and the three MPs, Green, Fulton, and Pearkes. Formation of a separate organization to deal with all federal affairs was announced soon after the Vernon meeting.

The fight was a public one and many bitter words were exchanged as first this Conservative and then another held press conferences. During the month of July, 1954, newspapers reported almost daily incidents evidencing the split. An editorial in *The Vancouver Province*, headed "Suicide at Vernon," expressed a commonly held view of the affair:

> So far as the public knows, the vote at Vernon was based on nothing but the charge that George Drew and his federal party supporters were interfering with the provincial politicians. There was no major issue of policy. It was strictly a domestic row over the kitchen sink.
>
> By resolution, George Drew stands condemned, not because he failed in matters of national policy, but because he butted in on Mr. Finlayson, the seatless leader of a seatless party.[5]

Throughout the constituency associations, an ever-widening gulf became evident as supporters of both sides sought to put their group on record in support of either Finlayson or Drew. Those members of the constituency associations who found themselves in a local minority on the leadership loyalty question sometimes sought help from the headquarters of either faction to set up a new association, but more often they simply quit active party work. Premier Bennett claimed that large numbers of disaffected Tories were joining his Social Credit "movement." In August, the federal group began reorganizing in earnest; the three MPs divided responsibility for the province between themselves, established the Federal Council, and sought to ensure the loyalty of all the federal constituency associations. The executive of the Canadian association recognized the Federal Council as having sole responsibility for federal work in British Columbia.

Sporadic attempts at reconciliation were made, but without much apparent effect. The provincial association did not match the activity of the Federal Council in organizing, and although the Finlayson group claimed large numbers of supporters and carried on a vigorous press campaign, little that was tangible appeared to result. In March, 1955, the provincial wing published what it called *A Factual Documented Statement of the Conservative Party's Position in British Columbia and Some of the Reasons for the Motion of No Confidence in the National Leader*. This publication, which was widely distributed, presented a series of statements, letters, and parts of letters, tracing the difficulties back to 1942 and Green's appointment by Bracken. The statement purported to demonstrate that Green had sought undue power for himself in opposition to the only legally constituted association, and that the two federal leaders had systematically supported Green's attempts to divide the party. The publication reiterated the association's claim to be the sole legitimate embodiment of the party in British Columbia and attacked the federal wing for setting up the Federal Council. The charge of "a saw-off with Social Credit" was repeated and was made a formal resolution of the provincial officers. In the provincial election held a year later, 1956, the Conservative share of the popular vote stood at an all-time low. Virtually every newspaper's interpretation of the vote attributed the Tories' dismal showing to the internal party split.

Much debate in British Columbia swirled about the institutional manifestations of the central party within the province, that is to say, the post of personal representative of the federal leader and the Federal Council. Both institutions require examination.

The designation of a personal representative began with John Bracken, was continued by George Drew, and – with some modification – by John Diefenbaker. Considering the controversy about the post, it was somewhat surprising to discover that so slight was the importance attached to the post by its holders that they were unable to recall with certainty exactly who had held the appointment during what years. The representative's duties were always vaguely defined and his powers were even less definite. All four of the people who held the post have agreed, however, that the primary function was that of funnelling reliable information to and from the federal leader and the local organizations. From the time of the coalition government, the federal leaders were never convinced that much credence could be placed in situation assessments made by persons working closely with the Liberal Party or by an association long accustomed to co-operating with the Liberals and essentially unchanged since the coalition. It was primarily to fill this gap in information that personal representatives were appointed.

Formation of the Federal Council did not at first supersede the personal representative's work, for the Council was more concerned with associational work and less with the divination of popular feeling. But as the Federal Council largely completed its task of building loyal party groups in every constituency, the Council's president assumed the additional task of obtaining information as well. Diefenbaker utilized the system he inherited in British Columbia but began to supplement information supplied by the Council with that of other advisers.

The Federal Council of British Columbia was not unique in the country-wide scheme of Conservative Party organization, a consideration that received acknowledgement neither from the Council's opponents in the province nor from the press in its discussions of the party divisions. In 1959 the national organizer, Allister Grosart, gave the Federal Council an outline of party structures in other parts of the country. Quebec had a federal association overseeing three regional associations and "more than seventy-five riding associations, most of them fairly new." Manitoba had been organized on a strong federal-constituency basis after a coalition provincial government had resulted in the atrophy of many Conservative groups in the provincial ridings. Grosart said that the separate federal association was to be maintained in Manitoba until the provincial organization had been rebuilt and the two fields of work could be divided under one jurisdiction. A federal council was to be organized in Newfoundland in 1960. Grosart emphasized that no problems resulted wherever there was a strong provincial association and that separate federal organization was usually unnecessary. This situation was believed to obtain in Ontario, Nova Scotia, and New Brunswick. The federal organizer did not report on Prince Edward Island and noted that there were provincial but no federal associations in Saskatchewan and Alberta.

In other parties and in other situations, federal cabinet ministers have often been the party's effective chieftains within a province ruled by an opposition party. Where the party forms the provincial government, it seems safe to assert that the premier has had full control over all organizational work within the province – unless he has specifically declined interest in the federal work, as, for example, Ontario's Leslie Frost was thought to have done.

Today, ten years after the Vernon resolution condemning the federal leader, reconciliation has been effected between the two factions. The Federal Council has been disbanded, the two offices merged, and the provincial leader made responsible for all federal organization in the province; during the federal and provincial election campaigns of 1963 the most thoroughgoing co-operation of the two wings was evident to press observers. Without detailing the transformation, it may be well to suggest a few of its significant aspects.

It should be recognized that there was, and still is, some genuine conviction that the federal and provincial functions of a party can be prosecuted most efficiently by separate organizations; this was indicated in surveys of the constituency presidents made in 1958 and again in 1964. Most party workers, however, believed that a public façade of unified party activity was essential, and so it would appear – especially wherever party work is seen in ideological terms such as "the promotion of conservative principles and philosophy in all aspects of government."

The passage of time, the resignation or death of certain embittered individuals, and lack of success at the provincial polls eventually dissipated the provincial faction's resolution. The provincial leader, Finlayson, sought election a number of times but was unable to win a seat in either the Legislative Assembly or the House of Commons. He was confirmed as provincial leader by only a narrow margin in a 1958 challenge to his position by Desmond Kidd, whose bid was plainly sponsored by the federal wing. Selection of a new federal leader was significant for the provincial situation. Diefenbaker was generally thought to have given aid and comfort to Finlayson in the quarrel with Drew, and it was Diefenbaker rather than Fulton, the British Columbia Member of Parliament, who received the votes of provincial association delegates to the leadership convention. But while the new federal leader was on good terms with Finlayson, he did not disturb the organization of responsibility for federal work in the province. For their part, the Fulton-Green group constituted for the 1957 and 1958 general elections a campaign committee that included prominent members of the provincial faction. Members of the federal wing won election to the provincial executive while three of the MPs succeeded to cabinet posts at Ottawa. Finlayson, after another provincial election shut-out in 1960, resigned his post in despair. After a period in which the provincial leadership was deliberately left vacant, the Federal Council disappeared into a reconstructed provincial association. Within it were constituted two parallel committees, one charged with provincial responsibility and the other with federal duties. After helping to effect these changes, federal Public Works Minister Fulton answered an almost unanimous draft to become provincial leader. One respected newspaperman reported from the 1963 leadership convention that "even the most cynical delegate agreed that due to the Fulton touch a bitter split between federal and provincial wings of the party were dead, buried and soon to be forgotten." Later, he commented that "in the long run, final healing of the ... split may prove to be a more significant development politically than Fulton's tumultuous election as leader of the provincial Conservatives."[8] Head-table guests at the final luncheon included both Deane Finlayson and Herbert Anscomb. The new executive elected at the convention was composed of members who had not been associated with either of the two former factions.

As a summary of political difficulties in British Columbia, a few salient points should be noted:

(1) During the 1940s the Conservative Party as a whole was embarrassed by the anomaly of being in active alliance with the Liberals at the provincial seat of government and being in active opposition to them at Ottawa. (2) In the immediate post-war period, an organizational resurgence in the federal sphere was in marked contrast to the antebellum attitudes of the provincial leaders. (3) The established provincial faction was challenged unsuccessfully four times by leadership candidates enjoying the support of the federal wing. (4) While the dispute appeared to involve nothing more than the status of the provincial leader, the question embraced both the shape and control of all party organization in the province as well as the selection and final approval of candidates for both federal and provincial contests. (5) Even in the depths of electoral despair, the provincial faction

maintained a firm grip on the only legal Conservative association and with it was able to censure the federal leader. (6) During the 1950s, the federal faction was always better able to raise election funds than was the provincial faction; this situation further embittered the provincial partisans, but it does not seem to have been a significant factor contributing to the party division. (7) No aspect of the quarrel seemed to derive from differences over policy. (Can we attribute this to the lack of office-holding by the party, or does it simply confirm our impressions about the group's rather slight ideological commitment?) (8) Not until one of the two factions was able to attain public office were its representatives able to assimilate the other group.

This study has concentrated on British Columbia. While other students of Canadian politics will recall similar conflicts, perhaps particular attention might be directed to two. The first concerns the Ontario Liberal Party during the 1930s. Then, as is well known, the Liberal leader, Mitchell Hepburn, was engaged in a long and violent public quarrel with the federal leader, W.L. Mackenzie King. That neither King nor Hepburn could tolerate the other's personality seems to be well agreed, but were there not other causes underpinning the dispute? An inquiry into that situation might well cast further light on the impact of federalism on Canadian party life.

The second conflict concerned the Liberal Party in Saskatchewan during the early 1960s. This problem would appear to have issued in ideological terms primarily because of a tactical situation. In seeking to overthrow Saskatchewan's CCF government, the provincial Liberal leader, Ross Thatcher, carefully cultivated a strong right-wing "look" for his group, an attitude in notable contrast with that of the federal party. The right-wing provincial group organized the 1962 federal campaign in the province, but only one MP won election. "Mr. Pearson evidently found the Thatcher attitude unacceptable," reported Charles Lynch, because following the 1962 election, "the national Liberal leader ordered a change."[9] Dean Otto Lang of the University of Saskatchewan built a new organization that excluded the provincial leader's group and, when the 1963 election was announced, set about his task without consulting Thatcher. The result seems to have been that the provincial officers did little but look on with amusement while Dean Lang's forces battled futilely with those of John Diefenbaker.[10]

Whenever leaders of the same party are caught quarrelling in public, both supporters and commentators are wont to reduce the matter to a problem of differences in personality and to assert that the dispute lacks substantive content. This, for the leaders' part, may well be the most acceptable public face to put on the dispute if they are unable to deny its existence. The personality explanation has the attraction of simplicity and credibility, and it helps to reinforce Canadian reluctance to see important differences of principle as significant factors in the country's political life. Expressed as a general thesis, this explanation holds that federalism as such does not make an important difference to the leadership of the major parties, and that quarrels within them arise chiefly from natural jealousies and personality incompatibilities, just as they do in the parties of unitary states.

This thesis is, however, inadequate. While some of the internal disputes in Canada's federal parties do result from clashes of personality, something more than one man's inability to get along with another is required to split a party and range its members into factions. The divided organizational arrangements which manifested the Conservative split in British Columbia persisted for more than a decade and through three different pairs of federal and provincial leaders. It is, of course, reasonable to suggest that personality differences may trigger a dispute which rends a party in two. But if that division endures within a two-party or multi-party system, then we must look beyond the personalities for deeper conditions which themselves might have split the party eventually. Here we will probably find clues to the fissiparous forces which federalism attempts to contain.

Standing as something of an antithesis to the "personality" theory is the "party brokerage" theory. According to this idea, the successful party in a federal state serves as a broker or middleman between the provinces, which have diverse and often contradictory policy claims. Inter-factional quarrels are said to be reflections of these internal policy contradictions as the national party seeks to work out program compromises which are acceptable both to those primarily oriented toward the provinces and to those oriented toward the country as a whole. The validity of this theory is dependent upon finding substantive policy content behind the internal party disputations. While we do not have to disagree with the assertion that Canada's major parties very seldom display coherent and consistent philosophies or policy orientations, there is enough truth in the statement, and so little evidence of policy differences in the British Columbia conflict, that the brokerage explanation is also unsatisfactory.

A synthesis of these ideas may be more serviceable. It may be put this way: The Canadian outlook favours, and, indeed, sometimes requires, politics of pragmatism rather than of policies or ideology; internal party disputes represent, from time to time, conflicts of personalities, attempts to reconcile divergent provincial policy demands, and problems resulting from the often disparate organizational needs of two groups within the party, the one group seeking federal victory and the other seeking victory at the provincial capital.

So little do we know about the relationship between federalism and our political parties that it would probably be prudent to conclude with a series of "questions deserving further exploration." But few people seriously wish to add to their lists of unanswered questions. Consequently, some of the general propositions suggested by this study will be outlined instead. If this course seems incautious, it should be noted that the propositions are themselves cautiously phrased.

(1) Canada's major parties do not fit the model of unified country-wide parties with hierarchically inferior provincial subdivisions: major party supporters do not exhibit the necessary degree of commitment. (2) Both the structure and the internal operation of a major party resemble that of the Canadian system of government. The sovereignty of provincial party units is as real and extensive as that of the provinces with respect to Ottawa. (3) Just as the virtual independence of a provincial government's policy-making depends to a considerable extent on its provincial resources, so the effective control of provincial organization by the local officers depends upon the local unit's political resources in comparison with those of the central party; such resources are considered to be size and commitment of membership, financial capabilities, quality and appeal of leadership, and, of course, electoral success. (4) Party organizers must deal with three types of active members: those whose political interests are primarily oriented in provincial terms, those whose interests are multifaceted or else are concentrated on some aspect of political life comprehending both spheres of government – such as the attainment of ideological objectives or general governmental power for the party. (5) A party's policy objectives and organizational requirements in the federal and provincial arenas are often quite different, but both sets of leaders must rely in large measure on the same relatively small group of people and on the same resources for their field work. (6) The interests and energies of the party machinery within one province cannot be converted readily and with equal efficiency to both federal and provincial objectives. Attempts to treat the party as if it were readily convertible impose almost intolerable stresses on the organization, stresses which may be expected to become manifest in difficulties between the party leaders. (7) The public or private character of the expression and resolution of internal party differences is a reflection of the leadership skills and institutional machinery with which the groups are endowed, and of the party's electoral morale. (8) Even where a provincial party organization is controlled by relatively ineffectual persons, if they are determined in their leadership, representatives of the central party can undertake "corrective" action only at considerable risk. (9) The provincial party is a highly charged organism, with many internal stresses and tensions, which must be capable of frequent integration with as many as nine others of similar nature to produce a country-wide mechanism focusing its power on system-wide problems. (10) The pattern of authoritative relationships between central and provincial party groups will depend upon whether

public office is held by one, neither, or both of the two party groups. These relationships will also be affected by the nature of any "rehabilitative" process through which an out-of-office party faction may be going and by the degree of ideological and policy solidarity between the central and the provincial units.

Notes

1. Numerous points of similarity and differences between the Canadian and American situations will suggest themselves; it did not seem desirable to bring them within the scope of the present paper.
2. Much of this section of the paper is based on the writer's M.A. thesis, "The Progressive Conservative Party in British Columbia: Some Aspects of Organization" (University of British Columbia, 1960).
3. Reliance for the information of this section was placed on an extensive series of personal interviews and on newspaper and Conservative Party files. The sources are detailed in the M.A. thesis cited above.
4. [Allan J. McDonell, ed.] *A Factual Documented Statement of the Conservative Party's Position in British Columbia and Some of the Reasons for the Motion of No Confidence in the National Leader* (Vancouver, 1955), 20.
5. *The* [Vancouver] *Province*, July 20, 1954.
6. All four men were interviewed at length. Howard Green was the first representative appointed, but, except for times of election campaigning, his duties were largely performed by Leon J. Ladner. In December, 1951, Lt.-Col. C.C.I. Merritt, vc, was named as George Drew's personal emissary to whom all federal party matters in British Columbia should be referred. A. Leslie Bewley assumed the task in the late spring of 1953. Ladner remained intermittently active through these years. When the Federal Council was formalized in December, 1954, it chose Ladner as president, while Bewley worked on Drew's behalf until April, 1956. Drew did not name another representative, and the Federal Council president (Ladner) performed the task both for him and for Diefenbaker, who succeeded Drew in the winter of 1956.
7. This information on the other provinces was taken from Grosart's memorandum, which was on file in the Federal Council (now provincial association) offices in Vancouver.
8. Tom Hazlitt, "Fulton's Political Miracle," *The* [Vancouver] *Province*, January 28, 1963.
9. "Sask. Liberals in strange family squabble," *The* [Vancouver] *Province*, March 15, 1963. See also Don McGillivray, "Thatcher no star in Ottawa," *ibid.*, May 25, 1964.
10. Little assistance from the federal Liberals was evident in the party's successful campaign against the CCF government of Saskatchewan in the spring of 1964.

After the swearing in of Premier Ross Thatcher, Professor Norman Ward reported: "Even Liberals are not sure where their party stands. Those interested in the federal scene are frankly nervous about whether the province is on the verge of another King-Hepburn fiasco." "Saskatchewan in 1964: Which Thatcher Won the Election?" *Canadian Forum*, XLIV (June, 1964), 56.

11. HENRY JACEK
JOHN MCDONOUGH
RONALD SHIMIZU
PATRICK SMITH

The Congruence of Federal-Provincial Campaign Activity in Party Organizations: The Influence of Recruitment Patterns in Three Hamilton Ridings

Political scientists have often discussed the federal character of the Canadian political system and the relationship of political parties to the federal system.[1] How are the campaign activities of political party organizations affected by federalism? Do the parties differ in their responses to such a governmental system, and, if so, what are the reasons for partisan variations?[2] The main goal of this article is to help answer these questions by examining federal and provincial campaign activity among party workers. These party officials can be treated as both individual discrete units and components of aggregate party organizations. If party workers are treated only as individuals, then small group organizational effects are ignored. On the other hand, if there is emphasis only on party organizations themselves, then the investigator runs the risk of mistakenly inferring individual relationships from aggregate data.

Hypotheses and Operational Definitions

The study of political behaviour is marked by the use of data which can be divided into three different types: action; socio-economic characteristics; and psychological or attitudinal attributes. Explanations of behaviour sometimes give the impression that one type is paramount over the others while perhaps a stronger position is that all three types are interrelated in a complex fashion and that explanation by one type does not destroy the

---

Reprinted by permission of the journal and the author from *Canadian Journal of Political Science* (1972).

validity of explanation by another type. At the same time political scientists should recognize that variables of one type may be more proximate in influence to the behaviour under study.

In the case of campaign activity, one could expect an attitudinal attribute, incentives for continued political participation, to be the best predictor of activity. Another relevant attitude would be the orientation of party workers toward their immediate community. Some activists are primarily concerned with politics in their local community, which is essentially their world, while others have more cosmopolitan, more ecumenical, interests in the larger national and international communities.

An important behavioural component of organizational recruitment is the extent to which individuals are co-opted into a party organization. This variable should be closely related to the two previous variables but it should have an independent relationship with both party and campaign activity. Finally, the social characteristics of family income, education, occupation, father's birthplace, and religion should be related to the three previous variables as well as party but the social characteristics should be weakly related to campaign activity because these characteristics influence activity only through attitudinal variables and the behavioural variable of co-optation.

In order to test empirically the propositions listed above, the variables listed below will be used.

1. The major dependent variable in the study was the federal and provincial campaign activity of party workers. The respondents were asked to describe their political activities in the recent federal (1968) and provincial (1967) campaigns. On the basis of this information, workers were placed into one of four categories: highly active in both campaigns, highly active only in the federal campaign, highly active only in the provincial campaign, or low or no activity in either campaign.

2. To get at the incentives for political participation respondents were asked why they were active in political life. On the basis of the replies to this open-ended question, party workers were typed as either those who were primarily concerned with public policy issues or those who enjoyed mainly the social or material rewards of party activity.[3]

3. In order to understand the initial trigger event for becoming active politically, the party workers were asked to state their main reason for becoming involved in their first political campaign. The respondents were then placed into one of the three groupings: public policy or ideological concerns, attraction to candidate or party leader, or interpersonal influence.

4. Data on community orientation[4] were obtained by asking the party officers whether in general they were more interested in local community affairs or in political affairs outside the local community. On the basis of their replies the officials were defined as either locals or cosmopolitans.

5. In order to understand the method of political recruitment, respondents were asked to explain in detail the circumstances under which they

became members of the executive committee or key campaign workers. As the result of this information the party workers were classified as either volunteers (self-recruitment in that the main initiative came from the respondent) or as co-opted (the official was responding to an external solicitation from, say, a relative, friend, party worker, or candidate).[5]

6. Income was defined as total family income in 1968. Three categories were used: 0 to 10,000; 10,000 to 15,000; and more than 15,000.

7. The occupations of the respondents were divided into managers, including small businessmen, professionals, low-level clerical and skilled workers, semi- and unskilled workers, housewives, and students.

8. Respondents were asked to state the last grade or year they completed in school. Then four educational categories were established: elementary, high school, some university but no degree, and university degree.

9. Five religious groupings were used: Protestant, Catholic and Orthodox, Jewish, Unitarian and Universalist, and no religion.

10. Finally, we divided the place of birth of the respondent's father into four categories: North America, British Isles, continental Europe, and Asia and Africa.

Findings

In order to test our propositions the relationship of the variables is determined by the relatively conservative tau-alpha measure of association developed by Goodman and Kruskal (see Table 1). The major relationships are presented in Figure 1. Relationships included meet two criteria: (1) the coefficient is .10 or higher and (2) the independent variables are either directly or indirectly related to campaign activity or to a variable that is related in some way to campaign activity. The only variable that is directly related in an important way to campaign activity is that of partisan affiliation. In turn the major distinguishing characteristic of partisan recruitment is religion. The latter variable in turn is also related to method of recruitment, although the trigger event is a better predictor of recruitment method.

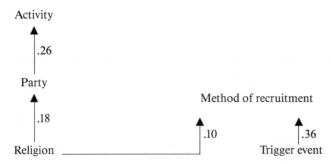

FIGURE 1. Relationships of independent variables to federal-provincial campaign activity

Table 1
Relationship* of Major Variables

		A	B	C	D	E	F	G	H	I	J	K
A	Activity	—										
B	Party	**.26**	—									
C	Incentives	.01	.06	—								
D	Trigger event	.03	.07	.05	—							
E	Community orientation	.01	.01	.01	.01	—						
F	Recruitment method	.02	.08	.06	**.36**	.03	—					
G	Income	.03	.08	.01	.01	.04	.02	—				
H	Education	.04	.03	.02	.02	.02	.05	**.15**	—			
I	Occupation	.03	.06	.07	.03	.04	.00	**.22**	**.24**			
J	Father's birth place	.02	.06	.01	.01	.01	.01	.02	.05	.03	—	
K	Religion	.02	**.18**	.05	.02	.04	**.10**	.04	.06	.05	.09	—

* The bivariate relationships are measured by Goodman and Kruskal's tau-alpha. Coefficients .10 or higher are set out in bold type so the reader can pick out more easily the strongest relationships. The coefficient derived measures the percentage increase in our ability to predict the dependent or alpha characteristics of units (for example, the campaign activity of party workers) when we know the distribution of units in each category of the independent or beta variable (for example, partisan affiliation). For a more extended discussion of the nominal measures of association developed by L.A. Goodman and W.H. Kruskal, see their "Measures of Association for Cross-Classifications," *Journal of the American Statistical Association*, XLIX (1954), pp. 732-64; Hubert Blalock, *Social Statistics* (Toronto, 1960), pp. 225-39; and Richard Neimi, "A Note of Clarification on the Term (Tau-beta)," *Social Science Information*, VII, 6 (1968), pp. 195-97.

Finally, income, education, and occupation are all interrelated but none of these three is related in an important way (defined by a coefficient of .10 or more) to the other five variables in the figure.

It is quite clear that the New Democratic Party has the most congruent party organizations (see Table 2). In every riding they have extremely high activity rates and little differentiation by governmental level. The Liberals, on the other hand, have higher federal activity rates than they do provincially and in two ridings the differences are very large. The Progressive Conservatives have a less consistent pattern and, unexpectedly, in two ridings, federal participation is higher than provincial activity.

If the officials are grouped by party without distinguishing between ridings the dimension of activity becomes even clearer (see Table 3). Over half of all officials are highly active at both levels of government and what specialization that does develop is in the direction of high federal activity alone. Eighteen officials are not highly active at either level. The NDP activists are highly consistent in their campaigning and interest and the few who are not do not reveal any particular bias. The Liberals, on the other hand, are the least congruent with 39 per cent highly committed to only federal politics. The Tories are a little more congruent but also show deeper interest federally than provincially. They are more likely, however, than any other party, to have provincial specialists.

Table 2
Percentage of Party Officials Highly Involved in
Federal and Provincial Campaigns

	Liberals	*Conservatives*	*NDP*
Hamilton East			
Provincial	23	57	100
Federal	100	100	100
N	13	7	9

Seat held provincially (Hamilton Centre) by NDP, federally by Liberals

	Liberals	*Conservatives*	*NDP*
Hamilton Mountain			
Provincial	86	100	92
Federal	100	60	100
N	21	15	13

Seat held provincially by Progressive Conservatives, federally by Liberals

	Liberals	*Conservatives*	*NDP*
Hamilton West			
Provincial	39	53	81
Federal	75	84	77
N	43	36	23

Seat held provincially and federally by Progressive Conservatives

Table 3
Party Officials and Their Levels of High Activity

High activity	*Liberal*		*PC*		*NDP*		*Total*
	%	*N*	*%*	*N*	*%*	*N*	
Provincial only	0	0	14	8	4	2	10
Provincially and federally	47	36	52	30	85	38	104
Federally only	39	30	27	16	4	2	48
At neither level	14	11	7	4	7	3	18
Total		77		58		45	180

Goodman and Kruskal tau-alpha = .26

Table 2 also shows interesting organizational differences in the size of the riding executives. In each riding the Liberals have the largest executive committee. The NDP, in contrast, has a relatively small number of riding officers. In addition, the size of the committees for all three parties is ordered perfectly by riding. Hamilton West has the largest groups while the smallest executives appear in Hamilton East.

One possible reason for this pattern may lie in the degree of competition in the constituencies (see Table 4). Competition is both very intensive and extensive in Hamilton West. Provincially, all three parties have a reasonable chance of victory while federally the relative difference in Liberal and Tory percentages is quite narrow. Although the NDP appears weak at this level, its percentage share of the vote may be due to a relatively weak candidate. In contrast, Hamilton East is the least competitive at both levels of elections. The Conservatives can mobilize only about 13 per cent of the enumerated voters regardless of governmental level. Provincially, the NDP has a fairly safe riding while federally Health Minister John Munro is not seriously threatened by the NDP. Thus, one might wish to conclude that intense party competition is related to the size of the party executives. The causal relationship between these two variables is not immediately clear and will be dealt with later.

Table 4
Percentage Distribution* of Votes in Hamilton Constituencies

	Liberal	PC	NDP	Non-voters
Federal, 1968				
Hamilton East	37	13	22	26
Hamilton Mountain	33	19	27	20
Hamilton West	29	30	15	26
Provincial, 1967				
Hamilton Centre	21	13	28	38
Hamilton Mountain	10	30	27	32
Hamilton West	20	24	20	36

* Percentages sometimes add up to less than 100 because of rounding, rejected ballots, and very minor fourth candidates.

Overall, the ridings do not differ in level of activity at various governmental levels, although some comparisons are interesting (see Table 5). First, all eighteen officials who are not highly active at any level are in Hamilton West party organizations. What appears to happen here is that large organizations for all three parties increase the probability that marginally active officials will be placed on executive committees. By having smaller execu-

Table 5
Party Officials Highly Involved in Federal and Provincial Campaigns
Within Each Riding

High activity	East		Mountain		West		Total
	%	N	%	N	%	N	
Provincially only	0	0	12	6	4	4	10
Provincially and federally	54	16	78	38	49	50	104
Federally only	46	13	10	5	29	30	48
Neither level	0	0	0	0	18	18	18
Total		29		49		102	180

Tau-alpha = .07

tive committees a party can produce 100 per cent high-activity levels for at least one type of campaign (see Table 2) but larger executives mean less electoral cohesion. In addition, of the eight provincial specialists among the Tories, six are in the Mountain organization. Finally, single-level activists are most likely to be found in non-competitive Hamilton East, all of which activists are federal specialists who nearly equal the number of officials active at both election levels.[6] It is also in this riding that the sharpest association occurs between party and levels of activity (tau alpha = .44).

The Recruitment Process

As was pointed out earlier, the most distinctive characteristic of partisan recruitment in Hamilton is that of religion. Most strikingly, party workers of Catholic-Orthodox background go into the Liberal Party (see Table 6).

Table 6
Party By Religion

	Protestant		Catholic-Orthodox		Jewish		Unitarian-Universalist		None		Total
	%	N	%	N	%	N	%	N	%	N	
Liberal	29	25	79	42	50	4	22	2	17	4	77
Conservative	48	41	15	8	25	2	22	2	21	5	58
NDP	23	20	6	3	20	2	56	5	62	15	45
Total		86		53		8		9		24	180

This recruitment along religious lines does form the basis for voter mobilization in election campaigns. A particularly striking example occurred on Hamilton Mountain in 1968. Here a great number of Knights of Columbus and Catholic secondary school students were activated for canvassing for the Liberal candidate, Gordon Sullivan. So close was the connection between church and party that the Catholic bishop of the Hamilton diocese met with the campaign organizers in the Liberal headquarters.

The Tories, on the other hand, can be viewed as a Protestant, especially Anglican, organization. Religious organizations provide important recruiting grounds for the Conservatives as well. Such is the case on Hamilton Mountain. Here over half of the executive is recruited from a single Anglican parish organization to work for an Anglican MLA. This particular recruitment process was accomplished by emphasizing the need to support a "respectable young man of high character." Thus, the incentive of candidate attraction was used to develop a strong social bond in the Tory organization. Because the unifying force is based on loyalty to a respected Anglican MLA, only a half-hearted attempt at campaigning occurred in the 1968 federal election for a Catholic candidate of Scottish background.

Finally, the NDP recruits heavily among those with no religion. In the case of the NDP the non-religious characteristics of their officials do not derive from recruitment among groups purposely organized along this dimension. Rather this characteristic is found among Hamilton-area trade unionists. In this case an economic association, the labour union, provides the setting for recruitment and the materialistic-class ideology of this environment is negative toward organized religion, viewed as an instrument of the societal elite to maintain their privileged position in the status quo.

The religion of a party worker also helps to predict the method of recruitment by which the respondents became members of the executive committee or key campaign workers (see Table 7). Those of Catholic-Orthodox background and Unitarians and Universalists are the most likely to be co-opted. On the other hand, the internally motivated volunteers are most likely to come from the ranks of the Jews and especially from those who profess to have no religion.

Table 7
Method of Recruitment By Religion

	Protestant		Catholic-Orthodox		Jewish		Unitarian-Universalist		None		
	%	N	%	N	%	N	%	N	%	N	Total
Co-opted	78	67	89	47	50	4	89	8	46	11	137
Volunteered	22	19	11	6	50	4	11	1	54	13	43
Total		86		53		8		9		24	180

The best predictor of recruitment method, however, is that of the initial trigger event for becoming politically active beyond mere voting (see Table 8).[7] The internally motivated volunteers are derived mainly from those

Table 8
Method of Recruitment By Initial Trigger Event

	Ideology		Candidate and leader attraction		Personal		
	%	N	%	N	%	N	Total
Co-opted	35	17	87	40	94	80	137
Volunteered	65	32	13	6	6	5	43
Total		49		46		85	180

activists who initially became active in the partisan political process because they were acting on ideological concerns. To these people questions of public policy were paramount in getting them active. In contrast, those activists who were pulled into party work because of an attraction to either candidates or party leaders, or, even more important, those activists who were initially brought into politics by personal solicitation, tended to be co-opted into the key party positions.

The Effects of Organizations

One of the more interesting findings of this research report is that many of the variables we initially thought would be related to campaign activity are not predictive when the respondents are treated as individuals. On reflection, however, we realize that the respondents are not merely isolated individuals. Rather, they are members of party organizations. Thus, it seems important to examine our originally hypothesized independent variables, but now measured as aggregate characteristics of nine party organizations, to see whether, at the aggregate level, these variables are related to campaign activity, also measured at the aggregate level. Specifically, we will look at incentives, methods of recruitment, and community orientation.

In treating the party workers as individuals we were surprised that incentives were not related to campaign activities overall. A re-analysis of the data was performed which grouped the respondents by party organization and then the two variables were collapsed into dichotomous variables. Campaign activity was divided into two categories for the respondents: (1) high campaign activity in both federal and provincial campaigns; and (2) all others. Incentives of respondents were divided into those with dominant ideological and public policy incentives, and those with either material or social incentives as the dominant motive. This analysis produced a pattern which is plotted in Figure 2. This figure appears to capture the small group effects of the influence of organization incentive structures on campaign activity.

Party officials highly involved

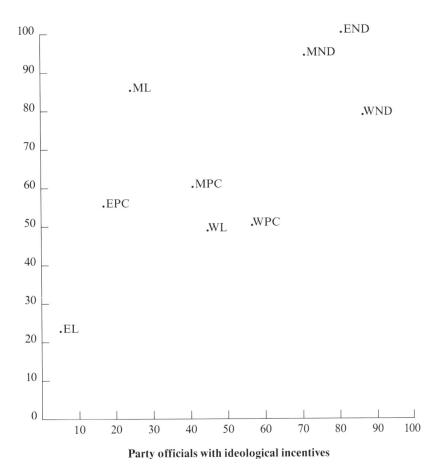

EL = East Liberals   WL = West Liberals   ML = Mountain Liberals
EPC = East Conservatives   WPC = West Conservatives
MPC = Mountain Conservatives
END = East NDP   WND = West NDP   MND = Mountain NDP

FIGURE 2. Percentage of Party Officials Highly Active at Federal and Provincial
Levels by Percentage of Party Officials with Ideological Incentives in
Each Organization

It seems clear that the ideological orientation of the NDP organizations is strongly associated with high behavioural campaign congruence in all three ridings. This strong ideological orientation produces a strong party loyalty which in turn creates a norm of intense campaign commitment regardless of governmental level. Since the bond holding the organization together is a primary loyalty to the party and its stated policy objectives, it is not surprising that the NDP is the first party in Hamilton to submerge personal loyalties to a number of city office-holders and to enter city politics with a party slate. The NDP activists are conscious of the distinctive reward structure of their party and see the NDP as very different in organizational character from the Tories to the Liberals. Thus, we must strongly disagree with Gad Horowitz when he says the NDP (CCF) "sees itself, and is seen by the public, not as a coterie of ideologists but as a party like the others...."[8] It is unclear how the public views the NDP as against the Liberals and Tories but the NDP officials in our study certainly realize that they are pursuing a concept of the public interest above all else, an incentive not viewed as predominant in the other two parties.

The Liberals, on the other hand, are more heterogeneous in their reward patterns. The percentage of ideological types is highest in Hamilton West, which has the best educated population, and lowest in the East, an area with a very poorly educated electorate. The Hamilton East Liberal organization is the least ideological of all nine party organizations and has the lowest percentage of two-level activists in all nine organizations. Social-material rewards seem to be very important. In addition, this riding organization is distinctive for two reasons: (1) only three of thirteen Liberals are active provincially, and (2) only one official can be viewed as motivated for ideological reasons. Most officials have been offered federal patronage and many have accepted it. The offers of patronage came quickly after the 1968 federal election and the standard question was "What do you want?" The organization keeps very systematic records of all favours performed, ordered by recipient, and the amount and effectiveness of campaign work performed. Thus, we agree with the NDP official who said: "Liberals expect to be paid for their party work" – to which a Grit official added: "and quickly." Overall, then, an organization heavily based on social and material rewards seems to produce a single-level orientation directed at the level of government where the party is in control and where ready access to patronage exists. Finally, the organizational bond of the Hamilton East Liberals is cemented by the deep respect and affection felt for Health Minister John Munro. In fact, the officials argue that the personal bond to the member is even more important than the federal patronage he produces.

The Hamilton Mountain Liberal organization is also based on social and material rewards but less so than the Hamilton East organization. The third Liberal organization, the one in Hamilton West, offers a good test of the relationship between incentives and activity level because there are almost equal proportions of ideological and non-ideological party activists. Within this organization non-ideological activists are more likely to be active at one level, in federal campaigns, than in both types of elections while ideological activists show the opposite tendency.

Although material and ideological motivations are sometimes present among Tory partisans, the dominant friendship satisfactions seem most responsible for the differentiation in their party organization. In two of the three ridings these friendship motivations centre on Conservative incumbents. The words and phrases used by Tories in describing their motivations differ considerably from the comments made by other party officials. These responses reflect the solidarity[9] nature of their organization. "Respect," "leadership qualities," and "good character" are frequently used by Tories to describe their orientation toward the incumbent and this attitude seems to be the major incentive. Statements about ideology usually are added on after the candidate-orientation statements and these policy views seem to be secondary.

A good approximation of the solidarity party is found among the Mountain Conservatives. Here, loyalty is directed to the MLA, John Smith, and six provincial specialists are present. Of these six, five are clear solidarity types. The two social conveners are considered to hold important posts and the major organizational activity between elections is the bi-monthly bridge night (it is very difficult to imagine the Liberal and NDP organizations getting together for a night of bridge). In Hamilton West, the Tories divide into two solidarity cliques, each focused around an incumbent. One group, which centres on the MP, consists of recent arrivals to intense political activity and these officials work primarily for the federal incumbent. The provincial clique has more experience and sees its main loyalty to the MLA. They do in fact work at both campaign levels although their hearts are really in provincial politics.

The Hamilton East Conservatives are a more difficult organization to understand. They are the smallest of the nine party organizations in this study and they recognize the non-competitive status of their party in the riding. Some are interested in material rewards and these are active provincially as well as federally. Because of their desperate situation electorally, material rewards may be a very important incentive that need not be used by the party elsewhere. To underline this generalization we can note that the Conservative candidate in the 1968 federal election was appointed a provincial judge soon after his dismal campaign. Tories with non-material motivations, however, are more likely to be federal specialists.

The character of Conservative expectations of material rewards differs considerably from those of the Liberals. While activists of the latter party expect to receive these rewards quickly after a campaign, Tories do not have these expectations. A relatively lengthy period of party work is first required for two reasons. First, the major patronage post is a judicial appointment. Judgeship vacancies occur gradually over an extended period of time and appointments appear to be given to older, more experienced party workers. Second, other Tory patronage is highly concentrated on older established Conservatives in contrast to the diffused federal

Party officials highly involved

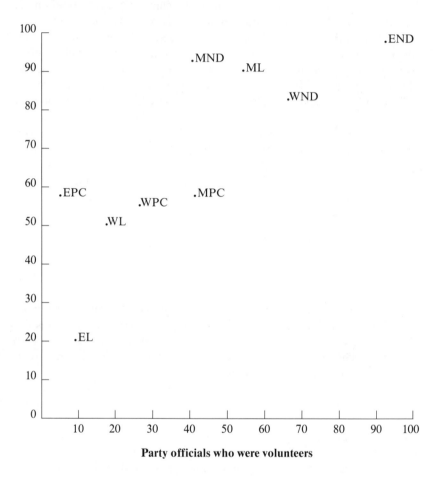

Party officials who were volunteers

FIGURE 3. Percentage of Party Officials Highly Active at Two Levels by
Percentage of Volunteers in Each Organization

patronage distributed by the Liberals. Thus, a young politician with expectations of a quick financial payoff would be attracted to the Liberals.

In treating the party workers as members of party organizations, the
method of recruitment also appears related to organizational activity patterns (see Figure 3). The more party groups are composed of volunteers,
the more likely the organizations are heavily involved in both federal and
provincial campaigns. This is especially true for the Liberal groups. Two of
the NDP organizations have the largest percentage of volunteers and the
third NDP group ranks in the top five in terms of volunteers. The NDP
organizations, on the whole, are the most congruent groups in terms of

campaign activity. The Mountain NDP is somewhat different than the other two in terms of volunteers because of external recruitment among trade union officials. Nonetheless, this pattern of recruitment does not produce single-level campaigning. The NDP emphasis on ideological volunteers seems to result from an ideological stance which deprecates the notion of co-optation. Rather, the process seems similar to recruitment into fundamentalist religions. The prospective activist first must be converted to the socialist creed and then his internal conversion will logically propel him to become active in party affairs and to proselytize others.

Co-optation, on the other hand, is the norm among the other two parties, especially the Liberals. Within this party the emphasis on external recruitment also seems to account for the relatively large size of the executive in each riding. Thus, in highly competitive Hamilton West is found the largest Liberal executive. Here the process of co-optation is consciously designed to better the organization's competitive position. A somewhat different form of co-optation occurs in Hamilton East. Here ten of thirteen executive members were personally given their positions by the incumbent MP and it is also here that we find the party organization that is most composed of single-level activists. On the other hand, the Mountain Liberals have a relatively low percentage of co-opted officials but the most integrated Liberal organization.

The Tory organizations are also composed of co-opted officials. The characteristic is strong in both the East and West for two apparently different reasons. In Hamilton East the competive position of the Tories is so poor no one appears ready to volunteer to work for a lost cause. In the West, however, recruitment seems to be the result of two Tory incumbents who recognize the need for strong organization in a highly competitive situation.

In light of the activity patterns and their apparent association with the recruitment process, one may suspect that the content of ideological views held by party officials may underlie and explain the patterns among the party organizations. But ideological views in and of themselves do not seem to have much impact on activity levels. It is true that the extent to which ideology of any kind is an organizational incentive does seem to relate to activity levels (see Figure 2). Specific ideological positions, however, do not.

Although ideological content was not systematically covered in great depth in our study, it is possible to comment on partisan differences of a general nature. By and large, NDP officials have views that fit within the broad spectrum of socialist thought. Policy views of Tories and Liberals, however, are somewhat different than previous literature would have us believe. The Tories are not really small "c" conservatives and in many ways they seem similar to traditional small "l" liberals. The Progressive Conservatives are strongly committed to the free enterprise market economy and view governmental interference, such as broad welfare policies, as an evil. Strong rewards for individual economic initiative are favoured and people with these characteristics should be the natural political elite.

Liberals, on the other hand, usually make very vague philosophical statements and class is usually seen as an irrelevant dimension by which one can understand politics. In fact, Liberals, unlike activists of the other parties, were often quite hostile to our questions on their subjective social class. Part of this hostility may be due to the competitive position of the NDP and Liberals. Some of the officials from the latter party see the NDP as attempting to take voters away from them by class appeals. Thus, in order to stymie the NDP threat, Liberals feel the need to play down class cleavage and the whole notion of class as a way of understanding political life.

Another important attitude of party officials is their orientation toward their immediate community. Some are primarily concerned with politics in their local community, which is essentially their world, while others have more cosmopolitan, more ecumenical interests in the larger national and international communities. In every riding the NDP organizations are much more cosmopolitan. On the other hand, the Liberals and Conservatives are more local in orientation. On the whole, cosmopolitan organizations appear to be highly active in both federal and provincial election campaigns while localism seems to reinforce the tendency toward single-level specialists (see Figure 4). While party organizations with large numbers of locally oriented workers tend to be more active in only one type of election, such organizations may be either federally oriented, such as the Hamilton East Liberals, or provincially oriented, such as the Hamilton Mountain Conservatives.

Conclusion

The purpose of this research report is to examine the impact of a federal system of government of the campaign activities of party workers. The investigation of nine party organizations in Hamilton shows that there is indeed a great deal of variation in the campaign activities of the 180 party officials in the study. Fifty-eight per cent are highly involved in both federal and provincial campaigns while 10 per cent are not highly involved in either type of election. On the other hand, 27 per cent are highly active only in federal campaigns while 5 per cent are provincial specialists. The best predictor of campaign involvement is political party affiliation. Party recruitment in turn is most influenced by religious cleavages within the community. Religion is also related to method of recruitment although the trigger event is a better predictor of recruitment method. Finally, income, education, and occupation are all interrelated but none of these three is significantly related to the political variables.

When the party workers are grouped into the nine party organizations, the organizations vary a great deal in the extent to which they are composed

Party officials highly involved

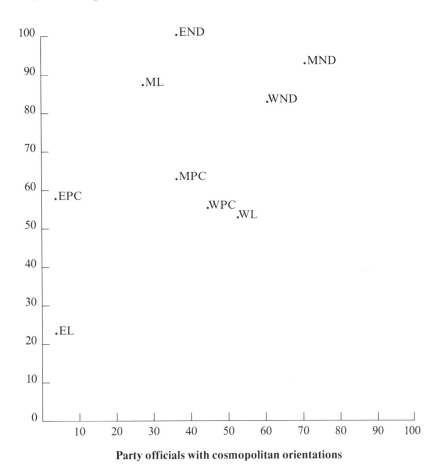

FIGURE 4. Percentage of Party Officials Highly Active at Two Levels by
Percentage of Party Officials with Cosmopolitan Orientations in
Each Organization

of party workers who are highly involved in both federal and provincial
campaigns. The range is from 23 to 100 per cent with four other organizations between 50 and 60 per cent and three other groups between 81 and 92
per cent. Three recruitment variables are related to the percentage of party
officials in each organization who are highly involved in both federal and
provincial campaigns. These recruitment characteristics include the degree
to which organizations rely on ideological incentives, the percentage of
volunteers for party activity, and the degree to which officials hold cosmopolitan attitudes. As organizations rely on ideological incentives, volun-

teers, and those with cosmopolitan attitudes, these party organizations are more likely to be composed of officials who are highly involved in both federal and provincial election campaigns.

Of the numerous variables associated with the study of party organizations, incentive structures appear most useful in understanding participation patterns. Organizations based on ideological incentive structures produce a high degree of electoral congruence while parties based on social and material rewards are more prone to federal and provincial specialists. Party competition seems to condition the operations of organizations based on social and material incentives but not necessarily parties based on ideological incentives.

The nature of the ideological images of the parties does not seem terribly relevant to participation. The degree to which the organization is made up of ideologically motivated workers does seem important but the specific content of these beliefs does not appear to influence activity patterns. A contrasting image, the brokerage model, is inaccurate for Hamilton parties because there are important ideological and social differences between the two major parties. Certainly the parties differ in social-group composition. The relationship of social differentiation to patterns of participation appears to be an indirect one. The intervening variables include incentives, attitudes, and techniques of recruitment.

Probably the most interesting dimension of Hamilton party organizations rests on the nature of party loyalty ties. Recently, James C. Scott[10] has outlined a model of change in party loyalty ties which divides into three phases. Scott views the characteristics of each phase as dominating all parties existing during the phase. In Hamilton, however, the partisan organizations appear to encompass all three loyalty patterns within the same time period. Thus, the Conservatives have the characteristics associated with Phase A:

> Political ties are determined largely by traditional patterns of deference (vertical ties) to establish[ed] authorities. Material, particularistic inducements to cooperation play a minor role except among a limited number of local power-holders.

The Liberals have the characteristics predominant in Phase B:

> Deference patterns have weakened considerably in a period of rapid socio-economic change. Vertical ties can only be maintained through a relationship of greater reciprocity. Competition among leaders for support, coupled with the predominance of narrow, parochial loyalties, will encourage the widespread use of concrete, short-run, material inducements to secure cooperation. The greater the competitive electoral pressures, the wider the distribution of inducements is likely to be.

Finally, the NDP seems to be a Phase C party:

> New loyalties have emerged in the process of economic growth that increasingly stress horizontal (functional) class or occupational ties. The nature of inducements for political support are accordingly likely to stress policy concerns or ideology.

The latter type of party, in this case the NDP, seems best able to perform at a high level of activity in both federal and provincial elections. The diffuse interest in both governmental levels as indicated by high participation rates seems important for strengthening the tendencies toward a strong national union. Empirically in this study, the one recruitment factor mitigating the NDP's high levels of participation is the party's inability so far to recruit working-class Catholics, especially those of southern and eastern European background.

The Phase B party, the Liberals, is more specialized in its behaviour, depending as it does on federal patronage alone. Thus, intense activity is present for federal politics but less so provincially. But on the positive side, activity is directed mainly at the national government, a more inclusive unit than any single provincial unit, and it is quite possible that specific legitimacy, engendered by short-run material payoffs, may over a long period of time result in diffuse support for the national community and regime.

Finally, a Phase A party, such as the Conservatives, seems least able to produce consistently high levels of campaign activity since its activists are united by loyalty to individual local candidates. Thus, the party is most prone to develop two wings, one oriented toward provincial politicians, the other toward federal ones. If the most talented and respected Tories in an area lose interest in a particular level of government, then given the Tory organizational bond the party is likely to become a single-level party. In Hamilton this specialization seems to have occurred already, except in Hamilton West. Thus, the Conservatives must now depend on their keeping control of the provincial government in order to maintain their organizational strength. As long as the Conservative Party forms the government in Ontario,[11] it is very unlikely that the Conservative organizations in Hamilton would disappear at the provincial level, however weak this party may be in federal elections.

Notes

Although most of the interviewing, upon which this article is based, was conducted by the authors, several key interviews were done by Ralph Joyce and Ronald Whyte.

1. See, for example, Edwin Black, "Federal Strains within a Canadian Party," in Hugh Thorburn, ed., *Party Politics in Canada* (2nd ed., Scarborough, 1967), 130-40. For the view that Canadian federalism has been a major factor in the purported decline in the policy-making importance of Canadian parties, see John Meisel, "Recent Changes in Canadian Parties," *ibid.*, 33-54. For a strong attack on the view that Canada's two major parties have integrated the federal system through brokerage politics, see Alan C. Cairns, "The Electoral System and the Party System in Canada, 1921-1965," *Canadian Journal of Political Science*, 1 (March, 1968), 55-80.

2. The specific data collected to help answer these questions is based on interviews with 180 party officials in the three federal ridings of Hamilton East, Hamilton Mountain, and Hamilton West. All these activists are members of riding executive committees except for four individuals who were included because they held very important positions in campaign organizations. These 180 officials represent 93 per cent of the intended population. The personal interviews were conducted in 1969 by means of a structured interview schedule designed to elicit information on campaign activity and recruitment variables.

3. This typology is similar to that developed by Peter Clark and James Q. Wilson; see their "Incentive Systems: A Theory of Organizations," *Administrative Science Quarterly*, VI (1961), 129-67; Wilson, *The Amateur Democrat* (Chicago, 1962).

4. This orientation is best explained by Robert Merton. He distinguished the localite – whose interest is "confined to his community," which is essentially his world, who is preoccupied with local problems, who is "parochial" – from the cosmopolitan – who is "oriented significantly to the world outside his community," who regards himself as an integral part of the world, and who is "ecumenical." See "Types of Influentials: Local and Cosmopolitan," in Edward Banfield, ed., *Urban Government* (New York, 1961), 390.

5. Methods of recruitment have been emphasized by political scientists studying the selection of candidates for office. See, for example, Lester Seligman, "Political Recruitment and Party Structure: A Case Study," *American Political Science Review*, LV, 2 (March, 1961), especially 85-86. Seligman distinguishes between two types of external recruitment, which distinction appears important in understanding candidate-selection but is less relevant in studying the involvement of political workers. The concept of recruitment methods has been used before in studying Canadian politicians. See David Hoffman and Norman Ward, *Bilingualism and Biculturalism in the Canadian House of Commons*, Documents of the Royal Commission on Bilingualism and Biculturalism (Ottawa, 1970), 61.

6. When level of activity is collapsed into two categories, single-and two-level activists, no overall association, however, with riding occurs.

7. A good understanding of the conservative interpretation of tables by the Goodman and Kruskal tau-alpha can be gained by examining closely Table 8. On the face of the table it would appear that there is a very strong relationship

between the two variables, yet our predictability is increased only 36 per cent. Three identical distributions of data with nominal, ordinal, and interval characteristics would produce far larger coefficients if ordinal or interval measures were used. Thus, when one uses the Goodman and Kruskal tau-alpha, an investigator is less likely to overestimate the strength of relationships than if he were to use other more common statistics.

8. Gad Horowitz, *Canadian Labour in Politics* (Toronto, 1968), 27.

9. Peter Clark and James Q. Wilson applied their system of incentives to organizations. Groups which rely upon material incentives are called *utilitarian* organizations. An organization in which status, prestige, and fellowship are the main benefits is seen as a *solidarity* group. Finally, a group with ideological incentives as the dominant reward is called a *purposive* organization. Wilson, in *The Amateur Democrat*, groups utilitarian and solidarity organizations into the professional category and calls the purposive group an amateur organization.

10. James C. Scott, "Corruption, Machine Politics and Political Change," *American Political Science Review*, LXIII, 4 (December, 1969), 1142-58, especially 1146.

11. The Conservative Party may be able to keep its organizational strength even if it fails to form the provincial government. A general demoralization may not set in until the party is in opposition for more than two consecutive terms. On this point, see John Wilson and David Hoffman, "Ontario: A Three Party System in Transition," in Martin Robin, ed., *Canadian Provincial Politics* (Scarborough, 1972).

12. K.L. MORRISON

The Businessman Voter

in Thunder Bay:

The Catalyst to the

Federal-Provincial

Voting Split?

Why do Canadians vote for one party to form the federal government and then so frequently vote for another to form the government in a provincial legislature? While the problem has been ably restated by George Perlin and Patti Peppin, a satisfactory answer still eludes us.[1] One widely regarded explanation, the so-called balance theory, appears to rest on the assumption that Canadian voters in the mass agree, by some mysterious process, to maintain a balance between federal and provincial powers.[2] Since this process is not spelled out, it must be regarded, as it stands, as a mere extension of the market mythology of classical political economy and, as such, of little value. A better explanation needs to be found. One unexplored possibility is that the very nature of the British North America Act creates tensions within the Canadian polity which find their expression in the contradictory voting patterns. Might, for example, the division of powers between the federal and provincial governments create different, and frequently contradictory and antagonistic, blocks of economic power, which would be most active politically either in the federal or the provincial sphere, and which would express their antagonisms by supporting opposing parties at the two levels of government?

The city of Thunder Bay in Ontario seemed to be an ideal place to explore this suggestion. The city's economy is fairly evenly balanced between the federally oriented grain-handling and transportation industries, and the provincially oriented forest and tourist industries. The area

Reprinted by permission of the journal and the author from *Canadian Journal of Political Science* (1973).

has a well-organized business community whose principal agency is the Thunder Bay Chamber of Commerce. The city is relatively isolated, being some 440 miles east and west from the nearest Canadian cities and 200 miles north of Duluth, Minnesota. Opinions expressed would thus tend to be those of the business leaders of the community itself and not mere echoes of some larger community nearby. Finally, and most important, the city (and its original constituent cities, Fort William and Port Arthur, after whom both the federal and provincial riding are named[3]) has a well-established pattern of voting one way federally, and then with a new party established in power in Ottawa promptly voting for candidates of the opposition parties to sit in Queen's Park (see Table 1).

The instrument used to test our hypothesis was a questionnaire mailed out to every fourth member on the Thunder Bay Chamber of Commerce and to every fourth lawyer not on this list.[4] Two questions were posed: one sought to uncover the businessman's conception of the importance of federal or provincial government activity to his economic well-being while the other, it was hoped, would uncover discernible federally oriented as against provincially oriented economic groupings. The first was a four-choice question on the importance of federal and provincial government activity to the businessman scaled from "Absolutely vital. They make or break me" to "On the level of the average citizen." It was assumed that if the difference hypothesized existed, it would show up here. No such difference appeared. With few exceptions those who felt that provincial government activities were "very important" or "absolutely vital" felt the same way about the activities of the federal government. Nor is there any evidence that those who put the activities of either level of government in the top two categories felt impelled to extra political exertions as a result. On the contrary, these respondents showed themselves to be slightly more politically quiescent than those for whom government activity was indicated as being less urgent.[5] Thunder Bay businessmen, at least, do not tie their political exertions to their perceived assessment of the importance of government activity to their business or professional life.

A second question that might have produced evidence of a strong federal or provincial orientation was an omnibus one covering the respondent's reasons for voting for the party of his choice in the most recent federal and provincial elections. For the provincial vote, each respondent was given the opportunity to indicate that the party chosen would best defend Ontario interests against federal encroachment. A strong provincial bias failed to appear. Only two respondents out of 82 gave this question first choice, and 10 others mentioned it at varying levels of importance. This reason ranked tenth among the 14 possibilities with a weighted score of 19, and so cannot be considered to be a matter of prime importance for those concerned.[6]

If there was not a strong anti-federal sentiment among respondents, neither was there a strong pro-federal sentiment insofar as this question-

Table 1
Thunder Bay Voting Patterns

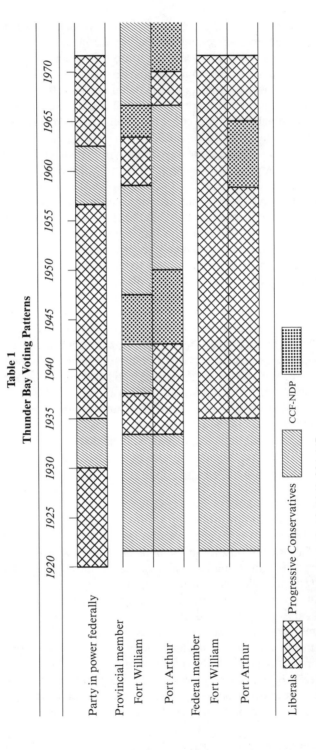

Party in power federally

Provincial member
  Fort William
  Port Arthur

Federal member
  Fort William
  Port Arthur

Liberals   Progressive Conservatives   CCF-NDP

SOURCE: *Canadian Parliamentary Guide 1969*, 294-447.

naire was a legitimate device of elicitation. Two questions touched on this matter. The first asked which party could best maintain national unity; and the second which party could best keep the provinces in line. Neither question received a first choice answer, and while 21 respondents indicated with variations in enthusiasm that their party could best maintain national unity, giving this question a score of 34 and a rank of 4, only nine backed the tougher question that the federal government kept the provinces in line, giving this question a score of 12 and a rank of the same number. Significantly, these replies referred to an election in which federal-provincial relations were considered to be an issue of the first rank.[7] One interesting figure in this area is the differing financial support offered provincial Conservatives as against federal Liberals. Twenty-nine businessmen indicated that they had contributed personally to the provincial party's coffers in 1971, while only 11 indicated similar support for the federal Liberals in spite of the fact that businessmen gave both parties almost equal voting support.[8] However, this may merely reflect the businessman's natural affinity to the Progressive Conservative Party, which is indicated by the fact that while provincially only 20 per cent of respondents identified with the Liberal Party, 63 per cent identified with the Conservatives. Federally, in spite of their propensity to cross party lines and vote Liberal, 35 per cent of respondents identified with the Progressive Conservative Party as against 48 per cent who identified themselves with the Liberals.[9] It may also reflect the fact that in the 1971 provincial election the NDP ran energetic campaigns in Thunder Bay which culminated in their taking Port Arthur. In the federal election of 1968, by contrast, the NDP ran a lacklustre campaign, with two previously defeated candidates running against popular and well-entrenched sitting members. It was not a circumstance to cause a businessman to give sacrificially.

Thus, while our survey failed to produce the expected information it did provide some interesting evidence that the business community does develop a consensus in the field of political activity and that this consensus is transmitted into support for the chosen candidate of an elite party[10] and is made manifest by the nomination of a Chamber-groomed candidate by that party – a person of substance and a "strong candidate" by reason of his professional or business success, public exposure, network of connections, and financial backing. In short, the perfect "available candidate."

The most striking evidence of this consensus and its political results has already been alluded to. In the federal election of 1968, 30 of the 82 respondents indicated identification with the Progressive Conservatives, including 15 who claimed party membership.[11] But in 1968 only 22 of these Conservative-leaning businessmen trooped to the polls and loyally supported that party. Eight, plus six from the ranks of the uncommitted, voted with the Liberals. The 10 defecting Conservatives included five party members, two of whom were among the rather select group of five who reported influencing a contribution to any party.[12] This tendency was evident in the federal election of 1963 when the Liberals out-polled the Conservatives 34 to 21 and became a stampede in the 1965 election when Robert Andras, the first president of the newly amalgamated Chamber, joined Hubert Badanai, a former president of the Fort William Chamber, on the Liberal ticket. This time the ratio was 52 to 16, and the NDP lost the seat formerly held by Douglas Fisher. With the NDP out of the way, Conservative strength picked up slightly in the election of 1968, but respondents still favoured the Liberals 54 to 22.

In the provincial arena a similar but reversed situation pertains. Here the Progressive Conservatives are the chosen party, and only 16 respondents identified with the Liberals. Of these, five voted Conservative, two contributed money personally, and two, including one of the contributors, took part in other pro-Conservative election activity.[13] Here again earlier voting trends were confirmed with the Conservatives receiving 61 of the respondents' votes to the Liberals 13, with six going to the NDP. Both in 1967 and 1971 voters were offered Chamber past presidents as Progressive Conservative candidates. If Dr. Charles Johnston had won Port Arthur, as he came close to doing,[14] all four sitting members would have been past presidents of the Thunder Bay Chamber of Commerce or its predecessors in the pre-amalgamation cities. Since the Second World War, four of the six successful elite party provincial candidates have been past presidents of one of the chambers and the two exceptions are instructive.[15]

This candidate and voting pattern suggests a possible answer to the problem already mentioned concerning the balance theory – its failure to identify the process by which ridings swing from one party in the federal field to another in the provincial and by cumulation swing a province against the federal party in power. Perhaps the businessman is the catalyst of the swing. Our data suggest that he is in a strong position to influence the results in many ridings and we would suggest that he has many and valid reasons for voting provincially against a federal party in power.

To begin with, a businessman is in a position to influence an election by his availability as a candidate, which must say something both about his appreciation of his chances of winning, including his appreciation of the support which may be forthcoming from his fellow businessmen, and also about his concern and commitment to a party and its policies. We have already noted the tendency of Thunder Bay businessmen to vote for a prominent Chamber of Commerce member and this support for the candidate was underlined both in comments on the returns and in private. Conversely, in Thunder Bay the non-chosen elite party finds it difficult to get a prominent businessman to run, certainly not one as prominent as a former Chamber president, and in the last federal and provincial elections the federal Conservatives and the provincial Liberals were reduced to running more or less token candidates who looked as if they came from the traditional NDP stable of preachers and teachers rather than from the traditional elite party stable of lawyers and businessmen.[16]

Even when not serving as candidates businessmen are very influential by their activity. With elections becoming increasingly expensive it is obvious that the candidate who has the support of those in the community with access to large sums of money is at a real advantage. We have already noted that many businessmen indicate their political support by financial contributions. But this is not the only, or perhaps even the most significant, aspect to their political commitment. Chamber members take their citizenship responsibilities seriously. Our respondents represented almost 40 per cent of the sample polled. Of the 82, only two in the last federal and provincial elections respectively did not vote. When one considers the pressures of business and the normal hazards of illness and disaster, this is a remarkable turnout. Again, 37.8 per cent indicated party membership. It is just possible that our questionnaire was returned by the most politically active and informed among Chamber members and that the other 60 per cent were relatively politically quiescent. Even at that, 125 of the 844 members considered would be party members. If the returns were not biased the number could be as high as 319. Since our best information indicates that even in the height of a hard-fought election the membership of all parties in the two city ridings does not exceed six thousand, the potential influence of Chamber members, aside from their influence as prominent citizens and employers, is considerable.

Moreover, their position as employers and civic leaders cannot be overlooked. At the time of writing nine out of 13 members of the Thunder Bay city council are members of the Chamber of Commerce. Businessmen and their families are traditionally prominent in service clubs, lodges, churches, and other community organizations. Inevitably many people look to them for political guidance or feel impelled to move their way.[17] It is probably safe to assume that counting family, friends, business associates, and employees who can be influenced or pressured, the average Chamber member can carry at least 10 people with him when his peers develop a policy, a political "line," and especially when, by whatever means, the business community decides to throw its weight behind one party and/or one candidate.[18] These 10 represent approximately one out of every eight voters in the city. When this fact is combined with the voting dedication of Chamber members, their party activity, and their economic strength, it is hardly surprising that candidates who receive their backing do so well.

Why do businessmen throw their support behind the candidate of one party and then another? One factor is doubtless the desire to be on the winner's side, and a bandwagon effect is created when one elite party or the other is seen to be the probable winner. With contracts, concessions, and a variety of other favours available to the businessman from the party in power, it would be amazing if shrewd calculating concerning probable election results was not a considerable pre-election preoccupation of many businessmen.

A second factor related to the above is the desire to keep the socialists out. Not only are the New Democrats less friendly to business than are the elite parties, but their history of always being to the left of the Speaker of the House at Toronto and Ottawa makes them even less desirable as members from a business point of view. Anti-NDP sentiment appeared to be an important factor in the 1971 Ontario provincial election where, as we have noted already, the NDP ran a strong local campaign while a series of election upsets of incumbent governments in other provinces gave some credence to the NDP slogan of "Ontario next." Twenty-eight respondents indicated that anti-socialist sentiment was a factor in their voting, giving this question a score of 49 and a rank of 5. Nine specifically named the New Democrats as the party they were voting against while only one indicated voting against another party, the Progressive Conservatives. Federal voters were not asked a specifically anti-socialist question, but five named the New Democrats as the party they were voting against, as opposed to two anti-Conservative votes, and one anti-Liberal vote.

A final factor affecting businessmen's voting habits can only be speculated upon since the questionnaire was circulated during a period when neither level of government was doing, or failing to do, anything which would particularly aggravate Chamber members.[19] This factor is related to the traditional business belief in free enterprise and in the mystique that state intervention in the world of business is evil or at least unwise. There can be no doubt that governments in the pursuit of the most desirable social objectives – a fair distribution of the tax burden, reasonable income minimums, reasonable standards of education and health, an unpolluted environment, and protection of the weak and handicapped – do create problems for business. It is hardly surprising that for many businessmen their dearest wish is that government would leave them alone.

But the businessman would be the first to protest, and loudly, if the government left him alone. He needs the aid and succour of government desperately and continuously – police and tariffs to protect him, subsidies to help him, contracts to sustain him, and regulations to control his labour relations and his market. It is hardly surprising to find that the businessman is very ambivalent in his attitude to government, and especially ambivalent in his attitudes to the federal government. This would seem to be reflected in the answers to our questionnaire where respondents showed much more enthusiasm for the federal party, its leaders and its candidates, than for their provincial counterparts, but much less enthusiasm for claims that the federal party had done a good job while previously in office, was best for business, or related questions (see Tables 2 and 3). In light of the responsibilities and taxing powers of the federal government under the British North America Act this is hardly surprising. The federal govern-

Table 2
Ranking of the Respondents' Most Pressing Reason for
Voting in the 1968 Federal Election

Reason	(Scores indicated in brackets)
1. This party offered the best local candidate.	(97)
2. The leader of the party of my choice would make the best Prime Minister of Canada.	(92)
3. I always vote federally for this party.	(48)
4. The party of my choice would best maintain national unity.	(34)
5. The party of my choice would best maintain Canadian independence and integrity.	(33)
6. The party of my choice had done a good job when last in office.	(31)
7. The party of my choice was best to maintain high employment and prosperity.	(26)
8. The party of my choice had the best platform.	(25)
9. The party of my choice was the most reform-minded.	(17)
10. The party of my choice was the best to deal with foreign affairs.	(15)
11. The party of my choice was the best for business.	(15)
12. The party of my choice would keep the provinces in line.	(12)
13. I voted to keep the candidate of — party from winning.	(14)
14. Other	(6)

ment is the big tax collector while, relatively speaking, the provinces are the big spenders.[20] Everybody loves the generous uncle, but few revere the Scrooge who accumulated the family wealth. Again, the types of taxes traditionally collected by the federal government – income and corporation taxes, succession duties, tariffs, and the federal sales tax – are all imposts to which the businessman is peculiarly sensitive, while the direct taxes traditionally levied by the provinces strike at a more oblique angle. Finally, the

Table 3
Ranking of the Respondents' Most Pressing Reasons for
Voting in the 1971 Provincial Election

Reasons	*(Scores indicated in brackets)*
1. The leader of the party of my choice would make the best Premier of Ontario.	(80)
2. This party offered the local candidate.	(76)
3. The party of my choice had done a good job when last in office.	(68)
4. The party of my choice could best act to maintain higher employment and prosperity.	(50)
5. The party of my choice was best able to keep Ontario from become more socialist.	(49)
6. The party of my choice is best for business.	(31)
7. The party of my choice had the best platform.	(29)
8. I always vote provincially for this party.	(25)
9. I voted to keep the candidate of — party from winning.	(21)
10. The party of my choice would best defend Ontario's interests against federal encroachment.	(19)
11. The party of my choice could best act to maintain good labour relations in the province.	(13)
12. Other	(10)
13. The party of my choice would help maintain national unity.	(9)
14. The party of my choice was the most reform-minded.	(7)

responsibilities of the federal government for the management of the national economy, including foreign trade, the money supply, interest rates, and the value of the dollar, are all matters of prime importance to business. Few of the areas of provincial responsibility strike the whole business community so directly and so urgently. It can come as no surprise, therefore, that in spite of the presence in the federal cabinet of such luminaries from the world of business as a C.D. Howe, a Wallace McCutcheon, a Robert Winters, or a Mitchell Sharp, it is a rare federal government indeed that is not charged with being insensitive to the needs of business. Provincial governments are less frequently so charged.

If a business community feels that the federal government is insensitive to its needs or is not acting to promote general business interest, what can it do? One answer is to vote in the federal elite opposition party at the next general election. But this has its difficulties. One is that the next federal election may be some time away, and meanwhile, irreparable damage could be done. The other is that opposition parties, once they have taken their place on the speaker's right, have notorious habits of acting very much like their predecessors in office. Might it not appear much more useful to elect the federal opposition party to provincial office at the next opportunity, which could come quickly as a result of the more frequent provincial elections? In power in the province such a party is not only more effective than Her Majesty's Loyal Opposition in checking the federal government, but it also has the power and patronage of provincial office at its disposal.

This is at least one logical explanation of the voting tendencies in Thunder Bay mentioned earlier. The community is peculiarly sensitive to the sins of omission and commission, real or imagined, of the federal government, dominated as the city is by two export-oriented industries, grain and pulp and paper. When something goes wrong there will be disenchantment and even backlash against the federal party in power. The temptation to register this disapproval by voting for the opposition party provincially, or at least to support the provincial wing of the federal party in power less enthusiastically, must be very strong. The result will either be a victory for the provincial wing of the federal opposition party, or a split in the ranks of the elite which will aid an NDP victory. In either case, it will appear as a contradiction to the federal voting pattern.

This then may be the kernel of truth behind the traditional balance theory explanation of the federal-provincial voting split. It is not that the voters in the mass decide that federal power is to be checked by provincial opposition, but that the business community for its own good and sufficient reasons tends to opt for this arrangement and to make it possible.

We do not suggest that our case is proven. Much more research in Thunder Bay and elsewhere will need to be done, especially in a period when party support by the business community is more fluid than at present. But we do suggest that Thunder Bay's businessman voter does indicate one reasonable explanation of the phenomenon that is worthy of further study.

Notes

1. George Perlin and Patti Peppin, "Variations in Party Support in Federal and Provincial Elections; Some Hypotheses," *Canadian Journal of Political*

Science [hereafter *CJPS*], IV (June, 1971). Also, John Wilson and David Hoffman, "The Liberal Party in Contemporary Ontario Politics," *CJPS*, III (June, 1970).

2. Perlin and Peppin, "Variations in Party Support," 282.
3. The constituency of Thunder Bay, federally and provincially, encompasses, in the main, the provincial District of Thunder Bay and is wholly outside the city by the same name. Both city ridings at one time included parts of the present riding of Thunder Bay. The larger urban populations so effectively dominated these ridings that past variations in riding boundaries can be safely ignored.
4. Our rationale for adding lawyers was the intimate connection between the legal profession and the business community and the traditional importance of lawyers as leaders in business-supported parties. The leaders of the Progressive Conservative Party of Ontario from 1943 to the present, for example, have all been lawyers. In the event, the addition was not significant. Only half-a-dozen names were added to the list and these could not significantly affect the results of the survey based on 211 questionnaires and 83 replies, or a 39.3 per cent return. One respondent tore off the sheet which contained the provincial questions and another ignored the federal page. We are thus effectively dealing with 82 returns.
5. In the provincial sphere, although 45 per cent of respondents reported donating to the party of their choice, only 38 per cent of the most government-affected businessmen did so. Federally, 21 per cent of respondents reported making donations, but only 16 per cent of those most government-affected did so. Distance from the federal election may have dimmed memories somewhat, although, as we shall see, our respondents showed a surprisingly strong memory for past political activity.
6. While respondents were invited to rank their reasons for voting as they did, the methods of responding to this question were so varied as to nullify useful tabulation based directly on respondent ranking. We therefore adopted a scheme of weighting the responses in order to produce a meaningful rank order of importance. First or only choices were given a weight of three; second and third choices, and one of three unranked choices, a weight of two, and all other indications of support a weight of one. On this basis the most popular choice was the local candidate in the 1968 federal election. He received 21 choices of the first category, 15 of the second, and 4 of the third for a score of 97. The most popular provincial choice was the provincial leader with a score of 80.
7. *Canadian Annual Review for 1968*, ed. John Saywell (Toronto, 1969), 41.
8. Sixty-one voted Progressive Conservative provincially, 54 Liberal federally; 7 contributed to the provincial Liberals and 4 to the federal PCs; 2 contributed to the NDP in both elections.
9. Or perhaps this is an indication of the claim that while the Liberals are able to depend upon "funds raised mainly from anonymous (so far as the public is

concerned) corporate donors" (George Bain, *The Globe and Mail*, February 10, 1972) the Conservatives depend more on small and medium-sized business-men.

10. Duverger uses the term "cadre" to describe parties which are "groupings of notabilities for the preparation of elections, conducting campaigns and main-taining contact with the candidates." Maurice Duverger, *Political Parties* (London, 1954), 64. Since "cadre" is not in common use in Canada we will use the more popular word "elite" for these parties and "the elite" to describe the "notabilities" who manage such parties.

11. Forty indicated that they were Liberal-inclined and four NDP; 14 of the Liber-als indicated party membership as did 2 for the NDP.

12. One to the Conservatives, the balance to the Liberals.

13. Fifty-two identified with the Conservatives, five with the NDP, and nine abjured party identification.

14. Dr. Johnston received 10,092 votes; Jim Foulds of the NDP received 11,461.

15. The exceptions are John Chapple (Liberal), the scion of an important local merchant family, and Ron Knight, also Liberal. Chapple was in the line of offices which would have led to a Chamber presidency when he fell out with his colleagues over the proposed amalgamation of the two cities and stepped aside (information supplied by Mr. Chapple personally). Knight achieved local fame as the host of an open-line radio talk show. His discernible political convictions would have made him an ideal Social Credit candidate, but as Social Credit has never been able to offer even a token candidate in Thunder Bay he had to look elsewhere. After the elite of the Fort William Liberal Association moved heaven and earth to deny him their nomination (according to a past president of that association) he moved over to Port Arthur and managed to become the choice of the candidate-hungry Port Arthur Liberals. (One of his nominators admitted ruefully to the writer later that neither he nor his wife listened to Knight's radio show and thus did not know what they were getting their party into.) Swept along by adoring housewives for whom his program provided a platform to articulate grievances and frustrations, Knight won the seat for the Liberals. But it was not a Liberal seat for long. He quickly fell out with his party's caucus at Queen's Park and ended up sitting as an independent, or as he preferred to call it as a "free" member. He did not seek re-election. It is significant that both of these "deviants" were Liberals, the unchosen elite party provincially, both lasted only one term, and both were succeeded by CCF/NDP. In both cases it may be noted that the PCs started with candidates who lacked status in the business community. In Fort William in 1963 the candidate was C. Assef, a local billiard hall owner and school trustee who was Lebanese by origin, not a large ethnic group in the Lakehead. In Port Arthur in 1971 the PCs started with Gordon Crompton, owner of a fried chicken concession, but shortly before the election was called switched to Chamber past-president and physician Dr. Charles Johnston. The palace

revolution involved is known to have created dissatisfaction among rank-and-file PCs and undoubtedly aided the hard-running NDP candidate to slip in.

16. Three were teachers and one was a mildly maverick dentist, school trustee, and Chamber member. Twenty-five per cent of the city's dentists are Chamber members. Similarly, 13 per cent of the doctors and 25 per cent of the lawyers belong. However, many doctors are in clinics and many lawyers in firms, both of which by the Chamber constitution only register a limited number of their personnel as members. As a result, these figures do not indicate the full measure of Chamber support from among these professions. In the 1968 federal election, the Ontario candidates of the NDP included 27 school teachers or university instructors, 9 clergymen, 9 businessmen, and 5 lawyers. In the same campaign successful Liberals in Ontario numbered in their ranks 26 lawyers and 14 businessmen out of a total of 64 and successful Progressive Conservatives included 3 lawyers and 8 businessmen from 17 winners. Six teachers won for the Liberals and four lost, but the Conservatives appeared to offer teachers and housewives only to lost causes; all of them, six and two respectively, lost. The provincial pattern is much similar with the Conservative winners including 17 lawyers and 32 businessmen. Winning Liberals included 7 lawyers and 9 businessmen out of 21. Both parties elected 3 teachers. Sources: *28th General Election 1968. Report of the Chief Electoral Returning Officer* (Ottawa) and *Canadian Parliamentary Guide*. Not all members list occupations so the Ontario statistics which depend on the *Guide* are incomplete.

17. When the writer lived in the Ottawa area he was impressed by the number of public servants who felt impelled to vote, federally and provincially, for the party in power lest a hint of deviation threaten their jobs or their promotions. This in spite of the well-established secret ballot and the equally well-established political activity of the wives of some "non-political" civil servants. We feel that it is safe to assume that at least some of the employees of a politically committed employer will feel pressed to go his way. (Some, of course, will deliberately vote against him as has been the tradition in Cardinal, Ontario, where the main employer was a prominent Conservative and the town Liberal). Similarly, a colleague tells how during the 1930s his father habitually went through his factory on the day before election inquiring after the voting plans of his employees. After the event he carefully checked the poll returns looking for "liars." This was more possible in days gone by and in small open-shop communities than in the unionized urban centres of today, but we suspect this type of political pressure is not entirely absent even now.

18. Federal election 1968:

	Percentage of popular vote	Percentage of Chamber vote
Liberals	45.4	67.5
NDP	30.7	5.0
PC	23.4	27.5
Other	.5	0

Provincial election 1971:

Liberals	16.0	16.3
NDP	38.4	7.4
PC	45.6	76.3

The closeness of the Chamber vote to the popular vote for the non-chosen elite party candidates in federal PCs and provincial Liberals is striking. It would seem to indicate that the hard-core party faithful among Chamber members is very similar to that of the general population, while the less-committed Chamber members swing sharply one way and then the other.

19. The time was January, 1972. Provincially the Progressive Conservatives had just been returned to the great satisfaction of the business community. Federally, the government was taking a number of measures to assure business of its good will. A business delegation was met and was assured that tax reform measures would be modified to meet businesses' most serious objections; Mr. Benson was the hero of the hour for his handling of the international monetary crisis as it affected Canada, and federal-provincial relations were quiet. Locally, the grain boats had been standing off in the harbour like members of a wartime convoy all season signifying an almost-record grain shipping year. Thunder Bay businessmen had little to complain about concerning either level of government.

20. In 1962 the federal government collected $6.5 billion in taxes while the provinces collected under $3.6 billion. The provinces spent $3.4 billion against the federal government's $6.8 billion. This provincial spending power was assisted by $279 million from the federal government in transfer payments for which the federal government probably had the odium of collecting while the provinces received the kudos for spending. Recent fiscal arrangements whereby the provinces are getting increasingly into income and corporation taxing, succession duties, and the like may modify business attitudes toward the two levels of government in time. Source: *1967 Canada Yearbook* (Ottawa).

13. DAVID M. RAYSIDE

Federalism and the

Party System: Provincial

and Federal Liberals

in the Province of Quebec

Any large or geographically diverse country is bound to experience inter-regional tension. Varying geographic endowments generate divergent and often conflicting political interests, and political loyalties to smaller and more familiar communities are tenacious, whatever the benefits of combination with other regions. But if misunderstanding and conflict are normally the product of diversity, how much more likely is conflict to result from a federal system in which autonomous and financially self-sufficient regional governments are established, each with a leadership cadre interested in increasing the power and prestige of the government to which it is attached? As David Truman has observed:

> The basic political fact of federalism is that it creates separate self-sustaining centers of power, privilege, and profit which may be sought and defended as desirable in themselves, as means of leverage upon elements in the political structure above and below, and as bases from which individuals may move to places of greater influence and prestige in and out of government.[1]

The tension inherent in a federation clearly affects the party system, and the party system in turn affects the relationship between regional governments and central authorities.[2] In principle, parties play an important role in the articulation of popular preferences and demands, so that a consider-

---

Reprinted by permission of the journal and the author from *Canadian Journal of Political Science* (1978).

ation of the divergent interests that form part of the politics of federalism necessarily deals with the role of parties in articulating and aggregating regional interests. An examination of that role requires attention to the degree to which the party system itself is federalized – that is, structurally divided along regional lines and divided between federal and regional arenas. If the party system is federalized in either of those ways – and it is almost inevitable that the coexistence of two relatively autonomous levels of political authority would lead to such federalization – what is the relationship between the organizations and elite groups of the federal and provincial parties? And what if any divergence is there between the outlooks of representatives of the provincial parties and their federal counterparts? Answering questions such as these will provide clues as to the "centripetal" and the "centrifugal" roles that parties and party leaders play in a federation such as the Canadian.

Within the Canadian federation, it is particularly important to focus on the province of Quebec, since the most serious challenges to the maintenance of the Canadian union have come from nationalist forces in that province. Although Quebec is not the only site of alienation and regionalist sentiment in the country, it is in that province that the separatist option has gained the most legitimacy. Even those observers who argue that much of the support for the Parti Québécois is not a separatist vote would have to agree that a substantial percentage of the Quebec electorate supports the separation of the province from Confederation, and a much larger percentage might well acquiesce.

Quebec is a particularly interesting province in which to examine the relationship between federalism and the party system because it is in that province that relations between federal and provincial parties have been most consistently strained. The Progressive Conservatives have had little or nothing in the way of a provincial party since the 1930s, although they have at times formed an *entente cordiale* with the Union Nationale. The Quebec wing of the New Democratic Party has had a history of difficult relationships with the rest of the party, and there is little if any activity in provincial politics. Provincial Liberals formally separated from their federal brethren in 1964 and since then there have been almost no observable links between the two parties other than the party label itself. No other provincial party system in Canada is as distinct from the federal system as Quebec's.

The relationship between Liberals in Ottawa and Quebec City is worthy of particular attention. For most of the last two decades, the Liberals have been governing parties in both capitals, so presumably there is a close connection between the relationship of the two parties and the relationship between the federal and provincial governments in general. By understanding the patterns of contact between the two parties and the points of ideological divergence in their leadership groups, we will have gone a long way toward understanding the present strains in Canadian federalism, and we may pave the way for a reasoned judgement of the "performance" of the party system in representing regional concerns and helping to accommodate regional differences.

This analysis of Liberals in Quebec will rest in part on an historical survey of the relationship between the federal and provincial parties. But it will also rest on a survey of parliamentary backbenchers and party activists conducted at the two levels in 1973. Interviews were conducted with 36 federal Liberal MPs and 26 provincial Liberal MNAs, in each case representing approximately 50 per cent of the backbench contingent (including all of the Anglophone contingent in Quebec City), and questionnaires were mailed to and received from 179 local activists in the Liberal Federation of Canada and 94 in the Liberal Party of Quebec. The federal and provincial respondents included constituency association presidents and local campaign managers for the preceding national election. (All presidents and managers received questionnaires, and in all about 40 per cent of the federal activists and 46 per cent of the provincial activists responded.)[3]

It would be natural to expect some divergence in the perspectives of federal and provincial representatives, at least with regard to regional and constitutional questions. Political actors tied to one or the other level of government would be expected to defend the jurisdictional prerogatives of that level, if only because their own prestige is partially dependent on the authority of the decision-making centre to which they are attached. Particularly in Quebec, we would expect highly nationalist politicians to direct their ambitions toward the provincial arena. French Canadians who believe strongly in the worth of federalism may choose either arena, but those who are less enthusiastic about the benefits of Confederation are unlikely to be interested in federal politics. That sort of self-screening does not invariably occur in federal systems, as even a quick glance at American federal politics would indicate. However, it is likely to occur in a system such as the Canadian, where political authority is more evenly balanced between national and regional governments, and where recruitment to provincial office is less likely to be seen as simply a stepping stone to national office. The pattern of self-screening being described here may not exist in all provinces at all times, of course. In those areas in which the provincial Liberal or Conservative Party fares a great deal better or worse than its federal counterpart, the ambitious politician in a given party may elect the more favourable arena despite any prior inclinations to federal or provincial politics. But that would not be the case in Quebec, where the Liberals have enjoyed substantial success in both electoral arenas.[4]

Before exploring attitudinal differences between federal and provincial arenas, we should embark on an examination of the organizational federalization of the Liberal Party of Quebec. To use Donald Smiley's terminology, we should determine the degree to which the Canadian party system is "confederal" rather than "integrated."[5] An important part of the Smiley analysis rests on three essentially structural questions: the degree to which federal and provincial parties are autonomous in the organization of elections and the determination of policy; the extent to which federal and provincial parties are financially independent of one another; and the degree to which the politically ambitious switch from one level to another in their political ascent. But an understanding of the relationship between federalism and the party system demands attention to more than the connections between federal and provincial parties: it also requires an examination of the centralization or decentralization of federal parties themselves, if in fact they are separate from their provincial namesakes. It is to the latter question that we first turn our attention.

The Federalization of the Liberal Party of Canada

The Liberal Party, along with other Canadian parties, has been organizationally decentralized for most of its history. Before Confederation, Rouges from Canada East and Grits from Canada West often seemed to form only a grudging alliance, and even after 1867, the alliance was apparently little more than an *entente cordiale* – able to choose a common leader only in 1872.[6] The two major national parties at that time were coalitions of sectional groups more than the organized parties that we are familiar with today, and their extension into the Maritime and western regions was particularly fragile. As parliamentary discipline engulfed the large contingent of ministerialists and tied all MPs more firmly to the front-bench leadership of each party, the policy formulation and decision-making functions of Canadian parties became more centralized, but the organization of the party remained relatively decentralized. Provincial parties formed the structural base of the Liberal Party, for example, and election organization and patronage distribution were supervised by regional or provincial luminaries in the federal cabinet, some of them operating with considerable autonomy from the national leader.

Even as the cabinet began to withdraw from its intensive involvement in organizational matters, decentralization was still characteristic of Liberal electioneering. The central office of the Liberal Federation assumed some of the organizational burden, but it remained a relatively small outfit and still perceived itself as relying on the provincial associations. The federal campaign committee was centralized in its appointment, in the sense that all of the provincial chairmen were appointed by the prime minister, but for most elections each chairman worked relatively independently with the provincial organization in his province. And increasingly, each provincial committee has been financially self-sufficient, less dependent on the resources gathered by the Toronto and Montreal "collectors."

There is, to be sure, some variability in the decentralization being portrayed here. In some elections, a great deal more than the campaign tour of the party's leading luminaries is tightly organized by the central campaign committee, while in other years, most of the decisions are left to the provincial committees and the organizations working under them. As a generalization, Donald Smiley's characterization of the federal Liberal Party as a centralized organization is probably somewhat overstated.[7] He successfully argues that the provincial and federal parties are increasingly separate, but it is quite another thing to argue that the remaining federal organization is highly centralized.

Even if the overall organization of the Liberal Party – during and between elections – is becoming more centralized, federal Liberal organization in Quebec has at most times been peculiarly separate. When the central office was first established in Ottawa, the Quebec organization was reluctant to give it any support, apparently on the grounds that Quebec had no need of a central headquarters. When, for example, Sir Wilfrid Laurier asked for assistance in 1917, Senator Raoul Dandurand replied in the following manner:

> Nous sommes toujours de même avis sur l'inutilité de cet établissement pour ce qui concerne notre province. Nous sommes aussi convaincus qu'il ne nous a rendu aucun service appréciable dans la plupart des autres provinces.
>
> Nous croyons que chaque province doit avoir son organisation distincte. . . .
>
> Et puis, la situation de notre parti est telle que nous ne pouvons dire quels seront nos alliés de demain. Dans ces conditions nous croyons que nous devrions donner plutôt notre aide à notre bureau de Montréal qui nous rend des services réels. Si dans les autres provinces on est incapable d'en faire autant c'est qu'il n'y a rien à ésperer d'ici à ce qu'il se produise un évènement d'importance majeur. Nous ne saurons qu'après la guerre si le parti libéral anglais nous reviendra avec la presse anglaise. Ce n'est pas l'action du Central Liberal Information Office qui influencera son retour.[8]

Much has changed in party organization since 1917, but the special position of Quebec has not completely disappeared. In the first place, the transfer of authority over party organization from the cabinet to extra-parliamentary bodies has not fully taken place in Quebec, where the "regional cabinet minister" system has been largely retained. Reference is still made to a "Quebec leader" in the cabinet, whereas analogous expressions for other provinces are now virtually unknown. The position is not as formally constituted now as it once was, in part because the incumbent prime minister is himself a Quebecer, but the label persists in current informal usage. In the second place, the national campaign committee has usually been led by two co-chairmen – one from Quebec, who focuses his attention on that province, and one from elsewhere, who is responsible for the "English" provinces. Thirdly, it has remained true until very recently that the Quebec organization has participated only marginally in the central office's functioning and financial sustenance – regarding it essentially as the central office for the other provinces. One effect of that traditional isolation was that no French Canadian ever presided over or directed the Liberal Federation of Canada until 1973, when a Manitoban of French-Canadian descent was elected president. It is noteworthy, however, that this first Francophone was not from Quebec.[9]

The special status of Quebec is due not only to the language barrier and to the resulting convenience of dividing the task of preparing and distributing election materials, but also to what many Liberals see as a different style of political organization. The following exchange with a member of the central office personnel in 1973 reflects that image.

> Q: Traditionally, is the pattern to restrict contact with the Quebec organization more to the top echelons and then have it funnelled down; or to go down lower in this office and have lateral contact all the way?
> A: I think the standard traditional pattern is the first one – to have contact at the upper echelons and then to rely on that. And that sort of fits the Quebec culture, doesn't it? You know, you talk to Jean Marchand and it's as good as talking to two or three thousand militants out in the field – because you get just as good results or better results.[10]

There is a danger of overstating the uniqueness of Quebec's image, since similar assessments could have been made of other regions at one time or another. In the 1940s and 1950s, the Prairie provinces' Liberal organization was at least as dominated by a single strong personality (Jimmy Gardiner) as Quebec has been in recent times; although it bears restating that this highly personalized pattern has remained longer in Quebec than elsewhere.

There is one other respect in which the province of Quebec is set apart from almost all other provinces in the Liberal fold. It was until 1975 the only province in which federal and provincial Liberals were formally separated into two distinct extra-parliamentary organizations, ostensibly with no ties between them. But that story deserves telling in detail.

The Organizational Relationship Between Federal and Provincial Liberals[11]

There is some separation between federal and provincial Liberal parties in almost all of the Canadian provinces, even if it is not always officially recognized in constitutional statutes.[12] If only because constituency boundaries at the two levels rarely correspond and elections are never held at the same time, separate organizations are often required. But in addition, the principal parties opposing one another in provincial politics are frequently not the same parties that oppose one another in federal elections. And in some provinces, voting at one level is usually incongruent with voting at the other.[13] In that light, it is not surprising that in 1970, Jacek, McDonough, Shimuzu, and Smith found that less than half of the Liberal Party activists polled in Hamilton worked at both the federal and provincial levels.[14]

As elsewhere, federal and provincial Liberal parties in Quebec were once almost indistinguishable. Up to the 1920s certainly, it was possible to assume at virtually every level in the party hierarchy that if one were Rouge in Quebec City one was also Rouge in Ottawa. Between 1912 and 1931, for example, an electoral organization headed by Philippe Paradis was used in federal as well as provincial contests.[15] Rewards for party workers were granted by both federal and provincial governments, when controlled by Liberals, regardless of whether the worker paid more attention to one or the other electoral arena. (Paradis himself was rewarded with an appointment to the Legislative Council in Quebec and later with an appointment to the Canadian Senate.) And since provincial contracting was more malleable than federal, Quebec government patronage was often used to help Members of Parliament in preparing for the next election.[16]

In the 1930s, provincial elections were heavily infiltrated by federal Liberal personalities. Paradis's successor in 1931 was a federal MP (Chubby Power) who continued the habit of failing to differentiate the two arenas. The Quebec leader in the federal cabinet, Ernest Lapointe, was very active in the provincial election of that year and talked about federal issues a great deal of the time. In 1935, members of the provincial Liberal cabinet returned the favour by openly participating in the federal election. There were some strains between federal and provincial leaders at that time, arising in part from the continuing ties between Quebec region federal Liberals and the breakaway Action Liberale Nationale, but the tension was relatively short-lived.[17] The 1939 provincial election provides the most obvious and frequently cited example of the unity between federal and provincial Liberals at the time. The Union Nationale premier, Maurice Duplessis, had called the election and by that call had launched a direct challenge to the federal government's war involvement. Federal Liberals felt obliged to participate in the campaign, and along with his colleagues Chubby Power reasoned as follows:

> If the federal Liberal Party was to be seriously involved it should direct the campaign, and this we undertook to do. I took over the entire provincial organization in the district of Quebec.... To all intents and purposes I eliminated the people of purely provincial interest from the organization.[18]

The federal Liberals exercised some influence in the selection of candidates and in the collection of funds. Much of the electoral fund, in fact, was gathered by Jimmy Gardiner, federal Minister of Agriculture, from such areas as western Canada and Toronto!

J.A.A. Lovink claims that until this time, the federal Liberal influence on the provincial Liberals was all-pervasive.[19] Provincial leaders acquiesced in part because of the beneficial coattail effect. They felt able to capitalize on the overwhelming support given to the federal Liberals in Quebec since the time of Laurier and often asked voters to support a party in Quebec City that was "in tune" with Ottawa.[20]

By the end of the decade, relations between federal and provincial Liberals had deteriorated. According to some provincial Liberal leaders at the time, the federal Liberals set the provincial party adrift, and as early as the 1948 election it was evident that some federal Liberals were cementing non-aggression pacts with the provincial Union Nationale.[21] The divorce continued through the 1952 election, when, in the view of one provincial leader, federal MPs were always somewhere other than in the constituency of their provincial counterparts. The great strength of the provincial Union Nationale, of course, provided the federal Liberals with an incentive to avoid involvement, for fear of retaliation in federal campaigns. The non-aggression pacts between some federal MPs and their Union Nationale counterparts were a source of considerable irritation to provincial Liberals, and in the 1956 congress of the Liberal Federation of Quebec there was substantial support given to the suggestion that the provincial party declare its independence of the federal Liberals.[22]

It was becoming especially important at that time for the Liberals to portray themselves as independent of the federal Liberal Party. The Union Nationale had based part of its electoral appeal on a national and anti-federal stance and had frequently railed against the Liberal opposition as a pawn of the federal Liberals. As a provincial party with no formal ties to any federal party, the UN could easily capitalize on such a charge, and its electoral success in the 1950s suggested that the appeal was a potent one.

In the 1950s, then, provincial Liberals had some grounds for resenting their brethren in Ottawa, and some incentive to take their distance. That was especially in the case for the left wing of the party, where one would have found the greatest resentment of the federal party's seeming approval of the Duplessis government's economic and natural resources policies, and where one would therefore have found the most resentment of the federal party's equivocation in supporting the provincial Liberals. It was also among the leftists that the bulk of the party's fervent nationalists were found, and they would clearly be interested in accenting their independence of a federal party which was organizationally dominant over them and apparently centralist in its views on federalism.

The 1957 and 1958 federal elections delayed a confrontation between Liberals. The weakening of federal organization which defeat entailed increased the need for co-operation between federal and provincial politicians. But the 1960s created new pressures for a change in the relationship. The 1960 provincial election brought the Lesage Liberals to power and the 1962 election reinforced their hold on governmental power. At the same time, the 1962 federal election confirmed the federal Liberals' weakness. The provincial Liberals no longer seemed to gain from unity with their federal colleagues. Also, among the provincial ranks, there was a zeal and elan that formed a part of what came to be called a Quiet Revolution, which did not seem to have impregnated the federal party's ranks. The emergence of younger elements, led by people such as François Aquin, the new president of the Quebec Liberal Federation, seemed to accentuate generational and policy differences between Ottawa and Quebec Liberals. René Lévesque was part of the regeneration, and he began pushing for a separation of the federal and provincial parties in 1963. He argued that the Quebec Liberal Federation must serve Quebec alone and that the principle of double allegiance to the federal and provincial parties was unfair to those who felt attached to one of them. Since the two parties often seemed opposed on policy, Lévesque and Aquin could logically argue that it was difficult to be "black and white" at the same time. That was an especially plausible argument with the federal Liberals' accession to power in 1963. The Quebec government's assertiveness during this time, and its calls for a substantial increase in the province's autonomy, now pitted a provincial Liberal government against a federal Liberal government. Hard bargaining marked most meetings between representatives of Quebec and Ottawa (although often not as hard as Lesage portrayed to the press), and many partisans began to feel that simultaneous affiliation with the two parties was increasingly incompatible.

There was a potent financial argument in favour of separation. The importance of corporations that were increasingly falling under provincial jurisdiction added to the election-funding independence of provincial parties through the country, particularly in those provinces such as Ontario and Quebec which contained a large number of corporate head offices and resource industries. In the early days of Confederation, most industries were under federal jurisdiction or subject to federal regulation, and they were therefore interested in flattering federal politicians. But now a large number of firms owe their sustenance to provincial governments or depend on provincial regulation in some degree. The financial capabilities which the expansion of the provincial sector has implied for provincial parties has decreased the dependence on federal collection networks. Independence was increased even more in Quebec with the introduction of an electoral law which envisaged state funding of political parties. Khayyam Paltiel has argued, in fact, that the Lesage government's legislation was motivated in part by the desire to make the provincial Liberals financially independent of the federal party.[23]

In the first half of 1964, the campaign for disaffiliation was taken up in earnest and soon had two prestigious allies: Jean Lesage and Guy Favreau (an important member of Prime Minister Pearson's cabinet in Ottawa). A special congress was called for July 5 of that year, for the express purpose of effecting a structural distinction between the National Liberal Federation and the Quebec Liberal Federation, and the selection during that spring of Guy Favreau as Quebec leader in Ottawa virtually assured federal concurrence.

The special congress approved disaffiliation. And at that congress, both Jean Lesage and Guy Favreau gave voice to a common theme – namely, that a federal system was in some respects incompatible with a union of national and regional parties. Lesage argued that

> ... l'essence même du fédéralisme canadien est de mettre en présence des gouvernements constamment appelés à s'affronter. Et ceci est davantage vrai depuis que l'on parle de fédéralisme coopératif. Or, le caractère même du fédéralisme coopératif, tel que je l'entends, accentue, à mon point de vue, la necessité pour les partis politiques – premièrement, de réfléter aussi fidèlement que possible la dualité de gouvernements établie par la constitution; deuxièmement, d'exercer leurs activités dans leurs domaines respectifs, suivant leurs juridictions propres. En d'autres mots, il est devenue évident que la réalité canadienne exige de plus en plus que les partis politiques qui oeuvrent sur le plan fédéral soient distincts des partis provinciaux et vice versa.[24]

The following year, the federal Liberals worked intensively to establish federal associations in most constituencies. Although most party activists remained tied to both parties, separate infrastructures had to be set up and, in most cases, the personnel involved in leading the federal party in Quebec, at the riding and the provincial level, was different than that which headed the provincial Liberal structure.

But did organizational disaffiliation also mean an elimination of contact between them? Was the break as complete as it seemed on the surface and as complete as most Liberal leaders proclaimed? The 1965 federal election campaign at first seemed to indicate that it was. Lesage declared himself neutral, and few of the provincial leaders were open participants in the campaign. But at the last minute, the provincial prime minister did come out in favour of the federal Liberals, something which is not always characteristic of provincial premiers, even when formally linked to federal parties.[25] And at the constituency level, many federal and provincial candidates exchanged campaign favours.

There is also some contact between elections. To ensure that his constituency gets the best of two worlds, the Liberal legislator will often keep in touch with his Liberal counterpart in the other capital (if there is one) in order to coax government money into the area. Judicial and other government appointments at the two levels of government also occasion some inter-Liberal consultation. Jean Chrétien, for example, owed his rapid early rise in Ottawa politics to a recommendation from Jean Lesage to Lester Pearson.

Long before the federal and provincial Liberal parties broke their formal ties, recruitment to elective office at the two levels of government became highly differentiated. Although during the early decades of Confederation it was common for provincial legislators to enter federal politics and for some politicians to hold office at the two levels simultaneously, that is now an increasingly rare occurrence in all provinces. Few legislators at either level of government have had experience at the other level, and since most municipal elections are not infiltrated by the national party system, there is no common local base for recruitment to the provincial or national arenas.[26] This is in some contrast to the American system, and to some extent the West German. In the United States, the climb to political power very frequently entails shifting from state to federal politics and back; in part, David Truman argues, because the separate election of the chief executives at the federal and state levels multiplies and renders ambiguous the lines of succession and recruitment for each.[27] The unequal prestige of state and federal politics also plays a role. In Canada, there is not the same imbalance in political power and the concomitant imbalance in the political prestige of office-holders that exists between the American state and national governments, so that it is unusual for one arena to be viewed as simply a stepping stone to more prestigious office elsewhere.

The size of the regional components in the Canadian federation and the scope of their jurisdictions contribute to the separation of federal and provincial party systems. There were circumstances in post-war Quebec which particularly exacerbated tensions between federal and provincial Liberals, but the growth of provincial government jurisdictions and spending powers across the country has generated intraparty strains elsewhere as well. In addition, there are features of the parliamentary system that Canada has inherited from Great Britain which are likely to compound that organizational and recruitment separation of the two levels with differences in outlook on important regional and constitutional issues. Party discipline in federal parties inhibits the open expression of regional interests in the national political arena, thus forcing provincial governments and provincial parties to assume a disproportionate amount of the burden in articulating regional points of view. In almost any political system with more than one tier of government, we would expect most politicians to defend the prerogatives of the government to which they were attached, but in a system such as the Canadian, the defensiveness of each set of legislators is increased by party discipline. That discipline helped to exacerbate the strain between federal and provincial Liberals in Quebec during the early 1960s, since it was difficult even for those parliamentarians who might have sided with the position taken by the *other* protagonist to sympathize openly with it. An American congressman or senator would not be as constrained by party doctrine or by the decisions taken by congressional or presidential leaders, so there is less likelihood of tension developing between him and his colleagues in the state legislature.

The fact that neither Liberals nor Conservatives are bound together by a firm commitment to a consistent ideology leaves considerable room for a division between federal and provincial parties on questions of provincial rights or on other matters touching regional interests.[28] Socialist or Catholic parties in the European mould might well stay firmly tied across different levels of government, since they are in many cases fighting fiercely for a fundamental alteration in the ownership of the means of production or for a defence of Catholic schooling; but it is difficult to conceive of similar issues which would create firm bonds among Liberals (or Conservatives), particularly in the post-war period.

Reflection on the federalization of the Canadian party system, as it is manifest within the Liberal Party of Canada and in the relations between federal and provincial Liberals in Quebec, suggests that disagreement and perhaps some tension exists between federal and provincial politicians. Although Quebec still occupies a special position in the federal party's organization, the tensions between federal and provincial wings in the 1950s and 1960s, culminating in separation, seemed to indicate a clear divergence in perspective on federalism. To explore such attitudinal differences, and the attitudinal mix within each party structure, we now turn to the sets of parliamentary and activist respondents questioned in 1973, which were introduced earlier. We will begin with a brief analysis of social background differences between them and will then proceed to an examination of attitudinal differences.

Attitudinal Differences Between Liberals in Quebec and Liberals in Ottawa

The focus of our attention here lies with Quebec MNAs and MPs, although the attitude of federal Liberal MPs from other provinces will not be ignored. The set of respondents being analysed here roughly reflected the composition of the federal caucus as a whole in 1973 and, as Table 1 indicates, about half of the federal parliamentarians came from the province of Quebec. About half, too, were Francophone, although some came from other provinces. At that time, just as at the present time, the Liberals drew disproportionate strength from central Canada and were badly underrepresented in the West. The array of Anglophone attitudes in the

Table 1
Federal Liberal MPs and Activists:
Number of Respondents, by Language Group and Region

		Maritimes	*Quebec*	*Ontario*	*West*
MPs:	Francophones	1	16	3	0
	Anglophones	1	3	10	2
Activists:	Francophones	1	49	5	0
	Anglophones	18	3	55	48

caucus may in part reflect that imbalance, but in due course that can be checked with suitable controls.

If disagreements between federal and provincial Liberals appear, few are likely to be explained by differences in social background. The only noticeable difference is a generational one. Largely because of the sudden increase in the Liberal legislative contingent arising from the 1973 provincial election, that caucus is on average four years younger than the federal caucus and its members have on average two to three years less parliamentary experience. In light of the rapidity of the change in attitudes about Confederation that has taken place in Quebec in the last decade and a half, that generational gap may play an important role in the interpretation of attitudinal differences between the two caucuses.

The most obvious issue areas in which to look for federal-provincial differences are those that touch directly on governmental centralization and on Quebec's status in Confederation. Other areas that warrant an immediate examination are those which concern the status of the French language in Quebec and the sort of measures that might be contemplated for protecting that status. The latter is particularly interesting because of the difference in approach taken by the federal and provincial governments. The federal Liberal leadership has placed a great deal of emphasis on bilingualism, whereas the Quebec government (under Liberal leadership as well) has taken at least symbolic steps toward unilingualism in the operations of the provincial government itself. The contrast between government action in the two arenas has been greatly overdrawn by most observers, for in fact the provincial Liberal approach, as embodied in Bill 22, leaves substantially intact the existing English-language rights, but there is a decided difference in emphasis.

Table 2 presents the responses of federal and provincial parliamentarians of both language groups to a wide variety of constitutional, regional, linguistic, and socioeconomic questions, and it indicates that there are some of the expected differences in outlook on only some of those issues. The small number of Anglophone MNAs introduces a note of caution in any comparison of English-Canadian attitudes, so that our clearest indica-

Table 2
Federal and Provincial Liberal Parliamentarians:
Responses to Constitutional, Regional, Linguistic, and
Socioeconomic Questions, by Language Group

Agreeing with item:	Percentages				
	Francophones			Anglophones	
	Prov.	Fed. (Que.)	Fed. (all)	Prov.	Fed. (all)
Constitutional and regional items					
"Quebec has a right to special status"	67	31	25	40	7
"Canadian federation too centralized"	76	44	45	20	38
"Quebec economic development not sufficiently stimulated by Ottawa"	67	60	58	0	21
"Prairie economic development more than sufficiently stimulated"	47	44	37	40	57
Language items					
"Quebec should force immigrant children to French schools"	74	43	33	20	7
"Residents of Quebec should be able to speak French"	95	79	74	80	50
"French Cdns. have essentially obtained most of demands"	57	43	42	60	53
"Logical that more FCs speak English than ECs speak French"	52	47	42	40	67
"English is inevitably language of business in Quebec"	20	13	12	60	19
"Quebec government should move to protect French language"	95	94	95	40	60
Socioeconomic items					
"Too much state intervention in economy"	19	19	16	80	25
"Rapid industrialization requires increased state intervention"	57	50	47	20	81
"Right to strike in essential services needs limiting"	95	94	89	100	81
"Compromise dangerous – risks betraying one's own side"	14	17	20	0	7
N*	21	16	19	5	16

* These numbers represent the sample sizes in each category. For some questions, one or two respondents did not indicate a reaction, but in none of the above categories of respondents were there more than two parliamentarians who failed to answer any given question.

tion of attitudinal differences at the two levels of government lies within the Francophone group.[29] Subtracting the percentage agreement among federal Quebec Francophones from that of their provincial colleagues gives an indication of the divergence of view between the caucuses. By that measure, there was little major disagreement between federals and provincials in most issue domains. On matters concerning state intervention, the right to strike in essential services, and the art of compromise, the two caucus groups did not substantially differ. Within the linguistic domain, there was also a wide measure of agreement. An overwhelming majority of the Francophone respondents agreed that the Quebec government should take steps to protect the French language, although most were vague in specifying the necessary steps. The great majority also agreed that English was *not* inevitably the language of business in Quebec. As to whether or not it is logical that more Francophones in Canada speak English than Anglophones speaking French, there was more ambivalence, but equally so in the federal and the provincial contingents. In the realm of regional economic imbalances, there was also relatively little federal-provincial disagreement – somewhat surprisingly in the case of Quebec economic development. Many Francophones in the federal Liberal Party were prepared to argue that the federal government has been insufficient in its assistance to Quebec – only a slightly smaller percentage of them than of their provincial counterparts.

Table 3
Federal and Provincial Liberal Parliamentarians:
Differences in the Percentages of Quebec Francophone Respondents
Agreeing with Selected Questionnaire Items

	Difference in % agreeing
"Quebec has a right to special status"	36
"Canadian federation too centralized"	33
"Quebec should force immigrants to French schools"	31
"Residents of Quebec should speak French"	16

Nevertheless, there were some issues which did elicit different reactions – issues which *did* engage some of the explicit policy perspectives of the federal and provincial governments or of their respective leaders. As expected, provincial Liberals were more decentralist than their federal counterparts. More than three-quarters of the provincial Francophones argued that the federation was too centralized, while less than half of their federal counterparts agreed. On this particular question, Anglophones disagreed, and that dissent was revealing of the peculiar status of Quebec's English-speaking population. Just as Francophone minorities in other provinces have on occasion looked to Ottawa as a defender of minority rights, the English in Quebec seem to be looking in the same direction for protection of their supposed rights. During the passage of Bill 22, the province's Anglophones seemed to expect the federal government to take judicial action against the Quebec government, and we might assume from that reaction that they would support the retention of a strong and assertive federal authority. The same sort of protectiveness toward the federal government is evident in reaction to the suggestion that the federal government has not sufficiently stimulated the economic development of the province of Quebec. In reaction to that claim, there were no significant federal-provincial differences among Francophones, but Anglophones in both caucuses differed substantially from their colleagues, particularly in the provincial caucus.

The issue of special status evoked significant federal-provincial differences in both language groups. Two-thirds of the French Canadians in Quebec City felt that their province warranted special treatment in Confederation, as compared to one-third of the Quebec French Canadians in Ottawa. Their argument of course is that Quebec is the *de facto* home of French Canada, containing as it does the vast majority of unassimilated Francophones in Canada. The argument has some logic behind it, but is vehemently opposed by the incumbent Canadian prime minister. Certainly, then, it is difficult for federal Liberal MPs to support openly the notion of special status. it is also unlikely for reasons of personal status that federal Quebecers would be as enthusiastic about the idea as their provincial counterparts, simply because special status would entail an unusually large transfer of jurisdictional authority from the federal government to the provincial government. Writing before his entry into politics, Prime Minister Trudeau argued that Quebec's representatives would be placed in a curious position with the advent of special status, for they could conceivably be legislating on matters that would have no bearing on their province and might consequently develop a second-class status among their colleagues.[30] It is possible in that eventuality that the weight of Quebec MPs in Ottawa would be reduced, and it would probably be difficult to find MPs from that province who would greatly favour a reduction in their own influence.

The more decentralist perspectives among provincial MNAs that Table 2 indicates should not be exaggerated. Informal probing among parliamentary respondents suggested that most Francophones held relatively moderate views on the subject. The following views were typical in that regard:

If the federal system that existed at the founding of Confederation was maybe valid and applicable at that time, one hundred years have passed. If today the provinces have different conceptions – if modern life is different from what existed before – why not leave more latitude to the provinces in certain fields of activity, while still retaining the federal regime.... There's no need to break up the country; but we know that people in Ottawa are centralizers by nature and try to justify the importance of the federal government by keeping as many domains of activity as possible in their hands. Federalism must be more flexible.[31]

I think it would probably be a lot easier in the social field if the provinces had complete jurisdiction.... But we've gained a lot, you know. Politics is the art of compromise. Castonguay for three years said that we wanted everything, and we only got part of it. But if we had not accepted that, I think we would have been very foolish, because there's never any question of all or nothing in politics. You ask for all to get half of what you ask for.[32]

The moment one accepts federalism, one must acknowledge that the federal government should have powers and the means to subsist; and that it has a right to a certain amount of taxation. If one accepts federalism, one must try to put oneself in the shoes of federal leaders. But the federal government should not be too rigid or too centralizing – it should elaborate general policies and leave the care of those policies to the province.[33]

The provincial Liberal Party is still a "federalist" party, despite its differences with Ottawa; although it does seem at times that the provincial Liberal image of a viable federation is a vague and uncertain one!

One of the issues included in Table 2 that elicited a major difference in perspective between language groups as well as between federal and provincial legislators was the linguistic issue or at least aspects of it. At the time of interviewing, Quebec's Official Language Act (Bill 22) had not yet been introduced, but some of the issues which it confronted were much in the air. The immigrant question was particularly contentious, with some French Canadians arguing that the tendency for immigrants to assimilate into the Anglophone milieu had to be stopped if the long-term survival of the French language was to be assured. The issue was barometric in some respects, because it involved forcing immigrants to install their children in French schools. For some Quebecers, therefore, it seemed to entail an element of coercion – a denial of the individual rights of a segment of Quebec's population in the interests of preserving the rights of the French-Canadian collectivity. In fact, relatively little coercion need have been in question, since any moves affecting immigrants could be tailored to affect only newcomers, who presumably could be warned in advance of the situation in Quebec and who would therefore be able to choose their province of immigration accordingly. But for most of the participants in the debate, the stakes were grand ones: collective rights versus individual rights; the insistence that Quebec was by and large a Francophone province versus the claim that the English language should be allowed unfettered growth. The "collective" or "territorial" perspective on language rights dovetails with calls for greater provincial autonomy or for a special status for Quebec, for it tends to equate French Canada and Quebec. On both the constitutional and the linguistic fronts, that perspective contravenes established federal Liberal policy, which tends to embody a more individualist perspective on French-English relations.

In that light we would anticipate differences in view between federal and provincial Liberals as well as between Quebec Anglophones and Francophones, and the reactions to the immigrant question tabulated above correspond to those expectations. Almost three-quarters of the Francophones in Quebec City were prepared to agree that immigrants should be forced to install their children in French schools. On the other hand, only 43 per cent of the federal Quebec Francophones agree with the provincial caucus majority, and only one-third of the entire Francophone contingent in Ottawa agrees. Most of the Ottawa-based French Canadians did show some concern for the problems facing their language, and most felt, if only vaguely, that some measures should be taken to protect it. Still, most were unsure that a legislative solution was possible: they tended to argue that you cannot legislate cultural development. Members of the provincial Assembly were more prone to argue that some government measures were possible, although few were prepared to put the issue at the top of their priority list.

The contrast between federal and provincial perspectives that has been examined here is not simply a product of age. It was noted earlier that a noticeable age difference does exist between the two caucuses. But age tends not to affect the outlooks of parliamentarians. There is some relationship between age and views toward the questions of immigrants and special status, but as Table 4 indicates, it is not sufficient to wash out the federal-provincial contrast. For both questions, younger respondents were

Table 4
Federal and Provincial Liberal Parliamentarians:
Reactions to Questions on Immigrants and Quebec's Special Status
Among Francophones, Controlling for Age

		Agreeing with item:			
	Age group	Fed. Libs.		Prov. Libs.	
		N	%	N	%
"Quebec has a right to	30-49	(6)	33	(8)	88
special status"	50-69	(13)	30	(12)	50
"Quebec should force	30-49	(5)	60	(8)	88
immigrants to French schools"	50-69	(12)	42	(11)	55

more prone to agree that Quebec warranted special status and that immigrants to Quebec should be nudged into the French-language educational system, but in both cases younger provincial members were more likely to adopt that argument than younger federal members.

What explains the difference in view? Two of the most important reasons that would explain much of the disagreement on both the constitutional and the linguistic domains have already been suggested. In the first place, party discipline and loyalty to incumbent leadership inevitably draw most backbenchers into agreement with established party policy, even in the intimacy of a confidential interview. Clearly, for example, MPs in Ottawa and MNAs in Quebec City are influenced to some extent by the attitudes expressed by colleagues and leaders in caucus. In addition, even if explicit policy has not been developed, there are some domains in which the desire to retain power and prestige effectively socializes the freshman MP or MNA. The Quebec provincial Liberals do not have to pronounce themselves officially in favour of increased provincial jurisdiction in order that most MNAs come to the view that it is desirable to give the provinces more authority or to give Quebec a special role in Confederation.

Donald Smiley elaborates on essentially a variant of this point, arguing that the milieu in which politicians find themselves affects their orientations in important ways:

> Somewhat like sovereign states, Canadian provinces have fairly durable and persisting interests. Whatever administrations are in power, Ontario is a large and wealthy province and Prince Edward Island a small and poor one. New Brunswick is inevitably more pre-occupied with bilingualism than is Alberta. Every Quebec administration since 1944 has put a higher priority on autonomy than have other provinces. It is safe to predict that despite their egalitarian commitments no NDP governments of British Columbia or Ontario would press for higher equalization payments to less favoured provinces.[34]

The negotiations between federal and provincial authorities on the Canada Pension Plan and the Quebec Pension Plan illustrate the point well. In 1964 a provincial Liberal government was locked in disagreement with the federal Liberal government, even though the two Liberal parties were organizationally linked at the time. The provincial cabinet succeeded in winning unanimous support in the legislature for its determination to establish a plan that was separate from the national pension plan; yet at the same time, most federal Liberals from Quebec were probably reluctant to make concessions on Quebec separateness (if we can take the reaction of several of the Quebec cabinet ministers in Ottawa to the final agreement worked out between federal and provincial authorities as indicative of the feelings in the caucus as a whole). When agreement finally came, it was not so much because of Liberal fraternity but rather the fears of growing nationalist sentiment in Quebec and the fears that Confederation itself may be endangered. Later, in fact, some federal leaders found the Union Nationale successor to Premier Lesage a great deal easier to deal with.

The third explanation for federal-provincial differences lies in the realm of self-selection. Before even entering the legislature and being subjected to socializing pressures in the federal or the provincial milieu, politicians aspiring to public office at one level or another are likely to be predisposed in different directions. As we suggested earlier, those who aim for provincial office are more likely to be preoccupied with the interest of Quebec and its population, whereas those who aim for federal office are more likely to concern themselves with problems of national unity and with the problems of Canada as a whole, in addition to the issues affecting their own province. No claim is being made here that one vocation is superior to the other, only that they are different. And if in fact they are different in the ways being argued here, we would clearly expect federal aspirants to be fearful of what they would claim was excessive provincial autonomy, especially in the case of Quebec, and we would expect them to be wary of the impact that a "unilingualist" linguistic policy in the province of Quebec would have in English Canada.

The organizational separation of the federal and provincial Liberals increases the likelihood that the opinions of political leaders at the two levels will differ, before and after entry into the legislature. The lines of elite recruitment are more sharply distinguished with disaffiliation, and the opportunities for "cross-pressured" socialization are reduced. A weakened sensitivity in the federal caucus to the social concerns and needs of one's own province or region and its government is the likely consequence.

But before coming to any definite conclusions about the impact of organization separation, or of pre-and post-recruitment socialization, it is worth extending the analysis to party activists. To this point, our focus has been on legislators, who are tied by party discipline to established federal or provincial policy, and who are influenced by intimate contact with other parliamentarians at the same level. Party activists are subject to neither the same discipline nor the intense contact, and we should find out if, in the absence of those forces, federal and provincial activists are of different minds on the sort of issues being examined here.

Party Activists

The party activists analysed here include some of the most active of party workers – constituency association leaders and local campaign managers. Because they are active and probably more integrated into party life and party norms than other party members, there may be only very slight differences between them and their legislative colleagues. But we should still expect some differences in perspective between those partisans who are out "in the field" and those enmeshed in legislative traditions and practices.

When we look at those issues which divided federal and provincial parliamentarians – Francophones in particular – we find that disagreement between federal and provincial Liberal activists is very minor or nonexistent. Federal activists, particularly those in Quebec, are more prepared than their legislative counterparts to argue that Quebec should force immigrant children to attend French schools, that Quebec has a right to some form of special status, and that Confederation is too centralized. Provincial activists, on the other hand, are less prone to take those stands than their parliamentary counterparts, though by and large only slightly less. The reactions of all four sets of respondents are summarized in the diagrams in Figure 1. The deviation of MPs from activists is clearer and more consistent than the difference between MNAs and their activist colleagues (among Anglophones as well as the Francophones portrayed in Figure 1), probably because federal Liberal policy on these matters was clearer in 1973 than provincial policy. The federal government had long been committed to a policy which emphasized individual rights and official bilingualism and which opposed Quebec's assertion of special status. In the absence of clearly stated views on these matters Quebec MNAs were less likely to be united and less drawn to a single policy. As long as no official policy exists, parliamentarians are less likely to differ in systematic ways from their militant followers.

Although we have no evidence that prospective legislators "start" from the same ideological point as their activist colleagues, the data encapsulated in Figure 1 would seem to point to the importance of post-recruitment socialization in generating federal-provincial contrasts in outlook on regional and linguistic issues. Most activist leaders such as those being polled here do seem to prefer working at the level they do: just over half of the federal Liberals and about two-thirds of the provincial Liberals expressed a clear preference for federal and provincial politics respectively. In that sense, they have made the same sort of choice that candidates for election office have, and may well do so for the same reasons – including a predilection for federal or national interests and not simply provincial interests. In that light, the self-selection explanation for policy differences between MPs and MNAs should apply to militants as well. Since that does not appear to lead to a difference in attitude, we may tentatively conclude that MPs and MNAs are tied into a set of perspectives by party discipline, friendly persuasion, or the self-interest that is linked to the prestige of one's government.

Notice what this may say to the students of "leader-follower" or "elite-activist-mass" ideological differences. Some writers have argued that extra-parliamentary activists are more ideological than legislators or members of the top echelons of their party's leadership.[35] John May draws on a

Figure 1
Francophone Federal and Provincial Liberal Parliamentarians
and Activists (Quebecers only):
Federal-Provincial Differences on Selected Linguistic and Regional Issues

"Everyone residing in the Province of
Quebec ought to be able to speak
French"

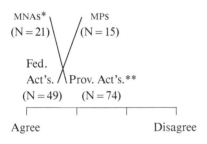

"The Quebec government should be
allowed to force immigrants to place
their children in French schools"

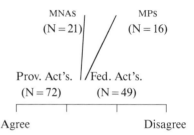

"The Canadian federation is too
highly centralized"

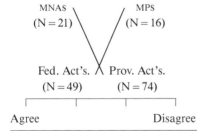

"Quebec has a right to some special
treatment or special status"

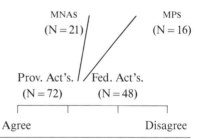

* These points represent the arithmetic means of the responses given on
  seven-point scales ranging from "strongly agree" (1) to "strongly disagree" (7).
  See Table 2 for the percentages of each category of respondent expressing
  agreement with each of these four questions.
** Federal Liberal activists (constituency association presidents and campaign
  managers) and provincial Liberal activists (also constituency presidents and
  managers).

great deal of literature on political parties and finds that the "special law of
curvilinear disparity," by which top leaders occupy an ideologically intermediate position between relatively extremist sub-leaders and less polarized followers, has wide applicability.[36] He cites Mosei Ostragorski, Henry
Pelling, Philip Poirier, David Butler, Samuel Beer, and Leon Epstein in
support of the argument that British parties fit into this pattern, and draws

on several American sources to make the same point in the case of U.S. parties. The phenomenon is an important one in his view, since sub-leaders often play a role in leadership selection, and even normally moderate incumbent leaders might be influenced by a more partisan activist corps if they believe that militants will form part of a future elite selectorate. Elites also rely to some extent on activists for campaign work and rely on them for clues about public opinion. Activists may as a result be deferred to on some issues, in part because they play a necessary role in manning the party's electoral machine, and in part because they act as part of the sensory nerve system of the party's parliamentary contingent.

A variety of explanations have been brought to bear on this model. Although all upper-level partisans are more intensively involved in politics than their followers and have more of an opportunity to acquire a consistent outlook on political issues, *elected* leaders are more regularly confronted with the need to compromise with political opponents, and may not be as fervent as party activists in defending party principles. The militant is less involved in confronting his own ideas with the supposed harshness of political reality and therefore has more opportunity to retain his ideological principles intact. Elected members are more likely to be preoccupied with success at the polls, and may be prepared to put ideological questions and fundamental principles to one side or prepare to allow their own ideological inclinations to be shaped by their electoral noses.

The data at hand in this study give pause to any attempt to generalize about inter-level differences, though, for we are confronted here with legislators who are hewing more consistently to party policy than are the activists. Whereas we might have expected MPs and MNAs to be more "moderate" or "centrist" than activists, they are not. It is not that the explanations for these particular findings are especially difficult, for we can explain legislator attitudes to some extent with reference to self-interest – the desire to increase power and prestige – but we are counselled by these data against too easy a generalization from the existing findings on party elites and activists. In one respect – one which has relevance for any discussion of politics in Quebec – the literature on inter-level differences is deficient. It tends to neglect the impact of electoral challenge. Elite-activist differences may be seriously altered in the face of an imminent threat to the electoral fortunes of the party or parties in question. For several years, prior to its victory in 1976, the separatist Parti Québécois had been making important gains, and although by all appearances most of those gains were at the expense of the Union Nationale, there are still grounds for suspecting that it had some impact on the Liberals, in particular since the PQ leader was himself once a Liberal. If we can assume that more actively partisan Liberals are less likely to defect from the party than less active ones, even when they share the same "deviant" views on questions such as the role of Quebec in Confederation, then the presence of a party such as the PQ might have some impact on the combination of outlooks to be found at various levels in the party hierarchy. Not only are legislators more actively immersed in politics than almost all activists, but they gain personal prestige and power from their involvement. Even those Liberal legislators who might normally find themselves sympathetic to some of the PQ's stands, then, would probably find it difficult to defect. The activist is not in the same position at all. He is less likely to be loyal, since his involvement is less intense and the costs of shifting allegiance are much less. For the full-time partisan, "loyalty," in Albert Hirschman's words, "would hold exit at bay," while for the activist, "exit" would be much more plausible.[37]

Not only would "deviant" provincial MNAs be less likely than activists to shift from the Liberal to other parties, but they are also more sensitive to electoral threats than activists. It is, after all, they who would lose their posts in the face of serious electoral challenge, and not the extra-parliamentary workers. The continued rise of the PQ could well have been sharpening the Liberal contingent's sensitivity to nationalist concerns and to questions of provincial autonomy, thereby increasing its attitudinal distance from the federal Liberal caucus. As a result, we find that Liberal MNAs were not more moderate than activists, but were instead very similar in their perspectives, and in one case more "extreme." The federal caucus diverged more from its activist corps, but as in the provincial setting, it is not at all clear that the findings in the elite-activist literature summarized by John May are replicated here. The combination of federal and provincial data suggests that careful note be taken of the effect of electoral threat on elite attitudes, in addition to the more commonly acknowledged post-recruitment socialization.

Conclusions

Those observers who began to think that difficulties in the relationships between French and English Canadians and between Quebec and the other provinces in the Canadian union were coming to an end have probably had a rude awakening since 1973 – or they should have. The strength of the separatist idea is as great as it ever was in Quebec, and the Anglophone resistance to any meaningful steps designed to strengthen the position of the French language, inside or outside Quebec, is as evident now as it has been since the end of World War Two. It may be an exaggeration to speak of crisis, but it is unmitigated folly to assume that interethnic or interregional relations are amicable.

The polling of Liberal partisans that is being reported here is important in elaborating on the nature of the present relationship between French and English Canadians and between Quebec and the central government. It is also important in judging the performance of the existing party system in the face of those relationships. The division of opinion is far from complete, but what division there is in the linguistic and the regional domains does lend credence to the argument made by Lipset and Simeon and others that the combination of a British parliamentary system and federalism inhibits the expression of regional or sectional interests within national parties and forces the expression of those concerns to the provincial level.[38] That system has also contributed to patterns of legislative and executive recruitment that reinforce the separation between federal and provincial arenas and, by separating recruitment, it has increased the stake that political elites have in the authority of the government to which they find themselves affiliated.

Even in the secrecy and in the free-flowing atmosphere of the cabinet room, federal politicians are likely to be preoccupied with the national arena and with policies that will contribute to the power of the federal government and the sustenance of the party to which they belong. Simeon, in arguing that the role of the federal cabinet in mediating and expressing regional interests is more limited than is commonly believed, suggests:

> Federal ministers operate in the federal environment. They are oriented to winning national office, to formulating national policies in areas of federal jurisdiction, and to survival in the House of Commons. Provincial governments are only a part of that environment. It would therefore be unrealistic to view the minister's chief role as that of regional spokesman.[39]

The differences in perspective between federal and provincial representatives might be reduced when they come from the same party or from the same "partisan family," but probably reduced to only a minor extent if that party or those parties are both governing at the same time. Although several factors were involved in generating the tensions between federal and provincial Liberals in Quebec, it was not simply coincidence that the final break came when the Liberal Party was in power in Ottawa and in Quebec City. Many Liberal leaders found it difficult to remain in the same party with leaders of another level of government whom they faced and fought in tough federal-provincial negotiations. Being in power accentuates the sense of responsibility felt by parties holding provincial power to represent provincial interests, and it accentuates the personal gain in prestige that comes of success in presenting regional concerns and in increasing provincial autonomy. What occurred in Quebec after 1964 seemed to occur in Saskatchewan after the provincial Liberals took power from the CCF. Although the personality and style of Ross Thatcher may have had something to do with the tensions between the federal Liberal leadership and the provincial leadership, their common tenure of governmental power contributed mightily to the difficulty of the relationship.

When in opposition, parties can often avoid establishing definitive policy on contentious matters and there is often a freer expression of dissenting opinion. One can, after all, criticize a government policy belonging to another party without always specifying what one would replace it with, and one can thereby satisfy a wide range of discontents. Federal opposition parties have also been more inclined to argue in favour of provincial rights, although not to the same extent as most provincial elites. The Liberals during the time of Macdonald, and the Conservatives during much of their time in opposition in this century, have frequently voiced some sympathy with provincial claims that the federal government was usurping provincial rights or unfairly infringing on the rights or interests of particular regions. That takes nothing from the general argument that federal politicians tend to be more federalist than provincial politicians and less preoccupied with regional interests, but it does argue that being in government sharpens the contrast.

In a curious way, the Canadian political system and party system accentuate regionalism, and then stifle the expression of regional concerns in the national arena. David Truman's argument, that in the American system the low temperature and domestic quality of political debate and the relative absence of major ideological divisions between parties accentuate localism and regionalism, can be applied with ease to Canada.[40] The absence of a socialist working-class party or a religiously based party in national politics allows for a greater preoccupation with regional interests.[41] Alan Cairns makes the additional point, of course, that the Canadian party system, operating under the single-member constituency electoral system, exacerbates regionalism and increases the temptation for national parties to regionalize their appeals.[42] He argues that the electoral system exaggerates the regional concentration of each party's support; and since the extra-parliamentary organizations of the two major parties remain weak, the fortunes of either party depend very much on the (distorted) results of the previous election. No permanent organization with active influence over policy is able to correct the parliamentary party's bias, and although it is possible for some leaders to concertedly correct the bias themselves, it is ordinarily easier simply to reflect those regional opinions most active in the party's parliamentary contingent.

But despite the regionalism that such a system provokes, it is unable to complete the cycle, for many regional concerns are inexpressible within disciplined national parties, and many of the personnel recruited into national politics are unlikely to give a sufficiently fierce and determined voice to such concerns. The combination of an electoral system that accentuates regional differences in national party politics and a party system that between elections cannot easily cope with the open channelling of provincial interests makes for a potentially explosive combination. When Quebec Liberals in Ottawa clearly disagree with their provincial counterparts, even while both parties claim allegiance to the idea of federalism, the meeting of minds can be a creative one but it can also be a needlessly destructive one –

one that may be more enmeshed with the self-interest of elected politicians than with the interests of the people of Quebec.

Notes

Financial assistance for the larger project from which this is drawn was received from the Woodrow Wilson Foundation, the Canada Council, and the Western European Studies Center of the University of Michigan. In the preparation of that project, invaluable advice was received from Samuel Barnes, Raymond Grew, Albert Verdoodt, and in particular Robert Putnam. In addition, for general support and encouragement, there are a few close friends based in Toronto, Kingston, Ottawa, and especially in London who know my undying gratitude.

1. David Truman, "Federalism and the Party System," in Aaron Wildavsky, ed., *American Federalism in Perspective* (Boston, 1967), 81-108. To the extent that federalism implies sectional diversity (which it need not always imply), it almost necessarily leads to a federalized party organization. In George Hougham's words, "Sectional diversity precluded the establishment of a unitary state in 1867. Sectional diversity has, likewise, precluded the establishment of unitary party organizations. . . . In the early years, indeed, both the Liberal and Conservative parties were nothing more than loose alliances of sectional groups." "The Background and Development of National Parties," in Hugh G. Thorburn, ed., *Party Politics in Canada* (2nd ed., Scarborough, 1967), 13.

2. Both William Riker, in a general theoretical context, and Donald Smiley, in the specific Canadian context, talk at some length about the close relationship between the party system and the operation of a federal system. See William H. Riker, *Federalism: Origin, Operation, Significance* (Boston, 1964); Donald V. Smiley, *Canada in Question: Federalism in the Seventies* (2nd ed., Toronto, 1976), especially ch. 4.

3. The author undertook a series of semi-structured interviews with backbench parliamentarians in both Liberal parties, alongside a similar series of interviews with parliamentarians in the Belgian Social Christian party (with response rates of about 80 per cent in each setting). In each party, interviews were conducted with about half of the backbench contingent in the lower house of each legislature, with some over-sampling of the minority language group in each case. Oral interviews were coupled with a relatively short written questionnaire, containing a variety of "agree-disagree" statements. Those written statements were included as well in a mail-out questionnaire addressed to leading party activists. It is difficult to know whether the 40 and 46 per cent of the federal and provincial activists polled who did respond to those questionnaires were different in systematic ways from those who did not, since relatively little is known about the latter. Their roles within their parties and their place of residence is known, and on that basis there appear to be no

grounds for fearing an unrepresentative sample. It is true that among federal activists, constituency association presidents responded more frequently than the average, and campaign managers less frequently – 49 and 30 per cent respectively – but there were no indications that either category of respondent had markedly distinctive perspectives on the issues probed here. For more details on the study from which this analysis is extracted, see David M. Rayside, "Linguistic Divisions in the Social Christian Party of Belgium and the Liberal Parties of Canada and Quebec" (Ph.D. thesis, University of Michigan, 1976).

4. Smiley, *Canada in Question,* 102.
5. *Ibid.,* 84-85.
6. Escott M. Reid, "The Rise of National Parties in Canada," in Thorburn, ed., *Party Politics*, 16.
7. Smiley, *Canada in Question*, 93-94.
8. Laurier papers: Dandurand to Laurier, January 4, 1918, quoted in Peter Regenstreif, "The Liberal Party of Canada: A Political Analysis" (Ph.D. thesis, Cornell University, 1963), 128.
9. By some accounts, the Quebec organization is now more involved in the activities of the central office in Ottawa, and Quebec personnel are more fully integrated with those from other parts of Canada. But there is still a certain separateness in the relationship between the Montreal and Ottawa offices, and despite appearances there is probably still some feeling that a disproportionate amount of the Ottawa office's activities are oriented towards the English-speaking provinces.
10. Interview C35, July 27, 1973.
11. The relationship between federal and provincial Liberals and the split between them are described in detail in Gérard Bergeron, *Du duplessisme à Trudeau et Bourassa, 1956-1971* (Montreal, 1971). For the 1940s and 1950s, George-Emile Lapalme, *Mémoires*, Tome II, *Le vent de l'oubli* (Montreal, 1970), and Jean-Marie Nadeau, *Carnets politiques* (Montreal, 1966), are useful sources of information and opinion.
12. This argument is presented by Ernest E. Harill, "The Structure of Organization and Power in Canadian Political Parties: A Study in Party Financing" (Ph.D. thesis, University of North Carolina, 1958), 280-87; Richard Simeon, *Federal-Provincial Diplomacy: The Making of Recent Policy in Canada* (Toronto, 1972), 34.
13. Smiley marshals an impressive amount of evidence in this regard, although he takes care to note that the distinctiveness of federal and provincial voting patterns varies by region and province. *Canada in Question*, 85-92.
14. Henry Jacek, John McDonough, Richard Shimuzu, and Patrick Smith, "Federal-Provincial Integration in Ontario Party Organization – The Influence of Recruitment Patterns," paper presented to the 1970 Annual Meeting of the Canadian Political Science Association, 102. Cited in Smiley, *Canada in Question*, 93.

15. Norman Ward, ed., *The Memoirs of Chubby Power: A Party Politician* (Toronto, 1966), 312.

16. *Ibid.*

17. This is the assessment of Reginald Whitaker in an extraordinarily comprehensive and insightful analysis of the relationship between federal and provincial Liberals in Quebec, contained in "The Quebec Liberals: Federal-Provincial Aspects of Party Organization, 1921-1964," mimeo, 1976, 56.

18. Ward, *Memoirs*, 347.

19. J.A.A. Lovink, "The Politics of Quebec: Provincial Political Parties, 1897-1936" (Ph.D. thesis, Duke University, 1968), 98-149. Whitaker argues that the provincial organization was the dominant partner during the 1920s, at the height of Premier Taschereau's power, although that might have been more short-lived than Whitaker claims. "The Quebec Liberals," 50-51.

20. Consistency was not always maintained along these lines. In 1931, when the federal Liberals were in opposition, Premier Taschereau urged on Quebecers the importance of electing a government in Quebec that was not of the same party as the federal government!

21. Interview, March 21, 1969.

22. *La Réforme*, November 21, 1956.

23. Khayyam Z. Paltiel, "Federalism and Party Finance: A Preliminary Sounding," in K.Z. Paltiel *et al., Studies in Canadian Party Financing* (Ottawa, 1966), 1-21.

24. From "Le Rapport du congrès spécial de la Fédération libérale du Québec, tenu au Motel des Laurentides à Beauport, le dimanche, 5 juillet 1964."

25. Smiley, *Canada in Question*, 93-94.

26. According to Roman March, for example (*The Myth of Parliament* [Scarborough, 1974]), about 49 per cent of all MPs in Ottawa who served between 1867 and 1873 had at least run for provincial office. Between 1874 and 1899, the figure was about 28 per cent, and for 1911-39, it was 22-23 per cent. By the 1959-64 period, only 6.7 per cent had run for provincial office (32-33). According to Smiley's count of the 1974 House of Commons, only 4.9 per cent had ever held provincial seats and only 13.3 per cent had ever even contested provincial elections. The figures for the Liberals were 2 per cent and 4 per cent respectively. *Canada in Question*, 97.

27. Truman, "Federalism and the Party System," 102.

28. Smiley makes the same point, arguing that the unprogrammatic nature of Canadian parties, coupled with a reliance on personality-based electoral appeals, reduces the ties binding federal and provincial politicians of the same partisan stripe. *Canada in Question*, 96.

29. Among provincial Liberals there were 21 Francophone MNAs, in addition to 94 local activists of both language groups.

30. For opposing views on this subject, see Daniel Johnson, "Speech in the Quebec Legislature, April 23, 1963," in Frank Scott and Michael Oliver, eds.,

Quebec States Her Case (Toronto, 1964), 31-40; and Pierre Elliott Trudeau, *Federalism and the French Canadians* (Toronto, 1968), 3-51.

31. Interview Q12, November 29, 1973, author's translation.
32. Interview Q13, November 29, 1973, author's translation.
33. Interview Q24, December, 1973, author's translation.
34. Smiley, *Canada in Question*, 108.
35. Representative of this literature are the following: Rodney P. Stiefbold, "Segmented Pluralism and Consociational Democracy: Problems of Political Stability and Change," in Martin O. Heisler, ed., *Politics in Europe: Structures and Processes in Some Post-industrial Democracies* (New York, 1974), 117-78; Maurice Duverger, *Political Parties: Their Organization and Activity in the Modern State*, trans. by Barbara and Robert North (New York, 1963), 182-202; Herbert McClosky, Paul J. Hoffman, and Rosemary O'Hara, "Issue Conflict and Consensus Among Party Leaders and Followers," *American Political Science Review*, 54 (1960), 406-29; Edmond Costantini, "Intraparty Attitude Conflict: Democratic Party Leadership in California," *Western Political Quarterly,* 16 (1963), 956-72; and Thomas A. Flinn and Frederick M. Wirt, "Local Party Leaders: Groups of Like-Minded Men," *Midwest Journal of Political Science*, 9 (1965), 77-98.
36. John D. May, "Opinion Structure of Political Parties: The Special Law of Curvilinear Disparity," *Political Studies*, 21 (1973), 135-51.
37. Albert O. Hirschman, *Exit, Voice, and Loyalty: Responses to Decline in Firms, Organizations, and States* (Cambridge, Mass., 1970), especially ch.7.
38. For variations on this theme, see Stephen Muller, "Federalism and the Party System in Canada," in J. Peter Meekison, ed., *Canadian Federalism: Myth or Reality* (Toronto, 1968), 154; Seymour Martin Lipset, "Democracy in Alberta," in John C. Courtney, ed., *Voting in Canada* (Scarborough, 1967), 182-85; and Simeon, *Federal-Provincial Diplomacy*, 27-29, 303.
39. Simeon, *Federal-Provincial Diplomacy*, 28.
40. Truman, "Federalism and the Party System," 104.
41. John Porter argues something of the reverse, namely that it is the preoccupation with regionalism that has reduced the "temperature" and the ideological coloration of political debate in Canada. There are, however, several good explanations for the weakness of working-class parties and the present-day absence of the sort of clerical parties that characterize European party systems that do not rest on the argument that contemporary national parties are preoccupied with regionalism and with questions of "national unity." See John Porter, *The Vertical Mosaic* (Toronto, 1965), ch. 12.
42. Alan C. Cairns, "The Electoral System and the Party System in Canada, 1921-1965," *Canadian Journal of Political Science*, 1 (1968), 65.

PART FOUR

Intergovernmental

Relations:

Past and Present

K.C. Wheare, in his classic book on federal government, defined federalism as a system with two levels of government, each of which is independent of the other level in relation to the matters over which it has jurisdiction.[1] If Wheare's definition is taken literally one might imagine, in theory, a federal state in which there was no need for any interaction between the two levels of government. In practice, of course, no such version of federalism has ever existed. Jurisdictions can never be allocated so precisely as to avoid overlap between the responsibilities of the two levels of government. The activities of each level of government inevitably affect those of the other. Both levels are likely to respond to new subjects of concern that are not referred to in the constitution, so that co-ordination of their respective policies becomes necessary. In addition, it is difficult to distribute revenues between two levels of government in such a way that each has exactly enough to perform the tasks assigned to it by the constitution, particularly if economic development is unevenly distributed across the country. For all of these reasons, federalism inevitably implies intergovernmental relations, and these have tended in all federations to become more important and more complex over time. The essays in this concluding section explore different aspects of the relations between federal and provincial governments in Canada.

J.A. Maxwell's article, published more than half a century ago, traces the history of federal grants to the provincial governments. Because the provinces could not impose tariffs or excise taxes after Confederation, federal grants to them were provided for in the BNA Act. The amount of these grants was intended to be fixed, but almost immediately it began to be modified by special arrangements for particular provinces. As new provinces entered Confederation they were also favoured with additional financial inducements, increasing the discontent of the original provinces. Subsidies to all provinces were increased in 1873, in 1884, and in 1907, with the last of these increases being entrenched in the constitution. In addition there were, according to Maxwell, twenty-six instances of "better terms" to individual provinces. By 1928 Ontario, Quebec, and British Columbia were virtually self-supporting, but the remaining provinces were all heavily dependent on subsidies from the federal government. By the time Maxwell's article was published the economic depression had increased the financial difficulties of all Canadian governments, and fiscal federalism seemed on the brink of collapse.

Maxwell's main criticism of fiscal federalism was that the escalation of grants to the provinces had resulted from political expediency rather than economic rationality. Provinces were given "better terms" to secure their support in federal elections or to repay their governments for support in previous elections. Provinces governed by the party that held office in Ottawa were far more likely to receive additional grants than provinces governed by the major opposition party. Concessions to one province would cause others to increase their demands. Although demands were usually accompanied by claims that the province was in need, or that it was adversely affected by the economic policies of the federal government, the distribution of grants that resulted from this process could not be justified by either criterion. Maxwell recommended that grants to provinces be distributed in a way that removed partisan politics from the process.

To a large extent this has now been achieved. Since 1957 the federal government has made equalization payments to all provinces whose ability to raise revenue falls below a certain standard, and since 1982 the obligation to make such payments has been entrenched in the constitution. The eligibility of a province for equalization payments and the amount it receives are determined by a mathematical formula applied to all provinces and normally revised every five years.[2] Provincial budgets have been largely immunized from the effects of political expediency at the federal level. The greater independence of the provinces in this regard has probably contributed to the separate development of their party systems, as described in Part Three of this book.

The next two essays both deal with major issues of federal-provincial relations in the 1960s, issues that continue to have relevance today. The issue of offshore mineral resources, as described by Neil Caplan, produced considerable conflict between the federal government and provincial governments. The issue of the funding of public welfare programs, as described by Rand Dyck, created a large amount of co-operation and very little conflict. The fact that these issues were prominent on the intergovernmental agenda at the same time suggests the complex nature of federal-provincial relations, which involve both conflict and co-operation.

Caplan's article identifies the factors that determine the outcome of federal-provincial conflicts, using the dispute between the federal and British Columbia governments over offshore minerals as a case study. The relative balance of power between the contending governments, their beliefs about the issue and about one another, and the personalities of the politicians and officials in both governments are all discussed. Caplan mentions another factor he does not discuss, namely, the role of private interests that are affected by the outcome of the dispute. Such interested parties, including business corporations and a variety of interest groups, might have a preference for one or the other level of government, or they might simply wish the issue to be resolved, one way or another. In some circumstances they might even wish the dispute to be prolonged, so that the two levels of government might compete for their support.

One interesting aspect of Caplan's article is his critique of what he calls the mystique of co-operative federalism. The federal government is often urged to negotiate with the provincial governments or is unfairly condemned for not doing so, but the provinces themselves may be quite intransigent and not prepared to make any concessions. Those who insist that the federal government should make concessions to the provinces are also usually reluctant to have issues resolved in the courts. Caplan suggests that such attitudes were not helpful in the British Columbia minerals dispute and may actually have delayed a settlement.

Offshore minerals remained a contentious issue even after the Supreme Court rejected British Columbia's claims, but attention shifted from the Pacific to the Atlantic coast. Nova Scotia, recognizing that the Supreme Court decision had weakened its bargaining power, eventually accepted an agreement that recognized federal ownership of offshore petroleum but allowed the province a share of revenues and limited participation in the management of the resource. Newfoundland argued that it was in a different legal situation from the other coastal provinces because of its allegedly independent status before 1949. This claim was finally rejected by the Supreme Court in 1984, but the Mulroney government nonetheless made an exceptionally generous settlement with Newfoundland, largely negating the effect of the Supreme Court's decision. Also in 1984, the Supreme Court ruled that British Columbia owns the seabed under the strait that separates Vancouver Island from the mainland, distinguishing this seabed from the continental shelf beyond the island. Somewhat ironically, in view of the conflict described by Caplan, no evidence of oil or gas has actually been found off Canada's Pacific coast.

Although Caplan concludes that federal-provincial relations are basically competitive rather than co-operative, Rand Dyck's article on the establishment of the Canada Assistance Plan provides some evidence for a contrary view. Conditional grants, a device by which the federal government assists in the funding of provincial programs that meet federally determined criteria, became an important aspect of Canadian fiscal federalism after the Second World War.[3] Initially at least, they were welcomed by most provinces and the CAP, one of the last major conditional grant programs to be established, was no exception to the rule. Dyck attributes the harmonious nature of the CAP negotiations to three factors: the initiative in seeking federal funding came from the provinces; federal politicians and officials involved in the negotiations were sympathetic toward the provincial governments; and the commitment of program specialists to the goals of the program transcended any rivalry that existed between the two levels of government. Although there were some conflicts over relatively minor details of the program, these were quite easily resolved.

In 1978, after Dyck's article was published, the federal government and most of the provinces agreed that the Canada Assistance Plan should be replaced with a block grant that would in effect leave each province free to spend the money as it pleased. Only Saskatchewan, which had an NDP government at the time, opposed this idea, and legislation to implement it was introduced in Parliament. Later the federal government had second thoughts, so that the legislation was never adopted. The Canada Assistance Plan still exists and federal contributions to it in the 1987-88 fiscal year were in excess of $4 billion.

At about the same time that the termination of the Canada Assistance Plan was under consideration major changes took place in the arrangements for funding two other shared-cost programs: health insurance and post-secondary education. The changes, and the arrangements that have generally remained in force ever since, are considered in the essay by George Carter. Carter begins by describing the evolution of federal-provincial fiscal relations from 1965, when Quebec accepted a federal offer to allow "opting out" from several existing programs, until 1977, when the arrangements now known as Established Programs Financing came into effect. During this period both the federal government and the governments of the larger provinces became increasingly dissatisfied with the conditional grant mechanism, although for different reasons. Despite this dissatisfaction, the termination of the programs was politically unthinkable, the provinces could not fund them alone, and the federal government lacked the constitutional jurisdiction to assume complete responsibility for them. The exceptionally complex arrangements devised to resolve this problem are described, as clearly as is possible, in Carter's article. Written very soon after EPF came into effect, the article concludes on a note of cautious optimism.

After a few years of experience with EPF the federal government (and much of the public) concluded that the new arrangements left the provinces with too much freedom to spend the money as they pleased, while the federal government had lost any influence over the operation of the programs. The Canada Health Act of 1984, which was supported by all three parties in Parliament, reimposed more rigid standards on provincial health insurance programs and provided financial penalties for provinces that failed to comply. At about the same time Parliament established a formal distinction between the health and education components of EPF. Despite the widespread support for the Canada Health Act, no comparable legislation has been adopted to extend federal influence over post-secondary education. In effect, the provinces have complete discretion over the funding of their colleges and universities.

The concluding essay, by Albert Breton, was originally published as a supplement to the report of the Royal Commission on the Economic Union and Development Prospects for Canada, of which Breton was a member. Breton, an academic economist now at the University of Toronto, was among the small group of Quebec intellectuals, including future politicians Pierre Elliott Trudeau and Marc Lalonde, who criticized Quebec nationalism during the Quiet Revolution. He has written extensively about federalism and related subjects. His statement is interesting because it challenges much of the conventional wisdom about federalism in Canada, and particularly the view that co-operation between federal and provincial governments is always desirable. Neil Caplan's critique of "the mystique of co-operative federalism" may be recalled in this connection, and closely resembles Breton's description of co-operative federalism as "a disguised ploy to shackle the federal government."

Breton uses the "public-choice" model, which has become an increasingly popular approach to political analysis in recent years. Public-choice theorists apply the methodology and assumptions of economics to the analysis of politics, on the assumption that significant analogies can be drawn between economic markets and political institutions. Voters use their votes to buy goods and services from governments just as consumers use their dollars to buy goods and services in the economy. The public-choice theorist assumes that both voters and politicians act out of self-interest, just as the economist makes the same assumption about the motives of consumers and entrepreneurs. Self-interest is considered desirable, however, as long as there is enough competition to ensure that no one controls the market. The market, Adam Smith's "invisible hand," will then automatically bring about the most efficient, and therefore desirable, use of resources.

Breton assesses the institutions of Canadian government from this standpoint and finds them only partially satisfactory. Parliamentary government produces less competition among political elites and institutions than the American system, but when it is combined with federalism, as in the Canadian case, considerable competition results. Federalism produces two kinds of competition: vertical competition between the two levels of government and horizontal competition among the provinces themselves. Federalism is thus desirable, and its desirability does not depend on any real or alleged cultural diversity among the provinces. However, and this is where Breton most clearly parts company with the conventional wisdom, the desirability of federalism is reduced when governments co-operate with one another. Co-operation means less competition and is thus detrimental to the interests of the voters, just as collaboration among firms to fix prices or control the supply of goods is detrimental to the interests of consumers.

In an interesting extension of this argument, Breton makes a fairly persuasive case for the proposition that an elected Senate with equal representation for each province would make Canadian federalism work better. In the last part of his essay he discusses five major issues related to Canadian federalism: Canada as an economic union, intergovernmental grants, tax collection agreements, the Charter of Rights and Freedoms, and the role of municipal government. Whether one accepts his conclusions or not, he has produced one of the most thought-provoking analyses of Canadian federalism ever written.

Notes

1. K.C. Wheare, *Federal Government* (4th edition, New York, 1964), 2.
2. A fuller explanation may be found in Garth Stevenson, *Unfulfilled Union* (3rd edition, Toronto, 1989), 140-45.
3. See *ibid.*, 151-76, for discussion of the history of conditional grants.

14. J.A. MAXWELL

Better Terms

The days of stress which have come upon us have made it plain that there must be a thoroughgoing revision of federal-provincial relations. There is, of course, nothing surprising about this; students of the problem have been insisting upon it for years, and there is evidence that the practical statesmen, through whom any changes must be put into effect, are not unaware of the situation.

The purpose of this article will be to examine the federal subsidy system, one feature of federal-provincial relations which emphatically requires reform. The system in Canada at present includes grants of two sorts: (1) unconditional sums, provided at Confederation and expanded at various times since, which are paid by the federal treasury to the provincial treasuries, without restriction as to how they shall be spent; (2) conditional sums – subventions – developed in the last twenty years, which are given in aid of specific provincial activities – highway construction, vocational training – and to which the Dominion attaches strings. Whatever the future may disclose, the former have been vastly more important in the past, and it is with them only that I am here concerned. But no attempt will be made to state what direction reform should take. It will suffice for the present to demonstrate that the system was a makeshift when initiated, that changes made in later years have been utterly illogical, and that the subsidy system as it now stands is a positive menace to the federal treasury and to good feeling between the various provinces.

Originally published in *Queen's Quarterly* (1933). Reprinted with permission of Mrs. Mary N. Maxwell.

The system of subsidies was written into our constitution because the Fathers of Confederation were practical statesmen, willing to compromise in order to accomplish their main object. When, at the Quebec conference in 1864, they began to divide governmental functions into those which should be performed by the Dominion and those by the provinces, and when also they divided sources of revenue, a most serious difficulty arose. At this time all of the old provincial governments, without exception, were drawing the bulk of their revenue from import duties. Yet it was perfectly clear that the new federal government must have control of external trade and have, therefore, the sole right of levying duties. Thus what had been the major source of income for the provincial governments would be taken away. However, as a counterbalance they would, under the new federal constitution, have less extensive functions to perform and less heavy expenditure to make; and if, for each province, the decline in revenues had been compensated by a decline in functions and therefore in expenditures, no problem would have arisen. But this was not the case. The old provincial governments in the Maritimes were, so it appeared, performing much more extensive tasks than the provincial governments in the Canadas. In the Maritimes the government had been a "nursing mother" to the localities, aiding them with their roads, schools, wharves; while in the Canadas a municipal system had been developed by which such tasks were put upon the local units themselves. A few figures will illustrate this point. In 1863 nearly 12 per cent of the current expenditure of the provincial government of Nova Scotia was for roads and bridges, while in Canada this expenditure was just about 1 per cent. The same point can be illustrated more forcibly in another way. The new federal government would, under the plan first proposed, have assumed 77 per cent of the existing expenditures of the Canadas, while it would have taken over only 45 per cent of those of Nova Scotia. In short, any uniform division of functions and of revenues between the new provincial governments and the Dominion which would balance the budgets of the upper provinces, would start the Maritimes with unbalanced budgets.

There were two possible solutions. A municipal system was a good thing. If the Maritimes adopted it, functions and expenditures would be shifted from the provincial to the local governments and the budgets of the former might be balanced. Some of the delegates at Quebec – notably Brown and Galt – favoured this solution, but obviously it was objectionable. Even granted that a municipal system was desirable, the people of the Maritimes ought not to be asked to accept both federation and municipal reform in one dose.

The other solution, and the one adopted, was that subsidies should be paid to the provincial governments from the federal treasury. After assent to this general proposition was secured, two important questions remained: On what basis and to what amount should subsidies be paid? To the first question there seemed at first sight to be a ready answer: subsidies, like representation, should be based upon population. Canada, with a population ten times that of New Brunswick, should get ten times as much subsidy. But when the delegates started to discuss what should be the *absolute* amounts of the subsidies, they once more ran up against the old difficulty – that governmental functions were differently distributed in the Maritimes than they were in Canada. For this reason, subsidies apportioned upon a uniform per capita basis, which would balance the budgets of the provincial governments of the Maritimes, would give Upper and Lower Canada large surplus revenues.

The dispute over these questions almost wrecked the conference. On the one side were those who, like Galt and Brown, believed subsidies at best to be a necessary evil and who therefore insisted that their amount be kept as low as possible. They urged, besides, that it would be unwise to place heavy annual fixed charges upon the federal treasury. On the other side were those who, like Tupper and Tilley, were without doctrinaire convictions about subsidies, but who saw the practical impossibility of launching provincial governments not possessed of adequate revenues. The problem was referred by the conference to a committee composed of the finance ministers of every province, and after long debate it formulated a series of resolutions.

The resolutions, so far as possible, used the population of 1861 as the basis for the distribution of subsidies. A yearly grant of 80 cents per capita was to go to the provincial governments, and the federal treasury was to assume a provincial debt equal to $25 per capita, e.g., Canada, with a population of 2,500,000, was to have a "debt allowance" of $62,500,000. Besides these general provisions, several exceptional grants were made. New Brunswick was promised an extra allowance of $63,000 a year for ten years because of its difficult fiscal position, and Newfoundland was promised an annual grant of $150,000, ostensibly for the surrender of its territorial rights to the federal government, but really as a way to give the colony a special subsidy. Thus even in the Quebec resolutions there was recognition that strict apportionment of financial favours according to population would not serve.

Before going farther, it will be well to indicate how the four men – Galt, Brown, Tupper, and Tilley – who framed the subsidy resolutions felt toward them. The former two made explicit pronouncements against the principle of subsidies and they both believed that the wisest, as distinct from the most practicable plan, would have been to make practice and principle coincide. Galt and Brown had these convictions partly because they had seen, in the operation of the municipal loan fund, the evils which grow out of distribution of revenue by superior to inferior governments, and partly because they were acquainted with and influenced by current English fiscal doctrine, which condemned grants-in-aid as economically unsound. What Tupper and Tilley thought is less clear. At no time did they defend subsidies as anything more than a convenient expedient and it is, I think, fair to assume that about the principle of subsidies they had no views.

Upon one further point contemporary opinion should be noticed. The Quebec resolutions provided for subsidies which were to be rigid in amount. It has, in later years, been asserted that this was an oversight and that the Fathers of Confederation had forgotten that fixed grants would become inadequate as population grew and expenditure of the provinces mounted. Such an assertion assumes that the men who framed the resolutions were financial simpletons, and they were not. The fixity of the subsidies was explicitly discussed in 1864 and vigorously commended. Galt insisted that the amount of the grants "should be definitely settled now and not doubled when the population of any province doubles." Such a plan would force provincial governments to exercise "a rigid and proper control" over expenditures, while any other would lead to unceasing demands upon the federal treasury.

This was the opinion which the delegates accepted, and they embodied in the Quebec resolutions a "finality clause" which declared that the subsidies were to be "in full settlement of all future demands upon the General Government for local purposes." There can be no doubt but that the declaration was literally meant and was literally given by the delegates.

The Fathers of Confederation left Quebec eminently satisfied with their labours and the reception given their resolutions in Canada was all that could have been hoped; but in the Maritimes, as is well known, there was a storm of protest and the most concerted assault fell upon the financial terms framed at Quebec. Even then neither Tupper nor Tilley ventured to appease the opposition or to calm their friends by declaring that the subsidies could be revised. They were, indeed, willing to ask that better terms be given their provinces, but they believed that the financial, like the other provisions of the resolutions, were binding.

At the opening of the year 1866 only the legislature of Canada had acted favourably upon the Quebec resolutions. Then came the elections of May and June in New Brunswick, which brought Tilley once more into power. The stage was set for progress toward union, but not through the adoption of the Quebec resolutions. Instead, first Tupper and then Tilley carried through their legislatures a resolution providing for the appointment of delegates to arrange with the Imperial government "a scheme of union" which would "effectually secure just provision for the rights and interests" of Nova Scotia and New Brunswick. This meant merely that they hoped to win some concessions, especially larger subsidies, beyond those agreed to in 1864. The anxiety manifested by Tupper and Tilley to secure alteration of the resolutions before they were enacted into law is clear evidence of their belief that thereafter change would be next to impossible.

By the deliberations at London the financial demands of Nova Scotia and New Brunswick were met in two ways. First, for them the calculation of the grant of 80 cents per capita was to be, not upon population in 1861, but upon actual population, as established by each decennial census, until it amounted to 400,000 persons. Since the populations of Nova Scotia and New Brunswick in 1861 were respectively 330,900 and 252,000, this provision gave them an extra subsidy for the future above that provided by the Quebec resolutions and above that given to Ontario and Quebec. In the second place, new subsidies – the so-called grants for the support of government – were agreed upon. These amounted to $80,000 for Ontario, $70,000 for Quebec, $60,000 for Nova Scotia, and $50,000 for New Brunswick. Clearly, upon a per capita basis, the two smaller provinces were favoured. Thus at the London conference the annual subsidy payments of the Dominion to the provinces were increased immediately by $260,000 and prospectively by a further sum which, at its maximum, would be $173,700. By these changes undoubtedly some friends had been won in Nova Scotia and New Brunswick, and although George Brown, who was not at London, attacked them bitterly through the *Globe*, the breach made in the Quebec terms did not seem to be serious. Moreover, at London, as at Quebec, the grants were declared to be "in full settlement of all future demands" and the same words were embodied in the British North America Act itself.

Beyond all dispute the policy of the Fathers of Confederation was to fix the subsidies at a minimum and to make them final and unalterable. It is, of course, one thing to show that this was their policy and quite another to assert that this policy was correct. Judged by a pragmatic test, then certainly the Fathers were wrong, because the financial terms of the British North America Act have been altered almost beyond recognition.

As everybody knows, the first alteration was made in 1869 as a result of Joseph Howe's anti-Confederation campaign. Nova Scotia was given an increase of $1,186,800 in its debt allowance and an additional subsidy of $82,700 a year for ten years. To Sir John A. Macdonald this step was justified as a way to calm the storm raised by "that pestilent fellow Howe." But the remedy was dangerous, for it set an unfortunate precedent and made a breach in the constitution not yet repaired. Provincial governments saw that pressure upon Ottawa, skillfully applied and not stopping short of the threat of secession, would secure "better terms." They have been acting upon that knowledge ever since.

If any further elements of confusion were needed in order to bedevil the situation, they were supplied within the next few years by the financial terms given Manitoba, British Columbia, and Prince Edward Island when they entered Confederation. For example, the per capita grant of 80 cents and the debt allowance given British Columbia in 1871 were based upon an *estimated* population which, even including 30,000 Indians and Chinese, was nearly twice actual population as disclosed by the census of that year. British Columbia was also given a special subsidy of $100,000 a year, ostensibly because it was to hand over a strip of land – the "railway belt" – to the Dominion; Manitoba, admitted a year earlier, had been given no such subsidy, although all its land was retained by the Dominion; and Prince Edward Island, admitted in 1873, was given a special subsidy of $45,000 a year because it had no land at all. Prince Edward Island was also given a debt allowance at a rate per capita twice that of the four original provinces. From this medley doubtless no consistent principle could have been evolved. Certainly the better terms given since have been governed by no other rule than haphazard.

The grants of better terms have been numerous and yet in many cases amazingly petty. There have been three general revisions affecting all the provinces. By the first, coming in 1873, the debt allowances were scaled up approximately 17 per cent over what they had been at union. By the second, in 1884, the debt allowances were again scaled up by about 8 1/2 per cent, with some variation from province to province. By the third, in 1907, the grants in support of government were roughly trebled, and the limit of population, upon which 80 cents per capita was to be paid, was raised to 2,500,000, while upon population in excess, payment was to be at the rate of 60 cents. Besides these general revisions, better terms of one sort or other have been conceded to individual provinces on no fewer than twenty-six occasions, and in every year since 1867 provincial governments have been ferreting out claims and stirring up local sentiment as steps toward a raid upon the federal treasury.

One result of the frequent concessions has been that subsidies are now distributed on a very different basis from that which appealed to the Fathers of Confederation. The basis which they favoured was population, and although at London there was some departure from it, nevertheless, in 1867 the per capita payments from the federal treasury to the four original provinces were not far apart. The situation at present is very different, as Table 1 illustrates.

Why has this disparity arisen? What are the reasons which have served as a warrant for better terms? If we look behind the screen of excuses thrown up by provincial governments, it will be found that the inspiration of most agitations for better terms has been fiscal need. A provincial government, either because of the relative poverty of the resources from which it can draw revenue, or because it has been extravagant, finds its budget unbalanced. It appeals to Ottawa for assistance and on numerous occasions the appeal has been favourably received. Only a few examples need be cited. When Sir Leonard Tilley, in 1884, presented a bill scaling up the provincial debt allowances, he defended it as a means by which the financial embarrassments of many provinces would be relieved. Sir Thomas White, in 1912, when giving an extra subsidy to Prince Edward Island, used a similar

Table 1
Per Capita Payments from the Dominion

| | Omitting interest on debt allowances | | | Including interest on debt allowances | |
	1864*	1867	1928-29	1867	1928-29
Nova Scotia	$ .76	$ .89	$2.70	$ .74	$2.79
New Brunswick	1.01	1.15**	2.96	.97	3.10
Ontario.	.76	.78	.79	.60	.83
Quebec	.78	.83	.81	.61	.86
Manitoba	. .	. .	2.16	. .	2.74
Saskatchewan	. .	. .	3.13	. .	3.59
Alberta	. .	. .	3.06	. .	3.68
British Columbia.	. .	. .	1.20	. .	1.25
Prince Edward Island . . .	. .	. .	5.32	. .	5.78

* Payments planned by the Quebec conference.

** The figures for New Brunswick are high because of the special grant of $63,000 given it for *ten* years.

justification. The Duncan Commission, reporting upon Maritime claims in 1926, stated explicitly that larger federal subsidies should be given because the revenues of Nova Scotia, New Brunswick, and Prince Edward Island, small provinces with a stationary population, were not a "sufficient minimum" to balance their budgets. The general adoption of the basis of fiscal need, so interpreted, would have far-reaching significance. Subsidies would become, in effect, poor relief, and the poorer a provincial government was, the larger would be the grants it should draw from the Dominion.

But although fiscal need has usually been the real, it has not always been the ostensible reason behind an agitation for better terms. Indeed, provincial governments have often presented a case in which every sort of grievance has been given a place and the whole past history of a province has been falsified in the hope of satisfying the urgent necessities of the present. The purpose behind recital of these matters, which on their face have no apparent connection with better terms, has been to give the impression that in many ways the particular province has been badly used; and besides there has been in the background the suggestion that the grievances had their price. If larger subsidies were forthcoming, the grievances would be endurable. As a result the federal government has frequently given better terms in order to buy off agitation, taking care in most instances to deal with provincial governments which conformed with it in political faith. The instability of any such arrangement is obvious. The grievances are not removed by the larger subsidy and the way is open for political opponents to charge both that a bribe has been taken and that the bribe is too small. It has always been easy to win public opinion in a province over to either belief and the outcome has been that the government has been forced to begin agitation anew, or that it has been turned out of office and a new administration, committed to a more clamorous campaign for provincial rights, has come in. The "rights" have, in time, been again commuted into better terms.

A prominent feature of many agitations has been the assertion that, in some way or other, the province in question has been the Cinderella of Confederation – that it has, because of federal policy, been put in a position of "inequality" with its sister provinces. For example, when Manitoba in 1905 discovered that both Saskatchewan and Alberta had been given a larger area than it possessed, as well as a larger subsidy in lieu of land, there was an uproar. Why, asked Premier R.P. Roblin, should Manitoba, the pioneer province of the West, be at an "inequality" with *parvenu* Saskatchewan and Alberta? The agitation went merrily on until 1912, when the government of Sir Robert Borden enlarged the boundaries of Manitoba, increased its subsidy in lieu of land, gave "arrearages" as compensation for its previous position of inferiority and, in general, placed it upon an "equality" with Saskatchewan and Alberta. For a time there was silence, but soon the Prairie provinces, with Manitoba in the lead, discovered another "inequality." In contrast to the other provinces, their public domain was held by the Dominion. To be sure, a generous subsidy in lieu of it was being received and federal land policy had been wholly in accord with the wishes of the West. But considerations of this sort were brushed aside and the Prairie provinces demanded that their public domain be returned to them and also that, after the return the subsidy in lieu of land be continued without diminution. To most people the demand seemed outrageous and, using diplomatic language, successive prime ministers – Sir Robert Borden, Mr. Arthur Meighen, Mr. Mackenzie King – so expressed themselves. Yet in 1930 the federal government conceded everything which the Prairie provinces had asked. The domain was handed over, the land subsidies were continued, Manitoba got a new award of arrearages, and Saskatchewan and Alberta were assured that later they also would receive an award.

One other instance of successful use of the "inequality" plea should be noticed. During the recent Maritime Rights agitation, the Maritimes contended that, viewing Dominion policy as a whole – with respect to subsidies, tariffs, transportation, immigration – they had been unfairly treated and that, as a consequence, they ought to be given better terms. Again results were secured: in 1927 the federal government almost doubled the subsidies which it was to pay them. Here is an argument which will never become obsolete, because some provinces will always be more prosperous than others and the prosperity or lack of it can be attributed, rightly or wrongly, to federal policy.

I come now to the prime reason for the sorry state of affairs into which this phase of federal-provincial relations has fallen. It is that most agitations for better terms have been predominantly political by-play and most grants of better terms have been of the nature of political rewards. It is not mere coincidence that, of the twenty-six concessions made since 1867 to individual provinces, only five have gone to governments definitely of an opposite political faith. Moreover, all the important concessions have been made immediately before or immediately after a federal election. Thus the first general revision of financial terms was made in 1873 at the first session of a new Parliament; the second was made in 1884 at the second session of Parliament, and the reason for the slight delay was that Sir John A. Macdonald took the step unwillingly and only after his hand was forced by his supporters from Quebec; the third was made in 1907 at the last session of Parliament. It was, furthermore, not because of the unique nature of their claims that Conservative governments in Manitoba and Prince Edward Island received larger subsidies in 1911-12 from the new Borden administration. And one need not be a chronic cynic to see a connection between the appointment of the Duncan Commission upon Maritime claims in 1926 and the fact that, by reason of disaffection in the Maritimes, the very existence of King administration was precarious; or between the passage of natural resources legislation, in 1930, eminently favourable to the Prairie provinces, and the proximity of a general election. Evidence could be multiplied, all going to show that in the majority of cases the grant of better terms has been to pay political debts or to win political support. In such case one does not expect to find principles uppermost.

What is the danger in the situation? It might, of course, be averred that any situation as bemuddled as this is bound, sooner or later, to cause trouble; but the danger is more immediate for two reasons. In the first place, the events of the past few years have aggravated the subsidy question; in the second place, for some time to come most provincial governments are going to be in desperate financial straits and they will look to Ottawa for salvation. The significance of the second reason is obvious; that of the first ought to be shown.

In 1926 the Duncan Commission on Maritime claims recommended that the federal government make important concessions, notably a large increase in subsidy, to Nova Scotia, New Brunswick, and Prince Edward Island. To many westerners these recommendations appeared outrageously excessive, and although the King administration implemented most of them, it did so in the face of much hostile feeling among its western supporters. There is, moreover, clear evidence that the westerners understood, tacitly at least, that if they did not block the grant of better terms to the Maritimes, the claims of the West would next receive favourable consideration. So it proved. In 1928 the so-called Turgeon Commission was appointed to consider the natural resources question and its recommendations, in turn, granted practically all that the Prairie provinces had ever asked. In the same year the Martin Commission, appointed to report on a claim of British Columbia with respect to railway lands, presented its recommendations and again a complete concession was made to the demands of the province. Both sets of recommendations were acted upon favourably by Parliament in 1930.

These results serve to illustrate what is an old story – that subsidy concessions to any province or group of provinces lead inevitably to concessions to other provinces. So it has always been in the past and so it will be so long as the present method is followed. It must not be thought, once concessions are made to particular provinces, that thereby their particular claims are quieted. Just the opposite is true. The demand for better terms is insatiable; it grows with its growth; and the blundering way in which claims are handled continually creates just opportunities. For example, the Duncan report advised payment of larger subsidies to Nova Scotia, New Brunswick, and Prince Edward Island; but these sums were only to be "interim" payments and it went on to recommend that the federal government give "immediate consideration" to a more complete revision of its financial relations with the Maritimes. Obviously the deliberations of the Commission, instead of providing a solution, had left the Dominion with a new subsidy question on its doorstep. Similarly, the natural resources terms did not satisfy the provincial government of Saskatchewan. It raised a constitutional question – which is also financial – concerning the right of the Dominion to hold domain, and although it was rebuffed by the courts, this in no sense means that the claim is politically extinct.

The plain truth is that each and every province has a number of dormant claims for better terms which are at least as good as those favourably received in the past. Whenever a political party in a province lacks an issue, it can patch together these fragments, wave the crazy quilt before the eyes of the electors, and stir up local feelings by a demand for provincial rights. Judged by experience no plan is more likely to receive acclaim and none is more certain of ultimate success.

Surely it is time to put a check on this procedure. In nothing have the Fathers of Confederation been more justified by events than in their belief that, at best, unconditional subsidies were a dubious financial device. It is, of course, futile to ask for absolute curtailment of subsidies in Canada just now, but further expansion on the present basis ought to be checked. Complete revision must come. As to how it should proceed I shall venture only the negative suggestion, that whatever has been done since 1867 be considered an unfit guide for future policy.

15. RAND DYCK

The Canada Assistance
Plan: The Ultimate in
Co-operative Federalism

"Co-operative federalism" is the term that has generally been used to categorize Canadian federal-provincial relations in the 1960s. Although it has been given many definitions by academics and politicians alike,[1] the concept is commonly accepted to refer to an intense degree of intergovernmental consultation, to the basic equality of the relationship, and to the decentralizing nature of the results in this period. In these respects federal-provincial relations in the 1960s were distinct from the federal dominance, the centralization, and the lesser degree of interaction which characterized Canadian federalism up to that time.

While co-operative federalism implies a spirit of co-operation, we know that federal-provincial relations in the 1960s were not entirely free of conflict. In fact, two basic models of Canadian federalism in the period could be suggested. The first, which emerges from analyses of the Canada Pension Plan, medicare, financial relations, and vocational training,[2] emphasizes the conflict and bargaining involved. The other, first noted and most thoroughly documented by Smiley, stresses harmonious executive relationships – genuine co-operation.[3] Yet to be discussed in any detail in this context is the Canada Assistance Plan, another significant product of this period and the one which probably best exemplifies the genuine co-operative federalism process.

The Canada Assistance Plan began as a means of improving existing federal-provincial public assistance programs. It was developed over a

Originally published in *Canadian Public Administration*, 19, 4 (1976). Reprinted with permission of the Institute of Public Administration of Canada.

three-year period beginning in 1963 and was designed to consolidate, extend, and replace the Unemployment Assistance Act and the three existing "categorical" programs – the Old Age Assistance, Blind, and Disabled Persons Allowances Acts. It provided for federal contributions for the first time to all provincial mothers' allowance schemes, to provincial costs in providing health services to the public assistance recipients, to rehabilitative and preventive welfare services, and to the administrative costs of such programs. The Canada Assistance Plan also shared in provincial child welfare expenditures, and, where the provinces so used it, in work activity projects and Indian welfare programs. At the option of the provinces, it could also be used to assist those working part- or full-time, if such persons continued to be in need. In return, the Plan required that provincial assistance programs be based on a needs or budget deficit test, that they incorporate an appeals procedure for recipients, and that any residence requirements for eligibility be removed.

In this article it will be seen that five aspects of the Canada Assistance Plan combined to distinguish it as perhaps the most harmonious product of the co-operative federalism period.[4] Two of these aspects concern the conception stage of the Plan; two, the formulation stage; and one has to do with its implementation. In each case brief contrasts will be drawn between CAP and other measures developed in the 1960s. Some attention will then be devoted to the conflictual aspects of the Plan, as insignificant as these were, in order to ascertain the relevance of the Simeon bargaining model to this case.

Conception

The first distinctive aspect of the Canada Assistance Plan was the nearly simultaneous recognition by both levels of government that it was a desirable move. The realization struck many of the provinces first, but their sporadic, isolated early demands produced no effect. Almost as soon as they began to demand such a measure in a concerted, forceful manner, however, the federal level indicated its willingness to take action.[5]

It is not difficult to account for the provincial demands. They were primarily based on the desire for greater federal financial assistance. To them it seemed that obvious gaps remained in federal cost-sharing under the Unemployment Assistance Act: mothers' allowance payments, the cost of medical care of persons on social assistance, and the administrative costs of welfare programs were all borne entirely by the provinces. They were generally anxious to have this financial burden shared by Ottawa.

That the federal response to these demands was so prompt and generous can be attributed to a variety of political and bureaucratic factors. At the official level, health and welfare administrators were first anxious to help develop more effective provincial welfare programs which could be achieved with more federal money combined with high federal standards.

Secondly, they recognized the need for a unification of the administration of unemployment assistance and categorical assistance programs which could result from a new initiative of this kind. In the third place, they looked forward to experiment with new concepts in dealing with the chronically unemployed and to modernize other aspects of welfare administration. Finally, Indian Affairs officials hoped to develop improved welfare services for the native population through a new co-operative effort with the provinces.

The federal political response also involved several different factors. One was the realization that after the adoption of the Canada Pension Plan there would need to be certain changes made to related welfare measures. In its initial stages, CAP was not seen as a major innovation, but merely as a "tidying up" exercise in the wake of the CPP. Subsidiary to this motive was the Pearson government's general willingness to proceed with new ventures in the welfare field – "to complete the welfare state" as the Prime Minister sometimes put it. Thirdly, the Pearson cabinet, especially in its first few years, was particularly sensitive to provincial demands and could hardly bring itself to reject one which was expressed with such force and unanimity and which at first did not appear to be costly. Later, as the scope of CAP expanded, so did the federal cabinet's appetite for reform in this area. The Canada Assistance Plan fell neatly within the Pearson-Kent conception of a Canadian "War on Poverty," under which guise the cabinet was persuaded to accept a measure of considerable breadth.

The second distinctive aspect about the conception of CAP was the degree to which both levels of government were involved in establishing the basic outline of the Plan. Once the decision had been made to go ahead, the Plan was deliberately developed on a joint basis and a concensus on its main components was easily and almost spontaneously achieved.

What the Plan should contain was first discussed by federal and provincial welfare officials, chiefly deputy ministers, in February, 1964. The participants at this initial meeting were unanimous in the belief that the federal government should begin to cost-share provincial mothers' allowance payments. On most other issues there was widespread agreement, coupled with a certain amount of indecision.[6] Being left to such officials to discuss the basic content of the Plan in the first instance, it is not surprising, perhaps, that a large degree of harmony prevailed. As Smiley has convincingly established:

> federal-provincial administrative relationships have been harmonious and constructive to the extent that they have been dominated by program specialists ... the attitudes, procedures and values common to particular groups of program specialists ... provide common standards to which officials from federal and provincial levels defer.[7]

Such was clearly the situation here, as welfare officials from both levels of government together discussed the form of a joint program that would improve the entire welfare system and which, in the process, would reflect their professional norms.

To a large extent, the norms to which they were all deferring had been set down clearly by the Canadian Welfare Council in its 1958 document, "Social Security for Canada." In that statement, to which many of the officials at the 1964 meeting contributed, the CWC laid down a blueprint for welfare reform which the eventual Canada Assistance Plan reflected almost word for word.

Federal-provincial co-operation was also facilitated by the mutual acquaintanceship, often friendship, of many of the participants at the meeting. In addition to their participation in CWC activities, prior intergovernmental interaction and old social work "school ties" put most of the deputy ministers and other officials on a first-name basis.

A final aspect of the joint conception of the Plan, and another measure of the influence of the "buureaucratic elite" in the welfare field, was the rapidity with which welfare *ministers* absorbed the norms and attitudes of their departments. After the deputy ministers returned home to further consider the issues raised and to discuss them with their political "lords and masters,"[8] the welfare ministers met and readily approved the basic features of the Plan meetings in May, 1964, and April, 1965.

To reinforce the distinctiveness of the conception of the Canada Assistance Plan in terms of both timing and design, reference can be made to some of the other federal-provincial measures developed in the same period. In the case of adult occupational training, for example, Dupré demonstrates that the new plan was sprung on the provinces by the federal government when the former were not conscious that any significant change was needed. He also documents a clash of two very different "grand designs," an economists' design developed in Ottawa in isolation from an educationists' design formulated in Toronto. Somewhat similarly, the Canada Pension Plan and medicare were precipitated upon the provinces by the federal government at a time and in a form that some provinces at least found unacceptable. That this process of joint conception was distinctive can also been seen in contrasting CAP with the Unemployment Assistance Act, predecessor to CAP, which evolved ten years previously. At that time, in a period of "federal dominance" prior to co-operative federalism, the federal government was responding to provincial demands, but then designed a measure unilaterally and presented it to provinces almost as a *fait accompli*.[9]

Formulation

In the formulation stage of the Canada Assistance Plan, there were also two striking features which reveal a particularly congenial process of co-operative federalism at work. The first of these was the hyper-sensitivity of federal officials to provincial demands for flexibility. It must be remembered that CAP was a shared-cost program developed at precisely the time that both the Quebec administration and the federal Liberal government had declared themselves opposed to any additional measures of this kind. It was only to be expected, therefore, that certain federal officials would be highly sensitive to Quebec's reaction to the proposal and anxious to avoid the strict federal standards and controls which were the marks of most earlier joint programs.

Quebec raised the issue of contracting out of CAP as soon as serious discussion of the measure began, and continued to voice its intention to do so throughout the formulation process. Similarly, but in a less extreme way, other provinces demanded more flexibility than under predecessor programs. Federal welfare officials were not particularly forthcoming in reaction to these provincial attitudes. They believed that to achieve maximum effectiveness, fairly stringent federal standards and controls would have to be incorporated. Instead, it was officials of the Department of Finance, the Treasury Board, and the Privy Council Office who were most concerned about this problem. A.W. Johnston, assistant deputy minister of finance, and R.B. Bryce, the deputy minister, were the main protagonists of this point of view.

The prevailing philosophy of the Finance Department was that such measures should be as flexible as possible and contain as few conditions as necessary – only enough to satisfy Parliament and to maintain an element of federal financial control. This attitude resulted partly from a new recognition at the federal level that the provinces were getting stronger and better staffed and managed all the time, and partly from the increasing resentment expressed by the provinces about inflexibility in joint programs. Johnson, an ex-deputy minister at the provincial level, did not feel it was up to the federal government to force reform on the provinces. These sentiments were reiterated by officials of the Federal-Provincial Relations section of the Privy Council Office. The Prime Minister's policy secretary, Tom Kent, also urged the strongest supporters of CAP and welfare reform among the federal bureaucractic and political elites to adopt a more flexible attitude toward the provinces.

While most provincial officials responded appreciatively to the maximum flexibility which Johnson, Bryce, and Kent were offering them, others at the provincial level valued high federal standards. Such standards were regarded by some provincial deputy ministers as a device to achieve progress within the province, progress normally retarded by conservative cabinet ministers. In the end, however, flexibility carried the day.

The second aspect of the formulation stage that marks the Canada Assistance Plan as perhaps the ultimate in co-operative federalism concerned the extensive consultation which took place among the federal and provincial officials on the details of the Plan. Judy LaMarsh, the federal welfare minister at the time, accurately predicted that "detailed technical consideration will be the key to success in developing this program."[10]

Federal officials were initially concerned about how far they could go in revealing their intentions to the provinces. Later, they decided to discuss the measure on the basis of the instructions they had drawn up for the use of the Department of Justice in the eventual drafting of the new legislation. Federal political authorization of these drafting instructions was apparently considered unnecessary.

A closely knit three-man team was formed in the new Canada Assistance Plan Division of the federal Welfare Department to visit each province. This group usually spent two or three days in the provincial capital, engaged in fairly intensive discussions in a "semi-informal" atmosphere. The session lasted all day long with the provincial deputy minister of welfare and a varying number of other officials present. In some cases the provincial minister was visited briefly, but this was only in the nature of a courtesy call or as part of generous provincial hospitality. The officials went through the drafting instructions in each province, point by point, acquainting provincial authorities with federal thinking and plans, getting feedback from the provinces on their thoughts, and then working this into the consensus of the overall plan. They would ask, for example: "If CAP were written in this way, what would be your province's reaction to it?" "Do you feel that this provision would adequately cover your situation?" "If you foresee problems, what are they?"

There were basically three kinds of consultation involved in this process. The first area was where federal officials willingly enlarged their original proposals in order to accommodate under the Plan unanticipated worthwhile provincial programs and practices. For example, on the question of health care for welfare recipients, the new measure was expanded to cover practices and agencies already involved in this area in the provinces, even if administered by a health rather than a welfare department.

A second area was where federal officials reluctantly conceded to provincial objections or demands. While the hope had been, for example, to avoid identifying specific causes in defining a "person in need," provincial resistance to this open-endedness led to a compromise on this definition, as follows: "a person who, by reason of inability to obtain employment, loss of the principal family provider, illness, disability, age or other cause of any kind acceptable to the provincial authority, if found to be unable ... to provide adequately for himself ...." On this set of issues, then, federal officials were conciliatory, but did not entirely abandon their original objectives.

A third kind of consultation consisted of a simple exchange of information. To illustrate, federal officials told their provincial counterparts what they meant by a "work activity project"; the latter agreed to supply a list of all welfare institutions in the province to the federal department.

The extent of such intimate federal-provincial consultation prior to the final drafting of the measure was highly unusual. Also extraordinary was a supplementary special trip which federal officials made to Nova Scotia in order to study a typical welfare system in detail and to determine exactly how federal proposals would work in practice. Less surprising, but equally conducive to the success of the Plan, a process identical to that described was followed on the drafting of the regulations and the agreements under the Plan. The same three-man team criss-crossed the country on these two other occasions before the regulations were issued and before the federal-provincial agreements were signed.

It is not surprising, in the light of all this consultation, to find that the reaction of provincial officals was highly laudatory. It was said that the Plan was developed in the "very best of co-operation and assistance"; the federal officials involved were called "princes of men of great personal integrity and ability"; and the Plan was termed the result of the "best arrangements of any federal-provincial program that ever came into being."[11]

It may be wondered, however, why the federal government was willing to invest so much time and effort in this consultative process with the provinces. To this question there appear to be three main answers: jurisdictional, informational, and personal.

The federal level trod lightly in dealing with the provinces over CAP for several jurisdictional reasons. As mentioned above, Quebec was feeling highly sensitive about its own jurisdiction in the welfare field, and was at the same time arousing the consciousness of other provinces. Both the Quebec and federal governments had declared their opposition to new shared-cost programs. Furthermore, there had been general provincial criticism expressed about the rigidity of predecessor measures. Extensive provincial consultation was therefore considered essential because the federal government was expanding its role in an area of provincial jurisdiction.

A second reason had to do with the limited experience and information available at the federal level. To design a measure that would intimately affect ten distinctive provincial welfare systems obviously necessitated close consultation with the directors of those systems. Moreover, in the attempt to introduce entirely new concepts into welfare programs, the advice of provincial administrators was highly advantageous. Such interaction became all the more essential given the lack of practical experience in the delivery aspect of welfare programs on the part of federal officials, who sometimes referred to themselves as "babes in the woods."[12]

On a personal level, federation officials were already well acquainted with their provincial counterparts and realized that the success of the new Plan would depend upon future congenial relations between them. Besides hoping to influence provincial actions in certain directions, they wanted to help the provinces gear up to the Plan and generally to provide a means for the fullest mutual reaction before either side was cemented into position. For these reasons, then, extensive consultation in the formulation stage was considered the appropriate, advisable, and courteous course to follow.

What has been said about the formulation of the Canada Assistance Plan shows it to be a classic example of Smiley's description of "executive federalism." It probably goes a step further, however, than even he has documented previously. Again, the distinctiveness of CAP when contrasted with the other prominent federal-provincial measures of the day, is quite striking.

Dupré demonstrates, for example, that in the adult training program it was only after the clash of the Ottawa and Ontario "grand designs" that federal concessions were made. Similarly, the Canadian Pension Plan was salvaged by last-minute secret summit diplomacy with Quebec only after repeated clashes of grand designs in this field. The federal level showed no reluctance to reform provincial medicare programs which did not comply with Ottawa's conditions. In that case, provincial objections were simply ignored, for the most part, until the financial incentives involved forced the provinces into submission.

Implementation

The extensive federal-provincial interaction out of which the Plan emerged provided a model and a disposition for a continuation of such intimate intergovernmental consultation once CAP was adopted and implemented. This consultation took the form of daily contact between provincial officials and federal consultants and field representatives, less frequent reference of problems to federal head office personnel, and periodic meetings of ministers and deputy ministers of welfare. In this respect, too – in the harmony of such contacts – CAP was distinctive among the federal-provincial measures of the period.

Under the Canada Assistance Plan one or more federal field representatives were appointed to be located in each provincial capital. These officials usually occupied an office in the midst of the provincial welfare department and were in constant communication with provincial welfare administrators. They had two main functions. One was to control the operation of the Plan to ensure that the province carried out its responsibilities, met federal conditions, and made valid claims on the federal treasury. The other was a liaison function between the federal and provincial departments, to advise both levels on issues raised, to report on current or expected developments in both directions, and to solve or minimize potential problems. These field officers were more than financial auditors, and were not necessarily concerned to minimize federal contributions. In many instances they showed a province where cost-sharing was available but was not being claimed. The good relations they developed with the provinces often led to invitations to attend provincial welfare meetings.

At the same time, the federal department appointed consultants in some fifteen welfare fields such as child welfare and community development. They were available to travel to any province to offer advice on problems in their area of expertise. Without exception, the provinces found their services very useful.

While small problems could generally be solved through the use of consultants and field representatives, however, some issues required the attention of more senior personnel. Here, too, the contact was frequent, immediate, and friendly. Finally, the issues which still remained unresolved were brought to the attention of the federal minister or deputy minister, who discussed them at federal-provincial meetings at those levels. Ministers of welfare met five times between 1968 and 1971, and deputy ministers an additional four times, to deal primarily with matters relating to CAP. By 1971 the program was operating with virtually no significant problems.

This congeniality of the implementation process contrasts sharply with Dupré's account of adult occupational training. In that case, the federal level had a much larger staff in the field – primarily the Canada Manpower Centre managers and economists. While the total number of federal-provincial contacts may thus have been greater than in the case of CAP, they were invariably indifferent to antagonistic in tone. Much of the contrast between the two sets of relationships can be explained by the Smiley conception of shared norms among officials. Federal and provincial social workers and other welfare administrators – even financial auditors connected with welfare – were able to work harmoniously with each other; on the other hand, federal economists and manpower officials shared few norms with provincial educators and educational administrators, whether located in provincial ministries or in institutions in the field. It is also important to note, however, that the basic orientation of federal and provincial programs in adult training was very different, while in welfare the orientation was essentially identical.

Areas of Conflict

This somewhat idyllic account of spontaneous unanimity on most aspects of the Canada Assistance Plan should not obscure the fact that certain areas of federal-provincial conflict did arise from time to time. These can be found in one basic feature of its conception, in two main facets of its formulation, and in two principal issues in its implementation.

As far as the general conception of CAP was concerned, the only conflict of any magnitude developed with respect to Quebec's desire to contract out. Even this presented no major problem once the federal government clarified its thinking on what "contracting out" meant, in the form of the Established Programs (Interim Arrangements) Act of 1965. Under that Act a province could contract out of the four predecessor measures to CAP and ultimately the same provisions applied to CAP itself. If this issue was not long one of substance, however, it did provide the Quebec delegation at many welfare conferences with an opportunity to emphasize its sovereignty in the welfare field, to denounce new federal inititatives, and to insist on alternative financing arrangements being written into the Plan. The federal decision to accede to the contracting-out demand rendered most of this rhetoric unnecessary.

Two more substantive issues arose in the formulation stage of the Plan: child welfare services and the cost-sharing formula, although even these were not clear-cut federal-provincial disputes. Throughout the formulation stage, the extent of federal cost-sharing envisaged in the child welfare field had been ambiguous. Once it became clear that federal contributions would be limited, a number of provinces demanded more. Ontario, acting on its own, and British Columbia, trying to construct a provincial alliance on the issue, managed to get the federal level to review the extent of shareability in this field and eventually to expand federal contributions considerably. Here was a logical request, unopposed at the provincial level,[13] and not meeting any particular resistance at the federal level, once the demand was clearly made.

On the cost-sharing formula, the initial assumption among all participants was that a straight 50-50 federal-provincial division of costs would be adopted. As time went on, however, the Atlantic provinces began to see that such a cost division would leave all provinces in their existing relative condition. Led by Nova Scotia, and particularly by its deputy minister of welfare, the Atlantic provinces began to demand a differential sharing formula based on provincial need. This demand was put most forcefully at the Welfare Ministers' Conference in January, 1966. The federal level did not respond so readily in this case, however, as there were two strong opponents of the request. On the one hand, the richer provinces were opposed to any distinction in the cost-sharing formula from one province to another. On the other hand, the federal Department of Finance was adamant that regional disparities would be dealt with through general equalization payments rather than by differential formulas in specific joint programs. The Federal Welfare Department's intervention on behalf of the Atlantic provinces was to no avail, as the Finance Department insisted on the 50-50 division of costs across the board.

The two main disputes that developed in the first few years of implementation of the Plan were more genuinely federal-provincial ones. These conflicts centred on appeal procedures and on paying social assistance to persons on strike. The Act required each province to establish an appeals procedure for dissatisfied welfare recipients within one year of signing a CAP agreement. Although most provinces had some kind of appeal system even prior to CAP, federal officials did not regard these as adequate in most cases. They soon became impatient with provincial inaction in improving them and made known their unhappiness to provincial officials and ministers on several occasions. Later, they issued guidelines on the kind of appeal system they considered adequate. It was only after a good deal of further prodding that all provinces adopted satisfactory appeal procedures.

In the case of persons on strike, the federal viewpoint was that everyone in need was entitled to assistance, regardless of the cause of need. In several provinces or municipalities, however, authorities refused to give assistance to those in need on account of strike action. This refusal was based on a reluctance "to interfere in labour-management disputes" as well, of course, as on a desire to save money. After pressure from federal officials and upon the personal intervention of the minister on occasion, provincial and municipal authorities have usually softened their stand, at least when the issue obtained real prominence.

Relevance of the Bargaining Model

Up to this point it has been suggested that the policy development involved in the Canada Assistance Plan can best be understood in terms of Smiley's discussion of shared norms among program administrators. The main alternative – the bargaining model – appears to be less relevant because of the small degree of conflict involved in this case. Nevertheless, it is instructive to apply a bargaining model to the areas of dispute involved, however small their proportions. Such a model, as outlined by Simeon in his *Federal-Provincial Diplomacy*, for example, characteristically emphasizes the issues, resources, and strategies that make up the bargaining process. Having dealt with the few significant issues of conflict which arose under CAP, we may turn directly to resources and strategies.

The main political resources involved in the Canada Assistance Plan were legal authority, money, and expertise. Because it was agreed that public assistance was primarily a provincial responsibility, few federal controls on the provinces were ever proposed. Moreover, most of the remainder gave way under the combined resistance of Quebec, some other provinces, and federal Finance officials. The very significant role of Quebec in this regard hardly requires further comment. Depending heavily on that province for its support, and being deeply committed to keeping Quebec within Confederation, the Pearson government was quick to respond to the demands of the Quebec provincial government, especially on issues it could claim were within provincial jurisdiction. It thus readily acceded to Quebec's demand to opt out.

Against the provincial resource of jurisdiction, the federal government held the power of the purse. Federal fiscal capacity, based on its unlimited powers of taxation and its domination of joint tax fields, was an important resource in dealing with what were, in most cases, impecunious provinces. The federal cabinet had the last word on which new services or programs it would help to finance, though provincial demands were rather restrained and it hardly had to exercise this ultimate power.

As far as provincial size and wealth are concerned, in this connection, two points of view have been expressed. Is it the larger, wealthier provinces or the smaller, poorer ones which carry more weight in federal-provincial negotiations? Simeon suggests that the latter is often the case; that "wealth in some circumstances may be a positive disadvantage in ... negotiations."

> One of the strongest arguments the provinces can make in financial discussions is their great need for funds. For the Maritimes the need is obvious, and ... Ottawa is strongly committed to help alleviate the need.[14]

As far as CAP is concerned, however, it was the other point of view that held sway. Repeated pleas from the Atlantic provinces, supported by federal welfare officials, for a differential sharing forumula based on provincial need were overridden by an intransigent Finance Department supported by some of the larger provinces.

A third political resource is information, skill, or expertise. It has now been widely accepted in Canada that one of the reasons for federal dominance in the 1945-60 period was the skill of the Ottawa bureaucracy (and to some extent, politicians) compared to that of the provinces. By the early 1960s the average provincial civil service was of increasing competence and in the welfare field almost every province had at least a deputy minister and a few officials with considerable training and experience. At the same time, the federal officials immediately involved were, despite impressive credentials, operating somewhat outside their area of expertise. None was familiar with the nuts and bolts of an operating welfare program. In this situation, with experience heavily on the provincial side, it is not surprising that a large number of original federal ideas were modified in the process of consulting the provinces as to their practicality.

It is sometime suggested that solidarity is another political resource of some importance. In the case of the Canada Assistance Plan, however, beyond the original consensus on the part of all those involved to go ahead with the measure, this factor was of little account. There were divisions both within the federal side and among the provinces on the questions of the conditions to be required of the provinces and of the sharing formula. The eventual unanimity of the provinces on the child welfare matter, however, did provoke federal acquiescence, even though the expenditure of additional federal funds was involved.

On the question of strategies and tactics, Simeon suggests that these are used covertly, that participants in federal-provincial negotiations claim to engage in "discussion" rather than "bargaining."[15] Few if any of those involved in the development of CAP regarded it as a bargaining process, but certain strategies and tactics can be detected, at least at the provincial level.

First of all, there was the provincial alliance. This strategy was used on two occasions in particular. One was the widespread interaction of Atlantic welfare ministers and deputy ministers out of which came the united front against the 50-50 sharing formula. On the child welfare issue, British Columbia tried to develop a common provincial point of view before going into the January, 1966, Minister's Conference. Otherwise, provinces were content to put forward their views on an individual basis to federal-provincial conferences or in discussions with the federal team of officials.

A second provincial tactic that can be identified is therefore simple preparedness, having information at hand, or at least giving the appearance of being prepared. Quebec's formal written briefs at federal-provincial conferences, for example, were first admired and then imitated by certain other provinces which had previously made only an informal, verbal presentation.

This is closely related to a third provincial tactic used with great effect in this development: taking a parochial point of view. More accurately, it was to ensure that the other side was fully aware of the province's local policies, practices, and concerns. It was precisely this knowledge of local problems and procedures that the cross-country tours of federal officials were designed to achieve. Given their flexible attitude in most cases, the more local peculiarities they were informed of, the more general and all-encompassing the final proposal became.

A final strategy involved in the federal-provincial aspects of the measure was the threat. Though it could not be used effectively in this situation as in the three cases Simeon deals with, Quebec could and did threaten to have no part of the Plan unless an opting-out provision was included and federal conditions were left virtually impotent.

Alliances, preparedness, parochialism, and threats can therefore be identified as provincial strategies and tactics used in the development of the Plan. While the first and third of these are somewhat at odds with Simeon, it must always be recalled within what a restricted scope they were used.

Once the Act was passed and federal-provincial agreements signed, there were minor modifications in this pattern of resources and strategies. The Act, regulations, and agreements were themselves resources on the part of the federal government since the provinces were now committed to meeting the federal conditions established. The power to contribute or withhold funds continued to be a significant federal political resource and this was now complemented by the vast amount of expertise amassed at the federal level in the process of formulating and implementing the Plan.

The provinces' chief resource remained their legal authority in the welfare field. In spite of the agreement they had signed, they could continue to complain, where it suited their purposes to do so, of federal interference in an area of provincial jurisdiction. As at the federal level, most provinces were also continually increasing their stock bureaucratic skill.

In respect to strategies and tactics in the implementation process, these were for the most part very civilized and unspectacular. Both federal and provincial officials made use of persuasion as they engaged in courteous negotiation. On rare occasions the federal minister threatened to cut off contributions, but no one took such threats very seriously.

Conclusion

While it was not without elements of conflict and bargaining in several minor respects, the development of the Canada Assistance Plan was undoubtedly the most harmonious major product of federal-provincial relations in the 1960s. CAP stands in sharp contrast in this respect to the other significant federal-provincial initiatives of the period: the Canada Pension Plan, medicare, financial relations, constitutional review, and vocational training. Three main reasons for this contrast can be advanced.

The first relates to the dominant place which the norms of program administrators occupied in its development. Federal and provincial deputy ministers of welfare essentially determined the scope of the measure in the first instance and they and their leading officials went on to play the major role in formulating its details. A measure of this magnitude naturally requires a large degree of political input as well, but this is a case in which ministers of welfare and cabinets in general were usually willing to go along with the recommendations of their advisers.

A second reason for the harmonious nature of CAP's development is that the initiative came largely from the provinces, rather than from the federal government. While the federal level almost simultaneously arrived at the same realization of its need, there was no "grand design" unilaterally created in Ottawa. Instead, the federal government was prepared to provide what the provinces demanded in the wake of the Canada Pension Plan and even anxious to take action along these lines as part of the "War on Poverty."

The attitude of federal officials toward the provinces is the third major distinguishing feature of the Canada Assistance Plan's development. Partly because of friendship ties, partly because of previous provincial experience, and partly because of provincial objections (Quebec in particular) to the old-style shared-cost programs, federal officials dealt with their provincial counterparts in a most conciliatory way. While welfare officials wished to impose certain standards on the provinces, they were also anxious to develop a flexible, workable program. Finance and Privy Council officials were even more conciliatory and insisted on keeping federal conditions to a minimum.

These three factors were embodied in the doctrine of co-operative federalism as espoused by the Liberal Party of the period. The Canada Assistance Plan therefore stands as a product of the co-operative federalism process as it was officially enunciated. The surprise is perhaps not so much that it reflected such genuine co-operation as that so few other major federal-provincial programs developed in the 1960s were consistent with stated political objectives.

Notes

1. See, for example, "The Liberal Program (1962)," reproduced in D.O. Carrigan, comp., *Canadian Party Platforms 1867-1968* (Toronto, 1968), 262; Jean-Luc Pepin, "Cooperative Federalism," *Canadian Forum* (December, 1964); and D.V. Smiley, "Public Administration and Canadian Federalism," *Canadian Public Administration*, 7, 3 (September, 1964).

2. The analytical model as well as much documentation is provided by Richard Simeon, *Federal-Provincial Diplomacy* (Toronto, 1971). J. Stefan Dupré *et al.* have furnished a case study teeming with conflict in their study of adult occupational training, *Federalism and Policy Development* (Toronto, 1973).

3. Among his voluminous work on the subject, see in particular, D.V. Smiley, "Public Administration and Canadian Federalism," and Smiley, *Constitutional Adaptation and Canadian Federalism since 1945* (Ottawa, 1970).

4. Parts of this article are extracted from my Ph.D. thesis, "Poverty and Policy-making in the 1960s: The Canada Assistance Plan" (Queen's University, 1973). The material on which it is based includes interviews with a large number of federal and provincial policy-makers and most of the confidential documentation involved, courtesy of certain broad-minded public servants.

5. The early, sporadic provincial demands addressed to the Diefenbaker government were not given much response. The more forceful demands made upon the Pearson government led to federal action for reasons noted below.

6. *Meeting of the Federal-Provincial Working Group on Welfare Programs*, Ottawa, February 14 and 15, 1964.

7. Smiley, "Public Administration and Canadian Federalism," 378.

8. An expression used frequently by the deputy ministers at their meeting.

9. Dyck, "Poverty and Policy-making in the 1960s."

10. Position Statements of the Minister of National Health and Welfare on the Agenda Items of the Conference of Ministers of Welfare, April 8 and 9, 1965.

11. Expressions used in interviews with provincial welfare officials.

12. Interviews with federal welfare officials.

13. Except by a few provinces which, while anxious for additional funds, were reluctant to press for them in the fear that this would jeopardize some of the gains already made.

14. Simeon, *Federal-Provincial Diplomacy*, 219.

15. *Ibid.*, 229.

16. NEIL CAPLAN

Some Factors Affecting
the Resolution of a
Federal-Provincial
Conflict

I

Federal-provincial conflicts may be seen to pass through a number of stages, at each of which resolution of the dispute may or may not emerge. When a settlement is ultimately reached, making successive phases unnecessary, we then have a crude measure of the effectiveness of the available means for conflict-resolution within the federal system, namely, in terms of an early or late settlement. A second such measurement involves ascertaining whether federal and provincial actors succeeded in resolving the dispute with a minimum loss of mutual goodwill.[1]

The offshore mineral rights dispute in Canada has been with us as an open confrontation between governments since 1960. A *de facto* claim by British Columbia in 1949 was challenged by proposed (but soon abandoned) federal legislation in 1957;[2] an effective "counter-claim" came in the form of federal orders-in-council in 1960 and 1961.[3] "Consultations" took place by correspondence between 1960 and 1962,[4] and "negotiations" were attempted in 1963 and 1964.[5] Finally, in 1965, the federal government, by-passing provincial reluctance and even hostility, submitted specific legal questions relating to British Columbia offshore areas to the Supreme Court of Canada.[6] The Court's advisory opinion handed down on November 7, 1967, was unanimous, favouring the federal argument on all five questions asked.[7], Some optimism has since been voiced, suggesting that fruitful negotiations may soon take place to work out an equitable accommodation with the provinces, but this stage has yet to be reached.[8]

Reprinted by permission from *Canadian Journal of Political Science* (1969).

The present article focuses on some of the factors that shaped the outcomes of the various confrontations between the two levels of government on the offshore mineral rights issue. Some of these factors seem to be (a) the relative balance of power, (b) the prevailing beliefs operating on both sets of actors, (c) the personalities involved, and (d) the role of certain private interests which interact with each level of government.[9]

A. The Relative Strength of the Contestants

The history of the federal-provincial conflict over offshore mineral rights suggests the need to investigate the fundamental factor of the relative strength of the parties involved. Just as the final outcome of any conflict will reflect the unequal strength of the opponents,[10] so too will intermediate confrontations be a function of this factor. The closer the contestants are to being nearly equal in strength, the less likely will one easily predominate over the other, and the more likely will a deadlock develop or persist.

In the case of the offshore dispute, the following hypothesis is suggested: After the post-war era of "co-operative" – but clearly centralizing – federalism, there has emerged a "co-operative" – but relatively decentralizing – pattern of relationships. In the process of this transition, the relative strength of the two levels of government has been altered, but not without causing ambiguities in the perceptions of the new balance of power.[11] These ambiguities have caused each party to misjudge and underestimate the strength and resolve the other, while at the same time rendering its own position more inflexible. The anxiety not to "lose ground" during a very uncertain and crucial period transformed the stands taken on this single issue into a more general test of strength for each level of government.[12]

This explanation is more readily understood in the light of an historical outline. Both before and since the advent of "co-operative federalism" we could see a "balanced tension"[13] in Canadian federalism, pulling in the direction of either centralization or decentralization.[14] Judicial interpretation by the Privy Council swung the "pendulum" from its initial position of would-be centralization to one of decentralization, especially from 1896 to 1937.[15] The initial period of "co-operative federalism" (1939-60), on the other hand, was based on wartime emergency, post-war reconstruction, and an increasingly sophisticated federal bureaucracy;[16] not unnaturally, this period has been labelled a "one-way street" toward greater centralization.[17] However, the resurgence of the provinces in the 1960s[18] has made less clear which level of government is profiting more from co-operating with the other in the "grey areas."[19] Many are of the view that it is now the provinces that have become dominant.[20]

Against this background it is not difficult to see why the actual pattern of the offshore rights dispute was characterized by frequent deadlocks.[21] Following the federal "counter-claim" of 1960, and the absence of legal certainty, both sides were able to consolidate strong *de facto* positions, with neither party strong enough to intimidate the other into backing down. The federal government was confident in the soundness of its legal claim,[22] while British Columbia felt sure that its prior occupation and ability to rally the other provinces should have convinced Ottawa to withdraw its claim. To agree to federal suggestions for an interim arrangement for the issuance of permits, "without prejudice to their respective claims," would have been tantamount to a provincial admission that there existed some doubt as to ownership.[23]

When both sides finally recognized the need for *an* agreement, each insisted that the final settlement should be realized only through *the* particular procedure which gave it the best advantage.[24] Neither side was able to convince the other to accept amicably the procedure it preferred. Each party was so sure of victory on its own terms that it stood firm, waiting for the other to capitulate. The federal government knew that, as a last resort, it could submit a reference to the Supreme Court of Canada, with or without provincial agreement (although the former was to be preferred). The provinces, on the other hand, were certain that under the guise of "negotiations" their united front, amid much publicity, would prevail to force the federal government into making a "political" transfer of its claim to offshore mineral rights. The deadlock was ultimately broken, but not without the loss of the little goodwill that remained.

B. Prevailing Beliefs: The Mystique of "Co-operative Federalism"

In any period there will tend to be certain widespread views on what is "right" and what is "wrong," on what behaviour is acceptable or "legitimate," and what actions are frowned upon as "illegitimate." The era of "co-operative federalism" has developed its own particular set of prevailing beliefs, chief among which is the often uncritical veneration of "negotiation." Some politicians, many commentators, and the public generally have shown themselves to be "true believers" in this mystique. But an examination of this ethos as it applies to the offshore mineral rights dispute reveals that deadlock and mistrust often resulted from a lack of real understanding, and occasional deliberate misuse, of this set of prevailing beliefs.

In contrast with the hypothesis suggested above, most commentators have taken a different view. Edwin R. Black interprets events as demonstrating that, "the Pearson administration, having failed to win its case through political negotiation, decided it had nothing to lose by trying a reference to the [Supreme] court."[25] Ronald Atkey shares a similar viewpoint: "The justices of the court will be forced to answer questions which the federal government was unable to resolve by political negotiation with the provinces.[26] Both commentators agree that, "in recent years, competing levels of government in Canada ... have exhibited a reluctance to take their important revenue and resource conflicts to court";[27] but, from this descriptive statement they leap to the *prescriptive* implication that governments should (and can) always resolve their disputes out of court.

To these observers the offshore mineral rights conflict is a deviant case in this respect. Furthermore, the implication is clear that it was simply the federal government's "weakness at the bargaining table" that forced the issue out of the "political arena" – where it belongs – and into the laps of the jurists:[28] "The breakdown of political negotiations should not automatically, or at the whim of only one of the adversaries, render a controversy of this nature justiciable before a court of law, particularly the highest court in the nation.... Surely, then, this is one controversy that should be resolved in the political arena of Dominion-provincial negotiation.... One can only wonder why Prime Minister Lester Pearson chose to stall negotiations by going to court in the first place."[29]

In addition to the exaggerated distinction between the political and the judicial, the above interpretations may be challenged for their naive understanding of the concept of "negotiation," and for the unwarranted assumption that *real* negotiations ever had, in fact, an opportunity to take place. Just as in international relations the "pacific settlement of disputes" has become a norm making negotiations a universal ideal, so too has the mystique of "co-operative federalism" elevated negotiation to a pedestal in federal-provincial relations. Iklé wisely observes that, "Given the prevalence of [the] views [ascribing so many beneficial affects to negotiation], governments are reluctant to refuse negotiation, no matter how unlikely or undesirable an agreement. They fear that such refusal would impair the goodwill of other groups important to them – their own parliament, the public.... These audiences may judge quite superficially in praising those willing to negotiate and censuring those who refuse ... [and] may have only a vague notion as to what negotiating means and how it relates to the merits of the issue."[30]

The applicability of this observation to interpretations of the offshore rights dispute is glaringly evident. As in the case of the term "co-operative federalism" itself,[31] the word "negotiation" has been invoked indiscriminately by commentators and participants alike; in the latter case, this uncritical usage may be held responsible for delaying an ultimate settlement. Iklé defines "negotiation" as "a process in which explicit proposals are put forward ostensibly for the purpose of reaching an agreement on an exchange or on the realization of a common interest when conflicting interests are present.[32] Maurice Duverger describes the process as follows: "The conflicting parties gather round a table and, *at the cost of mututal concessions*, attempt to define the terms of an agreement which will take their respective interests into account."[33]

It seems clear from the definitions that only one of the necessary ingredients for negotiation – that is, conflicting interests – was present in the offshore mineral rights dispute. The continual absence of a second prerequisite – the existence of even minimal "negotiables" or potential concessions – rendered dubious any reference to the federal-provincial confrontations of July, 1963, June, 1964, October, 1964, and July, 1965, as "negotiations." On July 26, 1963, British Columbia officials came to Ottawa, where it was decided that (a) British Columbia would prepare a statement of its legal claim[34] for Ottawa's consideration and reciprocal reply, while (b) the federal government would draft a suggestion for some administrative arrangement, without prejudice to jurisdictional rights, which would minimize the difficulties being faced by oil companies.[35] It had been expected that the ministers responsible would have met again, having completed the agreed exchanges, in October or November that year. However, the meeting was twice postponed, while some friction developed owing to the federal government's delay in providing British Columbia with a reciprocal statement of its legal position.[36] When federal and provincial ministers did meet in 1964, their joint press release of June 15 seemed to indicate that both sides had agreed on the necessity of a reference to the Supreme Court of Canada,[37] but the required cabinet endorsement did not come from Victoria. The federal-provincial conferences of October, 1964, and July, 1965, witnessed a united and determined effort on the part of the provinces to prevent the issue from being put before the court. But the federal government remained firm by insisting that legal uncertainties be removed before going any further.[38]

A close examination of correspondence and public statements of the period suggest that the real[39] provincial stand could be interpreted as follows: "These rights are totally ours; there is nothing to compromise; we will use negotiations (read: political pressure) to force you to abandon your claim."[40] The corresponding real position of the federal government may be stated as follows: "These rights are totally ours. Since you don't seem to believe us, we'll have to ask the courts." By private correspondence[41] and public statements[42] provincial politicians goaded the federal government into staging "negotiations" long after the latter had realized the futility of the negotiating process in the context of the positions taken. Ottawa was forced to react to provincial "public relations" stigmatizing its resort to the Supreme Court of Canada as a "violation of co-operative federalism."[43] Although there was no basis for real negotiation, the federal government was forced to go through the motions of negotiating in order to avoid censure in the era of "co-operative federalism."

While it may be that a greater degree of co-operation and administrative pragmatism has reduced the primacy of judicial litigation in the resolution of federal-provincial controversies,[44] this provides no justification for the view that this "traditional" process of conflict-resolution has (or ought to) become obsolete in the era of "co-operative federalism." Peter Russell observes that,

... despite the emergence of ... 'co-operative federalism' ... the atmosphere of competitive jurisdiction has remained an enduring feature of Canada's political landscape. The first question that Canadians are still most likely to ask of any new subject of legislation is, 'Does it come under provincial or federal jurisdiction?' [He warns against] dismissing too categorically the importance of the constitutional text and its application by the courts.... In any of the issues that arise in federal-provincial relations, those who are responsible for working out the policies and strategies of the governments involved, not matter how pragmatic and flexible they may appear to be in dealing with the division of powers, must operate on some assessment of the constitutional power which could be found to sustain the positions they wish to assume.[45]

In view of the silence of the constitution on the subject of offshore mineral rights, the contentiousness of the legal claims, and the frustrating experience of negotiation attempts, it seems hardly illegitimate that one party should have used its ability to gain a court opinion on the subject.

This "red herring" about "violation of co-operative federalism" served only to embitter and stiffen the respective stands of the opponents. In addition, increasing public interest and awareness aroused by the vigour of provincial politicians soon transformed the dispute into a larger test of strength for both levels of government. By winning control over offshore rights, the Bennett administration could face its legislature and electorate as their staunch defender against a federal "steal."[46] By not giving in to provincial pressure, the Pearson administration could face Parliament and its electorate as the guardian of the "national interest" against the disturbing trend of "provincial erosion" of federal power.[47]

If the possibility of arriving at real negotiations without a court opinion was slim enough in view of the above considerations, there are additional and perhaps stronger reasons why negotiation was destined to fail. Despite the skilful manipulation of the mystique of "co-operative federalism," actors in the federal-provincial dispute showed an almost complete lack of appreciation for the basic "rules of accommodation ... whose violation would almost invariably terminate [a] friendly relationship."[48] By running through the following partial list of such rules, it is not difficult to see why goodwill between federal and provincial participants deteriorated: "Honour partial agreements."[49] "Maintain flexibility."[50] "Refrain from flagrant lies."[51] Do not impugn the motives of your opponent.[52] "Avoid emotionalism and rudeness."[53]

The alleged violation of the July, 1963, agreements seemed to arouse the most bitterness among the participants. While the obligations incurred by both parties seem reasonably clear,[54] the interpretation of their fulfilment has caused considerable confusion and resentment. On the one hand, the provincial view was that the federal government was continually stalling for time, for lack of a "hard" legal case.[55] The federal government, on the other hand, contended that British Columbia's twenty-two-page submission of August, 1963,[56] "could not be called a legal brief. In essence it was an historical résumé of the colonization of Vancouver's Island and the mainland of British Columbia and a review of various statements appearing in Hansard and made before a Senate committee, and ended with a statement of claim on behalf of British Columbia."[57] The meeting on June 12, 1964, between federal and provincial resources ministers, Arthur Laing and Donald Brothers, was regarded by the former as having "extinguished any 'commitment' that might have existed."[58] As late as February, 1966, Mr. Kiernan – then Minister of Recreation – was still referring to Mr. Laing's unfulfilled promise, refusing to deal with him on that account.[59]

Thus it seems clear that in addition to a lack of appreciation for the "rules of accommodation," uncritical veneration and tactical usage of "negotiations" resulted in continued deadlock and increasing bitterness. The mystique of "co-operative federalism" has, in the offshore mineral rights dispute, prevented both federal and provincial actors from achieving a useful and sound understanding of the basic principles necessary for harmonious and productive federal-provincial relations.

C. Personalities

The *mésentente* between Mr. Laing and Mr. Kiernan discussed above suggests a third closely related factor influencing the resolution of federal-provincial conflicts. The evolution of Canadian federalism from its more "traditional" to its newer "co-operative" form has, of necessity, elevated the importance of the personality factor. Co-operation must take place between people (a truism), and requires interpersonal understanding. J.A. Corry notes that the initial complaints of those administrators working in the areas of federal-provincial "over-lap" had to do with "personality difficulties." While he went on to ascribe the occurrence of clashes more to situational factors than to personality, he nevertheless had to account for this factor in his conclusion: ". . . except when a personal vendetta develops between the higher officials, a progressive improvement in the administrative relationship in fields jointly occupied by the Dominion and the provinces will emerge."[60]

While professionalism among administrators has reduced the problems likely to arise from personality factors,[61] it does not appear correct to say that this is also true of the political actors. In the case of the offshore mineral rights dispute, Edwin Black has noted that "the intergovernmental talks were fraught with partisan and personality differences. . . . Under both Conservative and Liberal regimes at Ottawa, the offshore oil conflict involved politicians noted for personal as well as partisan difficulties with Premier Bennett's imperial protectorate."[62]

Among the federal ministers having most to do with the conflict were (a) Alvin Hamilton, who openly regarded the continental shelf as "the key to the struggle over the encroaching powers of the provinces upon the federal government," and who referred to the provinces as having "larcenous hands which reach out to take what belongs to all of Canada, not just to the people of a single province";[63] (b) E. Davie Fulton and (c) Arthur Laing, who, as former leaders of the defeated provincial Conservative and Liberal parties of British Columbia, were old antagonists of Premier Bennett. The styles of the British Columbia politicians engaged in the controversy were especially prone to focusing on personality. Mr. Bennett made no secret of his interpretation of the federal stand: "I have it on good authority that the Pearson cabinet is divided. Half want to be fair to B.C.; the other half, led by Laing, say 'Don't give Bennett anything out there.' "[64] On another occasion he said, "The Liberals and especially Arthur Laing ... started a court case to take these resources.... If we give ground on this, the next thing he'll take our other resources."[65] The advent of M. Jean-Luc Pepin to the federal Energy, Mines and Resources portfolio in 1966 marked a new détente in the dispute. Provincial officials seemed unanimous in their respect for him generally, and for his approach to the issue in particular.

It seems reasonable to suggest that an important variable affecting the process of conflict-resolution in Canadian federal-provincial relations is the basic hostility or sympathy of the actors as measured on a "centralist/provincialist" spectrum.[66] While Mr. Pepin may be classified as leaning toward the "provincialist" pole, previous federal ministers seem decidedly more "centralist." It is with this latter group that the necessary cordiality and goodwill for federal-provincial relations broke down.[67] It would seem that, in an era of increasing interaction between officials of both levels of government, federal appointments to cabinet posts requiring good rapport with provincial politicians should be made to those qualified men on the "provincialist," rather than the "centralist," half of the spectrum.

Thus, we may conclude that the settlement of the offshore mineral rights dispute seems to have been delayed and hampered by (a) uncertainty about, and near-equality of, the relative strength of the opponents, (b) a tactical misuse of the mystique surrounding, and a basic lack of understanding of, "co-operative federalism" as a pattern of intergovernmental relations, and (c) an unfortunate confrontation of incompatible personalities. The primacy of these factors as determinants of the resolution of other federal-provincial disputes remains, of course, to be tested.

II.

Periodic disputes, like the one over offshore mineral rights, are a reminder that the basic nature of federal-provincial relations is *competitive*, rather than co-operative.[68] Corry, in 1939, chose the phrase "rival centres of power" rather than "eager co-operators for the fulfilment of a grand national purpose" to illustrate the nature of early attempts at federal-provincial collaboration.[69] In 1958 he observed generally that "Federal-state co-operative arrangements are not undertaken except where there are special and compelling reasons."[70] Writing in an earlier period, L.M. Gouin and Brooke Claxton saw the problem as follows: "A consideration of the constitutional conflict ... shows both the Dominion and the provinces insisting upon their rights, stretched to the ultimate limits allowed by the courts. ... The failure of the Dominion and the provinces to co-operate to deal with such matters as insurance and company legislation, having little or no political implications, shows how unlikely it would be for the Dominion and the provinces to co-operate to deal with any important or controversial question."[71] Despite the fact that successful co-operation in many fields has rendered this forecast unduly pessimistic, there is no evidence to suggest that the underlying "tug-of-war" relationship implied in the above quotation has changed significantly. In 1967 a federal senior civil servant and former high provincial official observed that:

> The inevitable frictions that accompany the side-by-side existence of federal and provincial programmes have been exacerbated by alleged invasions of provincial jurisdiction and *vice versa*. The federal power has been used knowingly and intentionally to alter provincial priorities. It has sometimes been used, too, unknowingly and unintentionally – in such a way as to affect the very administration of provincial programmes. Similarly, the provinces, or certain of them, have sought by hard political pressure and negotiation to lay claim to jurisdiction long accepted as being federal – the mineral rights of Hudson Bay, for example, and certain aspects of international relations.[72]

This enduring and inescapable competition can also be seen in a pronouncement by the late Quebec premier, Daniel Johnson: "We cannot afford to take any chances with Ottawa in spite of the apparent goodwill which is manifesting itself there, and of the magnificent talk that some of them proffer."[73]

While it is difficult to answer the question, "Why is competition (conflict) between the two levels of government inevitable?" perhaps a valuable insight may be gained from Corry, who attempted to answer the question by posing another: "Is it possible for two bureaucracies (using the word in a purely descriptive sense with none of the sinister connotations sometimes attached to it) responsible to separate and independent authorities, to co-operate efficiently and harmoniously over a long period of time?"[74] A parallel question may be posed with regard to political actors: Is it possible for two sets of elected officials responsible to different electorates, elected on different issues, emphasizing different priorities, and subject to different intragovernmental forces and institutions (including the bureaucracies to which Corry refers) to "co-operate efficiently and harmoniously over a long period of time"?

One point arising out of the above discussion of the offshore mineral rights dispute is that we should not allow the mystique of "co-operative federalism," with all its connotations of amicability, compromise, agreement, and absence of conflict, to obscure the basic fact that both levels of government have yet to renounce their interest in securing new areas of jurisdiction and new sources of revenue as these become available.[75] The expansion of the number and the scope of areas where governmental activity has been co-ordinated and conflicts resolved by means of the newer patterns of "co-operative federalism" may very well have reduced the *litigious* resolution of federal-provincial disputes. It has not, however, brought about any major change in the basic competitive nature of federal-provincial relations.[76]

In addition to reminding us of the essential competitiveness of federal-provincial relations, the offshore rights dispute, occurring as it does in the era of "co-operative federalism," also offers an illustration of the limitations of negotiation and the continuing relevance of the courts in the resolution of serious controversy. The newer patterns of conflict-resolution cannot be said to be *per se* the only legitimate (or even the best possible) ones to use for every case. While negotiation may be the preferred technique today, it is clear from the history of this dispute[77] that it can sometimes turn out to be a very unreliable procedure. A federal system must have alternative methods of conflict-resolution available to compensate for the possible failure of negotiations. Resort to the Supreme Court, while perhaps lacking "flexibility and ... easy adaptability to the dominant moods of the country,"[78] would seem to have the advantage of certainty in producing – albeit sometimes "forcing" – some form of settlement.[79]

Notes

I am particularly indebted to Professor Michael Stein, formerly of Carleton University, for valuable suggestions in discussing earlier drafts of this paper, which is adapted from my unpublished M.A. thesis, "The Offshore Mineral Rights Dispute in Canada" (Carleton University, 1968).

1. A detailed history of the dispute can be found in the author's "Offshore Mineral Rights: Anatomy of a Federal-Provincial Conflict," *Journal of Canadian Studies*, v, 1 (February, 1970), 50-61.
2. Bill "L," "An Act to Amend the Territorial Lands Act," introduced in the Senate on October 29, 1957, and referred to the Standing Committee on Natural Resources which held hearings on November 21 and December 11, 1957, and January 9, 1958.

3. *Canada Oil and Gas Regulations*, PC 1960-474; superseded by *Canada Oil and Gas Lands Regulations*, PC 1961-797 and subsequent amendments.
4. Most of the correspondence exchanged was made public in the "Case" submitted to the Supreme Court of Canada in 1965.
5. The first ministerial meeting took place in Ottawa on July 26, 1963. This meeting was followed by only one other, which took place almost a year later, June 12, 1964.
6. PC 1965-750, April 26, 1965.
7. *Reference Re Ownership of Off-shore Mineral Rights* (1968) 65 DLR [2d] 353. For a discussion, see the author's "Legal Issues of the Offshore Mineral Rights Dispute," *McGill Law Journal*, XIV, 3 (Sept., 1968), 475-93.
8. For the initial federal optimism and proposals see, e.g., *House of Commons Debates,* March 15, 1968, 7670; Dec. 2, 1968, 3342–43; and March 4, 1969, 6171. Evidence of the continuing dispute may be seen in the provincial hostility to these federal proposals. See, e.g., *Le Devoir*, 3 déc. 1968; *Globe and Mail*, Dec. 4, 1968.
9. This last set of factors, while of no small importance, will not be discussed in the present article owing to the difficulty of penetrating the secretive oil firms involved. For an interesting exposé of the role of oil interests in the United States "tidelands" controversy, see Robert Engler, *The Politics of Oil* (Chicago, 1961), esp. 86-95.
10. Maurice Duverger, *The Idea of Politics* (London, 1966), 171.
11. This was complicated further by the fact that judicial interpretation since the Second World War was tending to favour the central government, while informal political relationships seem to have benefited the provinces more (see n. 20 below). In addition, further confusion resulted from the misunderstood and misused "mystique" of "co-operative federalism" (see section B below).
12. This suggests that perhaps single issues periodically serve as foci for the frustrations encountered in a variety of unresolved federal-provincial problems.
13. James Ross Hurley, "Federalism, Co-ordinate Status, and the Canadian Situation," *Queen's Quarterly*, LXXIII (Summer, 1966), 151. Cf. A.W. Johnson, "The Dynamics of Federalism in Canada," *Canadian Journal of Political Science*, I, 1 (March, 1968), 24.
14. Carl Friedrich has suggested the notion of federalism as a "process" of continuous differentiation and integration. "New Tendencies in Federal Theory and Practice," mimeo., 1964; see A.H. Birch, "Approaches to the Study of Federalism." in A. Wildavsky, ed., *American Federalism in Perspective* (Boston, 1967), 59-60. A related notion in Canada can be seen in P.E. Trudeau, who speaks of the oscillation between times of federal and times of provincial dominance. "The Practice and Theory of Federalism," in his *Federalism and the French Canadians* (Toronto, 1968), 134ff.; cf. his "Quebec and the Constitutional Problem," *ibid.*, 37-39. Black and Cairns refer to the "cyclical swings from centralization to decentralization and back again." E.R. Black and A.C.

Cairns, "A Different Perspective on Canadian Federalism," *Canadian Public Administration*, IX (1966), 29. See also Johnson, "The Dynamics of Federalism in Canada," 20-21.

15. See, e.g., D.V. Smiley, *The Canadian Political Nationality* (Toronto, 1967), 20-21; J.A. Corry, "Constitutional Trends and Federalism," in A.R.M. Lower, F.R. Scott *et al.*, *Evolving Canadian Federalism* (Durham, N.C., 1958), 118; Black and Cairns, "A Different Perspective on Canadian Federalism," 30-31; A.R.M. Lower, "Theories of Canadian Federalism," in Lower, Scott *et al.*, *Evolving Canadian Federalism*, 40; Jean Beetz, "Les Attitudes changeantes du Québec à l'endroit de la constitution de 1867," in P.-A. Crépeau and C.B. Macpherson, eds., *The Future of Canadian Federalism/L'Avenir du fédéralisme canadien* (Toronto, 1965), 119.

16. See, e.g., Smiley, *The Canadian Political Nationality*, 39-41, 51-52; Black and Cairns, "A Different Perspective on Canadian Federalism," 31-33.

17. The levelling of jurisdictional barriers resulted in a 'fused federalism' characterized by involvement of the federal administration in virtually all of the provincial areas of 'exclusive' jurisdiction." Black and Cairns, "A Different Perspective," 33. Cf. D.V. Smiley, "Public Administration and Canadian Federalism," *Canadian Public Administration*, VII (1964), 385-86; Smiley, *The Canadian Political Nationality*.

18. See, e.g., Black and Cairns, "A Different Perspective," 34ff.; Smiley, "Public Administration and Canadian Federalism," 380ff.; Johnson, "The Dynamics of Federalism in Canada," 22-23; Trudeau, "Quebec and the Constitutional Problem," 38-39.

19. "Il reste en effect à savoir si la pénombre s'étendra sur les compétences provinciales ou sur les pouvoirs fédéraux." Jacques-Yvan Morin, "Vers un nouvel équilibre constitutionnel au Canada," in Crépeau and Macpherson, *The Future of Canadian Federalism*, 144. It is suggested that both observers, like Mr. Morin, *and* political actors themselves are unable to clearly assess the "direction" of contemporary "co-operative federalism."

20. For example, Black and Cairns, "A Different Perspective," 36; Johnson, "The Dynamics of Federalism in Canada," 23-24. However, J.-L. Pepin believes that "constant co-operation is what might save Canadian federalism in the future from swinging, as in the past, from excessive centralization to excessive decentralization." Speech of March 13, 1967, to the Association of Real Estate Boards, mimeo., 10.

21. A deadlock situation may be seen as one in which either (a) both parties prefer non-agreement to the kind of agreement which each feels is available from the other, or (b) one party is perfectly willing to allow the state of non-agreement to continue, while the other in unable to coerce or convince the former into *wanting* to come to an agreement at that particular time. See, e.g., Fred Charles Iklé, *How Nations Negotiate* (New York, 1964), 68ff.

22. "The provinces have not been asked [their opinions on the proposed amendment to the Territorial Lands Act (see n. 2 above)]. If they were to challenge it,

I presume they would do so in the courts." R.G. Robertson, deputy minister of northern affairs and natural resources, *Proceedings* of the standing committee on natural resources (Senate of Canada), Nov. 21, 1957, 8. "Any reversal of [our] position would depend upon the advice of the courts." W.G. Dinsdale, minister of northern affairs and natural resources, *House of Commons Debates*, Sept. 11, 1961, 8153.

23. For example, Premier Lesage said, "Nous continuerons d'émettre nos propres permis et les reconnaîtrons comme seuls valides. Il n'est pas question d'émettre conjointement des permis." *La Presse*, 22 juillet 1965.

24. In such situations it may be expected that each party will (a) hold out for as long as it can in order to arrive at a settlement which will offer it the best "available" terms, and (b) always seek to bargain from a position of strength. See, e.g., Iklé, *How Nations Negotiate*, 59-62.

25. "Offshore Oil Troubles the Waters," *Queen's Quarterly*, LXXII (Winter, 1965-66), 602.

26. *Globe and Mail*, Dec. 9, 1966.

27. *Ibid.* Cf. Black, "Offshore Oil Troubles the Waters," 590, and below. Russell, in contrast to these opinions, says that the "inclination of governments to refer constitutional questions directly to the courts is especially marked in the modern period." Peter H. Russell, ed., *Leading Constitutional Decisions* (Toronto, 1965), xxiv-xxv.

28. Atkey, *Globe and Mail*; Black, "Offshore Oil Troubles the Waters," 602.

29. Atkey, *Globe and Mail*. Although his diagnosis is similar, Black dissents from this conclusion (although with some internal inconsistencies to his own argument, it seems to me) by stating that ultimately, if negotiation in good faith has continued fruitlessly for some time, an outside referee becomes essential where the controversy is of some public consequence." "Offshore Oil Troubles the Waters," 603.

30. Iklé questions the conventional wisdom concerning negotiation: "Is this always the best way to settle a conflict? . . . both sides make concessions, [but] according to which law?" He also challenges several platitudes on the subject: "If both sides negotiate in good faith (Who judges 'good faith'?) they can always find a fair solution (And what is 'fair'?) . . . A good negotiator should never make a threat he is not prepared to carry out (What is wrong with successful bluffing?)." *How Nations Negotiate*, 1-2, 53-54.

    In the present case, see *House of Commons Debates*, March 12, 1962, 1708ff.; December 12, 1962, 2580; February 25, 1965, 11719; February 26, 1965, 11759; June 25, 1965, 2842-43; February 21, 1966, 1540-41.

31. Rejecting the idea of a reference case to the Supreme Court of Canada, Premier Bennett publicly called for the resolution of the dispute "by co-operative federalism." Vancouver *Sun* and Victoria *Daily Colonist*, Aug. 5, 1964; Vancouver *Sun*, Aug. 6, 1964; cf. comments by John Diefenbaker, *House of Commons Debates* (unrev.), Aug. 7, 1964, 6525. Also, on May 4, 1965, Premier Bennett accused the Liberal government of hypocrisy for hav-

ing violated its pledges of "co-operative federalism," because it was going ahead with the reference case. Vancouver *Sun*, May 4, 1965. See also n. 43.

32. *How Nations Negotiate*, 3-4.

33. *The Idea of Politics*, 169-70. Emphasis added.

34. "Statement Regarding the Position of the Province of British Columbia With Respect to Offshore Mineral Rights," Aug. 20, 1963, dispatched to Ottawa, Sept. 24, 1963.

35. *Ibid.*, 20; correspondence between Laing and Kiernan, July 31, 1963, Aug. 21, 1963 (confidential).

36. See, e.g., Kiernan's statements reported in Vancouver *Sun* and Victoria *Daily Colonist*, Jan. 3 and May 1, 1964.

37. Press release 201-5609, Monday, June 15, 1964: ". . . After a review of the possibility of administrative arrangements and a review also of their respective legal positions, both Ministers were of the view that the only way the matter could be reconciled was by a reference to the Supreme Court of Canada. . . ."

38. For reports of these conferences see *Globe and Mail*, Oct. 15, 1964; *Victoria Daily Times*, Oct. 21, 1964; *Financial Post*, Nov. 21, 1964; *House of Commons Debates* (unrev.), Nov. 4, 1964, 9740-41; John T. Saywell, "Federal-provincial Conferences," in Saywell, ed., *Canadian Annual Review for 1965* (Toronto, 1966), 61; *Globe and Mail*, July 22, 1965; Vancouver *Sun* and *Victoria Daily Times*, July 21, 1965; *La Presse*, 22 juillet 1965; Vancouver *Sun*, July 22, 1965.

39. It is to be expected that in a bargaining situation a distinction can be made between one's *real* and one's *stated* positions. In an ideal situation, one deliberately overstates the latter, so that concessions which are not inimical to one's *real* stand may be made, if necessary. In the present case, British Columbia's seemed to leave no such room for manoeuvring, asking for the maximum and being satisfied with nothing less. For example, ". . . so far as mineral rights in B.C. are concerned, they are ours and that's all there is to it." W.A.C. Bennett, quoted in Vancouver *Sun*, Aug. 14, 1961.

40. "Imaginez-vous bien les mots que j'emploierai le 19 juillet [1965] alors que je serai entouré des premiers ministres [*sic*] qui ont les mêmes interêts que les miens." Premier Lesage, quoted in *Le Devoir*, 25 juin 1965. Cf. the alarm expressed in a *Montreal Star* editorial of June 29, 1965: "What is implied in M. Lesage's statement is that, if a substantial number of provinces back him . . . Ottawa should give way."

41. See, e.g., the replies of the provincial premiers to Lester Pearson's letter of Dec. 11, 1964, which announced his definite intention to proceed with a reference case. Sessional Paper 356, tabled in the House of Commons, Feb. 26, 1965.

42. Even when the dispute was relatively obscured from the public spotlight, provincial premiers have gone on record as listing Ottawa's resort to the Supreme Court on this issue as one of their main grievances. See, e.g., Premiers Stanfield and Robichaud, interviewed by Peter Newman, reported in *Ottawa Journal*, Jan. 24 and 31, 1967. See also Premier Stanfield's comments in *Globe and Mail*, Aug. 3, 1967.

43. Premier Bennett saw withdrawal of the reference as "the real test of the Liberals – if they really believe in co-operative federalism or are just out to grab everything the provinces own." Quoted in Vancouver *Sun*, May 4, 1965. Mr. Laing's reactions were forthcoming in a three-page press release 1-6559, May 7, 1965.

44. See, e.g., Corry, "Consitutional Trends and Federalism," 96, 115-18, 120-21. Smiley has noted the "federal aspects of the Canadian constitution . . . have come to be less what the courts say they are than what the federal and provincial cabinets and bureaucracies determine them to be." "The Rowell-Sirois Report and Provincial Autonomy," *Canadian Journal of Economic and Political Science*, XXVIII (Feb., 1962), 59, quoted in Russell, *Leading Constitutional Decisions*, xxvi. Russell goes on to agree that "co-operative federalism" in the post-war period had "been much less a litigious struggle between Ottawa and the provinces to defend and expand their own enclaves than a matter of political compromise and administrative pragmatism"; but he imposes important qualifications (see below).

45. *Leading Constitutional Decisions*, xiv, xxvi.

46. For example, "British Columbia was never a willing bride in Canada. Ottawa talks with a forked tongue. . . . They think of us as a goblet to be drained. . . . Ottawa's trying to steal our offshore minerals, but they never will, because that would shake this country as nothing has shaken it before." Premier Bennett, interviewed by Peter Newman, *Toronto Daily Star*, Feb. 18, 1967.

47. Mr. Pearson saw the problem as follows: "If federal compromises in the interest of agreements which are valid and wise . . . merely increase the appetite for concessions that would not be valid or wise, and if the feeling develops that the federal government will always give way when pressed, then this country is in for serious trouble." *House of Commons Debates*, Jan. 20, 1966, 73. Cf. Mr. Diefenbaker's doubts about "that so-called new federalism that has brought about so much division" (*ibid.*, June 25, 1965, 1843) and Mr. Hamilton's view, n. 63.

48. Iklé, *How Nations Negotiate*, 87. Cf. "Co-operation is a two-way street. It has obligations as well as benefits. Sometimes it has appeared that our various representatives have failed to consider it in these terms." R.M. Burns, "The Machinery of Federal-Provincial Relations, II," *Canadian Public Administration*, VIII (1965), 532.

49. Iklé, *How Nations Negotiate*, 99ff. In addition, it is possible to view the sequence of events from 1957 to 1960 as constituting a broken pledge of sorts. When testifying before the standing committee on natural resources on January 9, 1958, federal ministers specified (in an about-face after an initial hostile reception to Bill "L" by the senators) that the amendment to the Territorial Lands Act was "not applicable to land under the sea on the east or west coast." Alvin Hamilton, *Proceedings* . . . . Jan. 9, 1958, 46; cf. 47, 52, 56. Yet in 1960 a federal order-in-council (n. 3) made possible the federal granting of offshore exploration permits in these areas. (See correspondence cited in n. 4.)

50. Iklé, *How Nations Negotiate*, 102ff. Cf. above, esp. n. 39.

51. *Ibid.*, 106ff. Immediately following the announcement of the order-in-council asking the opinion of the Supreme Court, British Columbia's attorney-general, Robert Bonner, publicly claimed that neither he nor his officials had been consulted, and pointed out that "this reference has got off to a very bad start." Vancouver *Sun*, April 30, 1965. Mr. Pearson quickly dispatched (and released to the press) a stern wire expressing his astonishment at the attorney-general's statement, which was undoubtedly erroneous. CN Wire, May 1, 1965.

52. Iklé, *How Nations Negotiate*, 109-11. For instance, Mr. Laing charged Mr. Bennett with preventing exploration by greedily demanding exorbitant fees. *Calgary Herald*, Oct. 6, 1964; Victoria *Daily Colonist*, Oct. 7, 1964 ("Bennett to Laing: 'Keep Hands Out' "). Also, British Columbia did not hesitate to imply "thievery" on the part of the federal Liberal party; cf. n. 43, n. 46

53. Iklé, *How Nations Negotiate*, 114ff. For example, "Federal officials are trying to butt in, but they have no more chance of getting offshore mineral rights in British Columbia than they have of getting them on the moon.... They'd better keep their cotton-pickin' fingers off our resources." W.A.C. Bennett, quoted in *Globe and Mail*, Oct. 15, 1964. It is difficult, of course, for both the observer and the politicians themselves to draw a definite line between personal "colour" or "flair" on the one hand, and downright arrogance or rudeness on the other.

54. Cf. page 429, above.

55. "Our repeated efforts to get a stated case from the Federal Government, however, have on each occasion received only the bland reply that the Federal Government is advised by its law officers that they have jurisdiction. We do not know to this day and are unable to find out on what, if anything, the Federal Government bases its assertion. From this failure to state their case we can only further conclude that they have in fact no case at all." W.K. Kiernan, "Excerpts from an Address in the Legislative Assembly during the 1962 Session," mimeo. (n.d.), 3. See also Victoria *Daily Colonist* and Vancouver *Sun* for Jan. 3, 1964; *Victoria Daily Times*, Aug. 8, 1963; Vancouver *Sun*, Nov. 2, 1965.

56. Cf. n. 34.

57. Arthur Laing to W.K. Kiernan, March 21, 1966 (used with permission).

58. *Ibid.* When, in December, 1964, Mr. Bennett continued to press for the federal brief, Mr. Pearson immediately replied that his letter of December 11, 1964, fulfilled any obligation which his government might have had. Sessional Paper 356.

59. See, e.g., Vancouver *Sun*, Feb. 18, 1966. Mr. Laing, also in a different portfolio at the time, wrote Mr. Kiernan to review once again the history of the dispute as he saw it.

60. *Difficulties of Divided Jurisdiction*, Study prepared for the Royal Commission on Dominion-Provincial Relations (Ottawa, 1939), 9-10.

61. Smiley, "Public Administration and Canadian Federalism," 375-77. It should be noted that the animosities generated during the offshore mineral rights dispute remained, as in the case of other disputes, only at the level of the political actors, and did not seep down to the stratum of senior civil servants.
62. "Offshore Oil Troubles the Waters," 590, 602.
63. *House of Commons Debates* (unrev.), May 24, 1966, 5462.
64. Newman interview, *Toronto Daily Star*, Feb. 18, 1967.
65. Quoted in Vancouver *Sun*, Oct. 23, 1965; see also *ibid.*, March 19, 1965.
66. "Like any human beings, officials who play a role in negotiations have their emotions, personal frailties, and quirks ... [and] are all influenced by their own sympathies or hostilities...." Iklé, *How Nations Negotiate*, 143. In Canada it seems possible to classify most politically aware people on the basis of their "centralist" or "provincialist" sympathies.
67. Edgar Gallant underlines the importance of the "process of getting to know one's counterparts in other governments, to the extent that a sense of *rapport* and conviviality is established. This ... helps to oil the channels for smoother intergovernmental consultations in future." "The Machinery of Federal-Provincial Relations, I," *Canadian Public Administration*, VIII (1965), 524.
68. This is suggestive of Bertram Gross's choice of the term "struggle," rather than "adjustment" or "bargaining," to describe the American legislative process. The rejected terms, he feels, unrealistically suggest either a balanced outcome or a willingness to compromise. The *Legislative Struggle* (New York, 1953), 4-7.
69. *Difficulties of Divided Jurisdiction*, 9.
70. "Constitutional Trends and Federalism," 124.
71. *Legislative Expedients and Devices Adopted by the Dominion and the Provinces*, Study prepared for the Royal Commission on Dominion-Provincial Relations (Ottawa, 1939), 8-9.
72. Johnson, "The Dynamics of Federalism in Canada," 24. Manitoba seems to be the province referred to in the case of Hudson Bay. See Sessional Paper 356.
73. *Montreal Star*, May 8, 1967.
74. *Difficulties of Divided Jurisdiction*, 9. Smiley is more explicit in paraphrasing Corry's main contention: "... if the provincial official shows himself to be relatively passive in the face of his federal collaborators [or vice versa, for that matter], he is demonstrating to his superiors that he has lost his originality. Conflicts thus [can] be attributed to ... factors inherent in the situation and are more likely than otherwise to occur when able and zealous people are involved.... It is almost inevitable that federal and provincial officials will disagree on the objectives of particular public policies and the most appropriate means by which they may be attained.... When administrative conflict between two independent bureaucracies occurs there is no hierarchical superior by which the dispute may be expeditiously resolved." "Public Administration and Canadian Federalism," 375-76.

75. There has been a very recent pragmatism expressed by some federal politicians suggesting that, where functionally justifiable, there should be strong federal *and* strong provincial governments (i.e., the strength of one level does not necessarily mean the corresponding "weakness" on the part of the other). See, esp., the suggestions of Pierre Elliott Trudeau for "un seul critère: l'efficacité." *Réponses* (Montreal, 1968), 42-43. Jean-Luc Pepin suggests the principle, "à chaque ordre de gouvernement selon ses aptitudes." "Le fédéralisme coopératif," in Institut canadien des Affaires publiques, *Le Canada face à l'avenir* (Montreal, 1964), 118. Whether this philosophy is truly practicable and to what extent it will be practised are interesting questions for future observation.
76. Cf. n. 44, n. 45.
77. For a more detailed account, see the author's "Offshore Mineral Rights: Anatomy of a Federal-Provincial Conflict."
78. Corry, "Constitutional Trends and Federalism," 121.
79. This is not to suggest that arriving at a solution guarantees that *the* settlement arrived at will be "equitable" and "satisfactory" in the eyes of all concerned. This is a "value" question focusing on the *content* of the settlement, which is a different and subtler dimension of conflict-resolution.

17. GEORGE E. CARTER

Financing Health and

Post-Secondary

Education:

A New and Complex

Fiscal Arrangement

The treasury planner [belongs to] a species which survives at a particular altitude in our community, living in communion with the binominal theorem, tending carefully square and cube roots, [his work] comprehensible only to the other groups of similar planners.[1]

Fiscal arrangements between governments in a federal state have never been simple, yet it is hard to conceive of arrangements more complex than those recently adopted for financing health and post-secondary education. The Federal-Provincial Fiscal Arrangements and Established Programs Financing Act,[2] covering the five years from 1977 to 1982, contains no less than ten sections. While several important changes have occurred in the overall fiscal package, the present analysis relates only to the three so-called "established" programs – hospital insurance, medicare, and post-secondary education.[3] Indeed, the complicated new formula for financing these major programs, Part VI of the Act, is the most significant – and contentious – departure from former practice. Moreover, the "Revenue Guarantee" (Part IV) is not examined here, although in the course of bargaining, this controversial element became entangled with the federal transfer for "established programs financing" (hereinafter referred to as EPF).

Originally published in *Canadian Tax Journal* (1977). Reprinted with permission of the Canadian Tax Foundation.

The Established Programs

Hospital insurance, the oldest and most costly program, began in 1958, and the post-secondary education transfer and medicare date from 1967 and 1968.[4] The designation "established" implied that a federal presence was no longer thought needed to ensure their continuance; any sharp provincial reduction in the level or quality of provision, especially of health services, would bring a storm of public protest.

Federal conditional grants to the provinces covered 50 per cent of the costs of hospital insurance and medicare deemed sharable by Ottawa. While the federal government also paid 50 per cent of provincial expenditures on post-secondary education, such assistance took the form of a complex fiscal transfer.[5]

Table 1 bears witness to the dramatic growth of the federal contribution to the three programs over the decade, 1967-77. By fiscal 1976-77, the federal outlay had expanded almost fivefold to $5,269.2 million, representing roughly two-thirds of total federal payments to the provinces under the previous fiscal arrangements, and just over 15 per cent of federal budgetary revenue. The hospital insurance program claimed more federal dollars in 1977 (51 per cent of the total spending on the three) than medicare (18 per cent) and post-secondary education (31 per cent) combined. Beyond question, the alarming growth in the magnitude of the sums involved largely explains the federal government's determination to end these open-ended grants if an acceptable fiscal substitute could be devised. A short account of the events behind this important development follows.

Moving Toward a Fiscal Alternative

Mounting dissatisfaction of the provinces, especially Quebec, over shared-cost financing led to the creation of a unique fiscal alternative. What had been called the Pearson proposals became, in 1965, the Established Programs (Interim Arrangements) Act under which provinces were allowed to opt out of several "established" programs. As expected, Quebec alone, having spurned the federal grants, opted out of several programs, including hospital insurance.[6] Fiscal equivalence originally took the form of a federal tax abatement of 20 percentage points of personal income tax. The abatements were equalized to the level of the per capita yield in the two highest-yield provinces. The advantage to Quebec was purely nominal, since *ex post* adjustments would ensure that the value of the fiscal transfer would be identical to the value of the grants foregone.

Although only one province had opted out, the 1965 provisions made the future role of shared-cost programs in the other nine provinces a matter of some speculation. Even more clearly presaging the present fiscal arrangements, in 1966 the federal government had actually urged the provinces to follow Quebec in opting out. Indeed, in his statement to the Tax Structure Committee in 1966, the then Minister of Finance, Mitchell

Table 1
Federal Contributions to the Three Established Programs, 1967-77
($ millions)

Year*	Hospital Insurance**	Medicare	Post-Secondary Education	Total†	Percent Change over Previous Year (%)
1968	673.9	—	421.5	1,095.5	—
1969	799.7	33.0	527.4	1,360.1	24.2%
1970	920.9	181.0	650.4	1,752.2	28.8
1971	1,040.1	400.5	788.8	2,229.4	27.2
1972	1,218.8	576.5	922.0	2,717.3	21.9
1973	1,358.9	630.8	987.0	2,976.7	9.5
1974	1,495.6	677.9	1,066.7	3,240.3	8.9
1975	1,868.2	762.7	1,217.1	3,848.0	18.8
1976	2,380.0	795.8	1,340.3	4,515.7	17.4
1977††	2,691.5	958.8	1,619.0	5,269.2	16.7

* Fiscal years ending March 31 of year shown.
** Includes the value of Quebec's federal abatement of 16 points of personal income tax and cash adjustments under the Established Programs (Interim Arrangements) Act.
†May not add to totals, because of rounding.
††Department of Finance.

SOURCES: Public Accounts and Department of the Secretary of State, *Review of Educational Policies in Canada* (Ottawa, 1975); and Department of the Secretary of State, *Annual Report* (Ottawa: Information Canada, 1975).

Sharp, made clear the federal government's intention to end conditional grants for "certain well established and continuing" programs with the expectation that the provinces would assume "full responsibility" for them.[7] In fact, the provinces were offered, as a substitute for two major grants[8] (hospital insurance and a Canada Assistance Plan), a federal tax abatement of 17 percentage points of the personal income tax, equalized to the national per capita average. Moreover, this proposed formula would also contain "adjustment" payments which would be tied to the annual growth in personal income.

More noteworthy than the striking resemblance between this early proposal and the one recently adopted, however, is that the 1966 offer was firmly rejected.[9] To be sure, a decade ago Quebec alone pressed for opting out of shared-cost programs. The view held by the other provinces was best summed up by Ontario's premier when he stated that "any proposal to hand back to the provinces total responsibility for mature programmes, in exchange for additional tax capacity . . . offers no real gain to the provinces."[10] The fundamental and obvious fear was that the value of the fiscal transfer would not keep pace with the growth in program costs. Evidence for 1960-69, a decade of remarkable cost increases in hospital insurance, proves that these fears were realized.[11]

Further attempts by Ottawa to secure provincial approval of an opting-out scheme were postponed until reform of the federal income taxes, then imminent, was accomplished. But notice was served in the White Paper, *Proposals for Tax Reform*, that a revised offer would follow tax reform when "the value of tax points and the costs of the major, continuing joint programs can be better appraised."[12]

It is worth noting that the federal announcement to launch a major new program to assist post-secondary education came only one month after provincial rejection of the 1966 opting-out offer.[13] Growing provincial hostility toward conditions attached to shared-cost grants, coupled with the federal determination to end existing ones, explains why this new assistance took such a complex form. And, as noted later, the fiscal transfer component – federal tax reductions in the two income taxes – has been fully incorporated into the 1977-82 arrangements.

Following the 1971 tax reforms, the federal government renewed its efforts to find a provincially acceptable substitute for financing health and post-secondary education. Accordingly, in 1973 Ottawa proposed a variant of the 1966 formula which would restrict the federal contributions to the annual growth rate in GNP.[14] It was promptly rejected by the provinces. Once again the provinces feared the risk inherent in any scheme under which the federal committment would no longer be fully tied to program costs. Meanwhile, the federal government imposed a 15 per cent ceiling, effective from 1973-74, on the annual growth of its payments to post-secondary education. Similarly, federal contributions to medicare were limited to an annual growth rate of 14.5 per cent in 1976-77 and to 12 per cent in 1977-78; at the same time, federal notice was officially given to terminate the Hospital Insurance agreements at the earliest possible date (1980).[15]

These developments set the stage for the federal government's important policy statement at the Federal-Provincial Conference of June, 1976. Prime Minister Trudeau indicated that underlying the proposed substitute for the shared-cost programs were five objectives. These objectives, essentially consistent with similar policy statements of the past decade,[16] were as follows:

1. to maintain across Canada the standards of service to the public under these major programs, and to facilitate their improvement;

2. to put the programs on a more stable footing, so that both levels of government are better able to plan their expenditures;
3. to give provinces flexibility in the use of their own funds which they have been spending in these fields;
4. to bring about greater equality among the provinces with regard to the amount of federal funds they receive under the programs;
5. to provide for continuing joint policy discussions relating to the health and post-secondary education fields.[17]

Following these principles, which were broad enough to gain general acceptance, the details of the federal proposal were spelled out at a meeting of provincial finance ministers in July, 1976. Subsequent events amply demonstate the fascinating and often circuitous process of intergovernmental bargaining before agreement can be reached.[18] First, in order to assess the revenue impact on provincial revenues, the ministers met several times in the following months. At these meetings four provinces presented counter-proposals,[19] and, without precedent, consensus was reached by the provincial ministers on the overall fiscal arrangements; as spokesman, the Alberta treasurer took this proposal to the federal government.[20] It should be noted that consensus required a major concession on the part of the four Atlantic provinces and Saskatchewan. These provinces, now the sole supporters of cost-sharing, agreed to reverse their stand and to accept instead equalized tax points, which they had always viewed as a risky substitute for the former. After the finance ministers failed to secure federal approval of their proposal, the matter was left to the provincial premiers. Finally, on December 14, 1976, the provinces "reluctantly"[21] agreed to a modified federal offer.

The Fiscal Anatomy of EPF

The new fiscal transfer is divided into two parts: "tax points" and cash payments. The first part consists of a federal reduction of 13.5 personal and one corporate income tax points[22] in order to permit the provinces to increase their tax rates by an equivalent amount. Since the yield of the tax points differs widely from province to province, an equalization payment is included to raise the value of the tax points to the per capita national average.

The second part, of approximately equal value, is a cash payment, the calculation of which is highly complicated. Five determinants are involved: (1) the national average per capita contribution for the three programs in the "base" year, 1975-76; (2) provincial population; (3) an "escalator" consisting of a three-year moving average of the annual growth rate of per capita GNP; (4) "levelling" adjustments to remove existing interprovincial disparities in per capita federal contributions: provinces whose per capita contribution was *below* the national average in the base year would be brought up to the national average in three years and provinces *above* would be brought down to the national average in five years; and (5) "transitional" adjustments to those provinces where the value of the tax transfer plus associated equalization falls short of the value of the basic cash payment.

Estimated EPF transfers to the provinces are shown by component for 1977-78 in Table 2. In the first year under the new arrangements, the federal contribution is expected to total $6,460.8 million, representing an impressive 43 per cent increase over the previous year. Unfortunately, the fiscal gyrations performed in determining the total federal transfers are several and demand effort to be understood. Much vexation can be spared, however, if the reader can remember that the foundation from which the transfer begins – and grows – is the national average per capita, federal contribution to the three "established" programs in 1975-76. This historical per capita sum, adjusted upward through time by growth of GNP and population, defines the limit of federal support. And half of this amount is the Basic Cash Payment, translated into dollar amounts from its original per capita calculation (top line, Table 2).

Moving next to the tax component (lines 7 through 11), the value to the provinces of 13.5 personal income and one corporate income "tax points" plus associated equalization (for the seven recipient provinces) is shown.[23] Significantly, the basic cash component exceeds the value of the total tax transfer (line 11) for all provinces except the two "have" provinces, Ontario and British Columbia (and Quebec for a special reason).[24] The obvious reason for this disparity is the relatively more productive income tax fields in these two provinces.

Returning to the more intricate cash payment, it may be instructive to compare the position of a "have" province (Ontario) with that of a "have-not" province (Newfoundland). Starting with the "basic" $80.5 and $1,210.4 million (line 1),[25] move next to line 2, which indicates that Newfoundland qualifies for a transitional payment; only Ontario and British Columbia do not. The rationale is that in the short run, such payments will be needed to lift the value of the equalized tax room to the level of the basic cash component. The provinces are thus assured that the aggregate federal transfer under the cash-tax formula will at least be equivalent to what they would have received had the entire transfer consisted simply of cash. In the longer run, however, such transitional adjustments will disappear because revenues from the personal income tax, by virtue of progressive rates, grow faster than GNP. And, as already indicated, growth of the cash transfer depends on the latter rate of growth.

A more curious element in the formula, the levelling adjustment (line 3), is designed to eliminate, gradually, the interprovincial disparities in the per capita federal cash contribution. For provinces whose per capita contributions in the base year (1975-76) were below the per capita national average,

Table 2
Estimated EPF Transfer to Provinces, by Component, 1977-78
($ millions)

	Nfld.	P.E.I.	N.S.	N.B.	Que.	Ont.	Man.	Sask.	Alta.	B.C.	Total
1. Basic Cash Payment	80.5	17.5	120.2	100.0	898.6	1,210.4	148.0	135.7	266.8	365.4	3,343.1
2. Transitional Cash Payment	6.8	1.5	10.1	8.4	75.8	—	12.5	11.4	10.5	—	137.0
3. Levelling Cash Payment	-10.5	-3.4	-8.3	-13.8	-8.6	+0.8	-10.6	-15.5	+4.8	-39.0	-104.1
4. Quebec Abatement*	—	—	—	—	-393.7	—	—	—	—	—	-393.7
5. Tax Transfer Recovery	-6.0	-1.3	-8.9	-7.4	-28.6	-105.1	-11.0	-10.0	-20.7	-31.1	-230.1
6. Total Cash Transfer	70.8	14.3	113.1	87.2	543.5	1,106.1	138.9	121.6	261.4	295.3	2,751.8
7. 13.5 Personal Income Tax Points**	36.9	7.3	70.2	51.7	1,081.9	1,213.6	106.4	95.1	227.6	363.5	3,254.2
8. Associated PIT Equalization	32.0	7.7	32.7	33.9	80.7	—	20.3	21.0	—	—	228.3
9. 1 Corporate Income Tax Point	2.0	0.4	3.6	3.2	42.9	86.0	7.3	5.4	28.7	21.5	201.0
10. Associated CIT Equalization	2.9	0.7	3.6	2.8	11.1	—	1.6	2.8	—	—	25.5
11. Total Tax Transfer	73.8	16.1	110.1	91.6	1,216.6	1,299.6	135.6	124.3	256.3	385.0	3,709.0
12. Total Cash and Tax Transfer	144.6	30.4	223.2	178.8	1,760.1	2,405.7	274.5	245.9	517.7	680.3	6,460.8

* Under Part VII of the Act, Quebec receives a federal tax abatement of 8.5 personal income tax points to replace the 7.723 points received formerly under the Established Programs (Interim Arrangements) Act.

** The tax transfer to Quebec includes the value of the 8.5 points abatement, which is not equalized. Quebec's tax transfer therefore is not comparable with the amounts shown for the other provinces.

SOURCE: Department of Finance.

their cash contributions will be raised to the national average over three years; for provinces above the national average, their cash contributions are reduced to the national average in five years. Hence the − $10.5 million for Newfoundland means that fewer federal dollars per capita than the national average had been received by that province; the amount shown is subtracted lest the full disparity be eliminated in a single year (1977-78). By contrast, Ontario, having received slightly above average federal assistance on a per capita basis, needs a small (+ 0.8 million) adjustment. (The only other province whose per capita federal transfer had exceeded the national average is Alberta.)

A final complicating feature, though minor, is the provision of a recovery payment (line 5) in the first two fiscal years. For the convenience of administrators and taxpayers, the new federal tax reduction (and corresponding increases in provincial rates) was made effective from January 1, 1977, although the new arrangements would not supersede the existing shared-cost agreements until three months later (April 1). The federal treasury will therefore correct for some of this double-counting by subtracting part of the resultant excess amounts from each province's total transfer. The patient reader who has persisted through this fiscal labyrinth will be relieved to reach, finally, total cash transfers on line 6 ($70.8 and $1,106.1 million for Newfoundland and Ontario).[26]

To complete the fiscal package, Part VI of the Act also launches a new conditional grant, the value of which is not included in Table 2. While the details of the grant are yet to be spelled out, federal funds will go to the provinces for nursing-home care, residential care for adults, health aspects of home care and other health services not previously covered under the Hospital Insurance program. Called the Extended Health Care program, the grant is non-matching and is apportioned simply on the basis of population. Beginning with $20 per capita, the amount will be escalated by the same GNP growth index applicable to other cash payments in order to determine the grant for 1977-78 and subsequent years. The new grant gives the federal government two advantages: (1) it silences provincial criticism that some of these costs (especially nursing homes) were not shareable under Hospital Insurance; and (2) it ends all open-end cost-sharing programs in health care since some of these services to needy persons were formerly covered under the Canada Assistance Program. At the time of writing, not all the provinces have agreed to participate in the program. Nevertheless, on the assumption that they will do so, the program will cost the federal government approximately $500 million in 1977-78.

Tax Points and the Taxpayer

What effect, if any, does the federal transfer of tax points to the provinces have on the taxpayer? The purpose of this fiscal instrument, like federal tax credits in the United States, is to enlarge provincial tax revenues at the expense of the federal treasury. The provinces then seize this opportunity to raise their own rates to take up the tax room vacated by the federal government. Neutrality with respect to the overall position of the taxpayer is thus intended; he pays less to Ottawa, more to his provincial government. Moreover, the real costs of taxpayer compliance are unaffected. Under tax collection agreements, in nine provinces the tax base on which provincial rates are applied is uniform; the provincial tax liability can thus be easily calculated on a single form. Only in Quebec, which continues to collect its own tax, does the taxpayer need to make two independent determinations on separate forms.

For the nine provinces under tax collection agreements, Table 3 shows the increase in their own tax rates necessary to occupy the new tax room. Accordingly, the 1977 provincial rates incorporate the federal transfer of 9.143 *new* tax points and are expressed as a percentage of federal basic tax.[27] Since the legislation requires that the new rates be rounded to the nearest one-half percentage point, the provincial rates enacted in 1977 are also shown. Notice that seven provinces merely raised their rates enough to pick up the released tax room, while the rates in Newfoundland and Saskatchewan go beyond this level. Yet the relevant point here is that the effect of the new EPF transfer on the taxpayer is neutral (except for some slight increases from rounding).

Table 3
Provincial Personal Income Tax Rates (1977) Required to Occupy
Tax Room Vacated by Federal Tax Reduction
(percent of federal tax)

Province*	1977 Rate	1977 Rate (after federal tax transfer)	Actual 1977 Rate
Nfld.	42.0	56.289	57.5
P.E.I.	36.0	49.686	50.0
N.S.	38.5	52.437	52.5
N.B.	41.5	55.739	55.5
Ont.	30.5	43.632	44.0
Man.	42.5	56.840	56.0
Sask.	40.0	54.088	58.5
Alta.	26.0	38.680	38.5
B.C.	32.5	45.834	46.0

* Excludes Quebec. As noted, Quebec is not under a tax collection agreement, but levies its own tax on personal income independent of federal rates.

SOURCE: Budgets (1977) of provincial governments.

Provincial Reaction

As outlined above, provincial agreement to the EPF proposal had been secured only after long and difficult negotiations. By far the most enthusiastic province was Ontario, which stands to gain the most revenue from the additional tax room. Moreover, Ontario's objections to cost-sharing, exceeded only by those of Quebec, had intensified in recent years. Of the familiar list of complaints, the most vexing were: (1) provincial expenditure preferences were distorted by inflexible rules over which service costs were eligible for federal sharing (especially within the broad area of health); (2) federal auditing procedures demanded an excessive bureaucracy; (3) long delays, experienced before final settlement of provincial claims; and (4) unilateral federal termination of a grant program, or the imposition of limits on the federal contribution, left the provinces with an unexpected burden.[28]

Quebec, long the archenemy of conditional grants, has, however, expressed dissatisfaction with the size of the tax transfer.[29] At issue is the technical fact that the number of tax points to be transferred was determined on the basis of the yield in the two provinces where the per capita yield is the highest. Consequently, only in these provinces did the tax transfer equal half the per capita national average federal contribution in the base year.[30] As explained, transitional payments prevent the other provinces from receiving less than they would receive were the whole amount a cash transfer linked to GNP growth. Since the value of the equalized tax points will grow faster than the GNP-escalated cash component, transitional payments are expected to diminish over time and disappear in about a decade. But different rates of increase in the two components mean that in the interim the whole federal contribution to eight provinces will grow in proportion to GNP. Only Ontario and British Columbia will, at the outset, reap financial gains from the tax component.

A related and not unexpected complaint voiced by the Atlantic provinces and Saskatchewan is that associated equalization to the per capita national average is inadequate. They argue that the tax points should be equalized up to the level of the top-yielding provinces. Indeed, Saskatchewan's Minister of Finance asserted that: "It would be illogical to equalize to the national average if the number of points to be transferred were calculated with reference to the province with the highest per capita yield."[31] The theoretical merit of this argument is examined below. To be sure, such interprovincial disparities would disappear with equalization to the top. Although sympathetic, the Prime Minister claimed that: "Such an approach would call on the federal government to pay out larger sums of money from a tax base which would itself have been reduced by the tax transfer."[32]

An indication of the financial difference between equalizing the taxes involved to the top-yielding provinces and the per capita national average is provided by Table 4. As expected, equalization to the highest per capita

Table 4
Estimated Cost of Equalizing Tax Transfer to Top Province's
Per Capita Yield Compared to National Average
Per Capita, 1977-78
($ millions)*

	Equalizing 13.5 Personal Income Tax Points to National Average (1)	Equalizing 1 Corporate Income Tax Points to National Average (2)	Total (1+2) (3)	Equalizing 13.5 Personal Income Tax Points to Top (Ontario) (4)	Equalizing 1 Corporate Income Tax Points to Top (Alberta) (5)	Total (4+5) (6)
Nfld.	29.7	2.8	32.5	41.9	6.7	48.6
P.E.I.	6.8	0.7	7.5	9.5	1.5	11.0
N.S.	31.1	3.5	34.6	47.3	9.2	56.5
N.B.	32.4	2.8	35.2	45.9	7.6	53.5
Que.	75.6	11.0	86.6	201.2	53.2	254.4
Ont.	—	—	—	—	44.2	44.2
Man.	18.9	1.5	20.4	39.2	8.5	47.7
Sask.	20.1	2.8	22.9	39.2	9.2	48.4
Alta.	—	—	—	37.8	—	37.8
B.C.	—	—	—	2.7	23.2	25.9
Total	214.6	25.1	239.7**	464.7	163.3	628.0

* Note that the above figures pertain only to the equalization of the tax points, and ignore the resultant reduction in certain adjustment payments. Hence these amounts do not represent the *actual* additional cost to the federal government (see text).

** This amount differs from the amount shown in Table 2. For convenience, the figures above were calculated from the earlier estimates ("Lilac Book").

SOURCE: Department of Finance, *Financial Assessment of Established Programs Financing Proposal* ("Lilac Book"). Calculations are based on "standard price estimates" (70-75) and population projections (66).

provincial yields (Ontario and Alberta) would increase the federal outlay by a substantial $388 million (161 per cent), raising the equalization entitlement to $628 million in 1977-78. It is important to note, however, that this estimate is exaggerated; it relates only to the equalization of the relevant tax points isolated from the other adjustments involved in determining the final transfer. (Transitional adjustments would, of course, vanish, thus reducing significantly the net cost to the federal treasury.)

Finally, British Columbia's harsh criticism of Ottawa's withdrawal from the former cost-sharing arrangements is noteworthy. The bone of contention was that the federal government, by "unilaterally" limiting its grants to post-secondary education (1972)[33] and medicare (1976), had "abrogated" its initial 50:50 commitment to these programs.[34] It seems fair to conclude, therefore, that at least one "have" province – Alberta's position is less clear – keenly regrets the end of cost-sharing.

In short the disenchantment expressed first by Quebec, and later by Ontario, over the shared-cost programs was not really representative of *all* the provinces. In fact, the Saskatchewan finance minister expressed a widely held conviction when he declared that, "The problems that exist, however, are not inherent in the cost-sharing mechanism itself; they are defects in the program design, and they can be corrected."[35] And most assuredly, the poorer provinces only agreed begrudgingly to give up grants in exchange for more tax room. Not only would 9.143 points of personal income tax, even after equalization to the national average, yield 17 per cent less per capita than in Ontario, but they feared the financial risks implied in the new arrangement. As Newfoundland's finance minister lamented: "The days of the 50-cent dollar have passed," and warned that the growth rate of revenue would make it more difficult for his province to "catch up" to national standards.[36]

Appraisal

Most certainly, the adoption of the EPF transfer as a substitute for cost-sharing raises several important questions and theoretical issues. Some of the more crucial ones are examined here.

Foremost among questions raised by provincial officials is whether federal contributions will, in future, fall short of the former level of federal support (50 per cent of program costs). Table 5 compares federal contributions under EPF projected to fiscal 1982 with those under the previous shared-cost arrangements. According to these projections, prepared by the federal government, every province will register significant gains under the new system. Not only are per capita contributions more generous, but much greater interprovincial uniformity is attained.

Underlying these projections are several assumptions with respect to the growth of GNP, population, prices and wages over the next five years.[37] The data presented in Table 5, especially projected costs of shared-cost programs (assuming their continuation under the former arrangement) must, therefore, be treated with extreme caution. Unfortunately, the provincial fear that the growth of program costs might outpace the increase in the EPF transfer cannot be dismissed on the basis of projections.

It might prove instructive to examine the shared-cost programs and the EPF transfer in terms of the theory of intergovernmental grants. Essentially two fundamental problems are inherent to any federal state.[38] Differing fiscal strength of the various provincial governments will result in pronounced interprovincial differences in the provision of public services.

Table 5

Comparing Estimated Federal Contributions to the Three Established Programs Under EPF With Those Under the Former Shared-Cost Arrangements, Projected to 1981-82

	Nfld.	P.E.I.	N.S.	N.B.	Que.	Ont.	Man.	Sask.	Alta.	B.C.	Total
Shared-Cost Arrangements ($ millions)											
1977-78........	133.3	26.7	208.4	161.5	1,625.6	2,194.5	255.4	233.0	471.0	600.7	5,900.1
1978-79........	149.5	29.7	230.6	180.3	1,810.6	2,453.1	283.9	246.3	525.4	673.4	6,583.8
1979-80........	165.2	32.8	253.7	199.7	1,984.9	2,716.2	311.5	271.8	584.6	752.8	7,273.2
1980-81........	181.5	36.2	277.3	220.0	2,163.0	2,986.1	340.6	298.4	646.8	837.1	7,987.0
1981-82........	197.4	39.3	300.4	239.8	2,337.3	3,251.0	368.6	324.7	707.6	920.1	8,686.2
EPF ($ millions)											
1977-78........	144.6	30.4	223.2	178.8	1,760.1	2,405.7	274.5	245.9	517.7	680.3	6,460.8
1978-79........	171.8	36.7	260.1	214.1	1,988.3	2,760.5	319.1	292.2	599.3	809.3	7,451.4
1979-80........	202.6	44.2	300.6	253.4	2,233.6	3,123.9	368.8	342.8	687.5	948.0	8,504.9
1980-81........	224.5	48.7	332.9	281.7	2,462.7	3,486.4	406.4	381.3	768.5	1,066.4	9,459.5
1981-82........	247.5	53.9	365.7	311.3	2,696.6	3,870.0	445.4	420.8	852.8	1,193.0	10,457.1
Shared-Cost Arrangements ($ per capita)											
1977-78........	237.19	218.85	248.39	231.38	259.23	259.80	247.24	235.48	252.95	235.57	252.89
1978-79........	263.20	241.46	272.90	254.66	287.35	286.51	273.51	256.56	276.38	257.91	278.73
1979-80........	287.80	262.40	299.77	278.13	313.52	313.00	298.37	279.63	301.34	281.53	304.22
1980-81........	312.93	287.30	322.44	302.20	339.93	339.48	324.38	302.94	326.50	305.62	329.93
1981-82........	336.29	307.03	346.08	324.49	365.20	364.26	348.72	325.03	349.60	327.67	354.03
EPF ($ per capita)											
1977-78........	257.25	249.79	266.19	256.05	280.66	284.80	265.78	259.63	277.99	266.84	276.92
1978-79........	302.46	297.89	307.66	302.36	315.54	322.43	307.30	304.53	315.57	309.97	315.51
1979-80........	352.96	354.16	356.65	352.87	352.78	359.99	353.20	352.60	354.34	354.54	355.72
1980-81........	387.00	385.28	387.27	386.79	387.06	396.34	387.08	387.07	387.99	389.37	390.77
1981-82........	421.78	420.76	421.50	421.02	421.35	433.59	421.46	421.18	421.34	424.75	426.61

SOURCE: Department of Finance.

Only by accepting above-average tax burdens could the residents of poorer provinces enjoy an average bundle of services. Undeniably, equity demands that all provinces, by average fiscal effort, be enabled to provide some "foundation" or average level of services. The appropriate and efficient fiscal instrument to resolve this problem is the unconditional grant. And the Canadian practice of equalizing provincial-local government revenues to the per capita national average is praiseworthy. These grants go to all provinces except Ontario, Alberta, and British Columbia and are expected to reach $2.5 billion in 1977-78.

The second problem – and the one relevant here – is recurrent: provincial expenditure functions expand faster than revenues, compared to the opposite situation at the federal level. Logically, this vertical imbalance could be corrected by an appropriate shift of revenue sources from the federal government to the provinces. But the relief provided by this approach would be temporary: in time, the new division would grow outmoded. To avoid the difficulties of restructuring a federal framework, the conditional grant was devised. When the federal government perceives a national interest in specific provincial functions (health and higher education), federal funds, through conditional grants, can be directed to expand them or improve their quality.

Federal grants to the two health programs and to post-secondary education fit the theoretical framework that rationalizes such grants in terms of spillovers (or externalities). Benefits (costs) from these programs are not confined to the province providing them, but spill out to residents of other provinces. Sub-optimal program levels would thus result if their supply were left to the provincial governments alone. Optimality (i.e., the supply representative of the national interest) calls for the internalization of such spillovers by the federal government through specific purpose grants. Matching grants are suitable, with the federal share equal to the ratio of external to total benefits. The operational validity of this theory, however, is limited by the fact that many spillovers defy precise measurement.

Another important feature of "optimizing" grants is that they be closed. This means that the federal government must accept the difficult task of determining the size of its contribution at the outset. That all three programs under discussion were open-end was a major fault; moreover, the ensuing move by Ottawa to regain control over its own spending by restricting assistance to two of them was bitterly resented by the provinces. Indeed, the open-end feature gave the federal government a powerful incentive to end these programs.

Finally, while grants should possess clearly defined national objectives, narrowly defined conditions are often inappropriate. Some important national priorities had been specified in the health field, but, surprisingly enough, national objectives in the area of higher education had never been articulated. More contentious, the conditions attached to the hospital insurance grants were overly rigid for a mature program; more flexibility concerning eligibility of shareable costs would have encouraged greater efficiency in the use of provincial funds within the broad field of health care.

The EPF Transfer

The new transfer, half financial, half fiscal, poses a conceptual problem. As in the case of the previous transfer for post-secondary education, it can be argued that only the cash component constitutes a federal contribution; the provinces have a constitutional right to income taxes. Yet the slice of federal revenue given up was meant as compensation for the grants withdrawn from three specified areas of provincial expenditure. It is useful to split the transfer into its two components. The cash payment is a block grant, non-matching, and having only a few general restrictions over its use. Provinces are required to maintain minimum standards in the health services,[39] but are free to set their own standards and priorities in their system of higher education. The cash element also has one key advantage over its antecedents: it is *closed*, the annual grant being automatically determined by an objective formula.

In sharp contrast, the tax component may be viewed either as an unconditional grant or as provincial own-source revenue. Either interpretation reveals at least two serious faults: (1) once the size of the equalized tax points comes to exceed that of the cash grant in all provinces, the association the tax transfer now has with a specific area of provincial expenditure will vanish; and (2) the short history with tax abatements demonstrates that this part of the EPF transfer is inflexible and irreversible; provinces will argue that they have a constitutional right to a permanently larger share of income taxes, independent of future changes in federal-provincial fiscal arrangements.

More basically, the device of a tax transfer is a poor substitute for a federal grant because per capita yields from a uniform slice of federal income taxes differ widely from province to province. As already mentioned, the "have-not" provinces argued correctly that, even after equalization to the national average, the tax transfer would have no advantage to them over a cash grant until its value eclipses the value of the other component. Estimated interprovincial disparities in the per capita yields of one personal and one corporate income tax point for fiscal 1978 are shown in Table 6. The range is striking: from $4.18 (less than half the national average per capita) in Prince Edward Island up to $10.02 (17 per cent above the national average) in Ontario for one point of personal income tax. As predicted, differences in the per capita yields of one corporate tax point are even more dramatic. Again, Prince Edward Island is in bottom place with a mere $2.97 (only 35 per cent of the national average) and Alberta is in top place with $15.19 (an astonishing 79 per cent above national average).

Table 6

Interprovincial Disparities in the Per Capita Yields of One Personal Income Tax Point and One Corporate Income Tax Point, 1977-78 (Estimated)

	Value of One Personal Income Tax Point ($ per capita)	Per cent of National Average (%)	Value of One Corporate Income Tax Point ($ per capita)	Per cent of National Average %
Nfld.....................	4.59	53.7	3.45	40.7
P.E.I.	4.18	48.9	2.97	35.0
N.S......................	5.84	68.3	4.27	50.4
N.B.	5.17	60.5	4.46	52.6
Que.	7.66	89.6	6.74	79.5
Ont.	10.02	117.2	10.03	118.3
Man....................	7.18	84.0	6.99	82.4
Sask....................	7.00	81.9	5.57	65.7
Alta....................	8.53	99.8	15.19	179.1
B.C.	9.95	116.4	8.31	98.0
National Average	8.55	100.0	8.48	100.0

SOURCE: Same as Table 4.

Finally, two different interpretations of equity – one relating to a provincial complaint, the other to a federal objective – merit comment. First is the Saskatchewan complaint that the tax points should be equalized up to the per capita yield of the top-yielding provinces. But apart from the federal cost involved, the tax points in question are part of an overall system of revenue equalization involving a comprehensive list of provincial-local revenue sources. If fiscal equity does indeed demand equalization to the top – a dubious concept – then the *general* equalization formula should be modified; differential treatment of a slice of income tax revenues would be arbitrary and unwarranted.

Secondly, the major federal objective of achieving uniformity in its per capita contributions to the provinces over five years conveys a different meaning of equity. As indicated in Table 7, marked interprovincial disparities in federal per capita contributions to the three programs in fiscal year 1976-77 existed. These disparities are especially notable in post-secondary education, since the federal contribution was equal to 50 per cent of a province's own operating costs (expenditures). The differences ranged from Newfoundland's low $56.24 to Alberta's high $75.34, with a per capita national average contribution of $70.19. Such disparities are less pronounced in the case of hospital insurance because only half the federal payment was determined by a province's *own* costs.[40] With a national

Table 7
Interprovincial Disparities in Federal Per Capita Contributions
to the Three Established Programs, 1976-77
($ per capita)

	Hospital Insurance	Medicare	Post-Secondary Education	Total*
Nfld.	113.61	41.56	56.24	211.13
P.E.I.	100.14	41.56	56.98	199.17
N.S.	114.59	41.56	69.09	225.36
N.B.	112.56	41.56	56.41	210.60
Que.	116.78	41.56	73.94	232.27
Ont.	118.33	41.56	74.13	234.02
Man.	119.30	41.56	62.47	223.25
Sask.	112.24	41.56	60.97	214.64
Alta.	115.28	41.56	75.34	232.20
B.C.	115.89	41.56	58.37	215.86
National Average	116.68	41.56	70.19	228.43

* May not add to totals because of rounding.

SOURCE: *Financial Assessment of Established Programs Financing Proposal*, 51-53.

average of $116.68, the federal payments vary from Prince Edward Island's $110.14 per capita to Manitoba's $119.30. Only with respect to Medicare were the per capita grants uniform, simply because the whole federal contribution was based on per capita national average costs.

Obviously, in adopting the EPF system, equity demanded that the federal contributions be put on an equal per capita footing; otherwise, the disparities would be built in to the new federal *cash* payments, and carried into the future as the GNP escalator was applied to them. The federal government had also grown sensitive to the charge that cost-sharing was responsible for such unequal per capita grants. Such disparities, of course, were the inevitable outcome of open-end grants having a 50:50 matching provision. The "have-not" provinces were at a relative disadvantage; they simply could not afford to expand their program levels to equal those of richer provinces, and thus picked up smaller grants.[41]

Nevertheless, the distribution of federal grants among the provinces on a uniform per capita basis is subject to criticism. Assuming the grants *are* intended for specific purposes, is population alone an adequate indicator of program *need*? Surely other factors – especially the distribution of population by age and labour costs – account for provincial differences in program need, and hence expenditures. Moreover, the allocation of grants should not take into account interprovincial differences in per capita income. Provincial *revenues*, through a set of general equalization grants, have already been brought up to the per capita national average. Additional equalization would thus be vulnerable to the charge of invoking an exaggerated notion of equity.

Conclusion

The new arrangements for financing health and higher education constitute a major development in intergovernmental fiscal relations. Shared-cost financing (conditional grants), defective in design and administration, had been losing their credentials as fiscal instruments. Both the opting-out provision in 1965 (taken up by Quebec) and the post-secondary education arrangement, two years later, had anticipated the new approach to financing "established" programs.

In theory, the provinces would be enabled to assume full financial responsibility for the programs by a federal transfer to them of the appropriate tax room. But this obvious (and much simpler) approach was rejected for two important reasons. First, through the cash grant (although unrelated to actual program costs), a federal presence would be retained. And the high national standards achieved in the health field could be imputed to several specific federal objectives. Secondly, the acceptance by most provinces of the whole federal contribution in the form of a tax transfer was unlikely. After all, a uniform number of tax points yields very different amounts of revenue from province to province. Indeed, a principal fault, already explained, is that only Ontario and British Columbia benefit initially from the transfer of tax room. Until the value of the equalized tax points surpasses that of the cash component, the *whole* federal contribution to the other eight provinces will grow in proportion to GNP. While conversion of the whole contribution into a block grant would have avoided this problem, a concession in the form of income tax points had become politically imperative. Such a concession is, however, more inflexible and less able to be reversed than one in the form of a block grant.

On the positive side, the federal government has regained control over a sizable slice of its own expenditures by eliminating the three largest open-end grants. In addition, the removal of conditions under which costs were eligable for federal sharing may result in more efficient provincial expenditures *within* the health field. But it is unfortunate that the extraordinary complexity of the EPF transfer has left out all but a few treasury economists in the Stygian darkness.

Notes

1. *House of Commons Debates*, February 18, 1977, 3200 (Hon. Donald Macdonald, Minister of Finance).

2. Bill C-37, sc 25-26 Eliz. II, c. (1977).

3. The most significant change *not* discussed here concerns the refinement of the general equalization formula, increasing from twenty-two to twenty-nine the number of provincial-local revenue sources for equalization, and for eighteen of these, redefining the indicator or base. (Part I of the Act.) For a general discussion, see David B. Perry, "The Federal-Provincial Fiscal Arrangements Introduced in 1977," *Canadian Tax Journal*, XXV (July-August, 1977). See also Bank of Nova Scotia, *Monthly Review* (March-April, 1977).

4. No detailed description is offered here; for a description and a review of the issues, see George E. Carter, *Canadian Conditional Grants Since World War II* (Toronto, 1971).

5. For an analysis, see George E. Carter, "Financing Post-Secondary Education Under the Federal-Provincial Fiscal Arrangements Act: An Appraisal," *Canadian Tax Journal*, XXIV (September-October, 1976), 505-22.

6. For a detailed account see Carter, *Canadian Conditional Grants*, ch. 5.

7. Federal-Provincial Tax Structure Committee, *Report* (Ottawa, 1966), 19.

8. Also lumped into the offer was the continuing portion of the national health grants which involved relatively small amounts for professional training and public health research.

9. Carter, *Canadian Conditional Grants*, 93ff. This earlier offer, antedating both medicare and the post-secondary education transfer, pertained to hospital insurance, two small health grants (professional training and public health research), and, interestingly enough, the Canada Assistance Plan. Though well "established" CAP is conspicuously missing from the new EPF arrangement. Exclusion is because social welfare programs have recently been undergoing review which may well result in a major overhaul of the welfare system. For an indication of new directions in this major area, see Canada, Department of National Health and Welfare, *Working Paper on Social Security in Canada* (2nd ed.), April, 1973 (known as the "Orange Paper").

10. Tax Structure Committee, *Report*, 41.

11. Carter, *Canadian Conditional Grants*, 96-101.

12. Hon. E.J. Benson, Minister of Finance, *Proposals for Tax Reform* (Ottawa, 1969), 81.

13. *Federal-Provincial Conference*, October, 1966 (Ottawa, 1968).

14. Prime Minister Pierre Trudeau, "Established Programs Financing: A Proposal Regarding the Major Shared-Cost Programs in the Fields of Health and Post-Secondary Education" (Statement tabled at the Federal-Provincial Conference, Ottawa, June 14-15, 1976).

15. These arrangements actually ended three years earlier (March 31, 1977); their termination was a mandatory condition of the 1977 EPF proposal.

16. Cf. Tax Structure Committee, *Report*, 13-14.

17. Trudeau, "Established Programs Financing," 2.

18. Unfortunately, no published accounts exist of the several federal-provincial meetings which were held in camera. Information must therefore be drawn

from budget speeches of provincial governments, *House of Commons Debates*, press releases, and so forth.

19. New Brunswick, Quebec, Ontario, and Saskatchewan.

20. The Hon. Merv Leitch, "Federal-Provincial Arrangements: The Provincial Proposal," statement on behalf of all provincial ministers of finance and provincial treasurers, December 6-7, 1976. (This address is contained as an appendix in British Columbia, *Budget* [Victoria, January 24, 1977].) Also at this stage the "revenue guarantee" became entangled in the EPF proposal; as compensation for withdrawal of the guarantee the provinces demanded an additional federal transfer of 4 personal income tax points. As noted later, the provinces finally settled for half this amount.

21. The agreement was so characterized by the Ontario premier. See "Budget Paper B," *Ontario Budget*, Toronto, April 19, 1977, 9.

22. The net provincial gain in "tax room" actually amounts to 9.143 per cent of the federal personal income tax, since 4.347 per cent of this tax and the 1 per cent of the corporate income tax base had already been secured under the former arrangements for financing post-secondary education. Moreover, of the 13.5 points of personal income tax, 1 equalized point plus its cash equivalent were added late in negotiations as partial compensation for the so-called Revenue Guarantee.

23. The number of tax points transferred is, in the last analysis, the outcome of intergovernmental bargaining; however, it seems that the value of 12.5 personal income tax points and 1 corporate tax point in the two highest-yielding provinces (Ontario and Alberta) was approximately equivalent to half the national average federal contribution to the three programs in the base year. As noted, the additional 1 personal income tax point together with an equal amount in cash came later as part of the Revenue Guarantee settlement. The value of 1 such point in 1975-76 was $7.63 per capita (section 19 of the Act).

24. The value of Quebec's tax transfer is inflated by the value of 8.5 points of personal income tax, an extension of the opting-out arrangement. The inclusion of the value of this federal tax abatement for EPF means, of course, that Quebec's tax transfer is not comparable with those of the other provinces.

25. To repeat: these amounts represent one-half the national per capita average of the federal contribution to the three programs in the base year (1975-76) escalated by the per capita growth index and multiplied by the estimated 1977 population.

26. The most significant contrast between these two provinces is, of course, that Newfoundland's basic cash component (line 1) accounts for 55.7 per cent of the total transfer (line 12), while the corresponding ratio for Ontario is only 50.3 per cent. These ratios underscore the important distinction made earlier that tax points, even after equalization, are worth more to the "have" provinces than they are to the "have-nots."

27. To clarify, the provinces (except Quebec) levy their personal income taxes on the federal basic tax; when this base originated in 1972, it was expressed as 100

"tax points." Hence the federal tax reduction of 9.143 points, *ipso facto*, shrinks the provincial tax base to 90.857 points. Therefore, Ontario, for example, must increase its rate simply to prevent revenue loss. Since the old 100-point base was 110.063 per cent of the new, smaller base of 90.857 points, Ontario's old rate (30.5 per cent) must be grossed up to 33.57 per cent (30.5 per cent × 1.10063). For the same reason (the reduced provincial tax base), the 9.143 tax points gained must be grossed up to 10.06 per cent (9.143 per cent × 1.10063). Table 3 therefore shows Ontario's new tax rate (before rounding) as 43.632 per cent (33.57 per cent + 10.06 per cent).

28. Ontario, 1977 Budget, "Budget Paper B" (Toronto, April 19, 1977), 6.

29. Quebec, *Budget Speech*, "Supplementary Information" (Quebec City, April 12, 1977), 42. Manitoba and Saskatchewan have registered the same complaint. See Manitoba, *Budget Address*, Appendix E (Winnipeg, April 22, 1977), 6, and Saskatchewan, *Budget Speech* (Regina, March 10, 1977), 66.

30. Ontario and British Columbia; although (as mentioned before) Alberta's per capita yield from 1 corporate tax point is in first place.

31. Saskatchewan, *Budget Speech*, 69. Significantly, the provincial proposal to Ottawa had actually provided equalization to this level. Doubtless, this was the major concession made to the poorer provinces before they would relinquish their customary support for some form of cost-sharing. See "Federal-Provincial Arrangements: The Provincial Proposal."

32. Trudeau, "Established Programs Financing," 13.

33. British Columbia felt especially shortchanged by the federal ceiling to its commitment, since it had begun to expand the province's system of post-secondary education at about the same time.

34. British Columbia, *Budget* (Victoria, January 24, 1977), 12.

35. Saskatchewan, *Budget Speech*, 68.

36. Newfoundland, *Budget* (St. John's, April 22, 1977), 12.

37. *Financial Assessment of Established Programs Proposal*, 66-69.

38. For a full theoretical treatment, see particularly George G. Break, *Intergovernmental Fiscal Relations in the United States* (Washington, 1967); Wallace E. Oates, *Fiscal Federalism* (New York, 1972); James A. Maxwell, *Specific Purpose Grants in the United States: Recent Developments* (Canberra, Australia, 1975); and R.L. Mathews, ed., *Responsibility Sharing in a Federal System* (Canberra, Australia, 1975).

39. Originating in the former Medicare legislation, these are: comprehensiveness of coverage with respect to services, universality with respect to people covered, portability of benefits, accessibility, and non-profit administration by a public agency.

40. Accordingly, in provinces with below-average costs, the federal grant would cover a larger proportion of its total program costs. This has been called "implicit" equalization, the logic of which has been called into question. See Carter, *Canadian Conditional Grants*, 47-50.

41. Of course, smaller federal grants per capita would also result if a province

(British Columbia in the case of post-secondary education) simply chose not to expand its expenditures as far as other provinces. It is interesting to note that Spearman coefficients of rank correlation by province between per capita income (1975) and per capita federal payments (1975-76) show significant positive correlation. For the three programs combined, the Spearman coefficient is $+0.6970$.

18. ALBERT BRETON

The Theory of
Competitive Federalism

I. Introduction

I hold with considerable conviction to the notion that the mechanisms which discipline and constrain democratic politics, especially democratic politics in federal states, operate with as much force as those which discipline and constrain economic life. That is not a widely shared view, though it is one that is gaining ground. The traditional and more conventional view is that economic mechanisms are so constraining as to be essentially deterministic, while politics, being the exercise of power, can be set in motion or stopped, as it were, at will. In that view, politics is always capricious and beyond rational explanation.

To my knowledge, Commissioners never held to the traditional view of politics, but it is fair to say, I believe, that neither did most of us accept the notion that political mechanisms are as constraining as economic ones. Over the last two and a half years, our views of politics, and especially of democratic politics in federal systems, have moved quite far away from the traditional concept, as readers of the Commission's Report will have been able to witness for themselves. However, in my opinion, the movement has not been sufficiently great. In a way, that is understandable because breaking away from traditional modes of thought, even in the face of dire necessity, is never easy.

From the *Report of the Royal Commission on the Economic Union and Development Propects for Canada* (1985). Reproduced with permission of the Minister of Supply and Services Canada.

The discussion that follows, submitted as a supplementary view to the Commission's Report, is therefore a clarification and an extension of the theory of democratic politics in federal states, a theory which I call the theory of competitive federalism. To put if differently, in what follows, I provide a brief but more extensive analysis of the mechanisms of competitive federalism, indicate some reforms that are necessary if we wish these mechanisms to be more efficient, and draw a few implications of the theory for certain key issues. I insist that there is still much research to be done in this area and many problems to be resolved. However, I believe that what can be defended seriously at this moment should be present in the debates which the Commission's Report will no doubt engender. Hence this document.

The following discussion is divided into four sections. After this Introduction, Section II examines the nature and properties of competitive politics in a federal state. In Section III, I derive implications of that analysis for a number of questions such as those of the economic union, intergovernmental grants, and municipal governments. Section IV concludes my statement.

II. Theory

It has been and, to a large extent, remains conventional wisdom that the two pillars which define Canada's political institutions – parliamentary government and federalism – lack congruence.[1] That view springs from an *a priori* abstract and formal definition of what constitutes parliamentarism to which is added a no less abstract and formal notion of federalism. The presumed lack of congruence has had enormous influence, not only on the way Canadians think about politics, but also on the way they have conditioned the evolution of their political institutions. It is true that for almost a century and a quarter Canadian parliamentarism and federalism have co-existed in more or less harmonious fashion, but the general tendency – still present in the Commission's Report – to set parliamentary institutions and federalism in opposition, or if not, to view them as separate and unrelated to one another, is at the root of many of our difficulties.

From the beginning of their history as a country to the present, Canadians have reflected on their political institutions with one eye on the United Kingdom and the other on the United States. England was and remains a unitary-parliamentary system, while the U.S. was and is a federal-congressional structure. Hence the following questions: Could a federal-parliamentary system work? Should priority be given to parliamentarism or to federalism? With which one of these two pillars is democracy more closely associated?

I wish to argue that parliamentarism and federalism are congruent; that the issue of having to give priority to either in opting for democracy is a false one; and that it is possible to reform our national and federal institutions in ways that increase their effectiveness, while remaining true to their fundamental genius. A clarification of these issues is necessarily an intellectual exercise, one which requires the selection of a particular language. Being an economist by training and by preference, I feel more at ease formulating and discussing issues, even those outside the traditional frontiers of economics (problems of politics and of society, the traditional domains of political science and of the other social sciences), in the language of that discipline. At the same time, such a strategy makes it easier to draw on the powerful methodology of economics. There is, finally, a third bonus that comes from stating the issues of politics in the language of economics: it makes it easier to go from political to economic real-life questions and issues and makes it easier to formulate a theory of politics that is "compatible" with economic theory. I know from having worked with sociologists and political scientists over many years that the translation from one language to another is a relatively easy matter and that nothing substantive is altered in the process.

Parliamentary (that is, responsible or party) government was not designed. It evolved in response to pressures and influences applied first to monarchs by powerful interests and then, throughout history, to those in office by new emerging centres of power. The dynamics of parliamentarism are appropriately, if somewhat summarily, encapsulated by the expression "elite accommodation."

There is not much competition (or not many "checks and balances": the kinds of behaviour associated with political competition within governments, as distinguished from competition between governments) in such a system. There are, of course, the checks and balances that come from powerful interests, whether economic (like business and labour, though these are not usually of equal strength), religious (churches), intellectual (academics and research organizations), and so on. There are also the checks and balances that come from the Question Period in the House of Commons, from the log-rolling that takes place in caucus, and from public opinion. Finally, and very importantly, there is competition that originates in the requirement of popular support elicited in contested elections at more or less regular intervals.

All in all, however, competition is quite weak, especially when cabinet is supported by a good parliamentary majority. The weakness of the checks and balances that come from the lack of separation between the executive and legislative branches is aggravated by the "independence" of the judiciary, an independence which is reflected in the doctrine of "parliamentary supremacy," as contrasted to the doctrine of "judicial review." (I return to this question below [Section III.4], when I discuss the place of the Charter of Rights and Freedoms in Canadian politics.)

A necessary implication of the foregoing is that the preferences, aspirations, and opinions of the public, unless they are adopted by the power elites, are not likely to be represented as vividly as they would be in a system in which competition was more vibrant. This overly schematic description of parliamentarism would be even more incomplete if I did not immediately add that the system is susceptible to improvements. The system is capable, as history documents, of absorbing further checks and balances, while at the same time remaining faithful to its own virtues and genius.

The Report contains recommendations which go in the direction of improving competition, such as those aimed at removing budget secrecy and at reforming the Senate, recommendations that I support, although I will have more to say on Senate reforms below. But one could go further. I would suggest that in addition *serious consideration should be given to finding ways of reducing party discipline in the House of Commons and, to the extent that it exists, in parliamentary committees as well, for all matters, except budgetary ones.* If that was done – slowly, but deliberately – the power of elected representatives would be increased, their ability to voice the opinions of their constituents would be enhanced, and the capacity of constituents to influence governments would be augmented.

Responsible or party government in unitary states, however fine-tuned to better reflect the preferences of citizens, remains a weak mechanism in the performance of the task I have just noted. But when responsible government is married to federalism, that job is done much more effectively. I must hasten to add that some marriages are more successful than others and that some federal structures are better designed than others. I will explore these issues in the pages that follow and indicate what I believe are the ingredients of a good federalism and of a good marriage of federalism with party government. However, the central proposition holds: parliamentary government combined with federalism give the citizens of a country a more effective set of institutions for reflecting their will, preferences, and aspirations. Responsible government is democratic government; but responsible government plus federalism is extended democracy, simply because there is more competition.

I must, therefore, address two preliminary questions: How does federalism introduce more competition in any system of government, more particularly, in a system of responsible government? Is competition a "good" thing, that is, something we should want in our political institutions? I will seek to answer these two questions in Sections II.2 and II.4 below. As an introduction to that discussion – and in recognition of the fact that competition is so central to my view of politics and of democracy – I must devote some space to clarification of the meaning I give to the word "competition."

1. Competition

The development of mainline economic thought in the Anglo-American tradition – by any measure the overwhelming tradition – has systematically restricted the notion of competition to price competition. This tradition has come to focus on the conditions under which this kind of competition leads to (Pareto) efficiency, that is, to that state in which no one individual can be made better off without someone else being made worse off. Significantly, this neo-classical tradition has not associated any particular behaviours or activities with its definition of competition.

Since the conditions under which competition is optimal in one sense or another will be examined later on for the case of competitive federalism, it may be worth noting that it is only in the case of price competition that the conditions are known under which competition is Pareto optimal. In other words, under certain conditions, Adam Smith's "invisible hand" allocates resources efficiently for the case of price competition. Although there has been much discussion in the literature on advertising and quality competition, and less, though still a respectable amount, on competition involving research and development expenditures, innovation, and technology, it is not known if these various forms of competition are socially efficient. Until recently, the weight of opinion in the profession would have been, I believe, that they were not. Things have been changing in recent years, but no consensus, not even a minimal one, has emerged.

I mention this to underscore that even if it is not possible to specify all the conditions – those that are necessary as well as those that are sufficient – under which political competition in a federal state is optimal, that does not constitute a basis for rejecting such competition, any more than our inability to specify necessary and sufficient conditions for economic competition to be efficient is a satisfactory ground for rejecting market organization.

Price competition must be contrasted to other kinds of competition, which have from time to time retained the attention of economists and others. There are a number of strands in the literature associated with such labels as "working competition" and "countervailing power." One of the more important of these is the notion of *entrepreneurial competition*, sometimes also called Austrian or Schumpeterian competition. In the early 1900s an important number of (to become distinguished) Austrian economists (notably Joseph Schumpeter, Ludwig Mises, and Frederick Hayek), seeking to come to grips with the crucial Marxian question of the dynamics of capitalism, proposed theories of economic development in which that particular notion of competition played a central role.

In the words of Schumpeter, one of the ablest analysts of this kind of competition:

> In capitalist reality as distinguished from its textbook picture, it is not that kind of competition (price competition) which counts but the competition from the new commodity, the new technology, the new source of supply, the new type of organization ... competition which

commands a decisive cost or quality advantage and which strikes not at the margins of the profits and the outputs of the existing firms but at their foundations and their very lives. This kind of competition is as much more effective than the other as a bombardment is in comparison with forcing a door, so much more important that it becomes a matter of comparative indifference whether competition in the ordinary sense functions more or less promptly; the powerful lever that in the long run expands output and brings down prices is in any case made of other stuff.[2]

Notwithstanding that fact that barriers are sometimes erected to soften the impact of entrepreneurial competition, one must acknowledge that in seeking to understand the economic factors that determine how resources are allocated, as well as the forces that have shaped the broad development of capitalism, the Austrians' notion of competition is more useful than that of mainline neo-classical theory.[3]

It is not an accident that the extension of the analytical tools of economics to politics was initiated by Schumpeter (although Niccolo Machiavelli and John Stuart Mill, among others, had anticipated the possibility): it was a natural outgrowth of his work on entrepreneurial competition. Politicians, in that view, are entrepreneurs who compete for resources by introducing new policies, by developing new forms of organization, by heralding new unifying symbols, by structuring a new social consensus, etc. Recent writers have characterized entrepreneurial competition as "alertness to opportunities."[4] If that is a good definition of entrepreneurship, it cannot be limited to the realm of economics, but extends naturally to politics and to other areas of life. To be sure, the "*modus operandi* of competition" (to use a Schumpeterian expression) will vary between business and political entrepreneurs, but their behaviour will have enough in common to be called competitive.

Having said that, it must be recognized that not much is known about competitive processes. Earlier, in referring to intra-governmental competition – the competition between political parties, between the executive, legislative, and judicial branches of government (when such competition exists), between the various departments and bureaus that constitute the bureaucracy of a particular governmental unit, such as that of Quebec or Saskatchewan – I used the American expression "checks and balances." These words correspond to more or less specific and precise behaviour and are useful in characterizing that kind of competition. In his study of *American Capitalism*,[5] Galbraith used the evocative term "countervailing power" in an effort to describe a particular process of competition. Recently, Nelson and Winter[6] have sought to model entrepreneurial competition in terms of two activities: "do research" or "do imitation." A friend of mine, having read an earlier draft of this statement, suggested that the behaviour associated with federal-provincial competition was "complement and countervail." To illustrate, if the federal government chose to subsidize post-secondary education by giving money directly to students instead of giving it to provincial governments, these latter could "complement" by targeting their spending on education more closely to their own priorities, or "countervail" by taking the money away from students.

This area of study is in its infancy. I cannot therefore associate particular competitive processes with the various kinds of entrepreneurial competition that I will discuss below. Because it is appropriate, I use the words "checks and balances" for intra-governmental competition; otherwise, for politics as for economics, I use the word "competition," having in mind entrepreneurial competition, but no particular behavioural process.

2. Federalism

At its simplest, that is, before introducing real-world complications into the picture – a task to be undertaken later – a federal state can be formally defined as a type of political organization in which there are at least two levels of jurisdiction – in Canada, national and provincial – between which the entire set of constitutional powers is divided. The assignment of these powers between the governmental levels is not made by one level alone. That distinguishes federalism from confederalism, a system in which the assignment of powers is made by the provinces alone, and from unitary states, structures in which powers are assigned by senior governments acting in isolation. According to that definition, Canada is and has been a federation and never a confederation. The Canadian provinces, on the other hand, in their relationship with their municipalities, are unitary states.

The division of powers and the mode through which it is effected define federalism well, albeit in a way that is too formal to be very useful in understanding how such a system actually works. From that point of view, what is much more important are the implications of any division of powers for the operations of, and relationships between, the governments of the federation, all of which are responsible governments. The central and most important implication is that in the search for popular support – something that is as needed for the effectiveness of governing parties as revenue is essential for the effectiveness of business firms – the governments of a federation will find themselves competing with each other. Federalism thus adds more competition to that already present in responsible or party government.

One point needs emphasis. Political competition is not something that politicians choose or want, whatever their commitment to federalism and, more broadly, to liberty and to democracy. In that respect, they are exactly like business entrepreneurs who do not want competition either. Competition arises from the necessity to respond to the actions of others; it is "forced" on people by the environment. One does not even have to be aware that one is competing to be competitive. A business firm that adopts a new technology to reduce its costs is acting competitively; one that advertises and places some of its output on sale is acting in a competitive fashion; someone who supports a particular social movement or a particular lobby is competing; as is the politician who seeks harmony with provincial governments by removing the contentious questions from the agenda of federal-provincial encounters.

There is so much mystification about this that I must dwell on two corollary points, at the risk of seeming to insist on the obvious for those who have seen their way clear on the subject. First, there is the whole bag of issues that are best summarized by the words "co-operative federalism." What is co-operative federalism and how is it to be distinguished from other types of federalisms? To my knowledge, the expression has never been formally defined. That may not be a lacuna because we all have, from practical experience and observation, a good intuitive idea of what is meant by these two words. Two or more persons working together to lift a heavy object; two or more persons engaged in a search for something lost; two or more persons removing snow from the road: these are examples of the kind of behaviour we have in mind when we think of co-operation. In other words, someone helping someone else achieve a certain goal or objective.

Co-operative federalism by analogy would exist if all the politicians of a federation worked together to achieve some collective end. Instead of working on their own for citizens, governments would work together for the betterment of all "the people." Before examining what is meant by co-operative federalism in more detail, I would like the reader to ask him or herself why it is that we do not, as societies, organize the search for justice on a co-operative basis, but instead set defence against prosecuting attorneys in courts of law? Why do we not organize the working of party politics on a co-operative basis, but instead pit political parties against each other in grand electoral contests? Why do we not organize the search for truth on a co-operative basis, but instead require scholars and scientists to compete for research funds and for limited space in research publications? And, finally – though the list could go on – why do we not organize the production of goods and services on a co-operative basis, but instead implement laws that make co-operation an offence?

These examples underline the fact that in some areas, co-operation is *not* the efficient principle of social organization and that it is less efficient than competition, essentially because co-operation can easily degenerate into collusion, conspiracy, and connivance and that this is not necessarily good! In the case of federalism, would co-operation be a better principle of social organization than competition? I will only begin to answer this question here; the answer will be completed in Section II.5. To answer the question, it must be recognized that co-operative federalism is aimed at removing the competition which is a natural by-product of federal organization. Consequently, to be able to answer the question, it is necessary to know whether competition is a "good" feature of political organizations. I do not address this issue before Section II.4.

I have posed the question here, however, because I wish to stress that the notion of co-operative federalism is part and parcel of the politics of "elite accommodation" which plays such an important role in the dynamics of party governments. Indeed, in practice, co-operative federalism is nothing but executive federalism. This has been defined by Smiley "as the relations between elected and appointed officials of the two orders of government in federal-provincial interactions and among the executives of the provinces in interprovincial interactions."[7] I will argue later that there is a place for a limited executive federalism. The executive federalism contemplated by co-operative federalists, however, effectively extends to all the areas of federal-provincial contact. It transfers to executive and bureaucratic bargaining and negotiation what properly belongs to the realm of the political.

Co-operative federalism does not necessarily eliminate federalist competition, but by moving it into executive and bureaucratic offices and corridors, it mutes its public manifestations and its effectiveness. The heart of co-operative federalism is secret deals, not the stuff on which a lively democracy thrives! There are other implications of the doctrine of co-operative federalism; I mention two.

A first is a by-product of drumming into the psyche of Canadians the belief that federalism is or should be co-operative. Once that is achieved, it provides a fruitful background for the arguments of those, sometimes in one province, sometimes in another, who wish to promote and foster separatism. Indeed, a process that is inherently competitive, even if it is called co-operative, is bound to throw up incidents which separatists – themselves competitive individuals – will use to argue that "the system does not work," because on a particular matter the politicians of a province have been rebuffed or have simply lost in the competitive game. It would be relatively easy to document that the rhetoric of Canadian separatists is often based on the notion that federalism is not as co-operative as one had been led to believe it should be. I cannot undertake that documentation task here. I simply note that if Canadians had been helped to understand that federalist politics, like all politics, is inherently competitive, the propaganda of separatism would have fallen on more barren ground.

A second implication of the doctrine of co-operative federalism relates to the condemnation, by those who adhere to it, of unilateralism, that is, of independent action by any one government of the federation. Unilateral action by one government is, of course, a derogation from co-operation, since when one is acting alone one is not co-operating. Consequently, those who espouse co-operative federalism decry unilateral action on the part of any government in the federation. Although in principle the condemnation applies to all, in practice it strikes much harder at the federal government, simply because the provinces, if they want to act in unison, have to come to an agreement – something that is not easy to do for essentially competitive entities. To put it differently, in the normal course of affairs, the central government is likely to act unilaterally more often than the provinces, to the extent that these wish to act as one, because the costs of co-ordination are positive. A condemnation of unilateralism, if enforced, would therefore affect the central government more than the provinces.

Co-operative federalism, because it proscribes unilateral action, is therefore a disguised ploy to shackle the federal government, to prevent it from addressing the problems it alone can resolve and is constitutionally responsible for resolving. Indeed, condemning federal unilateralism is condemning the federal government for acting constitutionally! This is so true that if one takes the trouble to go behind the language of co-operative federalism, to the reality of the arguments which it seeks to convey, one discovers either confederalism or a conservative view which seeks to reduce the role of the federal government and, indeed, of all governments in society.

In concluding this argument, I note that the condemnation of unilateralism is also a denial that the division of powers between orders of government is essential to federalism. That indeed is the crux of the matter. Co-operative federalism, if it came to pass, would deny federalism itself. Those who seek co-operative federalism and labour for its realization, seek and labour for a unitary state, disguised in the trappings of federalism, but from which competition would have been reduced to a minimum or even eliminated.

The second corollary point related to the mystification surrounding the notion of political competition pertains to the language of competition and of federalism. Competition in the marketplace, in courtrooms, in parliaments, on hustings, in university seminars, and wherever it takes place is sometimes smooth, so smooth that one could be led into believing that it is not there. But at other times, it is rough, so rough that outsiders are often at a loss in trying to understand why so much energy and effort are displayed, why opponents are characterized in such vile fashion, why the parties become uncouth and impolite in the process of competing. In describing this second circumstance, it is not uncommon for the outsiders, who would have no problem with "well-behaved" competition, to describe the situation in terms of conflict, rancour, combat, suspicion, disharmony, and so on, and to attach to these expressions a negative connotation. The stage is then set for appeals to co-operation and for a rhetoric that praises the virtues of co-operative federalism.

Words have emotional content. For that reason, debates and disagreements are sometimes resolved by using a different language. It is important, however, that the change in vocabulary be only that, not the occasion for unnecessary changes in institutions. When competition is acrimonious one may wish to reduce its acrimoniousness; that can be a legitimate objective. But it is not because we choose to relabel a competitive process by some other name, such as conflict, disharmony, or rivalry, that we have improved things. Indeed, if relabelling leads to the search for unwarranted institutional changes, we may have worsened the situation. Prosecuting and defence attorneys may be uncouth and antagonistic to each other; things could possibly be better if such behaviour did not exist, but surely justice would not be well served, if, to remove such behaviour, courtroom procedures were transformed from competitive into co-operative ones!

Many a time I have been struck by the fact that those who resist the notion of competition and its reality in fact take offence at the language of competition. The question of how a language can be made more genteel and gracious is an interesting and difficult one. It may be possible to have a genteel and graceful competitive federalism, but whether it is or not has little bearing on whether competitive federalism is desirable or not.

Before moving on to a discussion of the costs and benefits of political competition and to an overall evaluation of its worth, I must deal with two subjects that are likely to be of most interest to specialists of co-operative federalism, but which must be cleared up if what I call competitive federalism is to be understood. For that reason, I encourage even those who are not co-operative federalists to stay with me through the next section.

3. Not Co-operation and Not Anarchy

The "proof" that co-operation in federations is beneficial has traditionally been based on sentimentalism and romanticism. Many people do not mind this, but scholars have generally sought to extract themselves from such clutches; consequently they have searched for a rigorous theory of federalism that would provide them with the desired proof. One of the theories used by these scholars derives from an application to federalism of the theory of games, specifically an application of the theory of the non-co-operative game known as "prisoner's dilemma,"[8]

That theory is a representation of a situation in which non-co-operative behaviour on the part of individuals leads to an outcome than is inefficient, in that if the individuals could enter into a pre-game binding agreement to co-operate, they would choose another outcome than the one that obtains in the absence of co-operation. In the words of Luce and Raiffa, the prisoner's dilemma game can be characterized as follows:

> Two suspects are taken into custody *and separated*. This district attorney is certain that they are guilty of a specific crime, but he does not have adequate evidence to convict them at a trial. He points out to each prisoner that each has two alternatives: to confess to the crime the

police are sure they have done, or not to confess. If they both do not confess, then the district attorney states he will book them on some very minor trumped-up charge such as petty larceny and illegal possession of a weapon, and they will both receive minor punishment; if they both confess they will be prosecuted, but he will not recommend less than the most severe sentence; but if one confesses and the other does not, then the confessor will receive lenient treatment for turning state's evidence whereas the latter will get "the book" slapped at him.[9]

If they could co-operate, the two suspects would decide not to confess. But being separated and held incommunicado, they will both confess, each to "receive lenient treatment," and both will get "the book." This serves to show that non-co-operative behaviour is inefficient.

The queston is whether the prisoner's dilemma game is an appropriate model to think about and to analyse federalism. In other words, will the co-operative behaviour which would lead to efficient results in the prisoner's dilemma game also lead to efficient results in the case of federalism? The answer must be a resounding no. The prisoner's dilemma game is simply not an appropriate model for federalism. Why? For two reasons.

The first and most obvious is that the governments of federal states are not kept incommunicado. In Canada, with close to one thousand federal-provincial meetings per year, it is hard to assume that the parties are separated.

The second reason for the inapplicability of the prisoner's dilemma model to federalism is more basic. As the Luce and Raiffa narration makes clear, there are no gains from competition in a prisoner's dilemma model: there are only gains from co-operation. To understand the full burden of this point, assume that the parties in the game are not criminal suspects, but ordinary oligopolists. Would we also conclude that they should co-operate (collude?) to improve their position? The logic of the prisoner's dilemma model would seem to push us in that direction. In this "oligopolist's dilemma" game, it is our instinct as economists – for those of us who are – which keeps us in check; we know that the logic of co-operation appears correct only because consumers are left out of the game. Once their presence is acknowledged, it is easy to understand that competition is for their benefit. We must conclude that co-operation benefits the oligopolists, while competition serves consumers. That is why the prisoner's dilemma model cannot be used to analyse oligopolies.

It is essentially for the same reason that the prisoner's dilemma game cannot be used to analyse federalism. In this case, citizens are left out of the picture. They are the ones who benefit from competition. If that is the case, how are thoughtful scholars led to adopt a completely inappropriate model to analyse federalism? The answer must be that underlying the use of the prisoner's dilemma model is the (tacit) assumption that provincial governments perfectly embody the interests of the people and their respective provinces. There is no role for competition because each provincial government is assumed to be serving its people perfectly! All models of co-operative federalism in fact make the same assumption.

We are therefore back to competition and to competitive federalism. But competitive behaviour is not unconstrained or anarchical behaviour; indeed, competition would not survive, still less be efficient, if such behaviour was the rule. In fact, competitive behaviour is restrained and disciplined behaviour.

One thing that can discipline competition is legally enforced property rights. One of the best definitions of these is that provided by Dales. I quote:

> In everyday conversation we usually speak of "property" rather than "property rights", but the contraction is misleading if it tends to make us think of property as *things* rather than as *rights*, or of ownership as outright rather than circumscribed. . . . When you own a car, you own a set of legally defined rights to use the vehicle in certain ways and not in others; you may not use it as a personal weapon, for example, nor may you leave it unattended beside a fire hydrant. Among the most important rights you do have are the right to prevent others from using the vehicle, except with your permission and on your terms, and the right to divest yourself of your ownership rights in the vehicle by selling them to someone else. We may say, then, that ownership always consists of (1) a set of rights to use property in certain ways (and a set of negative rights or prohibitions, that prevent its use in other ways); (2) a right to prevent others from exercising those rights, or to set the terms on which others may exercise them; and (3) a right to sell your property rights.[10]

Property rights extend beyond physical objects like cars, to things such as bonds, shares of stock, and money. They extend to one's time (which can be sold as labour or consumed as leisure); it is important that they extend to roads, canals, air waves, and, as the Law of the Sea Conference made abundantly clear, especially during the last four or five years of negotiations, to the oceans and the seabeds.

It is important to stress that property rights may or may not be related to private property. Indeed, property rights can be vested in individuals, in groups (such as corporations), and in government or other public bodies. That is, property rights can be private or collective. On August 8, 1983, *The Globe and Mail* reported on a debate in the Department of External Affairs in Ottawa on whether the Antarctic should be considered the "common heritage of mankind" or be assigned to "a select group of nations that already have scientific and commercial interests in Antarctica" (p.9); that is a debate about property rights.

But sometimes legally enforced property rights do not exist. That may result from failures in legislation or in law enforcement, but it may also derive from intrinsic problems as in the case of public goods, intellectual property, common property, and so on. In such instances, substitutes have to be found if they do not "spontaneously" arise; otherwise competition will be inefficient. I cannot here analyse all the – sometimes nearly perfect, sometimes much less than perfect – substitutes for legally enforced property rights. I suggest two which I believe have a special role in disciplining competition in federal states. The first is trust, which, even if it is important, cannot be legislated and is less susceptible to improvement through institutional reform. I will, consequently, just mention it. The second is "monitoring,"[11] which I introduce here, but will discuss at length below, in Sections II.8 and II.9.

Trust can be a substitute for property rights. It need not, obviously, be a perfect substitute for them, in the sense that both trust and legally enforced property rights can co-exist. Trust is a substitute for property rights if the competing parties are confident (i.e., trust, believe) that each will abide by the rules of the game. The parties compete, but there are certain behaviours and activities which are proscribed – possibly only through tacit understanding – and to which neither party will resort.

Another substitute for property rights (and for trust) is "monitoring." The function of property rights is to define penalty-reward structures which, if they are efficient, ensure that one party does not, through his or her actions, impose costs on others that are out of proportion to the benefits he or she derives for these actions. A "monitor" can obviously do this. A "monitor" can be a person, but it can also be an institution. I distinguish below between horizontal and vertical competition. The first refers to interprovincial competition, while the second relates to federal-provincial competition. I will argue that the federal government and a number of "self-regulating" federal institutions are natural "monitors" of horizontal competition. I will also argue that the natural "monitor" of vertical competition is a reformed Senate. Before I can do justice to that problem, there are a number of issues that must be cleared up.

One point needs to be emphasized immediately, however. Property rights are never perfect, trust is never absolute, and "monitors" as well as "monitoring" devices are all of human fabrication. Because of this, competition is never absolutely efficient. It will sometimes attain its maximum efficiency, which may be far from the ideal; at other times it will even attain less than the maximum. That is true in politics, as it is in economics.

There is no doubt that at times competition in the Canadian federation has been less than efficient, possibly even destructive. The problem of economic union, which are at the centre of the Royal Commission's mandate, raise this question with urgency. Are certain policies adopted by governments in the pursuit of local objectives, but which impede the free flow of resources, inefficient competitive policies? I address this and other like questions below.

It is important, however, when faced with a situation of inefficient competition not to conclude that competition is always inefficient. When such situations arise, we must turn our attention to the property rights, the trust and the "monitoring" which are supposed to guarantee the efficiency of competition, and seek ways to strengthen all of them or any of them. I try to do this in the pages that follow.

4. Checks and Balances

The remainder of section II deals with the benefits and the costs of competition: this subsection with intra-governmental competition and the next five with intergovernmental competition. In this section I ask and seek to answer the following question: Are checks and balances a "good" thing? There are at least two different ways of answering this question: one which is more formal, in that it focuses on structural features of political institutions, and a second one which is more behavioural in that it concentrates on the mechanisms and responses which characterize institutions marked by checks and balances, compared to those which are not. Because there is an element of truth in both lines of inquiry – although it will soon transpire that I accord more importance to the second – I will look at each in turn.

As the words "checks and balances" indicate, a system in which they plan an important role is one in which more barriers have to be opened, more hoops jumped, more obstacles circumvented, and more impediments negotiated in an effort to obtain the passage and implementation of a piece of legislation, than would be the case in a system in which they played a lesser role. From a static short-run point of view, checks and balances reduce the legislative and executive efficiency – defined as the ratio of laws passed and implemented to the time and effort put in passing them – of political institutions.

Looked at from another point of view, the reduced efficiency of law-making bodies is nothing but the greater popular control over the exercise of political power which is automatically achieved by the fact that checks and balances exist. In terms of this formal way of looking at the problem, one's view about the costs and benefits of checks and balances – and about whether they are "good" – centres one's conception of the role and importance of political power for the conduct of public affairs on the one hand, and on the extent to which that power should be controlled for the greater blossoming of individual and collective liberty on the other.

The virtues of efficiency versus control are not as easily described as the above formulation may inadvertently signal. Indeed, in some instances, liberty is guaranteed by a swift and unequivocal exercise of political power.

For this reason, constitutions which recognize that there is a genuine trade-off between political power and liberty nonetheless acknowledge that that trade-off is not always "well behaved" – that, in other words, it is sometimes subject to exemptions – by vesting in constitutions clauses which permit the rapid employment of power in emergency situations, such as that pertaining to "peace, order, and good government" in the Canadian constitution.

From a structural point of view, parliamentary systems, such as the Canadian system, are characterized by far fewer checks and balances than are congressional systems such as the American. Thus from a short-run static or formal point of view, the Canadian political system, if we disregard its federal dimension, would seem to be more efficient at "making laws" than the American system, again neglecting the federal dimension. Or to put the point differently, political power is more controlled in the American political system than the Canadian system.

However, the effective differences in the law-making efficiency of the two systems are not as great as one would have to conclude from an analysis of their stuctural characteristics. Should one impute the similarities in the two systems to characteristics of federalism or should one look elsewhere? There is little doubt that federalism has an important role to play in explaining the *de facto* similarity in the law-making performance of the two systems, but the second aspect of checks and balances that I noted at the beginning of the section is also of great importance.

The second aspect pertains to the dynamics of checks and balances. A system which places barriers and other impediments to the passage of legislation at the same time and in the very fact of forcing people to deal with the barriers and with the other impediments, stimulates discussion and debate on the matters to be legislated. It is as if the items remained longer on the agenda and consequently attracted the interest – voiced approval or disapproval – of a larger number of persons.

The people who develop an interest in discussing and debating matters kept on the agenda by the checks and balances are not only those who have a professional or para-professional concern for the matter – politicians, bureaucrats, lobbyists, and others like them – but members of the general public, including academics, freelance intellectuals, writers, social critics, organized groups, and others. The greater involvement in public affairs which checks and balances generate will, in general, not be limited to haphazard intervention, but will stimulate the publication of magazines and other periodicals intensely concerned with the evolution of policy. It will, in other words, stimulate organized interest in public affairs.

Strong checks and balances will also mean that those citizens who get involved in public discussions and debates will want to engage in meaningful participation and consequently will seek to acquire more information on public affairs than professionals would of themselves freely choose to make available. The pressures for more information imply that over the longer term, the presence of more checks and balances leads to less secretive political institutions.

As a consequence, checks and balances, by raising the level of political involvement on the part of citizens, increase the legitimacy of the political process. Checks and balances still act to control the exercise of political power, but because, from a dynamic point of view, they raise the legitimacy of that political power, they make its exercise more efficient. The dynamic longer-term effects of checks and balances partially or even completely reverse the static shorter-term effects.

I wish to emphasize that the foregoing argument about dynamic effects reversing the static ones does *not* mean that law-making will be more rapid in systems with more checks and balances compared to those with fewer. The efficiency of checks and balances must be sought elsewhere. I mention two possible areas.

In a system with more checks and balances there should be fewer policy reversals over time. That is, changes in governments as a result of elections should produce fewer returns to the *status quo ante*. It is possible to argue, for example, that the cycle of nationalization and denationalization of certain industries which has taken place in Britain would not have happened if the British parliamentary system had had more checks and balances. This is a blatant case; the reader can surely provide some possibly less blatant but still spectacular cases in Canada.

A second area of increased efficiency of checks and balances due to the long-term effects overturning the short-term one pertains to social consensus. More social consensus means that the differences between majorities and minoritites have less saliency. As a consequence, other things being equal, it is easier to enforce laws. (The "other things being equal" relates to the desire or will of the population to have laws enforced, as revealed, among other things, in the amount of resources they choose to allocate to that task.)

The dominance of long-term over short-term effects is important. It provides part of the basis for the recommendation I made earlier for a reduction of party discipline in the House of Commons and in parliamentary committees for all non-budgetary matters. The reduction of party discipline would slow down the passage of legislation but, in the longer run, the benefits of this slowdown will be a more politically involved citizenry and policies and programs that are more broadly accepted by citizens. It is for that reason that I support the recommendations of the Commission's Report that are aimed at reducing and even eliminating the secrecy surrounding the budgetary process. I also support, for the same reason, the establishment of a permanent Economic Policy Committee of the House of Commons, which would hold annual pre-budget hearings and whose proceedings would be televised. In short, I support both recommendations because they increase checks and balances.

I deal with Senate reform later. I simply note here that any reform which increased the legitimacy of the Senate would automatically increase its ability to check and balance. Again, that would sometimes slow down the passage of legislation, but in the long run, through the process described above, it would increase the involvement and the participation of Canadians in public affairs. That must be deemed a net benefit. Checks and balances within our national institutions, as long as they are designed with care and prudence, are therefore of overall benefit.

What about the competition that is introduced in the political system through the medium of federalism? Is it also of overall benefit? That is the question to which I now turn. To proceed with the analysis, I distinguish between the competition which organizes the relationship of federal and provincial governments and that which structures the relationships of the provinces with each other. I call the first vertical competition and the second horizontal competiton. I examine each of these under different aspects in the next five sections.

5. *Division of Powers*

Competition plays no role in the conventional approaches to federalism, whether these approaches derive from political science, law, or economics. Competition is (unwittingly) removed by two assumptions which are both, in my view, unacceptable. The first of these, which will occupy my attention in this section, rests on a confusion between what could be called the *de jure* and the *de facto* division of powers. The second assumption, which I will analyse in Section II.7, relates to what may be called the territorial basis of interests and, hence, of community: the idea that federal states rest or are based on territorially more or less well-defined communities.

There can be little doubt that from a *legal-constitutional* point of view, an optimal assignment of powers is one in which the degree of concurrency, of overlap, or of joint occupation of any one power has been reduced to a minimum. Constitutions that embody such an assignment are sometimes said to be the hallmark of "classical federalism." The need for the smallest possible degree of *de jure* concurrency does not originate in a desire for neatness, nor is it a relic inherited from the long-dying nineteenth-century conception of political sovereignty enshrined in early definitions of federal countries as states constituted of two "sovereign and independent orders of government."

Instead, a minimal degree of *de jure* concurrency is required by the necessity of "judicial accountability," Ultimately, when things come to a crunch, a court must be able to decide whether a government has the authority to implement a particular policy or not; whether it is acting *intra vires* or *ultra vires*. If there is no "compartmentalization" within which legal authority can be exercised, there will be no basis on which a court can make decisions and, in fact, no meaning to a juridical division of powers. I will insist below that courts, and in particular the Supreme Court, are often called upon to act as "monitors" of federalist competition and to ensure that competiton is efficient. They cannot play that role unless the degree of *de jure* concurrency is small, for if it is significant, the courts would find it harder to impute responsibility to one or the other government involved.[12] The fundamental democratic principle that Parliament must be accountable becomes meaningless.

That much seems incontrovertible. But at the political or *de facto* level things are different: there, concurrency is the rule. We have to be clear about what that means if we do not want to become victims of the confusion between *de jure* and *de facto* concurrency which pervades the literature and which is used to argue against competitive federalism.

Before examining why an airtight *de facto* division of powers is not possible in principle, let me illustrate the nature of the problem with a few examples. Consider the (welfare) economist's standard classification of powers into allocation, redistribution, and stabilization, to which may or may not be added a revenue power, depending on how the first three have been defined. Now assume that for whatever reason, the redistribution and stabilization powers *de jure* are assigned to the federal jurisdictional level while allocation is somehow, again, *de jure*, divided between the federal and provincial levels. If the division of the allocation powers is airtight, we have a "classical" assignment of powers.

Now suppose that some provincial governments decide to use some of their allocation powers – those in areas such as education, transportation, or urban land use – in ways that fully respect the constitution, but which change the distribution of income in a direction that the federal government does not like, so that the government feels obliged to implement policies of its own to "re-establish" the distribution of income it desires. Would not the air-tight separation of powers have *de facto* been broken? I believe so, since the federal government's actions are now governed by decisions taken at the provincial level.

Consider a second case. Suppose that to stabilize the economy the federal government increases or reduces some or all of the expenditures resulting from policies implemented under the allocation powers juridically assigned to it in a way that is respectful of classical federalism's dictum regarding concurrency. But, from a behavioural point of view, will it still be respectful of that division? Not if there is any relationship between federal and provincial policies, because if there is, decisions by the federal government will impact on the provinces, and, what is even worse, not equally.

We can now turn to general principles. As I hope the examples have made clear, the various day-to-day policies which can be implemented by the governments of a federation under the powers which have juridically been assigned to them, stand in all sorts of relationships to each other. In the way citizens look at these policies (formally, in the utility functions of citizens), some will be independent, while many others will be either substitutes or complements to each other. On the other side of decision-making, in the way politicians and bureaucrats look at policies (formally at the technical level of "production" and implementation), policies will be independent, substitutes, or complements, but not necessarily in the same way as they are for citizens.

That is the reason why *de facto* all powers tend to be concurrent. It is important to be clear about what that means and what it does not mean. It does not mean that both orders of government will, at the same time, legislate in the same policy area. It simply means that governments at the two jurisdictional levels, will, in general, be legislating in policy areas that are closely related to each other. As noted, that "closeness" has two possible sources: the preference of citizens and the technical properties of production and implementation technologies. In other words, policies can be related to each other in one fashion or another because of the way citizens value them; or they can be related, because their production and implementation connects them to each other. These connections create the *de facto* concurrency.

Once this is acknowledged, it is impossible not to recognize at the same time that governments at different jurisdictional levels will be in competition with each other. The competition originates in the desire of governments to obtain the support of citizens by providing them with the policies they want. Since these policies will not have the same relationships in the preferences of citizens and in the technical structure of the implementation technologies that they have in constitutional documents, governments at one level will be implementing policies which are substitutes or complements to policies that are the responsibility of governments at another level, hence the competition.

Does this *de facto* concurrency – the outcome of characteristics of policies and of the political process – imply that constitutions do not matter? That the juridical division of powers is meaningless? That any *de jure* division of powers would be equivalent to any other? The answer to these questions must be an emphatic no. There are better and there are worse *de jure* divisions of powers. There is a view – the outcome of the confusion between *de jure* and *de facto* concurrency – which holds that the best constitutional assignment of powers is the one which leads to the smallest degree of competition possible. The bookshelves of Canada's libraries are littered with constitutional blueprints aimed at working out a division of powers that would eliminate *de facto* concurrency, so as to eliminate federalist competition.

Such constitutional blueprints are impossible to design for the only reason that people and the environment change. A blueprint that succeeded in assigning powers so as to suppress competition today would be obsolete, in that respect, tomorrow. What then is the optimal constitutional division of powers? To answer that question would take me too far afield. In addition, it is not, for the issues that concern me here, of prime importance; consequently I skip over the question.[13]

6. Executive Federalism

The discussion of the last section clearly acknowledges the existence of interdependence. Indeed, it associates interdependence with two prime sources: the preferences of citizens and the characteristics of "production and implementation" processes. The question I address here is whether that interdependence calls for federal-provincial co-operation and co-ordination.

The question is easy to answer. To the extent that interdependence originates in the properties of the preferences (utility functions) of citizens, there is no need for formal institutionalized co-ordination. Indeed, one should rely on vertical competition between governments at different levels to deal with the co-ordination problem. The rule is the same for market co-ordination. That is one reason why in its day-to-day operations federalism tends to be "messy," but one should keep in mind that it is this messiness which is the secret of its efficiency!

When we turn to the interdependence on the production and implementation side, there is a strong case for formal federal-provincial co-ordination. That is the limited case for executive federalism. The co-ordination activities are embodied in federal-provincial committees which involve various levels and various departments of governments, all of which seek to find better ways to "produce" and implement the policies which have been decided upon and designed by the political arm of governments.

There is a real temptation, reinforced by the internal logic of parliamentary government, to extend executive federalism beyond production and implementation questions to the elaboration, formulation, and design of policies. If the temptation is not resisted – and it must be acknowledged that many times in the past it has not been – executive federalism serves to reduce the beneficial effects of competition.

For this reason, I believe it is important that federal-provincial consultation on virtually all matters follows, not *precedes, debates in the House of Commons and in provincial parliaments. Parliamentary debates should extend to a specification of the areas that could be reasonably co-ordinated and those which should not be.* This kind of sorting is currently undertaken at the cabinet level. Bringing these matters before Parliament would increase checks and balances and hence democracy. It should be favoured on that ground. Furthermore, *it is essential that such matters be debated publicly if a reformed Senate is to perform its "monitoring" role efficiently.* To those who argue that this will slow down the decision-making process, I reply with the argument developed earlier, that such a procedure will increase public involvement in public affairs and, over the long term, will make for a more politically mature citizenry.

But a more intense involvement of Parliament in the policy design of federal-provincial matters and a restriction of executive federalism to "production" and implementation of policies are not sufficient for efficient competition. *Efficient competition also requires that more information be available to the public*, not only on the federal-provincial and provincial-provincial policies that are co-ordinated, but on the nature and form of the co-ordination. At present, in the Access to Information Act, federal-provincial communications are accorded a status equal to that of national security. That is ludicrous and should be changed.

7. The Territorial Basis of Interest

The search for a basis that would make it possible to define a community has absorbed much time and effort in the last two or three centuries. Such a search has had many motivations, some more noble than others. One of these has been the belief that some notion of community was a necessary adjunct to the definition of the still dominant, and not receding, idea of the nation-state. Community was therefore sought along cleavages or lines of demarcation between people such as race (colour, blood, and cranial measurements having been the most important indexes of race), language, ethnicity, religion, and in more recent times, culture and "society," these defined in purely socio-institutional terms.

Much of the reflection on federalism developed in juxtaposition to that on the nation-state. In addition, federalism appeared to some as a way of salvaging the idea of community, based on whichever cleavage was cherished at that moment, together with the notion of some minimum efficient size of country. It is not an accident, therefore, that in much of the literature on federalism – even fairly sophisticated literature – federalism as a "community of communities" or as a compact, a confederation or an alliance of communities based on particular cleavages, keeps coming up.

In Canadian thought, this intellectual atavism has nourished two dominant views of what may be called communitarian federalism and a number of minor derivatives which it would serve no purpose to even acknowledge. The first of these dominant traditions, and by far the one with the highest profile, asserts – in language that has changed as times and circumstances have changed – that Canada is made up of "two peoples," "two races," "two cultures," or "two societies." According to that view, the fact that there are ten provinces in Canada is seen either as an illusion – a way of shifting attention away from the cherished dichotomy – or as a sinister ploy to deprive one of the peoples-race-cultures-societies of its identity (one that is re-defined as the terms of the dichotomy are re-defined).

The second major tradition of Canadian communitarian federalism acknowledges the fact that there are ten provinces in the country, and goes on to assert that they constitute ten communities. History has played havoc with the first "dichotomy" tradition as the constant change in language indicates. But things are worse for the "ten-provincial-communities" tradition, if only because any definition of society and culture that has the barest elements of operational significance will not be applicable at the same time to the provinces and to the nation. In other words, if one adopts a definition of culture or society that makes Alberta, Ontario, Quebec, and Newfoundland – the provinces most often mentioned – into distinct communities based on cultural or societal dimensions, then on that definition Canada will not be a community.

Before indicating why we must divest ourselves of these atavistic intellectual notions, let me note one implication of the doctrine of communitarian federalism. Since the communities are based on race, language, culture, or whatever, there is no place for horizontal competition between the various provincial governments, because a provincial government, which is assumed to be catering to a community of individuals whose preferences are assumed to be defined by communal characteristics, will be able to do very little, if anything, of interest for individuals of another community whose preferences are defined on an altogether different set of communal characteristics. And, I may add, as a matter of logic, the federal government is superfluous in that system. It is true that it has a role to play in the "dichotomy" tradition where it is seen as the government of one people-race-culture-society, replacing the nine other superfluous provincial governments!

Horizontal competition has no role to play in a model of communitarian federalism because that notion of federalism is always used as a device to collectivize interests. To put it differently, the notion of community is used as an interest to make the interest of Manitoba dominate those of Manitobans and the interests of Prince Edward Island those of individual Islanders. Consequently, only the government of the community can know the interests, preferences, and aspirations of the community. Other governments, not being of the "proper" race, blood, language, religion, or culture, are by definition strangers to these interests. It is a neat assumption to use to remove competition.[14]

It is essential to acknowledge that provinces are made up of people, some of whom have traits that are similar to those of other people in the same province and in other provinces, but also of some who have dissimilar traits. There is no province in Canada that is made up of a homogeneous mass of people and there is no province in Canada in which the interests, preferences, and aspirations of all the people are the same. And it is to be hoped there never will be.

But even if there were, even if the people of Canada were subdividable into x or y homogeneous globs of humankind, that would not furnish us with a rationale for a federal state. That rationale, as the *Federalist*[15] in the great debates that preceded the Philadelphia Convention of 1787 recognized, is to provide the political system with more (additional to those in each government) competition to ensure that over the long run, political power is exercised both efficiently and legitimately in the interests of citizens. In a political system based on parliamentary rules of the game, the importance of additional competiton cannot be over-emphasized.

The foregoing is *not* a denial of the existence of communities. I recognize that these exist and they play an irreplaceable role in the life of people. Without the communities provided by families, professions, workplaces, churches, associations, and groups of various sorts, anomie, disintegration, and even a Hobbesian "war of all against all" would be the norm. I am only saying that there is no independent definition of community that can serve as a guide to the design of federal structures and to their governance. *The task of governments is to meet the preferences of citizens who happen to be in the provinces or in the country they have been elected to govern.* Meaningful provincial communities do not exist, except as provinces.

8. Nation-Building and Province-Building

Earlier, in Section II.3, I noted that unless property rights are well defined, unless trust is sufficient or unless "monitoring" is efficient, competition will not produce the beneficial results which it can be expected to produce. I repeat that it is possible to have property rights that are so inappropriately specified and/or so poorly enforced, to have such a lack of trust, or to have "monitoring" that is so inefficient, that the effects of competition will be perverse. This is therefore a central issue. In this subsection, I look at some of the factors that govern or at least should govern horizontal competition. In Section II.9 I turn my attention to the same question for the case of vertical competition. I must insist immediately on two points: first, as I have already noted, it is not possible, given the present state of knowledge and research, to describe all the conditions – those necessary and those sufficient – that make for efficient horizontal political competition in a federation; second, in the discussion on the division of powers (Section II.5), on executive federalism (Section II.6), and on the territorial basis of interest (Section II.7), I have already indicated some of the conditions that are necessary for efficient competition. Those that follow are additional.

The first of these conditions pertains to a notion of "competitive equality." To be sure, efficient horizontal competition does not require that all competing units be of equal size any more than efficient competition in markets requires that firms be of equal size. But it must be that the large units are not in a position to continally dominate, coerce, and in other ways prevent the smaller units for making independent autonomous decisions; nor are they in a position to inflict "disproportionate" damage on them. The smaller units must be able to compete with the strong on an equal footing. This problem is more acute in some federations than in others, and is certainly an important one in the Canadian federation in which the disparity in the size of provinces is large and possibly growing.

The responsibility for ensuring that the smaller units are able to compete against the larger ones cannot lie elsewhere than with the federal government. That is a first reason why the central government is different from provincial governments. How does the central government play this role or fulfil this responsibility? Before answering this question, let me note that it cannot be an easy role to play, because, as I have already indicated, the federal government also competes with the provinces. We are faced with the situation in which a government, competing with those at another level, must act to ensure that the competition between the latter is "fair" and "productive." That is necessarily a difficult task, one that cannot be left exclusively to the day-to-day push and pull of politics, but must be institutionally entrenched. I discuss the problem in Section II.9.

Conventional wisdom about public policy in Canada is overlaid with the words "nation-building" and "province building." When the view is not made explicitly, it is implicit that nation-building is the business of the central government, while province-building is that of the provinces. I would like to suggest that a look at the record would indicate that the attribution is largely wrong: the central government in Canada (and I would submit in other federal countries also) has been and continues to be engaged in province-building as much, if not more in certain instances, than the provinces themselves. That is one of the ways it acts as a "monitor" of horizontal competition.

How does the federal government foster province-building? It is not possible in this brief statement to indicate all the ways this is done. It will do if I give examples taken from various modes of interventions to illustrate what I mean; the reader will then be able to provide more examples for him or herself.

One notorious example of federal province-building was the creation of the Borden Line, the line which forced a differential price in oil and oil products, such that the prices east of the Ontario-Quebec border were lower that those west of that line. The policy permitted the development of an oil industry in western Canada at a time when the pure economics of the case would not have permitted that to happen. Although it was not called province-building, nor labelled regional policy either, there can be no doubt that the policy played that role, and quite effectively so.

A second example of province-building is the entire set of policies which have come to be labelled regional policies and over which there is still so much uncertainty and controversy. An analysis would indicate that the federal government has always pursued regional policies: it has always tailored or adjusted relevant policies to regional or provincial realities. However, the modern development or regional policies begins in the post-war period, more exactly in the 1950s, and continues to expand and grow until the present. This is not an accident. If one of the roles of regional policy is to ensure that the smaller and least favoured provincial governments are able to compete with the larger and more favoured ones, it must be that regional policies will grow and acquire more significance as the intensity of competition increases. The most casual observation confirms that the extent and the degree of horizontal competition in the Canadian federation have grown enormously in the post-World War Two period as the provinces have "come of age." This coming of age has manifested itself in a number of ways, not the least of which is the increase in the size of provincial budgets – relative to the total of public expenditures – and the development of competent, mature provincial bureaucracies.

A third example of province-building policies by the central government – that is, of policies which make all provincial governments, if not equal, at least capable of horizontal competition that is efficient and productive – is equalization payments. These grants, to which I devote some discussion in Section III, are primarily an instrument aimed at improving the competition position of the weaker *governments* of the federation and ameliorating the productive features of the competition in which they are engaged vis-à-vis other provincial governments. They are not instruments aimed at achieving "horizontal equity" between the inhabitants of the provinces. This does not mean that considerations of equity and of narrow (neo-classical) economic efficiency do not enter their design. But these grants would be of minor importance if their primary role of acting as province-builders was set aside. That is why it was appropriate for the federal government, after the increase in the price of crude oil that made the Ontario government a "have-not" government, to change the equalization formula so that government remained a "have" government: in the competitive game, it is hard to imagine that the Ontario government is not a "have" government.

One could continue giving examples, (for example, transportation policy, procurement policy, etc.), but the point, I hope, is made. Before moving on, I stress two subsidiary points. First, the fact that the various programs I have listed to illustrate the nature of province-building by the federal authorities exist, does not mean that they cannot be improved. Therefore, the fact that the federal government engages in province-building activities does not tell us whether it does too much or too little of it. The second point, which I mention only to remove all ambiguity, is that even if the federal government pursues province-building policies, this does not mean that the provincial governments do not also pursue policies aimed at the same end. Furthermore, province-building policies, whether federal or provincial in origin, contribute to nation-building. These obvious points have to be made only because the conventional dichotomy between nation-building and province-building tends to obscure them.

Besides competitive equality, another condition, this one pertaining to the appropriability of costs and benefits of public policies, must be satisfied. (A not dissimilar condition must also rule in markets if competition there is to be efficient.) The condition requires that the benefits and costs of decisions made by the government of a province be borne by the people living in that province, and, therefore, by the government of the province. This condition is particularly relevant for costs, so let me re-state it with respect to that variable. In competing to attract business to its jurisdiction, either by supplying particularly attractive local public goods, such as theatre, concerts, or dance, by offering tax advantages, or by buying part of the output of the sought-after enterprises, the government of a province should not be able to shift the burden of the offered amenities to the citizens of other jurisdictions. It is clear that otherwise the competition would be inefficient. There is already considerable machinery in place in Canada to ensure that benefits and costs are appropriated by decision-makers themselves. This is particularly the case in the field of taxation. But there is room for improvement. I will return to this question when I address the issue of "economic union" in Section III – a matter that is important enough in our terms of reference to have given the Commission part of its name.

Were I engaged in writing a formal treatise instead of presenting a broad framework that can help decide on appropriate policies, I would devote considerable space to another condition for efficient competition which could be called "entry." For competition to be efficient, those who can elicit more support should be able to enter the competitive arena and those less effective at doing that should have to leave it. Although there is some evidence – mostly American – that the life expectancy of political incumbents has been increasing, it is not known whether that phenomenon is "natural" or contrived.[16] Should future research indicate that anywhere in the Canadian federation, entry by existing or new political parties to the apparatus of state is reduced by artificial contrivances, that would be a matter for serious concern, because that would greatly reduce the competitive nature of Canadian politics, not only between parties, but overall.

The matter is particularly important in respect of electoral rules, because these may, under certain circumstances, prevent the representation of groups of citizens in political institutions. There is some weak evidence that the operation of electoral rules in Canada, both nationally and provincially, may be artificially lengthening the tenure of incumbents. If that is ever seriously documented, these rules should be altered.

9. Who Monitors the Monitor?

"Who monitors the monitor?" is the most fundamental question of economic social, and political organization. It was raised in the first century of our era by Juvenal (*nam quis custodiet ipsos Custodes?*) and continues to be asked to this day.[17] It is a fundamental question, but, ironically, it is one that possesses no satisfactory logical answer. For, indeed, if one finds a monitor (guard) who will guarantee that an appointed monitor (guard) will do an assigned job well, how are we to know that the first monitor will do his or her job the way it should be done? Economists have been somewhat cavalier with the question, and, given how hard it is to answer, they are somewhat justified. They have usually assumed that the state should monitor property rights, competition, and market behaviour, but have seldom asked who should or would monitor the state. Economics, indeed, has no worthwhile theory of politics.

I suspect that it is this fundamental question, lurking in the back of people's minds, which is the biggest impediment to an acceptance of the obvious fact that democratic politics is competitive. The idea of competition is, of course, intimately related to the notion that individuals pursue their own interest. If politics is competitive and driven by self-interest, who will monitor politics? To assume that politics is not competitive, or should not be, has been the classical way out of the problem. The assumption will not do and, indeed, has never done.

Historians report that when the Fathers of the Canadian federation met in Quebec City and in Charlottetown in 1864 and 1867, as well as when the Constitutional Convention met in Philadelphia in 1787, the debates on the division of powers in both cases took very little time. Agreement was reached almost immediately on the conviction that the proposals envisaged were reasonable, and that in any case, marginal changes in the division of powers could be achieved subsequently either formally, informally, or by judicial interpretation. The wisdom of both groups of Fathers has been vindicated by history.

What required much time and debate and was the source of intense bargaining in both cases was the Senate. To my knowledge, why things happened that way has not been considered, nor has an explanation been provided of why the structure of the Senate mattered so much to these wise men. The explanation, I wish to suggest, rests on the fact that senates play an absolutely central role in "monitoring" the vertical competition that exists in federations – the competition between the federal and provincial (state) governments. Because of that central role, it is desirable that senates be designed so as to guarantee that competition is as fair and as unbiased as possible. In my view, the Americans understood this,[18] whereas the Canadians did not; they were too British in their outlook to understand federalism and the role of a senate in that form of political organization.

The Senate acts as a "monitor" of vertical competition by injecting a provincial dimension in the central government. In a well-functioning federation, although it would always be an integral part of the central government, a senate would in some important sense be related to both orders of government. The Supreme Court was therefore right, and revealed a profound understanding of federalism, when it recently argued that the federal government could not alone, that is, without the provinces, change the basic structure of the Canadian Senate.

It is interesting to note, in passing that the New Democratic Party as well as its predecessor, the Co-operative Commonwealth Federation, has consistently favoured, not the reform of the Canadian Senate, but its abolition. One must also acknowledge that these parties – less so in recent years than in the past – have often been lukewarm vis-à-vis federalism as a way of organizing politics.[19] I find great logic in that position, and, to me at least, it confirms that in a federation, a senate has an important "monitoring" role to play. To the extent that federalism becomes absorbed in the interstices of NDP thought, I would expect that party to move from abolition to reform of the Senate.

A senate can only play a "monitoring" role if it has legitimacy, and, in our time, *that can be achieved only if it is popularly elected*. Comparisons with the House of Lords in the United Kingdom are beside the point. The United Kingdom is not a federation and therefore whether the House of Lords has legitimacy or not cannot be an impediment to a role of "monitor" of vertical competition.

However, legitimacy is not enough. If a senate is to inject a provincial dimension in the federal government and thus become capable of "monitoring" vertical competition efficiently, *that basis or representation must be provincial*, not regional, as in current practice. The persistent confusion between provinces and regions that one encounters in the literature and in public debates is a close cousin, I believe, to the notion that interests are communal. The size of provinces and the location of their frontiers are not "rational" in any real sense of that term, but they are there and they determine the jurisdictions of provincial governments.

There is a growing recognition in Canada that the basis of representation in the Senate should be provincial, but there seems to be no rationale underlying this developing awareness. Because the notion of provincial representation is not derived from a well-structured theory of federalism, but appears to be no more than a component of the current Zeitgeist, it could be as fleeting as all Zeitgeists It is therefore important to know why provincial representation is better than regional representation.

The House of Commons is elected on the principle of popular representation: that is as it should be. But if the Senate is to "monitor" vertical competition efficiently, it must be elected on a different basis. *The best rule would be, as is the most common practice in other federations, to make all provinces equal*. Thus, each province could elect ten or twelve senators. The current practice is not only inefficient, it is perverse, since it gives more, considerably more, senators to the large regions (provinces), thus adding to the "competitive inequality" that is inherent in size differences, however measured. It is hard to imagine that the larger and more powerful provincial governments – Ontario and Quebec – would accept changes in the rules of the game that would oblige them to compete more fairly with Manitoba and Prince Edward Island; but without being an incurable dreamer, one can hope that the genuine sense of fairness that characterizes Canadians may, one day, induce these governments to adopt such a change.

The primary role of the Senate should *not*, therefore, be that of a "chamber of sober second thought," although it would continue to play that role. *Its primary role should be to give saliency to the provincial dimensions of public policies.* I stress that this is not essentially a representation role; it is a "monitoring" function. In other words, in the competition over resources and policies that takes place in the national government, it is imperative, if the competition is to be efficient, that provincial interests be competing with each other on an equal footing. It is not sufficient, to put it still differently, that provincial interests be represented appropriately in national debates. They must be able to vie with each other on a basis of "competitive equality"; otherwise the checks and balances that characterize national politics will be biased against the weaker provinces, even if their points of view are represented. A capacity to compete is more than a capacity to talk; it is also, and radically, a capacity to exert a real influence on decisions. That is the real meaning underlying the notion of "monitored" competition.

To fulfil its "monitoring" role, the Senate should keep some distance from the House. This would be achieved *if the Senate was not elected on the same basis as the House.* I have already noted that the basis should be provincial and that equal representation of the provinces should be the objective. In addition, *it would be best if the Senate was elected on the basis of proportional representation, at fixed intervals and for fixed periods.* If these were the rules, the distance between the House and the Senate would be great enough to ensure that the Senate could "monitor" vertical competition effectively. If the distance was any less, it would be too much a creature of the House of Commons to do effective "monitoring."

It has often been suggested that the Senate be given a six-month suspensive veto. That raises a difficult problem. A suspensive veto, it would seem, is not consistent with legitimacy acquired at the ballot box. Elected senators are unlikely to be satisfied with a temporary delay, especially if the matter of confidence in the cabinet with the House. What should be done? I think that it would be best if the Senate was not given a suspensive veto. *Instead, a bill that was amended or defeated in the Senate should be passed anew by the House of Commons.* That would leave the ultimate power with the House, and would be conducive to bargaining between MPs and Senators. A suspensive veto does not encourage compromise.

The Senate is not the only national body that serves to "monitor" vertical competition. That is also done by the Supreme Court. It is that body which interprets the division of powers and determines the competitive behaviours which, from a legal point of view, are constitutional and those which are not. In the absence of an efficient Senate, the burden which must be carried by the Supreme Court, in its role of "monitor" of vertical competition, tends to be heavy. However, the remedy for the problem is *not* to reform the Supreme Court, as some have proposed, but to reform the Senate.

III. Applications

A theory of competitive federalism, such as the one adumbrated in the foregoing pages, has great power not only in providing an integrative and unifying framework to matters which otherwise appear not to have any meaning and consequence, but also in making it possible, as I hope I have already shown, to address matters of institutional reform in other than a purely *ad hoc* fashion. That is true in respect of Senate reform, a matter that has provoked countless suggestions, not many of which, however, are anchored in a strong rationale related to the purpose or role of that body. That is also true for the institutions of executive federalism and for regional development policy, a subject to which I return below.

In the discussion that follows, I wish to demonstrate the power of the theory by applying it to sundry issues that have been raised in one locality or another during the Royal Commission's hearings. These are usually matters on which there is considerable debate, that is, matters which are difficult to discuss because of the lack of a consistent framework of analysis. Applying the theory of competitive federalism to these questions and deriving the recommendations for reform which seem to follow from it will shed more light on the approach.

I will look at five questions which are "natural" questions for a theory of competitive federalism. Because neither time nor space allow an extensive and detailed treatment, I will only sketch the problems and point to the solutions. The reader will have to supplement the development with his or her own insights. I will examine the following five questions in the order indicated, although that order is not an index of significance or of saliency: 1) economic union; 2) intergovernmental grants, that is, equalization payments and established program financing; 3) tax collection agreements; 4) the Charter of Rights and Freedoms; and 5) municipal governments.

1. Economic Union

Economic development policies, of which industrial and regional policies are a subset, now play an important role in the policy arsenal of every jurisdiction. Many times, of course, they are not called by that name; they may even be implemented as a part of other policies. For example, it has been said that industrial and regional considerations play a significant role in the defence and military expenditures of the United States government;[20] it is, in any case, a fact that the Pentagon publishes yearly a map which displays defence expenditures by congressional districts!

These economic development policies are, as I have already argued, the product of federalist competition, but in two different senses. First, some of these policies are responses by federal and provincial governments to opportunities created either by the demands of citizens or by comparative public entrepreneurial capacity. For simplicity, I will call these demand-supply development policies. Secondly, some policies are implemented, mostly by the federal government, but not inappropriately also by both orders of government acting together, to ameliorate the degree of "competitive equality" between the provinces of the federation in order that competition between them be more efficient and productive.

It is absolutely essential to keep the above distinction in mind in analysing industrial and regional policies, and, more generally, economic development policies. The distinction is a feature of federations which is absent from unitary states. In the latter, indeed, the only source of economic development policies is demand and supply considerations; the establishment of property rights aimed at making federalist competition efficient is, by definition, absent in these political structures.

Though it is important to distinguish between the two identified "sources" of development policies, it is also indispensable to keep in mind that they are not independent of each other. The relationship between them can be put in the following way: the more efficiently designed the economic development policies that serve to promote "competitive equality" and thus to "monitor" federalist competition, the higher the benefit-cost ratio of development policies implemented in response to demand-supply considerations.

To see why that must be so, we must first identify the benefits and the costs of the development policies I have called demand-supply policies. The benefits are easily ascertained, at least for those who assume that when governments respond to what people want, they raise the well-being of these citizens.

The costs arise because economic development policies almost invariably create impediments or barriers to the free movement of goods, services (for example, the services of lawyers, nurses, etc.), labour, capital, and entrepreneurship. These barriers – in the present discussion solely a by-product of responses to the demands of citizens – reduce the specialization that would otherwise be achieved in the use of scarce resources. It is these barriers that constitute the "economic union problem."

The affirmation made above that if the economic development policies designed to "monitor" federalist competition are efficient, the ratio of the benefits and costs just defined would be maximized, rests on the notion that federalist competition is a self-corrective mechanism. To put it differently, federalist competition, like all competition, if it is well "monitored," is efficient in the sense that it will economize on scarce resources in achieving the objectives willed by people. Indeed, efficient "monitoring" means, among other things, that costs imposed on others in the competitive pursuit of a target must be proportionate to the benefits obtained. In addition, self-correction or restraint is brought about by the fact that under efficiently "monitored" federalist competition, the benefits of economic development policies are closely related to thier own costs.

If the above analysis is correct, it has one empirically testable implication: there should be more inefficient barriers to the free flow of resources in unitary than in federal states. In unitary states, indeed, the discipline of competition is much weaker, and the obligation to meet the preferences of citizens less constraining. I should insist that to test the proposition, one must focus on demand-supply development policies, and exclude from the analysis those policies implemented to make federalist competition efficient. It is not an easy proposition to test, but my own casual observation of both unitary and federal states supports the proposition.

In the Canadian context, "monitoring" is not as efficient as it could be, not only because the Senate does not interject the "proper" provincial dimension in federal institutions, but because executive federalism is too "encompassing," and because of other reasons, some of which have been noted above. Consequently, the economic development policies that should serve to improve "competitive equality" and to make federalist competition more productive are less than optimal; and the benefit-cost ratio associated with demand-supply policies is lower than it could be.

What should we do to correct that situation? The best solution is to reform the Senate and the institution of executive federalism along the lines recommended earlier, as well as implement other measures, such as those suggested in this supplementary view, that would make federalist competition more efficient. If this was done, the only other things that would be needed would be to implement the recommendations of the Commission's Report pertaining to section 121 of the Constitution Act and those relating to interprovincial trade.

If significant institutional reforms cannot be achieved, then *as a second-best solution*, I support the Report's recommendation that a Federal-Provincial Commission on the Economic Union be established to implement a "Code of Economic Conduct" that would be a "monitor" of the economic union. My own version of the code would, however, require that the distinction made above between what are in effect "framework" policies and demand-supply policies be entrenched and respected. The code would then be aimed at restricting the implementation of demand-supply development policies that have an "obviously low" benefit-cost ratio. The code should seek to achieve through administrative and bureaucratic means what, in a more ideal situation, would be the "automatic" outcome of the operations of Parliament, federal-provincial machinery, and federalist competition.

2. Intergovernmental Grants

All theories of intergovernmental grants reflect or are derived from some theory of federalism. That thought may seem obvious, but it bears repeating, because there are many theories of government grants which present themselves as independent of any conception of federalism. I do not have the time or the space to demonstrate that point here; that will have to wait. It will be clear, however, that the theory of grants that follows is an integral part of the theory of competitive federalism. It does not rest on such intractable and pious notions as "Canadians are a sharing people" or "Canadians are compassionate"; it does not, in other words, derive firstly from notions of equity, because if equity was the basis for governmental grants, one would be led immediately to the view that transfers should be made to persons, not to governments.

I have already indicated that the role of government grants is the promotion of "competitive equality" between the provincial governments of the Canadian federation. The purpose of this section is to amplify this point. I consider equalization payments first, and then turn my attention to the financing of established programs.

I must repeat that in a federation, the competition that I have called horizontal takes place between the *governments of the federation*. Equalization payments are aimed at making that horizontal competition work more efficiently. That rationale is not inconsistent with section 36(2) of The Constitution Act, 1982, which says the equalization payments are made "to ensure that provincial governments have sufficient revenues to provide reasonably comparable levels of public services at reasonably comparable levels of taxation."

An efficient equalization formula redistributes tax revenues between provincial governments but, importantly, it does so according to certain (temporarily fixed) rules and thus acts as an "automatic monitor" of horizontal competition. Equalization payments, therefore, allow weaker provincial governments to "hold their own" vis-à-vis stronger ones in federalist competition; but also, they serve to deter any provincial government from engaging in competitive actions that would be privately beneficial to itself, but socially inefficient and destructive.

Let me give an illustration of this last point. Suppose that a provincial government sought, through predatory behaviour, to attract the head offices of corporations to its province, so as to increase corporate profits in the province and hence revenues from that source. In the absence of an equalization formula (or of other "monitoring" devices), such action, even if destructive, could be profitable to the province. But an efficient equalization formula would produce a reduction in equalization payments to the province and would thus deter such predatory behaviour. It is clear that the deterrent should not be absolute; indeed, it should be incremental. It is also clear that an efficient equalization formula need not subject all provinces to the same marginal deterrence. The current formula, based on a five-province standard, is different in that respect from the older formula which was based on a ten-province standard, but it is not necessarily inferior to it. To come to a decision on the matter requires a judgement about the relative competitive ability of provincial governments.

Equalization payments do redistribute income but their primary rationale and their prime function is allocational. It is because of this allocational role that equalization receives the support of all provincial governments, those of the "have" and those of the "have-not" provinces. It is also because of the allocational function that equalization payments have to be unconditional; if they were not, they would suppress federalist competition.

In this regard, it is important to stress that an efficient equalization formula should "monitor" competition, not seek to eliminate it. Suppose, for example, that a provincial government, as a result of some fortuitous or deliberately sought event, benefits from a windfall revenue which would permit it to compete more effectively with other provinces for resources and people; should the equalization formula redistribute all of this windfall between the provincial governments and thus impede federalist competition? Certainly not. Such a provincial government is indeed in the same position as a firm which, following a favourable event, is able to expand its clientele at the expense of other firms.

Those who would suppress federalist competition in that way usually embrace a Benthamite notion of government, according to which governments act in the public interest because the public interest is their business, and because to be in public life is to be motivated by the public interest. When governments are assumed to always maximize social welfare functions, why have competition, indeed, why have governments in the first place?

I note in passing that the view of equalization grants advanced here is, broadly speaking, the one to be found in the *Report* of the Royal Commission on Dominion-Provincial Relations, commonly known as the Rowell-Sirois Report. It is true that the Commission's conception of federalist competition appears to be different from mine, at least on a first reading: it seems to be arguing that federalist competition is essentially destabilizing and destructive. That Commission's views reflect the analysis of the realities of interprovincial fiscal competition during the 1930s, as well as the prevalent idea of the period which viewed competition as generally inefficient even in markets.

The "monitoring" role of the federal government in the 1930s was by any reckoning quite limited. It is intriguing that Rowell-Sirois recommended the introduction of National Adjustment Grants (NAG), admittedly different from, but close in spirit to, the present equalization grants which I argue make competition more productive. The Commission also recommended that the NAG be unconditional. The rationale for its recommendation, though shunning the language of competition, is so suffused with its spirit that it is worth quoting at length:

> It should be made clear that while the adjustment grant proposed is designed to enable a province to provide adequate services (at the average Canadian standard) without excessive taxation (on the average Canadian basis) the freedom of action of a province is in no way impaired. If a province chooses to provide inferior services and impose lower taxation it is free to do so, or it may provide better services than the average if its people are willing to be taxed accordingly, or it may, for example, starve its roads and improve its education, or starve its education and improve its roads – exactly as it may do today. But no provincial government will be free from the pressure of the opinion of its own people and if, when it applies for an increased adjustment grant on the basis of need, it has to produce figures which indicate that although it might, without specially heavy taxation, have provided better education but did not do so, it has, of course, to justify this to its own voters.[21]

But, given the Zeitgeist of the period, the Rowell-Sirois Report could not imagine that, even after the implementation of the NAG, the federal government would become a true "monitor" of horizontal federalist competition. For that reason, it proposed dealing with competition by re-assigning taxation and significant expenditure powers to the federal government. That was the solution adopted everywhere at that time. It rested on a confusion between competition and the mechanisms that ensure its efficiency: property rights, trust, "monitoring," and so on – a confusion which still today is far from fully exorcised.

That notwithstanding, there is still something we can learn from the Rowell-Sirois Report and from section 36(2) of the Constitution Act which reflects that Commission's view of NAG. To put it as simply as possible, the current equalization formula reflects only the revenue needs of provincial budgets. *Competitive equality would require a formula designed to reflect expenditure needs as well*, but only if the costs of incorporating the expenditure side in the equalization formula do not exceed the benefits.

Equalization grants are negotiated grants; the negotiating parties are the federal and provincial governments. Because these grants are aimed at improving "competitive equality" between the provinces, the role of the federal government cannot be symmetrical to that of the provinces, for if it was, the outcome of the negotiations could easily be more competitive inequality instead of more competitive equality. Indeed, a neutral role on the part of the federal government would eliminate the "monitoring" function that must be played by the central government. In some circumstances, it may even be necessary for the federal government to act unilaterally as it did a few years ago, that is, to forgo all negotiations with the provinces.

The Established Program Financing agreements, as they currently exist, are of a class and kind that is altogether different from the equalization payments. Their intent and purpose is to limit and even to eliminate interprovincial competition in certain areas. Whether that is good or bad is not at issue here. (In fact, I support the recommendation of the Commission's Report that the mode of financing of education be changed with the aim of increasing interprovincial competition at the level of postsecondary education.)

But if, for any reason, the federal and provincial governments choose to restrict horizontal competition in certin domains, such as is presently done in health and education, *then the grants used for that purpose must be conditional grants.* The situation in which we currently find ourselves regarding this matter derives from the fact that the grants are unconditional. Unconditionality, in turn, is the product of a reliance on a theory of intergovernmental grants in which the decision-makers are neither real governments nor competitive.

The problem which unconditionality creates is analogous to a "free rider" problem. By agreement and by choice of financial instruments, federalist competition is suppressed in, let us say, post-secondary education. The device used to suppress competition is "national standards" or "minimum standards." Since competition is eliminated, unconditional money will not be spent in that area, but will tend toward areas where competition is greater. Consequently, "national standards" are not achieved, federalist competition is distorted, and federal-provincial relations soured.

3. Tax Collection Agreements

There are substantial real economies of scale in tax collection. It is not clear and certainly not known whether these economies persist over all the taxable units in the country. But it is not impossible that they do. There are therefore advantages, possibly large, to the tax collection agreements whereby the federal government collects personal income taxes for all provincial governments (except that of Quebec), and also collects the corporation income tax (except for the governments of Alberta, Ontario, and Quebec).

The economies of scale derive from many sources. Not unimportant among them are the following: the tax bases used by all parties must be defined in the same way and, secondly, though tax rates can differ, they cannot differ by much. The tax collection agreements therefore serve as a way of reducing tax competition between the provinces and possibly between the provinces and the federal government. The economies of scale in tax collection are not, therefore, dissimilar to the economies of scale that would result if dress manufacturers were to sign a fashion standardization agreement whereby dress styles and designs would be restricted and differences in them greatly limited.

The analogy is appropriate not only in illustrating how the tax collection agreements restrict competition, but in indicating why so many tax experts think they are a good thing! It is, indeed, only recently – some thirty to forty years after the introduction of "monopolistic competition" as a model of markets in which businesses compete with each other through the medium of fashion and product characteristics – that economists openly acknowledge that product differentiation may raise economic welfare instead of always reducing it.

The point can be put differently. There are often costs, in addition to advantages, in exploiting economies of scale. In the case under consideration – the tax collection agreements – the benefits of standardized tax bases and (to some extent) rates are readily appreciated. The costs resulting from restriction of competition and over-standardized bases and rates are, however, no less real even if less direct and palpable.

The foregoing does not mean that tax collection agreements should not exist. But the advantages must be balanced against the costs. After study, it may be decided that collection agreements should bring together the provinces in three or four subsets in which the federal government would not be involved. The bulk of the economies of scale could thus be exploited and the benefits of tax competition reaped.

Whatever is done, it is well to stress that tax competition would not necessarily produce large differences in tax bases and rates. Indeed, to the extent that there are no differences in preferences of citizens and in technologies of production, competition would operate to eliminate differences in tax rates. However, if there are real differences, especially in the preferences of citizens, competition would guarantee that these are not forgotten. Since differences in preferences between provinces are not absolute (see Section II.8), there is a "natural" limit to the extent to which competition would lead to differences in tax bases and rates.

4. The Charter of Rights and Freedoms

Everybody who has made it into the twentieth century and who pronounces on the matter supports rights and freedoms. The issue, if there is one, is not there; it is instead with the notion of a charter that has constitutional strength. The argument is sometimes made that a charter of rights and freedoms encroaches on parliamentary supremacy by allowing the judicial branch of the government to pass judgement on and to review matters that have been decided by Parliament (as well, of course, as on other matters).

The flavour of the argument that a charter of rights and freedoms is not congruent with parliamentarism resembles, in many ways, the one to the effect that federalism and parliamentarism are not congruent. In fact, there is enough resemblance between the two lines of reasoning that one can venture the hypothesis that those who in 1981-82 opposed a charter for Canada, would in 1864-67 have opposed the formation of the Canadian federation.

However that may be, let me ask if a charter and parliamentary institutions really lack congruence. The answer suggested by the theory of competitive federalism is that a charter and parliamentarism are congruent, because a charter makes the whole political system more competitive. It does this by bringing the courts, more especially the Supreme Court, more effectively into the competition that characterizes the political process. First, it sharply increases the competition between the judiciary and the two other branches of government – the executive and the legislative. That, by itself, is a major contribution of the Canadian Charter, for inevitably, over the longer term, the competition will tighten the democratic link between governments and citizens, by giving more importance to citizens, as citizens, in the political process. One implication of this is that the Charter will heighten the degree of competition between the public and the private sectors and to the extent that the latter responds, will truly raise the well-being of Canadians *by increasing market competition.*

It is important to note that the closer government-citizen link that the introduction of the courts in the political process will foster is not limited to the federal government, but will affect all the governments of the federation. To put it differently, the interests of citizens will, henceforth, not be met and served by eleven parliaments only, but also by the courts since citizens will be able to use the courts to be better served by parliaments. Through this second channel, the Charter of Rights and Freedoms will stimulate horizontal competition in the federation. This has already begun: through the courts, interests in one province are challenging rulings and laws in another. That can only serve the public good.

There is a third channel through which the Charter will affect the working of the political process, namely, by strengthening the ability of the Supreme Court to "monitor" vertical competition between the central and the provincial governments. This is achieved through the ability of governments at each level to appeal to the courts if they believe that decisions of governments at one level bias the workings of competition in an unfair and inefficient way. As I have already noted, that role of the courts, and again especially of the Supreme Court, is likely to be considerably larger than it should be unless the Senate is reformed in a way that introduces an effective provincial dimension in the federal Parliament.

The Supreme Court, of course, already "monitors" vertical competition. The reason why that role is likely to grow in the future derives from the fact that with the Charter, the pressure of citizens on their governments will increase and, consequently, governments will vie with each other more aggressively.

To the question of whether the Charter of Rights and Freedoms is a real third pillar of political institutions in Canada, congruent with parliamentarism and federalism, the answer must therefore be a resounding yes. The Charter, by bringing citizens more directly into the political process, increases the degree of competition in the system and, by making "elite accommodation" more difficult, will force the system to be more attentive to the preferences of all citizens.

5. Municipal Governments

Municipalities, as the saying goes, are creatures of provincial governments. This means that the government of a province can unilaterally alter the boundaries of municipal jurisdictions, alter the division of powers between itself and municipalities, and overrule decisions made locally in all areas of policy. As time passed, there has been a tendency for the provinces to consider and to treat municipal governments in many important areas as *de facto* administrative bodies. It is noteworthy that this has been going on at the same time that provincial politicians, in their dealings with the federal government, were arguing in favour of more decentralization.

Should municipalities be creatures of the provinces, or would Canadians be better off if municipalities were more autonomous decision-making bodies, thus more capable of reflecting the preferences of their citizens and of adjusting to local circumstances? In other words, would the allocation and distribution of resources be more efficient if the municipalities stood vis-à-vis the provinces more or less as the latter stand vis-à-vis the federal government?

The standard case against an entrenched division of powers between the provinces and the municipalities is that it would lead to a recapitulation at a lower level of the problems encountered at a higher level: on the one hand conflict, rancour, and disharmony, and on the other, overlap and duplication. At this point, the reader will not be surprised if, in relation to the first point, I simply say that in my language that means competition, something which, if well "monitored," I hold to be beneficial. With respect to the second point, I simply note that duplication and overlap are, in practice, what competition implies, whether we have market or political competition in mind. The point is readily grasped in the context of competitive markets: how could they be competitive if only one firm supplied a particular product?

The above objection to an entrenched division of powers between provincial and municipal governments is based on a misconception of federalism. Another objection is more simple-minded: it is that provincial governments will be opposed to the idea and consequently that it has no chance of being implemented. The objection is simple-minded because it is obvious that the provinces will be opposed to the notion; no one likes competition when that competition is directed at him or her; no elite with power readily gives it up! One should therefore expect provincial officials to marshal all available arguments – including ridicule – against the idea that if municipal officials were given entrenched powers, the country would be better governed.

Canadians would be better served if municipalities had entrenched powers. Such entrenchments would be provincial-municipal matters. They would be different from province to province. In some cases, a provincial entrenchment law might state that (say) the division of powers between the two orders of government would require some direct participation of municipalities. In other cases, the entrenchment might be more limited, so that changes in the division of powers (say) would be legislated in the provincial legislature, but require a two-thirds majority to pass. Other forms are possible.

No entrenchment can be meaningful unless municipalities are provided with tax bases that can generate revenues capable of matching expenditures. There would, of course, still be "equalization grants" to help "monitor" horizontal intermunicipal competition, but the present total mismatch of revenues and expenditures would have to be corrected.

If one province chose to promote the well-being of its citizens by giving entrenched powers to its municipal governments, it should be aware that the problems that it would face would be no different from those that have to be resolved in federalism as we now know it. In acting as "monitor" of the horizontal competition that would exist between the municipalities, it would have to face the issues of competitive equality, of the appropriability of benefits and costs of local decisions, and others like them. These are not trivial problems, nor are they problems that the highly competent officials now employed at each of the two levels of government – provincial and municipal – could not resolve, if they chose to.

When we come to the matter of "monitoring" vertical competition – that between the provinces and the municipalities – I would suggest that this could be more economically and more effectively done by the federal government than by any other body. That role could be fulfilled by a department, such as the now defunct Department of Urban Affairs, which would develop "municipality-building" policies. The reason for placing the responsibility with respect to vertical competition with the federal government is simply that municipal governments will compete not only with municipalities located in the same province, but with municipalities everywhere in the country. In view of that, it appears difficult to avoid the conclusion that however difficult such a role would be for the central government, no one else can substitute for it.

IV. Conclusion

In the introduction to this document, I stated my conviction that the mechanisms that discipline democratic politics, especially in federations, are as constraining as the mechanisms that discipline economic behaviour. I trust that the discussion in the two preceding sections, which has outlined a theory of competitive federalism, has gone part of the way in showing that this conviction can be held rationally. I also believe that further developments of the theory of competitive federalism will reinforce the rational basis for such a conviction.

To conclude this already long document, I ask the following question: what does it mean to say that the mechanisms of democratic politics and those of economics are equally constraining? At its most simple, it means that there are not one but two broad arenas in which people seek to obtain the things which increase their well-being: markets and governments. Markets, when they are well structured and competitive, do a good job over the longer term in allocating resources in ways that maximize the well-being of the population. That is a generally accepted proposition and one in which I strongly believe. What is less accepted, but an idea in which I nonetheless believe just as strongly, is that governments, when they are well structured and competitive, do as good a job as markets, and like them over the longer term, allocate resources in ways that maximize the well-being of people.

I must therefore reject the *a priori* notion that markets are more efficient, more flexible, and more responsive to change than governments. In some circumstances and in the performance of certain tasks, that is certainly the case. However, unless one specifies the circumstances and the tasks – an undertaking which requires the use of comparable theories of politics and of economics as well as solid empirical comparative research – affirmations to the effect that governments are less efficient, less flexible, and less capable of responding to change than markets add up to little less than propaganda.

If comparable[22] markets and governments do equally well, why not suppress one and give all the responsibilities and the kudos to the other? The reason is that they do not weigh the preferences of people in the same way and do not perform the same tasks equally well. There are some jobs which markets do better and others which governments are best at performing, although it is difficult, *a priori*, to sort them out. There is an enormous literature[23] devoted to that question, but it is not, on the whole, a very helpful one.

It is known,[24] however, that to solve this assignment problem on the basis of principles, one must contrast the relative efficiency of governments and markets in the performance of the tasks to be assigned. That is more easily said than done, because as just noted, comparisons must, at the very least, start with two theories, one of politics and one of economics. Furthermore, the two theories must have enough in common to make the comparisons possible and meaningful.

Conventional welfare economics – the most common theory used by economists to address the assignment problem – lacks a theory of politics; instead, it uses the assumption that governments seek the "common good."[25] It therefore "solves" the assignment problem by assumption. Indeed, if governments pursue the common good and if one can demonstrate "market failure," one must conclude that the tasks which markets fail to do perfectly should be assigned to the state. In recent years, a "reverse logic" has been used to generate the opposite conclusion. In that case, the assumption is made that markets always allocate resources efficiently. It then suffices to demonstrate "government failure" to argue that those tasks which governments fail to do perfectly should be assigned to markets.

That reverse logic model also solves the assignment problem by assumption. Why? First, because the work on market "imperfections" – on the increasing returns to scale of many technological processes, on the declining marginal revenue of many business enterprises, on the often less than arm's length relationship in transfer pricing, on the incidence of tie-in sales, on the presence of entry-deterring strategies by oligopolists, on the downward stickiness of many prices (including, of course, the price of labour), on price-fixing arrangements, on racial, gender, and other forms of discrimination, and on other market imperfections – is not usually brought to bear on the matter. Second, because that model also lacks a theory of politics; it demonstrates "government failure" by reference to market mechanisms alone.

The search for a solution to the assignment problem based on first principles is probably beneficial, although that is not certain. My own view of how modern societies work is that the assignment question is "resolved" through competition between governmental and market institutions and that competition, in turn, is shaped and conditioned by the demands of the public and by the supply of entrepreneurial talent to each sector. Consequently, a growing government sector reflects first the fact that people want not only the things governments supply better, but also those things which governments provide differently than markets, and second, the fact that more aggressive and talented entrepreneurs have found their way in that sector. A declining government sector reflects opposite tendencies. If I am allowed a conjecture, I would suggest that a number of things which are done by governments in Canada could have been done privately, if private-sector entrepreneurs had been more imaginative and more aggressive. In that sense, the success of business lobbies in preventing the implementation of an effective competition policy has contributed to the growth of the public sector in Canada.

However that may be, if markets and governments are two competing arenas for meeting the preferences, objectives, and desires of people, it is no longer possible to hold to the view, so dear to those who adhere to a Benthamite notion of politics, that all taxes, regulations, subsidies, and other forms of intervention by public bodies always cause "distortions."

The notion of distortion is not an easy one to work with. Consider the simplest possible case, that is, the case of an economy made up of perfectly competitive neo-classical markets in which the cost of a unit of resources allocated to any use – producing goods and services, moving them around, informing people of their quality, etc. – is exactly equal to the social value of that unit of resources. In such an economy, there are no distortions by construction. The presence of monopolies, pollution, sticky prices, and of taxes, quotas, subsidies, regulations, and other public interventions *may*, by introducing a wedge between private and social valuations of resources, create distortions. But they may not. If we acknowledge that governments can influence monopolies, pollution, regulations, and taxes, it is essential to know why interventions take place before calling them distortions. It would indeed be a perversion of language to put the name distortion on a deliberately sought policy objective.

An illustration may help. Suppose that the population of a jurisdiction unanimously agrees to ask its government to levy a tax on alcoholic beverages, because, assuming that these are harmful to health, it believes that people could not resist the temptation of drinking more if prices were lower. If the government levies the demanded tax, it would simply be wrong to say that the tax is a distortion; it is an efficient instrument used in the pursuit of a particular objective, which it is hardly the business of analysts or observers to approve or condemn.

The situation would be different if the demand for the tax was not unanimous. Those who found themselves in the minority, unlike the others, would face a distortive tax. It is, therefore, impossible to know if public intervention is distortive or not without a theory of politics. Given that fact, declarations to the effect that the tax system should be neutral, that industrial policy should mimic the market, or that Crown corporations should be privatized, unless they are grounded both in economics and politics, may cause serious distortions, if ever implemented, by preventing the political system from doing its job effectively.

I have run out of time and space and so rest my case. I hope that the theory of competitive federalism which I have suggested above, both as a model of what actually goes on in the Canadian political arena and as a guide to institutional reform, serves as a useful clarification and extension of the discussion of these matters in the Commission's Report and that it helps nourish the public debates which that Report will stimulate.

Notes

1. To these two pillars, a third, in the form of a Charter of Rights and Freedoms, has been added in 1982. I will consider its implications in Section III.
2. J.A. Schumpeter, *Capitalism, Socialism and Democracy* (New York, 1942, 1975), 84-85.
3. Mainline neo-classical theory is a very large building. There are consequently almost always some more or less obscure rooms in it in which little-talked-about subjects are being worked at. Work on research and development, on innovation and invention, on technical change, and even on economics of entrepreneurship has been carried out by someone or other at all times. Much of this will surely be re-interpreted and given new life in the light of the recent re-discovery of entrepreneurial competition.
4. I. Kirzner, *Competition and Entrepreneurship* (Chicago, 1973).
5. J.K. Galbraith, *American Capitalism, The Concept of Countervailing Power* (Boston, 1962).
6. R.R. Nelson and S.G. Winter, "Simulation of Schumpeterian Competition," *American Economic Review* (February, 1977).
7. D.V. Smiley, *Canada in Question: Federalism in the Eighties*, Third Edition (Toronto, 1980), 91.
8. A research paper done for the Commission also uses that model. See J.A. Brander, "Economic Policy Formation in a Federal State: A Game Theoretic Approach" (1984). Brander rationalizes the use of the prisoner's dilemma model on the basis of what he calls the "public interest" approach to politics. But it is essentially a "collectivist" or "organicist" assumption. See below.
9. R.D. Luce and H. Raiffa, *Games and Decisions* (New York, 1957), 95. Italics added.
10. J.H. Dales, *Pollution, Property, and Prices* (Toronto, 1968), 58-59. Italics in the original.
11. There is no good word to identify that activity or the role of "monitor." I use this word because it seems to me to be the most neutral. I would take any acceptable synonym as a substitute.
12. *De jure* concurrency is often inevitable. Such cases have led to the development of doctrines such as that of "paramountcy" that help settle the accountability issue.
13. The reader, if he or she desires, can form an impression (but no more) of how I would address the question by referring to A. Breton and A. Scott, *The Economic Constitution of Federal States* (Toronto, 1978), which is largely concerned with that matter, but in a different framework of analysis.

14. Earlier, in condemning the use of the prisoner's dilemma model as a model of federalism, I noted that it was this very same assumption which had led to its adoption. From the point of view of classical political science doctrine, the assumption derives from "organicist," as contrasted to "non-organicist" or "personalist" approaches to behaviour. The lure of organicist assumptions, even on the best minds, is always somewhat a puzzle to me.

15. A. Hamilton, J. Jay, and J. Madison, *The Federalist* (New York, 1937 [1787]).

16. It is possible that the life expectancy of "incumbents" is also increasing in the marketplace.

17. Juvenal's question is: "For who will guard the guards themselves?" Among the more important contemporary students of the question are J. Rawls, *A Theory of Justice* (Cambridge, 1971); R. Nozik, *Anarchy, State, and Utopia* (New York, 1974); and J.M. Buchanan, *The Limits of Liberty: Between Anarchy and Leviathan* (Chicago, 1975).

18. The Americans did not understand that role for the Senate perfectly. They designed a Senate to which senators were appointed by the states. That proved to be a disaster. Their present elected Senate, giving equal weight to all the states, is as close to the ideal as one can hope to come in designing an efficient "monitor" of vertical competition.

19. A classic exposition of that view is F.R. Scott, "Social Planning and Canadian Federalism," in M. Oliver, ed., *Social Purpose for Canada* (Toronto, 1961). The resistance to federalism is, in effect, a traditional feature of democratic socialism. That case is nowhere better put than in H.J. Laski, "The Obsolescence of Federalism," in A.N. Christensen and E.M. Kirkpatrick, eds., *The People, Politics and Politicians* (New York, 1941).

20. R.B. Reich, "An Industrial Policy of the Right," *The Public Interest* (Fall, 1983).

21. Canada, *Report of the Royal Commission on Dominion-Provincial Relations* (Ottawa, 1940), Book II, 84.

22. The kind of problems raised by Mancur Olson in his *The Rise and Decline of Nations* (New Haven, 1982) can affect markets and governments equally. For that reason, they are neglected in the following discussion. It would be easy to incorporate them in the analysis.

23. I have in mind the literature of welfare economics. At one time, that literature even served as a basis for the formulation of a theory of government. See W.J. Baumol, *Welfare Economics and the Theory of the State*, 2nd Edition (Cambridge, 1969).

24. See, for example, G.S. Becker, "Competition and Democracy," *The Journal of Law and Economics* (October, 1958).

25. In modern welfare economics, governments are assumed to be maximizing a social welfare function. The "common good" is then defined by choosing a particular degree for the elasticity of substitution among the utilities of persons in society.

from

Constitution Act, 1867

(as amended)

VI. – Distribution of Legislative Powers

Powers of the Parliament

91. It shall be lawful for the Queen, by and with the Advice and Consent of the Senate and House of Commons, to make Laws for the Peace, Order, and good Government of Canada, in relation to all Matters not coming within the Classes of Subjects by this Act assigned exclusively to the Legislatures of the Provinces; and for greater Certainty, but not so as to restrict the Generality of the foregoing Terms of this Section, it is hereby declared that (notwithstanding anything in this Act) the exclusive Legislative Authority of the Parliament of Canada extends to all Matters coming within the Classes of Subjects next hereinafter enumerated; that is to say, –

Legislative Authority of Parliament of Canada.

1. Repealed. (44)
1A. The Public Debt and Property. (45)
2. The Regulation of Trade and Commerce.
2A. Unemployment insurance. (46)
3. The raising of Money by any Mode or System of Taxation.
4. The borrowing of Money on the Public Credit.
5. Postal Service.
6. The Census and Statistics.
7. Militia, Military and Naval Service, and Defence.
8. The fixing of and providing for the Salaries and Allowances of Civil and other Officers of the Government of Canada.
9. Beacons, Buoys, Lighthouses, and Sable Island.
10. Navigation and Shipping.
11. Quarantine and the Establishment and Maintenance of Marine Hospitals.
12. Sea Coast and Inland Fisheries.
13. Ferries between a Province and any British or Foreign Country or between Two Provinces.
14. Currency and Coinage.

---

(44) Class 1 was added by the *British North America (No. 2) Act, 1949*, 13 Geo. VI, c. 8 (U.K.). That Act and class 1 were repealed by the *Constitution Act, 1982*. The matters referred to in class 1 are provided for in subsection 4(2) and Part V of the *Constitution Act, 1982*. As enacted, class 1 read as follows:

1. The amendment from time to time of the Constitution of Canada, except as regards matters coming within the classes of subjects by this Act assigned exclusively to the Legislatures of the provinces, or as regards rights or privileges by this or any other Constitutional Act granted or secured to the Legislature or the Government of a province, or to any class of persons with respect to schools or as regards the use of the English or the French language or as regards the requirements that there shall be a session of the Parliament of Canada at least once each year, and that no House of Commons shall continue for more than five years from the day of the return of the Writs for choosing the House: provided, however, that a House of Commons may in time of real or apprehended war, invasion or insurrection be continued by the Parliament of Canada if such continuation is not opposed by the votes of more than one-third of the members of such House.

(45) Re-numbered by the *British North America (No. 2) Act, 1949*.
(46) Added by the *Constitution Act, 1940*, 3-4 Geo. VI, c. 36 (U.K.).

15. Banking, Incorporation of Banks, and the Issue of Paper Money.
16. Savings Banks.
17. Weights and Measures.
18. Bills of Exchange and Promissory Notes.
19. Interest.
20. Legal Tender.
21. Bankruptcy and Insolvency.
22. Patents of Invention and Discovery.
23. Copyrights.
24. Indians, and Lands reserved for the Indians.
25. Naturalization and Aliens.
26. Marriage and Divorce.
27. The Criminal Law, except the Constitution of Courts of Criminal Jurisdiction, but including the Procedure in Criminal Matters.
28. The Establishment, Maintenance, and Management of Penitentiaries.
29. Such Classes of Subjects as are expressly excepted in the Enumeration of the Classes of Subjects by this Act assigned exclusively to the Legislatures of the Provinces.

And any Matter coming within any of the Classes of Subjects enumerated in this Section shall not be deemed to come within the Class of Matters of a local or private Nature comprised in the Enumeration of the Classes of Subjects by this Act assigned exclusively to the Legislatures of the Provinces. (47)

Exclusive Powers of Provincial Legislatures.

92. In each Province the Legislature may exclusively make Laws in relation to Matters coming within the Classes of Subject next hereinafter enumerated; that is to say,— *Subjects of exclusive Provincial Legislation.*

---

(47) Legislative authority has been conferred on Parliament by other Acts as follows:

1. The *Constitution Act, 1871*, 34-35 Vict., c. 28 (U.K.).

2. The Parliament of Canada may from time to time establish new Provinces in any territories forming for the time being part of the Dominion of Canada, but not included in any Province thereof, and may, at the time of such establishment, make provision for the constitution and administration of any such Province, and for the passing of laws for the peace, order, and good government of such Province, and for its representation in the said Parliament.

3. The Parliament of Canada may from time to time, with the consent of the Legislature of any province of the said Dominion, increase, diminish, or otherwise alter the limits of such Province, upon such terms and conditions as may be agreed to by the said Legislature, and may, with the like consent, make provision respecting the effect and operation of any such increase or diminution or alteration of territory in relation to any Province affected thereby.

4. The Parliament of Canada may from time to time make provision for the administration, peace, order, and good government of any territory not for the time being included in any Province.

5. The following Acts passed by the said Parliament of Canada, and intituled respectively, – "An Act for the temporary government of Rupert's Land and the North Western Territory when united with Canada"; and "An Act to amend and continue the Act thirty-two and thirty-three Victoria, chapter three, and to establish and provide for the government of "the Province of Manitoba", shall be and be deemed to have been valid and effectual for all purposes whatsoever from the date at which they respectively received the assent, in the Quenn's name, of the Governor General of the said Dominion of Canada.

6. Except as provided by the third section of this Act, it shall not be competent for the Parliament of Canada to alter the provisions of the last-mentioned Act of the said Parliament in so far as it relates to the Province of Manitoba, or of any other Act hereafter establishing new Provinces in the said Dominion, subject always to the right of the Legislature of the Province of Manitoba to alter from time to time the provisions of any law respecting the qualification of electors and members of the Legislative Assembly, and to make laws respecting elections in the said Province.

The *Rupert's Land Act, 1868,* 31-32 Vict., c. 105 (U.K.) (repealed by the *Statute Law Revision Act, 1893*, 56-57 Vict., c. 14 (U.K.) had previously conferred similar authority in relation to Rupert's Land and the North Western Territory upon admission of those areas.

2. The *Constitution Act, 1886*, 49-50 Vict., c. 35, (.U.K.).

1. The Parliament of Canada may from time to time make provision for the representation in the Senate and House of Commons of Canada, or in either of them, of any territories which for the time being form part of the Dominion of Canada, but are not included in any province thereof.

3. The *Statute of Westminster, 1931*, 22 Geo. V, c. 4 (U.K.).

1. Repealed (48).
2. Direct Taxation within the Province in order to the raising of a Revenue for Provincial Purposes.
3. The borrowing of Money on the sole Credit of the Province.
4. The Establishment and Tenure of Provincial Offices and the Appointment and Payment of Provincial Officers.
5. The Management and Sale of the Public Lands belonging to the Province and of the Timber and Wood thereon.
6. The Establishment, Maintenance, and Management of Public and Reformatory Prisons in and for the Province.
7. The Establishment, Maintenance, and Management of Hospitals, Asylums, Charities, and Eleemosynary Institutions in and for the Province, other than Marine Hospitals.
8. Municipal Institutions in the Province.
9. Shop, Saloon, Tavern, Auctioneer, and other Licences in order to the raising of a Revenue for Provincial, Local, or Municipal Purposes.
10. Local Works and Undertakings other than such as are of the following Classes: –
    (a) Lines of Steam or other Ships, Railways, Canals, Telegraphs, and other Works and Undertakings connecting the Province with any other or others of

---

3. It is hereby declared and enacted that the Parliament of a Dominion has full power to make laws having extra-territorial operation.

4. Section 44 of the *Constitution Act, 1982*, authorizes Parliament to amend the Constitution of Canada in relation to the executive government of Canada or the Senate and House of Commons. Sections 38, 41, 42, and 43 of that Act authorize the Senate and House of Commons to give their approval to certain other constitutional amendments by resolution.

(48) Class I was repealed by the *Constitution Act, 1982*. As enacted, it reads as follows:

1. The Amendment from Time to Time, notwithstanding anything in this Act, of the Constitution of the province, except as regards the Office of Lieutenant Governor.

the Provinces, or extending beyond the Limits of the Province;

(b) Lines of Steam Ships between the Province and any British or Foreign Country;

(c) Such Works as, although wholly situate within the Province, are before or after their Execution declared by the Parliament of Canada to be for the general Advantage of Canada or for the Advantage of Two or more of the Provinces.

11. The Incorporation of Companies with Provincial Objects.
12. The Solemnization of Marriage in the Province.
13. Property and Civil Rights in the Province.
14. The Administration of Justice in the Province, including the Constitution, Maintenance, and Organization of Provincial Courts, both of Civil and of Criminal Jurisdiction, and including Procedure in Civil Matters in those Courts.
15. The Imposition of Punishment by Fine, Penalty, or Imprisonment for enforcing any Law of the Province made in relation to any Matter coming within any of the Classes of Subjects enumerated in this Section.
16. Generally all Matters of a merely local or private Nature in the Province.

Non-Renewable Natural Resources, Forestry Resources and Electrical Energy.

Laws respecting non-renewable natural resources, forestry resources and electrical energy.

92A. (1) In each province, the legislature may exclusively make laws in relation to

(*a*) exploration for non-renewable natural resources in the province;

(*b*) development, conservation and management of non-renewable natural resources and forestry resources in the province, including laws in relation to the rate of primary production therefrom; and

(*c*) development, conservation and management of sites and facilities in the province for the generation and production of electrical energy.

Section 45 of the *Constitution Act, 1982*, now authorizes legislatures to make laws amending the constitution of the province. Sections 38, 41, 42, and 43 of that Act authorize legislative assemblies to give their approval by resolution to certain other amendments to the Constitution of Canada.

(2) In each province, the legislature may make laws in relation to the export from the province to another part of Canada of the primary production from non-renewable natural resources and forestry resources in the province and the production from facilities in the province for the generation of electrical energy, but such laws may not authorize or provide for discrimination in prices or in supplies exported to another part of Canada.

Export from provinces of resources.

(3) Nothing in subsection (2) derogates from the authority of Parliament to enact laws in relation to the matters referred to in that subsection and, where such a law of Parliament and a law of a province conflict, the law of Parliament prevails to the extent of the conflict.

Authority of Parliament.

(4) In each province, the legislature may make laws in relation to the raising of money by any mode or system of taxation in respect of

Taxation of resources.

(*a*) non-renewable natural resources and forestry resources in the province and the primary production therefrom, and

(*b*) sites and facilities in the province for the generation of electrical energy and the production therefrom, whether or not such production is exported in whole or in part from the province, but such laws may not authorize or provide for taxation that differentiates between production exported to another part of Canada and production not exported from the province.

(5) The expression "primary production" has the meaning assigned by the Sixth Schedule.

"Primary production"

(6) Nothing in subsections (1) to (5) derogates from any powers or rights that a legislature or government of a province had immediately before the coming into force of this section. (49)

Existing powers or rights.

Education

93. In and for each Province the Legislature may exclusively make Laws in relation to Education, subject and according to the following Provisions: –

Legislation respecting Education.

(1) Nothing in any such Law shall prejudicially affect any Right or Privilege with respect to Denominational Schools which any Class of Persons have by Law in the Province at the Union:

(49) Added by the *Constitution Act, 1982.*

(2) All the Powers, Privileges, and Duties at the Union by Law conferred and imposed in Upper Canada on the Separate Schools and School Trustees of the Queen's Roman Catholic Subjects shall be and the same are hereby extended to the Dissentient Schools of the Queen's Protestant and Roman Catholic Subjects in Quebec:

(3) Where in any Province a System of Separate or Dissentient Schools exists by Law at the Union or is thereafter established by the Legislature of the Province, an Appeal shall lie to the Governor General in Council from any Act or Decision of any Provincial Authority affecting any Right or Privilege of the Protestant or Roman Catholic Minority of the Queen's Subjects in relation to Education:

(4) In case any such Provincial Law as from Time to Time seems to the Governor General in Council requisite for the due Execution of the Provisions of this Section is not made, or in case any Decision of the Governor General in Council on any Appeal under this Section is not duly executed by the proper Provincial Authority in that Behalf, then and in every such Case, and as far only as the Circumstances of each Case require, the Parliament of Canada may make remedial Laws for the due Execution of the Provisions of this Section and of any Decision of the Governor General in Council under this Section. (50)

---

(50) Altered for Manitoba by section 22 of the *Manitoba Act, 1870*, 33 Vict., 3 (Canada), (confirmed by the *Constitution Act, 1871*), which reads as follows:

22. In and for the Province, the said Legislature may exclusively make Laws in relation to Education, subject and according to the following provisions:–

(1) Nothing in any such Law shall prejudicially affect any right or privilege with respect to Denominational Schools which any class of persons have by Law or practice in the Province at the Union:

(2) An appeal shall lie to the Governor General in Council from any Act or decision of the Legislature of the Province, or of any Provincial Authority, affecting any right or privilege, of the Protestant or Roman Catholic minority of the Queen's subjects in realtion to Education:

(3) In case any such Provincial Law, as from time to time seems to the Governor General in Council requisite for the due execution of the provisions of

this section, is not made, or in case any decision of the Governor General in Council on any appeal under this section is not duly executed by the proper Provincial Authority in that behalf, then, and in every such case, and as far only as the circumstances of each case require, the Parliament of Canada may make remedial Laws for the due execution of the provisions of this section, and of any decision of the Governor General in Council under this section.

Altered for Alberta by section 17 of the *Alberta Act*, 4-5 Edw. VII, c. 3, 1905 (Canada), which reads as follows:

17. Section 93 of the *Constitution Act, 1867*, shall apply to the said province, with the substitution for paragraph (1) of the said section 93 of the following paragraph:–

(1) Nothing in any such law shall prejudicially affect any right or privilege with respect to separate schools which any class of persons have at the date of the passing of this Act, under the terms of chapters 29 and 30 of the Ordinances of the Northwest Territories, passed in the year 1901, or with respect to religious instruction in any public or separate school as provided for in the said ordinances.

2. In the appropriation by the Legislature or distribution by the Government of the province of any moneys for the support of schools organized and carried on in accordance with the said chapter 29 or any Act passed in amendment thereof, or in substitution therefor, there shall be no discrimination against schools of any class described in the said chapter 29.

3. Where the expression "by law" is employed in paragraph 3 of the said section 93, it shall be held to mean the law as set out in the said chapters 29 and 30, and where the expression "at the Union" is employed, in the said paragraph 3, it shall be held to mean the date at which this Act comes into force.

Altered for Saskatchewan by section 17 of the *Saskatchewan Act*, 4-5 Edw. VII, c. 42, 1905 (Canada), which reads as follows:

17. Section 93 of the *Constitution Act, 1867*, shall apply to the said province, with the substitution for paragraph (1) of the said section 93, of the following paragraph:–

(1) Nothing in any such law shall prejudicially affect any right or privilege with respect to separate schools which any class of persons have at the date of the passing of this Act, under the terms of chapters 29 and 30 of the Ordinances of the Northwest Territories, passed in the year 1901, or with respect to religious instruction in any public or separate school as provided for in the said ordinances.

2. In the appropriation by the Legislature or distribution by the Government of the province of any moneys for the support of schools organized and carried

Legislation
for Uniform-
ity of Laws in
Three Prov-
inces.

Uniformity of Laws in Ontario, Nova Scotia and New Brunswick.

94. Notwithstanding anything in this Act, the Parliament of Canada may make Provision for the Uniformity

---

on in accordance with the said chapter 29, or any Act passed in amendment thereof or in substitution therefor, there shall be no discrimination against schools of any class described in the said chapter 29.

3. Where the expression "by law" in employed in paragraph (3) of the said section 93, it shall be held to mean the law as set out in the said chapters 29 and 30; and where the expression "at the Union" is employed in the said paragraph (3), it shall be held to mean the date at which this Act comes into force.

Altered by Term 17 of the Terms of Union of Newfoundland with Canada (confirmed by the *Newfoundland Act*, 12-13 Geo. VI, c. 22 (U.K.)), which reads as follows:

17. In lieu of section ninety-three of the *Constitution Act, 1867*, the following term shall apply in respect of the Province of Newfoundland:

In and for the Province of Newfoundland the Legislature shall have the exclusive authority to make laws in relation to education, but the Legislature will not have authority to make laws prejudicially affecting any right or privilege with respect to denominational schools, common (amalgamated) schools, or denominational colleges, that any class or classes of persons have by law in Newfoundland at the date of Union, and out of public funds of the Province of Newfoundland, provided for education,

(*a*) all such schools shall receive their share of such funds in accordance with scales determined on a non-discriminatory basis from time to time by the Legistlature for all schools then being conducted under authority of the Legislature; and

(*b*) all such colleges shall receive their share of any grant from time to time voted for all colleges then being conducted under authority of the Legislature, such grant being distributed on a non-discriminatory basis.

See also sections 23, 29, and 59 of the *Constitution Act, 1982*. Section 23 provides for new minority language educational rights and section 59 permits a delay in respect of the coming into force in Quebec of one aspect of those rights. Section 29 provides that nothing in the *Canadian Charter of Rights and Freedoms* abrogates or derogates from any rights or privileges guaranteed by or under the Constitution of Canada in respect of denominational, separate or dissentient schools.

of all or any of the Laws relative to Property and Civil Rights in Ontario, Nova Scotia, and New Brunswick, and of the Procedure of all or any of the Courts in Those Three Provinces, and from and after the passing of any Act in that Behalf the Power of the Parliament of Canada to make Laws in relation to any Matter comprised in any such Act shall, notwithstanding anything in this Act, be unrestricted; but any Act of the Parliament of Canada making Provision for such Uniformity shall not have effect in any Province unless and until it is adopted and enacted as Law by the Legislature thereof.

Old Age Pensions.

94A. The Parliament of Canada may make laws in relation to old age pensions and supplementary benefits, including survivors, and disability benefits irrespective of age, but no such law shall affect the operation of any law present or future of a provincial legislature in relation to any such matter.(51)

Legislation respecting old age pensions and supplementary benefits.

Agriculture and Immigration.

95. In each Province the Legislature may make Laws in relation to Agriculture in the Province, and to Immigration into the Province; and it is hereby declared that the Parliament of Canada may from Time to Time make Laws in relation to Agriculture in all or any of the Provinces, and to Immigration into all or any of the Provinces; and any Law of the Legislature of a Province relative to Agriculture or to Immigration shall have effect in and for the Province as long and as far only as it is not repugnant to any Act of the Parliament of Canada.

Concurrent Powers of Legislation respecting Agriculture, etc.

---

(51) Added by the *Constitution Act, 1964*, 12-13 Eliz. II, c. 73 (U.K.). As originally enacted by the *British North America Act, 1951*, 14-15 Geo. VI, c. 32 (U.K.), which was repealed by the *Constitution Act, 1982*, section 94A read as follows:

94A. It is hereby declared that the Parliament of Canada may from time to time make laws in relation to old age pensions in Canada, but no law made by the Parliament of Canada in relation to old age pensions shall affect the operation of any law present or future of a Provincial Legislature in relation to old age pensions.

VII. – Judicature.

Appointment
of Judges.

96. The Governor General shall appoint the Judges of the Superior, District, and County Courts in each Province, except those of the Courts of Probate in Nova Scotia and New Brunswick.

Selection of
Judges in
Ontario, etc.

97. Until the laws relative to Property and Civil Rights in Ontario, Nova Scotia, and New Brunswick, and the Procedure of the Courts in those Provinces, are made uniform, the Judges of the Courts of those Provinces appointed by the Governor General shall be selected from the respective Bars of those Provinces.

Selection of
Judges in
Quebec.

98. The Judges of the Courts of Quebec shall be selected from the Bar of that Province.

Tenure of
office of
Judges.

99. (1) Subject to subsection two of this section, the Judges of the Superior Courts shall hold office during good behaviour, but shall be removable by the Governor General on Address of the Senate and House of Commons.

Termination
at age 75.

(2) A Judge of a Superior Court, whether appointed before or after the coming into force of this section, shall cease to hold office upon attaining the age of seventy-five year, or upon the coming into force of this section if at that time he has already attained that age. (52)

Salaries etc.,
of Judges.

100. The Salaries, Allowances, and Pensions of the Judges of the Superior, District,and County Courts (except the Courts of Probate in Nova Scotia and New Brunswick), and of the Admiralty Courts in Cases where the Judges thereof are for the Time being being paid by Salary, shall be fixed and provided by the Parliament of Canada. (53)

General Court
of Appeal,
etc.

101. The Parliament of Canada may, notwithstanding anything in this Act, from Time to Time provide for the Constitution, Maintenance, and Organization of a General Court of Appeal for Canada, and for the Establishment of any additional Courts for the better Administration of the Laws of Canada. (54)

---

(52) Repealed and re-enacted by the *Constitution Act, 1960*, 9 Eliz. II, c. 2 (U.K.), which came into force on the 1st Day of March, 1961. The original section read as follows:

99. The Judges of the Superior Courts shall hold Office during good Behaviour, but shall be removable by the Governor General on Address of the Senate and House of Commons.

(53) Now provided for in the *Judges Act*, R.S.C. 1970, c. J-1.

(54) See the *Supreme Court Act*, R.S.C. 1970, c. S-19, and the *Federal Court Act*, R.S.C. 1970, (2nd Supp.) c. 10.

from

Constitution Act, 1982

PART III

Equalization and Regional Disparities

Commitment to promote equal opportunities

36. (1) Without altering the legislative authority of Parliament or of the provincial legislatures, or the rights of any of them with respect to exercise of their legislative authority, Parliament and the legislatures, together with the government of Canada and the provincial governments, are committed to

(*a*) promoting equal opportunities for the well-being of Canadians;
(*b*) furthering economic development to reduce disparity in opportunities; and
(*c*) providing essential public services of reasonable quality to all Canadians.

Commitment respecting public public services

(2) Parliament and the government of Canada are committed to the principle of making equalization payments to ensure that provincial governments have sufficient revenues to provide reasonably comparable levels of public services at reasonably comparable levels of taxation. (96)

Reproduced with permission of the Minister of Supply and Services Canada.

(96) See the footnotes to sections 114 and 118 of the *Constitution Act, 1867.*

PART V

Procedure for Amending Constitution of Canada
(99)

38. (1) An amendment to the Constitution of Canada may be made by proclamation issued by the Governor General under the Great Seal of Canada where so authorized by

(*a*) resolutions of the Senate and House of Commons, and

(*b*) resolutions of the legislative assemblies of at least two-thirds of the provinces that have, in the aggregate, according to the then latest general census, at least fifty per cent of the population of all the provinces.

(2) An amendment made under subsection (1) that derogates from the legislative powers, the proprietary rights or any other rights or privileges of the legislature or government of a province shall require a resolution supported by a majority of the members of each of the Senate, the House of Commons and the legislative assemblies required under subsection (1).

(3) An amendment referred to in subsection (2) shall not have effect in a province the legislative assembly of which has expressed its dissent thereto by resolution supported by a majority of its members prior to the issue of the proclamation to which the amendment relates unless that legislative assembly, subsequently, by resolution supported by a majority of its members, revokes its dissent and authorizes the amendment.

(4) A resolution of dissent made for the purposes of subsection (3) may be revoked at any time before or after the issue of the proclamation to which it relates.

39. (1) A proclamation shall not be issued under subsection 38(1) before the expiration of one year from the adoption of the resolution initiating the amendment procedure thereunder, unless the legislative assembly of each province has previously adopted a resolution of assent or dissent.

General procedure for amending Constitution of Canada

Majority of members

Expression of dissent

Revocation of dissent

Restriction on proclamation

---

(99) Prior to the enactment of Part V certain provisions of the Constitution of Canada and the provincial constitutions could be amended pursuant to the *Constitution Act, 1867*. See the footnotes to section 91, Class 1 and section 92, Class I thereof, *supra*. Other amendments to the Constitution could only be made by enactment of the Parliament of the United Kingdom.

Idem

(2) A proclamation shall not be issued under subsection 38(1) after the expiration of three years from the adoption of the resolution initiating the amendment procedure thereunder.

Compensation

40. Where an amendment is made under subsection 38(1) that transfers provincial legislative powers relating to education or other cultural matters from provincial legislatures to Parliament, Canada shall provide reasonable compensation to any province to which the amendment does not apply.

Amendment by unanimous consent

41. An amendment to the Constitution of Canada in relation to the following matters may be made by proclamation issued by the Governor General under the Great Seal of Canada only where authorized by resolutions of the Senate and House of Commons and of the legislative assembly of each province:

(*a*) the office of the Queen, the Governor General and the Lieutenant Governor of a province;

(*b*) the right of a province to a number of members in the House of Commons not less than the number of Senators by which the province is entitled to be represented at the time this Part comes into force;

(*c*) subject to section 43, the use of the English or the French language;

(*d*) the composition of the Supreme Court of Canada; and

(*e*) an amendment to this Part.

Amendment by general procedure

42. (1) An amendment to the Constitution of Canada in relation to the following matters may be made only in accordance with subsection 38(1):

(*a*) the principle of proportionate representation of the provinces in the House of Commons prescribed by the Constitution of Canada;

(*b*) the powers of the Senate and the method of selecting Senators;

(*c*) the number of members by which a province is entitled to be represented in the Senate and the residence qualifications of Senators;

(*d*) subject to paragraph 41 (*d*), the Supreme Court of Canada;

(*e*) the extension of existing provinces into the territories; and (*f*) notwithstanding any other law or practice, the establishment of new provinces.

(2) Subsections 38(2) to (4) do not apply in respect of amendments in relation to matters referred to in subsection (1). — Exception

43. An amendment to the Constitution of Canada in relation to any provision that applies to one or more, but not all, provinces, including — Amendment of provisions relating to some but not all provinces

(*a*) any alteration to boundaries between provinces, and

(*b*) any amendment to any provision that relates to the use of the English or the French langauge within a province,

may be made by proclamation issued by the Governor General under the Great Seal of Canada only where so authorized by resolutions of the Senate and House of Commons and of the legislative assembly of each province to which the amendment applies.

44. Subject to sections 41 and 42, Parliament may exclusively make laws amending the Constitution of Canada in relation to the executive government of Canada or the Senate and House of Commons. — Amendments by Parliament

45. Subject to section 41, the legislature of each province may exclusively make laws amending the constitution of the province. — Amendments by provincial legislatures

46. (1) The procedures for amendment under sections 38, 41, 42 and 43 may be initiated either by the Senate or the House of Commons or by the legislative assembly of a province. — Initiation of amendment procedures

(2) A resolution of assent made for the purposes of this Part may be revoked at any time before the issue of a proclamation authorized by it. — Revocation of authorization

47. (1) An amendment to the Constitution of Canada made by proclamation under section 38, 41, 42 or 43 may be made without a resolution of the Senate authorizing the issue of the proclamation if, within one hundred and eighty days after the adoption by the House of Commons of a resolution authorizing its issue, the Senate has not adopted such a resolution and if, at any time after the expiration of that period, the House of Commons again adopts the resolution. — Amendments without Senate resolution

(2) Any period when Parliament is prorogued or dis- — Computation of period

solved shall not be counted in computing the one hundred and eighty day period referred to in subsection (1).

Advice to issue proclamation

48. The Queen's Privy Council for Canada shall advise the Governor General to issue a proclamation under this Part forthwith on the adoption of the resolutions required for an amendment made by proclamation under this Part.

Constitutional conference

49. A constitutional conference composed of the Prime Minister of Canada and the first ministers of the provinces shall be convened by the Prime Minister of Canada within fifteen years after this Part comes into force to review the provisions of this Part.